D1563332

VICTORY'S SHADOW

VICTORY'S SHADOW

CONQUEST AND GOVERNANCE IN MEDIEVAL CATALONIA

Thomas W. Barton

CORNELL UNIVERSITY PRESS
Ithaca and London

First published 2019 by Cornell University Press

Printed in the United States of America

Library of Congress Cataloging-in-Publication Data

Names: Barton, Thomas W., 1976– author.
Title: Victory's shadow : conquest and governance in
    medieval Catalonia / Thomas W. Barton.
Description: Ithaca : Cornell University Press, 2019. |
    Includes bibliographical references and index.
Identifiers: LCCN 2018042957 (print) | LCCN 2018044225
    (ebook) | ISBN 9781501736186 (pdf) | ISBN
    9781501736179 (epub/mobi) | ISBN 9781501736162 |
    ISBN 9781501736162 (cloth: alk. paper)
Subjects: LCSH: Catalonia (Spain)—History. | Catalonia
    (Spain)—Religion. | Spain—History—711–1516. |
    Christianity and other religions—Islam—History—
    To 1500. | Islam—Relations—Christianity—
    History—To 1500.
Classification: LCC DP302.C65 (ebook) | LCC DP302.C65
    B37 2019 (print) | DDC 946.702—dc23
LC record available at https://lccn.loc.gov/2018042957

For Whitney

❦ Contents

❦ ACKNOWLEDGMENTS

This book has undergone dramatic changes over the years since I began it at Yale University. Paul Freedman initially suggested the topic, helped me get situated with my archival research in Catalonia by drawing on his extensive network of colleagues, and assisted me in countless invaluable other ways throughout the project's long development. I would like to recognize Teo Ruiz for being such a warm and caring mentor, friend, and role model for life. Carlos Eire and Adam Kosto were also instrumental—and Carlos has continued to support me with boundless encouragement ever since. I remain deeply grateful to my undergraduate professors at Princeton University. Numerous other colleagues have provided camaraderie, assurance, and assistance over the years, including Ibrahim Al-Marashi, Michelle Armstrong-Partida, Pere Benito, Jeff Bowman, Karen Burgess (CMRS), Nancy Caciola, Brian Catlos, Albert Curto, Andrew Devereux, Rowan Dorin, Daniel Duran i Duelt, John Eldevik, Gemma Escrivà, Hussein Fancy, Benjy Gampel, Rodrigo García-Velasco, Pat Geary, Claire Gilbert, Piotr Górecki, Matthew Herbst, Michelle Herder, Maya Soifer Irish, Bill Jordan, Marie Kelleher, Arash Khazeni, Mat Kuefler, Kristina Markman, Susan McDonough, Sara McDougall, Ted Melillo, Mark Meyerson, Maureen Miller, Greg Milton, David Nirenberg, Natalie Oeltjen, Laurea Pagarolas, Stéphane Péquignot, Gwen Rice, Erin Rowe, Mike Ryan, Flocel Sabaté, Alyssa Sepinwall, Dan Smail, George Trumbull IV, Lucas Villegas-Aristizábal, Ed Watts, Scott Wells, Ken Wolf, Matt Wranovix, and Antonio Zaldivar. I also acknowledge friends in Catalonia, including Marta Herreras, Xavier Sanahuja and Helena Garrigós, Teresa Julià, and Edgar Vergara. The California Medieval Seminar, Spain-North Africa Project, Mediterranean Seminar, and UCLA's CMRS served as vital venues for learning from other experts and for testing out many of the ideas presented in the following pages. I also recognize the helpful archivists and staff members of the ACA, ACL, ACT, ACTE, ADM at Poblet, AHN, AML, Arxiu Nacional de Catalunya, and Biblioteca de Catalunya. Thanks are due to my wonderful History (and non-History) colleagues at the University of San Diego as well as to my supportive deans, Noelle

Norton, Kristin Moran, and Ron Kaufmann. I'm especially grateful to Colin Fisher for assisting me as department chair with numerous reviews, grant and fellowship applications, and other responsibilities. Damian Smith has been a source of encouragement and support and provided vital constructive feedback on the manuscript. I have also benefited from kind and supportive correspondence with Larry McCrank, whose important scholarship on many of the topics addressed in this book has been an invaluable resource to me. I am grateful to my editor at Cornell University Press, Mahinder Kingra, for taking a chance on this manuscript and offering insightful suggestions on how to improve it, to Bethany Wasik, Carmen Torrado Gonzalez, and Karen Laun for assistance with the manuscript preparation and marketing, Deborah Oosterhouse for wonderful copyediting, and Kate Mertes for help with the preparation of the index.

Numerous grants and fellowships provided vital financial support, which I acknowledge with gratitude: the Andrew Mellon Graduate Fellowship, the Yale Graduate Fellowship, a Fulbright Fellowship, an Allan Sheldon III Memorial fellowship (Yale), a Heckman Research Scholarship (Hill Museum and Manuscript Library), a Grant-in-Aid fellowship (Oberlin College), an ACLS Fellowship, and numerous International Opportunities grants and Faculty Research grants from the University of San Diego. Publication costs were offset by a generous grant from the College of Arts and Sciences of the University of San Diego. Chris Woolgar and the *Journal of Medieval History* graciously allowed me to use some of the research already presented in "Lords, Settlers, and Shifting Frontiers in Medieval Catalonia," vol. 36 (2010): 204–52, in chapters 5 and 7.

For friendship over the years, I would also like to recognize Audrey and Kevin Barrett, Ed Batts and Robyn Hudgens, Beth Brett, Jordan Cohen and Sheila Gujrathi, Juliana and Scott Draper, Scarlett Freund, Shilpi and Anand Gowda, Henri Dolset and Patrick Leroy, Chris Kelley, Daniel Mason and Sara Houghteling, Rich and Koki Reasons, Jeff and Heather Slosar, Yi Sun and Gary Boggs, John and Tammy Unikewicz, Ben and Julie Waltzer, and Manasi Watts. I owe a huge debt to my parents and step-parents, who inspired me to enter academia and have supported me throughout the long journey. I'd especially like to acknowledge my father, Doug Barton, who encouraged me to study history at Princeton and was a powerful, ever-positive role model throughout my life. I'd also like to thank my extended family, Greg, Julie, Rachel and Lucy Barton, Jamie and Laura Barton, Betty Barton, Joe and Candee Lee, JJ Lee, Denise Tu and Bryan Wardlow, and Kristl and David Tu. My wife, Whitney, deserves recognition for picking up the slack during all of my research trips and long absences over the years. I lovingly dedicate this book to her. Thank you for always and unconditionally supporting my strange passion for premodern history. My three daughters, Mele, Koa, and Nanea, are my other great source of joy. I look forward to learning someday what they think of this mysterious book that took up so much of my time and attention as they were growing up.

✒ ABBREVIATIONS, NAMING, AND COINAGE

Generally, only the most reliable version is cited in the case of duplicate archival sources or multiple editions. In addition to the acronyms specified in the bibliography, the following abbreviations are used throughout the notes: Arm. (Armario), c. (carpeta, calaix, capítol), chap. (chapter), doc. (document/o), C (Cancillería Real), fol(s). (folio), leg. (legajo), no(s). (número), n (note), perg(s). (pergamí/pergamino), Reg. (Registre/o).

The names of individuals that appear in the chapters that follow generally reflect the linguistic cultures of their home regions, whenever distinguishable. For example, a Latin document referring to a certain "Jacobus" clearly deriving from the town of Salou, in Catalonia, would appear as Jaume, whereas a "Jacobus" from Zaragoza or Toledo would be named Jaime. Similarly, due to their dynasty's long-standing identification with Catalonia, the count-kings of Barcelona and Aragon have Catalonian naming (Alfons, Pere, Jaume, etc.). Catalano-Aragonese monarchs following the merger with Aragon are numbered according to Catalonian tradition: for example, Alfons I "El Cast" (r. 1154–96) and Pere I "El Catòlic" (r. 1196–1213). Generally, the names of individuals appear as spelled by scribes without diacritical marks. However, well-known Jewish or Muslim historical figures, such as Muḥammad ibn Abī ʿĀmir (al-Manṣur) or ibn Ḥazm, appear in their standard printed forms. Place-names that are commonly anglicized will appear as such throughout the text: for example, Catalonia and Aragon, not Catalunya and Aragón. Lesser known place-names will appear in their native forms: for example, Lleida and Zaragoza. Terminology such as *aljama*, *lleuda*, *pedatge*, and *prohoms* will be defined or explained when first employed. Since there are relatively few of these terms, this book does not utilize a glossary.

Although this study does refer to various distinct types of coinage and seeks to show how coinage could serve as a political tool, a detailed understanding of the Iberian Peninsula's complicated history of coinage is not necessary to follow its argumentation. It will suffice to appreciate that a number of roughly equivalent silver *solidus* coins circulated throughout the realms of the Crown of Aragon. As was the case with all currencies, the purchasing

ABBREVIATIONS, NAMING, AND COINAGE

power of these *solidi* varied from year to year, but each, nevertheless, was subject to the traditional Carolingian ratio of one pound to twenty *solidi* to twelve *denarii*. Similarly, although the *morabetin* coins mentioned throughout this book fluctuated in value, each was worth about nine Catalonian *solidi*, and three *morabetins* were roughly equal to five *masmudines*.[1]

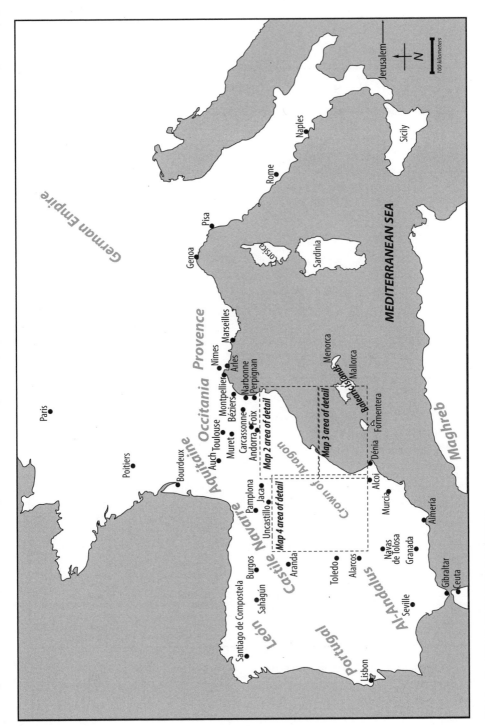

MAP 1. The Western Mediterranean and Europe

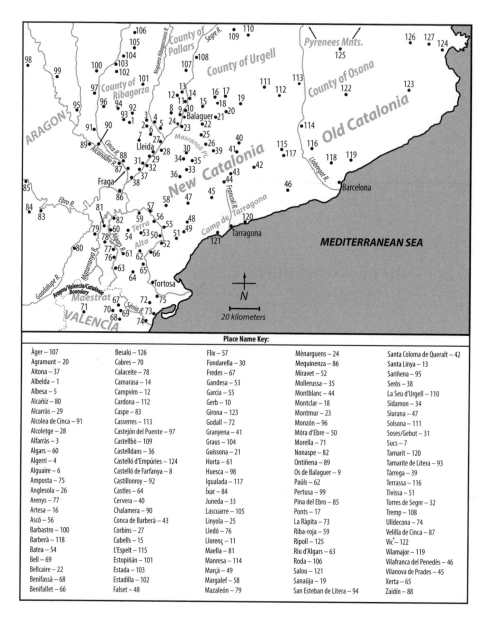

Place Name Key:

Àger – 107	Besalú – 126	Flix – 57	Mènarguens – 24	Santa Coloma de Queralt – 42
Agramunt – 20	Cabres – 70	Fondarella – 30	Mequinenza – 86	Santa Linya – 13
Aitona – 37	Calaceite – 78	Fredes – 67	Miravet – 52	Sariñena – 95
Albelda – 1	Camarasa – 14	Gandesa – 53	Mollerussa – 35	Seròs – 38
Albesa – 5	Campvim – 12	Garcia – 55	Montblanc – 44	La Seu d'Urgell – 110
Alcañíz – 80	Cardona – 112	Gerb – 10	Montclar – 18	Sidamon – 34
Alcarràs – 29	Caspe – 83	Girona – 123	Montmur – 23	Siurana – 47
Alcolea de Cinca – 91	Casserres – 113	Godall – 72	Monzón – 96	Solsona – 111
Alcoletge – 28	Castejón del Puente – 97	Granyena – 41	Móra d'Ebre – 50	Soses/Gebut – 31
Alfarràs – 3	Castellbò – 109	Graus – 104	Morella – 71	Sucs – 7
Algerri – 4	Castelldans – 36	Guissona – 21	Nonaspe – 82	Tamarit – 120
Alguaire – 6	Castelló d'Empúries – 124	Horta – 61	Ontiñena – 89	Tamarite de Litera – 93
Amposta – 75	Castelló de Farfanya – 8	Huesca – 98	Os de Balaguer – 9	Tàrrega – 39
Anglesola – 26	Castillonroy – 92	Igualada – 117	Paüls – 62	Terrassa – 116
Arenys – 77	Castles – 64	Íxar – 84	Pertusa – 99	Tivissa – 51
Artesa – 16	Cervera – 40	Juneda – 33	Pina del Ebro – 85	Torres de Segre – 32
Ascó – 56	Chalamera – 90	Lascuarre – 105	Ponts – 17	Tremp – 108
Barbastro – 100	Conca de Barberà – 43	Linyola – 25	La Ràpita – 73	Ulldecona – 74
Barberà – 118	Corbins – 27	Lledó – 76	Riba-roja – 59	Velilla de Cinca – 87
Batea – 54	Cubells – 15	Llorenç – 11	Ripoll – 125	Vic – 122
Bell – 69	L'Espelt – 115	Maella – 81	Riu d'Algars – 63	Vilamajor – 119
Bellcaire – 22	Estopiñán – 101	Manresa – 114	Roda – 106	Vilafranca del Penedès – 46
Benifassà – 68	Estada – 103	Marçà – 49	Salou – 121	Vilanova de Prades – 45
Benifallet – 66	Estadilla – 102	Margalef – 58	Sanaüja – 19	Xerta – 65
	Falset – 48	Mazaleón – 79	San Esteban de Litera – 94	Zaidín – 88

MAP 2. The Northeastern Crown of Aragon (detail from map 1)

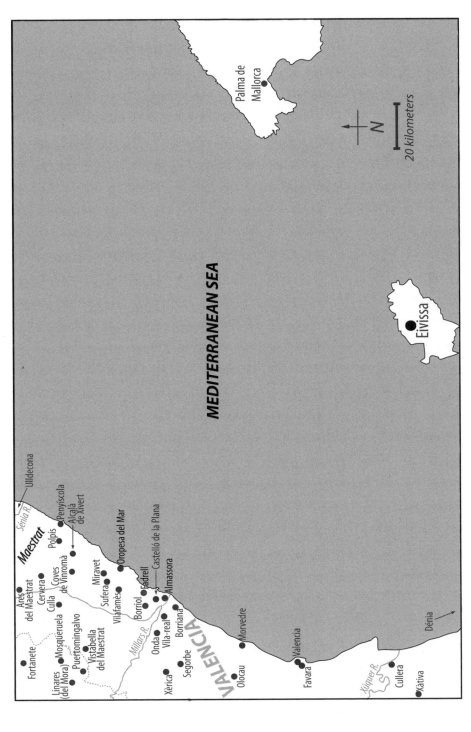

MAP 3. The Western Crown of Aragon (detail from map 1)

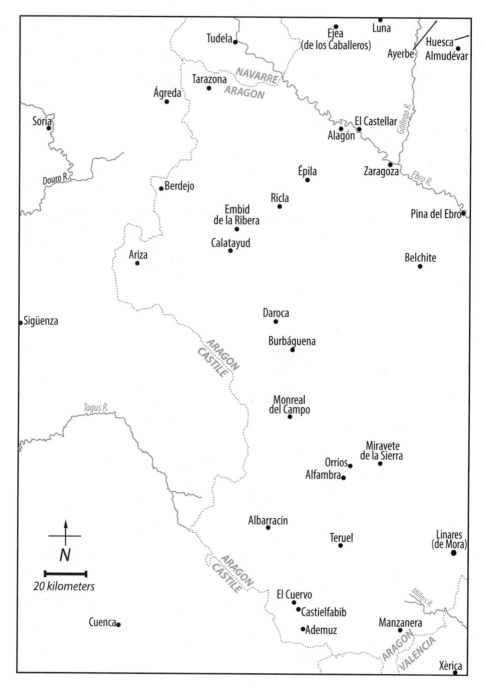

Luna
Ejea
(de los Caballeros)
Tudela
Ayerbe
Huesca
Almudévar
NAVARRE
Tarazona
ARAGON
Ágreda
El Castellar
Alagón
Soria
Zaragoza
Épila
Douro R.
Berdejo
Ricla
Pina del Ebro
Embid
de la Ribera
Calatayud
Belchite
Ariza
Sigüenza
Daroca
Burbáguena
ARAGON
CASTILE
Tagus R.
Monreal
del Campo
Miravete
de la Sierra
Orrios
Alfambra
Albarracín
Teruel
Linares
(de Mora)
N
Millars R.
20 kilometers
ARAGON
CASTILE
El Cuervo
Castielfabib
Cuenca
Ademuz
Manzanera
ARAGON
VALENCIA
Xèrica
Gallego R.
Ebro R.

MAP 4. The Southeastern Crown of Aragon (detail from map 1)

 VICTORY'S SHADOW

Introduction

In 1296, Jaume II (r. 1291–1327), count-king of the composite monarchy known as the Crown of Aragon, appointed the bishop of the Mediterranean port city of Tortosa to investigate a claim by the citizens of Narbonne that they held a full exemption from all levies on their trading in Tortosa. The king had good reason to scrutinize these privileges. Narbonne's traders moved a great deal of commerce through the port, and this exemption cost the government a significant stream of revenue. In this case, however, the royal administrators' aims were frustrated by Narbonne's procurators, who appeared before the bishop to furnish the original charter of enfranchisement issued by none other than Jaume II's distant ancestor, the count-prince Ramon Berenguer IV (r. 1131–62).

Only with vital financial and military assistance from the Narbonnese, the bishop noted, had Ramon Berenguer "extracted Tortosa from the hands of the Muslim enemies."[1] In preparation for the siege and as a means of securing their vital support, Ramon Berenguer had promised these allies these potentially lucrative trading exemptions as well as a monopoly over an enfranchised trading outpost (known as a *fondaco*) in the city that would only take effect upon the success of the venture.[2] Even though the conquest had transpired nearly 150 years before this court appearance, the Crown was legally bound to recognize the continued validity of Jaume's great-great-grandfather's perpetual privilege. Accordingly, within the year, royal administrators were

1

in the process of purchasing these concessions from the Narbonnese in an attempt to eliminate the liability once and for all.[3]

Such perpetual privileges were common during preparations for conquest and left durable marks on the political, economic, and juridical landscapes of captured territories. Ramon Berenguer IV's desire to secure these lands and need for assistance were so great that he signed away future revenue sources and landed rights to enlist and incentivize supporters. At that time, he and his advisors could not comprehend the true cost of the endeavor to the economic and political health of his domains, possibly concluding that they had nothing to lose and everything to gain from the acquisition of these territories.

These sorts of concessions initially reduced already limited revenues from these lands. They also constrained the count-prince's ability to mount the pressure on neighboring Islamic territories necessary to defend his conquests and capture lands to the south. Over the coming decades, the difficulty of making these acquisitions economically and politically viable within the governmental context of the Crown of Aragon would threaten the stability of this dynasty's political supremacy and hold over security throughout its realms. Given these apparent considerable short- and long-term challenges that repeatedly plagued victorious regimes, how can we account for this insatiable drive to conquer and expand? What implications did these difficulties and setbacks have for the integration and redevelopment of these acquired lands and for their evolving relationships with the societies that had seized them?

Numerous studies have underscored the importance of conquest and colonization throughout the medieval period for the creation of the cultural, economic, and political expanse that came to be known as Europe. Robert Bartlett, for example, asserts that expansion along Christendom's external frontiers was "a process of replication, not differentiation" in which "codifiable blueprints" from the core were implanted in the peripheries.[4] He contends that "the legal and institutional blueprints or models which were easily exportable and adaptable but also resistant" in "new circumstances . . . could be modified and survive, but they also transformed their surroundings."[5] While sharing in his view of the central importance of expansion for medieval European history, subsequent work has critiqued Bartlett for overemphasizing the homogeneity of the cores and peripheries and the resulting "deepening cultural uniformity of the Latin West." Nora Berend, for example, prefers to emphasize the adaptability of the models implanted along the shifting frontiers of a Christendom that "diversified as it expanded."[6]

Bartlett does acknowledge the potential for greater heterogeneity when it comes to the orchestration of territorial integration. Far from an orderly process conducted by an established and uncontested sovereign based in the core, he perceives that structures developed within these peripheries under the direction of numerous competing, "many-headed," nonroyal authorities with the capacity to be more spontaneous and less risk averse than the average king. "The knightly-clerical-mercantile consortium, not the apparatus of kingly power," he writes, "orchestrated the most characteristic expansionary movements of the eleventh and twelfth centuries."[7] Indeed, Bartlett has proposed that the strengthening of royal authority around the turn of the fourteenth century in some cases may have served as "some kind of brake on the expansion of Latin Europe." "The absence of political masterminding in the colonial ventures of the Middle Ages," he suggests, "is illustrated not only by the prominent role of these eclectic consortia, that is by the agents of expansion, but also by the distinctive nature of the forms of expansion."[8]

This book engages with these and related debates over the mechanisms and implications of territorial expansion through the analysis of Catalonia's interaction with neighboring Muslim-ruled states to the south. Our long-term scope, combined with the richness of this region's source materials, enables us not only to identify, with considerable detail, the societal elements that helped motivate territorial acquisition but also to evaluate the implications of expansionism for the lands undergoing colonization as well as for the conquering host society itself. As we shall see, various institutions that took root within these new lands became, either by design or through development, distinct in notable ways from those of settled Catalonia to the north. At the same time, the processes of acquisition, integration, and assimilation would exert profound and enduring influences on the economy, demography, and most notably the political affairs of both the captured lands and the conquering entities.

Catalonia's Southern Frontier

Wedged between the Pyrenees and the Mediterranean in northeastern Iberia, Catalonia emerged in the early Middle Ages as a conglomeration of counties, viscounties, and other lordships of varying shapes and sizes. Over the eleventh and early twelfth centuries, it gradually fell under the control of the counts of Barcelona. After these magnates secured title to the kingdom of Aragon by the mid-twelfth century, Catalonia developed into the political and cultural core of the expansionist Crown of Aragon.[9]

Between the eleventh and thirteenth centuries, Catalonia bordered to the south the Muslim-ruled Upper Frontier of Al-Andalus, which was chiefly administered by the Andalusi cities of Tortosa (Ṭurṭūša) and Lleida (Lārida). This region underwent a dramatic shift in the mid-twelfth century. Occupying the prized fertile valleys of the lower Ebro and Segre Rivers in a sector of northeastern Iberia now known as New Catalonia, these Muslim states succumbed to two distinct coalitions of Christian forces led by Ramon Berenguer IV. These conquests had materialized after many unsuccessful attempts by successive regimes punctuating generations of relatively peaceful interaction. Although religious fervor, emboldened by the Second Crusade, encouraged and invigorated these campaigns, political, demographic, and economic shifts on either side of the frontier more significantly influenced the timing and outcome of the conquests. Christian and Muslim rulers and warlords were chiefly interested in asserting their control over wealth and resources, and their activity was less motivated by religious identification. Exhortations to conquer by the papacy and local church leaders who were eager to restore churches on Muslim-held territory could influence these stakeholders at opportune moments, however, especially when there were worldly incentives at play to justify promoting the ecclesiastical agenda.[10]

These captured territories along the lower Ebro River valley represented the very edge of Christendom in this region for roughly eighty years following this conquest. After ardent campaigning into northern Valencia and only modest territorial gains under Ramon Berenguer IV's son and grandson, the so-called count-kings of Barcelona and Aragon, Alfons I (r. 1162–96) and Pere I (r. 1196–1213), Jaume I (r. 1213–76) orchestrated the effort that culminated in the fall of Muslim Valencia. This victory, and the resulting effort to pacify, settle, and restructure Valencia, further buffered the former Ebro frontier from Muslim-ruled lands and thereby accelerated the ongoing, painstaking effort to consolidate territory along these former limits of Christian control.

The political challenges and fiscal crises experienced by the monarchy in these two generations between the conquests of New Catalonia and Valencia simultaneously shaped and were colored by the dynamics of this turbulent border region with the Islamic world. Economic and demographic fluctuations may have helped generate these campaigns, yet once the battles were over, this vast landscape, with its sizeable population of Muslim inhabitants and high exposure to frontier danger from neighboring Al-Andalus, presented its captors, and anyone who sought to capitalize on it, with formidable organizational challenges. The new territorial rulers, despite being able to draw on resources from their domains in Catalonia and Aragon, lacked the subjects, administrative experience and capacity, and resources to quickly and decisively stabilize and assimilate the captured territories. Over time, as the war effort they struggled to maintain failed to sustain sufficient momentum to yield significant new conquests, the count-kings of Barcelona and Aragon had to reevaluate their goals. They weighed whether their wealth and political capital would benefit more from investing further in this southern frontier than in other costly projects they had inherited from their predecessors.

From the very beginnings of Christian rule, this frontier landscape's institutions, demography, and political framework were distinct—in some respects by the rulers' explicit design—from those of the core society that was attempting to colonize it. More than previous work has recognized, this frontier zone was also internally diversified and only became more differentiated with the effort to settle and develop the territories.[11] For example, the consolidation of these lands witnessed a sharp dichotomy between urban and rural areas. Urbanized cores were much more rapidly invested with Christian institutions due to a comparatively sizeable influx of Christian settlers (and small minority of Jews) stimulated by generous privileges and exemptions. Rural spaces, on the other hand, especially those more exposed to Muslim attack from across the frontier, naturally witnessed sparser settlement and resisted acculturation by Christian-ruled society, even after additional conquests distanced the boundary with Islamic society.

Such diverse territorial conditions encouraged jurisdictional differences that grew over the course of consolidation. Ultimately the expansion of Catalonia's southern frontiers held mixed outcomes for the monarchy and wider society. The attempt to settle, develop, and integrate these captured territories was haphazard. It was hampered by the monarchy's failure to implement its emerging sovereign ideology and to apply sophisticated, efficacious techniques of consolidation. Over the latter decades of the twelfth century and early years of the thirteenth, the ambitious but weak count-kings would increasingly delegate administration of much of the acquired territory to a range of lords as they struggled to maintain control over public order throughout the realms.

Although New Catalonia has a reputation for lacking the peasant servitude that came to afflict Old Catalonia to the north, the postconquest, colonizing dynamic along the Ebro frontier did witness the concentration of resources by the rapid crystallization of oligarchies that worked to the detriment of the local Christian and Muslim peasantry. This was no Turnerian landscape, and as Josep Torró notes, "there was, therefore, strictly speaking, no *tabula rasa* of equality of opportunities."[12] Most of the powerful or ascendant members of these frontier societies secured their privileged positions within this landscape owing largely to connections and resources they brought with them. Furthermore, if we look at Catalonia as a whole, we can appreciate how the idea of liberation could promote marginalization elsewhere.[13] According to Paul Freedman, the push by lords from the later twelfth century to lay down legal barriers to peasant mobility in Old Catalonia was partly prompted by their concerns that their tenants might relocate to what they assumed were more favorable tenures within the conquered territories of New Catalonia.[14]

Long after their time on the shifting frontier with Islam had passed, these communities of the lower Ebro valley still lived under the dark shadow of this victory. Considerable research has demonstrated how the manner in which individual cities, towns, villages, and regions were integrated and the extent to which they sought to maintain preconquest infrastructure and patterns could exert a powerful influence over their subsequent development.[15] The frontier foundations of their society remained highly noticeable. Many residents and their collectives also clung to the customs, policies, and practices instituted chiefly by the monarchy in the early years of consolidation even as they fell subject to increasingly pervasive seigniorial domination. As this landscape developed, and Europe transitioned from the booming yet rudimentary twelfth into the administratively top-heavy and labyrinthine thirteenth century, it became the site of greater institutional conflict. In the years leading up to the mid-thirteenth century, the monarchy experienced a great infusion of wealth and an accompanying boost in prestige and resources due to the long anticipated definitive conquests of Valencia and Mallorca. By this point, much of the former Ebro frontier had developed into a landscape of quasi-autonomous lordships held by both lay and religious lords. For a variety of reasons, these entities became the target of the ascendant monarchy. Empowered by their recent territorial enrichment, significant improvements in their governmental administrative apparatus, and an emboldened ideology of sovereignty, the later thirteenth-century monarchs sought to subjugate or eradicate these seigniorial autonomies to restore the direct governance once carefully guarded by their predecessors over a century earlier.

The inherent conservatism of medieval society made the timing of this enterprise even more significant. The territorial organization and societal institutions imposed by the monarchy, lords, and settlers, sometimes emulating Muslim precedents, formed a blueprint for the future history of the region. Within the broader framework of European growth and development, this book thus argues for more enduring, highly individuated legacies carried by each swath of consolidated frontier territory, and accordingly a more locally diversified picture of European society and culture. Expansionism on the frontiers did implant increasingly homogenized European social institutions, as Latin Christendom became more interconnected under the growing authority of monarchies and extralocal potentates like the papacy. Yet the human and institutional memories and vestiges of conquest and consolidation rendered these new lands institutionally and culturally distinct from those of their colonizers, despite not being administered as or considered colonial regimes. These differences, however, ultimately owed more to the course of territorial development than to any enduring crusader or conqueror identity among the settlers.

When Europe emerged as a colonial power in the fifteenth century, it may itself have been a product of conquest and colonization, as Bartlett has remarked, but its most active principalities remained, in Thomas Bisson's words, more "federative than integrative."[16] The Crown of Aragon, in particular, persisted as federative because it remained "a cluster of lordships."[17] Thus, in contrast to Bartlett's belief in a general rising trend of homogeneity throughout Europe and its peripheries, this book presents the view that heterogeneity was enhanced rather than diminished by centuries of expansionism and indeed remained the norm rather than the exception throughout as well as beyond the medieval period.

At the realm-wide level, this book asks whether engagements with these lands, culminating in conquest, strengthened or destabilized the power relationships between the ascendant rulers in Catalonia, the counts of Barcelona, and their competitors within and beyond the region, which included assertive nobles as well as a number of other comital families, not to mention the kings of Aragon and Castile. After the conquest, were Ramon Berenguer IV and his successors able to capitalize on these victories by effectively consolidating the spoils and using the new frontier as a staging point for raiding and capturing additional territories? Did such territorial accumulation facilitate further centralization throughout the conquering regime or did it help foster the creation or empowerment of rivals determined to undercut royal authority? Did governmental centralization under a single ruler or king promote or deter territorial expansionism?

At the local level, we must evaluate how the count-kings drew on the resources derived from conquest to increase their prestige and administrative capabilities, consequently reducing the autonomy of diverse lords throughout Catalonia. Furthermore, we will examine to what extent these conquerors replicated their institutions when integrating captured territory. Did the imposition of certain "blueprints" have a lasting influence on the development of societies taking shape on these lands?

Methodology and Structure

Controversy surrounds the concept of frontiers, with some scholars proposing to do away altogether with use of "frontier" as a term within the context of medieval society.[18] As with other baggage-ridden terms employed by medievalists (in many cases, reluctantly), such as "feudalism" and "othering," "frontier," when not employed with precision or attention to historicity, does run the risk of complicating the situations it seeks to describe. These problems originate not only in the application of models that may not suit the historical situations in question, but also in the use of the same term to characterize societies that were arguably exceedingly different from one another.[19] The approach employed here is to utilize "frontier" and descriptions of space in precise ways that are consistent with the historical evidence in order to facilitate analysis and enhance reader comprehension. As we shall see, medieval documents from Catalonia recognized frontier regions as a distinct category of landed space known as a *marchio* that could be claimed as a political territorial unit by a potentate. Sources also occasionally did employ the term *frontera* to refer to the political boundary with Islamic territory that rendered the neighboring Christian-ruled lands dangerous and unstable,[20] but much more frequent references use other words, such as "desert" and "waste," that seem to evoke the untamed and vacant frontier wilderness envisioned by Turner, which could serve as "a gate of escape from the bondage of the past" for intrepid settlers.[21] However, as many scholars now recognize, these references in fact often described a wilderness devoid not of people but of inhabitants who were part of the Latin Christian social order or power network. Indeed, they could, within the crusader mentality, have served as means to deny those who maintained independent existences or who did not recognize the sacred authority of Christians and their church the right to occupy their lands legitimately.[22] Nuanced readings of the sources, rather than merely models and theories imported from other fields and time periods, will guide our observation and interpretation of the dynamics of this frontier environment.

In its methodology and design, this project seeks to contribute to scholarship on both Iberian and wider European expansionism. Previous work on Iberia has tended to focus chiefly on conquests and their immediate aftermaths, thereby giving short shrift to the preconquest developments that often had important implications for the course of land capture as well as the dynamics of the ensuing consolidation. In limiting their treatments to the first generation of Christian rule, these studies have rarely been in a position to observe the long-term gestation of the frontier landscape.[23] This book, by contrast, traces over 150 years of postconquest societal development in order to consider how the nature of New Catalonia's conquest and ensuing colonization exerted a sustained yet variegated influence on this region's organization and administration. Those projects that have studied long-term societal change have primarily been interested in the interaction of ethno-religious minority groups, a process still referred to as *convivencia* by many scholars even as that term has increasingly fallen subject to criticism.[24] Due to this focus, much of this work has not been equipped to examine the broader social context surrounding such interfaith relationships.[25] Scholars have also been attracted to thirteenth-century conquests when royal administration was more dominant and capable and, accordingly, produced more systematic documentation.[26] As a result, they have often neglected the study of twelfth-century conquests when the contest between royal and seigneurial power was more volatile and when techniques crucial to later expansionism into the Balearic Islands, Valencia, and the wider Mediterranean were still in the early stages of development.

Historians of medieval Iberia have tended to grant conflicts with neighboring Muslim societies, and the diverse, piecemeal, and often disconnected efforts to conquer the lands under their control, traditionally known as the *Reconquista*,[27] a central position in the historical narrative.[28] Given this tendency, it is somewhat surprising that the broader political and institutional history of Catalonia's southern limits during these centuries has yet to be examined in depth by a modern study in any language. Although Catalonia's development is admittedly not well accommodated by the nationalistic, Castile-centric conceptualization of the *Reconquista*, its frontier history has nevertheless long been viewed by Catalan historians as a formative golden age during which its social fabric and *país* were forged.[29] Moreover, the vast local archives in Tortosa and Lleida, a core documentary focus of this project, have been left virtually unexplored by previous scholarship. Prior work has tended to study individual settlements within New Catalonia in isolation or focus on a single institution or collective rather than viewing them within the broader societal context of the conquered region.[30] In keeping with these objectives, historians of conquest also often rely primarily on one type of documentation (e.g., royal, municipal, ecclesiastical, monastic, or noble), which can promote skewed historical perspectives. This project instead seeks to present a multidimensional social history of consolidation by relying on documents from each of these points of view and from a diversity of archives.

This book's focus on the administrative implications of territorial expansion has necessitated a deliberately Eurocentric approach that should not imply that I consider the history of non-Christian groups to be less relevant to this history.[31] Indeed, this book is deeply connected, in terms of both its underlying research and argument, to other work I have recently published, most notably my first monograph, *Contested Treasure: Jews and Authority in the Crown of Aragon*, which examined how the changing policies of the monarchy and local lords within this conquered landscape influenced the administrative conditions and status of Jewish communities within Tortosa and other centers and areas within the Crown of Aragon and wider Europe.[32] *Victory's Shadow* contextualizes the case study of Tortosa by showing how the administrative patterns it assessed were related to broader trends in Christian-ruled society's efforts to manage these frontier territories. Due in part to the pronounced shift in the historiography toward the study of Andalusi systems and the experience of ethno-religious minorities following conquest over the past several decades, the implications of the transfer from Muslim to Christian control on the society and government of Christian-ruled Catalonia to be addressed here has received less recent attention and remains less well understood.

Another aspect of this history that this book contextualizes but will not address in detail is the restoration and development of the dioceses of Tortosa and Lleida. The establishment of these sees was part of a broader process of organizing the ecclesiastical space of the captured territories and ordering the relationships between the bishoprics and other newly founded religious institutions within these lands that is the subject of a third, in-progress monograph related to this line of research, *From the Hands of the Infidels: The Christianization of Islamic Landscapes in Europe*.[33] Readers should approach these books as a loosely interconnected trilogy, despite their order of publication. This present volume engages in the long-term analysis of the development, conquest, and consolidation of this frontier that serves as a framework for the other two more focused monographs.

This study frames its analysis using two interrelated and interwoven narratives. First, it presents and assesses the intricate political and military history of the conquest of New Catalonia over the course of the eleventh and twelfth centuries and numerous attempts to push that frontier further southward into Valencia that would witness limited success until the unprecedented campaigns of Jaume I in the 1230s. Second, it examines in detail how the emerging governmental structures within Catalonia confronted, and were influenced by, the trials they faced in managing the conquest and the consolidation of the Ebro valley frontier as well as the subsequent war effort along that front with Valencia. Each of these ongoing enterprises were, in turn, linked to formidable challenges to their rule by a range of rivals, from petty castellans and frontier warlords to more powerful counts and viscounts.

There is naturally inherent value in reconstructing and analyzing the history of the integration of Catalonia's understudied southern territories. It is my hope that this book will offer more by providing a complicated perspective on the relationship between a core and periphery to readers interested in comparing the gestation of frontiers and encourage them to further nuance their generalized models. Catalonia's southern boundary was internally variegated across time and space, and its influences on the rest of the region were similarly diverse and dynamic. Far from being peripheral and distanced from the important turning points faced by the colonizing society, this frontier zone remained integral to the political developments that shaped the entirety of Catalonia, and the Catalano-Aragonese culture that pervaded it.

🍂 Part I

Interaction and Conquest

🍃 CHAPTER 1

Parias and Churches along the Eleventh-Century Frontier

Scholars have long been perplexed and intrigued by the coexistence of conflictive and collaborative modes of behavior in the interactions of Christian- and Muslim-ruled societies within the premodern Iberian Peninsula. Their dealings were often aggressive and exploitative and usually culminated in territorial conquest. They could also feature mutually beneficial collaboration and even friendship that feel out of place in reference to the traditional view of Christian–Andalusi relations as chiefly a religiously defined war.[1]

Potentates who held lands that bordered the Islamic world faced a heightened potential of invasion or extortion at the hands of their Muslim neighbors. At the same time, direct access to the Andalusi world facilitated vital alliances with these Muslim rulers and increased opportunities for enrichment and expansion.[2] Territorial lords themselves recognized the importance of these interfaith relationships, so much so that they became accustomed to adopting titles over their frontiers as honorific distinctions and as testaments to the fact that they were members of an upwardly mobile elite group of frontier potentates.[3]

At the same time, there can be no question that frontier interaction had a religious bent to it. Documentation, especially the sources produced by church leaders, underscores the religious dimensions of the campaigns to regain formerly Christian territory that had stood under Muslim rule since the Arabs wrested the bulk of the Peninsula from Visigothic control centuries earlier.[4] Fixated as they were on the Christianization of the landscape, popes showed little interest in or comprehension of the political divisions of the Upper Frontier of al-Andalus that were fundamental to territorial accumulation by Christian regimes. When Urban II outlined the effort to Pedro I of Aragon in the 1090s, for example, he relied exclusively on ecclesiastical markers, ancient dioceses held captive by the "domination of the Muslims" (*sarracenorum dominacio*), to describe Andalusi territory.[5]

Although papal and local church sources issued from the later eleventh century onward are helpful for piecing together the ecclesiastical context of Christian campaigns into the Ebro valley, they can also provide a skewed picture of the involvement of other factors linked to developing political affairs in the region. Such documentation can lead us to overemphasize the extent to which the restoration project dictated Christian interaction with Muslim societies. It is not always clear that rulers saw their world exclusively, or even predominately, from this religious perspective.[6] Their frequently opportunistic decisions to violate alliances with Muslim counterparts in order to push for territorial conquest were surely the result of numerous complicated factors, only one of which was a sense of religious calling or the desire for spiritual favors.

As the first in a series of three chapters constituting the initial part of this study, the pages that follow will begin our examination of the interactions between Christian- and Muslim-ruled lands that took place many decades before Christian forces would embark on the campaigns that would realize the definitive conquest of the Ebro River valley. In order to set the stage, this initial chapter will pursue a line of argument that follows two main threads. First, it will assess the extent to which political survival in the Christian territories of the northeastern Peninsula depended on interaction with Islamic peoples to the south. Although scholars have long recognized the significance of such contact for the political entities and forces within this region in general, they have not explored in detail the full implications of communication, collaboration, and conflict across the Ebro frontier preceding the mid-twelfth-century conquest by Christian forces. This analysis will be relevant to our discussion later on in the book when we will observe how the dynamics of this jockeying for positions and influence along the frontier would, in certain respects, have powerful repercussions for the nature of the capture and consolidation of these lands. Second, we will examine how church leaders, based locally in the northeastern Peninsula and further afield, sought to campaign for the cause of restoring the "captive" churches and dioceses by pressuring rulers and their allies to view interaction with Muslim-ruled society exclusively through an ecclesiastical lens. As we shall see, these two modes of interaction were not always in direct opposition to one another and at times could be surprisingly complementary.

Frontier Engagement and Political Development in the Eleventh Century

In 1038, just three years into his tenure as count of Barcelona, Ramon Berenguer I (r. 1035–76) gave two of his men "vacant land" (*terra nostra erma*) at the far limits of his county of Barcelona. This territory would eventually come to be known as the Conca de Barberà, and within two centuries of this donation it would be situated at the core of Catalonia and the Crown of Aragon. In 1038, however, as Ramon Berenguer was careful to stipulate in his charter, this "barren" land, "where no man lives or sheep graze," faced the "Ishmaelite peoples." The count mandated that, in addition to inhabiting and working the land, these two men would have to build a castle to defend the position against these Muslims. The donor and recipients had already surveyed the territory and identified a "hill that they call Forés" as the ideal spot for the fortification.[7]

An increasing proliferation of these sorts of transactions by the counts of Barcelona and other rulers and magnates with a frontier presence during the eleventh century served to strengthen their hold over the furthest reaches of their claimed territories and support assaults against Muslim fortifications and settlements to the south. This new trend contrasted sharply with the circumstances that had predominated in this region over the past few generations. Aside from the "unofficial" expansion caused by the unregulated migration of settlers to the fringes of Christian territory, the frontiers of the "Catalan" and "Aragonese" counties of Barcelona, Osona/Manresa, Cerdanya, Urgell, Pallars, Ribagorza, Sobrarbe, and Aragon with the Islamic world had barely moved since around 950.[8]

During the early decades of the eleventh century, the upsurge in the Muslim offensive during the career of the powerful chamberlain known as al-Manṣūr (r. 977–1002) seemed poised to disrupt this stasis. Al-Manṣūr's activity had augmented the prestige and military dominance of the caliphate through twice-yearly campaigns against the petty Christian states clustered along the frontier. The Christian rulers across the Peninsula had once again found themselves on the defensive. Caliph al-Ḥakam II al-Mustanṣir had died in 976 with only one young son, Hishām. Muḥammad ibn Abī ʿĀmir, later known as al-Manṣūr, had worked to effect Hishām's accession and subsequently rose to prominence as his most important advisor, known officially as *ḥājib* or "chamberlain."[9] The most famous of these devastating raids, in 985, culminated in the defeat of Count Borrell II (r. 947–92), the sacking of his administrative base in Barcelona, the enslavement of part of its population, and the destruction of the comital archives.[10] Barcelona alone was besieged or infiltrated by Muslim forces no less than five times during this period (in 978, 982, 984, 985, and 1003).[11]

Al-Manṣūr's campaigns were not confined to the Christian lands of the northeast.[12] His armies also afflicted many of the major Christian principalities bordering Muslim-ruled territory, burned Christian monasteries and holy sites, and carried off large amounts of booty (including, infamously, church bells) from as far north as Santiago de Compostela.[13] Although these raids penetrated deeply into Christian territory and inflicted significant damage, they secured no notable lasting territorial gains for al-Manṣūr.[14]

When they were not having to fend off Muslim raiding, these Christian principalities had their own internal struggles and the integrity of their frontiers with Christian-ruled neighbors to preoccupy them.[15] The political map of this region underwent many alterations during this period, and by the mid-eleventh century, the autonomous Christian principalities along the frontier with al-Andalus were much reduced in number. Only the county of Barcelona, with its affiliate county of Osona / Manresa, the county of Urgell, and the kingdoms of Aragon and Navarre remained of what had once been an extensive patchwork of independent states.[16]

Despite winning many battles against the Christians, al-Manṣūr's focus on these campaigns, to the exclusion of other considerations, eventually lost him the war. His fixation on reforms meant to increase the caliphate's military strength at any cost transformed al-Andalus into a land whose nativized inhabitants were subject to a foreign Berber soldier elite transplanted from North Africa. Increasingly, internal conflicts arising from political discontentment distracted him from his military preoccupations.[17]

This political reorientation by non-native elements was not limited to the early eleventh century. It was a pattern that would continue to influence al-Andalus in subsequent generations, most notably with the entrance of the centralizing North African Almoravids and Almohads beginning in 1085 and 1147, respectively.[18] And just as the late caliphate's reliance on transplanted Maghrebian forces was inherently unstable, these later dynasties, as we shall see, would never be able to maintain stable rule over the lands of al-Andalus for long. Even so, al-Manṣūr's death did not in itself foment the dissolution of the centralized state of al-Andalus. His son and successor, ʿAbd al-Malik (r. 1002–8) struggled to maintain these military efforts against the Christians every year until his death in 1008. The effective power of the Umayyad caliphate of Córdoba was ultimately reduced to nothing during his weak reign.[19] Numerous constituencies within and outside Córdoba sought, unsuccessfully, to control the deteriorating caliphal office. As the authority of the caliphate rapidly disintegrated with the civil war (*fitna*) following al-Manṣūr's death in 1002, the decentralizing forces of the disparate regions overwhelmed any further attempts to hold al-Andalus together in one piece.[20] After another Umayyad emir failed to resuscitate the caliphate and ended up fleeing to Lleida to the north, the vizier Abū Ḥasm ibn Jahwar, who headed the leading men of Córdoba, proclaimed the caliphate officially abolished.[21] The cities of North Africa detached themselves from Córdoba, and Muslim-ruled Iberia shattered into a multitude of separate autonomously administered states known as *taifas* (from the Arabic *ṭāʾifa*, "party" or "group").[22] Although the caliphate initially broke up into at least thirty-eight individual *taifa* states, their composition would vary over the coming years.[23]

The Upper Frontier of al-Andalus (or *Thaghr al-ʿAqsa*), which occupied much of the length of the Ebro River valley, was less affected by this process of fragmentation due to its ingrained political organization and administrative culture.[24] During the emirate and caliphate, Córdoba had practiced a policy of periodically changing governors in order to discourage any tendencies to establish local bases of independent power. This practice did not become normative in the *Thaghr*, however, where permanent military governors (*qāʾid*) tended to administer each major urban center (*madīna*).[25] As early as the ninth century, this emerging pattern was fostering the development of local ruling dynasties.[26] The dominance exercised by the Banū Hūd family over the eastern *Thaghr* during the latter half of the eleventh century, for instance, was based on the governmental structures already well in place during the final years of the caliphate.[27] Following the dissolution of the caliphate, the governmental structures of al-Andalus would never again attain such a high degree of administrative cohesion. The forces of political entropy remained too powerful for any centralizing group to counteract for long. When it fractured into the *taifa* states of Zaragoza, Lleida, and Tortosa, the *Thaghr* came to mirror the segmented political units constituting the former Carolingian "Spanish March" to the north. Despite sharing similar cultures, religious creeds, administrative structures, and languages,[28] the *taifas* were locked in competition with each other that compromised their collective struggle against the Christian principalities to the north.[29]

Some degree of localized centralization did occur within the *Thaghr* during the eleventh and early twelfth centuries. Under this same Banū Hūd family, most notably, Zaragoza developed into arguably the most powerful *taifa* kingdom in al-Andalus. From the 1040s, Zaragoza achieved even greater influence. Under this dynasty's most significant rulers, Aḥmad ibn Sulaymān al-Muqtadir (r. 1049–81) and his descendants, Yūsuf ibn Aḥmad (r. 1081–85) the and Aḥmad ibn Yūsuf (r. 1085–1110), the Hūdids temporarily exercised authority over the whole of the eastern *Thaghr*.[30] They incorporated Huesca sometime in the first half of the eleventh century and acquired Lleida in 1139–40. Tortosa fell under Hūdid influence in 1060.[31]

When the emirate and caliphate had been at their peaks of power, they had been able to demand large tribute payments from exposed Christian polities in return for peace. As al-Andalus decentralized, however, Christian rulers reversed this relationship and extorted similar payments (*parias*) from different *taifa* kingdoms.[32] Count Ramon Berenguer I of Barcelona was among the earliest to be able to secure such tribute by developing castral positions along the limits of his lands during the early years of his reign.[33]

By the mid-eleventh century, the influx of gold via *parias* into Ramon Berenguer's coffers, and those of rival Christian rulers, had greatly heightened the stakes of interaction with the *taifa* states, putting at risk the independence of any Christian principality that did not participate in this enrichment. From this point forward, frontier rulers found themselves pitted in fierce competition to appear as the most imminent threat to neighboring Muslim frontier potentates. These Christians magnates appear to have understood well that the success of this delicate, diplomatic zero-sum game depended on their ability to control the men they delegated to guard the castles within striking distance of Muslim territory. They sought to exercise this control via tightly worded written agreements that were littered with security clauses. In one representative agreement from 1076, Counts Ramon Berenguer II (r. 1076–82) and Berenguer Ramon II (r. 1076–96) appointed Bonafill Oliba to fortify a holding at Puig de Anguera, on Barcelona's furthest limit (*marcha extrema*) at the north of Tarragona's *camp*. The rulers not only restricted Bonafill from selecting another lord or alienating the holding but also claimed full authority over his right to make peace or war with the Muslims.[34]

Given the instability of this political environment, rulers seeking to consolidate their power and nobles desiring to enhance their autonomy often preferred the quick gains of plunder and tribute over costly and more risky campaigns aimed at conquering territory.[35] The chancery records of Ramon Berenguer I of Barcelona are peppered with documentation concerned with maintaining or regaining payments of tribute. In 1058, for example, he promised Ramon Guifré, count of Cerdanya, an annual payment of gold and other pecuniary concessions as an aid for increasing the "marca d'Oluges" toward Muslim territory. In exchange, Ramon Guifré swore his fealty to the count and promised to help him obtain *parias* from Lleida and Zaragoza as well as to maintain Tortosa's established payment of tribute.[36] As with any other right or possession, present and future *parias* could be shared or pledged, as Ramon Berenguer did to his wife, Almodis, along with a long list of frontier castles, in 1056.[37] Ramon Berenguer's successful tactics earned him 9,000 *mancus* annually from Lleida, Tortosa, and Zaragoza between 1050 and 1060.[38]

Far from being mutually exclusive, projects to expand territorial boundaries and establish new fortified positions supported this growing interest in maintaining the flow of tribute. Conquests and castles could improve defensive and offensive capabilities, which, in turn, could serve as means to extort more effectively further tribute over the competing ambitions of Christian rivals. For example, when the first king of independent Aragon, Ramiro I (r. 1035–63), attacked Zaragoza's town of Graus in 1063, the *taifa* was at that time already a tributary of Ramiro's half-brother, King Fernando I of Castile-León (r. 1037–65).[39] Fernando was keen on protecting Zaragoza, and thereby monopolizing its tribute, until its resources were exhausted or he were able to conquer it. Accordingly, Fernando quickly dispatched an army, led by his son and Rodrigo Díaz, the future Cid, to assist Zaragoza's ruler, al-Muqtadir, in mounting a defense against the Aragonese. These allied forces soon confronted the Aragonese, killing Ramiro I and compelling his men to lift their attack on Graus and take flight.[40]

Such competition over *parias* and territory frequently occasioned these sorts of complicated interfaith alliances. Two decades later, in 1082, for instance, Count Berenguer Ramon II of Barcelona organized a major coalition composed of Aragon, Navarre, and his tributary, al-Mundhir ibn Aḥmad, ruler of the affiliated *taifas* of Lleida-Tortosa, against al-Muqtadir's successor, al-Mu'tamin of Zaragoza. Yet again, a federation of Muslim and Castilian troops commanded by Rodrigo Díaz moved in to defend Zaragoza. They defeated Berenguer Ramon's coalition at Almenar, north of Lleida.[41] Undeterred, Berenguer Ramon continued to engage in careful diplomacy with an eye to maintaining the flow of *parias* from his tributaries that was vital to his ongoing struggle to strengthen his authority over his rebellious vassals. He soon sought to help this same dependent, al-Mundhir, gain control of Valencia in order to buffer al-Mundhir's territories from erosion by the combined forces of Zaragoza and Castile. After numerous expeditions

targeting Valencia in the late 1080s, however, Berenguer Ramon again suffered defeat by the forces of Rodrigo Díaz in 1090 at Tévar. By then, Rodrigo
had been appointed the protector of King al-Qadir of Valencia, effectively
eliminating the count of Barcelona's chances to capture Valencia and furthermore losing him the *parias* of Lleida, Tortosa, and Zaragoza. This turn
of events also hurt Berenguer Ramon's reputation among church leaders
because it raised doubts regarding his ability to secure the restoration of the
archiepiscopal see of Tarragona.[42] By the late 1080s, after being accused of
fratricide, Berenguer Ramon II had been demoted from count to serving as
quasi-regent to the young Ramon Berenguer III (r. 1086–1131), a position he
held until 1097.

Rodrigo Díaz had counterparts in Aragon and Catalonia, who similarly
negotiated between Christian and Muslim rulers on either side of the frontier
in order to enhance their own authority and enrich themselves. Mir Geribert,
one of the most prominent nobles in open rebellion against Count Ramon
Berenguer I of Barcelona in the 1050s, was in frequent, independent negotiation with the *taifa* rulers. In 1058, for example, when messengers from the
count came to meet with Mir Geribert, they discovered that he was already
engaged in his own talks with the Muslims of Tortosa.[43] Such activity frustrated attempts by ambitious dynasts like Ramon Berenguer to dominate
contact in the region with the *taifa* rulers in order to monopolize the flow of
tribute. Following this encounter in 1058, this count went so far as to invoke
a judicial tribunal to force Mir Geribert to swear an oath that he would not
interfere with Ramon Berenguer's *"paria* from Spain (*Ispania*)." Rulers like
Ramon Berenguer already faced difficulty protecting their share of Muslim
tribute against incursions by other sovereign rulers. This combined internal
and external competition for *parias* constituted a significant threat to the fiscal health and overarching authority of comital governments.

Muslim and Christian religious leaders alike held such interfaith collaboration in bitter contempt.[44] Popular vernacular works, such as the well-known,
eleventh- or early twelfth-century *Song of Roland,* advertised the dangers of
fighting alongside Muslims. Successive popes, together with religious leaders situated outside of Rome, reinforced the messages conveyed by such
writings through their firm exhortations to Christian warrior aristocrats to
dispense with their rivalries and ally together against the common religious
enemy.[45] For their part, church leaders in Catalonia sporadically punished
what they viewed as nonconstructive behavior by lay magnates whenever
it was politically feasible and expedient, such as when they forced Count
Ramon V of Pallars Jussà (r. 1047–98) to perform penance for allying with
Muslim troops.[46]

The development of theories of holy war by religious elites on either side of the confessional divide appears to have intensified their respective views on the sacrilege committed by coreligionist opportunists who nonchalantly allied with infidels to achieve worldly goals.[47] This trend is especially notice-able within the Muslim context. In the mid-eleventh century, for example, the administrator and jurist ibn Ḥazm lamented the vices that, in his view, had become increasingly rampant among the opportunistic rulers operat-ing the fragmented environment of the *taifas*. "By God, I swear that if the [*taifa*] tyrants were to learn that they could attain their ends more easily by adopting the religion of the Cross, they would certainly hasten to profess it!" He claimed to yearn for the days when a more centralized political system had allegedly reined in such abuses.[48] Similarly, some years later, the poet al-Sumaysīr scathingly denounced these same *taifa* overlords for the damage their self-centered agendas had inflicted on the shared Islamic cause: "You have handed over Islam into enemy captivity . . . since you have given your support to the Christians . . . so that you have even broken the bonds of the community of the Prophet!"[49] Such feelings of betrayal by Islamic religious leaders would only intensify after the fall of Toledo in 1085. High-profile losses to the Christian enemy encouraged a broadening of the critique that often bordered on lament. A poem mourning the loss of Toledo blamed the defeat on the entire Andalusi Muslim community for failing to adhere to the principles of Islam: "Can we be sure that vengeance will not fall upon us, when corruption has combined with license among us?"[50]

Even though Muslim and Christian religious leaders continued to voice these sorts of denunciations, interfaith collaboration remained common and continued to define the shared sociopolitical environment of the frontier. On the Christian-ruled side, this phenomenon persisted in no small part because *parias*, and consequently diplomatic relations with the *taifa* states and their Christian allies and protectors, were so crucial to the economic and politi-cal viabilities of the Christian principalities of the northeast. According to now classic work by Pierre Bonnassie, the economic evolution of Catalonia between 980 and 1050 was largely fueled the continual, "massive" influx of Muslim *dinars*.[51]

A Double-Edged Sword: The Frontier and Political Crisis in Eleventh-Century Catalonia

Although the proximity of Muslim territory did offer Christian principali-ties economic stimulus that could be vital for regime stability and survival, it simultaneously threatened their political viabilities. This tension between the positive and negative repercussions of the frontier's presence heavily weighed upon the political climate of the northeastern Peninsula. Catalonia's state of affairs following the death of Count Ramon Borrell of Barcelona (r. 992–1017) will serve as a useful case to illustrate these varying pressures.

Although significant disagreement remains over the extent of the disruption, scholars now commonly agree that Ramon Borrell's demise, in 1017, generated a political vacuum that caused the progressive erosion of comital authority over the following several decades.[52] The ineffectual reign of Berenguer Ramon I (r. 1017–35) seems to have done little to slow this trend. During the minority of Ramon Berenguer I of Barcelona, which lasted until 1041, comital administrators had little choice but to entrust frontier defense to a number of noble warlords: Guillem de Mediona was active within the county of Osona, Arnau Mir de Tost oversaw the county of Urgell, and Mir Geribert dominated the county of Barcelona. These men appear to have used this period of instability to assert independence from comital authority that they then hoped to maintain once Ramon Berenguer I assumed his majority. Such independence entailed making agreements, transactions, and enfeoffing their holdings to dependents without comital involvement or approval.[53]

Many counties in the region were affected by these phenomena, including Pallars, Cerdanya, Urgell, and Barcelona. Arnau Mir de Tost, for example, was able to carve out a considerable territory that included some thirty castles along the Muslim boundary zone with Urgell. He then made preparations to pass these territories along to his descendants without comital approval, as if they were his personal property.[54] The situation was difficult to manage for the different Catalonian counts because they depended on these men to assist in the defense of their territories as well as to support offensives against the Muslims. For example, Ramon Berenguer I's reliance on warlords such as Arnau to stage raids into Muslim territory is made clear by an agreement (*convenientia*) from 1050 in which the count commended him with the castles of Camarasa and Cubells. These fortifications were key staging points for raids against Muslim centers along the Segre River valley above Lleida. Ramon Berenguer also promised Arnau half of the castle and town of Muslim Balaguer on the condition that he support the successful campaign. He not only reserved access these castles and the right (known as *potestas*) to reclaim them at will but also mandated how much military service Arnau and his men would have to provide. Although he was defensive about reserving his entitlement to these holdings and Arnau's service as his man, Ramon Berenguer positioned himself carefully so as not to encroach upon the liege status already held by Count Ermengol III of Urgell (r. 1038–66). Arnau would only be required to accompany Ramon Berenguer as his supporter on campaigns from which Ermengol was absent. If the count of Urgell were participating, then Arnau would ride with Ermengol and Arnau's son would accompany Ramon Berenguer in his place. Arnau would, furthermore, be obliged to solicit counsel from Ramon Berenguer for any independent expeditions he chose to undertake.[55]

Ermengol of Urgell was sufficiently concerned about this developing relationship between Ramon Berenguer and Arnau Mir de Tost to formulate two *convenientiae* of his own in 1058. In the first charter, Arnau recognized that he held the castle of Casserras (in the Ribagorza) from the count and promised to use it and his other resources to defend his lord against all enemies and obtain tributaries in return for two-thirds of all *parias* obtained. For his part, Ermengol would supplement Arnau's expenses for maintaining the castle from the *parias* he received from Zaragoza and Lleida and would take over responsibility for the castle guard during set periods in the future. The second agreement, in addition to reiterating Arnau's duty to support the count of Urgell, directed special attention at hardening the former's preferential relationship with the latter to the exclusion of Ramon Berenguer. It explicitly barred Arnau from expanding on his relationship with Ramon without Ermengol's prior consent. He could not, for instance, accept Ramon's offer to take command of the frontier castle of Estopiñán or agree to a marriage alliance unless Ermengol first approved of it. In addition to emphasizing Arnau's obligation to aid him, as his liege lord, over the count of Barcelona at all times, the count of Urgell also reserved his right to modify the aforementioned earlier *convenientia* between Ramon Berenguer and Arnau regarding the castles of Camarasa and Cubells without any input from Arnau.[56]

Both the origins of and the solution to the crisis of comital authority thus appear to have lain in the opportunities presented by the Islamic frontier. Each of these counts sought, via these sorts of agreements, to direct and delimit the activity of these castral lords so that it would empower rather than undermine the counts' diplomatic and governmental strategies. Effectively managing conflicts with these men was essential for maintaining not only public order but also profitable relationships with Muslim tributaries. In his confrontation with the insubordinate Mir Geribert, for example, Ramon Berenguer I of Barcelona had to manage a war against his rebellious defenders of the frontier while simultaneously putting on a good face for his Muslim neighbors so as not to raise their suspicion regarding his ability to attack. He continued to launch periodic campaigns and organize profitable truces with these Muslim rulers, all the time struggling to maintain the façade of normalcy in order to encourage the continued flow of *parias*. In 1051, when the Muslims could or would not or pay tribute, Ramon Berenguer decided to launch a punitive raid despite the continuing rebellion of Mir Geribert. Fortunately for this count, the expedition was both short and successful, and in 1052 he was able to resume his efforts to subdue this warlord without significant loss of ground.[57]

Certain Muslim rulers appear to have intervened strategically in these engagements, presumably in hopes of prolonging such conflicts. In the late 1060s, for instance, Count Ramon V of Pallars Jussà lost his domains to his cousin, the aforementioned Arnau Mir de Tost, and sought assistance with this desperate situation from the *taifa* "king" known as "Alzagib." Ramon eventually regained his county but later submitted to pressure to perform public penance for this interfaith alliance.[58] In the subsequent record of dispute between Ramon and Arnau Mir, the count appears to have reordered and recontextualized events in order to make his alliance seem more palatable. Ramon defended his alliance with the Muslim ruler on the grounds that it was a peace treaty that his cousin had then broken without authorization, thereby causing "great damage" to his interests.[59]

Just like *paria* gold, the existence of Muslim potentates willing to commit their troops to conflicts between Christians could be a double-edged sword for Christian political leaders. Accordingly, Christian rulers utilized their power of lordship to monopolize these diplomatic resources and put their delegates in compromised positions. After having relied on Muslim support to regain control of his county, for example, this same Ramon V of Pallars Jussà ordered thirty of his most important supporters to take oaths that they would not make similar alliances.[60] Similarly, when Ramon Berenguer I's men performed homage to him, they were obliged to swear not to enlist Muslim agents against their lord.[61]

Imposing these sorts of requirements came at a price, however. Ramon Berenguer I lacked the political capital during much of his rule to advance all of his comital interests at the expense of the powerful warlords within his domains. In addition to submitting to pressure to share his *paria* incomes, this count had to concede to these warlords a certain degree of jurisdictional autonomy.[62] The breakdown of comital "public" authority during Ramon's tenure featured the domination and privatization by these warlords of expanses of formerly free peasant lands.[63] Steadily over the course of many years, the peasantry had been migrating southward to settle unclaimed lands in the interstices between Islamic and Christian principalities that did not fall under the jurisdiction of any seigniorial authority. Many scholars continue to believe that this process of unregulated, independent settlement contributed nearly as much as conquest to the expansion of Christian-held territory.[64] Gradually, however, these allodial settlers lost their freedom, and they were subjugated by lords, integrated into their seigniorial domains, and made to pay to arbitrary levies and submit to restrictions on their mobility.[65] In most locales, this "privileged moment," as Bonnassie termed it, when the peasants had enjoyed their own surpluses and relatively free movement within the agrarian market economy, appears to have been brief.[66] Similar conditions would not be witnessed in Catalonia until the capture of new lands from Muslim Tortosa and Lleida in the mid-twelfth century, a period of expansion that would be followed by yet another cycle of declining comital capacity for authority, increasing seigniorial autonomy, and a corresponding deterioration of settler conditions, as we will see.[67] According to Freedman, this incorporation of large sectors of sparsely settled land ended up worsening circumstances for most peasants in Old Catalonia. Fearing that their tenants might relocate to more favorable tenures on lands captured from the Muslims, many landlords imposed legal restrictions to curtail peasant mobility.[68]

Due to this ratcheting back of comital oversight, administrative conditions at the lowest levels of society were therefore growing less regulated. Among the upper echelons, however, we can perceive a contrary trend, as the counts reconstructed their authority using new foundations. As Adam Kosto and others have demonstrated, written agreements redefining mutual obligations between lords and agents were instrumental in reestablishing and strengthening comital supremacy over certain sectors. From the later eleventh century onward, these enactments gradually established a rudimentary hierarchy of fidelity in support of this renewed comital authority.[69]

Military operations that eroded the fringes of Muslim-held territory mounted pressure on the *taifa* regimes, inducing more frequent and larger *paria* payments and increasing the likelihood of successful conquest. In the meantime, as a significant by-product, these territorial gains could assist rulers in Catalonia with their ongoing political challenges by shifting the frontier line and thereby distancing the castral lordships held by rebellious warlords from Muslim territories. As he was still attempting to surmount these challenges to his authority, in 1050, Ramon Berenguer I sought to accomplish these intertwined objectives via an agreement with his brother-in-law Berenguer, viscount of Narbonne. In an effort to prevent Mir Geribert from spreading his rebellious activity beyond the Penedès into the no-man's-land to the west of Tarragona (now known as the Camp de Tarragona), Ramon isolated Tarragona jurisdictionally, and further broadcast his claim to it, by refashioning its territory as a county. The agreement stipulated that Berenguer would mount the city's capture, reside there for a minimum of ten years, provide naval support, manage defense and launch further attacks against the Muslims "in Ispaniam" from its castle, and render all but a portion of any *parias* he received in the meantime to the count of Barcelona.[70] Aside from establishing the tradition of jurisdictional separation that would culminate in the papal enfeoffment of Tarragona as a principality to the Norman Robert Burdet in 1129, this agreement demonstrates how the count of Barcelona sought to form an alliance with new noble agents in opposition to his entrenched and rebellious frontier castellans.[71] Although this particular project never developed past the planning stage, it nevertheless continued to cast a shadow over subsequent dealmaking by the count. In 1060, for instance, Ramon Berenguer and Countess Almodis invested Bernat Amat de Claramunt, who had formerly served her as ambassador to Muslim Dénia, with the castles of Tamarit and Ullastrell with the understanding that he would use these positions to occupy and populate Tarragona as titular viscount of the city.[72]

There are no indications that either of these initiatives ever developed into campaigns targeting Tarragona. Yet, throughout the remainder of his reign, Ramon Berenguer nevertheless continued to strive to maintain a strong claim to the city and its surrounding county, which extended all the way to the Ebro River delta, in part by maintaining tight control over the most important frontier castles along the borders of the counties of Barcelona and Osona. He did not acquire all of these positions by force. In some cases, he had invested political capital or precious monetary resources to gain control, as when he took advantage of Ermengol III of Urgell's financial need and loaned him one thousand gold *mancus* in return for control of his castle of Toló, located to the northeast of Balaguer.[73] As evidenced by his will from 1076, Ramon Berenguer advanced broad claims to territories and castles across the southern and eastern borderlands toward the limits of Aragon and Urgell. He did this calculatingly, if unrealistically, to maintain a foothold for future territorial expansion and a claim to *parias* in these areas in the face of competing claims and military activity by other rulers. Ramon Berenguer also claimed all *parias* from Spain for himself and his sons, rights to Menorca (which he had asserted rights to since his expedition in 1058), the most important castles of Osona, and all of the castles leading up to Monzón.[74] Although they did not similarly make such sweeping general claims to Andalusi tribute, Ramon Berenguer II and Berenguer Ramon II did enumerate all of the *parias* they aspired to collect in an agreement with Ermengol III from the late 1070s. In addition to the tribute their father had habitually obtained from Lleida, Tortosa, and Zaragoza, they listed specific monetary goals for the *parias* from Murcia, Valencia, Dénia, and Granada.

They enlisted the count of Urgell to assist them in establishing or growing these payments, and in particular winning the war against Zaragoza in order to reestablish its tributary status, in return for a hefty one-third share plus an advance payment of 15,000 *mancus*.[75]

Economic Effects of the Frontier

Purely through the lens of the political development of the counties of Catalonia in the eleventh century, then, we can recognize the clear importance of the presence of neighboring Islamic states.[76] Other types of interaction, including cultural contacts and the transmission of learning and technology, were also of course notable and vital. It is worth considering in greater detail how the economic influences of the frontier on the neighboring Christian-ruled principalities during this period served as conduits or facilitators for these other modes of interchange. The opportunities for land accumulation, *parias*, and trade could fluctuate dramatically and had the potential to stabilize as well as disrupt. Yet both Christian and Muslim rulers had little choice but to seek to control them to their respective benefits.

The economic development of these Christian territories was equally tied to the frontier with Islam, yet in a more sophisticated manner than simply a one-way transmission of tribute.[77] During the eleventh and twelfth centuries, much of the gold received by Christian states passed back into al-Andalus as Christian traders used it to buy a range of Andalusi goods.[78] Moreover, even before *parias* became regularized into annual payments, gold and moveable property flowed into Christendom as conquest booty. Tellingly, around 1018, the county of Barcelona became the first principality within all of Europe to issue gold coinage since the Merovingians.[79] Landed frontiers with al-Andalus may have been chiefly a local concern, but the trade that penetrated them arguably had far-reaching, extralocal implications.

Rulers on either side of the frontier adopted varying policies regulating these sorts of routine, quotidian economic interactions. In 1069, for example, Sancho IV of Pamplona (r. 1054–76) established a treaty with al-Muqtadir of Zaragoza in which the rulers agreed to collaborate to keep the roads between their kingdoms "secure and safe, so that no impediment or harm come to any [of the people] who travel along them."[80] Evidence of tolls collected on overland trade across Muslim-Christian borders, particularly in the western kingdoms, furthermore, suggests that many Christian rulers were aware of this interaction and sought to take advantage of it.[81] Arabic terms for weights and measures came into dominant use in the Christian principalities across the Iberian Peninsula, attesting to the great importance of adapting to be compatible with the Muslim trading world.[82] Andalusi coins and goods circulated as far as northern Europe, via both land and sea routes. Genoese merchants, in particular, developed a thriving sea trade throughout the Christian and Muslim Mediterranean, including the Iberian Peninsula, and signed numerous treaties ensuring and protecting their involvement in Islamic trade.[83] Not only gold and goods, but also slaves, Muslim and Christian, variously passed across the frontier, seized by raiders and conquerors, with notable infiltration throughout European societies.[84] In other instances, however, certain rulers outlawed such economic engagement outright. The *Usatges de Barcelona*, for instance, which developed over the course of many years and were ultimately compiled in the twelfth century, deemed Christian trading with the *taifa* states to be dangerous and treasonous and prescribed considerable fines for Christians who sold food, weapons, or information to the Muslim states.[85]

Papal Influence on Frontier Dynamics

This strict opposition to Christian–Muslim interaction in the *Usatges* may have had more to do with the military objectives of the count-prince of Barcelona when the codification was compiled in the mid-twelfth century.[86] Nevertheless, the increased intervention of extralocal church leaders into the Iberian political landscape also exerted an influence over policy-making regarding these sorts of interactions between Christian and Muslim principalities. These authorities did their utmost to direct the attention of lay rulers to a series of ecclesiastical objectives, the most important of which was the push to regain control of putative diocesan territory that remained under Muslim control. As a means of pursuing these goals, numerous successive popes worked to develop relationships with various noble, comital, and royal factions within the northeastern Peninsula over the second half of the eleventh century.[87] Concurrently, they and their supporters developed papally centered religious justifications of expansion into formerly Christian territories occupied by Muslims.[88]

Papal correspondence with Aragon from the reign of Sancho Ramírez (r. 1063–94) onward dedicated special attention to territorial conquest and ecclesiastical restoration along and around the central Ebro River valley, to the south of Aragonese territory.[89] Various popes hailed the kingdom as the preeminent champion of Christian expansion in eastern Iberia.[90] Aragon would continue to enjoy this preferential status as it dominated the race for territorial acquisition in the lower Ebro region until its assumption by the house of Barcelona in 1137. Sancho Ramírez and his successors, Pedro

(r. 1094–1104) and Alfonso (r. 1104–34), empowered their political aspirations to acquire Muslim territory, and thereby enrich and strengthen their kingdom, by linking them to these ecclesiastical goals. Adherence to the ecclesiastical message would earn them powerful papal advocacy and a strategic moral advantage over their rivals. Such papal influence may have been responsible for the notable shift in official documentation of this period from raw descriptions of raiding and conquering to an image of a Christian struggle to restore the Muslim-dominated Christian ecclesiastical institutions and free the captive and suffering Mozarabs.[91] The papacy, in turn, seems to have allowed its influence to be utilized by these rulers in order to increase its authority within the Peninsula. By establishing such rulers as dependents, these popes could more effectively further their reform agenda and shape the course of ecclesiastical restoration throughout Iberia.[92]

Further strengthening this alliance, Sancho Ramírez forged a new dependent relationship with the papacy as he guided his kingdom into a more expansionist phase.[93] In 1068, this king traveled to Rome, where he attended the Holy Week celebrations in the company of Alexander II.[94] At the end of his visit, he formally placed himself and his kingdom under God's protection and into the hands of Saint Peter. With this commitment, he also promised to pay the Apostolic see an annual tribute of five hundred *mancus*.[95] We lack sufficient evidence to reconstruct fully Sancho Ramírez's motivations for agreeing to establish this papal suzerainty over his kingdom in this way.[96] As I. S. Robinson has noted, the relationship between kings like Sancho and Saint Peter may have seemed less overtly threatening because, according to the very words of these transactions, it involved not simply feudal subordination but rather "protection": *patrocinium, protectio, defensio, tuitio, tutela*. In this respect, such papal suzerainty was "developed by analogy with the protection which the vicar of St Peter had accorded since the mid-ninth century to religious houses."[97]

Although the ceremonies and ritual performed during Sancho's visit to the papacy established a fitting religious element to the bond, circumstantial evidence suggests that certain recent developments along his kingdom's boundaries with Muslim territory could have made Sancho feel politically vulnerable and in need of papal support to defend his interests against competitors. In 1064, Count Ermengol III of Urgell had launched a formidable campaign that utilized a contingent of northern knights and succeeded in temporarily capturing Barbastro, a Muslim town that had long sat within Aragon's sphere of influence.[98] The Barbastro campaign has become the subject of considerable controversy. Scholars disagree over the implications of this involvement by northern knights as well as whether the papacy, in fact, promoted the effort, which would have implications for Barbastro's place in the history of crusading within Iberia.[99] Whereas there are clear signs that Norman fighters did indeed support the campaign, there are no indications that Aragonese forces participated.[100] The Muslims of Barbastro quickly regrouped and launched a counterattack that cost Ermengol his life and drove the Christian occupiers from the town. In the aftermath, Sancho Ramírez had reason to be concerned about the implications of this failed attempt. Even though Urgell's victory had been fleeting and Ermengol's death had subsequently destabilized his county, his victory and heroic martyrdom helped establish Urgell's independent claims to conquering Barbastro and neighboring targets in the future, especially since Aragon had not involved itself in the campaign. The victory, however momentary, also served to cement the reputation of Ermengol's dynasty as containing serious contenders for Muslim territory and committed supporters of the church's cause. Given these developments, by subjugating himself and his kingdom to the papacy in this dramatic, ritualized fashion, Sancho Ramírez implicitly challenged any claim the counts of Urgell or other rivals could make that their expansionism aligned so closely with the goals of the church.[101]

Throughout the remainder of Sancho's rule and the reigns of his successors, the kingdom of Aragon maintained this symbolic subordination to papal lordship, receiving apostolic favor and protection in return.[102] As scholars widely recognize, the practice of submitting to papal lordship had become well established for ecclesiastical institutions since the early days of Cluny and would continue to be useful for certain religious orders troubled by property ownership.[103] It is likely that, for the kings of Aragon, as had been the case for Cluny, the symbolic submission of his lands and titles to a distant papal authority was a price worth paying in return for the acquisition of a potent ally who claimed to exercise eminent domain over the Peninsula's Muslim-ruled territories. It is clear from royal diplomas issued during this period that Sancho drew his sense of regnal legitimacy from his descent from his grandfather, Sancho III, and from the fact that, modeling himself after his namesake and the Old Testament exemplars of David and Solomon as warrior-kings, he expelled the Muslims from his lands. He underscored this feat as the primary factor in fueling his ascent to the apex of his power.[104] Such a conception of his rulership stood to benefit greatly from a papal alliance because his subordination to apostolic authority would reinforce his identity as a Christian warrior. Such submission was not without danger for the Aragonese monarchy, however. Even though Ramírez's regnal ideology was self-contained in that it was based on his dynastic ancestry, infeudation to the papacy carried with it significant religious and political liabilities. The papacy, much to the annoyance of subsequent monarchs, would increasingly exploit these vulnerabilities over the coming decades.

Although Aragon was the first Iberian principality to submit to papal lordship, other rulers in the northeastern Peninsula soon followed its example, thus reducing to some degree the potency of its precocious designation as papal feudatory. According to Paul Kehr, the biggest threat to Aragon's special status arguably came from Castile, with Catalonia assuming a secondary position.[105] In any case, successive popes increasingly viewed papal suzerainty as normative, and under Gregory VII and Urban II, papal pressure on rulers to follow suit mounted to unprecedented levels. As an archdeacon, Hildebrand had been instrumental in shaping the policies of Alexander II and may have helped concoct the very concept of Aragon's enfeoffment.[106] Hildebrand certainly had a hand in implementing major changes concerning the Roman rite in Aragon that took place in 1071, before the commencement of his pontificate.[107] After he was elected as Gregory VII (1073–85), his views became increasingly colored by the escalating Investiture Controversy to the north.[108] He likely saw the vague arrangement with Aragon, and his success in establishing the Roman rite there, as an opportunity to assert a canonical degree of papal authority over the whole of the Iberian Peninsula, especially given the apparent resistance to the Roman rite in various Castilian and Leonese monasteries and churches during these years.[109] While asserting papal administrative authority over ecclesiastical requirements, Gregory VII also worked to craft a firmer canonical foundation upon which he could fashion a more expansive interpretation of papal suzerainty.[110] In a letter to the "Christian princes of Spain" in 1073, he referenced the "well-known" fact that all the land and *honores* of the ancient kingdom of Spain, occupied by the Muslims, pertained to the Apostolic see.[111] Since royal authority in Iberia, from Gregory's perspective, was therefore wholly dependent on papal donation, enfeoffments of Iberian principalities to the papacy rightly reaffirmed the supremacy of papal spiritual and temporal power.

Even though their lands contained bishops who were amenable to increased papal involvement, rulers in Catalonia tended to enter into or renew dependent relationships with the papacy with caution and careful calculus. The marginalized counts of Besalú, for instance, submitted to papal suzerainty in 1077 only after they could muster no further delays.[112] At that time, Besalú's more formidable neighbors were threatening its independent status, which it had enjoyed since the late ninth century. Papal suzerainty, however, could not prevent Besalú's eventually subjugation to the county of Barcelona after Ramon Berenguer III of Barcelona married off his eldest daughter, in 1107, to Count Bernat III of Besalú, who died just three years later.[113]

Berenguer Ramon II of Barcelona similarly found himself in a compromised position. He was delegitimized by his alleged murder of his twin brother and coruler, Ramon Berenguer II, and eventually reduced to serving this brother's heir, the young Ramon Berenguer III.[114] As discussed earlier, Rodrigo Díaz had routed and captured Berenguer Ramon II at Tévar and then ransomed him for an enormous sum. This ransom was not the most damaging aspect of this defeat for Barcelona, however. It also cost Berenguer Ramon II the *parias* of Lleida, Tortosa, and Zaragoza and effectively ended any lingering hopes he may have had of capturing the *taifa* of Valencia.[115] With the restoration of Tarragona not yet approved by the papacy, the risk was now even higher that Alfonso VI of Castile-León might try to assert control over the restoration as well as potentially impose on Ramon Berenguer III during his minority.[116] If the challenges facing Berenguer Ramon were not enough to motivate him to emulate these other principalities and submit to the papacy, he may also have reasoned that increasing Urban II's involvement would accelerate this pope's approval of Catalonia's ecclesiastical restoration plan. Indeed, it seems likely that Bishop Berenguer of Vic and others involved in Ramon Berenguer III's regency pressured Berenguer Ramon to agree to papal suzerainty over Barcelona's territories, which he officially did in 1090.[117] According to the agreement with the papacy, Berenguer Ramon, following the Aragonese kings' example, would pay tribute signifying that everything pertaining to the counts of Barcelona was held "through the hand of the prince of the Apostles, Peter, and of his vicar, lord Urban the second, pope, and of his successors."[118]

During this period, papal legates and Iberian church leaders sought desperately but unsuccessfully to coordinate the offensives of the Aragonese, Castilians, and counties of Catalonia to serve the ecclesiastical reform effort. Indeed, church authorities increasingly had to content themselves with symbolic influence rather than direct control. Papal correspondence with Sancho Ramírez and his successors boldly, yet only vaguely, urged them to push ahead with territorial expansion within their sector of the Peninsula.[119]

Popes were so eager to stimulate territorial conquest that they facilitated use of church property and offices in a manner that openly violated the core tenets of the Gregorian Reform. For example, both Alexander II and Gregory VII conferred on Sancho Ramírez and his successors the right to distribute the churches they could conquer from Muslim territory or construct in their kingdom.[120] Even though these popes explicitly excluded from these concessions authority over the restoration of bishoprics, lay rulers neverthe-less continued to influence greatly (and in some cases largely monopolize) the postconquest establishment of dioceses. Direct papal involvement in such restorations in the eastern Peninsula was generally sporadic and chan-neled through lay rulers as much as via church leaders.[121]

Thus, after working systematically to advance the concept that these Ibe-rian principalities and their ecclesiastical institutions belonged to Saint Peter, popes and other extralocal church authorities were obliged to defer control over the dynamics of territorial expansionism and diocesan restoration to rulers and local church leaders. Although certain popes did remind these potentates that tithes, first fruits, and other ecclesiastical incomes should belong to churches, they made few attempts to dictate or regulate their poli-cies. Accordingly, tithe usurpation and other abuses quickly developed into a rampant and ingrained problem within both existing and restored dioceses.[122]

The Politics of Restoration: Tarragona

Authorities within and outside northeastern Iberia had long harbored strong opinions regarding the possibility of restoring the archiepiscopal see of Tar-ragona. Since the ninth century, it had remained a controversial objective due to its alignment with the aspirations of lay and religious leaders in the region. For differing reasons, these authorities longed to detach themselves from the metropolitanate of Narbonne, which had exercised temporary jurisdiction over the counties and churches of Catalonia and Aragon since Tarragona had fallen under Muslim control in the eighth century.[123] Tarragona's cap-ture and official restoration as an archbishopric therefore represented a core political and ecclesiastical objective for major stakeholders within this wider region.[124] Rulers and church leaders in the northeastern Peninsula deployed carefully selected religious ideological constructs to support their expansion-ist objectives in their campaigns to accomplish this goal.[125]

For its part, the archbishopric of Narbonne was naturally disinclined to support this restoration, which would dramatically reduce the size of its province and strip away its most valuable tithe-producing territories. Succes-sive archbishops consequently did their utmost to obstruct repeated earnest attempts to carry out this restoration.[126] As Lawrence McCrank and others have demonstrated, the implications of this potential shift in the ecclesias-tical landscape evolved considerably over the long history of attempts to restore Tarragona.[127] Even though Christian rulers clearly saw the merits of legitimizing their Peninsular policies by fitting them within ecclesiastical reform objectives, they nevertheless remained resistant to forming alliances with their Christian frontier rivals as they sought to guard and realize their competing claims to Muslim territories.[128]

So eager were various constituencies within the northeastern Peninsula to establish their own archdiocese that they made a series of attempts to restore Tarragona before the city had even been conquered. The most serious first effort to elect an archbishop occurred during the later tenth century under the oversight of Count Ramon Borrell of Barcelona.[129] Ramon Borrell's involvement had been chiefly motivated by the rising power of the viscounts of Narbonne, who were extending their political control over the archbishop and using this influence to marginalize the county of Barcelona and other principalities to the south. McCrank suspects that Ramon Borrell foresaw that the viscounts were intending to meddle with the upcoming archiepiscopal election, leading him to spring into action.[130] Rather than seeking to counteract these moves locally, the count circumvented the archbishop altogether by directly lobbying Pope John XIII to authorize Tarragona's restoration. John XIII ultimately consented and issued a bull in 971 that conferred Tarragona's archiepiscopal title to Bishop Ató of Vic and established his authority over the other bishops to the south of the Pyrenees. Ató died after only eight months, however, and a botched election suddenly sent the archiepiscopal see into a schism. After much wrangling, Tarragona's archiepiscopal status was allowed to lapse, and this territory once again fell subject to Narbonne's jurisdiction, although John XIII's bull was never formally annulled.[131]

Such campaigning for Tarragona's restoration thus was clearly intensified owing to this desire for political independence. At the same time, efforts by Catalonian and Aragonese bishops to separate their dioceses from Narbonne's archiepiscopal jurisdiction were heavily influenced by the new sensitivities generated by the emerging Gregorian Reform.[132] The corruption and misbehavior of certain Narbonnese prelates, in blatant violation of the core tenets of the reform movement, added a sense of urgency and attracted papal support to this cause. In 1051, Archbishop Guifré de Cerdanya of Narbonne defiantly sought to maintain his office even after being excommunicated by Pope Victor II.[133] It was not apparent to anyone that Catalonian stakeholders would succeed in separating from Narbonne's long-held hegemony.

Only after decades of campaigning did Catalonia's ecclesiastics manage the break that had eluded church and lay leaders alike for so long. At last, in 1078, a group of (chiefly Catalonian) bishops finally succeeded in securing a break from Narbonnese control at a legatine council convoked at Girona. Here they rejected the legate's urging that they reconcile with the archbishop and officially declared their independence from Narbonne's authority.[134]

Their ability to garner the papacy's consent, even though the occupation of Tarragona continued to elude Christian forces, indicates that there was widespread acknowledgement of Narbonne's dysfunction.

Despite this promising development, another threat to the independence of the dioceses of the northeastern Peninsula remained. Toledo's restoration under Alfonso VI of Castile-León following its capture in 1085 made the issue of Tarragona's restoration all the more urgent. Catalonia's authorities were naturally wary that Alfonso would try to use Toledo's primacy as a pretext to impose its authority over Catalonia and the Ebro region while the bishoprics of the northeast remained disconnected from Narbonne. Toledo's primacy within the Peninsula was already well established before the end of the eleventh century. In 1088, Urban II issued a vague set of bulls that seemed to indicate that the provinces of both Narbonne and Tarragona, once restored, should be subject to it.[135]

Catalonia's rulers and prelates opted not to deploy their political capital to challenge this proposed hierarchy at this time but rather focused their efforts on pushing forward to establish Tarragona as their provincial head. They accomplished this goal in the 1090s. At that time, the city remained nestled in an uninhabited and war-torn no-man's-land, some distance from stable Christian control. This forward-looking restoration had its origins as a local campaign that developed under the leadership of Bishop Berenguer de Lluçà of Vic in the late 1070s.[136] The details of Bishop Berenguer's plan were controversial in that certain dioceses stood to lose territories to the restored diocese of Tarragona since canon law and papal policy dictated that dioceses conform to their ancient limits.[137] Various bishops had been operating under the assumption that their dioceses would extend southward with the frontier and had already invested in establishing parish networks in zones now intended for Tarragona. Following papal recognition of Tarragona's restoration, Cardinal Gualter confirmed that Tarragona's ancient diocesan limits had to be respected to the letter, even if this meant that neighboring dioceses would lose control over parts of their existing territories.[138]

In making his push for Tarragona's immediate, preemptive restoration, Berenguer de Lluçà appears to have reasoned that to delay would leave open the possibility that rivals such as Castile-León or Aragon might lodge their own claims to the archdiocese. After considerable politicking to secure sufficient support from both prelates and lay rulers throughout Catalonia, Berenguer traveled to Rome in 1089 to push for the archiepiscopal see's preemptive restoration. Although Iberian church leaders and rulers were naturally supportive of episcopal restorations, preemptively restoring an archdiocese in this manner was unprecedented.[139]

Urban II and his advisors were clearly well aware of the controversial nature of the political situation and thus proceeded cautiously. This pope manifested concern over Narbonnese opposition as well as over the flagging Catalonian front with Islam.[140] Accordingly, he requested documentation confirming Tarragona's ancient status from Bishop Berenguer de Lluçà and his supporters as well as guarantees from the rulers of the region that they had to means to capture Tarragona in short order. In addition to other authoritative documentation, the Catalan bishops presented John XIII's bull of 971, which had incontrovertibly established Tarragona's restoration. The sitting archbishop of Narbonne at that time, Dalmace, was so desperate to overturn this bull that he or one of his supporters went so far as to forge a contradictory papal bull by Stephen V.[141] If these assurances and evidence were not sufficient, Berenguer Ramon II of Barcelona's willingness to submit to papal suzerainty apparently settled the issue for the pope, who issued the bull officially approving Tarragona's restoration on 1 July 1091. As a reward for his efforts and a testament to his leadership role in the campaign, Bishop Berenguer de Lluçà became interim metropolitan of the new archdiocese.[142]

This papal confirmation did not end opposition from Narbonne and certain Catalonian bishops who stood to lose diocesan territory and independence from the arrangement. Ecclesiastical affiliates were not so different from lay potentates in the region. For them, territorial expansion was tremendously politicized and caught up in the rivalries of the day. Although most religious leaders in the northeast promoted the papal reform agenda and supported the goals of territorial expansion and ecclesiastical restoration, some experienced tensions due to the landed wealth of their foundations.[143] Papal involvement, while helpful in empowering certain agendas, such as securing independence from Narbonne, could also serve to undermine these localized episcopal plans for ecclesiastical growth that had been developed hand-in-hand with local magnates.

As Urban II had feared, the capture of Tarragona ultimately required many more years of campaigning.[144] Unstable occupation of the city, permitting the metropolitanate's formal restoration, was only achieved in 1129. Periodic prodding by the papacy struggled to mobilize the local and the trans-Pyrenean military aristocracy. In spite of crusade obligations and spiritual concessions, these men often found it difficult to work together with rivals to seek to implement the papacy's vision for ecclesiastical restoration. Furthermore, the frontier Muslims' capacity for self-defense waxed and waned throughout the period, and sometimes the enterprises proved too much for Christian forces, even when a considerable number of magnates could collaborate.

A similar mixture of constraints would influence Christian campaigning in the region during the first half of the twelfth century. The course and timing of the Catalonian and Aragonese conquests that ultimately extended Christian territorial control beyond the course of the Ebro River valley were likewise conditioned by lay and ecclesiastical goals that were not always neatly aligned. Ultimately, papal sponsorship and local ecclesiastical advocacy and involvement, although certainly significant, were not sufficient in and of themselves to bring this expansionist campaigning to a successful conclusion. As we will see over the next two chapters, political and economic developments within both Muslim and Christian-ruled societies would largely determine the timing and nature of these decisive expeditions.

❧ CHAPTER 2

Competition along the Frontier

Building on the groundwork accomplished thus far, this chapter examines the rivalry between Aragon, Urgell, and Barcelona over interaction with the Upper Frontier of al-Andalus during the later eleventh and early twelfth centuries. In the pages that follow, we will witness how each of these powers sought to capitalize on the opportunities afforded by the neighboring Muslim-ruled regimes. Although these rulers clearly aspired to conquer the Ebro River valley, few managed to launch serious campaigns, and those efforts that did materialize fell far short of realizing their objectives. Here we will assess why these earlier attempts failed and begin to map out their implications for the successful expeditions and postconquest consolidation of the mid-twelfth century.

For the sake of clarity, the chapter separates analyses of the fronts with Lleida (including neighboring or dependent centers such as Zaragoza and Fraga) and Tortosa (including Tarragona) into distinct subsections, which have been labeled accordingly. As a result of this division, the discussion does not follow a rigid chronology but rather backtracks as necessary in order to explore the two developing relationships thematically. Occasional common subsections address shared influences and overlapping dynamics.

Lleida: Aragonese Intervention

Sancho Ramírez of Aragon had signaled his intentions to exert influence over the *taifa* of Lleida early on when he granted the *almunia* of Tabac, near the castle of Alguaire "in the district of Lleida," to two of his knights in 1075.[1] This territory had temporarily fallen under his control following deep raiding into the Segre River valley. However, Aragon's tenuous control over these zones soon after succumbed to Muslim counterattack. This reversal may, in turn, have convinced Sancho to focus on the contiguous expansion of his fortified frontiers along the Cinca River rather than on establishing such isolated castral satellites. Following these setbacks, he took advantage of Sancho IV of Pamplona's death in 1076, which reduced the level of competition along the frontier. He also profited from the destabilization caused by the demise of al-Muqtadir of Zaragoza in 1082 by mounting a southeastern offensive. A series of expeditions garnered the Aragonese monarch a number of important Zaragozan border fortresses: Graus (1083), Estada and Estadilla (1087), Montearagón (1088), and Monzón (1089).[2]

It is unclear whether these gains should suggest that Sancho Ramírez was preparing to move against both Zaragoza and Lleida at this point. He may have been more interested in maintaining Aragon's reputation as the most serious threat among these Muslim rulers to motivate them to continue paying him *parias*. Similar to his use of Tabac and Alguaire to pressure Lleida, Sancho Ramírez employed his new fortifications nearby, such as El Castellar up the Ebro from Zaragoza, as staging points for raiding or as defensive centers for the consolidation and settlement of territory.[3] He also redirected his military activity in these zones spontaneously in response to diplomatic opportunities, such as when al-Mundhir ibn Aḥmad of Lleida sent Sancho Ramírez a plea for aid to help contain Rodrigo Díaz de Vivar (the Cid), who was ravaging the eastern sector of his realm early in 1084. This invitation drew the Aragonese king into northern Valencia where he confronted the Cid that summer at Morella, southwest of the Ebro delta.[4] Although the campaign was theoretically in the service of Lleida as an ally, it may, as an unanticipated byproduct, have encouraged Sancho Ramírez to consider more seriously undertaking enterprises into the lower Ebro.

The extent of Sancho Ramírez's expansionist ambitions became clearer as he developed a position for capturing Huesca in the early 1090s. Over these years, he increasingly manifested a desire to control the Ebro River corridor and open up a channel to the Mediterranean for his landlocked kingdom. Territorial gains by the Aragonese in the service of these goals would begin to influence the counts of Barcelona by crowding their formerly unilateral engagement with the Muslims to the south.[5] By coordinating an attack on Tortosa with Berenguer Ramon II's assault in 1093, Sancho Ramírez secured rights to a share of Tarragona and territories up to Salou along the Mediterranean coast. A preemptive grant by the king of a chapel in Tortosa and the castle of Salou that same year appears to reveal these ambitions to move into the Ebro valley.[6] As part of this same campaign, he also likely succeeded in capturing Lleida's important fortification of Almenar, to the west of Balaguer. This new position enabled the king to mount even greater pressure on Lleida.[7] According to Xavier Eritja, the Aragonese continued to exercise lordship over Almenar, and certain rights held by the counts of Urgell in its district derived from Aragonese royal donation.[8] This collaboration between Aragon and Barcelona was only a momentary reversal of their usual rivalry.[9] Despite their established status as papal feudatories, the kings of Aragon had no strategic reasons for aiding any Barcelona-directed restoration of Tarragona and, indeed, exhibited no further signs of supporting this effort in the future.

After failing to establish a foothold in the east via this far-reaching campaign in 1093, Sancho Ramírez pursued a strategy of more conservative, closer territorial accumulation that his sons maintained during their reigns. Collectively, these Aragonese kings consolidated fortifications and castral zones in conquered lands into their defense networks and used them as staging points for campaigns against the new neighboring areas of Muslim territory. Long-distance raiding became increasingly infrequent. Pedro completed his father's earlier near victory over Huesca in 1096. He then besieged Zaragoza and captured Barbastro in 1101.[10] These new positions helped to establish Aragon's dominance in territorial expansion along the eastern corridor and would serve as important bases for mounting pressure southward toward the Ebro. Pedro devoted most of the remainder of his ten-year reign to closing in on Zaragoza, a project that remained far from completion by the time his brother, Alfonso I, succeeded him in 1104.

Aragon's eastern front at the start of Alfonso's reign was concentrated in Sobrarbe and Ribagorza and extended along the Cinca River to Fraga and along the Segre River to Lleida. Like his predecessors, Alfonso remained committed to expanding into these Andalusi cities. He coordinated his efforts against Zaragoza with maintaining pressure along the corridors to the cities of Balaguer, Lleida, and Fraga. Along this latter eastern front, he and his allied barons had to contend with the activity of the counts of Barcelona and Urgell. They also had a competing interest in maintaining the independent *taifas* of Zaragoza and Lleida, which helped shield Aragon from the recently emergent Almoravids.

Lleida: Urgell's Sphere of Influence

The county of Urgell was bounded by Aragon, the Barcelona-controlled counties of Osona / Manresa and Berga, and the territory pertaining to Muslim Lleida. Although Urgell's counts felt pressure from these generally more well-endowed neighbors, they had greater reason to be alarmed by these advances by the Aragonese, which threatened to reduce or eliminate altogether their ability to engage with the frontier.[11]

The potential for competition and alliances within this environment arguably worked to Urgell's advantage. Throughout his reign, Ermengol III's strategy was to enrich himself and his barons with monetary and territorial gains, counterbalance the pressure from the Aragonese, stabilize his eastern frontier through cooperation with Ramon Berenguer I of Barcelona while at the same time keeping sufficient distance so as to maintain his county's independence. In addition to periodically swearing general oaths of fidelity to Ramon Berenguer,[12] Ermengol also subscribed to more specific agreements with the count of Barcelona that provided for mutual assistance and targeted precise opportunities within the frontier environment. In 1058, for example, the two counts agreed to coordinate their engagement and support one another in their mutual war with Aḥmad ibn Sulaymān al-Muqtadir of Zaragoza and not to forge peace with the Muslim ruler without the other's prior consent. The concord anticipated a future assault on Zaragoza and established that Ermengol would provide a third of the required troops and cavalry and, in return, receive a one-third share of whatever they conquered. The two men also decided what castles Ermengol would be permitted to build and man with his castellans and agreed to divvy up any *parias* they might collect from Zaragoza as the result of these endeavors, with the count of Urgell again receiving a minority one-third share. Because these castles to be built were associated with the existing towns of Pilzán and Purroy, located near Benabarre in the Ribagorza along the southwestern sector of Ermengol's frontier with Lleida, they enabled the count of Barcelona to compete with the Aragonese for territory that would otherwise have been inaccessible due to the positioning of his domains.[13] Ermengol and Ramon Berenguer updated their arrangement some time later, in 1064, the same year that Ermengol would launch his successful campaign against Barbastro. Here again, Ermengol established Ramon Berenguer as his superior lord and committed to respecting the boundaries and castles of his counties of Barcelona, Osona, and Girona and *"paria* from Spain" that, Ermengol self-servingly noted, "you have acquired through my counsel."[14]

Aragon's gains under the leadership of Sancho Ramírez likely encouraged Urgell's subsequent counts, Ermengol IV (r. 1066–92) and Ermengol
V (r. 1092–1102), to build upon this growing tradition of collaboration with
the counts of Barcelona. They did this as a means of intensifying their competitive engagement with the *taifa* of Lleida by pressing into the territories
claimed by its dependent town of Balaguer. When Ermengol IV established
a *convenientia* with Ramon Berenguer I during the final decade of the latter's
reign, between 1066 and 1076, he secured control of a group of strategically
important castles that included Àlos, Artesa, and Montmagastre. Ermengol
promised to join Ramon Berenguer annually on his first raid (*prima hoste*)
into al-Andalus. As an added motivator, Ermengol was expressly permitted to keep whatever booty he captured entirely for himself. By this time,
the aforementioned war with al-Muqtadir of Zaragoza had ended, with
him once again resuming his tributary status. Accordingly, the agreement
expressly excluded from this raiding his lands as well as those governed by
the *taifa* ruler of Lleida, Yusūf ibn Sulaymān al-Mudhaffar (r. 1046–85).[15]

Ermengol IV maintained a similar alliance with Ramon Berenguer I's twin
sons and successors, Ramon Berenguer II and Berenguer Ramon II, with a
backward-looking *convenientia* that was arranged during the first five years of
their shared government, between 1076 and 1081. Notwithstanding Ermengol's recent concord with Ramon Berenguer I, this agreement provided for
him to have the same arrangement as his father, Ermengol III, with respect
to land and *parias* obtained from the Muslims. The renewal was clearly necessary not only because of Barcelona's regime change but also because war
with al-Muqtadir of Zaragoza had flared up owing largely to intervention by
the Cid.[16] Ramon Berenguer's sons and their advisors must have thought it
prudent to ensure, contractually, Ermengol's support in this conflict. They
also likely wanted to guarantee that the count would coordinate his diplomacy with Andalusi rulers with theirs and, in particular, not sign any unilateral peace accords. Although these counts were renewing a time-honored
alliance, they continued to be wary of one another and sought assurances.
Here the twin counts of Barcelona demanded that Ermengol send them ten
hostages as a surety that he would deliver the *paria* gold he was supposed to
retrieve from Dénia.[17]

Owing to such partnerships, the Ermengol counts secured their prominence as players within the broader Christian-Muslim diplomatic scene and
reaped the rewards that came with that level of access. This politicking, and
the ongoing relationship with Barcelona, permitted them to continue to
advance their county's local frontier with Muslim lands. Over the course
of the eleventh century, various agents within the counties of Urgell and

Barcelona had captured and fortified the eastern portion of the plain of Mascançà, a zone of Andalusi origin that roughly corresponds with the Pla d'Urgell *comarca*, thereby pushing deeper into Lleida's sphere of influence.[18] Donations of lands within the zone, many of which were tellingly compartmentalized into fortified districts, serve as a rough measure of this advance.[19] Furthermore, the seizure of a number of Andalusi fortifications supported this expansion; these include Guissona (captured ca. 1010–24), Montclar (today Montclar d'Urgell, ca. 1030), Agramunt (1051), and Tàrrega (1058).[20] Joan Eusebi García i Biosca has suggested that pressure along the corridor running from Balaguer to Corbins to Lleida had an important east–west component emanating from Guissona and Montclar.[21] In 1079, for example, Ermengol IV granted one of his men an allod in the district of Balaguer, situated between the Segre River and the road leaving the town.[22] At the same time, the county of Barcelona had moved from its eastern position and pushed its limits into the south of the plain along the castral territories of Anglesola and Sidamon, a short distance from Lleida.[23]

Building on this piecemeal, decades-long advance, the Ermengols invested heavily in their frontier castle of Gerb over the 1080s and 1090s and used it in tandem with neighboring fortifications to support the accumulation and settlement of new territory to the north and east of Balaguer.[24] Ermengol IV, whose association with this fortification was so strong that he took the name "El de Gerb," granted one of these castles, Bellcaire, to the monastery of Sant Sadurní de Tavèrnoles in 1091. The charter of donation denoted the formerly Andalusi territory pertaining to Bellcaire's district, assigned the monks its tithes and first fruits, and obliged them to construct a castle-church. Such directives, however, proved to be overly optimistic as the monks of Sant Sadurní failed to settle Bellcaire's castral district. The earliest extant charter of settlement in fact dates from 1139, when Ermengol VI (r. 1102–54), rather than these monks, assigned Bellcaire's surrounding lands to six settlers.[25] Donations from this period tended to establish provisions for future settlement, even though the likelihood of it was rare due to the zone's insecurity. In the early 1090s, for instance, Ermengol IV awarded the bishop of Urgell the castle of Campvim, which bordered the castral districts of Os (today Os de Balaguer), Castelló de Farfanya, and Llorenç (today Sant Llorenç de Montgai) and the territory claimed by Muslim Balaguer. The bishop, in turn, enfeoffed Campvim to Guillem and Gombau Bernat in 1094, who were required to pay him half of any tithes they might collect there.[26]

Given the volatility of this environment over these years, these castles were naturally better suited for defense and raiding than for offering adequate protection to settlers. Urgell did succeed in maintaining pressure on Balaguer, as indicated by Ermengol IV's receipt of *parias* from the *taifa* of Lleida in 1081, 1090, and 1092.[27] Likely motivated by Lleida's failure to pay tribute as well as by these aforementioned Aragonese territorial gains, shortly after his predecessor's death, Ermengol V began a series of unsuccessful attempts to use these castles to mount expeditions to conquer Balaguer, first in 1092 and then again in 1101 or 1102. In 1102, however, Ermengol V lost his life fighting the Almoravids at Mollerussa, between Lleida and Tàrrega, leaving the fates of his young heir and county in jeopardy.[28]

Young Ermengol VI's regent and grandfather, the Leonese exile Pedro Ansúrez, secured control over his county and soon completed Ermengol IV's project by capturing Balaguer in 1105.[29] Pedro Ansúrez's regency was unusual in a number of respects that gave Ermengol better than a fighting chance to preserve his dynasty.[30] Not only did Pedro assume the title of "count of Urgell" and thus position himself as a coruler with the legitimacy to make major decisions on Ermengol VI's behalf. He furthermore steered Urgell's diplomacy in an entirely new direction by allying with Count Ramon Berenguer III of Barcelona and inviting him in the push to take Balaguer. Although this overture earned Pedro and young Ermengol the support that had so clearly eluded Ermengol V in his numerous campaigns leading up to his death, it was also risky because it forced Urgell to expose its already vulnerable castral positions pressuring Balaguer and the *taifa* of Lleida to a formidable competitor.

The counts of Urgell and Barcelona negotiated this alliance shortly before embarking on their successful campaign against Balaguer in 1105. The parties agreed that the count of Barcelona would receive half of Balaguer and its fortress (known as the *zuda*) as well as control and partial lordship over a number of the most strategically important fortifications in this zone: Llorenç, Gerb, Castelló de Farfanya, Alguaire, and Os.[31] Collaborating with Urgell in this fashion, during a phase of considerable instability for the Ermengol dynasty, was a shrewd strategic move for the count of Barcelona. Ramon Berenguer III not only ensured himself a prominent role in future territorial acquisitions by Urgell along its frontiers but also helped to reinforce his status as its overlord when the young Ermengol was just getting onto his feet.

As a further sign of the count of Barcelona's growing influence over Urgell and this sector of its frontier, Pedro Ansúrez and Ermengol refashioned their agreement with him in the wake of Balaguer's capture and confirmed his share of the acquisition.[32] In addition to renewing the divisions they had agreed upon before the conquest, they joined the viscount of Girona and Lower Urgell, Guerau Ponç II de Cabrera, and other nobles from the county in commending themselves as Ramon Berenguer's men, "with [their] hands . . . in homage (*hominio*)." They reserved only preferential fidelity to

"Count Pedro and his wife and grandson [i.e., Ermengol]." Ermengol also gave Ramon Berenguer control over one of the more strategically important castles in the zone, Albesa, which had not been addressed by their prior arrangement. Although Ermengol retained usufruct of this castle, the count of Barcelona received the right of *potestas* (i.e., the ability to reclaim it at will).

Ramon Berenguer and his advisors strategically crafted these agreements to enhance his county's access to the front with the *taifa* of Lleida. First, they reduced the risk that other parties (such as the Aragonese) might end up joining their alliance group or displacing them as Urgell's partners in these holdings. They did this by making Pedro Ansúrez and Ermengol promise to give Ramon Berenguer or his successors their rights to Balaguer should either of them die without heirs to inherit their stakes. In return, Ramon Berenguer pledged not to interfere in their lordship over Albesa or Balaguer against their will. This commitment was significant, particularly because it compromised the valuable right of *potestas* he had reserved. He also had Ermengol and Pedro agree that, in return for his laissez-faire stance on their administration of Balaguer, they would cede him power over Lleida. They were not to invite other magnates into its lordship without his express consent. Ramon Berenguer thus seems to have been content to consign unilateral control over Balaguer to Urgell in return for undiluted rights to engage with Lleida.

Lleida: Competition

Ramon Berenguer III's calculated effort to monopolize the strategic benefits of Balaguer's capture nevertheless failed to block Aragon from involving itself. Around 1109, without any apparent regard to the restrictions of his 1105 agreement with the count of Barcelona, Pedro Ansúrez granted Alfonso of Aragon his stake in the *zuda* of Balaguer along with shares of fortifications in its vicinity, including the aforementioned castles of Llorenç and Albesa.[33] This development was far from surprising, however. As Ramon Berenguer and his supporters must have been well aware, there were clear precedents for Aragonese influence over Urgell. In addition to marriage ties that had bound Urgell closely with Aragon since early in the eleventh century, Pedro Ansúrez, as regent and temporary "count" of Urgell, had already pledged his fidelity to Alfonso, as past counts had done to prior Aragonese monarchs. Ermengol VI would be expected to do likewise. At one point, Pedro I of Aragon had even considered the possibility of inheriting Urgell himself, via shared bloodlines.[34]

Fortunately for Ramon Berenguer III, however, direct Aragonese influence over the county of Urgell in general, and Balaguer in particular, was on the decline in the years preceding Alfonso's death and the ensuing union of Barcelona and Aragon in the mid- to late 1130s. By 1110, Alfonso had already divested himself of at least some of the holdings in Balaguer that he had received from Pedro Ansúrez around the time of the conquest.[35] Eritja has observed that the Aragonese involvement with Urgell nevertheless endured and imparted a more lasting influence over the systematization of defense around Balaguer and Lleida over the first half of the twelfth century. He credits the increased use of defensive territorial units known as *almuniae* along Urgell's frontiers, and the resultant reduction of so-called *quadrae* units in charters prescribing fortification and settlement, to Aragonese influence.[36] Indeed, Philippe Sénac has noticed that the first systematic use of *almuniae* appeared after the Aragonese conquest of Monzón in 1089.[37] These strong, time-honored ties with Aragon notwithstanding, Urgell was increasingly drawn into the crystallizing hegemony of the house of Barcelona over the early decades of the twelfth century as its nobility and prominent ecclesiastical institutions played a dominant role in Christian territorial expansion southward toward Lleida. This trend may explain why Urgell pulled away from further participation in the Aragonese conquests after Balaguer.[38]

Ramon Berenguer III persisted in his effort to establish a presence along this western front with Lleida. In addition to his collaborative dealings with Urgell, he forged a key alliance not long afterward, in 1113, with the same Guerau Ponç II mentioned earlier, who was viscount of Girona and Lower Urgell and lord over the important strongholds of Cubells, Camarasa, Casserres, and Estopiñán scattered to the north of Balaguer.[39] Ties with these castles dovetailed with Ramon Berenguer's existing positions in the area. Notably, castles in the southwest of the county of Manresa originally established by his grandfather, such as Anglesola (1079) and Tàrrega (1058), enhanced the count's access to Lleida.[40] As Alfonso conquered along the Ebro River, capturing Zaragoza in 1118 and Tudela in 1119, the count of Barcelona may have grown concerned that the Aragonese would soon seize Lleida and be in a position to push into the lower Ebro valley toward Tortosa. Possibly owing to such fears, Ramon Berenguer focused increasing attention on moving into and alongside Urgell's frontier and on developing contact with the territory of Lleida, furthering his movement away from his dynasty's one-time exclusive fixation on Tortosa.[41]

Tortosa: Early Campaigning

Before we further address Barcelona's growing interest in Lleida, we first need to explore how the county had developed its existing front with Tortosa over the preceding decades within the context of Tarragona's restoration campaign. Although this ecclesiastical project was certainly an important consideration for the counties of Catalonia in formulating their policies toward the Muslim territories of the lower Ebro valley, it was by no means the only one. In keeping with what we discussed in the last chapter, although papal and local church sources from the 1090s are essential for piecing together the ecclesiastical context of Christian campaigns into the Ebro valley, taken alone they provide a skewed picture of the involvement of other factors linked to developing political affairs in the region.

The pressure from Urban II and certain Catalonian prelates on Berenguer Ramon II and his men to furnish the military support necessary to complete Tarragona's restoration reached a climax during the late 1080s and early 1090s. As we have seen, Tarragona's nominal reinstatement as an archdiocese had relied on papal approval, which, in turn, had hinged on Urban II's sense of the achievability of the project. Accordingly, the Iberian cardinal-legate Rainer of Bleda, the future Paschal II, together with Bishop Berenguer de Lluçà of Vic and other regional church leaders, had sought certain specific guarantees from rulers such as Berenguer Ramon II of Barcelona and lesser magnates with strategic positioning along the southern and western fringes of the counties of Catalonia that they would contribute to Tarragona's capture and defense.[42] Already early in his pontificate, Urban II had written to the counts of Urgell, Besalú, Empúries, Rosselló, and Cerdanya to urge them to remain in order to fight to restore Tarragona rather than join the armies on the crusade to the Holy Land.[43]

Such prodding and encouragement by this diverse group of church leaders eventually yielded results. Tellingly, two memorial charters that were produced in Vic during Urban II's pontificate presented a plan for the Barcelona-led campaign to secure Tarragona. These documents were clearly colored by papal desires for a formidable assault designed expressly to support the restoration.[44] Collectively, they reveal the composition of the group of Catalonian knights and magnates willing to contribute to a future campaign led by the count of Barcelona to move on Tarragona. They also document the working plan for funding and managing the infrastructural demands of the restoration.

Unfortunately, the memorial charters shed little light on the aspirations motivating these men to participate in the campaigns. We cannot use them to confirm whether these agents conceptualized the restoration of Tarragona as a goal worth fighting for in and of itself. Other circumstantial evidence, however, does provide some clues. These fighters pledged themselves to the archbishop as vassals of the newly restored see of Tarragona and swore to fast as a penance until the archdiocese had been decisively restored. Their service would earn them the then-customary full remission of their sins and penance obligations.[45] The men inventoried in the Vic *memoriae* also must have been conscious of what they stood to gain, or lose, materially from participating in this campaigning. It was no accident, for instance, that Berenguer Domnuç, castellan of Terrassa, prepared his will before departing on the "hoste munita Tortosa . . . in partes Ispanie."[46] Most of them were from less well-established families and had already served with Berenguer Ramon II in his failed campaigns against the Cid leading up to their defeat at Tévar.[47] They were highly incentivized to engage in operations that stood to enlarge their territorial positions and garner them new lands within the Camp de Tarragona and beyond, toward the Muslim-controlled Ebro River valley. In his prospective infeudation of Tarragona to the papacy from this same time, Berenguer Ramon II had already planned for a division of the territorial spoils from the captured city.[48] In a separate enactment, he also pledged to these specific supporters the lands in Tarragona and its countryside that they, in turn, would be expected to help settle and defend.[49]

Even though these planning documents identified Tarragona as the primary target during their preparations for the campaign, there are reasons to believe that their architects also intended, from the outset, to engage with the *taifa* of Tortosa to the south. Although they had been abandoned, Tarragona and its *camp* nevertheless fell under Tortosa's claimed sphere of influence and were within easy striking distance of the *taifa*. Furthermore, given Tarragona's abandoned state, funding for the archiepiscopal see's reconstruction, which the count and his supporters had pledged to contribute in generous quantities from the plunder they expected to seize, was more likely to come from the bustling economy of Tortosa and its district.[50]

The count and his supporters may have had other reasons to target Tortosa at this time. Pere Benito has noticed that certain campaigns designed to capture territories from the Muslims followed periods of agrarian crisis.[51] It is possible that Berenguer Ramon II's campaign to stabilize Tarragona and its surrounding territories and push the county of Barcelona's extent into the fertile and productive lower Ebro valley cultivated by the *taifa* of Tortosa was tied to food shortages that same year. In the spring of 1093, just months before the count's campaigns commenced, sources document a famine afflicting the whole of the Christian Mediterranean region, from Italy to Galicia. In March of that year, for example, Catalan nobles exchanged lands in Aiguatèbia with the canons of the see of Urgell for lands in Galicia in what may have been an attempt to diversify their respective holdings in case of further food shortages.[52]

As the preparations proceeded, rather than merely fortifying Tarragona as Ramon Berenguer I had once sought to do, Berenguer Ramon II and his advisors envisioned a more aggressive and potentially devastating direct attack on Tortosa in 1093. One reference to the operation appears to connect the siege of Tortosa with the goal of restoration. Berenguer Ramon promised fifty thousand *nummi* to Tarragona from the plunder of the sacking of Tortosa (*ex expolia Tortosa*). This was perhaps an indication that he viewed the move against Tortosa as providing both the security and the material proceeds necessary to support the metropolitanate's restoration.[53] Broadening the effort to involve a direct attack on Tortosa naturally required more sophisticated planning. Berenguer Ramon and his supporters apparently decided that blockading the city from the Ebro would increase the likelihood of success, and thus commissioned a combined fleet of around four hundred Genoese and Pisan ships to establish a position in the river.[54] Such use of Italian naval forces would become a characteristic of all subsequent expeditions against the city, including the final, successful assault in 1148. Even though Barcelona possessed a considerable fleet of its own, which Berenguer Ramon and his brother had once enumerated in order to plan a joint campaign "per mare et per terram" in 1080, the Italian republics offered valuable skills, not least an unparalleled prowess in siege warfare.[55] Although Berenguer Ramon did ultimately launch the expedition in 1093, no documentation has surfaced to help us reconstruct what transpired. All we know is that Tortosa successfully resisted whatever assault Berenguer Ramon's forces were able to muster.[56]

In the years after he assumed full control of his county, Ramon Berenguer III of Barcelona continued to launch expeditions into the lower Ebro valley. He achieved some modest gains and was able to occupy some of Tortosa's northern lands, thanks in part to the Cid's disruption and later occupation of Valencia, which forced Tortosa's ruler, Sulaymān ibn Hūd, to concern himself with two fronts.[57] The limited evidence regarding these efforts offers only the sketchiest of details. For example, the last testament of the knight Guillem Lobaton indicates that he was mortally wounded and died near Tortosa on 14 October 1094. Guillem may have been part of a larger expedition or a small raiding party, or possibly he was merely attacked while traveling through the area.[58] We can confirm that, by January of 1097, the count of Barcelona was devoting his resources to acquiring a position in Amposta, an important Muslim defensive site a short distance down the Ebro from Tortosa.[59] It is unlikely that the Muslims had an existing fortress at Amposta. Arabic sources do not mention one, and archeological research dates the oldest parts of the castle of Amposta to between the second half of the eleventh and the early twelfth centuries.[60] The combination of archeological and textual evidence suggests that the Christians were the first to establish an important fortification on the site.

The young count was overburdened by this campaigning and soon sought to involve allies in the effort to establish and defend this position. The fact that the First Crusade had been called in the fall of 1095 likely reduced the availability of foreign knights and Italian naval forces.[61] Ramon Berenguer III was, however, able to enlist the war-seasoned count, Artau II of Pallars Sobirà, who employed his supporters to help establish Amposta as a fortified stronghold. Shortly following his aforementioned preparations, Ramon Berenguer prospectively enfeoffed the castle site to him along with the whole of the city of Tortosa and its *zuda* in a *convenientia* formulated in January 1097.[62] Nevertheless, only a few months later, after this castle had been built at Amposta, the count shifted course and granted the holding, its church, and a wide assortment of ecclesiastical holdings and prerogatives in the wider area to the monastery of Sant Cugat del Vallès.[63]

This charter of donation to Sant Cugat demonstrates that, despite papal exhortations to enact Tarragona's restoration, Ramon Berenguer III's policy, at this point, prioritized the more lucrative and strategically significant objective of Tortosa. Ramon Berenguer pragmatically utilized Tortosa's existing political boundaries to delimit the donation, in conferring, for example, "all churches, which are or were in the entire kingdom of Tortosa." At the same time, he stressed Tortosa's credentials as an ancient bishopric and its deplorable state, devoid of clergy and a congregation "on account of the destruction and oppression of the Muslims," which had earned it attention from Christian forces. The count used this alleged depopulation as a justification for investing San Cugat with full authority over the election of Tortosa's future bishop and temporary control of its churches and prerogatives. There is no evidence by this point to suggest that Urban II was supportive of this strategy that viewed the capture of Tortosa as vital to Tarragona's stability or as a comparably pressing cause in its own right.[64] None of this pope's letters mentions Tortosa or the offensives managed by the count of Barcelona and other magnates to capture it. Furthermore, the aforementioned *memoriae* of Vic describing Berenguer Ramon II's initial venture, which had been crafted with the papal agenda in mind, did not acknowledge Tortosa as an objective of the count's army.

Lleida: Activity after Balaguer

During the early decades of the twelfth century, as the counts of Barcelona were continuing to develop, and justify ecclesiastically, this campaign to secure Tortosa, they were also engaged in extending increased influence over the counts of Urgell. By the time of Ramon Berenguer IV's reign, Urgell would find itself co-opted into Barcelona's frontier engagement with neighboring Muslim territories. This emerging dependency did not, however, automatically signify that Urgell would become directly involved in the conflicts with Tortosa. Faithfully dedicated as they were to the expansive operations elaborated by their ancestors since early in the previous century, the twelfth-century counts of Urgell remained focused on the traditional conflict along their local boundary with Muslim territory and, in particular, on engagement with Lleida.[65] Yet this focus did not prevent them from collaborating on extralocal projects. On occasion they did participate in such campaigns, such as the expedition to the Balearic Islands in 1114 coordinated by Ramon Berenguer III and the defensive measures taken against the *walī* of Zaragoza's subsequent raid into the plain of Barcelona. Furthermore, as suggested by these *memoriae* of Vic, castellans entrusted with important fortifications along the *marca* of the county of Urgell, such as Gerb, had pledged to participate in the Tarragonian restoration effort.[66]

A shift in Count Ermengol VI's regency, with the departure of Pedro Ansúrez in the early twelfth century, served to increase Urgell's exposure to Barcelona's influence. Up to this point, Pedro Ansúrez had continued to assist the young Count Ermengol VI with the customary distribution of conquered lands that reinforced his ties with important nobles and ecclesiastical institutions within his county.[67] During Pedro Ansúrez's tenure, Urgell had warded off lasting changes in its relationships with Aragon, Castile-León, and Barcelona and carefully maintained a neutral and relatively independent position among these larger and threatening neighbors.[68] When Pedro Ansúrez departed for Castile in 1109, Guerau Ponç II de Cabrera, the viscount of Girona and Lower Urgell, assumed the regency. His connections with the county of Barcelona were well established, and his advisory role during the remaining years of Ermengol's minority helped steer the county toward forming bonds with Ramon Berenguer III and away from Aragon and Castile-León to the detriment of its fragile neutrality.[69]

As he assumed greater control over his county during these early years of the twelfth century, Ermengol VI set to work consolidating and reconstructing his new defensive line to the south of Balaguer. He introduced new castellans into his castral network, such as Ramon Arnal, who received the tower of Afif (near Agramunt) from the count from 1120.[70] Nevertheless, Ermengol made few territorial or even strategic advances before 1122, when he captured the long sought-after castle of Albesa, located directly north of Lleida and close to the Noguera Ribagorzana River.[71]

Forces already directly allied with Barcelona witnessed more significant gains in this zone, which, in turn, served as an inroad for Ramon Berenguer III to enlarge his presence there. Ermengol VI's former regent, Guerau Ponç, for example, captured the castles of Os, Llorenç, Algerri, Almenar, and Castelló de Farfanya between 1115 and 1116. These victories enabled him to establish control over the zone in between Balaguer and the Noguera Ribagorzana River and stabilize the east–west line of defense. Although the fidelity Guerau Ponç had pledged to Ramon Berenguer III in 1106 may originally have been based on his holdings in the viscounty of Girona, before long the count of Barcelona was imposing on these new acquisitions around Balaguer.[72] With the viscount's newly formed castral network as a fallback, Ramon Berenguer III soon made the bold move of seizing the castle of Corbins, which was seated at the junction of the Noguera Ribagorzana and Segre Rivers just a few kilometers from Lleida.[73]

Thus, already some time before Urgell's capture of Albesa around 1122, Ramon Berenguer III and his close allies had accumulated castles that were arguably as well positioned to mount pressure on Lleida as the fortifications under Ermengol VI's control. Charters from this period document the count of Barcelona's careful management of these positions. In 1118, for example, he granted Arnau Berenguer d'Anglesola the castles of Alcoletge and Corbins ("per fevum") along with two-thirds of each castle's territory and incomes. In addition to honoring the count's right to lodge in the castle (*statica*), Arnau Berenguer promised to support him with raiding (*hosts, cavalcadas*) and other sorts of engagements with the Muslims of Lleida positioned just a short distance from each castle.[74] Similarly, the following year, Ramon Berenguer gave Guillem Dalmau de Cervera a large share of the lordship of Castelldans and full rights to Gebut, to the south of Lleida, with comparable terms.[75] These agreements presupposed that castellans would attempt to populate their castral zones. Such work would supplement the settlement projects outlined by other extant charters that sought to consolidate portions of the deserted buffer zone between Christian and Muslim territory, which extended along the *marca* of Urgell and continued to the south of Tàrrega along the northern fringes of Tarragona's *camp*.[76]

Further to the west, Alfonso of Aragon was busying himself with campaigning down the Ebro valley, sometimes in collaboration with Norman troops. Such French knights were attracted to campaigns in the Peninsula by a combination of preaching publicizing the potential spiritual rewards, the promise of booty, and diverse propaganda in the form of *chansons de geste* and other vernacular genres.[77] Since the conquest of Balaguer, Alfonso had maintained and occasionally extended his positions around Lleida with castles such as Tamarite (de Litera) and San Esteban (de Litera), both of which fell under his control in 1107.[78] These new acquisitions served to buffer the Aragonese front from rival fortifications like Castillonroy, a short distance to the east. Although the Aragonese had long been blocked by competitors from conquering southward along the Noguera Ribagorzana River, Alfonso had cultivated an area of advance facing Lleida and Fraga along the Cinca River that he had stabilized by drawing settlers to centers like Alcolea (de Cinca).[79]

Aragonese military activity around Lleida during the years leading up to the 1120s was minimal, especially in comparison to Aragon's tremendous progress against Zaragoza, further up the Ebro, that culminated in that city's capture in 1118. Alfonso's troops were spread thin in the effort to balance the two objectives. At the same time, they were challenged by forces from Barcelona and Urgell, which did their utmost to impede Alfonso's expansion down the Cinca and Segre River valleys. For their part, Barcelona and Urgell benefited from Aragon's campaigning to the west, and not only because it distracted Alfonso from fully competing with them against Lleida. The disruption and alarm caused by Alfonso's successful capture of Zaragoza likely helped them extort further tribute from Lleida, Tortosa, and Valencia beginning in 1118.[80]

Tortosa and Lleida: The Almoravids

The influence of the Almoravids over the zone of the Upper Frontier of al-Andalus can help explain why Christian forces did not achieve even greater territorial gains during these early decades of the twelfth century. Resistance managed by the Banū Hūd, who governed or exercised influence over the Muslim societies along the Ebro valley, initially buffered the Catalans and Aragonese from the approach made by these centralizing North Africans. This situation may even have served as a further disincentive for Christian principalities in the northeastern Peninsula to push hastily to conquer either Tortosa or Lleida, which would have increased their exposure to this volatility within al-Andalus. The continued receipt of gold tribute also must have played a role. Tortosa's ruler, for example, paid *parias* consistently over the years leading up to the Almoravid takeover (in 1091, 1095, 1096, 1098, and 1099).[81]

Following the fall of Toledo in 1085, fearful of further defeats at the hands of the Christians, Andalusi specialists in religious law (*faqīh/s*) and local judges (*qāḍī/s*) within the *Thaghr* had naively appealed to the Almoravids for aid.[82] Before long, these North Africans had moved in rapidly to capitalize on this situation. Over the space of about a decade, they would assume control over all of the Hūdid *taifa* states of the Upper Frontier. Although the Cid's occupation of ʿĀmirid Valencia between 1094 and his death in 1099 sheltered that kingdom for a time, it too eventually fell prey to the Almoravids, in 1102, when forces under the command of Alfonso VI of Castile-León evacuated his widow.[83]

This consolidation of the *Thaghr* under Almoravid power quickly confirmed the worst fears of the Christian rulers and potentates in the northeastern Peninsula. Indeed, when the North Africans assumed the governance of Tortosa, their forces continued to raid further to the north and eventually pushed Barcelona's forces back to the Gayá River, not far from where they had retreated during the later tenth-century campaigns of al-Manṣūr.[84] A charter from 1107 documenting a pious donation to the monastery of Sant Cugat del Vallès by Ramon Berenguer III evoked the turbulent nature of these times. The count beseeched that "omnipotent God grant me victory over the Muslims invading our territories."[85] In 1108, the Almoravids launched a raid that penetrated as deeply as the Penedès, south of Barcelona.[86] Paschal II wrote an urgent letter to Bishop Garcia of Burgos, a former papal legate, in 1109 in which he noted that the attempt to recover Tarragona had failed and that the city was once again overrun and uninhabitable. He lamented the setback dealt by the Almoravids to the overall effort to reclaim and restore ecclesiastical territories in Iberia.[87]

Tortosa was the first of the *Thaghr taifas* to succumb to Almoravid control, around 1099.[88] Hūdid-controlled Zaragoza was able to coordinate its defense for another decade but eventually succumbed in 1110. The last ruler of the Banū Hūd, Sayyid al-Dawla, died in 1102, but Lleida was not formally assumed by the Almoravid, Muhammad ibn al-Hajj, until 1111.[89] Each of these cities then naturally served as staging points for assaults on Christian-ruled territories.

On the other hand, this disruptive transition from the long-serving Hūdid dynasty to Almoravid control increased Zaragoza's vulnerability to Christian attack. Furthermore, not long after assuming power, the Almoravids imprudently pushed on with further raiding rather than devoting their attention to defending and consolidating their new acquisitions. When the Almoravid *walī* of Zaragoza launched a costly and unsuccessful campaign directed at Barcelona in 1115, for example, Count Ermengol VI of Urgell met and routed that Muslim army with the help of a coalition that included troops from Barcelona.[90] In spite of such miscalculations, the Almoravids would nevertheless continue to control the vast majority of the *Thaghr* until the arrival of the Almohads shortly before the midpoint of the twelfth century.

Tortosa: Rallying Support for a New Campaign

These changed conditions would ultimately help realign the formerly divergent policies and objectives of the papacy and local rulers regarding the war
effort in the northeastern Peninsula. In the aftermath of Berenguer Ramon
II's operations in the 1090s, the papacy had gradually come to terms with the
fact that the capture of Tortosa needed to be an integral part of the movement to secure Tarragona's restoration. Although papal authorities were no
doubt influenced by the justifications that Berenguer Ramon and his supporters had made to broaden that campaign, Paschal II's prior experiences as
the Iberian cardinal-legate also must have played a role in this shift. He surely
started his pontificate in 1099 with an unusually finely grained understanding of the political situation.[91]

The plan for the ecclesiastical reconstructions of Tortosa and Lleida, as
well as the composition of the military campaigning that would make those
restorations possible, evolved out of coordination and preparation over the
early years of the twelfth century. As we witnessed in the last chapter, Archbishop Berenguer de Lluçà of Tarragona had been the primary architect of
the political and ecclesiastical enterprise of territorial expansion into the
Ebro valley and, accordingly, a key orchestrator of the failed campaigns of
the 1090s. Building on that mixed legacy, Oleguer Bonestruga, first as bishop
of Barcelona and later (from 1118) as archbishop of Tarragona, proved
instrumental in coordinating a refreshed ecclesiastical plan for expansion
in the northeastern Peninsula with Ramon Berenguer III's preparations to
restructure offensives against Tortosa and Lleida.[92]

Even though Bishop Oleguer and Ramon Berenguer III were both
deceased by the time a successful campaign captured the Andalusi territories
of the lower Ebro and Segre valleys, their preparatory work would heavily
influence the successful campaigns of the late 1140s as well as the organization of the restorations of the episcopal sees of Tortosa and Lleida. Their
work to strengthen ties with trans-Pyrenean ecclesiastical institutions and
noble families was especially fundamental, as each of these groups would
exert considerable influence over the conquests. Ramon Berenguer III succeeded in adding the county of Provence to his titles in 1110, a union that
would further stimulate the involvement of knights in this area in Peninsular campaigns waged by Barcelona.[93] Bishop Oleguer was initially reluctant
to face the challenges inherent in the role of archbishop and temporarily
fled Barcelona to the north to serve as abbot of Saint Ruf in Avignon after
he was tapped by Ramon Berenguer III. This detour incidentally helped
establish the influence of this reformist house over Catalonia's ecclesiastical

restorations and development in the twelfth century, as the first bishops and canons implanted at Tortosa and Lleida would be drawn from this house of Saint Ruf.[94]

Ties with military resources in the wider western Mediterranean also bore fruit and continued to influence the campaigns organized by Ramon Berenguer III and his successors throughout the twelfth century. This count's expedition in 1114 against the Balearic Islands of Eivissa (Ibiza) and Mallorca, for instance, relied heavily on Pisan naval support and involved a diverse list of noble and municipal supporters from Narbonne and Rosselló, the dioceses of Beziers, Nîmes, and Montpellier, and many localities in Provence. The Pisans may have deliberately excluded the Genoese from this effort, as relations between the two city-states had grown less friendly during these years. The two republics began warring soon after the expedition and would not arrive at a formal peace until the 1130s.[95]

This offensive against the Balearic Islands was orchestrated by mercantile powers chiefly to curtail pernicious Muslim piracy in the western Mediterranean. Given our reliance on ecclesiastical sources to reconstruct these preparations, we should be skeptical of their common contention that these lay participants were solely motivated by unmitigated desires to effect ecclesiastical restorations.[96] Indeed, according to William Purkis, this campaign was one of the first instances in which "a crusade was launched without expectation that its achievements would directly contribute to the defence of the Holy Land."[97] Like many other Christian principalities, the Italian city-states engaged in conflict and interaction with Islam largely out of material considerations. The Genoese, for example, had long sought to expand their commercial activity and raiding in the Iberian Peninsula.[98] The same year as this Balearic expedition, the count of Barcelona granted the Genoese complete freedom "to make peace and war on the Saracens as they wish" in return for periodic passage duties.[99] Similarly, the Treaty of San Feliu de Guixols, which was signed between Ramon Berenguer III and the Pisans on 7 September 1113 and subscribed by Abbot Oleguer during his brief tenure at Saint Ruf, indicated that the primary objective of the impending campaign against the Balearics was the "deliverance of Christian prisoners" captured by pirates and held in captivity at Mallorca.[100] Indeed, an influential chronicle drafted in the aftermath, the *Liber Maiolichinus*, depicts the campaign as part of a continuum of activity in the western Mediterranean rather than as a facet of the recent, "miraculous" conquest of the Holy Land.[101]

The siege of Eivissa lasted thirty days and succeeded in August 1114, when its Muslim settlements were sacked, Christian captives freed, and fortifications largely destroyed. The following February, Christian forces breached neighboring Mallorca's defenses and disturbed a number of its settlements.[102] Before his forces could secure the island, however, Ramon Berenguer III had to depart hastily for Barcelona to defend against the invading troops of the Almoravid *walī* of Zaragoza as they raided toward Barcelona. He left the Pisans to hold their fortified position on Mallorca, but the arrival of the Almoravids there soon forced them to withdraw as well. Not long thereafter, activity by Muslim pirates against Christian maritime commerce in the zone had apparently already surpassed previous levels.[103]

Despite its mixed success, scholars nevertheless view this campaigning against the Balearics as foundational for demonstrating to church leaders Ramon Berenguer III's capacity as a conqueror.[104] The campaign put the count in the company of tested papal champions like Alfonso of Aragon. Ramon Berenguer did not wait long to capitalize on this status. In 1116, after he and his allies had narrowly rescued his domains from Almoravid attacks, he personally embarked on an embassy to Rome. En route, he made calculated stops in Provence and northern Italy to reaffirm the naval and ground support that had served him so well in 1114. In the south of France, he received the homage of important nobles whose support would be instrumental to the success of future campaigns launched into the Ebro region leading up to the victorious conquests of Tortosa and Lleida.[105] He also visited with leaders in Genoa and Pisa. Once in Rome, Ramon Berenguer formally requested help from Paschal II for the campaign to capture Tortosa.[106] Paschal II agreed on the condition that the count consent to renewing papal suzerainty over his realms, which Ramon Berenguer did in May of 1116. The pope used this occasion to note that he had been impressed by this recent success in the Balearics, however temporary.[107]

It is clear that Paschal II had the recent Almoravid incursion in mind when he made these arrangements with Ramon Berenguer III. In the charter reestablishing his papal suzerainty over Barcelona's domains, Paschal distinguished between the North Africans (*moabitas*) and the Andalusi inhabitants of Tortosa (*mauros*) but nevertheless mandated that both groups be "expelled" from these "parts of Spain."[108] The pope's sense of urgency and strong desire for progress are palpable in the document. He was clearly determined to ensure that his preemptive restoration and showing of apostolic support for an attack on Tortosa would not fail and cause him embarrassment, as they had for Urban II in the 1090s. Accordingly, in contrast to his predecessor, Paschal was no longer content to support the competing aims of regional rulers. Paschal's firsthand knowledge of Iberia had helped him and his advisors reach the difficult conclusion that decisive victory over the Almoravids would require a coalition involving both Aragon and Catalonia. Accordingly, the pope dispatched his cardinal-legate, Boso, to assess the potential for an Iberian Christian alliance against the Muslims.[109] Boso spent the better part of 1117 traveling around the Christian-ruled Peninsula and attending numerous church councils, including a council at Girona in the county of Barcelona, and appears to have found little to no backing for such collaboration.[110]

Much to Paschal II's likely dismay, Ramon Berenguer III, like his Christian rivals, continued to strengthen his position unilaterally during these years. He actively managed his defensive positions along the west of the Camp de Tarragona and Lower Urgell and intervened whenever he or his officials perceived weaknesses among his delegates. In 1119, for example, he discovered that Bernat Amat, viscount of Cardona, had not been fulfilling his duties of guarding and maintaining the important castle of Tamarit in the Camp de Tarragona. He consequently stripped the viscount of the fief and awarded Tamarit to a certain Fortún and his wife, Beatrice.[111] Around this same time, Ramon Berenguer also saw fit to delegate the management of the city of Tarragona to an invested and capable party, Bishop Oleguer.[112] Oleguer had already established a commitment to preaching the crusade effort throughout Iberia by this point.[113] When he preliminarily established Oleguer as archbishop, Ramon Berenguer III charged him with the tasks of settling and developing Tarragona's district and *camp*, thus liberating himself to focus on pressing military matters to the south and west.[114] Shortly afterward, on 21 March, Gelasius II consecrated Oleguer as Tarragona's new archbishop.[115]

These efforts to maintain his defenses along the frontier were furthermore supported by Ramon Berenguer's acquisition of Provence in 1112, through his marriage to the Countess Douce, and the counties of Besalú and Cerdanya in 1116 and 1117, respectively, which enabled him to draw from a larger pool of military resources.[116] These relationships were arguably more important for Barcelona's growing rivalry with Toulouse, however, than for its conflicts with the Almoravids to the south.[117]

Lleida: Alliance and Assault

Although the Almoravids had managed to launch some formidable raids into Christian-held lands in the northeastern Peninsula, their vigor soon waned. Following the Almoravids' loss of Zaragoza to the Aragonese in 1118, their governor in Lleida soon buckled under the pressure from the Christians' castral network and began paying tribute for peace.[118] In 1121, however, for mysterious reasons, Ramon Berenguer III moved to establish Lleida as a subordinate ally through a lopsided arrangement with the its *qāʾid* (*alcaid*), "Avifelel" (Abū Hilāl).[119]

In what took the form of a standard feudal agreement, Abū Hilāl agreed to serve the count, his "better lord" (*meliori seniori*), as his "faithful man and associate" (*fideli homini et amico*), a pledge that he secured by giving Ramon his sons as hostages.[120] In return, Ramon Berenguer offered to supply Abū Hilāl with twenty ships to shuttle two hundred of his troops safely through Christian and Muslim lands to Mallorca. The agreement does not indicate what Ramon Berenguer hoped to gain from this expedition, but it is possible that he had the understanding that the *alcaid* would conquer the island as the count's delegate.[121] Abū Hilāl also submitted to the count a long list of fortifications mainly along the Cinca River valley northwest of Fraga. Some of these, including Alcolea, Chalamera, and Zaidín, had formerly been held by the Aragonese but had since fallen into Muslim hands. Alcolea, for example, had been under Aragonese control since before 1103,[122] and Gebut and Castelldans had already been enfeoffed to a Christian castellan by the count of Barcelona in 1118.[123] Abū Hilāl retained only the castle of Soses, on the Segre River in between Lleida and Fraga, as well as Lleida's mills.[124]

As added incentive for his support of the count's military pursuits, the Muslim ruler would be entitled to half of any future *parias* paid to the count. Presumably this arrangement was designed to help compensate the *qā'id* for all that he was granting as well as to enlist him as a motivated agent within Barcelona's frontier coalition. Abū Hilāl also promised to render to Ramon Berenguer any castles or cities he might acquire in the future as well as to support him in any engagement with Tortosa or other Muslim regimes in Iberia. Although Abū Hilāl retained Lleida as an enfeoffed lordship, Ramon Berenguer would have the ability to reclaim it at will. As a further marker of Abū Hilāl's bond to the count as one of his faithful vassals, he would have the option to receive lands in Barcelona and Girona from the count.

It is worth considering what each side expected to gain from this arrangement. Abū Hilāl likely lacked sufficient resources to render further *parias* and had to resort to pawning off his possessions to one of his Christian aggressors. He also may have sought an upper hand in his rivalries with his Muslim neighbors. For his part, Ramon Berenguer must have recognized that these castles would, in fact, support his present objectives better than further tribute. Controlling them would give him a competitive advantage over his rivals in the pursuit of Lleida and Fraga when the time came to conquer them.[125]

If these were indeed the respective goals of Ramon Berenguer and Abū Hilāl, they appear to have backfired. This emerging partnership in fact appears to have prompted Alfonso of Aragon to intensify his military engagement against this sector of the *Thaghr*.[126] The following year, in 1122, he moved to secure his western border with Castile. He appears to have first targeted Fraga in February 1123, and there are signs that he occupied it (as well as neighboring Mequinenza) by April of that year.[127] He then undertook a major offensive against Lleida. Alfonso arrived there in the late winter and constructed the fortification later known as Gardeny on a hill above the city.[128] The Aragonese succeeded in using Gardeny to blockade Lleida temporarily, trapping its inhabitants and cutting off supplies normally delivered via the Segre River that runs alongside the city.[129] The siege ultimately failed, however, possibly due to intervention by Ramon Berenguer III, and Alfonso eventually withdrew his troops.[130] At some point, Alfonso also lost control of Fraga, Mequinenza, the castle of Alcañiz, and the whole of the Guadalupe River valley south of the Ebro town of Caspe to the Almoravids.[131]

Despite these mixed results, Alfonso's campaigning appears to have accelerated preparations by the Catalonian counts for a decisive push to capture Lleida before the Aragonese could manage to extend their recent gains. By 1122, even though conflicts in Occitania remained unresolved, Ramon Berenguer III and his allies were already planning seriously to make their own attack on both Lleida and Tortosa.[132] Then, in October 1122, Ramon Berenguer took a major step toward organizing a major assault on Lleida. He signed an expansive agreement (*convenientia*) with Count Ponç Hug of Empúries in which Ponç pledged to aid Ramon as a faithful vassal in the conquest or defense of territories up to and including Fraga, Lleida, and Tortosa. In return, Ponç would receive lordship over this expanse of Muslim territory as an *honor* held from the count of Barcelona.[133] Ramon Berenguer also obtained financial and spiritual support from institutions such as the monastery of Solsona, to which he pledged Lleida's main mosque.[134]

Archbishop Oleguer had been hard at work over the past several years to breathe new life into the restoration effort and must have been encouraged by Ramon Berenguer III's decision to abandon his diplomatic relations with Lleida and mount such an expansive campaign.[135] Already at the council of Toulouse in 1119, Oleguer had participated in the proclamation of a crusade against the Almoravids. Zaragoza's capture the previous year had been supported by a crusading bull from Gelasius II, and this council of Toulouse's directive may have sought to reapply it to Tortosa.[136] At the same council, Oleguer also campaigned for the papacy to reestablish the crusade status of Iberian conflict with Muslims, thus rendering it equivalent to crusade service in the Holy Land. While Oleguer was in Rome for the First Lateran Council in 1123, Calixtus II issued a new bull promoting the crusade to restore churches in Iberia and prescribing excommunication for the nonfulfillment of any crusader vow within a year.[137] The pope was clearly frustrated about the numerous delays to the Lleida-Tortosa campaign. His bull targeted the restorations of Tarragona and Tortosa specifically and seems to have been crafted in response to Ramon Berenguer III's preparations. In recognition of Oleguer's advocacy, Calixtus appointed him as the papal legate charged with managing the crusade effort.[138]

We know exceedingly little about the details of the ensuing attack, which, scholars hypothesize, took place in 1126.[139] After only a few months and little apparent progress, the Almoravids defeated the Christian forces resoundingly at a battle near the castle of Corbins, to the north of Lleida.[140] This Muslim offensive pushed back the extreme defensive line established by the count of Urgell between Albesa and Termens and opened up the northern territory of Ribagorza to raiding. Even Lascuarre, northeast of Barbastro, experienced an attack.[141]

Tortosa and Lleida: Further Attempts

The debacle at Corbins, together with Alfonso of Aragon's recent failure to capture Lleida, appears to have raised further serious doubts concerning the potential for success of any unilateral attempt to vanquish the Almoravids. The collective sense among the stakeholders seems to have been that the unilateral Aragonese victory at Zaragoza had likely been the product of the disruption of the Almoravid takeover and was the exception rather than the rule. Accordingly, around 1126, the bishops of Huesca and Roda, a group of important Aragonese lords, and Alfonso of Aragon met with Ramon Berenguer III and his supporters. Here, the rulers tentatively agreed to join a common war against the Muslims of the Upper Frontier.[142]

Although this tentative alliance did not immediately yield united campaigns into Muslim territories, it may have induced Alfonso to postpone further assaults into the territory surrounding Lleida until around 1131, soon after Ramon Berenguer III's death.[143] Other factors could have prompted this delay, however. Alfonso continued to be distracted by conflicts with Castile along his western boundary.[144] He was also preoccupied with other military campaigns against the Muslims. For instance, after raiding to the south to attack Dénia and other settlements in 1125–26, possibly in an attempt to isolate the Upper Frontier from further Almoravid support, Alfonso tried, unsuccessfully, to capture Valencia in 1129.[145]

By contrast, the alliance did not exert any noticeable influence on Ramon Berenguer III's military policies. Ramon Berenguer provoked Alfonso when he seized Monzón from the Aragonese between 1127 and 1130 in order to strengthen his position in the west.[146] He also began organizing a second assault against Tortosa, without Aragonese involvement, in early 1127, less than a year after agreeing to coordinate military efforts with Alfonso. For this new attempt on Tortosa, Ramon Berenguer again drew upon non-Peninsular alliances by enlisting the aid of his cousin, King Roger II of Sicily, and Guilhem VI of Montpellier, among others. Yet again, Archbishop Oleguer was instrumental in resolving disputes involving Guilhem in order to facilitate his cooperation with Ramon Berenguer III's campaign. Indeed, Oleguer appears to have worked as peacemaker between the different magnates of the northeastern Peninsula and southern France in an effort to unite disparate noble collectives into larger coalitions against the *Thaghr*.[147]

Archbishop Oleguer conducted this work alongside his assistance of Ramon Berenguer's independent campaign against Tortosa. In particular, he pressed for support at the council of Narbonne that was convoked in 1127. Although the numerous assembled bishops did not explicitly support this plan to capture Tortosa, they did voice their official advocacy for Tarragona's restoration that had implicit connections to that effort. They also founded a larger confraternity to co-opt the multiple confraternal associations already in existence in the provinces of Tarragona and Narbonne and direct them toward the effort to restore the archiepiscopal see.[148] All the clergy and monks of these provinces were declared members, and laymen were encouraged to join the confraternity in support of the objective as well. The confraternity would receive apostolic protection from the papacy as well as monetary support from its members. It was to hold periodic meetings that honored its membership with special masses and rites.[149]

Details are sketchy regarding the failed campaign that Ramon Berenguer III managed to carry out in 1128. Rather than engaging solely in a landed siege, he simultaneously targeted Tortosa via the mouth of the Ebro River using naval resources. Like the naval expedition to the Balearics in 1114–15, the campaign was arguably most significant for the alliances and relationships it fostered that would help shape Tortosa's successful midcentury conquest. Both Narbonne and Montpellier contributed naval support to the effort as they would later with the 1148 operation.[150]

Although the Pisans had served the count in his campaigning against the Balearic Islands, neither Pisan nor Genoese sailors assisted in the 1128 campaign. Despite its absence, Genoa nevertheless was in the process of developing a closer relationship with Barcelona during these same years. Not long before this failed attack on Tortosa, for example, in 1127, Archbishop Oleguer, acting on Ramon Berenguer III's behalf, had established new agreements with the Genoese consul, Caffaro, over Genoa's docking and trading within Barcelona's claimed jurisdiction between Nice and Tortosa. Ramon Berenguer accused Genoa of trading along the coast of Muslim Spain without his approval. When Barcelona and Genoa reconciled in November of that year, the count felt able to guarantee security to Genoese ships wishing to land along the entire Mediterranean coast, from Nice down to the Ebro delta.[151]

This concord also recognized Salou, to the south of Tarragona, as the county's most southerly port. The agreement even went so far as to establish a toll and levy system for Genoese trafficking within the zone. Each Genoese ship would have to pay ten *morabetins* to the men of Barcelona on money and products they brought from Muslim-ruled lands and traded between Nice and Salou. Furthermore, ships that landed between the Ebro delta and Nice would be under the count's protection so long as they paid ten *morabetins* to the men of Barcelona or to the church of San Feliu de Guixols. Those ships that neglected to pay would not be able to sail along the coast nor enjoy the count's protection. The document also stipulates that ships from Barcelona or Provence would have reciprocal rights at the ports of the Genoese republic.[152]

It is highly unlikely that Salou, to say nothing of the Ebro delta, had fallen under Christian control at this point when Tarragona still remained too unstable for habitation. Perhaps Ramon Berenguer was anticipating that his imminent campaign against Tortosa would succeed in pushing the coastal line of defense southward to buffer Tarragona. Grants of lands below the Penedès along the coast north of Tarragona or into the valley of the Francolí River are exceedingly scarce for these years.[153] Castles in the southern stretches of the counties of Barcelona and Osona/Manresa continued to be described as sitting in the "far frontier" (*extremo marche*) into the early 1130s.[154] The important castle of Tamarit along the northern coast of Tarragona had lain in ruins since the Almoravid invasion of 1115. It would be rebuilt in the 1120s, but its new castellan did not man the fortification until 1134.[155]

Following the failure of Ramon Berenguer III's most recent effort against Tortosa in 1128, it is not surprising that Archbishop Oleguer soon delegated responsibility over the settlement and defense of Tarragona, with which he had been entrusted by the count a decade earlier, to a more capable party. In 1129, the Norman warlord Robert Burdet assumed control as "prince of Tarragona" (*princeps Tarraconensis*). Robert would hold Tarragona and its surrounding district in fief from the church. As prince, he was expected to manage, develop, and defend the city and its district from nearby Muslim strongholds.[156] He also retained all the churches, ecclesiastical rights, and churchmen (and their families) in the city and district, as well as all tithes.[157] Oleguer worked diligently in the charter of donation to justify his authority to assign Tarragona to Robert, but it is curious that the enactment did not invoke or involve the count, who must have authorized the infeudation. Before assuming full responsibility, Robert first traveled to Rome to obtain Honorius III's confirmation of the infeudation.[158]

Robert Burdet was a shrewd choice for Oleguer because he and his family had a history of involvement with Aragon's and Barcelona's interactions along the Ebro valley in the 1120s.[159] His new status as prince of Tarragona gave him a major advantage over other lords in the race to extend deeper into the *Thaghr* and would encourage him to invest more of his resources and political capital in the military northeastern Peninsula. This attention would draw greater numbers of Norman knights. Even though Ramon Berenguer III did not subscribe the donation, this lack of consent was likely a byproduct of his preoccupation with his fronts with Tortosa and Lleida at this time and not a sign of his discontentment with the concord. The count likely welcomed Robert's takeover at Tarragona, given Oleguer's negligible progress with settling the zone over the past decade. Indeed, shortly after the donation of 1129, the count entered the city with Robert, Oleguer, and many other prelates and associates. The few settlers that were already established in Tarragona at that time received a privilege that exempted them from tithes and first fruits, guaranteed their property, and subjected them to Robert's jurisdiction.[160] These developments did not go unnoticed within the *Thaghr*. In 1129, an embassy from Tortosa to Marrakech complained that Tarragona had been permanently occupied by the Christians and pleaded for Almoravid reinforcements.[161]

Holding Tarragona by no means precluded Robert Burdet's participation in Aragon's rival expeditions. He had already been involved in Aragon's territorial expansion for many years by this point. Indeed, it is not surprising to note that he assisted in Alfonso's final expedition into the Ebro valley beginning in November 1132.[162]

Tortosa and Lleida: Alfonso's Final Campaign

Following Ramon Berenguer III's death in 1131, Alfonso of Aragon, more than any other Christian ruler, arguably possessed the resources to penetrate, disrupt, and occupy the whole of the Ebro valley. Other potentates, by comparison, seemed to be working harder to juggle internal and external security concerns. That same year, for example, Ermengol VI of Urgell appointed Ramon de Torroga as castellan of Olius near Solsona and supported him with men drawn from the castles of Pons and Agramunt, both of which lay closer to the frontier. Ermengol made it clear that he expected these knights to perform multiple duties. For instance, he simultaneously assigned Ramon de Torroga responsibilities in the consolidation and defense effort along the frontier zone around Balaguer.[163]

Possibly owing to this clear strategic advantage, Alfonso proceeded slowly and cautiously with arranging his renewed offensive into the Andalusi Upper Frontier. He had other distractions to contend with: his lingering conflict surrounding the succession of Alfonso VII of Castile-León (r. 1126–57) drew him to confront the monarch's half-brother, Count Alphonse Jordan of Toulouse, and forced him to campaign north of the Pyrenees in 1130 and 1131.[164] While besieging Bayonne in October 1131, Alfonso of Aragon issued his last testament. In it, he confirmed that he hoped to conquer Tortosa: "If God gives me Tortosa, all of it will belong to the Hospitallers of Jerusalem."[165]

Rather than targeting Lleida directly as he had in 1123, Alfonso sought to isolate it and its dependent cities from Almoravid aid by conquering further down the Ebro valley beginning in 1132.[166] After occupying Horta (de Sant Joan) and temporarily capturing Godall, to the south of Tortosa, by January 1133, Alfonso besieged and captured Mequinenza in June.[167] By the middle of that year, the Aragonese held nearly the entire right (southwesterly) bank of the Ebro, from Mequinenza down to Riba-roja. A line of fortifications along that bank, including Batea, Nonaspe, Algars, and Horta, appeared to defend these acquisitions.[168] From these castral centers, Alfonso and his allies must have sensed their capacity to conquer the whole of the Ebro valley and northern Valencia, finally fulfilling the license granted by the papacy for the restoration of these lands so many years earlier.[169] The Aragonese coalition also seems to have anticipated that the successful campaign would pressure Muslims further south to maintain tribute payments. When Alfonso's ally, Ermengol VI of Urgell, drafted his will early in 1133, for instance, he was confident enough to draw on "my *paria* from Spain" to fund a pious donation to the cathedral of the Seu d'Urgell and even capped the gift at an impressive two hundred gold *morabetins*.[170]

When Alfonso laid siege to Fraga later that same year, he received significant support from his French allies.[171] The city put up firm resistance, however, thus prolonging the offensive to over a year and threatening the resolve of the assembled Christian forces. The official in charge of guarding Fraga, Saʿd ibn Mardanīš, eventually appealed for aid from the governor of Lleida, ʿAbd Allāh ibn ʿIyāḍ, as well as from Almoravid governors further south. Yaḥyā ibn Gāniya, the governor of Murcia and Valencia, received his call and must have recognized the threat that an Aragonese capture of Fraga would pose to the stability of the entire *Thaghr*.[172]

If the often unreliable, anti-Aragonese *Chronica Adefonsi Imperatoris* can be believed, other military activity by Alfonso may have emboldened the Almoravid response. For instance, Alfonso had allegedly recently massacred the local population and captured numerous slaves at Almería.[173] The *Chronica* also recounts that ibn Gāniya sent two sets of reinforcements to rescue Fraga and Lleida. The first was defeated by the Christians and fled. The second, gathered from all around al-Andalus and led by ibn Gāniya himself, supposedly arrived on the eve of Fraga's surrender and contributed to Alfonso's defeat. Determined as the *Chronica*'s anonymous author was to blame the defeat entirely on Alfonso of Aragon's failings, its account must be interpreted with great caution.[174]

After the Almoravids broke the siege on Fraga in a major battle in July 1134, they launched a counterattack that obliterated Alfonso's forces. The onslaught led to the capture or deaths of a great many knights, nobles, and clerics.[175] Alfonso quickly retreated and struggled to regroup after the defeat in the face of a growing Almoravid offensive. Profoundly affected by this sudden upset, however, he soon fell ill and died in early September 1134, shortly after confirming his will.[176] Many of the territorial gains achieved by Alfonso and his predecessor, Pedro, over the past decades were soon lost to Almoravid forces. Ṣa'd ibn Mardanīš and ibn Gāniya regained control of Mequinenza as well as Monzón, Pomar de Cinca, and Lizana.[177] Troops under their command also attacked Zaragoza and even forced the Christian citizens of Barbastro to evacuate temporarily.[178]

Intervention by Aragon's opportunistic neighbor, Alfonso VII of Castile-León, as well as the heightened involvement of southern French nobles, however, prevented the permanent repossession of Zaragoza and its territories by Almoravid forces.[179] Alfonso naturally did not intervene out of a sense of altruism or any overriding commitment to rescuing the Christian cause. Rather, his primary interest appears to have been seizing for himself what remained of Aragon's conquests. Castile's frontier with Islamic lands bordered and thus stood within striking distance of Zaragoza's territories along the Ebro valley. A similar agenda clearly preoccupied both García Ramírez, who would soon assume the title of king of Pamplona/Navarre, and Count Ermengol VI of Urgell. Each of these rulers would involve themselves in Aragon's dealings by making liaisons with Alfonso of Aragon's brother and successor, Ramiro.[180]

From the middle of the reign of Sancho Ramírez in the mid-1080s to Alfonso's death in 1134, the Aragonese monarchy had marshaled local and foreign noble agents to further aggressive territorial expansion southeast along the Cinca and Ebro River corridors into the territories of Lleida, Fraga,

Valencia, and Tortosa. While these ambitious and resource-hungry kings may have gradually elaborated a military and diplomatic strategy to take advantage of opportunities to extract tribute or seize territory from the Muslims at the expense of rivals such as the counts of Barcelona, it is clear that they did not always implement well-considered strategies with long-term objectives.[181] In many respects, they were playing the part of opportunistic raiders. Desirous of additional lands and incomes, they charged and, with luck, conquered first, and only later faced up to the challenges of territorial assimilation. The tenuousness of Alfonso's hold over his rapidly acquired territories along the Ebro valley and to the northwest of Lleida was made evident when these areas so easily succumbed to Almoravid invasion following his failed siege of Fraga in 1134.

As we will see in the next and final chapter of part I, the counts of Barcelona ultimately would be more successful at assimilating their acquisition of Tortosa and Lleida, partly out of good fortune and partly due to a lack of serious rivals by that point thanks to the demise of the Aragonese dynasty. They had learned from Aragon's example to be cautious and disciplined and wary of conquering more than they could defend. Barcelona's territorial advance had been slow and supported, at every step, by deliberate, extensive castral development. Furthermore, its counts had anticipated and prepared for the organizational challenges to be brought by the decisive conquests of Tortosa and Lleida after the mid-twelfth century. They had issued prospective property grants followed by waves of postconquest donations to barons, petty castellans, monasteries, and military orders alike that served to delegate the hefty burden of defense and settlement.

✒ CHAPTER 3

Unification and Conquest

The successful mid-twelfth-century conquests of Tortosa and Lleida were generations in the making. Observers of this dramatic political shift in the history of the region must have recognized that these definitive campaigns built upon the patterns of Christian–Muslim frontier interaction that had marked the region for over a century, as we ourselves have witnessed throughout the previous two chapters. At the same time, this shift in governance was also influenced by novel political, religious, and economic developments on either side of the frontier that ultimately helped shift the balance in the Christians' favor.

The unification of Barcelona and Aragon was fundamental to the success of these expeditions. Count Ramon Berenguer IV of Barcelona and Petronilla, the daughter of Alfonso of Aragon's brother, Ramiro II, were betrothed in 1137. Even though their marriage was not finalized until 1151, well after these conquests had taken place, this pending confederacy was vital for investing Ramon, as count-prince of Barcelona and Aragon, with the resources, legitimacy, and entitlement to extend his territory into the Ebro valley and absorb Muslim-ruled Tortosa and Lleida. Furthermore, Barcelona's unification with Aragon not only eliminated its main rival in engagement with the Upper Frontier; it also heightened the perceived urgency to complete Tarragona's restoration, since its archdiocese, according to Nikolas Jaspert, now roughly represented "an ecclesiastical prefiguration of the nascent political entity."[1] Although the union made strategic sense in many respects, it was also naturally controversial for certain powerful constituencies. The Aragonese nobility, for one, would not fully support the dynastic merger. Ramon also faced stiff competition from other rivals, most notably the monarchs of Castile and Navarre.[2]

In this chapter, we will examine the evolution and characteristics of this merger of the house of Barcelona with the troubled Aragonese dynasty. We will trace how Ramon Berenguer IV and his supporters capitalized on Aragon's situation and warded off competitors in order to orchestrate the successful conquests of Tortosa and Lleida. As we will see, accomplishing the conquests was not the only objective, however. Ramon and his advisors also had to concern themselves with integrating the lands and with looking poised for further expansion into Muslim-ruled lands to help keep these rival regimes at bay.

Aragon after Alfonso

Alfonso's last testament had mandated the donation of his entire royal patrimony to the military orders of the Hospital, Temple, and Holy Sepulchre.[3] Within a month of Alfonso's death, however, his brother had taken control of Barbastro and entered Zaragoza, where he was proclaimed king and given the name of Ramiro II.[4] During this period, Ramiro routinely assumed the title of king of "my father's kingdom," ostensibly as a means to circumvent these inconvenient provisions of Alfonso's will and assert the legitimacy of his claim to the throne.[5] Given that Ramiro had been a monk serving as bishop of Roda-Barbastro at the time of his brother's untimely death, the likelihood was high that his accession to the throne would be rejected by the pope.[6] Indeed, due to the fact that he had seemingly only renounced his monastic vows and given up his position as bishop in order to rescue the dynasty from crisis, stakeholders viewed his reign as, at most, transitional. As multiple claimants circled, the question became not whether Ramiro would remain king for the long term. Rather, it was whether Ramiro would be able to hold on to power for sufficient time to produce an heir and thereby establish a succession favorable to his family and the Aragonese kingdom.[7]

Not surprisingly, Ramiro's accession was immediately rejected by Navarre, whose nobles soon elected García Ramírez (r. 1134–50) as their king in an effort to remove themselves from Aragonese control during this period of dynastic instability.[8] Following some heated exchanges between the two rulers, Ramiro ultimately agreed to recognize García Ramírez's status as an independent king, albeit with some degree of subordination. In this "adoption," Ramiro established himself as the "father" and García Ramírez as his "son."[9] This arrangement appears to have led García Ramírez to believe that he would inherit Ramiro's throne as his adoptive heir. When Ramiro later rejected this expectation, however, García Ramírez turned to ally with Castile and established himself as Alfonso VII's vassal, by May 1135.[10] As the great-grandson of Sancho III of Aragon, Alfonso also pressed his own claim to the Aragonese throne. Forces under his command soon displaced the Aragonese from Zaragoza and temporarily took control of much of its territory.[11]

These maneuvers did not dissuade Ramiro from doing his utmost to perpetuate his dynasty.[12] By 1135, the new king and his supporters had discovered a potential solution to this dynastic crisis. Ramiro had agreed to take Agnès of Aquitaine, the daughter of an established ally, Duke Guilhem X, as his queen.[13] The primary obstacle for this plan was obtaining papal approval. As papal suzerain, Innocent II exerted considerable influence over the Aragonese kingdom. Although he was inclined to allow Ramiro assume leadership of his dynasty, he prohibited this ambition to marry.[14] He also tellingly circulated a letter to Iberia's princes warning Aragon's claimants that he would reject any attempt to deviate from the stipulations of Alfonso's will.[15] Alfonso VII of Castile-León, arguably the most serious threat to Ramiro, did not resist the pope's ruling and promptly withdrew his claim.[16]

Despite such clear papal opposition to their union, Ramiro and Agnès nevertheless did marry. Yet this decision to ignore Innocent II's mandates does not appear to have engendered any hostile response from the papacy. When Agnès bore a baby girl instead of a male heir, rather than waiting for their daughter to approach the proper age, the couple quickly planned for Petronilla's future marriage in order to resolve the question of succession.[17] Ramiro effectively passed sovereignty over Aragon to the house of Barcelona when he promised Petronilla in marriage to Ramon Berenguer IV in August 1137.[18] The king commended his barons to the count, who pledged to him their fidelity and swore to guarantee and uphold the stipulations of their agreement. These important nobles furthermore agreed to act as guarantors for Ramiro and to serve Ramon Berenguer as their new sovereign lord.[19] The arrangement was specifically engineered to prevent the reopening of the succession crisis, even if it meant effectively ending the Aragonese dynasty. It stipulated that if Petronilla were to die early without progeny while Ramiro still lived, Ramon Berenguer IV would still retain full rights to the kingdom.

Ramon Berenguer IV's bestowal of homage to Alfonso VII as *impera-tor* in 1135 must have made this outcome somewhat more palatable to the Castilian-Leonese ruler.[20] Alfonso had already further backed away from his claim to the Aragonese throne by this time by confirming Ramiro's title to the kingdom of Zaragoza and agreeing to hold it from him in fief for his life-time.[21] In 1137, intervention by Archbishop Oleguer of Tarragona may have convinced Alfonso to retreat further by awarding him the "lands of Zara-goza" and other disputed holdings in the south of Aragon. Alfonso had estab-lished authority over these lands during the first year of Ramiro's weak rule to the count of Barcelona.[22] In return for this exodus and for Alfonso's pledge of military support, Ramon Berenguer also established himself as his vassal.[23]

As part of the transfer, Ramiro also defined Aragon's contentious western limits with its neighbors, Castile and Navarre, but seems to have deliberately neglected to demarcate the border with Catalonia.[24] It is unclear whether this omission was an attempt to present the territories as more contigu-ous, in keeping with the dynastic unification, or rather an effort to defer discussion of a potentially contentious issue until after the establishment of the merger. In support of this latter possibility, the parties also notably left unresolved the question of Aragon's and Catalonia's conflicting claims to future conquests of Muslim territory. Although the extant documentation makes no indication that territorial expansion into the Upper Frontier and beyond was even discussed, the transacting parties must have understood that the topic was critical and would complicate their relationship in the future. As we have seen, the kings of Aragon, like the counts of Barcelona, had enfeoffed their principalities to the papacy, and the popes had long sup-ported Aragonese expansion into Lleida and Tortosa without reconciling similar papal promotion of Barcelona's moves against Tortosa. The incerti-tude of the issue likely explains why these parties pragmatically agreed to postpone discussing it.

Carrying out these arrangements constituted Ramiro's primary achieve-ment during his brief reign. He was distracted by the vortex of powerful political forces in Aragon and by the defensive crisis following Alfonso's great defeat. His one diplomatic accomplishment with his Muslim neighbors was negotiating a truce in 1134 or 1135 with ibn Gāniya, governor of Valencia and Murcia. This agreement remained in force until late 1136.[25]

.   Following this alliance, Ramiro II retained his royal title but ruled only in a reduced capacity alongside Ramon Berenguer IV until around 1144, when he reestablished his vows and returned to religious life at the monastery of San Pedro in Huesca.[26] As Aragon's new monarch, "Prince" Ramon Berenguer was immediately beset with challenges as he sought to protect these additions to his patrimony.[27]

Alfonso's Will and the Military Orders

Ramon Berenguer IV had other concerns relating to the merger with Aragon that were arguably as formidable as garnering the support of Ramiro and the Aragonese nobility. He had to deal with the international military orders, the Templars, Hospitallers, and Order of the Holy Sepulchre, which had been collectively promised the kingdom by Alfonso's will. It is somewhat surprising that Ramon Berenguer IV was now having to contend with these military orders in this manner, given that he, his predecessors, and other rulers in both Aragon and Catalonia long struggled to involve the Hospitallers and Templars in the push to conquer the *Thaghr*. In the years before Alfonso's death, these two orders had initially established presences in northeastern Iberia solely to help support their operations in the east. At that time, they had been neither militarized nor involved directly in warfare against Muslim-ruled territories within the Peninsula.

The histories of each military order's gradual involvement in the affairs of the northeastern Peninsula have been subjects of controversy among scholars. Officially formed by the late eleventh century, the Hospitallers may have established themselves in Catalonia as early as 1111, although certain scholars have suggested that the order arrived at least a decade later.[28] Historians generally reject attempts to place the Templar Order in Catalonia and Aragon before 1130.[29]

Both orders had initially been resistant to efforts by rulers in both Catalonia and Aragon to involve them in the conflicts with al-Andalus. At the siege of Fraga in 1134, Alfonso had confirmed the property and rights of the Hospitallers, including castles, as well as "however much [the order] could augment, capture or add in all of my land." This enactment naturally would have motivated the Hospitallers to engage in the conflict in Aragon. We lack confirmation, however, that the order seized the opportunity at this time.[30] In Catalonia, Ramon Berenguer III had offered the Templars, described as a "confraternal association" (*societas confratris*), a frontier position at Granyena (today Granyena de Segarra), near Cervera, but here again there is no evidence that the order utilized the donation.[31] Count Ermengol VI of Urgell's 1132 grant of the castle at Barberà, bordering the north of the war-torn Camp de Tarragona, which he intended for the Templars to utilize "in the march against the Muslims," similarly languished.[32] In 1134, in search of further means to incentivize the Templars' engagement, Ramon Berenguer

IV, joined by numerous Catalonian lay magnates and prelates, extended the Truce of God to protect the order and all properties it held or might obtain in the future.[33] After assuming control of this same castle of Barberà from the count of Urgell, Ramon Berenguer IV renewed Ermengol VI's donation to the Templars in 1135. He emphasized that it was to be used to assist "our march against the Muslims."[34] The order appears to have done nothing with the castle since the initial grant three years earlier.

Even prior to formulating his will, Alfonso of Aragon had established himself as a generous patron of the military orders. Although his concessions may have been motivated partly by his devotion to these associations, they were also clearly structured so as to incentivize their increased engagement with Muslim-ruled states. He had, for instance, already exempted the Templars from the one-fifth tax customarily owed to the monarchy on any spoils of war it could capture from the Muslims.[35] His interest in these international military orders grew in the early 1130s, following the failure of his attempts to develop home-grown, Aragonese confraternities, Belchite and Monreal del Campo, over the previous decade.[36] These local orders appear to have collapsed before 1134; they go unmentioned in Alfonso's will that he made in 1131 and updated shortly before his death. During the final years of his reign, Alfonso continued to award the military orders potentially valuable exemptions and entitlements. Just days before being routed by the Almoravid counterattack during his siege of Fraga, for example, he confirmed the rights and possessions of the Hospitallers.[37]

Catalonia had witnessed no parallel effort to establish local military confraternities, but its rulers did manifest similar devotion to these international orders. Ramon Berenguer III, for instance, joined the Templars shortly before his death.[38] Ramon Berenguer IV made analogous attempts to entice these orders to support his military engagements with the Muslim regimes of the *Thaghr* in the years leading up to the unification with Aragon. In the "peace council" gathering of April 1134, he, Archbishop Oleguer of Tarragona, and an assortment of magnates and prelates extended an open invitation to any members of the Templar Order to come to reside and fight (*militare*) on their lands. As a pious donation in support of its efforts and a gesture of good will, Ramon Berenguer IV pledged to give the order twenty *morabetins* and two pounds of silver annually.[39]

The orders only agreed to renounce their rights to Aragon promised in Alfonso's will after extensive negotiations.[40] At the behest of the patriarch of Jerusalem, titular head of the Order of the Holy Sepulchre, the grand master of the Hospitallers negotiated the renunciations of the one-third share granted to each order. The resolutions reserved certain rights for each order, including entitlements in Barbastro, Huesca, Zaragoza, Daroca, and Jaca.[41] The Templars were the most resistant to compromise, but after painstaking deliberations, Ramon Berenguer IV obtained their renunciation, with substantial concessions, in 1143. The terms of this resolution established the Templars' prominent presence within the region for generations to come until its dissolution in the early fourteenth century. The order received the castles of Monzón, Mongay, Chalamera, and Belchite in Aragon, Remolins southwest of Lleida, the royal share of Corbins, and Barberà in Catalonia. Most every castle granted to the Templars sat at the fringes of Christian territory, and several had only recently been seized from Muslim control.[42] The order also received substantial incomes and entitlements to future acquisitions: one thousand *solidi* annually from royal incomes in Huesca and Zaragoza plus and additional one-tenth of royal revenues, exemption from various levies, and, perhaps most significantly, one-fifth of all future acquisitions of Muslim territory.[43] This fifth part "of the conquest of Muslim land" would serve to make the Templars the most domain-rich lords within New Catalonia and northern Valencia.

Not long after the successful conquests of Tortosa and Lleida, the Templars wisely invoked the papacy to ensure that Ramon Berenguer IV honored the full extent of his pledge and to protect the donation. Eugenius III confirmed the order's rights to these castles and incomes in a bull dated 30 March 1150.[44] For unknown reasons, the papacy withheld its full endorsement of the arrangement until 1156.[45]

Ramon Berenguer IV's resolution mandated that the Templars establish a local militia "for the defense of the western Church, which is in Spain." This shift was significant given that previously the order had solely been involved in enlisting recruits and obtaining property in the northeastern Peninsula.[46] The document also made clear that the Templars in Iberia would emulate their counterparts' military role in the East.[47] Ramon Berenguer had requested as much in his negotiations with the grand master: "insofar as you are able . . . send to us at least ten of your brothers, whom you think suitable for this task, by whom in our land knights and others of the faithful, who shall have given themselves to this armed force, may be governed and ruled."[48] The agreement established the order as a fully invested partner in the military engagements within the region, and Ramon Berenguer pledged to confer with its leadership before establishing any peace with the Muslims. This collection of key fortifications sprinkled across the Aragonese and Catalonian southern frontier and one-fifth share of future conquests all but ensured the order's participation in engagement with the Upper Frontier. The Templars would successfully maintain this share of future conquests throughout the remainder of the Aragonese territorial expansion into al-Andalus, receiving confirmations from each of Ramon Berenguer's successors until Jaume I.[49]

This early inclusion of these international orders by Ramon Berenguer IV may explain why Catalonia failed to generate or host Spanish military orders developed specifically for conflicts with al-Andalus, which were rising to such prominence elsewhere in the Peninsula.[50] Regardless of whether military orders were locally developed, there were clear advantages to enlisting such partners. Unlike many foreign knights who wished to fulfill their crusading vow and quickly enrich themselves with booty before returning home, these orders could be counted on to remain and contribute to the effort to defend and consolidate conquered lands.[51]

Land and Castle Management in Preparation for Another Assault

Even before his dynastic alliance with Aragon had been finalized, Ramon Berenguer IV was already preparing a new campaign against Tortosa around 1136. This time, he relied on naval support from the nobleman Guilhem VI de Montpellier, to whom he promised lordship over the city, "in fief," if successful.[52] As with earlier attempts, the count sought to implement naval forces to both blockade and attack Tortosa from the water in support of a land siege. Evidence has not surfaced to confirm that the campaign ever materialized.

Such expansionist activity proved to be the exception rather than the rule during the years leading up to 1148, however. As Flocel Sabaté has noticed, many potentates in Catalonia focused their attention more on fortifying, settling, and defending their border lands than on conquest.[53] Ermengol VI and his men, for example, devoted significant attention to the construction and improvement of fortifications within the territory of Balaguer, to the west toward the Noguera Ribagorzana, within the plain of Mascançà to the east, and southward toward Lleida.[54] In 1139, he established six men at Bellcaire and charged them with rebuilding the castle there. This project only imprecisely linked its primary defensive orientation with the distant goal of conquest. These men were to "defend against the Muslims and all bad men so that God might render Lleida to the Christians."[55] Several months later, Arnau de Pons granted a group of men the vacant land known as Bellestar in the plain of Mascançà near Linyola. He noted that the territory already bordered a number of defensive structures and stipulated that they were to build one of their own.[56] Similarly, when Ermengol VI of Urgell granted Ramon

Arnau d'Anglesola a *quadra* in the district of Balaguer in 1142 as a free allod, he required him to build a church as well as a castle there.[57] During this period, Ermengol also renewed or reassigned earlier transactions that had failed. In 1143, he enfeoffed the ruined castle of Faneca to the son of its former castellan who had received it as an anticipatory donation from Ermengol IV "in the time when the Muslims held Balaguer." Ermengol VI now ordered this son to rebuild it.[58] Certain existing fortifications were also manned with new castellans during these years. For example, in 1146, Pere Arnau de Castellserres, who had received the castle of Montmur (now La Rápita, near Balaguer) from the counts and viscounts of Urgell, established Guillem d'Ager and other men at the castle.[59] The military orders also became invested in these settlement and development projects, often due to their receipt of donations. In 1147, for example, Ermengol VI of Urgell piously granted the Templars some land near Balaguer with the right to build mills as well as access to the neighboring canal. A short time later, when a certain Mir Conill opted to join the Templars, he gave the order annual rents and a farm in Balaguer.[60]

In spite of these efforts to develop the defensive line above Lleida, the most significant Christian-held outpost, Balaguer, remained only marginally settled during these years. As with other militarized centers that formed the Christian principalities' chain of defense, such as Tàrrega, Cervera, and Tarragona, Balaguer's stability relied, to a great extent, on the capture of neighboring Muslim territory in order to buffer it from persistent attacks. Other castral zones in the area were likewise not able to shelter residents until after the conquests of Tortosa and Lleida. Permanent settlers do not appear to have been established at Bellcaire, for example, until after 1157.[61] This plodding pace of consolidation could help explain why rulers in Catalonia gradually developed a fixation on further territorial conquest during this period.

Warlords were able to acquire and assimilate territory along the frontiers of Catalonia and Aragon gradually by "castralizing" the landscape. This process served to orient, define, and often concentrate current and future settlement and land management around a fortification and its district.[62] After the frontier with Islam had been pushed southward by additional territorial conquest, the patterns inflicted on the distribution and organization of settlement by the further castralization of these new lands would persist and consequently continue to define and influence societal development within these zones.

Even though the clustering of castles situated between Balaguer and Lleida was dense compared with other areas of Catalonia, sometimes appearing as little as one kilometer apart, they do not appear to have interacted as a defensive network. Eritja has contended that, since most of these towers were situated in strategic, often inaccessible places, they may have operated more autonomously rather than as part of a defensive collective, and this orientation may have reduced settlement projects' chances of success.[63] This dynamic appears to have been the result of a lack of coordination at the castral level. Rulers viewed these castral districts as the basis for the feudal forces they needed to campaign against the Muslims as well as a means of coordinating the defense and settlement of a section of the landscape. Castellans, by contrast, despite participating in raids to plunder Muslim territory and capture new lands, possessed more localized awarenesses based on their defined and demarcated castral territories. These self-oriented perspectives naturally tended to encourage competition rather than cooperation with neighboring castles. The castral district of Almenar, for example, was hemmed in by numerous other fortifications and carefully demarcated by "signs and crosses" along every boundary that was not defined by some natural feature.[64] These neighboring towers were not merely markers but very much in use in the lead-up to the conquest.[65] Although proximity to Muslim-ruled territory certainly influenced the dynamic between Christian castles, a subset of which had been adapted from the remains of Muslim fortifications, the positioning of these castles did not alone condition the activity of their castellans.

As a result of his assumption of jurisdiction over Aragon, Ramon Berenguer IV now benefited from rather than competed against the Aragonese recuperation of fortifications and territory lost in the Almoravid counteroffensive of 1134. By 1141, Aragonese forces at Ramon Berenguer's command had regained control over Sariñena, Pina del Ebro, and Velilla de Cinca. The count-prince also made significant headway in the 1140s with restoring control over the Cinca River corridor with the capture of Alcolea de Cinca and Chalamera.[66] This river valley had served as an essential campaign route for Alfonso of Aragon for accessing both Fraga and Lleida. Then, in the spring of 1147, Aragonese forces led by Ramon Berenguer also seized Ontiñena, on the Alcanadre River not far upriver from its confluence with the Cinca.[67] The positioning of this group of fortifications enabled Christian forces to push, in particular, against Fraga, which sat at the western boundary of Lleida's territory.

There are signs that Ramon Berenguer IV had already by this point begun planning elements of what would become the successful attempt to capture Lleida. For example, he made two anticipatory grants of property belonging to specific Muslims in Lleida in December 1146.[68] The documents suggest that the noted Muslim property holders were known to be inhabitants of Lleida but that the count-prince lacked further information on the actual extent of their property holdings outside of the city. Such anticipatory grants remained common as Ramon Berenguer continued his preparations for conquest. In August 1148, for instance, he awarded to Arnau de Montpaó the castle of Vinfaro and the "capmàs" of "Asmed Asaragoci" situated within Lleida's walls.[69] In April 1147, Ramon Berenguer was clearly preparing for an assault when he relocated one hundred men from Balaguer to settle the castral district outpost of Almenar.[70] He crafted the grant to facilitate the unfettered participation of these men at this fortification. They had to be prepared to render defensive and offensive military services immediately, upon only two days' notice. Only "when God will have rendered Lleida in the power of the Christians" would the men begin to pay rents and duties for what they held within Almenar. Already by September of that year, his forces appear to have taken control of Gardeny, neighboring the southern walls of Lleida along the Segre River.[71]

Around this same time, certain warlords and castellans made their own preparations not simply for the conquest but also for its anticipated aftermath. In June 1147, for instance, Guerau de Jorba enfeoffed to Ferran a formerly Muslim tower ("que fuit de Pichato Mauro") he had received from Ramon Berenguer IV in the castral district of Alcarràs, a short distance from Lleida. Ferran would serve as Guerau's "man (solidus) for an entire century." The agreement did not mandate how Ferran was to use the fortification before or during the conquest. After Lleida's fall, however, he was to guard the tower continuously on his lord's behalf.[72]

The attention that Ramon Berenguer IV and his delegates directed at Lleida did not distract them from managing their front with Tortosa. Already by the later 1140s, there are indications that the count-prince and his advisors were planning to advance on these two remaining major centers of the *Thaghr* simultaneously or in quick succession. In February 1146, for instance, the count-prince designated Berenguer Arnau as the future castellan of Muslim-controlled Siurana, a hilltop fortification located to the west of Tarragona.[73] Ramon Berenguer was even claiming lordship over Tortosa before he secured its surrender in late December 1148. When he subscribed the aforementioned anticipatory grant of Muslim property within Lleida from August 1148, as the siege of Tortosa was still underway, he entitled himself "prince of Aragon and the march of Tortosa" (*princeps Aragonensis et Tortose marchio*).[74]

As the count-prince and his supporters anticipated these expeditions, it is possible that they were aware of, and emboldened by, signs of destabilization within the Upper Frontier. The renewed payment of tribute to the Christians indicates that Almoravid strength along the *Thaghr* was on the decline by this period. Governor of Valencia and Murcia, Muḥammad ibn 'Abd Allāh ibn Sa'd ibn Mardanīš, known as "King Lop" or "King Lobo," succeeded in breaking away from Almoravid control altogether and establishing himself as the independent ruler of Valencia, Murcia, and Dénia (r. 1147–72).[75] Archaeological work has furthermore uncovered evidence of the abandonment of dwellings in urban centers throughout the *Thaghr* during what would be the final years of Almoravid rule. Indeed, an Andalusi exodus appears to have been under way from these areas some time before the Christians launched their successful campaigns.[76]

Alliances Underlying the Conquests

Even though Tortosa and Lleida were conquered sequentially in a united campaign coordinated and led by Ramon Berenguer IV, it is important to recognize that these enterprises were distinct.[77] Tortosa's capture figured as part of the Second Crusade and thus featured the widespread participation of foreign knights.[78] The assault on Lleida, by contrast, remained a largely regional effort. This contrast between these expeditions would have lasting implications for the postconquest administration of Tortosa, Lleida, and their surrounding territories.

We lack contemporary narrative accounts of the conquest of the territory of Lleida. According to the sometimes unreliable sixteenth-century chronicler Zurita, the forces that took the Muslim city were composed almost exclusively of local Aragonese and Catalonian knights, in addition to Templar brothers stationed at Monzón and Corbins. To a certain extent, evidence of the postconquest *repartiment* of Lleida's territory confirms Zurita's reporting. He also noted that knights and "ricos hombres" of Aragon and Catalonia were led to battle by the "king" of Aragon.[79] The local orientation of this expedition was a surprising reversal of a well-established pattern of confrontation. As we observed in the previous chapter, under the Aragonese monarchs, Sancho Ramírez, Pedro, and Alfonso, the capture and restoration of Lleida had been well sponsored by the papacy. Plenary indulgences and ecclesiastical lobbying had promoted the influx of French knights, many of whom were already invested in the engagements through their long-standing ties to Aragon.

The knights who participated at Lleida probably understood the established papal policy that combat in al-Andalus and the Holy Land would be eligible for the same spiritual dispensations. Many of them were already invested as territorial lords in the region and had the further promise of lands and booty, plus possible allegiance to their count and monarch, to motivate them. Although the attack on Lleida was an extraordinary expedition, it was nevertheless part of the continuum of armed conflict with Muslims that had preoccupied the daily lives of warlords in the region for generations. In this respect, this final, successful attempt on Lleida paralleled more closely the expeditions that were typical throughout central and western Iberia, which only occasionally received extralocal aid.

The composition of Christian settlers in Lleida's territory during the first generations of Christian rule accordingly differed from those of settlements up the Ebro and of Tortosa, where significant numbers of foreign crusaders would obtain lands and entitlements.[80] Up to these mid-twelfth-century conquests, Aragon and Catalonia had been much more receptive of extralocal and crusader involvement in their engagements with Islamic lands. Yet this was a tradition that would be sharply curtailed from the later twelfth century. The Crown of Aragon, like the rest of Christian Iberia, would become much more reliant on its own forces. Iberian stakeholders enacted this reversal consciously due to the realization that foreign forces were less effective, less respectful of local rulership, and less committed to settling and defending the captured territory.[81]

This reduction of foreign involvement made it all the more important for Ramon Berenguer IV to ensure that his local allies were fully invested in the enterprise. Relations with Urgell were of particular concern following Barcelona's assumption of Aragon, which naturally had serious implications for that county's planned expansion into Lleida. Ramon Berenguer IV now exercised lordship over many of the most important castles bordering Lleida's territory and had the ability to isolate the county by cutting off access to areas of further expansion. Urgell was one of only a small number of entities in the region to have resisted absorption by Barcelona. Only Empúries, Pallars, and Rosselló remained independent. Of these, however, only Urgell possessed an Islamic frontier.

Just months before commencing the campaign against Tortosa, in May 1148, Ramon Berenguer IV and Ermengol VI of Urgell signed an agreement (*convenientia*) that detailed the terms of their cooperation against the Upper Frontier.[82] Most importantly, the concord assigned Ermengol a minority share of Lleida as well as lordship over it and over a number of Muslim-held castles that would constitute the new frontier zone following a successful conquest. Included among these castles was the strategically crucial fortification of Ascó. Situated at the right bank of the Ebro roughly one hundred kilometers south of Lleida, Ascó was a logical extension of the count of Urgell's territorial sphere of influence. Its inclusion was also possibly an indicator that the count, in emulation of Alfonso's assault on Fraga, was planning to use Ascó to blockade the Ebro in order to isolate both Lleida and Tortosa.[83] In return, the count of Urgell and his men were expected to perform military services ("ostes et cavalcadas") for the count-prince during and after the conquest. As had become customary for delegated castle lord-ships in Catalonia, Ermengol would hold everything in fief ("per fevum") from Ramon, who retained the power (*potestas*) to assert control at any time.[84]

The composition of the forces involved in the effort against Tortosa had grown more diverse as the commencement of the campaign drew nearer. Earlier on, in 1146, Ramon Berenguer IV seems to have envisioned, naively, that he would be able to manage the effort without such a long list of allies. That year, for instance, he had prospectively granted the noble Guillem Ramon I de Montcada full lordship over the city of Tortosa and its fortress (*zuda*), without qualification.[85] According to Gary Doxey, these donations were intended to set up Tortosa's future government under "the delegated leadership of the house of Montcada," thereby establishing a mechanism of colonization that would prevent a repeat of the outcome suffered at Mallorca in 1115.[86] Since local factors, rather than the pope's call to crusade, motivated this campaign, the count-prince had little way of foreseeing the extensive involvement of foreign crusaders en route to the Holy Land.[87]

Tortosa's orientation toward the sea, along the crucial Ebro fluvial axis, could explain why it attracted the interest of seafaring crusaders passing by. In sharp contrast to Lleida, Tortosa also remained of considerable interest to naval powers seeking trading outposts and depots along the Iberian coast. Earlier, we explored the evolution of Genoese links with Christian and Muslim Iberia and cooperation with Barcelona under Ramon Berenguer III. Due in part to their pursuit of trading access within Muslim- and Christian-ruled Iberia as well as Occitania, the Genoese, rather than the Pisans, would engage in this campaign against Tortosa and the ventures against Almería that preceded it.[88]

In the decades leading up to these successful engagements, Genoa sought to enhance its access to trading areas throughout the western Mediterra-nean. By the early 1130s, the Genoese had renegotiated their arrangements with Narbonne and gained the right to establish a fortified trading station on the Aude River, near Perpignan.[89] Furthermore, in 1138, Genoa had staked out its North African and Andalusi trade with a new fifteen-year treaty with the Almoravid emir in Morocco and successfully subjected most of the key ports of Provence's coastline as tributaries to Genoese authority.[90] The Pisans were involved in a number of Genoa's negotiations in the 1140s, which sug-gests the rivalry between the two city-states had reached a temporary lull after verging on full-scale war over their respective interests in Sicily, Cor-sica, and Sardinia in the late 1120s and early 1130s.[91] Side projects by the

Genoese served to draw other regional potentates into the effort. After the discontented men of Montpellier expelled their lord, Guilhem VI, in 1142, for instance, the Genoese helped him regain power the following year. This careful intervention helped establish Guilhem as a devoted ally and earned the Genoese valuable exemptions and privileges within his lordship.[92] Guilhem therefore was motivated to contribute his own ships to the campaigns against Almería and Tortosa alongside the Genoese not simply by the promise of a significant share of the spoils of conquest, based partly on his involvement in the aforementioned 1136 attempt. He also owed Genoa a debt of gratitude for helping to preserve his political viability within Montpellier.[93]

Other developments during this period served to involve the Genoese more deeply in the political struggles of the region, allying them with Guilhem and Ramon Berenguer IV of Barcelona in opposition to their mutual rival, Count Alphonse Jordan of Toulouse. In 1143, tellingly, Genoese goods were taken by the men of Saint-Gilles, located between Montpellier and Marseille, who were acting on behalf of Alphonse Jordan. A short conflict ensued, after which Alphonse Jordan capitulated. In the peace treaty, Alphonse promised the Genoese a considerable sum, a portion of which would be paid via exemptions on Genoese ships docking at Arles. Although Alphonse Jordan pledged to respect Genoese rights in Narbonne, he refused to relinquish his claimed judicial authority over Genoese and Pisans accused of certain crimes within his territories.[94] Alphonse Jordan's death in 1148 may help further account for why Ramon Berenguer IV waited until that year to launch his campaign against the Andalusi Upper Frontier targeting Tortosa, which drew heavily on resources and manpower in this contested region around Toulouse.[95]

In addition to previous agreements with the counts of Barcelona over trade along the Iberian coast, Genoa's dealings within Occitania and independent military pursuits served to pull the rising maritime power further into the Peninsular political arena.[96] In 1146, the Genoese had sent a fleet to raid against Almería, a well-fortified position located along the Peninsula's southern coast, which had long served as a base for pirates who menaced Christian merchants from Genoa and elsewhere. Although up to this time Genoese had been more motivated by monetary gains and trading concessions than the capture, rule, and defense of such zones that would put a stop to this activity, the republic moved in a new direction with these endeavors.

The *Chronica Adefonsi Imperatoris* asserts that the pirates of Almería had consistently raided the entire Christian Mediterranean "from one end of the Mediterranean to the other" including Barcelona, Genoa, and Pisa. It also claims that the joint campaign with Alfonso VII of Castile-León was proposed by the Genoese, and that only after deliberation did Alfonso agree to participate and finance the expedition.[97] Almería's thievery was one of the reasons for the expedition offered by the Genoese consul and historian Caffaro.[98] The success of this campaign, which was the product of much experience in long-distance raids on Muslim ports, enabled the Genoese to force the defeated Muslims of Almería to sign an unfavorable treaty and pay a massive twenty-five-thousand-*morabetin* fine.[99] Genoa's growing naval track-record enhanced the republic's importance as an ally for Peninsular rulers vying for territorial conquest. In addition, as Frederic Cheyette has noted, Genoa's value was due to "the lowly mechanical skills of carpenters and blacksmiths and rope makers that they brought to the bitter business at hand, skills we might imagine noble warriors treating with scorn but that were irreplaceable in the conduct of siege warfare."[100] Indeed, Caffaro's account suggests that the construction and operation of the siege engines were responsibilities managed primarily by the Genoese at Tortosa.[101]

Soon after the dust had settled from this wildly successful raid, Alfonso VII commissioned Genoa's navy to return to Almería in a major territorial expedition that he was preparing to launch under the umbrella of the Second Crusade the following year.[102] The Genoese promised the king that they would lend their naval support to an expedition that following May in exchange for one-third of the city and any land they helped to conquer as well as freedom from maritime levies within the ports and waters under his control. The pope had a hand in forging this alliance. Eugenius III had encouraged the Genoese to support the effort in late autumn of 1146.[103] Alfonso led a diverse coalition drawn from Castile, Barcelona, Aragon, Urgell, Provence, Navarre, Pamplona, and Pisa.[104] In spite of his collaboration, Ramon Berenguer IV was wary of further Castilian encroachment along the eastern coastline that he and his predecessors had long claimed. He accordingly pressured the Genoese to promise that they would not attack any settlement or castle between Almería and Tortosa in the future without his prior approval.[105]

Already by the time they had signed their accord with Alfonso, Genoa was in negotiations with Ramon Berenguer IV regarding his planned expedition against Tortosa. In a pair of agreements, Genoa's consuls pledged to assist the count-prince upon their fleet's return from Almería, with "siege engines and other [instruments of war]," with his planned expeditions against first Tortosa and then each of the Balearic islands, starting with Mallorca. In return, the republic would receive a third share of all of the "temporal" spoils of conquest and its church would obtain a third share of the "spiritual" incomes and property. They also obtained valuable exemptions from commerce levies throughout "all our lands and sea."[106] It is evident that the Genoese conducted a careful cost-benefit analysis before committing to either of these engagements. Indeed, when their representatives had signed the concord with the Castilians and Leonese, they made their participation conditional on their gaining the commission for Tortosa from Ramon Berenguer. Grouping the two conquests into a single year, wintering their ships and troops at Barcelona at the count-prince's expense, and reusing many of the siege engines and infrastructure they had built for Alfonso naturally made the ventures less risky and potentially far more enriching for the Genoese.[107] Ramon Berenguer's concerns that the calculating Genoese would fully deliver on their pledges after assisting Alfonso VII could explain why the Genoese took oaths to support Tortosa's conquest until it succeeded or was withdrawn before sailing from their home port and at the walls of Tortosa before launching the siege.[108]

Although there was clearly a strong rationale for enlisting the Genoese, the count-prince did have an alternate, potentially cheaper, source of naval support for these expeditions. Around the time that these negotiations were under way, the consuls of Pisa made an unsolicited request to Ramon Berenguer IV that he resist allying with their old rival, Genoa, and instead join them in resuming the engagements that they had nearly accomplished in collaboration with his father, Ramon Berenguer III, three decades earlier. They also sought to entice the count-prince by identifying Valencia as ripe for the taking, after eluding his father, and at serious risk of falling into the lands of an outsider (*extraneus*) if he did not move quickly to seize the opportunity.[109] Ramon Berenguer and his advisors must have sensed the palpable desperation of the Pisans' plea. They furthermore certainly had the wherewithal to observe that Genoa was better equipped to help this expedition succeed, in particular because it was already mobilizing to support this campaign against Almería. In any event, there are no signs that the count-prince ever deviated from his planning with the Genoese in order to pursue, or even investigate, this proposed alliance with Pisa.

The campaign against Almería proceeded smoothly, with the Genoese delivering their critical naval assistance as anticipated. Alfonso VII led his coalition's forces across the Peninsula to besiege Almería as Genoa's fleet approached from the sea. The combined forces captured the city, an enormous booty, and numerous Muslim captives on 17 October 1147.[110] The Genoese were little interested in assuming direct management of their share of the city, however. Instead, they preferred to infeudate their holdings, along with their share of any further territory acquired by Alfonso "from Dénia to Seville," to a local delegate, Ottone di Bonvillano.[111]

Soon after Almería's capture, the Genoese fleet sailed to Barcelona to pass the winter and prepare for supporting Ramon Berenguer IV's attack.

After reinforcements arrived from Genoa, the fleet sailed southward with the count-prince's forces. It reached the mouth of the Ebro on 1 July 1148 where it joined other forces and began the siege of Tortosa.[112] As discussed, the expedition involved allies from Occitania as well as northern Europeans who had sailed around the Iberian Peninsula en route to the Holy Land on the Second Crusade.[113] These crusaders had already assisted King Afonso Henriques of Portugal with his capture of Lisbon the previous year.[114]

The success of the Genoese in these partnerships attracted the interest of Pope Eugenius III. Just one Italian sea power, acting independently, had helped these Iberian rulers capture these elusive objectives so decisively, and the pope and his advisors must have dreamed of the impact that an Italian naval coalition could have. Accordingly, Eugenius soon counseled the Genoese and Pisans to end their quarreling once and for all in order to facilitate further engagement in the wars within the Peninsula. Representatives from the two city-states ultimately succumbed to this papal pressure and agreed to sign a long-term truce in 1149.[115]

The Genoese consuls were initially pleased with the outcome of their venture with Ramon Berenguer IV. They memorialized the victories over Almería and Tortosa through Caffaro's history and by commissioning a mural in Genoa's cathedral.[116] The Genoese also sought to develop their new Iberian acquisitions into profitable investments. In June 1149, the republic sought to make the most of its share of Tortosa by signing a ten-year peace with Muḥammad ibn ʿAbd Allāh ibn Saʿd ibn Mardanīš of Valencia, Murcia, and Dénia that guaranteed the safety of Genoese residents and traders in Almería and Tortosa and protected Genoese trading colonies in Valencia and Dénia.[117] Pisa had already enacted a truce with ibn Mardanīš, albeit without the trading outpost concessions, earlier that same year.[118] Despite careful attention to their expenditures and the reception of considerable property rights and exemptions, the debts incurred by the Genoese during the expedition were nevertheless already a cause of concern within months of Tortosa's capture.[119] They would sell their rights within the city by 1153 and subsequently refrain from any further involvement in expeditions within Iberia.[120]

Orchestrating the Conquests

This coalition secured lasting territorial gains that had eluded Ramon Berenguer IV's predecessors within both Catalonia and Aragon for generations. Tortosa fell, after a prolonged siege, in December 1148.[121] Lleida, along with its subject centers of Fraga and Mequinenza, surrendered to Christian forces in October 1149.[122] Military operations against Muslim strongholds further up the Ebro River, such as Miravet and Gandesa, and in the hill country around Siurana persisted for several years, until as late as 1153.[123]

As we have seen, in planning his expeditions, Ramon Berenguer IV had enlisted powerful allies whose compensation was naturally conditional on the success of the venture. When, as the sieges were underway, he found himself short on funds, Ramon Berenguer and his associates hastily worked out arrangements with less prominent associations and non-noble individuals. During the siege of Tortosa, for example, he and his closest Catalonian supporters went on a fund-raising campaign, seeking financial support from a range of backers. This effort may have been facilitated by a forty-day truce arranged by Tortosa's Muslims, who, according to Zurita, sought in vain to secure reinforcements from Valencia.[124] On 15 October 1148, he obtained a substantial sum of fifty pounds of silver from the cathedral of Barcelona "for the honor of God and the expansion of Christendom."[125] Almost two months later, when he was nearing the end of the siege and desperate for additional funding, the count-prince negotiated military and financial assistance from the burghers of Barcelona. In return, he pawned to them all of his mills and various levies. The charter for this exchange records amounts contributed by individual citizens of Barcelona ranging between four hundred and one thousand *solidi*, totaling 7,700 *solidi*.[126] The priory of Solsona had been more invested in the push into Lleida over the decades, but during the siege of Tortosa Ramon Berenguer promised its canons a manse in that city, presumably in exchange for some form of monetary support.[127] Later, in the midst of his campaign against Lleida in 1149, the count-prince gave the canons of the see of Urgell rights to the church of Llivia, near the Muslim-held city, in return for seven hundred *solidi*. In this charter, he cited his great necessity due to the expedition at hand and the aid already given by a great number of other ecclesiastical and monastic institutions.[128] Ramon Berenguer's lay and religious barons served as witnesses or guarantors for many of these transactions that helped him scrape the barrel in order to secure these victories. For their part, these men also made substantial monetary and military contributions to the campaigns.[129]

Successful conquest also naturally depended on ongoing diplomatic relations. Ramon Berenguer IV juggled numerous conflictive alliances and acted opportunistically when necessary for achieving his objectives. Probably because he was fearful that conflicts along Aragon's border with Navarre might distract him from capturing Lleida, the count-prince negotiated a peace with its king, García Ramírez, in July 1149, as he prepared to commence campaigns against the city.[130] Their restored relations and agreement to split future lands conquered from the Muslims were sealed by Ramon Berenguer's betrothal to Garcia Ramirez's daughter, Blanca. This commitment was contradictory, as Ramon Berenguer had of course been betrothed since 1137 to Petronilla of Aragon, as we have seen, who was still awaiting her coming of age. It is possible that Ramon Berenguer had duplicitously promised to annul his marriage alliance with the Aragonese in order to secure help from Navarre during this crucial moment in the push against Lleida. Later that same month, not knowing whether it would indeed lead to the long-awaited conquest, Eugenius III nevertheless congratulated the two monarchs on ending their conflicts, which threatened the "damage of churches, oppression of the poor, and much other injury."[131]

Making and breaking marriage deals was a common practice during this period. Under the circumstances, Ramon Berenguer may have contemplated the possibility of ending up with everything. He could have justified his claim on the basis that it derived from his agreements with the military orders rather than what he had arranged with Ramiro and Petronilla. The Aragonese and Navarrese nobility, of course, would have rejected such an outcome outright, but it would be surprising if Ramon Berenguer did not consider uniting all of the territories under his direct control. García Ramírez was quite advanced in years by this point and had only one son who, at seventeen, probably would have been unprepared to contend with rivals for his father's entitlements. In any case, after Lleida had been toppled with García Ramírez's assistance in 1151, Ramon Berenguer reverted to his original plan and married Petronilla, who by then had attained her maturity.[132]

Consolidation or Further Conquest?

Ramon Berenguer IV and other magnates invested in the conquest had their hands full with securing the huge territorial acquisitions and large Muslim populations who chose to remain under Christian rulership. It is not clear whether they deliberately sought to focus on consolidation or were merely forced to do so in spite of their inclinations to press on past the Ebro's right bank. Despite the retention of Muslim populations and fragments of their local economies, the conquerors did not inherit an immediately profitable, productive landscape. The economy of the postconquest Ebro River corridor appears to have been depressed and dysfunctional, especially when compared to the highly active and profitable character of the preconquest Andalusi landscape described by Muslim witnesses such as the geographer al-Idrīsī.[133] In many zones, the development necessary to harness the economic potential of the new territories would take decades to achieve.

Ramon Berenguer and his allies had waited generations for victories of this magnitude and had only accomplished a subset of the conquests he personally had envisioned when planning the Ebro valley campaigns. As we saw earlier, in 1146, the count-prince had identified as among his primary targets the islands of Mallorca and Eivissa, the coastal castle of Penyíscola, and other strongholds in northern Valencia.[134] On the other hand, he must have remembered clearly how Alfonso of Aragon and his kingdom had suffered due to overzealous expansion.

The pope and other church leaders sought diligently during these years to encourage Ramon Berenguer and his supporters to move onward to capitalize fully on their victories. In June 1152, for example, when certain strongholds north of the Ebro were still under Muslim control, Eugenius III urged faithful knights to assist with the Iberian situation rather than venturing to the Holy Land: "let them not hesitate to go with Count Ramon Berenguer."[135] Soon after assuming the pallium in 1153 or 1154, Anastasius IV added his support and urged continued campaigning.[136]

Even if Ramon Berenguer may have doubted his ability to push further southward, looking poised to continue his conquests into Valencia and the Balearic Islands did have obvious benefits. Indeed, with his siege of Lleida still underway, the count-prince used the moment to send his fiscal officer, Bernat de Castellet, to pressure neighboring Muslim rulers to pay tribute that he hoped to use to settle a debt.[137] In the aftermath of Tortosa's conquest, in 1151, Ramon Berenguer indicated that he anticipated an influx of such tribute payments when he endowed the see of Tortosa with one hundred *morabetins* annually from the "*paria* of the Muslims."[138] In May 1154, furthermore, he borrowed one hundred *morabetins* from the Barcelona burgher Arnau Adarró, to be repaid from "the *paria* of Spain" due to be received in September.[139] His frequent contact with such Muslim tributaries during this period is recorded in his accounts of his court's expenditures when it was encamped at Vilamajor, in western Catalonia near the border with Aragon. In November 1156, the *alcaid* of Muslim Borriana visited the count-prince at that court with "many other Muslim warriors." Ramon Berenguer's troops had escorted the embassy through Christian-ruled territory in order to guarantee its members safe passage. The *alcaid* and his entourage remained at the court for two days before returning to Muslim-ruled lands.[140]

In the zero-sum game of Peninsular territorial politics, appearing prepared to commence with further conquest, with active tributary relationships and both Muslim and Christian allies ready to support new expeditions, also permitted the count-prince to bargain most effectively with Alfonso VII of Castile-León over their respective partitions of future conquests in the eastern half of Muslim Iberia. The Treaty of Tudillén, signed by the two rulers in 1151, was the first of a series of concords aimed at minimizing quarrels over expansion. The agreement determined that Ramon Berenguer IV would have Valencia and its lands up to Tortosa and bordered to the south by the Xúquer (Júcar) River. Anything he could conquer further to the southwest or in Murcia, he would hold in fief from the emperor.[141] At this same meeting, Alfonso VII convinced Ramon Berenguer to abandon his aforementioned recent alliance with Navarre, thus reverting to the agreement they had made in 1141 at Carrión. Now that the count-prince was no longer in need of Navarre's aid, he agreed with Alfonso to conquer and divide up the kingdom of Navarre, with Ramon Berenguer receiving two-thirds and Alfonso receiving the remainder.[142] By decisively cutting out Navarre in this fashion, the Treaty of Tudillén established Castile-León and Barcelona-Aragon, once and for all, as the dominant players in expansion into Muslim territory in this eastern half of the Peninsula. In cooperating with Alfonso, Ramon Berenguer resolved conflictive open questions concerning Aragon's western border. He also earned formal recognition of his claim to the vast Muslim territories of Valencia and Murcia from the kingdom that had the greatest potential to disrupt Catalano-Aragonese southward expansion.

These diplomatic achievements in the wake of these considerable victories were certainly significant. For the time being, however, no matter how much he desired them, Ramon Berenguer IV lacked the ability to undertake additional territorial conquests. It is notable that prospective grants of prized objectives in northern Valencia from before the conquests of the lower Ebro valley, such as the donation of Penyíscola to Guillem Ramon I de Montcada in 1146, were not renewed after the count-prince had set to work consolidating his conquered lands.[143] The need for Muslim tribute and continued good relations with ibn Mardanīš of Valencia and Murcia made further conquest an unrealistic objective for the time being. Indeed, as we will see, ibn Mardanīš would assist Ramon Berenguer's victories at Tortosa and Lleida by ignoring calls for assistance from his coreligionists in the *Thaghr*. Such limitations, combined with the immense project of consolidating the Ebro and Segre valleys and continuing political complications concerning Barcelona's trans-Pyrenean possessions and titles, ultimately forced the count-prince to shelve any grand plans of conquest and prospective claims on the vast remainder of al-Andalus in the wake of his major victory over the Upper Frontier.

In the meantime, Ramon Berenguer IV and his magnates would devote themselves to this formidable task of developing this largest single territorial increase ever realized in Catalonia's history. As we shall see in part II of this study, this was a project that witnessed varying administrative techniques and mixed success. Ramon Berenguer's successors would manipulate the foundations he had established or coordinated in the initial decades following the conquests as they sought to confront new challenges and manage competing ambitions.

PART II

The Implications of Victory

✦ CHAPTER 4

Aftermaths

Constructing Authority within a Conquered Landscape

Successful conquest ushered in a phase of rapid redistribution as Ramon Berenguer IV fulfilled many of the pledges he had made before and during the campaigns. The count-prince's numerous obligations on his balance sheet did not oblige him to sacrifice his governmental authority within this conquered landscape, however. He was able to be strategic in his distribution of lands and rights. Most notably, he maintained dominant stakes in the most potentially lucrative urban lordships of Tortosa and Lleida while arranging for the most costly rural domains to be disseminated among and administered by lay and religious lords.

Within Lleida's district, Ramon Berenguer dispersed many of the surrounding castral territories. Evidence is lacking for the twelfth-century lordship of certain castral districts, but scholars generally assume that territories alienated by the monarchy at later dates had previously been subject to its authority since the *repartiment*. According to this logic and, in some cases, more reliable evidence of comital-royal possession, Ramon Berenguer retained five key castral territories that lay to the north and east of the city: Almacelles, Bell-lloc, Alamú, Puiggròs, and les Borges Blanques. A similar methodology is used to suggest that the count-prince continued to exercise control over the territories that would develop later into the barony of Aitona, which were defined by the castles of Aitona, Carratal, Seròs, Massalcoreig, and Escarp.[1] He also held the heavily fortified corridor that extended along the lower Segre River from Aitona to northeast of Mequinenza. He enfeoffed rather than alienated sectors of this expanse. For example, he granted the *almunia* of Almussara in fief to Ramon de Monells for service in the campaign.[2] In total, Ramon Berenguer distributed roughly two-thirds of Lleida and its district.[3]

Within the lower Ebro valley region, Ramon Berenguer's retained share amounted to a substantial sector running from Benifallet downriver past Tortosa to Amposta. The bulk of the count-prince's allocation of lands deriving from his share of the conquest from in and around Tortosa occurred within five years of the conquest.[4] In spite of this loss of direct control over these lands, Ramon Berenguer nevertheless continued to control a majority stake and carefully maintained and managed Tortosa's broader district. Preserving this level of control was essential since he and his supporters still hoped to resume campaigning beyond the Ebro River valley to the south.

The count-prince had surrounded himself with capable fiscal officers who would enable him to capitalize on these victories to further his ambitions for increased authority throughout greater Catalonia and Aragon. New documentary practices aided these efforts. The flurry of irregular parchments documenting the count's distribution of lands and rights may appear rudimentary and unsystematic in comparison to the "distribution books" or *Llibres de Repartiment* produced by Ramon Berenguer's great-grandson, Jaume I, following the thirteenth-century conquests of Mallorca and Valencia. Viewed as a corpus, however, these instruments were highly creative and effective for their time in advancing the count-prince's agenda. Similarly, although brief and haphazard, charters of settlement adequately outlined the juridical environments for the Christian, Muslim, and Jewish communities taking root in the two major cities and in certain of the smaller rural communities. The basic guarantees established by these documents were tailored to provide the exemptions and protections necessary to retain or attract present and future inhabitants to these environments.

This chapter will explore how the structuring of relationships and management of comital-royal rights in the new territories dovetailed with the administrative reforms that Ramon Berenguer IV and his fiscal officers were implementing elsewhere in his domains. As we will see, the unprecedented accounting surveys conducted by Bertran de Castellet and Ponç the Scribe within the comital domains in Catalonia in the decade following the conquest, in particular, generated novel instruments for itemizing comital property and officer obligations. As Bisson has observed, by subjugating wayward vicars and bailiffs, these surveys sought to improve the "efficiency of comital fiscal control" as well as to mobilize comital-royal credit, which permitted Ramon

Berenguer to capitalize immediately on some of his territorial acquisitions to the south rather than having to wait for the incomes to trickle in.[5] The new expectations of accountability informed the count-prince's prosecution of alleged abuses by representatives in New Catalonia as well. Indeed, Ramon Berenguer and his fiscal advisors seem to have understood that the efficacy of new instruments of comital authority depended on consistent oversight within his old and new domains alike.[6] Nevertheless, as we will observe, most of their ambitious reforms and policies enjoyed only mixed success in their application and efficacy during his reign as well as those of his immediate successors.

Distribution: Legal Frameworks and Implementation

There are some noticeable links between the administrative approaches implemented by the count and his fiscal officers from the 1150s toward Ramon Berenguer IV's patrimony in Old Catalonia and these new territorial acquisitions in the area that would eventually become known as New Catalonia. In both contexts, they sought to enhance accountability and reinforce comital authority. The surveys in Old Catalonia were coordinated by two of the count-prince's most influential and trusted officers at this time, Bertran de Castellet and Ponç the Scribe. These forays and the instruments they generated sought to reform the existing system of delegation, identifying and thus securing the comital-royal patrimony. Their initiatives sent a message to officeholders throughout Catalonia that their positions were not proprietary but owed allegiance and fidelity to Ramon Berenguer as their count-prince. According to Bisson, the court records they generated responded to two general administrative challenges: "malfeasance by incumbent vicars and bailiffs and the responsibility of securing comital rights and revenues in a land now abruptly and enormously expanded."[7]

As representatives of the count-prince and influential local landowners in their own rights, Bertran de Castellet and Ponç the Scribe each participated in many of the most important concords, divisions, and transactions involving lords, particularly around Tortosa, in the crucial first decade as the count-prince sought to establish administrative norms in the new territories.[8] In the aftermath of the conquest, Ramon Berenguer awarded houses and lands in and around both Tortosa and Lleida to each of these chief fiscal officers. Bernat de Castellet had been present at Tortosa's capture and retained annual incomes from the city given to him by the count-prince at that time.[9] He also appears to have been the recipient of the castle and settlement of Reus in fief from the archbishop of Tarragona and thus was also invested in the internal colonization of this zone north of the Ebro frontier.[10] In and of itself, the self-interest of these top-level advisors as landowners would have motivated increased oversight of the administration of these freshly captured centers.[11]

The legal language Ramon Berenguer IV used to take possession of and distribute these conquered lands implemented a strong governmental paradigm that supported the process of political "re-aggregation of the old counties of the [Carolingian] Spanish March" that was already in motion in Catalonia.[12] Rather than absorbing each conquered Muslim entity into Catalonia's existing territorial structure, he maintained Tortosa and Lleida as independent territorial units, each within its own independent frontier zone. By claiming title, first, to the "march of Tortosa" and then, after Lleida's fall, to the "march of Lleida and Tortosa" (*marchio Ilerde et Dertose*), Ramon Berenguer was not simply enjoying the honorific dimensions associated with the ancient designation of the "march." These territorial identifications also suggested the possibility of future expansion, the conscious assumption or adaptation of aspects of Andalusi organization, and the conquering regime's intent to construct upon the "clean slate" of these new territories the administrative framework it had not yet brought to fruition within Old Catalonia.[13]

This governmental paradigm positioned the count-prince at the top of the chain of authority within these lands.[14] Its underlying principle of organization aligned with what Bisson has identified as an attempt by Ramon Berenguer and his advisors to construct a new model of territorial power in the *Usatges de Barcelona*, which were promulgated shortly after the conquests.[15] Provisions within the *Usatges* called upon all subjects to assist the count-prince (*postat*) in protecting "his" public lands and thoroughfares against malefactors and common enemies.[16] In promoting the count-prince's roles as defender of the common good and chief arbiter, these laws sought to mitigate the relevance of the bonds between lords and their men when compared with the direct ties of fidelity that were purportedly owed to him by all subjects. Such legal principles would serve as a resource for expanding and strengthening comital-royal jurisdiction in the thirteenth century. During Ramon Berenguer's reign and those of his predecessors, however, these provisions remained relegated to the domains under his direct jurisdiction and even there faced resistance.[17]

Preconquest Pledges

Ramon Berenguer IV took possession of his new territories with numerous parties awaiting their shares for assisting in the campaigns. Most of these preconquest arrangements had pledged rights that amounted to the ownership of specific, delimited territories. Only the Templars garnered a set percentage of the conquests: one-fifth, per the arrangements regarding Alfonso of Aragon's will that we reviewed in chapter 3.[18] Although such a proportional obligation did represent a considerable ongoing liability, it also invested the count-prince with a certain degree of flexibility he did not enjoy with standard preconquest pledges. Ramon Berenguer could satisfy his commitment without awarding the order more than a minority share of any particular lordship, and he could give it less strategic or valuable holdings without being in breach of their contract. Similar to other beneficiaries, the Templars were also promised a number of specific holdings, but these represented a very small subset of their overall share.[19]

Examining the grants to the Templars in further detail illustrates how the count-king was able to shape this distribution to his advantage by delegating responsibility over the most burdensome and ostensibly least lucrative sectors while fulfilling his outstanding pledges and playing the part of the munificent benefactor. In 1153, he entrusted the order with extensive territories along the Ebro's course between Tortosa and Lleida before that zone had been fully conquered.[20] Although he did not broadcast their circumstances at the time, Ramon Berenguer and his advisors were likely well aware that pacifying and settling these war-torn, predominately Andalusi-populated lands promised to be a costly burden over the coming years. The manipulative language of this grant may have been crafted to convince the order's leadership that it was receiving lands worth having, likely to generate incomes in the near future. Ramon Berenguer emphasized, for example, that he was awarding them the "best property" (*maiorem hereditatem*) within the territories of Mequinenza, Flix, Ascó, Garcia, Móra, Marçá, and Tivissa.[21]

Although Ramon Berenguer usually honored the specific pledges he had made to the supporters of the campaigns, in some instances they were superseded, diminished, or modified to some degree by subsequent agreements. The successive campaigns against Tortosa had occasioned waves of anticipatory grants, many of which were written as if they had perpetual validity. Such outdated, unfulfilled pledges naturally came to conflict with subsequent donations that were generated to support new expeditions. Guilhem VI de Montpellier, for example, had been granted rights to Tortosa by Count Ramon Berenguer IV before the campaign in 1136. In his will from 1146, Guilhem indicated his belief that his claim to the city, "which the count of Barcelona gave to me in fief," remained in force when he awarded it to his eldest son.[22] Guilhem fought in the siege that toppled Tortosa and remained an important magnate in the lands surrounding it. His descendants possessed rights to lands and incomes in and around Tortosa that Guilhem

VIII later passed to his son Thomas (nicknamed "Tortosa") in 1202, but no evidence has surfaced to indicate that the family ever pressed for recognition of Ramon Berenguer's initial donation.[23]

Despite the overarching similarities in the general structure of the distributions of lands and rights in and around Tortosa and Lleida, it is not surprising to note, given their localized and individuated histories of conflict spanning generations, that these postconquest environments manifested differences that presented the comital-royal regime with distinct challenges.[24] Lleida's situation was of course heavily marked by the interests maintained by Count Ermengol VI of Urgell, which was a product not only of that dynasty's long engagement with that sector of the *Thaghr* but also of Ermengol's recent deal-making with Ramon Berenguer IV and subsequent support of the successful campaign. As we saw in the previous chapter, about a year before the conquest, the count-prince and Ermengol VI had negotiated their partition of lordship over that city.[25] Ermengol obtained the right to administer Lleida and its surrounding district (defined here as stretching from Corbins to Gebud), excepting the Templars' portion. He also would receive lordship of the castle of Ascó, once conquered. Ramon Berenguer reserved the right to reclaim this castle at will (i.e., the feudal right of *potestas*) as well as any rental incomes from its territories. Ermengol could appoint its castellan and receive two soldiers to defray his costs of manning the castle. The agreement clearly emphasized that, as one of the count-prince's most trusted barons, the count of Urgell would have to assist the count-prince with future raiding into Muslim territory.[26]

Perhaps owing to Ermengol's relatively independent status, his reception of administrative rights contained some peculiar features. Ramon Berenguer would select Lleida's first castellan, who would exercise lordship (*senioraticum*) over the shares of the city held by both the count-prince and count. At the same time, the castellan would hold this *senioraticum* as the count of Urgell's man (*homo solidus*).[27] Establishing the office in this roundabout manner—that is, investing the castellan with *senioraticum* himself rather than delegating this responsibility to the count—arguably enabled Ramon Berenguer to maintain greater control as overlord over the city and prevent any risk that the count of Urgell might try to increase his autonomy there. Only after the departure of the first castellan could Ermengol establish a man of his own choosing as castellan. This condition, and the aforementioned withheld right of *potestas*, invested the count-prince with greater control over Lleida during the transition to Christian rule.[28] The count of Urgell and his castellans would furthermore not exercise lordship over the Templar Order's one-fifth share, which consisted of the extramural castle of Gardeny and the neighboring suburb of Fontanet.[29]

This arrangement notably shifted some of the risk normally borne by the delegate to the grantor. Ramon Berenguer assumed responsibility over delays and mishaps that might postpone a successful conquest. Ermengol was to receive a considerable annual income of one thousand *morabetins* until Lleida's capture, to be paid out from Ramon Berenguer's *parias* or coffers. Ramon Berenguer had even guaranteed that this same level of income would continue from Ermengol's share of the city following the conquest, although there is no evidence to indicate that the count ever pursued this guarantee. In heavily favoring the grantee, the agreement attests to the difficulty the count-prince was having at that moment in 1147 in convincing his supporters that he would be able to succeed in this risky venture. This preconquest adversity translated into a meaningful reduction in Ramon Berenguer's postconquest control of Lleida's jurisdiction and resources.

In a similar vein, Ramon Berenguer IV's distribution of lands in and around Tortosa illustrates further how preconquest pledges, in the event that they were not proactively renegotiated, had the capacity to hamper the count-prince's postconquest administrative objectives, thereby necessitating adjustments. Conflictive anticipatory donations issued by Ramon Berenguer in his effort to enlist supporters in the campaign ultimately threatened to deprive him of his carefully managed controlling stake of the jurisdictional lordship over Tortosa. His grant to Guillem Ramon I de Montcada of lordship over the city and castle (*zuda*) and one-third of its incomes in 1146, for example, clashed with the full one-third share the count-prince later pledged to the Genoese in order to secure their naval support of the siege.[30] A record of the city's division enacted by the Genoese consul and Guillem Ramon de Montcada himself, intervening as Ramon Berenguer's delegate (seneschal),[31] shortly after the conquest, made no mention of Guillem Ramon's share: the count-prince received the western sector of the city bordering the riverfront (including the suburb of Remolins), the republic garnered the portion to the south and east, and they agreed to share ownership of Tortosa's *zuda*.[32] This omission was likely due to the fact that Guillem Ramon's stake by this point was being subtracted from the count-prince's and therefore was not germane to the division with the Genoese. This awkward division with Genoa persisted for only a few years, however. Soon, in 1153, fiscal considerations motivated its consuls to sell Ramon Berenguer its one-third stake.[33]

The count-prince's failure to satisfy his 1146 agreement with Guillem Ramon de Montcada did not develop into a conflict until several years after the conquest. Guillem Ramon may have been quieted by Ramon Berenguer's alleged promise to award him *senioraticum* over the Genoese third share if he ever recuperated it. The count-prince's subsequent refusal to carry out this pledge, however, together with other disagreements to be discussed later in this chapter, eventually sparked open conflict that was aired at the comital court around 1155. Guillem Ramon first pressed his claims for the full one-third share that he believed he was owed per the 1146 arrangement. Ramon Berenguer countered that Guillem Ramon's portion could only be computed from the rights to the city that he possessed after the distributions to the Templars and Genoese had been performed. Guillem Ramon, the count-prince pointed out, had himself approved and subscribed those anticipatory donations as seneschal. The court ultimately upheld the count-prince's reasoning, which prompted the noble to turn to the issue of Ramon Berenguer's alleged promise to award him Genoa's share. Yet Guillem Ramon proved unable to present written evidence or witnesses to confirm that the count-prince had indeed made this pledge. The court thus awarded the noble no change to his holdings within the city; this outcome amounted to a substantial decrease in the rights he claimed to have been promised a decade earlier.[34]

Ramon Berenguer's worsening relations with Guillem Ramon were clearly exacerbated by the noble's simultaneous service as the count-prince's lieutenant in Tortosa and role as a minority jurisdictional lord within Tortosa. These roles were not the true source of the conflict, however. In the end, it was Ramon Berenguer's determination to pursue his administrative goals even when they clashed with problematic preconquest pledges that generated tension with such beneficiaries.

Postconquest Donations

In contrast to the fulfillment of preconquest pledges, donations made from Ramon Berenguer IV's portion after the conquest could be tailored to support his developing local and realm-wide administrative objectives. As a result, so long as the count-king and his administrators did not award duplicate donations, the chances for conflict were considerably lower than they were for preconquest grants. While the immediate aftermath of the conquest ushered in an intensive period of comital-royal land donations, which in turn prompted dynamic rearrangement among the beneficiaries, distribution was an ongoing process of delegation that permitted Ramon Berenguer and his successors some degree of control in orchestrating the wider process of territorial development.

Early grants of individual parcels to lower-level supporters and subjects, as opposed to lordships passed to barons that were intended for their own settlement projects, tended to be confined to the major urban districts. Unlike Lleida and Tortosa, Ramon Berenguer did not award rights of lordship to Fraga in advance. He enfeoffed the city to Arnau Mir de Pallars by 1157.[35] The vast majority of the settlement grants within both Lleida and Tortosa were issued as heritable fiefs, usually termed *honores*. A subset of these carried with them expectations of predominately military service. Others invested the recipient with heritable allodial possession of lands subject to no service obligations save for lasting fidelity to the count-prince, in keeping with the nonfeudal tenor of the *Usatges de Barcelona*.[36] Such grants usually stipulated that they were being issued in return for services rendered. The assumption was that the knight would continue to serve the granting count or baron in return for further shares of conquest booty. Thus, although allodial grants were given free and clear, they could serve as a basis for ties of dependence and fidelity.[37] In a typical postconquest grant, Ramon Berenguer gave houses in Tortosa to Pere de Rajadell, who had fought in the siege. Although the count-prince noted that Pere would hold the houses "as his enfranchised and free heritable land," he also stipulated that he was making the transfer for services that Pere would continue to perform for him.[38]

Ramon Berenguer IV and his advisors expeditiously sought to ensure that donations within the urban cores would be utilized by their recipients rather than alienated or ignored. In one characteristic transfer from 1151, Ramon Berenguer gave the foreign crusader knight Guilabert Anglès (Gilbert, the Englishman) some houses and farmland in Tortosa on the condition that "you be a resident of Tortosa."[39] In this case, Guilabert retained the unrestricted ability to alienate these holdings to any party "except for knights (*militibus*) and clerics (*sanctis*)." Clauses to this effect would become a common notarial feature in comital-royal and ecclesiastical charters of donation; lords, like the count-prince, sought to maintain smaller grants among the subject population and prevent their accumulation by prominent landlords in the area.[40]

Strategic grants by the count-prince during the beginnings of the postconquest period awarded lordships within the zone defined by Tarragona, Lleida, and Tortosa to a range of lords. These recipients included the Templars and Hospitallers, ecclesiastical and monastic institutions, and an array of lay magnates. Such delegation spawned seigniorial charters of settlement that sought to attract residents to the rural lands beyond the reaches of the main urban districts.[41] Most of these grants of delegation were made during the 1150s when Ramon Berenguer IV was feeling the tension between frontier defense and obligations elsewhere in his realms. Such large distributions created the territorial divisions and allotments that would inform the withdrawal conducted by his successors, beginning in the mid-1160s during the regency of Alfons.[42]

Ramon Berenguer IV's defensive needs and interest in additional conquests recommended the involvement of the military orders in his distribution of the insecure lower Ebro River valley. In 1151, he gave the Hospitallers the strategically vital castle of Amposta, downriver from Tortosa and bordering the Ebro delta. Ramon Berenguer enlisted the order to use the castle "for the benefit of the church, the amplification of the Christian faith, and for the suppression and confusion of the Muslims."[43] Further donations of lands and castles by the count-prince, in 1157, increased the extent of the Hospitallers' exposure to the southern frontier with Muslim territories, which went a long way toward ensuring the order's augmented involvement in campaigning into Valencia. Ramon Berenguer also granted the order the caves of Remolins near Lleida, Sena and Sigena in Aragon along the Alcanadre River, and the castles of Cervera and Cullera in Valencia. In addition to consigning to the order one-tenth of any territories it helped capture, the count-prince furthermore promised it a tenth of any lands he conquered, even if the order failed to contribute to the successful expedition, so long as he managed the effort without the assistance of other allies. Although he was clearly interested in incentivizing the Hospitallers to engage themselves in these campaigns, Ramon Berenguer naturally wanted to avoid excessive reduction of his share of his conquests.[44]

Some of these charters echoed earlier donations performed by Ramon Berenguer's predecessors along the frontier with Lleida and Tortosa. These transactions appear to have mimicked or borrowed directly from known *formulae* to define the terms of tenure and service for these holdings.[45] The Genoese knight Bonifaci de la Volta, for example, received the castle of Flix in 1154 from Ramon Berenguer IV with terms that were virtually identical to those obtained by the Anglesola family from Ramon Berenguer I in 1079 for their eponymous castle of Anglesola and from Ramon Berenguer III in 1118 for Corbins and Alcoletge.[46] Bonifaci would hold the castle from the count-prince "in fief" (*ad fevum*) and render to him one-third of its incomes.[47] The conditions of this grant of Flix were notably more cautious and restrictive than, for example, those of the count-prince's anticipatory allodial donation of the nearby castle of Alguaire to the bishop of Urgell issued during the siege of Lleida.[48] How do we account for this differential in terms?

Unfortunately, charters rarely provide clues regarding what motivations informed their terms. For this case of Alguaire, Ramon Berenguer identified the donation as a pious one, but he may also have felt pressure to provide more favorable terms in order to secure additional financial and military support from the see of Urgell since the campaign against Lleida was evidently in its final stages. Furthermore, the relative undesirability of the holding could have helped dictate terms that conceded greater control to the recipient. In this instance, unlike Bonifaci de la Volta's castle of Flix, Alguaire not only remained under Muslim control at the time of donation, but its positioning to the south of Lleida significantly reduced the odds of its capture.

Unexpectedly, Alguaire fell under Christian control during that onslaught. This time, however, the favorability of the conceded tenurial terms did not yield the anticipated results. If the bishop of Urgell took possession of Alguaire, he seems to have done little with it. In fact, Count-king Alfons I eventually recuperated the holding and transmitted Alguaire to the Hospitallers in 1186.[49] In contrast, Bonifaci de la Volta's use of the castle of Flix to Ramon Berenguer's liking was likely what encouraged the count-prince to hand over a further one-third share of the fortification when he reinvested it to Bonifaci's son in 1158. Like other beneficiaries of Ramon Berenguer's postconquest distribution, Bonifaci awaited further donations from the count-prince to increase his holdings. He used his new domains as a springboard to enlarge his stake in the new territories through independent transactions, which included his purchase of the *almunia* of Matarranya and other properties in the area from the local Muslim *alfaqui* in 1158. When making these transactions, Bonifaci played the part of the deferential vassal by first seeking out the count-prince's confirmation.[50]

Ramon Berenguer IV (and his advisors) likely foresaw the potential for seigniorial aggrandizement among such a diversified pool of landholders. He remained sensitive to the subjection of smaller beneficiaries of the distribution to seigniorial authority, which threatened to weaken his authority as established by the landed grant. Accordingly, the count-prince sought to check the accumulation of holdings by larger lords, including his own officers. In 1154, he granted Pere de Santponç some houses as an allod, which, he added, neither "Ademar nor Guillem de Copons possessed, if you come upon [this issue] anywhere in the future." Guillem de Copons was the count-prince's local bailiff and a powerful lord in his own right. Here, Ramon Berenguer seems to have been warning Pere de Santponç that this plot of land had been involved in a dispute involving Guillem and Ademar, and that if they challenged his ownership, he should not be intimidated but rather seek legal recourse.[51] By maintaining settlers on their original lands, unfettered by local seigniorial authorities, Ramon Berenguer maintained their unadulterated ties of fidelity. Nevertheless, as we will observe in chapter 5 below, he and his successors could not prevent considerable settler failure in and around Tortosa that did ultimately facilitate the accumulation of lands by larger lords and seigniorial entities.

Religious Donations

Although religious institutions (monastic houses, military orders, and episcopal sees) were distinct from lay beneficiaries of the conquest, we should not draw too fine a line between them. Unlike the episcopal sees, monastic houses were not legally or customarily entitled to any share of the spoils of conquest but did, in many instances, receive contractual rights to significant landed holdings before, during, and after the successful campaigns. These contractual entitlements had no single origin but represented a complex mixture of pre- and postconquest pious grants made in return for spiritual benefits and distributions rendered for military or financial support for the campaigns.

We have witnessed at length how the Templar and Hospitaller military orders came to receive significant stakes in the conquests due to political negotiations or open-ended contracts designed to incentivize their collaboration in campaigning against Muslim territory. A parallel mode of contractual distribution rewarded the financial support of well-endowed religious institutions and associations that could be vital to the leaders of such costly campaigns. Owing to their assistance with these efforts, monasteries such as the Cistercian houses of Santes Creus and Poblet developed into significant landowners along Catalonia's expanding peripheries.[52]

The donations occasioned by the restoration and provisioning of the episcopal sees within conquered landscapes were distinct from the interests received by these religious houses since they were demanded by both ecclesiastical law and local tradition. Such ingrained guidelines did not, however, prevent the count-prince from improvising. Aside from the religious sentiments he must have experienced in playing this expected role, Ramon Berenguer IV had an interest in capitalizing on these opportunities in order to broadcast his roles as conqueror and ruler of greater Catalonia. The episcopal restorations and initial donations to endow these fledgling institutions must have been accomplished via highly scripted ceremonial acts designed to broadcast the authority and exalted stature of the count-prince. Although the archbishop of Tarragona and other prelates from the archiepiscopal province were present to authorize the enactments for Tortosa and Lleida, Ramon Berenguer IV assumed the primary public role as benefactor.[53]

With this distinction came the responsibility to sponsor the growth of diocesan infrastructure and personnel necessary to perform their ministry among the Christian settlers of the new territory. Accordingly, Ramon Berenguer IV, rather than the archbishop, was the primary target of Pope Hadrian IV's criticism and demands for greater support in 1156, after he received news that the see of Tortosa remained impoverished following its endowment.[54] The count-prince and his successors continued to respond to this expectation with mixed success, due primarily to the imprecision of the postconquest distribution, their inability to control their lords and the military orders, and their willingness to transgress their own donations and mandates when they conflicted with more pressing objectives.

Creating *Mudéjar* Communities

Like the charters of settlement for Christians and Jews that would serve as the foundations for the customary laws that would govern the recipient community for years to come, surrender treaties often served as social contracts between the conqueror (or his delegates) and his new Muslim subjects (known generally as *mudéjares*).[55] They defined the requirements that made life under Christian rule viable for the subject Muslim communities and, under certain circumstances, could be embellished or adjusted over time, just like any constitutional document.

These requirements varied according to societal setting and must have been shaped by the concerns felt by *mudéjares* regarding the conditions within their particular locality, as well as by the goals of the conquering collective.[56] In the charter of security granted to the Muslim communities of the Ribera d'Ebre (ca. 1153–58), for instance, Ramon Berenguer IV offered guarantees that had previously been granted to the Muslims of Tortosa and Zaragoza.[57] This was not a simple recycling of a contract that had already functioned to integrate other Muslim populations. The document was in fact tailored to suit a far less urban societal landscape, organized around inherited Andalusi fortifications, which were recognized as presenting different risks to the Muslim inhabitants. Unlike urban treaties, such as Tortosa's, for example, that usually required *mudéjares* to move to extramural neighborhoods within a year of the surrender, Muslims in these small communities were not required to relocate.[58] They could retain their mosques and all the property pertaining to them. In nearby Miravet and Benissanet, however, the Muslims were not granted this important exemption. A concord between the Templars and see of Tortosa, dated within several years of the conquest, mentioned that the mosques in these centers had already been vacated.[59] In the Ribera d'Ebre, the residents would nevertheless receive the customary year of exemption from most levies, excepting the tribute payable to the count-prince.

In certain respects that were acknowledged by the document itself, this continuity in settlement made the assumption of power by Christians potentially more disruptive. The Muslims involved in the agreement seem to have understood that their societal landscape was in fact more vulnerable because it was organized around fortified concentrations now occupied by Christian warlords. Consequently, the regulations appear to have been shaped so as to shelter these residents from some of the recognized dangers. The charter for the Ribera d'Ebre sought to institute powerful protections for the Muslim communities, presumably in order to entice these inhabitants to remain in an environment that would be slow to receive Christian migrants. It assured prospective *mudéjares* that they would not be abused by the Christian castellans occupying their fortresses, requiring specific courses of action in the event of violations: if the Muslim inhabitants of a castral district made a claim against an abusive castellan, for example, the count-prince promised to have him replaced. Tortosa's charter already contained detailed protections against unjustified violent searches of Muslim homes and property. This treaty further increased these safeguards. No "Christian" whatsoever could enter a Muslim's house by force regardless of who accompanied him.[60]

The Weight of the Andalusi Past on Consolidation

As surrender treaties reveal, the conquered landscape was anything but a blank slate. One of the most complicated aspects of the distribution was the manner in which the victors interacted with existing Andalusi patterns of organization. In establishing administrative guidelines for the new territories, Ramon Berenguer IV and other local potentates he invested were inclined to implement pragmatic rather than ideological measures regarding the transition to Christian rule. In many cases, as scholars have recognized, this rationale prompted them to rely heavily on Andalusi patterns of territorial organization and utilization.[61] Some degree of respect for the preconquest past was generally standard practice from the most expansive structural categories down to the smallest minutiae. The reuse of urban centers such as Tortosa and Lleida alongside lesser settlements in the region, from the Roman period up through the end of the Middle Ages, were clear cases of macrolevel territorial continuity.[62] At the micro level, Christian castles were developed out of Andalusi *ḥuṣūn*, villages from *alquerias*, towers from *almuniae*, dependent rural centers from *aldeas*, and municipal zones variously from *alfoces* (sing. *alfoz*, from the Arabic *ḥawz*, meaning district) or *mudun* (sing. *madīna*).[63]

Andalusi Land Organization

It is not always possible to reconstruct what motivated mentions of preconquest conditions or organization in documents dating from the years of

consolidation following the transfer to Christian rule. When Alfons I delimited his settlement charter for Horta and Bené from 1165 by reference to
Andalusi preconquest boundaries, for instance, he was not necessarily simply
attempting to retain Muslim residents.[64] The enactment tellingly made no
further moves to record any other aspects of preconquest use of the land.
Expediency rather than conservatism likely informed the inclusion of this
information within the grant, since honoring these boundaries did not prevent Alfons from manipulating the castral districts as he saw fit. Borrowing
these names and limits had the added benefit of facilitating the use of extant
infrastructure (dwellings, roads and bridges, agricultural systems, fortifications) by both Christian settlers and existing Muslim residents.

We can observe a similar mechanism with the restoration of the diocese
of Tortosa in 1151. Likely due to Tortosa's "partially captured" state, rather
than reverting to its Visigothic limits, the count-prince and archbishop temporarily arranged "that the episcopal see of Tortosa has and possesses without
any conflict all limits of its episcopate just as any king of Muslim times at any
time possessed, or ought to possess, the principality of Tortosa."[65] That the
subsequent restoration of the entire ancient see of Lleida from the lands captured by these same campaigns, by contrast, made no reference to Andalusi
boundaries reduces the possibility that Tortosa's arrangements were made
chiefly for symbolic reasons.[66] As witnessed by the Treaty of Tudillén, the
count-prince and his ecclesiastical collaborators anticipated that the momentum of conquest would soon yield territorial gains in northern Valencia, and
it appears that they planned to award Tortosa its ancient diocesan lands incre-
mentally as each Andalusi political unit succumbed to Christian control.[67]
Thus, as with Alfons's delimitation of Horta and Bené, authorities drew on
Andalusi organization to define ecclesiastical spaces as a temporary expedient that was compatible with their wider objectives. This pragmatic mode
of diocesan restoration even received papal approval in 1156.[68] Once Ramon
Berenguer IV's ambitions of further conquest languished and Alfons transitioned into a less aspirational policy concerning Tortosa's frontier, authorities generally shifted to relying on Visigothic boundaries.[69]

Although the settlement frameworks developed by lords and Christian
migrants in the new territories responded to postconquest conditions, they
were constrained to some degree by inherited Andalusi infrastructure. The
suddenness with which productive operations (such as mills, lime factories,
mines, and tanneries) appear in the postconquest sources suggests extensive reuse by the conquerors.[70] When grantors utilized existing place-names,
units, and limits to define their donations, these aspects of the Andalusi world,
in theory, enjoyed continued relevance within Christian society. However,

the persistence of Andalusi land organization into the Christian-ruled period ultimately relied on its ability to serve the interests of the new overlords and their administrators. As Sabaté has observed, the process of postconquest spatial organization was an extension of what had already been performed within neighboring integrated territory and had to correspond with physical, socioeconomic, and seigniorial constraints.[71]

Place-names endured in many cases, as did the locations of major settlements, even those that were depopulated during the conquest period. A grant from 1155, for example, referred to a village near Tortosa, "which the Muslims call Favarium [Favara], at the top of the mountain of Treseres."[72] In another case, following the conquest, the settlement called "Avincabacer" by Andalusis was renamed Vallclara, based on the foundation of the church of Santa Maria de Vallclara by the Premonstratensians of Montflabó. By 1158, the abbot transferred Vallclara, "which used to be called Avincabacer," to the see of Tortosa to administer as a parish church. Soon, the use of Vallclara was limited to refer to this religious foundation rather than to the general area.[73] When the count-prince confirmed the donation just a week later, he identified it only as "Avincabacer."[74] We can observe the distinction in a donation of land to this church by Arbert de Castellvell in 1164. He made the grant to "the church which is called of Vallclara," situated in the "terminus of Avincabecer."[75] Future charters nevertheless tended to refer to Avincabacer alone, usually without the Arabic prefix, as "Cabezeir" or "Cabacer," prefiguring its modern name, Cabacés.[76]

Shifts in place-names did not necessarily signify that the centers or lands in question had been put to different uses under new lordship. Even when the conquerors altered a place-name, their reuse of this node, together with the infrastructure and patterns of activity that surrounded it, constituted a form of continuity. Certain charters illuminate the linkages between the uses of holdings in Andalusi and Christian times. When Alfons delegated rights to the castral district of Ulldecona in 1180, for example, it remained in Andalusi hands. Nevertheless, the count-king indicated that the castle's boundaries and amenities would remain the same once it fell under Christian control.[77] Such preemptive donations helped ensure that castral districts like Ulldecona would enjoy a high degree of continuity. No recipient would accept alterations to the Andalusi circumstances unless beneficial to his rights.

Andalusi society tended to feature smaller, more regularized land units that were easily retained because they had analogues within Catalano-Aragonese society. Eritja and Sarobe have found that postconquest infrastructure incorporated *almunia*-tower zones by equating them to the *quadra* territorial structure that was well established within Christian-ruled society.[78] Like *quadrae*, *almuniae* could be granted individually to the petty nobility or amassed by more powerful noble barons into a larger castral district.[79] The use of conglomerations of received Andalusi fortification/population centers (predominately *almuniae*) further facilitated the process of provisional castralization. By consolidating these districts under their own compartmentalized jurisdictions, lords imposed new sociopolitical meanings on these organizational structures and rendered them operable for their immediate needs. Such expediency thus enabled lords to delay devoting attention to the internal reorganization of castral districts for years, if need be.[80]

The appropriation of Andalusi spatial organization similarly liberated rulers from having to stipulate boundaries in detail. In the aforementioned case of the 1165 settlement charter for Horta and Bené, for instance, the reuse of Andalusi boundaries by Alfons's advisors greatly expedited their transaction. Inheriting preexisting population centers and boundaries did potentially simplify both documentation as well as the settlement process itself. On the other hand, this simplification had the potential to complicate later boundary disputes since neither the written instruments nor the infrastructure itself retained sufficient detailed information regarding territorial limits. Such cases commonly had to rely on the memories of Muslims who had remained in Christian society. Reuse of Andalusi boundaries, in the manner in which it was executed by Christian-ruled society in this period, therefore could not be an enduring or durable model of territorial organization. It was innately subjective, prone to manipulation, and naturally difficult to sustain in areas that suffered a loss of their Muslim residents. In an illuminating case from 1154, just a year after the Christian capture of the mountain fortress of Siurana, Ramon Berenguer IV ordered two of his officers, Bertran de Castellet and Berenguer de Molnells, to obtain an official delimitation of that Andalusi castral territory from the former Muslim inhabitants who had since emigrated to Tortosa and Valencia.[81] These *mudéjares* were to assist their conquerors in taking stock of their former homelands in order to begin the process of distribution and consolidation. Through correspondence with the émigrés in Valencia and personal declarations from those in Tortosa, Bertran and Berenguer were able to determine the "proper" limits of Andalusi Siurana's district. These witnesses declared that these boundaries were more extensive than the count-prince and his administrators believed and in fact occupied almost the entire swath of territory separating the Ebro and Francolí rivers. Based on this testimony, Ramon Berenguer IV had cause to enlarge Siurana's castral domain, which benefited him since he exercised lordship over Siurana at this time. This increase came at the expense of neighboring seigniorial entities such as the Burdets' lordship of Tarragona, which lost a portion of its *camp* to Siurana's redefined district.

This redefinition would not endure, however. Arbert de Castellvell acquired Siurana in fief shortly after Alfons's accession. Yet, after Arbert's death in 1173 and before his young heir could be reinvested with the fief, various interested parties seized upon the family's vulnerability by lodging a complaint with the count-king that Siurana's official boundaries had been incorrectly drawn.[82] The claimants were a group of Christian magnates with holdings in the area. They appeared before Alfons and swore that the true Andalusi boundaries of Siurana had been manipulated. They produced "old Muslims from Siurana" who claimed to remember the preconquest organization. After taking Quranic oaths, they physically demonstrated these authentic boundaries. Siurana may have been a special case that welcomed manipulation due to the fact that the original donation was itself based on a survey. Siurana's redefined district came to include Falset, which, the claimants and their witnesses explained, had been sold by Siurana's Andalusi inhabitants to the residents of Garcia before their departure to the south. This addition did not benefit the Castellvell family, however, which already exercised lordship over Falset.[83] Overall, the new survey significantly reduced the extent of Siurana's territory held by the Castellvells from the limits originally established in the postconquest aftermath in 1154. These claimants, on the other hand, succeeded in enlarging their domains and in reducing the wealth and power of a local rival family.[84]

Evidence does not survive to compare the accuracy of the two surveys. Alfons's ambition to effect "the restoration and confirmation of the limits of the castle of Siurana" was a difficult enterprise.[85] Even had their memories served after two decades, the Muslims from the latter survey may have been pressured to alter their testimonies by the parties in the dispute. It is suspicious that the court asked them to confirm the boundaries that had already been publicly declared by the claimants rather than furnishing this information independently. Rather than correcting a deviation from Andalusi territorial conditions, these claimants may well have perpetrated one. Memories of the potentially useful yet often elusive Andalusi past were accordingly vulnerable to both inadvertent and intentional manipulation and manufacturing.

The importance of reusing infrastructure in urban zones could explain why boundary stipulations were treated more explicitly in settlement charters for cities and towns than for rural areas. Ramon Berenguer IV's charter confirming the rights and privileges of Tortosa's Christian settlers, issued within a year of the capture, entitled them to the natural resources and infrastructure that were vital to the city's future viability as a dense settlement and economic center. It also stipulated the limits of its district (comarca) in detail by naming the four cardinal points to define the space. Along the north, Tortosa's territory ran from the Roca Folletera (on the Ebro River, between Benifallet and Miravet) to the Coll de Balaguer (by L'Hospitalet del Infant on the Mediterranean coast). Along the south, it continued from Ull-decona (beyond the Ebro River's right bank) to the sea.[86] Such preservation of intricate spatial details in writing obviated the need to reference Andalusi delimitations and reduced the risk of subsequent boundary disputes.

However, cases where urban districts were not defined in such detail or where participants made implicit referrals to preconquest organization could experience disputes similar to what we have witnessed with Siurana. For instance, in his prospective grant of jurisdiction over Lleida to Ermengol VII of Urgell in 1148, Ramon Berenguer IV vaguely defined Lleida's limits as extending from "the limit of Gebut up to the limit of Corbins," and deliberately exempted castral territories within Lleida's district from the city's jurisdiction.[87] When the count-prince produced the city's population charter in 1150, however, he left its boundaries unspecified.[88] He may have reasoned that these limits would be defined by the developing seigniorial presence in the zone rather than by his implementation of a predetermined organization by fiat.

The imprecision of these guidelines created an opportunity for local potentates to lobby for a redefinition of Lleida's district based on its preconquest boundaries. As with Siurana, Lleida's Christian conquerors had researched and documented the city's Andalusi limits within a generation of the conquest.[89] Drafted around 1170, during the reign of Alfons, the *Termini Antiqui Civitatis Ilerde* recorded in detail what it purported to be "the ancient limits of Lleida when the Muslims left Lleida."[90] In this document, Lleida's territory was much larger than the district it had been assigned in the 1148 donation. It is unclear whether Ramon Berenguer had based his preconquest definition of Lleida's district in 1148 on its Andalusi *madīna* (urban zone) or on its *alfoz* (broader district). If he had referred to the former area, which was considerably smaller than the *alfoz*, it may have been a tactic to reduce the extent of the territory that would be subject to Ermengol's authority per the agreement. Furthermore, the limited information during the preconquest period regarding the limits of Lleida's *madīna* could explain why the boundaries of the 1148 donation were expressed so vaguely.

The *Termini Antiqui Civitatis Ilerde* notes that it was commissioned by Ermengol VII and Alfons but does not indicate their motives or, indeed, whether they conducted the exercise at the behest of other parties.[91] In the decades since the conquest, the two rulers may have come to understand that the durability of the 1148 grant depended on determining the true extent of Lleida's Andalusi district with greater accuracy.[92] Alfons had recently ascended the throne when the text was produced and may have planned to undo some of the erosion of Lleida's jurisdictional district through the development of exempt castral zones along its periphery as authorized by Ramon Berenguer IV. Alternatively, similar to Siurana's situation, lords holding domains located within Lleida's district could have demanded the new survey in hopes of escaping Ermengol's jurisdiction.

If the 1148 donation had been based on the boundaries of the *alfoz* rather than those of the *madīna*, and if Eritja is correct that Lleida's *alfoz* was actually smaller than the zone outlined in the *Termini* survey, then rival lords had a clear motive to push for a redefinition.[93] It is therefore possible that the circumstances of this belated survey of Lleida's Andalusi limits were similar to those surrounding the adjustment of Siurana's boundaries, save for the fact that the findings of the *Termini* were never implemented.[94] Even though they were based on third-party testimonies, these versions of past spatial orderings were analogously shaped and interpreted to service the objectives of the present. The mirage of the maintenance of preconquest conditions could veil and legitimize attempts to subvert authentic continuity.[95]

Although evocations of preconquest conditions could assist *mudéjar* communities in defending their customary land rights, they also could be utilized by lords as a means to enlarge their domains at the expense of neighbors. In a revealing example from 1209, the Muslims of Benifallet and Miravet won a case in Tortosa's municipal court that alleged that they had been displaced from two alluvial islands by the queen mother, Sancha, when she illegitimately seized the property.[96] Count-king Pere, who had been embroiled in disputes with his mother for years over property and prerogatives left by his father, Alfons, enlisted Guillem IV de Cervera and Ramon II de Montcada to investigate and see that these Muslims' rights, if determined to be valid, were restored.[97]

A year later, and before this intervention had achieved a resolution, the case was appealed to Tortosa's seigniorial court, which soon learned that there was more of a history to the dispute. The court discovered that, far from seizing the lands illegitimately, the queen had rightfully exercised lordship over the alluvial islands. If these Muslims had held ancestral rights to the lands, they ostensibly had not exercised them, since the lands had apparently sat vacant for over thirty years. Before the Muslims had lodged their complaint, the queen had rented the islands to two Christian tenants, Berenguer and Arnau Pinyol, who had "planted them well" and otherwise "improved" them. With this historical record established, this court sided with the queen mother and authorized Berenguer and Arnau to continue "working, harvesting, and improving the two places."[98]

Although the evidence leaves questions unanswered, it adds to our general sense of the relative importance of preconquest circumstances. Undergirded by the principle that protected the continuity of rights of *mudéjares* on rural lands, these Muslims had revived dormant claims or invented fictitious ones, purportedly based on a memory of Andalusi society, that directly benefited them and their lord. Their apparent fabrication that Queen Sancha had "seized" their ancestral lands illegitimately (in lieu of a more accurate description, i.e. the revocation of rights of usufruct due to absenteeism) does make it plausible that these Muslims had manipulated their version of the past in order to empower their complaint. The ruling by Tortosa's municipal court, and Pere's effort to carry it out at his mother's expense, may well have been motivated by factors other than a respect for ancestral Andalusi property rights. The reversal of this verdict, furthermore, may have hinged on the manner in which these Muslims and their lords based their claim: on rights of customary use rather than on the true Andalusi limits of Miravet and Benifallet. Did unrealized residual entitlement to usufruct trump utilized seigniorial rights? The judges were unwilling to redraw present boundaries based on these unsubstantiated claims by existing *mudéjar* constituencies. Theoretically static and definable limits, as they had existed at the time of conquest when Christians seized control and the initial distributions took place, remained the chief indicator for these kinds of disputes.

Andalusi Proprietorship

Alongside such ongoing efforts to document and negotiate preconquest boundaries associated with place-names and collective use, landlords were interested in recording prior individual landownership in the years following the Christian capture of Muslim territory. Many twelfth-century charters distributing land among new Christian property owners retain this information using formulaic clauses, usually starting with variants of the construction *"que fuit"* ("which belonged to"), that appear to reference previous Muslim owners by name, title, etc. Referring to former owners in this manner was a well-established feature of land charters in Aragon and Catalonia by this point that is also observable in documentation from other Iberian postconquest environments.[99] The characteristics of this body of evidence from Catalonia differ from those of twelfth-century postconquest sources that have survived from other areas, such as the interlineal, Arabic-Latin land charters from Tudela recently studied by Rodrigo García-Velasco Bernal. Although our *que fuit* documents may serve as evidence to support García-Velasco's contention that "the concept of land exchange and its implementation in the Christian Latin contracts was compatible with Andalusi models," the overwhelming majority of Catalonian land-transfer charters with *que fuit* clauses did not involve the Andalusis they mention.[100] Nevertheless, these haphazard and piecemeal records of proprietorship before or at the time of conquest allow us to explore the influence of the transition to Christian rule on indigenous residency and landholding and fathom how Christian attitudes concerning the recent Andalusi past during this formative period influenced their policies regarding integrating captured land.

The function and significance of these references remain a source of contention. Scholars, such as Sénac and Virgili, who emphasize the destructive nature of the Christian capture tend to view these references as evidence of exodus around the time of the conquest.[101] Historians whose research underscores the continuity between the Muslim and Christian rule, however, advance different interpretations. Brian Catlos, for instance, proposes that these clauses represent "merely a method of identifying a unit of land by eponymous reference to a former owner" and could well reflect voluntary Muslim relocation to elsewhere within Christian-ruled society.[102] This latter group accounts for the scarcity of evidence of *mudéjar* proprietorship by recalling the dramatic loss of preconquest Arabic-language documentation that would otherwise have been preserved by the Muslims themselves.

Neither side succeeds in convincingly marshaling the evidence in support of its model primarily because few of the charters indicate where these former proprietors went or when and for what reason they left. It is often difficult to confirm that these former proprietors were even Muslims. The irregular orthography of the names and frequent lack of other identifying information in the sources, combined with our limited record of preconquest inhabitants, generally makes it impossible to identify or locate these personages. Exceptional records yield more information, such as a transfer of an olive grove in Tortosa from 1156 that stipulated that the former Andalusi occupant "left and is (now) in Valencia."[103] Usually all that we can confirm is that departures purportedly took place. Standard *que fuit* documents also cannot indicate what proportion of these former Muslim occupants fled to Islamic lands compared with simply relocating to elsewhere in Christian-ruled society. Yet they do show plainly that the conquest fomented a process of land transfer in which a sizable proportion of Muslim-held properties fell under Christian ownership. *Que fuit* documents are thus useful for identifying individual cases of disruption in proprietorship and tenancy, and also, in some cases, continuity in territorial organization occasioned by the transition to Christian rule. Due to their sporadic production and survival, however, they are unsuited to measure statistically the proportions of Muslim exodus or displacement.[104]

Like the reuse of Andalusi boundaries, *que fuit* clauses were a product of expediency. Rather than detailing the boundaries of the lands being transferred, *que fuit* documents relied on the collective memory of past proprietorship. As a result, they rarely list the territorial limits or features of the transferred lands. Generalizing about this body of evidence is difficult, as the extent of the information recorded about the former proprietors varies dramatically from document to document. Only some of these charters make clear that the referenced Andalusi proprietorship predated the conquest, as when, in 1161, Christian parties exchanged a field in Palomera that "in the time of the Muslims . . . belonged to the Muslim named Abnalbaiub."[105] For the more typical *que fuit* clauses that mention a former Muslim owner without any time referent, these rights could postdate the onset of Christian rule. Such a scenario is especially plausible for charters that were produced some time after the conquest or for those with brief mentions of neighboring parcels to mark the boundaries of the property being transferred. A charter from 1166 noted that the land being sold terminated "to the west in the property which belonged to Avingalbo and Pere Alaman."[106] Typically, land-transfer documents would only transmit information regarding the ownership history for the specific parcels being sold and not for any neighboring properties. In 1179, for instance, Guillem de Salvanyac and his wife sold the see of Tortosa half of two olive groves but in this case used *que fuit* clauses to indicate only the former owners of their lands and not the parcels that shared boundaries with them.[107] These vendors and purchasers likely could have researched and included *que fuit* clauses for the properties surrounding their olive groves but presumably did not see the benefits of investigating and including that information.

Anticipatory grants issued before the transition to Christian rule reveal that the conquerors could obtain detailed information concerning the state of proprietorship in these territories and were already planning the reassignment of assemblages of property to Christian landlords. For example, the tense of Ramon Berenguer IV's grant to the nobleman Berenguer d'Anglesola, of "all of the property that Avialiez, Muslim, ever had or held (*habuit unquam vel tenuit*) in Lleida or in all of Spain," suggests that the participants considered this Muslim's proprietorship a thing of the past, even though they drafted the charter three years before Christian forces captured the city. The prospective nature of this transfer could have reflected Ramon Berenguer's knowledge that Avialiez, like many elites, had already fled Lleida in the face of impending Christian invasion. The count-prince's donation of all of Avializez's remaining property "in all of Muslim Iberia" suggests that his knowledge of the extent of this Muslim's property was incomplete. He was allowing for the possibility that additional titles could surface after the conquest.[108]

Some assemblages of property that derived from a certain proprietor were maintained intact, even when the lands were dispersed over a large area, during subsequent transfers among Christian owners. In 1167, for instance, Ramon de Copons bought all of the property from Tortosa up the Ebro valley to Miravet that had once belonged to a certain Muslim, "Abdela Abisandon."[109] Other transfers combined the lands of multiple Andalusi proprietors, as when, in 1152, the count-prince granted Pere Blanxard and his wife "those houses in Tortosa of the daughter Eicza Aluuazchi, wife of the son Aliaien de Miraved, and the honor of Azmeti, son of Alchoczen."[110] Again, this mode of transfer remained expedient so long as reliable memory persisted of what these properties constituted, since, like many other *que fuit* documents, this charter did not indicate the boundaries of these parcels pertaining to Abdela. Such cases where Christian landlords were supplanting the landholding relationships once maintained by Andalusi proprietors must have engendered an intricate process of fact-finding among the indigenous population following the conquest. In turn, beneficiaries of the distribution, such as the aforementioned Berenguer d'Anglesola, would have wanted to compile their own surveys as they sought to account for the extent of the patrimonies they had received. Unfortunately, in contrast to the aforementioned later inquests using Muslim witnesses, the process of verifying the details of preconquest proprietorship has not left any trace among the extant evidence.

In addition to helping to carry out transfers in an expedient fashion, *que fuit* clauses, by isolating ownership rights to identifiable former Andalusi owners, may also have served to legitimize postconquest recipients and limit their potential liability to claimants. This objective would explain why certain charters identified Andalusi proprietors or other parties with ownership rights by name or using other personal details.[111] A property sale in Arenys from 1159 referred to the Andalusi owner only as Galib, but added the defining characteristic that he had been a "scribe of the Muslims."[112] In 1178, a Christian vendor identified not only the former Muslim proprietor but also his wife.[113] When a certain Ermengarda granted to the see of Tortosa a property in Aldover in 1184, she disclosed that it had formerly belonged to a Muslim named "Xala Avinexme."[114] Another charter specified that the Andalusi owner with the common name of "Maomet" was the "son of Moaac."[115] Finally, a short charter of reconciliation from 1198 between the monastery of Poblet and an estranged *confrater* over the possession of houses in Tortosa's suburb of Remolins referenced the former Muslim proprietor by name three times.[116]

In other instances, vendors and purchasers could have interpreted properties' preconquest associations with notable personages as marks of value and prestige and thus worth recording. When Ponç the Scribe donated property to the see of Lleida less than four years after the capture of that city, he identified its former owner as an elite Muslim who had held the office of *qā'id* of Lleida.[117] The bishop of Lleida's sale of houses in Tortosa from 1190 similarly noted that the property had once belonged to the former *qā'id* of that city.[118] In 1154, Ramon Berenguer IV's donation to the bishop and cathedral chapter of Tortosa identified the *camp* of Bitem as once pertaining to the Andalusi "king . . . during the time of the Muslims."[119] At a time when he was receiving criticism from the pope for providing insufficient support to the impoverished see, the count-prince would have wanted to make the properties he was donating seem especially valuable.

Que fuit documents corresponded to an ephemeral stage in the transition from Muslim to Christian rule. The relevance of this information waned as distance from the conquest grew and the land market picked up pace. Once properties had changed hands several times, the identities of former Andalusi owners became less significant and were eventually dropped from the subsequent transfer documents. Charters indicating former Muslim proprietors more than one degree removed from the transaction at hand are therefore exceedingly rare, and, with few exceptions, *que fuit* clauses did not outlive the first postconquest generation. The parties involved in land deals were naturally interested in paying scribes to include only the most essential information for carrying out their transactions.

With variations in the self-interested objectives of Christian landlords came shifts and distortions in the perception and use of the Andalusi past. Certain elements of preconquest circumstances were already irrevocably lost in the transition to Christian rule. Others presented the conquerors with an array of choices concerning whether or how to maintain, adapt, or disrupt the continuity of Andalusi institutions.

Lordship, Accountability, and Comital Power: Two Cases

The delegation that was innate to the process of postconquest distribution was not only demanded by the supporters of the expeditions. It was also essential for effective settlement and defense of the land, which the count-prince lacked the capacity to manage himself. The resulting decentralization did carry some significant disadvantages. Most notably, it reduced the comital-royal government's direct control over some of the developmental dynamics of a portion of the new territories. Such distancing of this administration served to undercut the broader moves it was making to enhance its authority.

Although the *Usatges de Barcelona*, according to Bisson, promoted a notion of "pan-comital authority," Adam Kosto has shown that they remained "a work of comital propaganda" that enjoyed little respect from the barons of Catalonia in the years following the conquests.[120] The *Usatges* also contained conservative elements that could be employed by lords as a defense against comital impositions.[121] The count-prince lacked the adequate administrative tools and sufficient authority to impose upon the seigniorial domains within the conquered landscape. These circumstances reduced the relevance of many provisions of the *Usatges*, since their greatest novelty and utility was investing the count-prince with the legal right to subvert the authority lords exercised over their subjects outside his immediate jurisdiction.

Ramon Berenguer IV and his barons held divergent visions of the extent and implications of comital-royal authority. Within the limited zones under the count-prince's authority in New Catalonia, the administrative reforms set forth by the *Usatges* and implemented through the surveys conducted in areas of Old Catalonia by Bertran de Castellet and Ponç the Scribe informed efforts to protect his rights and hold his delegates accountable throughout his territories.[122] At the same time, the count-prince sought to defend his property and uphold his claimed control over public order in the face of what he viewed as unjustified appropriation. From the count-prince's perspective, these seigniorial actions were illegitimate and demanded his response as their lord and protector of the public peace throughout greater Catalonia. These lords naturally viewed their behavior as valid. It was justified by conventions with Ramon Berenguer and his predecessors or necessitated by misdeeds performed by the count-prince and his men. As a result, these lords responded with formal complaints (*querimoniae*) regarding alleged abuse of power by Ramon Berenguer and his officers.

Two embroiled conflicts that occurred within a decade and a half of the conquests will serve to illustrate how the dynamics of these administrative policies influenced the early years of consolidation. The first involved Ramon Berenguer's main lieutenant (or seneschal) and the minority lord in Tortosa, Guillem Ramon I de Montcada, and was arbitrated around the mid-1150s. The second, aired at Ramon Berenguer's court in 1162, concerned the noble Bernat d'Anglesola and actions perpetrated in and around Lleida. Although contrasting standards of legitimate conduct displayed in these cases were based on the dynamics of consolidation initiated by the comital distribution, their core disputes ultimately revolved around affronts to comital prerogatives and counterclaims of unjust lordship that were typical in *querimoniae* from the later twelfth century. Throughout Catalonia, the count-prince struggled to prevent privatization at the hands of lords and officers and to uphold the provisions for public peace and order informed by the influx of Roman law and promulgated by the *Usatges*.[123]

Guillem Ramon de Montcada in Tortosa

The court's arbitrators based their opinions on a range of considerations but focused their attention on the established facts of the case as well as mandates concerning future administration based primarily on constitutional documents that had served to construct seigniorial authority and local governance within Tortosa. These included the now lost charter of donation fulfilling the 1146 anticipatory grant to Guillem Ramon I de Montcada of "that *çuda* and *senioraticum* of that city and of that town and one-third part in the *dominium* of all incomes from that city and town and of all lands and appurtenances," the population charter for Christian settlers, and the charters of security for Muslim and Jewish residents.[124] The charter of donation naturally took center stage, as each side sought to defend its prerogatives by reading between the lines of the text to reduce its implications or advancing a more straightforward interpretation where it suited its interests. Although these were disagreements that could have surfaced among lesser lords and their men, the count-prince's wider efforts to revive elements of public authority that affirmed his sense of his own special prerogatives as conqueror and lawgiver heavily influenced the discourse of the proceedings with his seneschal. Ramon Berenguer and his advisors clearly believed that these presumed entitlements permitted him to redefine standard seigniorial rights and proper administrative conduct.

Since the conquest, Ramon Berenguer and Guillem Ramon had been operating with different visions of their prerogatives and obligations within Tortosa, a common disjunction between the count-prince and seigniorial authorities throughout the realms during this period.[125] When Guillem Ramon complained that Ramon Berenguer was not allowing him to exercise his rightful jurisdiction over his knights and foot soldiers resident in Tortosa, in violation of his prerogative of lordship (*senioraticum*), Ramon Berenguer countered that this *senioraticum* did not apply to Guillem Ramon because he was under the count-prince's direct lordship and therefore a member of "his household" (*sua familia*).[126] The court upheld Ramon Berenguer's interpretation of these limitations: he, as count-prince, retained the capacity to judge cases that might arise between his own men. Although it reduced the extent of the noble's jurisdiction over comital agents, this opinion tacitly established the competency of Guillem Ramon or his vicar to handle any cases involving citizens. With regard to Ramon Berenguer's authority, the ruling awarded an impressive level of immunity to his men by applying the logical elements of the archaic "personality of the law," revived since its erosion under Carolingian public authority by the "law of the land" (*lex terre*), to jurisdiction.[127] Here, the local customary laws of the city, as dispensed by the local lord and court officer, applied universally only to permanent residents, whereas the count-prince was able to maintain a separate legal culture for internal disputes among his resident men. This principle of parallel jurisdictional competencies within contiguous societal spaces served as a useful means for the count-prince to reserve jurisdiction over an important subset of his subjects. At the same time, it posed significant challenges to extending his authority and reviving the *lex terre*, even within his personal domains, given the governmental culture of delegation and endemic jurisdictional fragmentation throughout his realms.

Both men resisted the assignment of administrative prerogatives within the lordship. Even though Guillem Ramon had consented to the provision in the Muslim charter of security that established the count-prince's limited right to confirm the noble's appointment of the *zalmedina* (market official), he had nevertheless dismissed the sitting officer in preference for another without approval. Here the court again sided with the Ramon Berenguer and upheld the guidelines of the charter of security. The count-prince and the noble also clashed regarding Tortosa's market inspector, the *mostassaf*.[128] Guillem Ramon exercised jurisdiction over this officer, but when Ramon Berenguer sold the right of appointment to an elite citizen he gave the noble only part of the payment. When Guillem Ramon complained, the count-prince responded that, although based in Tortosa, the office serviced a much larger territory, and that the noble deserved only the fraction of the office assigned to his lordship. The court upheld the partial payment but added that the *mostassaf* should give the noble a portion of the incomes he earned in carrying out his duties (e.g., for his role in the sale of captives as slaves).

Other twists and turns in the case illustrate how Ramon Berenguer assigned costly administrative responsibilities while seeking to capture a larger share of the incomes to which Guillem Ramon was entitled as delegate. For example, the count-king deprived the noble of fines paid by townspeople in Tortosa for breaking the peace and truce with Muslims, which, the count-prince alleged, pertained to his "own personal right." Here, the court upheld the principle that these violations offended Ramon Berenguer's authority. The judges agreed that it was not customary to render any share to Guillem Ramon or other lords, as it was not practiced elsewhere in the region or during the previous generation.[129]

In general, Ramon Berenguer had sought to limit Guillem Ramon's jurisdictional competency while augmenting his obligations as seigniorial delegate. The count-prince claimed that Guillem Ramon had shirked his duties of "the guard and custody" of Tortosa's castle (*zuda*) assigned to him in that "fief and benefice," which Ramon Berenguer and his advisors estimated at the extraordinary sum of 60,000 *morabetins* (around 420,000 *solidi*). This number amounted to many times the annual output of all of the comital domains put together. Although the figure must have been a gross exaggeration, that Ramon Berenguer considered it to be within the realm of imagination indicates the perceived costliness of frontier castral lordship during this period.[130] The noble appealed to the wording of the charter of donation, which, he claimed, made no mention of his obligation to guard and maintain the castle.[131]

In making this defense, Guillem Ramon shifted attention to the count-prince's conduct as overlord. Was it not suspicious, he posed to the court, that Ramon Berenguer had never called him to court to answer for his alleged violation of their convention? Why should he be liable for these enormous damages when the count-prince had made no effort over this time to alert him to these unfulfilled provisions of their agreement? Ramon Berenguer lacked a reasonable explanation for the "delay," but this impasse led the court to place the onus on Guillem Ramon to prove that he had indeed made himself available during this time for the count-prince to express his discontentment. If the noble were able to defend himself using trustworthy witnesses, he would owe nothing, since, the judges concluded, "we [will then] know that the count was delaying, and there is always danger in delay (*mora semper ad se periculum trahit*)."[132] If unable to demonstrate that he had been receptive to any demand for justice (*fatiga*) issued by comital court, however, Guillem Ramon would be liable to repay Ramon Berenguer the expenses incurred for only his share of the *zuda*. The judges stipulated that costs for the castle guard should be shared in this fashion in the future.

Incomes produced by the lordship were also the subject of arbitration. This portion of the case record illustrates how city administration involved an inordinate number of complicating factors that could not have been resolved in an anticipatory charter of donation. Some of the courtroom reconciliations addressed the pressing need to stop making controversial ex post facto definitions to emend the exercise of lordship in the city. Guillem

Ramon's third share of "all incomes" had arisen as a *questio* among the noble and count-prince demanding specification by the court. The judges decided that the donation had indeed invested Guillem Ramon with a share of the various levies, and usages "on lands, vineyards, and orchards" that "pertain to the personal right (*ius proprium*) and fisc of the king" should be shared with his delegate. They determined that neither the noble nor the count-prince was entitled to shares of the general incomes produced by the properties held by the "clerics, knights, and burghers" within the city. The judges let Ramon Berenguer determine whether incomes earned by nonresident property owners would be partitioned among jurisdictional lords.

Even though the Crown's policies regarding Jews and Muslims remained inchoate at this point, the count-prince and his advisors clearly believed that the distribution or infeudation of rights of lordship should not encroach on the contract with Tortosa's non-Christian communities he had established in their charters of security.[133] Ramon Berenguer had reason to be defensive about his financial ties to these groups, since he was himself collecting an arbitrary levy (the *questia*) from Muslims and Jews in Tortosa without reserving a share for Guillem Ramon. He justified this monopolization by depicting these revenues not as taxes but as personal loans, "which he promised he would return to them," a highly unlikely outcome that Ramon Berenguer must have pledged disingenuously. The judges called the count-prince on this weak defense and ruled that, if he retained a portion of any proceeds from the lordship, then he should render the noble his contractual share. The very legality of these *questia* impositions by the count-prince remained in doubt, however, since the Montcada family was also collecting *questias* and judicial fines from Tortosa's Christians and Muslims during these early years.[134] Ramon Berenguer did not make issue of this parallel taxation by the Montcadas during these proceedings, possibly because he was sharing in them, but did question Guillem Ramon's imposition of "usages and new customs" that the count-prince deemed to be illicit, such as forcing the local Muslims to ferry goods up the Ebro and to permit him the use of their mills. In response, Guillem Ramon launched a bold defense in which he sought to strike down the very notion that Ramon Berenguer should enjoy exclusive prerogatives over non-Christian residents. He, as jurisdictional lord, should be solely entitled to any uses or customs enjoyed by the count-prince in Tortosa. There should, in other words, be no double standard of lordship. He thus joined other lords in taking offense to Ramon Berenguer's broader monarchical claim to exclusive financial and jurisdictional prerogatives as count-prince within any lordship. He flat rejected the notion, as Bisson has put it, that "vassalic and feudal structures, military and economic, were adjuncts to an authority built theoretically upon Romanist fidelity and majesty."[135]

In building his critique of Ramon Berenguer's conception of his authority, Guillem Ramon added that his alleged abuse of Tortosa's *mudéjares* was in keeping with local Andalusi tradition and thus did not require the count-prince's sanction. He explained that, in demanding these labor services, he was simply maintaining "those usages which these Muslims held in the time when they held the *zuda*, namely chickens, and firewood and certain other things." Ramon Berenguer, however, refused to let Andalusi custom set the standard for seigniorial conduct. Any novel imposition required the count-prince's "consent and will." Ramon Berenguer thus emphatically rejected the notion that lords like the Montcadas were equally invested with the authority to make policy.

This rejection of Guillem Ramon's autonomous handling of Tortosa's Muslim community was part of an overarching attitude expressed by Ramon Berenguer that independent noble action was arbitrary and illegitimate. He added further anecdotal evidence to convey the dangers of handing such policy-making over to the capricious whims of such lords. Guillem Ramon, for example, had allegedly killed Tortosa's Muslim *zalmedina* "out of hatred and ill-will." The noble, however, denied personal responsibility for the death. He explained that one of his men, Bernat de Bell-lloc, had beheaded the *zalmedina* not out of personal vengeance, but in accordance with sentencing rendered by the Muslim community's own magistrate, in keeping with the principle of autonomy enshrined in the charter of security.[136] Adding to this picture of the dysfunction of Tortosa's baronial administrative culture, Ramon Berenguer claimed that Guillem Ramon and his men had perpetrated "grave injuries and threats" against comital bailiffs and other officers based in Tortosa: "they beat them and, on account of these threats and the fear [they caused], the count lost his administration of justice and rights in the city."[137]

The strategy of Ramon Berenguer and this advisors throughout the proceedings seems to have been to expose unregulated baronial power as abusive and dangerous. The short-term goal was clearly to check Guillem Ramon's independence as comital delegate and thereby to reassert the count-prince's control over Tortosa's jurisdictional environment. Ramon Berenguer's apparent long-term objective was much loftier. He aimed to display the proper workings of his monarchical paradigm of governance as well as the benefits it offered to the common good by replacing irregular and unreliable vassalic structures with guaranteed, uniform administrative standards throughout the realms.[138]

In spite of the conflicts aired at court, Guillem Ramon was compliant in serving as the count-prince's faithful supporter in other respects. He subscribed transactions by Ramon Berenguer in both Tortosa and Lleida during these years and, in one notable instance, participated with other noble supporters in transferring one of the count-prince's sons as a hostage to guarantee the sums owed the Genoese for their share of Tortosa.[139]

The records for the case were eventually copied into the *Liber Feudorum Maior* (ca. 1194), a cartulary of conventions defining comital rights and prerogatives that was compiled at the end of Alfons's reign. The *Liber Feudorum Maior* was designed to empower control over the comital patrimony and the accountability of officers and other delegates. Such inclusion of these court transcripts in this collection suggests that subsequent officers viewed them as upholding a pertinent and favorable definition of comital-royal authority.

Bernat d'Anglesola in and around Lleida

The incremental growth of Catalonia's and Aragon's frontier with Muslim-ruled Lleida over the generations leading up to its conquest engendered local baronial independence that clashed with Ramon Berenguer IV's novel administrative initiatives in that area. A dispute with another noble family, the Anglesolas, that was aired at this same court several years later illustrates how particular features of the count-prince's distribution and infeudation of rights in and around Lleida exposed his administration there to unique challenges. In 1162, a collection of religious and lay barons, including Guillem Ramon de Montcada, assembled in Barcelona to judge the dispute between Ramon Berenguer and Bernat d'Anglesola.[140] Although we can certainly agree with Sabaté that the dispute represented a telling episode in the count-prince's struggle to secure a "preeminent position despite still emergent feudal relations and movements characteristic of seigniorial privatization and violence," our comparative approach will enable us to witness how the more mature and entrenched nature of seigniorial engagement with Lleida's territory, in contrast to Tortosa's, encouraged different strategies and distinct uses of documentation.[141]

Unlike the Montcada family, whose influence and holdings had become dispersed over generations of service to the counts of Barcelona, the Anglesolas had developed a localized presence along the frontier above Muslim Lleida from the eleventh century. This local family history served as the back story for the count-prince's first complaint. Ramon Berenguer IV claimed that Bernat d'Anglesola had invaded and seized property between their castle and town of Anglesola and Lleida's district that the count-prince had deliberately maintained under his direct control following its seizure from the Muslims.[142] Any lands within the captured territories, Ramon Berenguer made clear, automatically fell under his ownership and control as the conqueror *princeps*, even if he had not specifically claimed them. Newly acquired lands had to be distributed via an official donation and could not be occupied by any lord on his own authority. Bernat d'Anglesola did not challenge this legal principle and instead defended himself by arguing that the lands he had seized pertained to his family through a grant made by Ramon Berenguer's great-grandfather, Ramon Berenguer I. Here Bernat was likely referring to Ramon Berenguer I's transfer of the castle of Anglesola to Bernat's grandfather in 1079. As defined by this document, Anglesola's castral limits extended westward along the main road to Lleida where it intersected the domains of Mollerussa and Sidamon.[143]

The count-prince's response illuminates the fundamentally opposed perspectives of the two men. Before the court had demanded to see written certification of this donation, Ramon Berenguer initially denied that any such donation had ever taken place, based on the activity of Bernat's parents. Ramon Berenguer I could not have given them those lands because "that donation was never under the control (*potestas*) of [Bernat's relatives]."[144] Had Bernat been able to furnish evidence of the transaction, he would have easily overturned the count-prince's weak defense. The charter from 1079 confirms that Ramon Berenguer I had indeed handed over the castle and its domains to Bernat's grandparents as an allod under their lordship and control (*potestas*). In the absence of any proof to support Bernat's claims, the court ruled that the contested lands would remain under comital authority and that the Anglesolas would be restricted in their ability to select another lord. Had the judges been able to consult this original charter, the proceedings likely would have run a different course and taught us more about what the judicial panel, composed as it was of many lords who found themselves in a position similar to Bernat, thought about the count-prince's novel views regarding the extent of his authority.

Other complaints lodged by the count-prince fit into this theme of illicit seigniorial usurpation. Ramon Berenguer complained that Bernat had illegitimately expanded the district of his castle of Alcoletge beyond the limits of what the count-prince had formerly granted him and his father. Similar to his defense regarding the lands pertaining to Anglesola, here Bernat again countered that this enlarged territory fell within the boundaries of the castral district that he had received in fief. Yet again, however, the noble failed to present documentary evidence to substantiate his claim. In this case as well, the extant 1118 *convenientia* regarding Alcoletge (and another fortification known as Corbins to be discussed below) between Ramon Berenguer III and Bernat's father would have assisted Bernat with his defense.[145] As with the first complaint, the court ruled that Bernat needed to demonstrate his receipt of this enlarged castral district by submitting the charter in question or providing witnesses. Authentic records of both of these transactions exist today in the comital-royal chancery archives and presumably were available to the count-prince at this point in time. Given their contents, Ramon Berenguer had reason to appear as disorganized as his opponent, since Bernat's missing documentation obviously worked to his advantage.

Elsewhere in the proceedings, however, the failure of comital-royal administrators to produce documentation harmed Ramon Berenguer's claims, when the count-prince lodged a further complaint that sought to erode further at the patrimony possessed by the Anglesola family in and around Lleida. He claimed that the Bernat had enlarged the domains of his inherited castle of Corbins, to the northeast of Lleida, beyond what had been stipulated in the original donation to his father, Arnau Berenguer d'Anglesola. Once again, the court's ability to rule on the claim was hampered by the fact that neither party presented any supporting documentation for examination. It is not entirely clear what document Ramon Berenguer had in mind. Based on the aforementioned 1118 *convenientia*, we know that Bernat's father had indeed been enfeoffed with Corbins (as well as Alcoletge) by Ramon Berenguer III. Whereas this document did split the lands, properties, and tax incomes from the castles between Arnau Berenguer and Ramon Berenguer III, it did not detail the limits of their districts.[146] It seems likely that Ramon Berenguer IV was referring to this document, which he himself may have recalled or heard discussed by his advisors yet failed to locate and consult before coming to court. Because Ramon Berenguer had no evidence to present, the judges denied his claim. Such an experience was not entirely new; earlier counts had fallen prey to assertive lords and lost castles due to misplaced charters.[147] Outcomes like these must have helped motivate innovations such as the aforementioned *Liber Feudorum Maior*, or Great Book of the Fiefs, which brought together all of the most important charters relating to the comital-royal patrimony.[148]

Corbins was an unusual example of an earlier infeudation of a castle that was lost in the Almoravid counterattack before being reinstated upon its recapture, when Lleida succumbed to Christian forces in 1149. In the intervening period, the count-prince prospectively pledged his share of Corbins to the Templars as part of the compensation required for deviating from the dictates of Alfonso I's will in 1143.[149] Following Lleida's conquest, the order had transferred its stake in Corbins to Bernat d'Anglesola. This grant, Bernat explained, was what had enlarged his stake in Corbins, not any illegitimate expansion of its district. The court indicated that it would rule in Bernat's favor pending confirmation by the Templar commander.[150]

Ramon Berenguer also made allegations regarding illicit conduct by Bernat d'Anglesola and his men in the region. He claimed that Bernat, his recently deceased brother, and his subordinates had stolen sheep from his herds and committed violence against his men in the countryside and on the public roads. While such mention of public roads is reminiscent of the protections extended by the *Usatges* of Barcelona, Ramon Berenguer was not defending the public peace on behalf of a third party. In this case, he was being more conservative by simply advancing claims for damages suffered to his own seigniorial property and prerogatives.[151] Bernat's response to these allegations provides a rare window onto relations between rival lords in the early postconquest landscape. He explained that he had not attacked Ramon Berenguer's men but rather men of Lleida in the service of the count of Urgell, who had committed injustices against him. If Bernat's account can be believed, it seems that the count-prince's men and property had gotten caught in the crossfire of this seigniorial warfare. In an act of good will, possibly to curry favor with the Ramon Berenguer and attending barons against the count of Urgell, Bernat offered to pay reparations for the damage caused by his men or those of "his enemies." The judges recognized this commitment but decided that witnesses should still present testimony to determine if the Anglesolas were liable to repay the count-prince for other claims resulting from this violence.

In a surprising turn, the court also addressed Ramon Berenguer's ability to exercise justice throughout his lands. A claimant appeared in court while the proceedings were underway to press for three hundred *morabetins* that he alleged that Bernat still owed him for a loan he had made to the nobleman while he was en route to Santiago de Compostella. Bernat acknowledged the debt but argued that the matter did not concern Ramon Berenguer or the court because this man did not reside within his domains.[152] When the count-prince objected, the court upheld his position that anyone in his lands who had experienced injustice should fall under his protection, by comital-royal right.

For his part, similar to what Guillem Ramon de Montcada had voiced in the Tortosa dispute, Bernat accused the count-prince of being an unsupportive, or even unjust, lord while demanding extraordinary services. He claimed that Ramon Berenguer had not followed through with his promise to back him by supplying lawyers needed in a case defending his property rights. Reminiscent of the recent engagement regarding Tortosa's castle guard,

Bernat complained that even though Ramon Berenguer required that he campaign with him in Aragon, he had not reimbursed him, as promised, for the considerable expenses he had incurred during the expedition. The court decided that if Bernat could prove with legitimate witnesses that these promises were broken and that he was owed compensation for these services, then it would rule that the count-prince should reimburse him. In a final exchange, Bernat also claimed that men in the service of the count-prince had come to Anglesola and stolen money from his tenants there. After investigating the matter, however, the court determined that these tenants were indebted to the count-prince and that seizing this money from them was justified.

Unlike Guillem Ramon de Montcada, who had a special relationship with the count-prince as an elite officer, Bernat d'Anglesola was a local lord who simply held lands in fief from the count-prince. Although he seems to have been responsible for the kinds of violent seizures depicted in other disputes from this era, his intention was apparently not to steal from the local populace but rather to target the property of other lords: the stolen sheep belonged to the count-prince, and the attacks on the men of Lleida were part of his rivalry with the count of Urgell.[153] Ramon Berenguer had perpetrated similar behavior in pursuit or defense of his rights by having his men invade Bernat's lordship to collect overdue loans. In contrast to what we have seen in the case with the Montcadas over Tortosa's administration, the core issues addressed by the proceedings centered on seigniorial relations and did not address Ramon Berenguer's controversial claims to extraordinary authority.

Conclusions

Ramon Berenguer IV's efforts to secure and integrate the conquered territories had already made significant progress by the end of his reign in 1162. This count-prince mapped out a blueprint that would exert powerful influence over the handling of these territories by his successors. He established some of the most important socio-legal foundations within the conquered landscape and used this work to project an image of his authority and expectations regarding accountability for all of his realms. He also pieced together a plan for future territorial expansion into neighboring Muslim-ruled lands that was supported by the group of lay and religious lords in the new territories he invested through his postconquest distribution, who were eager to continue the push southward.

Although this distribution of lands deprived the count-prince of direct control over considerable expanses within this landscape, aspects of the process seem to have been engineered to serve his interests. For example, he retained direct lordship over the urban districts that were most likely to receive an influx of settlers, such as Lleida, or that were most important for continued engagement with Muslim-ruled lands, such as Tortosa. Overall, Ramon Berenguer retained what must have seemed to be the choicest assets. Outside of these sectors, he enfeoffed or alienated much of the landscape distanced from the major centers of population that promised to be harder to pacify and slower to attract new settlers.

These moves, however, could not prevent warlords and associations such as the military orders from accumulating lands within the more favorable zones that Ramon Berenguer had donated to landlords and settlers of more modest means who opted to sell their frontier holdings rather than make the effort to inhabit or develop them. Indeed, already by the end of Ramon Berenguer's reign, the signs were already in place that these conquered territories were falling ever more under the control of a relatively concentrated oligarchy of lay and religious lords. As we shall see in the next two chapters, this process would only accelerate due to the administrative withdrawal conducted by his successors in the coming decades.

𝄞 CHAPTER 5

Repositioning within the Lower Ebro Valley

Ramon Berenguer IV's successors, Alfons I and Pere I, built on the administrative practices we have already detailed in distinct ways in an effort to increase the accountability of officeholding throughout their domains. At the same time, they collectively overturned their predecessor's overarching strategic approaches to the conquered landscape. Lleida and neighboring castral territories situated to the north of New Catalonia, while highly leveraged, remained part of the count-kings' patrimony and under their direct governance, whereas the domains to the south, including Ramon Berenguer's closely guarded holdings within Tortosa and its district, were progressively alienated. This withdrawal generated an absence of comital-royal officials and delegates and, accordingly, a sharp decline in their regime's local administrative faculties.

The next two chapters should be read as a collaborative pair. The first focuses on Tortosa and the lower Ebro valley, whereas the following one will address the political circumstances in and around Lleida. Together, they assess to what extent, why, and by what means these count-kings, over the later twelfth and early thirteenth centuries, shifted their administrative relationships with these conquered territories away from the foundations established under Ramon Berenguer IV. They also collectively study how these new trajectories influenced the course of consolidation in these lands. As we will see, this partial divergence in policy regarding Ramon Berenguer's prized conquests was partly the result of deliberate decision-making and partly the inadvertent product of excessive leveraging.

Not all of these comital-royal domains became compromised for the same reasons. Some were chosen because they were income-producing, others because they were costly to maintain, and still others because these count-kings had no other options to satisfy their need for resources to finance other enterprises. These more pressing projects included attempts at further conquest along Catalonia's and Aragon's boundaries with Islamic territories and raiding elsewhere in the Peninsula as well as engagements to protect their trans-Pyrenean claims. Over the long term, these undertakings contributed to the successful conquests of Pere's son, Jaume I, and yielded considerable returns for the patrimony and for the strategic advantage of the monarchy as a whole. They also established valuable precedents that would serve as a foundation for the governmental centralization achieved under Jaume and his successors from the mid- to late thirteenth century. In the short term, however, these projects yielded few returns for the count-kings.[1] The end result was that a large portion of the conquered lands that Ramon Berenguer IV deliberately retained under his direct control fell into the hands of the Crown's major creditors. This shift in policy enhanced the abilities of the more significant seigniorial beneficiaries of the comital distribution to increase the size of their domains as well as their prerogatives in some cases.

Alfons's Minority

The beginnings of this withdrawal from the freshly conquered lands along the Ebro valley were partly inspired by the insecure circumstances of Alfons's early reign. Ramon Berenguer IV's sudden death from illness in the Piedmont en route to meet with the German emperor, Frederick Barbarossa, to renegotiate his interests in Provence in the late summer of 1162 left the dynasty in a compromised position.[2] Ramon Berenguer's heir, Alfons, was only five years old at the time. During the following years, Alfons's regents and supporters busied themselves with transactions calculated to defend the young monarch's entitlements from assertive barons and officers. These activities included conforming his image and titles to reinforce the merger between Aragon and Barcelona, establishing the subservience of the barons and other collectives, engaging in diplomacy and adopting a military policy to protect his inherited rights to expansion, and building on the administrative developments undertaken by his father's fiscal officers.

In spite of the arrangements following Alfonso's will and Ramon Berenguer IV's marriage to Ramiro II's daughter, Petronilla, in 1137, his claims to

Aragon had never been secure.[3] Petronilla had borne the title "reigning queen" of Aragon, whereas Ramon Berenguer, as we have seen, was only permitted the title of "prince" (princeps) by the defensive Aragonese.[4] One indication of Ramon Berenguer's frustration with the situation is that, after several years as co-ruler with Ramiro, he had surreptitiously begun subscribing charters independently as "prince" or "lord of Aragon" (Aragone dominum).[5] Ramon Berenguer's later reign featured cautionary measures to protect the dynastic merger. There was concern that the queen's premature death might foment rebellion among the largely discontented nobility throughout Aragon. The fact that Ramiro remained alive at this time and, moreover, continued to use the title of "king" while a monk made the situation even more unsettling for these ambitious dynasts.[6] Accordingly, in 1152, when Petronilla was preparing to give birth in Barcelona to their first son, Pere, she donated "the entire reign of Aragon . . . just as King Alfonso rightly held and had it" to her unborn child but entrusted it to her husband for his lifetime.[7] Petronilla gave birth to a second son, Ramon Berenguer (later known as Alfons), in Huesca in 1157.[8] When Pere died within a year of his birth, the monarchy moved quickly to establish the second son's claim. Already by 1158, the Treaty of Nájima with Castile identified Ramon Berenguer as the monarch's "firstborn son" (primogenito filio).[9] The count-prince confirmed this status when he granted his son the county of Barcelona and kingdom of Aragon in his final will from 1162.[10] As another cautionary step, the royal family carefully considered what regents and close advisors would be best equipped to assist the young heir upon inheriting the throne. Whereas the count-prince had named Henry II of England as one of his son's regents in his will, after his death, the dowager queen removed Henry in preference for local potentates.[11]

The royal family and these advisors sought to strengthen the new dynasty's legitimacy by emphasizing young Ramon Berenguer's connections to both dynastic lines. Even years after the union had been consummated and produced multiple offspring, Aragon's nobility remained unsupportive of the merger, and the Crown sought to make its heir apparent look more Aragonese. Not long after assuming the throne, Ramon Berenguer exchanged his birth name, which emphasized his connections with the county of Barcelona, for Alfonso (Alfons in Catalan-speaking lands), which broadcast his connection to the last monarch of independent Aragon. As the first monarch of this new dynastic merger, Alfons also adopted the title of "king of Aragon" that had eluded his father.[12]

Alfons's earliest known charters similarly appear to have been carefully crafted by his regents and closest advisors to garner him greater legitimacy.[13] Prepared in different major Aragonese cities and towns as the young king made his itinerary around the kingdom, these documents presented Alfons to his subjects as their legitimate ruler and displayed him fulfilling this role by confirming their customary privileges. Most of these early public enactments depicted Alfons as if he were acting alone and unimpaired as king, with his primary regent, Bishop Guillem de Torroja of Barcelona, and other court supporters appearing as passive participants among the other witnesses.[14]

Alfons's unimpaired involvement in these affairs, however, was a carefully constructed fiction orchestrated by his supporters for the consumption of subjects who were not in attendance as well as for documentary posterity. Alfons was only five years old at this time and could not have had much meaningful involvement in these momentous decisions. His supporters nevertheless used these opportunities to broadcast his title of "king" as well as the credentials backing that title. For instance, when he appeared with the "knights, burghers, and workers" of the city of Zaragoza in August 1162 and confirmed their privileges in writing, the charter clearly differentiated his titles from those of his father (who lay in "requiem") in both the text and the subscription: "I, Alfons, king of Aragon, son of Ramon, count of Barcelona and *princeps* of Aragon."[15] These meetings served as an opportunity for his advisors to advertise his lineage and remind his subjects that the blood of the kings of Aragon and counts of Barcelona mixed in his veins: "I confirm to you all of your *fueros* . . . [confirmed by] king Alfonso, my [grand-]uncle, and Ramiro, my grandfather, and my father, Ramon, . . . who lie deceased."[16] The ordering of these forebearers must have been carefully calculated to resonate with Aragonese audiences, with Alfonso I taking the primary position, followed by Ramiro II, and lastly Ramon Berenguer IV. Similarly, at the first meeting of the Aragonese court in Huesca in October 1162, the reading out of Ramon Berenguer IV's will confirmed to everyone present that the deceased prince of Aragon, with the blessing of his queen, Petronilla, had designated this new Alfonso as the legitimate heir to the throne.[17] During his visitations to Catalonian cities and towns, by contrast, the orchestrators broadcast Alfons's lineage much more selectively and seemed to downplay his association with Aragon. When Alfons personally confirmed Barcelona's privileges in 1163, for example, the charter simply identified his father, omitting any mention of his Aragonese forebearers who had held the most prominent positions in the Aragonese presentations. It instead devoted attention a sizeable list of Catalan baronial allies who constituted the new king's curia.[18]

Rare private transactions during these years conducted within Catalonia were more transparent about the king's compromised situation. In February 1163, for instance Alfons's regents met in Barcelona to execute Ramon Berenguer IV's long-promised donation of the church and tithes from Ascó to the see of Tortosa. Alfons was present, holding his first Catalonian court, but did not subscribe the charter.[19] Instead, the regents were the sole guarantors of the donation and noted that they would continue in this fashion "until Alfons, king of Aragon and count of Barcelona, becomes a knight and leaves his wardship."[20]

Dignitaries outside of the realms were willing to deal directly with Alfons during these years but did occasionally recognize his young age. His minority seems, for example, to have informed the Treaty of Ágreda signed with Fernando II of León (r. 1157–84) in 1162. As the two kings established pacts of mutual assistance and renewed their commitment to conquer and divide up Navarre, Fernando asserted the dominant position by adopting the Peninsular imperial title of "king of the Spains" (rex Ispaniarum) first claimed by his father, Alfonso VII. Alfons, in turn, accepted Fernando as an ally "in your defense and wardship of me and my land."[21] On the other hand, Alexander III seemed to presume that Alfons was fully capable of governing that same year, when he requested his support for the attendance of the prelates from his realms at an upcoming council at Tours. The following year, in 1163, this same pope solicited favors for his nephew from the young king by reminding him of the tradition of "fidelity and devotion" to the Holy See maintained by his father and other predecessors.[22]

Despite this early groundwork, even after Alfons had emerged from his minority, his legitimacy as inheritor of Alfonso I's kingdom, name, and title nevertheless continued to experience opposition.[23] An economic downturn in Aragon in the mid-1170s likely encouraged a longing for earlier days and wider popular support for the appearance of an "old man" claiming to be the true King Alfonso, still alive and well.[24] According to the fragmentary annal of Teruel, this man, who asserted that he was the "Don Alfonso . . . who besieged Zaragoza, Calatayud, and Daroca" and supported his claim with many "things that seemed true," was an imposter, a lowly blacksmith. Nevertheless, as he moved through Aragon, this resurrected King Alfonso was reportedly received by many localities "with great honor and great pomp."[25] Long-circulating popular legends that questioned the circumstances of Alfonso I's death emboldened these credulous subjects. Indeed, Rodrigo Jiménez de Rada's histories recounted stories that conflicted with the official account that Alfonso had been buried in the monastery of Montearagón. He noted that many in Aragon believed that the deceased king was still alive.[26] Another chronicle explained that Alfonso had felt such shame over his defeat at Fraga that he had fled to Jerusalem where he had lived and performed penance as a hermit ever since.[27]

Young Alfons and his advisors took the threat presented by this imposter and his followers very seriously. In March 1175 or 1176, he drew attention to his namesake's final resting place, thus taking aim at the story recounted by Jiménez de Rada, and asserted his own position within that dynasty by making a prominent donation to the monastery of Montearagón on behalf of "the soul of my uncle, King Alfonso, who lies in the church of Jesus the Nazarene of Montearagón."[28] Alfons's attempts to capture this pseudo-Alfonso failed, however, and late in 1178, he sent a letter to Louis VII claiming that the man had fled into the realms of France after he had caught wind of the warrant for his arrest. Alfons solicited the French king's aid in apprehending "this man who acts like a most fraudulent King Alfonso, my uncle."[29] By 1181, they arrested and executed the alleged traitor before a supportive Catalan crowd in Barcelona.[30]

Throughout this period, this beleaguered transitional dynast also suffered abuse from troubadours working in the service of his Occitan rivals. These authors directly targeted Alfons's qualifications to succeed both Alfonso and Ramiro as king of Aragon. In two poems from around 1183, Bertran de Born (ca. 1135–ca. 1215), reeling from the loss of his own castle during Alfons's campaigns against Raymond of Toulouse, accused this "cowardly, flaccid, weak, and lazy" upstart of having murdered the true Alfonso in order to seize the throne for himself.[31] Then, in an apparent effort to inflame the rivalry with Navarre, this troubadour lamented how García Ramírez of Navarre had formerly been robbed of control of Aragon following Alfonso's death. Bertran de Born counseled Navarre's current monarch, Sancho VI (r. 1150–94), that he could recover the kingdom easily, since "his merit is great and is more perfect than that of the apostate king."[32] In the employ of the wayward Viscount Arnau de Castellbò, the troubadour Guillem de Berguedà assailed Alfons, Bishop Arnau de Preixens of Urgell, and other opponents throughout the 1180s.[33] During the following decade, Giraut del Luc recounted similar stories that implied that Alfons's inability to achieve successful conquests against the Muslims was due to his poor leadership and corrupted will. Giraut purported to have uncovered evidence of Alfons's improper, amicable relations with the Muslims. He flagged as suspect, for instance, Alfons's sale of the castle of Polpís to the "Moroccan king" following its conquest in 1190 for far less than it was worth.[34]

Alfons commissioned royalist works from Cluzel, Giraut de Borneill, Arnaut Daniel, and Peire Vidal to counter these slanders.[35] Such groundwork in royal propaganda-making would later assist Pere's efforts to craft his own public image as an ideal prince. It also helped justify some of his more controversial policies in the early thirteenth century, as we will see.[36]

Settlement and Administration under Alfons

Ceremony and propaganda could only accomplish so much in the effort to stabilize this dynastic union. Alfons's legitimacy as the first king in a renewed line of conqueror monarchs also had to gain support from some tangible achievements. His ability to control his barons in Catalonia and Aragon partly hinged on his capacity to live up to the expectation that he continue the conquest of Muslim territory achieved by his predecessors in both dynasties. Accordingly, Alfons's successive failures to achieve new conquests exposed him and his policies to criticism. Lackluster outcomes in these ventures were clearly the result of multiple factors, only one of which was the count-king's lack of sufficient military might and wherewithal. Successful conquest would depend on Alfons's ability to control the resources within his own patrimony, on the lords' capacity to expand on castral positions, and on the count-king's power to command and mobilize those seigniorial reserves.

Managing the consolidation of the lower Ebro frontier to support this goal of further conquest was a complex enterprise. Before he could shunt resources away from this zone, Alfons first needed to ensure that it was pacified and, if not producing economic surpluses, at least self-sufficient. Upon his assumption of the throne, however, the vast majority of his sparsely settled lands within the lower Ebro zone, to say nothing of the predominately rural lands governed chiefly by his delegates, had barely attained the level of subsistence. As we have seen, Ramon Berenguer IV conducted the broad distribution of landed rights and engaged heavily in the settlement of the urban districts of Tortosa and Lleida yet had made scant progress in consolidating nonurban lands. The previous decade had witnessed few settlement projects beyond the Ebro's right bank and almost none outside of Tortosa's district. Furthermore, Ramon Berenguer's practice of delegating rural holdings to the military orders now made it difficult for Alfons to accelerate activity within these zones.

Early on in his reign, Alfons and his advisors turned their attention to fostering new nodes of settlement or revitalizing projects that appeared to be languishing within those areas that remained under his administration's direct control. Rather than simply repeating what had been done in the past, these new initiatives often implemented new tactics. Attempts during Alfons's minority tended to devote attention to inland zones that were buffered to varying degrees by the new territories and were theoretically easier to settle and develop.[37] One novel strategy sought to tap into new pools of potential migrants after Catalonia had proven unable to provide a sufficient supply. In 1165, Alfons tried to attract Aragonese settlers to the

districts of Horta and Bené by offering them the *fueros* of Zaragoza. As he
noted in the charter, his belief that the kingdom of Aragon extended along
that corridor due to Alfonso of Aragon's conquests and to the boundaries
of Andalusi Zaragoza helped justify this application of these *fueros*.[38] Alfons
also required that his delegates abide by these foral norms. When he gave
three knights lordship over Paüls, which bordered Horta and Bené to the
south, in 1168, he left the management of the lands largely to the discretion
of the grantees and dictated only that settlers here should similarly use the
fueros of Zaragoza.[39]

Such initiatives sometimes recuperated unsuccessful grants by Ramon
Berenguer IV by redelegating them or assigning them to comital-royal
officials. In February 1163, for example, Alfons terminated the donation
aimed at populating Villasalva in the *camp* of Tarragona that had languished
since its donation by his father. Rather than renewing the same project, the
count-king adopted a more ambitious approach. He authorized the establishment of the new town of Montblanc on the hill neighboring Villasalva
and appointed Pere Berenguer de Villafranca to serve as its vicar and bailiff.[40]

Alfons and his administrators sought to tailor these charters to include
terms that would increase the chances of success. Many of these grants were
more careful than earlier enactments to allocate the resources necessary for
viable settlement, particularly water, which permitted irrigation to boost
crop yields and provided a source of hydraulic power. In 1163, when Alfons
arranged for inhabitants to populate the tower of Moles, which neighbored
Alguaire along the Noguera Ribagorzana River north of Lleida, he assigned
the settlers full control over the waterway that fed the irrigated lands within
the tower's district.[41] The following year, he licensed the bishop of Tortosa to
build mills along the waterway coming from the mountains (likely the range
known as Els Ports) to the town and expanding the lands under the cathedral's lordship in the district of Castelldans.[42] The aforementioned settlement project for Horta and Bené from 1168 offered a number of concessions
that were calculated to increase the settlers' chances of prosperity. Alfons
awarded the grantees exemptions from commerce levies and established two
local officers to facilitate administrative assistance. An official known as the
çavaçequia would administer the waterways and irrigation systems, and the
zalmedina would manage the local market.[43]

It is likely that the count-king and his advisors referred to past experience
and the circumstances of other zones to guide them in the formulation or
adjustment of settler obligations. Only on rare occasions, however, did they
leave evidence of these sorts of considerations. Even though the domains of
Torre de Miró Torbaví had access to an irrigation canal, its tenants struggled

to generate sufficient yields from their agricultural production to satisfy their obligations. Rather than penalizing them for delinquency, in 1173, Alfons awarded them the exemptions from taxes and levies held by tenants on non-irrigated lands around Lleida. He thus relinquished temporarily some of his anticipated revenues in order to help these settlers establish themselves.[44]

Although direct causality is always difficult to establish for certain, there are indications that Alfons's handling of tenants on his domains inspired certain local lords to institute similar practices on their lands. In 1163, Count Ermengol VII of Urgell provided for settlement in neighboring Menàrguens under terms that were analogous to what Alfons had offered these settlers of Moles earlier that same year: he ensured their access to water for irrigation and obliged them to pay similar dues. The count strengthened his authority over the settlement by reserving jurisdiction and granting the customs held by Balaguer nearby.[45] Around that same time, Ermengol modeled his charter of enfranchisement to Almenar on the prerogatives received by Lleida. Such emulation could have sought to divert settlers from Lleida.[46] Alfons's success with Montblanc may have encouraged its castellan to develop a settlement project of his own within that town's immediate district. Ramon de Cervera established fourteen residents there under his personal lordship in 1166 on the condition that they assist him with the castle guard.[47]

Capitalizing on the economic potential of these lands required administrative development along the trajectories already set in motion by Ramon Berenguer IV. The twin initiatives of defining and capturing the revenue potential of the direct domains had commenced in the latter years of Ramon Berenguer IV's reign primarily as a means to "augment and stabilize his credit" essential for financing extraordinary expenditures, such as the campaigns into Occitania late in his reign.[48] Administrative growth under Alfons was similarly interested in harnessing the potential of his domains in order to be in a position to leverage them. In response to the development of his domains within New Catalonia, however, Alfons's leveraging increasingly targeted resources within these new territories as a basis for credit rather than relying exclusively on returns from Old Catalonia, as his father had been obliged to do.[49]

In his effort to maximize the profitability of his domains and prevent their illegitimate erosion, Alfons maintained his father's vigilance regarding his officers and delegates. In 1163, for example, he had to deal with unpleasant fallout from Ramon Berenguer III's final creative attempt to settle Tarragona when he had delegated the project to Robert Burdet and made him the "prince" of Tarragona in 1129.[50] Following Robert's death, Alfons vigorously defended his inherited share of lordship over the archiepiscopal city

against claims made by Robert's widow and son.[51] This conflict was reminiscent of aspects of Ramon Berenguer IV's dealings with Guillem Ramon
I de Montcada that we discussed in the previous chapter. The Burdet family
denied that Robert had ever transmitted two-thirds of that city and its district
to Ramon Berenguer, leaving them only one-third in fief. After Archbishop
Bernat Tort of Tarragona, Bishop Guillem de Torroja of Barcelona, and
the nobleman Berenguer de Castellet testified that they had witnessed this
very transmission by Robert, the court dismissed the Burdets' claim.[52] The
Burdets nevertheless resisted the ruling, thus initiating a period of aggressive infighting against the archbishop of Tarragona, who had come to hold
Alfons's portion of the city in fief. The court notably relied on third-party testimony rather than written documentation to define the count-king's holdings. At this stage, there were still no indications that the patrimony in New
Catalonia or elsewhere was being defended by the use of a well-organized
comital-royal archive.[53]

The tenor of this engagement with the Burdets was exceptional. Alfons
and his administrators were more accustomed to policing the patrimony and
upholding accountability through more routine engagements, such as audit-
ing officers in the spirit of Ramon Berenguer IV's surveys of the early 1150s.
Around 1165, to cite a typical instance, Bernat Bou de Girona appeared at
Alfons's court to defend his record as bailiff of Girona and its neighboring
villages since the days of Ramon Berenguer IV. In an effort to counter allegations that he had mismanaged his position, Bernat presented evidence that
he had increased revenues without any illicit "new usages" and contrasted
his results with the lackluster performance of his predecessor. Only Bernat's
presentation has survived, but the indications are that he was being held
against fiscal data that he himself was providing rather than a register maintained by fiscal officers at court.[54]

In addition to boosting efficiency through such measures, Alfons and his
advisors sought to enhance the institutional framework established by his
father's regime by creating new local administrative positions and revitalizing old ones. His officers not only bore the traditional responsibility over
managing royal properties but also in some cases served as creditors by paying Alfons advances on their collections. Emblematic of this phenomenon is
the Jew named Jafia, who first appeared as the count-king's bailiff in Lleida
in 1167.[55] The following year, Alfons recognized that he owed Jafia one thousand *morabetins*. He authorized this bailiff to collect repayment from the
incomes of his bailiwick, which he would accordingly continue to hold until
the loan was no longer outstanding.[56] Although Jafia may have been "more [of]
interest to the king as a creditor than as a steward," as Bisson has suggested,

local records also demonstrate that Jafia was heavily involved in comital-royal business in the area, appearing in numerous transactions as "royal bailiff" through the mid-1170s.[57] The incomes associated with these activities played a role in transforming Jafia into a major landowner in the area.[58] It is unclear how much Jafia had paid for the position or what he had been expected to render annually from its proceeds. By comparison, from the late 1170s, the Jews Vida and Azmel paid Alfons 1,500 *morabetins* annually for their shared bailiwick.[59]

Other early credit operations within the new territories naturally tended to be relegated to those districts that had experienced robust growth during the reign of Ramon Berenguer IV or Alfons's minority. Many of these loans were drawn from the Templars rather than from officers like Jafia. Bisson has determined that the Templars were the count-king's most significant creditor in Catalonia and advanced him at least 8,500 *morabetins* through 1177, some 13 percent of his total indebtedness.[60] Since many of the loans arranged with the order were based on incomes from Alfons's lands within New Catalonia, they collectively served to increase the extent of their investment along the Ebro valley frontier.

In the Templars' earliest known loan to Alfons, from 1168, the provincial master and other brothers provided him with five thousand *morabetins* to accommodate his "great affairs and necessities."[61] He pawned Ascó, Riba-roja, and Seròs, three of his most important castles along the Ebro–Segre corridor, to guarantee and repay the loan. Even though Alfons and his advisors may not have viewed this transaction as anything but temporary, pending the time required to repay the loan, transferring these castral districts to the order did amount to an administrative withdrawal and ultimately proved to be a permanent one. A clear sign of Alfons's desperation for funds is the lopsided nature of this agreement. Although these castles and their substantial incomes became the Templars' property, the order assumed all of the benefits and none of the risks of lordship. In taking possession of the domains, the Templars would have the right to replace whatever comital-royal officers were in residence with their own bailiffs and men. Whereas for Riba-roja and Seròs, the order would have to cover the expenses of castle maintenance and guard, Alfons assigned one-third of the revenues from Ascó for the order to keep, to reimburse it for these expenses. If the order lost the castles to Muslim raiding, its loans would be satisfied by drawing upon Alfons's reliable incomes from mills and other royal holdings to the south of Barcelona. Although Alfons did face continuing expenditures in the pursuit of his claims in Occitania following the death of Count Ramon Berenguer III of Provence in 1166, it is more likely that this early loan from the Templars was intended to finance his first expedition into Valencia.[62]

Alfons's Pursuit of Valencia

Before delving further into the nature and extent of Alfons's leveraging, we first need to explore the nature and extent of these southern campaigns. Alfons's first foray into Islamic territory took place in 1169 and followed failed peace and *paria* negotiations with Valencia and Murcia's ruler, Muḥammad ibn 'Abd Allāh ibn Sa'd ibn Mardanīš, the "King Lobo" mentioned in chapter 3 above, and a peace accord with the Navarrese the previous November.

In keeping with the alliance that had been arranged with Ramon Berenguer IV, ibn Mardanīš agreed to pay twenty-five thousand *morabetins* for two years of peace beginning the following May. As legate to the Muslim ruler, Guerau de Jorba pledged to remit five thousand *morabetins* to Alfons, with his son serving as a hostage for the sum.[63] The Muslim ruler would have until Christmas to remit payment of the remaining twenty thousand *morabetins*. Ibn Mardanīš had promised to remit what remained of this *paria* by Christmas but may have doubted the ability of the boy-king to act on his threats of attack.

Signs that ibn Mardanīš would have difficulty meeting this deadline likely motivated Alfons to sign a twenty-year peace treaty with Sancho VI of Navarre at Sangüesa on 19 December 1169. The two rulers committed to "capturing and acquiring in all the land of ibn Mardanīš and all other land of the Muslims" and dividing it equally, along with all resulting *paria* revenues.[64] Warming relations with the Navarrese reversed the Treaty of Tudillén that Ramon Berenguer IV had negotiated with the Castilians and Leonese in 1151 and the Treaty of Ágreda signed by Alfons in 1162. In these agreements, the allies had pledged to divide up Navarre between them. This shift that occurred at Sangüesa was likely the result of Alfons's desperate need for an ally to add credibility to his threats against ibn Mardanīš and to assist with his infighting with the Castilians. It is possible that Alfons's concord with the Leonese at Ágreda had worsened conflicts with Castile, culminating in Alfonso VII's destructive invasion throughout Lower Aragon, which had reached as far as Calatayud. Alfons and his regents had only been able to stop the raiding by launching a counteroffensive from Soria.[65]

There are no indications that the Navarrese assisted Alfons in his initial expedition into Valencia in 1169, as he made good on his threats against ibn Mardanīš and sought to display his credibility as heir to Ramon Berenguer IV and Alfonso I. Here, the Aragonese campaigned with a force composed primarily of brothers of the military orders of the Hospital and Calatrava in the watershed of the Guadalupe, Algars, and Matarranya rivers. The campaign expanded the territory of Lower Aragon and buffered the Ribera d'Ebre with the capture of numerous important positions, including Caspe, Favara, Nonaspe, Maella, and Mazaleón.[66] These acquisitions extended Christian control over the Baja Cinca, Matarranya, and Montsià, a territorial corridor running south of the Embalse de Mequinenza between Caspe and Alcañíz in the west and the Terra Alta in the east, possibly as far as Ulldecona. These gains superseded the positions Alfonso I of Aragon had temporarily acquired in the 1130s leading up to his assault on Fraga. Alcañíz had already received its settlement charter from Ramon Berenguer IV over a decade earlier and remained under Christian control until this renewed offensive.[67]

These territorial gains demonstrated Alfons's ability to challenge Castile's eastward expansion, and the abandonment of the Treaty of Sangüesa, due to disagreements with Navarre over the Pyrenean castle of Pau, led to peace between the count-king and Alfonso VIII of Castile (r. 1158–1214) with the Treaty of Sahagún in 1170. Following this diplomatic shift, Sancho VI of Navarre would repeatedly invade his border with Aragon, diverting Alfons's attention and resources from raiding into al-Andalus.[68]

The agreement at Sahagún largely reinstated the division of conquered Muslim territory established between the Castilians and Ramon Berenguer IV at Nájima, in 1158. The primary difference was that, at Sahagún, the Castilians received full entitlement to Murcia.[69] A supplementary agreement between the two monarchs, signed the same month, pledged mutual aid. Alfonso VIII of Castile promised Alfons that ibn Mardanīš would pay him forty thousand *morabetins* annually. He pledged to guard the peace for five years starting in 1171 and not to aid the Almohads in their attacks on the Valencian ruler.[70] Further solidifying this renewed alliance between the Aragonese and Castilians was Alfons's marriage to Sancha, Alfonso VIII's aunt, as he officially exited his minority in 1174.[71]

The momentum of Alfons's campaigning and the strategic value of his gains along the Catalano-Aragonese southern frontier in the years leading up to the Treaty of Sahagún were undercut, however, by the foundation of the independent lordship and church of Albarracín in northern Valencia by the knight Pedro Ruiz de Azagra around 1170. Pedro had made himself a feudatory of Valencia's ibn Mardanīš and refused to recognize the authority of the kings of Aragon and Castile. He had also restored the "ancient" see of Segorb, which earned papal approval despite inflaming the rivalry between the archbishoprics of Tarragona and Toledo.[72] Upon ibn Mardanīš's death in 1172 following several years spent heading the Andalusi resistance against the Almohads, his son and successor handed over the kingdom to the new Almohad caliph, Abū Yaʿqūb Yūsuf (r. 1163–84), but Albarracín was spared as an independent entity.[73] Its existence was furthermore supported by the now defiant Sancho VI of Navarre. Most problematic for its neighbors was the fact that Albarracín was seated inconveniently along the contested boundaries of Catalano-Aragonese and Castilian territorial expansion.[74]

Further campaigning in the early 1170s earned Alfons important fortifications in central and Lower Aragon, including Miravete de la Sierra, Alfambra, and Orrios, all of which the count-king subsequently issued to the military order of Mountjoy.[75] He may have sought to stabilize these gains and incentivize the push for more territory, while balancing out the castral holdings obtained by the Templars via their extension of credit, by also assigning some of these strategic holdings to the Hospitallers. Reenacting grants made by his father in 1158, Alfons gave the Hospitallers, "as soon as God renders them into Christian hands," the Valencian castles of Cervera and Cullera and La Ràpita, south of the Ebro Delta, in 1171. He lavished the order with the town of Ratera and land in the *camp* of Tarragona, in Montrubí, as enfranchised allods free from any "usage or service." He also pledged the order 1,000 *morabetins* annually from his "paria Hyspanie."[76] Although the charter treated the transaction as a pious donation, one suspects that this impoverished monarch may have been engaging in the veiled repayment of debts he owed the order with these transfers or possibly in a "pay-to-play" scenario. Indeed, such munificence is difficult to fathom given Alfons' desperate financial situation at this time. In a separate donation from this very same month, the count-king recognized his indebtedness to the order for a sum of 2,400 *morabetins* and promised to repay the Hospitallers through the application of these same tribute payments in precise payments of 1,200 *morabetins* at the first of the year for the following two years. In the charter, Alfons openly acknowledged the possibility that he could lose his *parias* at any time but assured his creditors by guaranteeing that his other properties would make up the difference if necessary. Furthermore, two of his barons, Guerau de Jorba and Blasco Romeu, subscribed the charter as guarantors if the count-king's arrangements proved insufficient to repay the debt. The detailed nature of this repayment plan made the count-king look far from a man with adequate resources to serve as a volunteer devotee of the order.[77]

After rallying support at the *Cortes* in Zaragoza in February 1172, Alfons and his supporters launched a major campaign in which they burned and pillaged parts of the kingdom of Valencia en route to besieging Xàtiva. Zurita reports that the new ruler of Valencia feared further damage and consequently established himself as Alfons's feudatory. The price for this alliance was considerable: he would have to pay Alfons twice the customary tribute and render him military and financial aid for his future campaigns against Murcia.[78]

Although the count-king had to shelve any immediate plans to resume his advance into Murcia due to a Navarrese attack along Aragon's borders, the threat alone was nevertheless sufficient to motivate the new ruler of Murcia to join his neighbor in Valencia as an Aragonese tributary.[79] Although these *paria* payments were considerable and represented a huge windfall for the count-king, alone they were insufficient to reverse his mounting financial challenges. Indeed, less than a year earlier, Alfons had acknowledged staggeringly large debt of 24,000 *morabetins* to Guilhem VIII de Montpellier. In the confirmation, he identified twenty hostages, who would secure the debt by traveling to Perpignan to remain in Guilhem's custody until the debt was satisfied. He also scheduled the repayment of the loan in dated installments over the following two years.[80]

Despite this looming fiscal crisis, Alfons and his advisors seem to have felt that they had little choice but to press on with campaigning to the south in competition with other principalities for Muslim territory and *parias*. Although sporadic engagements along Aragon's border continued with Navarre, these did not preclude Alfons's support of the Castilian siege of Cuenca in 1177.[81] This campaign by Fernando II was in response to extensive raiding by the Almohads in the years after their takeover of Murcia in 1172.[82] Zurita states that the kings enacted another agreement of mutual assistance at Cuenca against their common menaces of Pedro Ruiz de Azagra, lord of Albarracín, and Sancho VI of Navarre, a union later renewed in the second treaty signed at Ágreda in 1186.[83] Pursuant to this alliance, and in search of added support along Valencia's western frontier, Alfons entrusted the Castile-based Order of Calatrava in 1179 or 1180 with the castle and town of Alcañíz, a well-positioned staging point for raiding into Muslim territory.[84]

This modest progress in campaigning appears to have given Alfons and his supporters greater confidence that they were closer than ever to achieving Valencia's conquest. In 1176, Alfons prospectively granted Poblet the town of Cepolla near the city of Valencia. The monastery was commissioned to found an abbey for up to one hundred brothers and with sufficient territory to be worked by fifty pairs of oxen.[85] The following year, the count-king prospectively donated the Mozarabic church of San Vicente, in the city of Valencia, to the monastery of San Juan de la Peña.[86] In seeking to identify his legacy with these campaigns and this long-anticipated capture, Alfons turned away from the traditional burial places of his Catalan and Aragonese successors in Ripoll and Montearagón and arranged to be entombed at this new monastery in Cepolla if Valencia fell before his death.[87] Although Alfons later had a change of heart and decided instead to be buried at the Cistercian monastery of Poblet, this venue similarly broke with tradition and reinforced his legacy's connection with conquest and consolidation along Catalonia's southern limits.[88] At the consecration of Tortosa's new cathedral in November 1178, the count-king asserted his commitment to the conquest when he confirmed Tortosa's diocesan limits that extended into Muslim-ruled Valencia. The see itself was garnering a more prominent financial and military role in the advance. Alfons granted it the strategically important castles of Miravet and Zufere in northern Valencia that same year.[89] On the same day, Alfons and his queen also awarded the see of Tortosa the Valencian castles of Castelló, Fadrell, and Almassora.[90]

This confidence was premature, however, and Alfons would never succeed in organizing future expeditions that would accomplish more than securing modest improvements in his positioning along the militarized zone with northern Valencia. Ultimately, Alfons's campaigning and politicking throughout his reign proved more effective at sheltering settlement projects within the Ebro valley than at accumulating additional territory. Although his modest military successes did not enable the Aragonese to launch a viable campaign to conquer Valencia, they were nevertheless vital in convincing the Castilians that continuing their partnership was worthwhile.[91] Revisiting the partitioning of al-Andalus that had been arranged in the Treaty of Sahagún, the Treaty of Cazola between Alfons and Alfonso VIII in 1179 confirmed Castile's rights to Murcia and confirmed their shared commitment to conquering and dividing up Navarre.[92] In return, Alfons and his successors would be entitled to Valencia, freely and without any obligation to present and future Castilian monarchs.[93]

Although this division would prove to be definitive and enduring, at the time the signatories had reasons to fear revision, revocation, or violation of the terms and sought to secure their claimed territories as soon as possible. These concerns added further urgency to Aragonese campaigning over the 1180s and 1190s, when multiple smaller expeditions pushed further into northern Valencia. This activity led to the construction or capture of castles that helped make viable numerous new settlement projects positioned well beyond the Ebro River valley. Forces closed in on centers such as Morella and the coastal castle of Penyíscola while making occasional raids deeper into Valencia territory, such as an attack on Morvedre in 1179.[94] The Hospitallers received Olocau and Ulldecona in 1180 and managed to retain them both.[95] The Templars, by contrast, obtained the castle of Polpís in 1190 but soon lost the holding.[96] Alfons gave the neighboring castles of Fredes, Bel, and Benifassà to the see of Tortosa to guard and settle in 1195 on the condition that he receive half of its revenues.[97] The imminent threat presented by the nearby Muslim-held castles of Morella and Cervera stalled these projects, however.[98]

The count-king also sponsored the settlement of lands distanced from the militarized zones in hopes that these projects would have a greater chance of viability compared with earlier in his reign or during his father's rule. In a representative initiative from 1185, Alfons granted Montsant, between Castelldans and Ascó, on the condition that the recipient establish settlers there. He retained a majority interest in revenues from the town and its district while delegating administrative responsibilities.[99]

Although he had renewed his concord of mutual assistance with Alfonso VIII against Navarre in their strategically vital treaty of Cazola, the count-king nevertheless risked upsetting this delicate balance with Castile when he signed a treaty with Sancho VI of Navarre that ended their hostilities in 1190.[100] Alfons and Sancho established mutual accords with Portugal and León, thereby implicitly isolating Castile. Soon the Almohads under the direction of caliph Abū Yūsuf Yaʿqūb al-Manṣūr (r. 1184–99) defeated Alfonso VIII's forces at the well-known battle of Alarcos, on 19 July 1195. After advancing on the Castilian-held castle of Alarcos, the Muslim forces, with their superior numbers, forced the king to flee to Toledo and his troops to disperse throughout the countryside. After taking Alarcos and a number of other positions in the area, al-Manṣūr opted to withdraw his army to Seville after several weeks.[101] Nevertheless, this debacle forced Castile to shelve temporarily its grand ambitions for further conquest. Renewed gains against the Almohads would wait nearly two decades until the Christian principalities found the diplomatic means and papal support to reunite at the battle of Las Navas de Tolosa.[102]

Military Activity under Pere

Soon after assuming the throne in 1196, Count-king Pere quickly established himself as an even greater spendthrift than Alfons. Even though he did not suffer from the same legitimacy concerns as his predecessor, he was nevertheless a highly ambitious conqueror and directed his reign in pursuit of a larger-than-life legacy. During his nearly two-decade reign, his attentions and resources were heavily torn between trans-Pyrenean, broader Peninsular, and Mediterranean interests.[103] The pomp and circumstance with which he established himself as a tributary of St. Peter, when he was crowned by Innocent III in 1204 and pledged to pay an annual *census* of 250 *morabetins*, set the tone for the extravagant ambition of the rest of his reign.[104] More than his predecessors, Pere devoted his Peninsular efforts chiefly to long-range raiding. In keeping with Innocent III's efforts to broker a peace and promote alliances between the Iberian Christian rulers, Pere collaborated in campaigning with

Christian partners to the west. These relationships drew him to develop a different mode of engagement with Islamic territory in targeting territorial expansion in western Valencia, away from the Mediterranean coast.

In spite of Pere's clear ambition to establish a formidable reputation for conquest, he started his reign defending against Almohad offensives. After the fall of the Balearic Islands in 1203 to forces at the command of the new Almohad caliph Abū ʿAbd Allāh Muḥammad al-Nāṣir (r. 1199–1213), Pere sought unsuccessfully to organize campaigns against Mallorca with naval assistance from the Genoese. Innocent III also promoted the effort and prospectively restored the island's episcopal see on 16 June 1205.[105] On this very same day, with regard to the Catalano-Aragonese peninsular frontier, this same pope sought to enhance the extent of military-order support along the Lower Aragonese frontier with Muslim territory by encouraging the assistance of the military orders of Calatrava and Alcántara.[106] Indeed, the continued delegation of castral districts for settlement to stabilize the fringes of nominal Christian control—what later became the boundary between Lower Aragon and the northern Valencian province of the Maestrat (or Maestrazgo)—helped harden the line of defense there. During this same period, Pere assigned the development of numerous castral districts along this frontier to primarily Aragonese lay and ecclesiastical lords. The cathedral of Zaragoza received the castles of Linares (de Mora) and Puertomingalvo.[107] The Hospitallers obtained the castle of Fortanete, which was located "against the land of the Muslims." The count-king granted the noble Berenguer d'Entença the castle of Manzanera, "for the defense of my kingdom and for the disruption of the Muslims."[108] And the noble Arnaldo Palazín received the castle of El Boy, now in the district of Vistabella del Maestrat, to develop in order to support Pere and his successors as well as the castle of El Mallo, near Mosqueruela.[109]

After possibly campaigning in 1206, Pere united his armies at Monzón in the late summer of 1210 and marched into Valencia, where he captured the castles of Ademuz, Castielfabib, and Sertella.[110] By September 1210, he was already making attempts to establish settlers at Ademuz.[111] Aragon's frontier bishops (Zaragoza, Huesca, and Tarazona) as well as the Templars and Hospitallers were instrumental in supporting these efforts. Pere sought to assert greater control over these new holdings and the front with Valencia by drawing on his remaining rights within the Ebro valley. In return for their one-fifth share of these conquered castles, for instance, Pere restored the Templars' rights to Tortosa, Ascó, and Riba-roja, which were originally transferred by Alfons in 1182.[112]

Like his predecessors, Pere had to make pledges regarding future conquests in order to incentivize his supporters. He committed to give the Hospitallers the castle and town of Cabañas and the mosques of Borriana, once captured, and promised the Templars the *alquería* of Russafa by the city of Valencia in 1211.[113] Because he was overextended in foreign engagements and increasingly short on resources, Pere also encouraged his magnates with castral positions along the frontier to organize their own expeditions. Late in 1211, for example, he conceded to the bishop and see of Zaragoza rights to all the Muslim-held castles their foundation could conquer before a fixed date the following year.[114] Pere campaigned again in Valencia in 1212. He was with his troops in Xérica on 25 February and may have used this venture to capture the castle of Culla. The following year he granted the fortification and its district to the Templars with all of its Muslim, Christian, and Jewish inhabitants.[115]

Despite these modest successes, Pere contributed comparatively little to the consolidation of the Ebro valley or to the territorial expansion beyond it. Overall, Catalonia's southern frontier remained relatively static throughout his reign. As one indicator of this stasis, the castle of Cabres was likely taken by Alfons's campaigning in the 1190s. In 1210, when Pere gave it to Artal de Alagón, the castle still sat "on the frontier with Morella."[116] Instead of investing what resources were available to him into local projects of expansion, the count-king instead prioritized collaborative, long-distance campaigning against al-Andalus, prompted by forceful papal intervention, following the decisive Castilian defeat at Alarcos in 1195. His contributions to the victory at Las Navas de Tolosa in 1212, which largely benefited Castile, were financed by increasing his already crushing indebtedness to a range of creditors.[117]

Comital-Royal Borrowing and Administrative Shifts along the Lower Ebro River Valley

Just as his local campaigning would largely retrace the raiding conducted by Alfons, so too Pere's credit operations to finance his extraordinary expenditures followed patterns that had been established during his predecessor's reign, albeit on a much grander scale.[118] Accordingly, we must return our attention to the foundations of leveraging established by Alfons that we began to discuss earlier.

The transactions Alfons engaged in throughout his reign were heavily informed by those initial loans he had contracted with Jafia, the Jewish bailiff of Lleida, and with the Templars during his minority in 1168 and 1169, respectively. These were the earliest indications of his withdrawal from direct governance along the Ebro–Segre frontier in order to fund the acquisition of new territory. That loan from Jafia had been based on revenues he was to collect from his bailiwick. It was a modification of the standard sale of the office that provided the royal fisc with a lump sum and annual payments from future revenues.[119] Since the loan would be serviced by these annual payments, the count-king would receive nothing from the bailiwick until the debt was repaid.

This transaction with Jafia, based on incomes from Lleida, was similar in structure to what Alfons would contract with the Templars in 1169, using his castles of Ascó, Riba-roja, and Seròs.[120] The creditors took over local administration, and all of the revenues from the comital-royal rights were redirected to servicing administrative costs and the contracted debt. The Templar loan notably represented a much more sweeping withdrawal by the count-king, since the order assumed the roles of castellan, local lord, and bailiff, which, in Lleida, remained the responsibility of other parties.

Such loans represented a new, experimental form of delegation that redeployed capital to service new expansionist projects and reassigned administrative burdens. Following the conquest of New Catalonia, as we saw earlier, Ramon Berenguer IV distributed vast domains to the Templars along this exposed Ebro–Segre corridor to satisfy preconquest pledges that had uncertain financial values and high maintenance costs. Once these domains within the demesne were stabilized after several decades of Christian rule through the retention of indigenous populations or the installation of migrants, they could be drained of their capital via such indirect exploitation. The provisions of this loan from the Templars thus seem to have been designed to structure a longer-term relationship that would facilitate further leveraging. Although the order assumed lordship over these castles, its participation in this new paradigm of demesne exploitation was purely financial and had seemingly little to do with military service. As noted earlier, in addition to reimbursing the Templars for their costs of lordship, the count-king guaranteed their financial stake with safer demesne holdings to the north if the castles were lost.

It is impossible to ascertain whether Alfons and his advisors anticipated progressively leveraging these holdings when they originally structured the loan in 1169. Nevertheless, within a handful of years, they found themselves in further need of revenue to fund their costly initiatives and returned to these holdings, and tapped into new ones, to secure additional credit. In March 1175, Alfons added to his standing loan with the Templars on Riba-roja and established a new pledge on the castle of Castejón del Puente, located near Monzón, to the amount of five hundred *morabetins*.[121] Possibly he viewed basing a single pledge on frontier and inland holdings as a means of diversifying the loan's structure. In contrast to the initial 1169 loan from the order, Alfons did not offer other demesne possessions as collateral.

Perhaps territorial gains since the earlier loan had also made Riba-roja seem less exposed to attack to both lender and borrower, thus making such added assurances seem less necessary. The loan document from 1175 details that Alfons planned to utilize the received funds to purchase horses received in Lleida and Tortosa and repay outstanding loans. As with the loan from 1169, the count-king made it clear that the order assumed control of these castral positions through this transaction. On this occasion, he permitted the Templars to calculate its costs for the castle guard and then subtract them from the revenues, in contrast to earlier when he allocated a share of the incomes to cover these expenses.

An addendum to the charter written four years later indicates that over 225 *morabetins* remained unpaid. This sum did not take into account expenses incurred by the order for maintaining foot soldiers "that the king ordered be held there." Alfons furthermore authorized the Templars to administer these districts using their own bailiffs and thus collect taxes and levies from all of its inhabitants without reservation. He retained no rights for himself.

Alfons contracted another loan of six hundred *morabetins* from the order in August 1175 by pledging Almenar, situated to the north of Lleida. The Templars were concerned about the adequacy of Almenar's revenues, however, and required that the count-king identify and pledge alternate resources in advance. In response, Alfons gave the Templars access to his line of credit with his Jewish bailiff Jafia, presumably by further leveraging comital-royal incomes from his bailiwick of Lleida. In the event that both Almenar's revenues and Jafia's credit proved insufficient to satisfy his debt, the count-king authorized the Templars to collect additional revenues, as needed, from the pledges on Riba-roja, Ascó, and Seròs. As a final recourse, he assigned the order any tribute he might gain from al-Andalus to service the loan.[122]

Alfons also drew on his taxation prerogatives to fund lump monetary payments from creditors. In the mid-1170s, he assigned loan repayments from future collection of the peace tax known as the *bovatge*.[123] Then, in 1180, he awarded the Templars a perpetual exemption from various commercial levies from Christians, Muslims, and Jews resident in its castral district of Miravet. The order would receive total immunity from the *lleuda*, *passatge*, or any "usage in my entire land by land or by sea" in return for a seemingly modest payment: two good horses worth two hundred *morabetins*.[124] The fact that this transaction was couched as a religiously motivated donation, for which the count-king expected spiritual favors, may account for its lopsidedness. Alfons made numerous other pious donations during these years while leveraging his rights in order to raise funds. Earlier that year, he exempted the well-endowed monastery of Santes Creus from various levies on its holdings in Tortosa imposed by "my vicar, bailiff, or *saig*." These included redemptions for military service and required payments for maintaining the city's infrastructure and walls.[125] Similarly, he piously donated Santes Creus 140 *morabetins* from the incomes he received from Seròs's town and castle in 1181.[126] Fiscally, such enactments naturally worked against Alfons's other money-raising transactions during these years.

The Dynamics of Settlement and Lordship within the Postconquest Environment

This pattern of leveraging initiated by Alfons represented a deliberate deviation from the fiscal policies established by Ramon Berenguer IV. Other forces, however, that were not under Alfons's control, served to undermine the strategy his predecessor had carefully pursued with his distribution of territories following the conquests of Tortosa and Lleida by facilitating the accumulation of small-holder allodial property by larger seigniorial entities.

Settler failure remained common as the conquered landscape underwent consolidation, which played into the hands of those well-endowed lords who were eager to acquire more property. Within a decade of the conquest, the financial hardship of small landowners around Lleida facilitated accumulation by the Templars of Gardeny.[127] Many early sellers first borrowed on their properties, thereby incurring obligations that later forced them to sell. In a typical case, Guillem de Pomars and his family received allodial rights to a vineyard in Lleida's vicinity shortly after the conquest. In due course, they accepted the Templars of Gardeny as their landlord for the property for an undisclosed sum. Before long, the family sold its remaining rights to the vineyard to the order for one hundred *solidi* in 1159.[128]

Various factors could combine to provoke this phenomenon, including the availability of local markets, security, climate conditions, the extent of irrigation, poor decision-making, and plain misfortune. Some further anecdotal evidence will serve to illustrate how early migrants to these lands could succumb to the challenges of making ends meet in the postconquest environment. Ademar de Puig participated as a knight in the campaign against Tortosa and received some houses with land in its district. Within several years, he and his family fell into financial trouble and were forced to pledge these possessions for a series of loans. After Ademar died while campaigning in al-Andalus, his wife found herself in "great misery and grave poverty, labor[ing] most strenuously under this tribulation." They had to sell all of Ademar's property to satisfy this mounting debt and were ultimately left with just fifty *morabetins*.[129] In another case from 1158, a certain Raimbau pawned his lands to the Templars for five hundred *morabetins*. The order obtained the right to recover this debt from its use of his property until the following Christmas.[130] In a similar arrangement from 1163, Pere Guillem and his wife, Pareta, pawned two parcels they had received from Ramon Berenguer IV to the see of Tortosa for a total of sixty-nine *morabetins*. The arrangement established that the bishop and chapter would inherit full title over the lands once the husband and wife had passed away. In the meantime, the couple would receive an annual pension of one-fourth of the yields from the lands.[131] The see of Tortosa also seems to have earned a controlling interest over another parcel in Palomera that Pere and his wife had also received from the count-prince. When the couple established tenants on the land, they first obtained the "assent of the bishop and canons of the church of Tortosa" for the arrangement.[132] Although the sources do not stipulate if the limitations placed on this other parcel were a condition of Pere and Pareta's pension, forging an initial relationship with a seigniorial creditor for some of one's lands could have facilitated the progressive loss of independent control over the rest. Petty landowners experienced difficulty in the challenging frontier environment even decades after the conquest. In 1194, Maria, the widow of Dominic Iafia, had to sell her vineyard in Vilanova "on account of great necessity from hunger, neglect, and want."[133]

Arrangements that served to enlarge the domains under the control of larger lords did not always involve destitute small-holders, however. For example, Bernat d'Anglesola was a well-endowed noble from an eminent family and opted to pledge piously some of his lands to the Templars of Gardeny. He retained only future rights to the tithes and first fruits.[134] The transaction awarded Bernat a pension, similar to Pere's and Pareta's arrangement detailed earlier. Bernat was not personally working the lands when he made the commitment and would receive annual payments and spiritual benefits without any further responsibilities.

Although the evidence is too uneven to permit statistical analysis of settler failure, we can identify some broad patterns. In the half century following the transition to Christian rule, the environment in and around Tortosa witnessed a sharp increase in pawning of property and indebtedness by small- and medium-scale landowners between 1170 and 1180. The rate of failure and exodus declined slightly for the period between 1181 and 1190 before climbing again before 1200.[135] The trends appear to have been less dramatic in Lleida. Sabaté has determined that, by the end of the twelfth century, only around thirteen percent of rural properties in Lleida were under baronial control whereas over fifty percent of these properties were held by non-noble landlords.[136]

We need to be careful to differentiate between petty landowners, who were generally owner-occupants, and tenants (including peasants) who paid rent to landlords. Although harsh conditions facilitated the growth of large seigniorial domains at the expense of these petty landowners, as we have seen, they also made it more difficult for lords to retain successful tenants and attain high lease rates on their plots. Lords naturally had to respond to the challenges of the environment in order to attract and retain residents. In 1174, for instance, when the Templar Order rented land within Lleida's district to a group of settlers, it made arrangements for the worse-case scenario: "if it happens that all the other inhabitants of the farm leave, we have the right to recover these three *fanecades* of land."[137] Landlords often experienced difficulty with their tenants and did not always have the upper-hand when managing them. In a telling case from 1153, the Templars pressured Guillem de Partanai to hand over lands he occupied in Fontanet, near Lleida, on the grounds that he had obtained them unjustly. "Fearing trouble," the order decided not to press charges and paid Guillem three *morabetins* to leave quietly.[138]

Scrutinizing the dynamics of the establishment of new tenants on the domains of these larger lords can add meaning to these figures by helping us understand the pressures experienced by groups seeking to establish themselves. In general, the earliest settlers to arrive in New Catalonia benefited from more robust exemptions and higher-quality lands. In order to encourage migration to the new territories, the rents and obligations should have been lighter there in comparison to the crowded domains of Old Catalonia and Upper Aragon.[139] Indeed, Jordi Bolòs has determined from an early thirteenth-century Templar *capbreu* (record of account) concerned with lands around Lleida that the peasants with the most land paying the highest rents often derived from the first generation of settlers. A lower tier of peasants with smaller holdings paid substantially less rent. At the bottom, roughly one-third of the population possessed little and struggled to subsist.[140]

Other evidence shows how the Templars of the Terra Alta and Ribera d'Ebre, for example, established a system of distributing set amounts of land to each settler in the communities of Horta, Gandesa, Pinell, and Batea, which were granted population charters between 1192 and 1205.[141] Once the initial allotment was exhausted, subsequent settlers commonly purchased or rented fractional shares of these original parcels, which usually were sufficiently large to permit subdivision.[142] Arriving early did not guarantee prosperity, however. These early settlers needed to be industrious and enjoy good fortune in order to succeed. For many, obtaining large tracts was the easy part, followed by risky years of toil developing the lands. The extent of the work naturally hinged on the condition of the received plots, whether they had been occupied by Andalusi proprietors, and what sort of damage or disruption they might have suffered in the transition to Christian rule.

In sum, in spite of Ramon Berenguer IV's effort to distribute the comital-royal portion of these conquered lands among a sea of small-holders, all of whom would look to him as their direct overlords, by the later twelfth century much of this landscape had passed into the possession of an oligarchy of great lords.[143] This trend was the product of multiple causes that emerged within the postconquest land market, only one of which was the changing fiscal policies of his successors. The count-kings actually appear to have been aware of this trend and even sometimes took extreme measures to seek to counteract it. In an illuminating case from 1198, Pere, with dubious legality, intervened to reduce the tithe obligations for all of the residents of Tortosa, without qualification. He reasoned that they collectively merited the reduction "since they are on the frontier" and because they gain sustenance "with the utmost labor and danger to their possessions and bodies in Tortosa."[144]

Restructuring Tortosa's Administration

Throughout the years that witnessed these patterns of borrowing and alienation, Alfons initially appears to have maintained his father's policy of preserving Tortosa as an unleveraged, directly administered holding. In keeping with this strategy, he also built upon Ramon Berenguer IV's special protective relationship with Tortosa's residents. He devoted an unusual level of attention to the center, even micromanaging its administration at times. Unlike the confirmations of privileges Alfons made during the initial months of his reign, only in Tortosa did he receive the homage of every male member of the city's citizenry.[145] In June 1174, the count-king joined Tortosa's minority lord and castellan, the seneschal Ramon I de Montcada, in making a convention with the Muslim *aljama* that fixed the amount of its annual tribute at four hundred *masmudines* for four years. Although set at this general level, this sum would fluctuate with the *aljama*'s population size. Responsibility for these calculations lay with the *zalmedina* and *alcaydus*, both of which were appointed by the count-king, as well as with the *prohoms* ("leading members") of the *aljama*. This arrangement barred the lords and their officers from demanding labor services or payments from the community within the urban district.[146]

Despite these protective measures, Alfons had to respond to the "many complaints and clamors" made by the Muslim *aljama* of Tortosa in 1180 concerning the "many injuries and extortions which evil bailiffs and bad men exacted upon false authority." The Muslims accused his local bailiffs of running a peculiar scam in which they allegedly forced marrying Muslim couples to hire wedding singers who were in the officers' employ. Alfons agreed that this interference violated the provisions of the Muslims' surrender treaty and reiterated that no "Christian, Jewish, or Muslim bailiff" had the authority to manipulate the local customs of the *aljama*. He threatened future offenders with a one-thousand-*morabetin* fine and ruled that, in accordance with Ramon Berenguer IV's privileges, only the *zalmedina* and *alcaydus* could exercise authority over the *aljama*.[147]

Alfons also demonstrated his special interest in Tortosa's residents when he renewed the customary privileges and protections held by the Jewish *aljama* in 1182. His decision to invoke Ramon de Montcada at every guarantee could indicate that Ramon and his officers had been responsible for the recent abuses against the Muslim community, actions reminiscent of the abuses allegedly perpetrated by Guillem Ramon I de Montcada that we discussed in the last chapter. Given this track record, Tortosa's Jewish *aljama* may not have placed much stock in the value of guarantees issued by the count-king alone. They were aware that local lords tended to assert themselves in the absence of adequate royal oversight. Fearful of the abuses suffered by local Muslims and covetous of the confirmation of privileges they had subsequently received, Tortosa's Jews may have requested this joint charter that pledged to protect them from noncustomary services demanded by any lord or officer and safeguarded some of their rights of self-determination. The charter records how the count-king and Ramon de Montcada swore that neither their men nor those of any other lord in Tortosa would possess the right to open the doors of the Jewish quarter. Given how financially needy Alfons was at this time, it is not surprising that he included a confirmation of his own "customary" taxation rights over the community when issuing these guarantees. He also stipulated that unless the Jews were locked up in the *zuda* for their protection during a time of insecurity or otherwise prevented from accessing their monetary resources, they were not permitted to offer pledges for any levies or subsidies they owed the count-king. Alfons thus made it clear that he expected them to satisfy their obligations promptly and in full.[148]

While illustrating the dangers of investing local lords with more authority, these incidents also could have convinced Alfons that he no longer wished to be distracted by such local administrative matters. Engagements along the northern and southern frontiers of his realms must have seemed more pressing and a worthy cause for deviating from Ramon Berenguer IV's protective policy for Tortosa. Accordingly, in March 1182, Alfons transferred jurisdiction over the castles and centers of Tortosa and Ascó to the Templars and sold them Riba-roja outright.[149]

While modeled on the earlier credit transactions with the order to some degree, this arrangement featured some notably different elements. Although Alfons collected five thousand *morabetins* for the transfer of his rights to Ascó and Riba-roja, this amount was not a loan but rather compensation for the order's increased shares in these holdings. Unlike those earlier loans, which had been construed as short-term arrangements when initially contracted yet subsequently treated as open lines of credit, Alfons gave the Templars lordship over all three holdings with its attendant administrative responsibilities, as free allods, "in perpetuity." The arrangement was therefore deliberately engineered to transact a long-term transfer of control: Riba-roja now belonged entirely to the order. In Ascó and Tortosa, by contrast, the Templars had to render the Crown half of all revenues, including those from their additional one-fifth share received in 1175. This ongoing income-sharing arrangement would also apply to additional property acquired by either party. As with Alfons's castral pledges made in 1169, here the count-king agreed to subsidize the order's administration expenses for the holdings in which he retained an interest. Although the parties would share expenses for maintaining mills, ovens, and other obligations in Ascó, Alfons gave the Templars a one-time payment of four hundred *masmudines* to cover the costs of future infrastructure in Tortosa. As in the earlier arrangements, the shift to indirect administration reduced the need for a dedicated comital-royal bailiff, although one would nevertheless remain in Tortosa for several years to come.[150] Alfons indicated that "the [Templar] brothers should have their bailiff in the city . . . , who should faithfully collect all of the incomes of the city and its district."[151] Although the local vicar would remain a constant feature of the jurisdictional scene, in Tortosa this executive office, which oversaw the municipal court among other responsibilities, had customarily been appointed by the Montcada family and was not subject to comital-royal direction following the administrative transfer.[152]

With respect to Tortosa, the transaction brought about less of an absolute withdrawal than it might appear. Although Alfons assigned the order lordship over Tortosa, he withheld property rights (*dominicaturas*) that were not itemized in the primary charter of donation consisting of half of the city's incomes along with certain properties within its district. Furthermore, in both Tortosa and Ascó, Alfons retained "ecclesiastical rights which pertain to the royal majesty" as well as half of the proceeds from hunting and fishing when he or the queen were in residence.[153]

Two memorials from May 1182 and January 1184 tell us more about this retained royal property in Tortosa. The first document was necessitated by conflicts between the king and the Templars over the extent of his retained *dominicaturas* that arose as the Templars took over administrative control of the city.[154] Alfons claimed to have "discovered" properties belonging to him "when I gave Tortosa to God and the aforementioned house and brethren," and the Templars, fighting fire with fire, moved to itemize the specific properties they, in turn, had "discovered" within their share of Tortosa in order to secure their entitlement. The order also documented donations made by the count-king and Ramon I de Montcada prior to the transfer that were not subject to the division of revenues. As defined by the first memorial and confirmed by the second, the count-king and queen retained property and the Muslim marketplace in the nearby locality of Labar plus mills and cellars past the right bank of the Ebro that had belonged to Ramon Berenguer IV. The second memorial also confirmed comital-royal rights to resources that had not been mentioned in the earlier charters. When in residence, the count-king and queen could take as much firewood as they needed, while the comital-royal bailiff would additionally collect a shipload of wood on their behalf once a year. They also retained the right to sell the local Muslims vegetables and other produce from comital-royal lands at a "just price." These instruments confirm that the Templars were expected to facilitate the comital-royal bailiff's administration of the royal family's retained rights. Any disputes involving this bailiff would be judged in accordance with the customs of the city.[155]

A charter drafted several years after this transfer indicates that the count-king retained some of his levying rights within the city, which were ostensibly excluded from this division of revenues. A concord forged between the see of Tortosa and the Templars in 1185 over tithes dictated that the order would receive just one-fifth of any collected levies, in accordance with the "custom of Tortosa," which would be exempt from tithes. Alfons would be entitled to the remaining four-fifths share but would pay the see tithes from it.[156]

Queen Sancha and the Templars

When Alfons took Alfonso VII's daughter, Sancha of Castile, as his queen in 1174, he assigned her a substantial dower composed of an extensive collection of properties many of which were located within New Catalonia and Lower Aragon.[157] Cardinal Hyacinth attended the enactment at Zaragoza when Alfons established her dower with more than forty castles and towns and the county of Rosselló as a means to strengthen Aragon's alliance with Castile.[158] It is important to consider how these transactions with the Templars, and indeed all of the leveraging conducted by Alfons since his marriage to Sancha, were complicated by these rights that he had assigned to her dower. As we will see, the holdings assigned to this dower would later become a subject of considerable controversy following Alfons's death in 1196, when Sancha became entitled to at least some of them during the reign of their son, Pere.[159]

This list of property held by her dower included Alfons's interest in Tortosa and Ascó along with many other recently conquered holdings. These included Alfamén, Almenar, Barbastro, Boleia, Camarasa, Castelldans, Cervera, Cubells, Mequinenza, Pomar, Quart, Siurana, Tamarite (de Litera), Tarragona, Tàrrega, and Zaidín. Bisson has suggested that the list may represent a partial list of "the domain the king continued to exploit directly" rather than the holdings to be received by the queen.[160] Rather than assigning her title to these holdings, the dower contract instead established them as pledges to secure the incomes to which the queen would be entitled for her maintenance for the remainder of her life in the event of Alfons's premature death.[161] During this period, wives did not have the legal right to exercise control over their husband's handling of the property that pertained to their dowers.[162] This limitation could explain why Sancha did not take part in the credit operations from 1175 that concerned holdings (Almenar and Ascó) pertaining to her dower and why she did not subscribe the memorials concerning her *dominicaturas* in Tortosa.[163]

Taking full advantage of Sancha's legal impairment, Alfons leveraged her dower's holdings without her direct consent and substantially altered them. While the reorganization of a dower's portfolio could have been permissible so long as its holdings continued to support the minimum required revenue stream, in this case Alfons's actions were of dubious legality since they substantially reduced the dower's net value. Even if Alfons's intention had been to correct immediately any temporary reduction in the dower's overall value using other resources in the event of his premature death, the use of this capital to fund his regime's project still violated the spirit of the law governing the dower. It is unlikely that Sancha approved of these actions and possible that she used her husband's conflicts with her nephew, Alfonso VIII of Castile, to pressure him to reverse some of these steps and to begin to make her dower whole again. Relations between Aragon and Castile had worsened since their signing of the Treaty of Cazola in 1179, but they resolved their differences, temporarily and likely with Sancha's support, in the treaties of Ágreda and Berdejo in 1186, and once again agreed to ally against Navarre and Albarracín.[164]

In what may have been a move to start assigning more valuable holdings to Sancha's dower, in 1187, Alfons unilaterally redefined it as consisting of ten castles from Catalonia and Aragon, some of which had not been part of the assemblage established in 1174: Barbastro, Cervera, Daroca, Épila, Montblanc, Pina, San Esteban (de Litera), Siurana, Tamarite (de Litera), and Uncastillo.[165] In directly assigning Sancha these castles, Alfons notably excluded the holdings from the Ebro valley that he had leveraged over the past years. It is not clear from its language, however, that this grant was intended to supplant fully what had been established in 1174.[166] Instead, this alteration in 1187 may have been designed to grant Sancha direct control over a collection of property representing a fraction of her dower during her husband's lifetime. Sancha and her advisors likely would have preferred this situation over having this property stand as a pledge for incomes she would be owed only upon Alfons's premature death.

This 1187 enactment contained stipulations concerning Sancha's assumption of these castles and limitations on her lordship that had been absent from the initial marriage arrangements. Alfons wished for the men guarding these castles to be maintained by the queen and conceded that they should perform homage to her, but he also made provisions for the appointment of new personnel should she desire it. Seemingly conscious of the fact that these were strategically important castles, he reserved the right to commandeer them, if necessary, by claiming the right of *potestas*, which required her to render these castles to him upon request, "just as a vassal ought to do for his lord." Given his recent conflicts with Alfonso VIII, which would flare up again in 1190 when Alfons would form an alliance with Navarre, León, and Portugal against Castile, he inserted careful language reserving his rights to these properties. For instance, he made careful arrangements for the dower's eventual dissolution: upon her death, the dower's castles within Aragon and Catalonia would be restored to that kingdom and county, respectively.[167]

Evidence of direct administrative consequences of this donation exists for very few of these holdings. Ramon de Mercadal was serving as the queen's vicar by 1193 and was also her bailiff in Siurana from 1194 through at least 1200.[168] We have few indications, however, that Sancha was engaging in the appointment or management of castellans. Contrary to what Alfons had implied in the agreement, the queen must have received incomes from these holdings without exercising significant administrative responsibilities.

If the 1182 arrangement establishing Templar administration over Tortosa and Ascó remained in force, then these 1187 arrangements with Sancha that removed her connection to them, if executed as drafted, would have further liberated her husband to secure additional loans from the Templars, without any interference, by pledging his remaining half share of incomes from these lordships. Indeed, over the winter of 1189–90, Alfons contracted loans of 4,500 *solidi* and 700 *morabetins* in two separate charters, assigning repayment from his revenues from Tortosa and Ascó.[169] Templar administration facilitated his use of these incomes as a line of credit. Additional borrowing based on Alfons's share would decrease the annual portion received by comital-royal fisc.

In the end, we lack the evidence to confirm definitively whether the 1187 alteration was fully implemented or endured over the long term. The fact that the dower would remain a conflictive issue between Sancha and Pere following Alfons's death suggests that it did not address all of her complaints. Alfons's will of 1194 unhelpfully neither referred to the 1187 accord nor itemized the full dower to which the queen would be entitled.[170] Enigmatically, the distributions it called for drew heavily from some of the holdings originally constituting her dower yet strayed from the assemblage assigned to her by the 1187 agreement. Even though Sancha had received the "entire county of Rosselló" in 1174, for example, the will granted Pere unimpaired rights to it alongside his other inherited realms.

In making these final arrangements, Alfons implied that he did not consider the dower to be fully settled by the 1187 arrangements and that Sancha still deserved further compensation. Yet despite his presumption that the queen's entitlements would need to be allocated from other sources, he failed to identify any with specificity and laid out only a very rough plan for resolving any future conflicts following his death. Other matters, by contrast, he addressed in considerable detail. For instance, he appointed for debts to be repaid after his death from "my revenues" from Ascó and Tortosa as well as from Cervera, Tarragona, and Tàrrega.[171] Late in the document, Alfons noted that Sancha was entitled "without contradiction, [to] her dower that I made, gave, and conceded to her, just as is contained in the charter granted and confirmed by me." At the same time, he confessed that many of the distributions mandated by the will pertained to Sancha's dower and directed their heir, Pere, to render to her what she was owed "from my own incomes" so long as she remained unmarried. He thus empowered her to insist on receiving the holdings originally pledged to her dower without indicating how these assessed obligations would be calculated or funded. And after laying down these directives, Alfons washed his hands of the matter, leaving the details and heavy-lifting to Pere, who would have to "restore to her the aforementioned property of her dower," appropriating "my other incomes" as necessary.[172]

Although Alfons underestimated the potential for discord in these provisions, even before his death, Sancha was already playing a key role in ensuring that the early years of her son's reign would be mired in conflict. There are signs that she cajoled Alfons into safeguarding her authority in the event that he predeceased her. His will designated her as primary regent and extended Pere's minority for an uncustomarily long time, until his twentieth year.[173] By contrast, their younger son would remain under her custody for only sixteen years. When Pere signed a renewed peace accord with her nephew, Alfonso VIII of Castile, against Navarre and other mutual enemies in 1198, the queen mother inserted herself into the negotiations, winning assurances from each side that it would come to her aid if she ever had an unresolved dispute with the other party.[174] Sancha also engaged in dealings that had no direct connection to her own entitlements. She was instrumental in organizing further peace negotiations between Castile, León, Aragon, and Navarre and thus helped bring about Innocent III's mandates for united action against the Almohads.[175] No doubt with Sancha's encouragement, Alfons had already increased Castilian influence over his heir when he emended this will as he lay dying in Perpignan in April 1196, at a time when famine and plague were besetting the realms.[176] He had placed his wife, children, and "land" (*terram*) under the "custody and maintenance" (*custodia et manutenencia*) of Alfonso VIII.[177] He did not, however, revisit the issue of the dower on this occasion.

Although Pere officially stood under his mother's custody for two years following his father's death, he tried to resist her influence in the very early days of his rule.[178] Only a month into his reign, in 1196, Pere confirmed a number of important donations, privileges, and exemptions for major cities and towns in Catalonia and Aragon as "king" and "count" without involving Sancha or obtaining her consent.[179] Sancha quickly and effectively countered this attempt at independence by means that have not yet come to light. Her results, however, were decisive: later that year, Pere placed "myself and my entire kingdom [of Aragon] and county of Barcelona and my other counties and property under the direction and command of Doña Sancha, my celebrated Queen Mother." Sancha did more than grab power from her son on this occasion. She also prepared to extend her right to enjoy that authority beyond the already elongated period of Pere's minority. Rather than foreseeing an end to her custody, he recognized her full authority, "for as long as she might wish to rule and govern, promising firmly that on no occasion shall I seize or take away her power over the aforementioned [realms], nor shall I return without her counsel and command so long as it is her wish to have custody of them."[180] He also swore to uphold his father's guarantee that she receive all of the castles and property constituting her dower, which entailed freeing them from debt.[181] Such an obligation was in keeping with her rights, as outlined by her husband's will, but would have been no minor enterprise given the extent of Alfons's pledges on many of these holdings.

Despite the damaging implications of these concessions for Pere's authority, they had little apparent effect on his subsequent governmental activity or even his handling of Sancha's dower. Despite the prerogatives she had secured and her efforts to assert her authority, Sancha rarely involved herself in day-to-day governance and, in fact, exerted little apparent influence over her son. Pere's decision to be buried at the Hospitaller monastery of Sigena, which had recently been founded by Sancha, for example, could be a sign of her authority but also could have been an effort to honor Alfons, whose final donations to the Hospitaller Order were carried out by Pere in this same charter.[182]

Nevertheless, Pere's ongoing resistance against Sancha's rather hollow authority as regent eventually prompted her to appeal to the pope for assistance. Celestine III's response in the form of two highly calculated letters, sent on the same day in August 1196, advocated for the queen mother while using the opportunity to reestablish the monarchy's long-standing subordination to the Apostolic see. Although the letters sidestepped any direct mention of the conflict, they were clearly written to assist Sancha in her dealings with her son. One letter established apostolic protection over both Pere and his mother, while the other extended the pope's protection over Sancha and "especially [over] that which the former king of Aragon of glorious memory gave [you]."[183] Collectively, these letters sent the message that her importance to the kingdom and to its relationship to St. Peter were equal to that of her son. There are no indications that these letters accomplished anything to resolve the problematic relations within the comital-royal family, however, and Sancha subsequently appears to have backed away from her ambition to exercise authority once Pere attained his majority.

The dower issue, on the other hand, did not recede from view but instead increasingly took center stage as Sancha's principal disagreement with Pere. She soon lodged a new complaint with the new pope, Innocent III, who intervened first in 1199 and again the following year. As justification for his involvement, Innocent cited his obligation to defend the mandates of Alfons's will and to safeguard the rights of widows, in general, and Sancha's welfare, in particular, especially given her ongoing fidelity to the Apostolic see.[184] As Innocent implied, his interest in the conflict may well have been enhanced by Sancha's involvement with the Hospitaller house of Sigena, which she had founded and joined by 1197.[185]

Pere's desperate need for further borrowing forced him to cooperate with Sancha more than he might have liked during this tense period. Most importantly, he wanted to assign incomes from Seròs to supplement the repayment of a debt of five thousand *masmudines*. In order to arrange this loan, Pere first had to obtain Sancha's consent for the transaction, which she would only do after he had formally recognized the annual payment of one hundred *masmudines* she had the right to draw from Seròs.[186] He also recognized that five hundred *solidi* from the holding were owed to another creditor, Perfet de Prats. When it became established that Seròs would be used to repay this loan two months later, the charter of recognition prominently recognized Sancha's and Perfet's respective rights.[187]

Later in 1200, lay rather than clerical intervention was making progress toward a resolution. Sancha's nephew, Alfonso VIII of Castile, interceded to negotiate a compromise. The agreement, enacted in September 1200, clarified that the primary source of conflict between the two had been whether Pere would honor the original 1174 dower agreement by continuing to add to the assemblage of properties awarded to her in the modification of 1187, in keeping with the mandates of Alfons's will. Pere confirmed the majority of the castral districts already in Sancha's possession from that agreement: Barbastro, Cervera, Daroca, Montblanc, Pina, San Esteban, Siurana, Tamarite, and Uncastillo. He also included two lands that had not been part of either dower definition: Burbáguena and Íxar (Híjar).[188] In addition, Pere conceded two of the most conflict-ridden holdings from the 1174 dower: Tortosa and Ascó.[189] In return, Sancha granted her son the castles and towns of Ariza, Embid de la Ribera, and Épila, only the last of which had been assigned to her because of her dower, in the 1187 modification. She also gave him incomes from holdings in Aragon and Catalonia and confirmed his right to recover all of the transferred properties upon her death. The long list of rights and holdings received by Sancha included incomes from holdings in Calatayud, Huesca, and general incomes from Seròs, none of which had been assigned to her or her dower in the previous enactments.[190]

Somewhat surprisingly, the concord did not devote any attention to how the encumbered states of some of the transferred holdings affected their value to Sancha. Only a fraction remained of the original comital-royal interest in Ascó and Tortosa when the dower had been arranged in 1174. At this point, comital-royal incomes from Tortosa were also greatly reduced due to other obligations, such as annual incomes that had been consigned to the local cathedral, the Carthusians, and the nuns of Vallbona, "all of which," the agreement made clear, "the Lord Queen shall have to pay while she holds" the city. Enigmatically, the document made no mention of the seigniorial rights still possessed by the Montcada family in Tortosa. Likely anxious to secure full and uncontested rights to these holdings after such a long period of conflict, Sancha did not make an issue of these important details but instead quickly petitioned Innocent III for a renewal of apostolic protection, which she received in 1203.[191]

How were Sancha's confirmed rights to Ascó and Tortosa compatible with the Templars' jurisdictional powers as established by the 1182 donation? Information regarding the exercise of administration in Ascó is unfortunately lacking for these years. For Tortosa, however, the picture is clearer. In 1199, a dispute between the citizens and the Templars over jurisdiction adjudicated by Pere and his barons identified the Templars as the "lords of Tortosa" and indicates that the provisions of Alfons's 1182 transfer of the city remained in force at this point.[192] Other signs, however, suggest that the Templars' hold of the city was less than secure. Just months before Sancha and Pere resolved their differences, in March 1200, the order received confirmation of its one-fifth share that had been awarded by Alfons—a grant that should have been rendered moot by the prior transfer of lordship.[193]

Following this latest resolution with Pere, Sancha exercised some administrative rights within the Tortosa, although the full extent of her powers of lordship remains uncertain.[194] In 1202, the local Templar commander recognized her exercise of lordship when he acknowledged her lieutenant, Arnau de Siscar, "who at that time held the place of the lord-queen in Tortosa."[195] Sancha also exercised the right, via delegates, to appoint local officers. In 1207, with the consent of local lord Ramon II de Montcada, Guillem de Bonastre designated Ali Abinhaole as *alcaydus* of Tortosa's Muslim *aljama*. Guillem had served as Sancha's bailiff from around 1201 following a period as comital-royal and seigniorial bailiff in Lleida in the 1190s. His identification as simply "bailiff" when witnessing a transfer of property in Tortosa neighboring a parcel owned by him and his wife could suggest that he served multiple lords in Tortosa as he had in Lleida.[196]

Although no formal complaint from the Templars regarding Sancha's assumption of rights to Tortosa or Ascó survives, it is possible that the order exerted pressure on the count-king in some form that has not survived, thus leading him to issue a contradictory confirmation regarding its rights to Tortosa in July 1202.[197] If it had been executed, this confirmation would have been problematic since it violated rights he had just assigned to Sancha in their reconciliation. It is unlikely that this grant was enacted, however.[198] Additionally, even though his precise motives remain a mystery, there are reasons to doubt Pere's sincerity in making the confirmation. Although bearing all of the signs of a legal instrument, the charter lacked the subscriptions of any of the relevant local potentates (e.g., Sancha, Ramon II de Montcada, the bishop) or even a single Catalan magnate. The witnesses were exclusively

Aragonese lords who lacked clear affiliations to the city or even its surrounding region. The donations enacted by the document were also unrealistically vague in their revival of Alfons's initial transaction from 1182. They made no mention of the changes experienced by comital-royal or seigniorial rights in the interim. The charter also defined the order's jurisdiction over the city unrealistically as extending over all of its residents, Christian, Jew, and Muslim, with no apparent restrictions.

Furthermore, in purporting to recall the privileges ever given to the Templars by his grandfather and father, Pere's donation of this one-tenth share of all of his present and future domains was misleading and enigmatic. The charter was not confirming prerogatives that the Templars had ever, in fact, received. As we saw earlier, the 1143 resolution with Ramon Berenguer IV of the order's one-fifth share applied only to lands that it had helped conquer. While the 1182 transfer with regard to Tortosa had been annulled or modified prior to this arrangement with Sancha, it seems more likely that some of the Templars' rights to Ascó were reduced but not displaced altogether as a direct result of Sancha's new prerogatives.

Following his mother's death, Pere also made plans to restore the order's rights to Ascó per the 1182 agreement. According to their agreement with the count-king from 1204, the Templars were permitted to collect up to one thousand *morabetins* from Seròs through the sale of its incomes and render any additional income to the king. In return, Pere would receive the tithe incomes normally retained, according to papal exemption and comital-royal privilege, by the Templar brethren for incomes produced by their own labors throughout the kingdom of Aragon.[199] When Pere revisited this arrangement in 1206, he developed a precise estimate of the value of the Templars' original half stake in Ascó and determined that it had been worth only five hundred *morabetins* annually, which, again, the order would have the right to draw from the incomes of the lordship of Seròs.[200] A record of account submitted by the Templar Order to Pere in 1209 summarized its management of Seròs and Ascó for the past seven years and ten months. The order's continuous administrative control of these castral districts clearly facilitated the count-king's adjustments to these income-sharing conventions.[201]

In the days preceding Sancha's death on 9 November 1208, Pere authorized the donation of certain incomes from her dower holdings to the Hospitallers, in general, and her house of Sigena, in particular. He also held her to their prior arrangement by not allowing her to alienate permanently any castles or towns while she lay dying.[202] The Hospitallers could draw income from the castle and town of Siurana only until the collected sum amounted to 3,500 *solidi*, at which time the holding would revert to full comital-royal control.[203] This arrangement must have been satisfied quickly, since the count-king had already pledged his mother's former rights in and around Siurana to Gombau de Ribelles in partial repayment of a debt of 7,500 *masmudines* three months later, at the end of January 1209.[204]

Guillem de Cervera and the Templars

Just weeks after Sancha's death in November 1208, Pere granted the entire city and district of Tortosa, together with the nearby village of Benifallet, to the noble Guillem IV de Cervera, lord of Juneda and Castelldans.[205] Such a dramatic reversal of decades of policy-making regarding the zone further confirms our suspicions that Pere's donation of Tortosa to the Templars in 1202 had been insincere. For reasons that remain unclear, the count-king decided against making the order whole with respect to its long-promised rights to Tortosa. Instead, he invited further potential legal headaches by investing yet another interested party.

The rights to jurisdiction and revenues received by Guillem were much more expansive than what the Templars had been promised by Alfons back in 1182. In this 1208 arrangement, the count-king retained very few prerogatives: only military rights and fines for breaking the peace and the *questia* on Christian residents. In addition to all levies, judicial fines, and office incomes, Guillem would also possess, for his lifetime, all revenues from the castle, city, and village and all comital-royal property, "just as at any time Lord King Alfons, our father, and Doña Sancha, our mother, and we had, held, and possessed." As with the unexecuted donation to the Templars in 1202, Guillem received unrestricted jurisdiction over all Christians, Jews, and Muslims residing there. Elements of the grant are difficult to square with the convoluted transaction history up to that point. It made no mention, for instance, of the Montcada family's rights to the city. Unlike Pere's reconciliation with Sancha in 1200, no provisions were made for any prerogatives retained by the Templars.

One possible explanation for this odd reversal by the count-king is that the Templar Order itself might have been ambivalent, at this point, about assuming responsibility over the city. It could have viewed owning a controlling stake over Tortosa as an unwanted burden and backed away from increased responsibility. Tortosa, as represented by Pere in the charter of donation to Guillem de Cervera, remained a scarcely viable settlement, beset by insecurity from the proximity of Muslim territory. Indeed, the grant to Guillem depicted his assumption of the city as an honorable deed in the service of the count-king "for the honor of God and the defense of Christendom."

Neither the grantor nor the recipient appears to have viewed Tortosa as a lucrative asset at this point. Pere and Guillem were sufficiently concerned about Tortosa's ability to survive under its adverse conditions that they made special arrangements to import food and other essentials to keep it afloat under Guillem's lordship.

> Since the city of Tortosa and its territory are in the frontier and in the vicinity of the Muslims, and to this point they have not been able to obtain and have sufficient sustinence, we therefore give and concede to you, Guillem de Cervera, and to all men of Tortosa, Christians, Jews, and Muslims, present and future, . . . full license and authority to import as much grain, meat, and other foodstuffs, and as many necessities from Lleida, Tarragona, Zaragoza, and Barcelona and from all the other cities and towns and other places in our lands always, whenever and however often you and they need, enfranchised and free from any *leuda*, *pedatge*, usage, and custom and seizure.[206]

In the nearly two decades since Alfons had demanded a share of the revenues from the lordship, Tortosa's prospects thus appear to have fallen precipitously. More than a half century after the conquest, Tortosa continued to possess considerable strategic importance but was far from a profitable lordship. It threatened to drain rather than enrich whomever exercised lordship over it.

At this time, there was much to motivate Pere to distance himself from the Lower Ebro. First, he was preoccupied by the uncertainty of the war against the Almohads, diplomacy among the Iberian Christian principalities, and his pursuit of further gains from western Valencia along Lower Aragon's limits. Following his treaty with Alfonso VIII signed at Calatayud in 1198 that renewed their shared commitment to fight against the Muslims and divide up Navarre, Pere had joined the Castilians, in 1205, in a campaign to punish Alfonso IX of León and Galicia (r. 1171–1230) for his raiding along Castile's western border.[207] Pere was motivated to reaffirm this partnership following Innocent III's refusal to organize a crusade in 1204, due to the ongoing quarrels among the Christian principalities and the continued advance of the Almohads, who had recently captured Mallorca at the direction of the caliph al-Nāṣir.[208] Although Pere organized the aforementioned unsuccessful unilateral campaign to take Mallorca in 1204, he put more of his resources into this intensive collaboration with the Castilians (and later with the Navarrese) and would continue with the crusade against the Almohads that would culminate in Las Navas de Tolosa.[209] Second, he was investing heavily in his pursuit of his interests north of the Pyrenees at this time. Following his decision to sever his dynasty's long ties with Toulouse, he sealed his partnership with Montpellier through his marriage to Marie, daughter of Guilhem VIII de Montpellier, in 1204.[210] Pere was progressively drawn into affairs surrounding Montpellier in the years that followed.[211] At this point, in 1208, he was on the brink of becoming even more deeply and personally engaged in the situation there with the impending arrival of the Albigensian crusaders.[212]

Accordingly, just days before this donation of Tortosa, Guillem de Cervera received from the count-king the castle of Benifassà, which sat on the fringes of Christian control to the south of the Ebro River valley.[213] Taken together, these enactments indicated that the count-king was decisively moving away from reliance on the Templars for defending and administering the lower Ebro region. These transfers stipulated that Guillem de Cervera would not only fulfill military duties but also work to promote the stabilization of both holdings.

This first charter had sought to incentivize his activity by assigning him full rights to "all settlements you are able to establish in all of Tortosa at any time." Guillem would hold Benifassà directly from the count-king in fief per the customs of Barcelona, and Pere would retain the right to reclaim the castle at any time. Similar to what he would express regarding Tortosa, Pere recognized that maintaining Benifassà represented a considerable burden for Guillem de Cervera. When Alfons had invested the bishop of Tortosa with Benifassà and a number of neighboring castles in 1195, he had reserved half of the lordship's revenues for himself.[214] Here, by contrast, Pere obliged Guillem de Cervera to render nothing from whatever incomes he managed to generate from Benifassà. The count-king and his advisors likely hoped that Guillem would succeed in stabilizing Benifassà so that the fortification could offer a further layer of protection for Tortosa and the lower Ebro region and potentially serve as a staging point for expeditions into Muslim Valencia.

These considerations would help explain why Pere wanted to delegate responsibility over these holdings to a capable party, but it is worth pondering further why the count-king opted to assign this responsibility to Guillem de Cervera. He could have chosen another baron, such as Ramon II de Montcada, who already exercised minority lordship in the city and whose family, of course, had been involved in the administration of the region since the conquest. First, Pere's dealings with Guillem de Cervera regarding the lower Ebro valley were likely intertwined in some fashion with the noble's acquisition of rights of lordship in and around Lleida during these same years. Second, Guillem may also have further earned the count-king's trust and favor through his ardent support of Pere's campaigns against the viscounts of Cabrera.[215] We will devote attention to both of these topics in the next chapter. Third, even though the grants of Tortosa, Benifallet, and

Benifassà were not directly linked to the repayment of any loans, the trans-action was possibly related to the noble's role as a massive creditor to the Crown to cover Pere's extraordinary expenses during these years. In 1209, the count-king recognized that he owed Guillem 21,500 *morabetins* that had to be repaid by the following year before Pentecost in order to avoid a 20-percent interest penalty. Guillem received in pledge, and was to administer, a long list of royal domains from both Catalonia and Aragon (but not Tortosa or Benifallet) whose incomes were to pay down the debt.[216]

Documentation confirms that, following this investiture, Guillem de Cer-vera actively managed Tortosa, Benifallet, and Benifassà along the lines set forth by the count-king and his advisors. An illuminating case from 1209 that we touched on briefly in the previous chapter depicts the administration con-ducted by Tortosa's new lord. Guillem and co-lord Ramon II de Montcada, "for us and for the lord king," carried out a sentence delivered by the *prohoms* of Tortosa in favor of the Muslims of Benifallet, who claimed that Bernat and Arnau Pinyol illegitimately inhabited these alluvial islands for the queen mother, Sancha.[217] Less than a year later, in 1210, however, after much fur-ther disputing between the parties, these co-lords revisited the issue, likely owing to an appeal by the Pinyols, and ended up reversing the earlier ruling. It came to light that Sancha's bailiff, Guillem de Bonastre, had installed the Pinyols on these lands, in 1204, after they had been left vacant and barren by the local Muslim community for over thirty years, in return for one-fourth of the yields.[218] In the 1210 verdict, which was subscribed by the count-king, Guillem and Ramon ruled that, because Bernat and Arnau had since planted and otherwise improved the lands, they should be permitted to remain as tenants on the condition that they continue to improve them and render the lords of Tortosa the quarter of their yields they once owed the queen.[219] In making this shift, the co-lords were likely emboldened by the fact that the Pinyols were experienced agriculturalists in Benifallet. Indeed, in 1199, the bishop and prior of Tortosa rented Bernat and Arnau a different *algezira* in Benifallet for an annual rent in olive oil on the condition that they remain on the land and not pledge or transfer it for a minimum of twenty years. These men also contemporaneously held other lands in Benifallet. For example, also in 1199, they leased the *algezira* of Anastet from the see of Tortosa.[220] When Ramon and Guillem indicated, in establishing the right of the Pin-yols to occupy the islands, that they were acting "on behalf of the lordship (*senioraticum*) of Tortosa," it is unlikely they intended to include the Templar Order, which at this point still only possessed the fifth share of the city it had received following the conquest. Representatives from the order, further-more, did not subscribe the charter.[221]

Such public exclusion of the Templars from the profits of exercising authority, combined with the stabilization of Tortosa's circumstances, could have served to stiffen the order's resolve in opposing Pere's restructuring of the jurisdictions within the lower Ebro. We lack any evidence of the kinds of negotiations that ensued and are cognizant only of the outcomes. In September 1210, the count-king sought to implement yet another dramatic administrative reversal. He advocated the full restoration of the Templars' rights not only to Tortosa but also to Ascó and Riba-roja, as defined in Alfons's original donation from 1182.[222] Pere couched the grant as repayment for the order's service in the recent successful campaigns that had yielded the Muslim castles of Ademuz and Castielfabib. A transaction the following month indicated that the king was consigning Ascó to the order in return for its fifth share of these recently captured castles, in addition to El Cuervo and Sertella.[223] This subsequent charter also revealed other conditions that had not been stipulated in the count-king's grant a month earlier. In addition to withholding levying rights and two hundred *morabetins* annually from Ascó, Pere noted he had received five thousand *morabetins* from the order. This considerable sum could have been an entirely new payment meant to carry out this transfer. Alternatively, it could have been the amount required by the unexecuted 1182 agreement, which may never have been rendered by the order.

In making these provisions, Pere made no mention of the rights he conceded to Guillem de Cervera and that the noble was clearly already exercising by this point. This omission could have been reflective of the order's own efforts to subjugate Guillem as its castellan and vassal that were already in progress. When the Templar master and assorted brethren met with Guillem de Cervera before a panel of arbitrators the following month, the order claimed that Pere had commanded him to swear homage and fealty to them for Tortosa. Guillem, however, denied this responsibility, and noted that he held these rights from comital-royal donation. Apparently, once pressed by the order, Pere's solution to having granted rights to Guillem de Cervera that, in fact, should have belonged to the Templars was to recast that grant as an infeudation that could then be subjected to the order's authority as overlord.[224] Even though this reinterpretation ran counter to the language of the 1208 charter that had awarded Guillem these contested prerogatives, the fact that the count-king had restored the Templars' lordship as established in 1182 may have convinced the judges to rule in favor of the order. A month later, the Templars donated Tortosa to Guillem and his son, for their lifetimes, "in fief . . . just as you had the city and everything in fief from the donation of [the count-king]."[225] It is perplexing that the Templars fought so valiantly for control over Tortosa on this occasion after Pere's failure to execute the earlier donations left no trace of complaint by the order. In addition to illustrating Pere's incapacity to reverse such donations when challenged by a claimant, the episode seems to indicate that the Templars had come to view Tortosa as a more valuable concession that, for the first time, truly merited a legal battle.

Pere's sudden death, in 1213, may have encouraged the Templars to push harder to secure full control of the lordship.[226] In 1215, during the early years of Jaume I's minority, Guillem de Cervera exchanged the "castle and town of Tortosa and Benifallet" to the order for the minor rights it had received from Pere.[227] Guillem's custodian, Bernat Ermengol, held rights that he too rendered to the Templars on the same day.[228] Guillem's decision to retreat from direct lordship indeed may have been linked to the new political climate ushered in by this turn of events. He appears to have been unwilling to resist the Templars after having lost Pere as an advocate. Guillem did retain his rights to Benifassà, however, which he eventually ceded to Poblet when he joined that monastery near the end of his life, in 1229.[229]

Although the order's prerogatives within Tortosa remained unclear and in jeopardy for many years due to the monarchy's convoluted administrative arrangements, ultimately the contradictory transactions involving Sancha and Guillem de Cervera helped the Templars secure a much more significant share of the lordship. Their assumption of Guillem's rights must also have invalidated other aspects of the Templars' arrangement with Alfons in 1182 that was later revived by Pere in 1210. Given all of the conflicting exchanges, donations, and restorations, the extent of the order's rights over Tortosa from 1215 remained ill-defined.

The complexity of these transactions had repercussions for the conduct of lords and residents during these years of transition, as illustrated by further engagements over one of these alluvial islands in Benifallet. In 1211, the order may have been trying to challenge the validity of Guillem de Cervera's lordship over Tortosa and Benifallet when its local commander sought to recuperate Bernat Pinyol's *algezira* of Legem. After Bernat presented his rental contract from Guillem de Cervera at court, Tortosa's vicar determined that the commander had no right to take possession of the land.[230] Following Guillem de Cervera's transfer of lordship to the Templars, it took a further two years before Bernat Pinyol formally recognized the order's rights, as "lords of Tortosa," to "all that property of Legem, which I, with my brother, at one time obtained from the lord queen and lord king and Guillem de Cervera . . . with all of the improvements which I have made there."[231] It is possible that the delay was the result of Bernat Pinyol's incertitude regarding the identity of his lord. Perhaps he had even maintained the naïve hope that the confusion of the transfer of lordship might permit him to secure better terms to the property or even to own it altogether.

Conclusions

Within the postconquest environment, shifting comital-royal policy, difficult conditions, and acquisitive, well-endowed lords generated dynamics of territorial redistribution that generally served to increase the size and autonomy of seigniorial domains throughout New Catalonia. The dynamics of colonization as well as the proximity of the frontier certainly influenced this process, with profound implications for the practice of lordship and tenurial conditions.[232] Yet we should not be led to believe that such redistribution, that worked to the benefit of seigniorial authority and at the expense of comital-royal control, could not take place in other contexts. Sabaté's work, for example, has shown clearly how the creation of new, redefined, or enlarged baronial spaces was a phenomenon as familiar to the fourteenth century as it had been to the twelfth, even if it took place within the context of a more capable and expansive system of local royal administration.[233]

Ultimately, as this chapter has demonstrated, seigniorial control over Tortosa and other holdings in the Ebro valley emerged significantly tighter than Alfons must have ever envisioned. Pere and his advisors were likely more cognizant of the effects of these policies due to the fact that some of the repercussions were already noticeable during his reign. Nevertheless, he had continued his withdrawal from direct administration along this frontier, adding further distance from the policies of Ramon Berenguer IV while, tragically for the comital-royal regime's long-term fiscal situation, retaining far fewer financial prerogatives. As Bensch has observed, this progression afflicted other areas of Catalonia as well, as "the urgent need for credit overwhelmed the task of regular fiscal administration from 1204 to 1213, [and] entire bailiwicks, vicariates, and castellanies were given out as personal benefices to creditors."[234] During the disruptive years of Jaume's minority, as we will see later, the lords of New Catalonia appear to have asserted much greater independent authority than Pere and his administrators had intended. These developments would establish trends that would culminate in significant seigniorial jurisdictional struggles in the mid- to late thirteenth century, leading up to and following Jaume's successful capture of Valencia. Yet, before moving forward in time to explore those situations, we first need to look to the northwest to compare how Lleida and its surrounding areas fared under these same count-kings during this formative period, in contrast to what we have observed with Tortosa and the lower Ebro region.

❧ CHAPTER 6

Lleida and the County of Urgell

Compared with the lower Ebro region that encircled Tortosa, the Segre-Cinca watershed surrounding Lleida was more directly implicated in the major internal political struggles facing Catalonia during the reigns of Alfons and Pere. This increased level of engagement was prompted by Lleida's affiliation with the county of Urgell as well as by its positioning further to the north. Here, the city and its surrounding district were distanced from the frontier with Islam and situated much closer to the established core territories of Catalonia and Aragon.[1] This orientation signified that Lleida's development in the decades following its capture would be informed more by the political rhythms of the greater Crown of Aragon than by the peripheral frontier dynamics that so deeply colored Tortosa's development, as we have seen.

The counts of Urgell, who exercised lordship over both Lleida and neighboring lordships following the conquest, were tightly allied with count-kings throughout the reigns of Ramon Berenguer IV, Alfons, and Pere. As we will observe, although a number of factors encouraged this alliance, arguably most important were the count-kings' long, embroiled struggles with the viscounts of Àger and Castellbò and the count of Foix. Even though these rivalries were preexisting and centered on or around the domains of the county of Urgell to the north of the conquered lands, they came to involve the territorial dynamics of settling and developing Lleida and the

Segre-Cinca watershed largely because of the interests of the count-kings of Barcelona and counts of Urgell there. This chapter will explore how these disputes flared up in the 1180s during Alfons's reign and continued to cause trouble through Pere's reign. Our work here will also serve to preface our later discussion (in part III) of the transformation of these conflicts during the thirteenth century into a struggle for control of the entire county of Urgell that ended up playing into the hands of the later monarchs of the Crown of Aragon.

Alfons and Ermengol VIII

Both Alfons and Pere seemed to recognize Lleida's importance as a key military foothold south of the county of Urgell. Such a shared understanding could explain why both of these rulers sought to maximize their authority over the city and its district and resisted drawing on the financial resources of their demesne holdings there, especially as conflicts with these troublesome viscounts of Àger and Castellbò intensified. As demonstrated extensively in *Contested Treasure*, the persistent comital-royal presence in Lleida throughout this period is striking when compared with the distance these count-kings kept from Tortosa and the lower Ebro.[2] One telling illustration of this difference is how, shortly before Pere's death, not long after he had established Guillem IV de Cervera and the Templars in complete control of Tortosa, and in spite of his mounting debts, he nevertheless maintained a "castle of the king" in Lleida and continued to make generous provisions for the royal chapel housed within it.[3]

As with Tortosa and other areas of the conquered landscape, Ramon Berenguer IV had been obliged to share lordship over Lleida with his backers in return for their support. In this case, due to his 1148 *convenientia* with the count-prince that we discussed in chapter 3, Ermengol VI of Urgell received a minority share of lordship over the city as well as control over a number of important nearby fortifications.[4] Accordingly, there were contractual limits to the administrative control Ramon Berenguer and his successors could wield over Lleida. Enactments regarding the city and its populace were supposed to be issued jointly with the counts of Urgell as co-lords rather than unilaterally.[5] The count-prince had made provisions for Ermengol to assume responsibility over the position of Lleida's castellan after the initial appointment, but he, and later Alfons, nevertheless continued to exert some control over the post. Following Lleida's capture, for instance, Ramon Berenguer IV had established Guillem Ramon I de Montcada as the city's castellan, subject to the powers of lordship exerted by Count Ermengol. After Guillem

Ramon's death in 1173, his son, Ramon I de Montcada, had inherited this post but soon entrusted it, with its seigniorial capacities ("senioraticum et dominicum"), to Guillem de Cervera, this same nobleman who would later take control of Tortosa, Benifallet, and Benifassà.[6] In spite of Ramon de Montcada's ability to delegate these responsibilities, Alfons made it clear, in 1179, that he continued to oversee the position. He indicated that Guillem de Cervera would be entitled to one-sixth of all incomes from the city and district. These revenues were "things," he advertised, "in which the great castellans of this city receive part."[7]

A concord between Alfons and Ermengol VIII (r. 1184–1209) from June 1187 concerning the count's "fief of the city of Lleida" clarifies further how the rulers managed to share authority.[8] In confirming the provisions of the 1148 *convenientia*, Alfons reiterated his own right to appoint the castellan and assign him control over the royal two-thirds of Lleida. The office, he recalled, would exercise jurisdiction over the entire city, save for the one-fifth share held by the Templars. All of the powers of lordship received by the castellan, although granted by the count-king, would be held directly from Ermengol. The convention reestablished similar terms for Ermengol's military rights to the castle of Ascó originally awarded him by Ramon Berenguer IV as compensation for the one-fifth share of Lleida received by the Templars. Alfons also reiterated his right of *potestas* over both of the holdings, which enabled him to recover them at any time.

Lleida, Urgell, and the Viscounts of Castellbò and Cabrera-Àger

This 1187 renewal restored good relations between Alfons and Ermengol VIII after a rocky period following Ermengol VII's death while campaigning in Valencia in 1184 that requires some detailed explanation.[9] Ermengol VII's demise had created problems for both dynasties. His will from 1177, drafted as he prepared for an earlier expedition into Muslim territory, had named his son, Ermengol VIII, as his primary heir but also clarified that his daughter, Marquesa, would inherit the county if his son failed to marry or produce a legitimate heir before his own death.[10] At the same time, Ermengol VII had recognized the continued entitlement to his patrimony of his wife, Countess Dolça, who derived from the rival house of Foix. These reservations, combined with Ermengol VIII's relatively young age at the time of his father's demise, soon emboldened Marquesa's husband, Ponç III de Cabrera, viscount of Cabrera-Àger (r. ca. 1165–1199), to advance his own claims to the county. Lingering questions regarding the succession would furthermore later encourage Ponç's son, Guerau IV (r. 1199–1229), at the turn of the thirteenth century, to seek control over the county after Ermengol VIII died in 1209 with only a daughter to succeed him, as we will see later.[11]

It is difficult to measure the seriousness of Ponç de Cabrera's claim and the extent to which it represented a threat to Ermengol VIII. Ponç may have intended, initially at least, to exploit the situation to help him resist young Ermengol's authority over the castles and domains that he, the viscount, held in Àger. Indeed, during the previous few years, Ponç had already engaged in similar efforts to assert more independence in his relationship with the count-king, Alfons. Since inheriting his viscomital titles from his father, Ponç had made the reasonably good bet that Alfons's preoccupation with other affairs—in particular, establishing control over castral domains along the coast—would permit him to assert his autonomy from Barcelona without serious repercussions.[12]

While it is certainly true that Alfons's resources and attention were spread thin at this time, he may also have decided against escalating the conflict and asserting his authority over Ponç's castles by force for other reasons. During these years of uncertainty following Ermengol VII's death and preceding his renewal of Ermengol VIII's powers in Lleida, when relations with the House of Barcelona remained tense, Alfons in fact favored Ponç as the titular head of the house of Urgell, and he may have kept his distance in order to give the viscount freer rein to press his claims, thereby further compromising Ermengol's limited stability. Ermengol VIII was struggling to assume control of his domains in the wake of his father's sudden death, and it may have been unclear to observers that he would succeed. Furthermore, by this point, the counts of Urgell had an even more mixed track record as supporters of comital-royal initiatives than the viscounts of Cabrera-Àger. For example, whereas Ermengol VII had prioritized his county's independence over supporting Alfons's public peace constitutions, Ponç had subscribed Alfons's initial attempt to establish a comital-royal peace and truce along the border of the county of Urgell at Fondarella in 1173.[13]

Such considerations could explain why Alfons soon decided to ally with the viscount against Ermengol VIII after securing Ponç's release from Alfonso VIII of Castile in April 1186.[14] This moment of détente between the count-king and the viscount accomplished two ends. First, it corrected the problem of Ponç's insubordination. He swore his homage and fidelity to the count-king, admitted that he indeed held the disputed castles from the king according to the "custom of Catalonia," and conceded to Alfons the all-important right to recover them at will (*potestas*) that Alfons had formerly demanded in vain. Second, it established an alliance with a strong, viable claimant to the county of Urgell, whose probable success over Ermengol VIII, thanks to the military support pledged by the count-king, stood to resolve definitively Alfons's lingering issues with the county of Urgell's independence.[15]

Facing such formidable opposition during his uncertain early days as count, Ermengol was naturally desperate to form alliances with potential supporters who could help him survive his impending wars with the viscount and count-king. An appeal by the Viscount Arnau de Castellbò (r. 1185–1229) for assistance presented one such opportunity.[16] By the middle of 1185, Arnau had already married Arnaua de Caboet, heiress of the valleys of Cabó and Sant Joan and recent widow of Bertran de Tarascó.[17] Complicating this merger of the Caboet and Castellbò houses, these lordships of Cabó and Sant Joan had been part of Arnaua's dowry carried by Bertran de Tarascó and were held in fief from the bishop of Urgell, Arnau de Preixens. For his part, this bishop was reluctant to condone Arnau's reception of the valleys because Arnaua and her first husband had already produced a son, also named Bertran, who should have had the right to inherit them. Arnau de Castellbò therefore sought to circumvent the bishop's ruling by appealing to Ermengol VIII, who, in addition to needing allies, was eager to establish his own authority over the valleys. In two transactions from later in 1185, Arnau de Castellbò nullified the earlier donations of Cabó and Sant Joan by the Caboets to the see of Urgell using the pretext that the current bishop's predecessors had not received the necessary approval for these infeudations from the count, who in fact held personal allodial title to these lands. The bishop and see of Urgell would be able to maintain control over these valleys only on the condition that they use them to support Ermengol militarily and recognize his right of *potestas* over them.[18]

Within months, Bishop Arnau de Preixens of Urgell was doing his utmost to counter this perceived affront to his see's rights. First, he preemptively tightened his church's hold over the remaining lordship retained by the Caboets, the valley of Andorra, by receiving an oath from its residents that they would never recognize Arnau de Castellbò as their lord against the bishop's will.[19] Secondly, he offered Ermengol VIII a better deal than Arnau de Castellbò that recognized his comital authority and earned him financial reward. Bishop Arnau bought a concession from the young count for three hundred *morabetins*, which confirmed retroactively the donations the Caboets had made to his church.[20] Now that his convention with the count had been effectively counteracted, Arnau de Castellbò had no alternative but to submit to Bishop Arnau. In May 1186, allegedly out of respect for the wishes of Arnaua, the bishop consented to grant Arnau de Castellbò the valleys of Cabó and Sant Joan as well as Andorra in fief. Because the valleys had formed part of Arnaua's dowry, they would be inherited by Arnau's stepson,

Bertran, and retained by Arnaua if her marriage were ever dissolved. Arnau de Castellbò swore to be a faithful vassal by respecting the bishop's right to *potestas* over the valleys, supporting him in military conflicts, and upholding the privileges owed to the inhabitants.[21]

Emboldened by his apparent success in establishing authority over the viscount of Castellbò without alienating the bishop of Urgell and the legitimacy it conferred upon him, Ermengol then developed a more systemic response to this threatening convention between Ponç de Cabrera and Alfons, which had been in force since April 1186.[22] By the following May, 1187, Ermengol had taken a page out of Alfons's own playbook by promulgating his own peace constitutions for his county.[23] In effect, this enactment served to proclaim publicly Ermengol's independence and status as a peer, rather than a subordinate, of the count-king.[24] Furthermore, his choice of venue for the oath-taking in support of his comital authority, at the church of Castelló de Farfanya, northeast of Balaguer on Ponç de Cabrera's domains of Àger, sent a stern, provocative message to the viscount. In counsel with his leading men and magnates, Ermengol cited his desire to join the archbishop of Tarragona and bishop of Urgell in the effort to fulfill the mission of the Peace of God, "for the benefit of conserving justice for the honor of God and the comfort of all my territory."[25] As part of this peace concord, Ermengol reestablished his authority over Ponç de Cabrera and, antagonistically, extended his peace over some of the castles that the viscount had agreed to hold from the count-king in their arrangement from the previous year.[26]

While clearly informed by what Alfons promulgated at Fondarella, with its extension of protection over peasants, animals and other property, public thoroughfares, and religious places, Ermengol's provisions manifested some significant differences and, in some respects, arguably represented a more ambitious initiative. For instance, he invested comital bailiffs and vicars with the responsibility of enforcement and stipulated their right to fine violators sixty *solidi*. Offenders who did not render the sum to the vicar within fifteen days were threatened with excommunication and double fines.[27] Whereas the *Usatges de Barcelona* mandated that all knights assist the count in upholding peace and order, Alfons's peace of Fondarella had not provided for mechanisms of enforcement beyond enlisting bishops and comital-royal bailiffs to fine violators.[28] In this respect, Ermengol's peace was unprecedented within Catalonia in that it obliged his men to join him in upholding its statutes.[29]

These aspects made it all the more important that the provisions of the peace were supported by a sizeable group of the count's magnates, a long list of which swore oaths at the county of Urgell's principal center of Agramunt.[30] Ermengol reestablished his bond with Ponç de Cabrera by means of a separate oath. Here, the viscount pledged these castles in support of "this truce" and received money coined by Ermengol at Agramunt in return. This claimed right to coin money was itself a potent statement regarding Ermengol's independence.[31]

Judging from the extent of his magnates' participation, this enactment by the young count was impressively successful. Not only did he obtain a public acclamation by his magnates of his succession as ruler of Urgell, regaining, in particular, recognition of his lordship over Ponç de Cabrera's domains. He also successfully signaled the independence of his county from comital-royal control by supplementing (or perhaps even overriding) Alfons's peace constitutions with provisions specifically governing his territories.

With this contextual information laid out in detail, let us circle back to the *convenientia* concerning Lleida and Ascó forged by Ermengol and Alfons in June 1187, just a month after Ermengol had established these peace constitutions for his county. We can now appreciate how this agreement must have been made in response to the escalating tension between the count-king and count. Ermengol's concord with the viscount of Cabrera-Àger as well as with the viscount of Castellbò put the standing of the lordships he shared with the count-king, such as Lleida and Ascó, which were situated outside the limits of the county of Urgell, on uncertain terms. And given that Ermengol VIII had already served as count of Urgell for several years by this point, the parties could no longer delay in renewing the terms of his possession of these holdings. This *convenientia* between Alfons and Ermengol notably did not refer to these peace constitutions or to Ermengol's convention with Ponç, which had counteracted what the count-king had established with the viscount the year before. This omission suggests that these rulers were confirming the relationship they had inherited with respect to these important holdings with considerable caution. The delicacy of the situation recommended the conservatism of the confirmation.

The Broken Peace

While Ermengol VIII was successfully navigating the challenges of asserting his authority over his magnates and positioning himself favorably vis-à-vis the count-king during his early years as count, Alfons's policing of his own administrative rights was showing signs of deficiency. Over the preceding decade, probably owing to distractions elsewhere in his realms, he had let his authority over these same viscounts of Cabrera-Àger and Castellbò and their dependents slip. This lack of oversight had enabled them to engage in private warfare with impunity. One of the best examples of these circumstances is Viscount Arnau de Castellbò's "long contention and great war" with his knight, Arnau de Saga. This so-called "War of the Two Arnaus," as Bisson has termed it, unleashed destructive violence on more than twenty communities in the area.

The origins of the war appear to have been in a dispute over the castle of Toloriu (in the county of Cerdanya), which Arnau de Saga claimed to possess independently, to the consternation of Arnau de Castellbò.[32] According to a memorial documenting "the broken [royal] peaces and truces," these men and their knights attacked numerous localities and religious houses in the county, setting fire to homes, defiling wine, breaking chattels, capturing and ransoming residents, and otherwise terrorizing the local populations.[33] Neither the count-king nor the count of Urgell appears to have played a role in quelling the violence and reconciling the two Arnaus. The men negotiated an independent peace accord that took effect in June 1188. Only cathedral canons from the Seu d'Urgell and local castellans subscribed the convention, which reestablished Arnau de Saga as Arnau de Castellbò's man and asserted that he hold the castle of Toloriu from him on the condition that he not do "bad things" with it. Yet, if he were to violate his lord's trust with the castle—and, at this point, the scribe interjected, "But if by chance, let God avert it!"—Arnau de Saga would be obliged to repair whatever damage he had done within thirty days.[34]

It is notable that this concord did not invoke any outside authority figures for enforcement. Even had the Arnaus desired the count-king's assistance with keeping the peace, it is unlikely that Alfons would have had the means to do so at the time. Indeed, he did not actively reassert authority over the viscount's holdings in Cerdanya until September 1188, when Arnau de Castellbò confirmed Alfons's rights to three of his castles in Cerdanya (Sant Martí, Cheralt, and Miralles). In what may have been an attempt to emphasize Alfons's legitimacy as count-king and preempt further attacks by Arnau's troubadour ally, Guillem de Berguedà, Arnau was pressured to commend himself to Alfons as "my lord, who is son of the venerable queen, named Petronilla."[35] As a further check on Arnau's ability to act abusively in the future, Alfons received confirmation of his *potestas* over these castles from each of their castellans just days later.[36]

The memorial indicated that this violence occurred during the "first peace" of Fondarella.[37] Such a violation of Alfons's initial peace was likely the primary factor for prompting the count-king to seek to renew his peace constitutions at Girona and Villafranca del Penedès in August 1188, although

Ermengol VIII's competitive peace the previous year may also have played a role. Alfons was clearly concerned at this time about his relations with Ermengol. He feared specifically that the count might seek to press into his county of Cerdanya. Indeed, in Alfons's recent conventions with Arnau de Castellbò, Arnau had sworn to reinforce the count-king with knights from Cerdanya and five of his personal men led by his son "if you should have war with the count of Urgell" for as long as that conflict should last.[38] In this situation of ever-shifting alliances, the greatest offender of the count-king's peace had been restored, temporarily, to his proper place as a defender of comital-royal interests in the viscounty against potential incursions by great barons such as the count of Urgell.

Alfons's constitutions of peace and truce in 1188 did not merely repeat the ones he had passed, with considerable baronial support, at Fondarella in 1173. Some of their innovative features were also clearly borrowed from the count of Urgell's peace provisions that had been issued a year earlier at Agramunt and Castelló de Farfanya. Such emulation was likely a sign that Alfons was wary of Ermengol's continued assertions of independence in spite of their renewed convention concerning their shared lordships of Lleida and Ascó in 1187. He imitated, in particular, Ermengol's designation of vicars as the primary enforcers of the peace, authorizing them to organize a militia for enforcement, and imposed a scheme of fines that was nearly identical to what the count of Urgell had adopted.[39] Alfons also added a number of concessions to these constitutions in an apparent effort to encourage greater support from his barons. These dispensations included his personal promise not to impose the peace tax (*bovatge*) or to appoint any non-Catalan vicars. He furthermore agreed to adhere to "written usage in giving power over castles to his vassal lords." This guarantee made all the more important the individual instruments concerning enfeoffed castles that his fiscal officers were already organizing as the comital-royal archive and would compile into the *Liber Feudorum Maior*.[40]

In spite of these allowances, the count-king failed to win support for his constitutions. He had not convinced traditionally resistant potentates, such as the count of Urgell, nor customarily compliant families, many of which had formerly subscribed the provisions from Fondarella in 1173. Not a single baron swore to uphold his constitutions. Alfons was lone subscriber. They were likely taken aback by Alfons's assertiveness and attempts to force them to remain faithful and disappointed at the slow pace of the conquest of Muslim lands.[41] Exceptional resistance by a minority of the most powerful barons had spawned an unanticipated collective rejection by all of Alfons's magnates.[42]

Shifting Negotiations over Lleida

Alfons's failure to reinstitute the peace and truce in 1188 coincided with continued resistance by these same troublesome viscounts. Viscount Arnau de
Castellbò had respected his conventions with Alfons concerning his rights
within Cerdanya but had transgressed the authority of the count of Urgell
and his ally, Bishop Arnau de Preixens of Urgell. He had sought to construct
new castles without authorization and resisted Ermengol's right of *potestas* over existing fortifications. Hostilities must have been halted following
Alfons's intervention, on Ermengol's and Bishop Arnau's behalf, against any
further offenses by Arnau de Castellbò and his associate Ramon de Sant Martí
in April 1190.[43] In two conventions signed between Ermengol and Arnau
de Castellbò in October of that year, the count manifested his eagerness to
restore good relations with the viscount. Ermengol could have been fearful
that he might suffer violence similar to what the count-king had experienced
in 1188. In return for Arnau's recognition of his comital authority, Ermengol
let the viscount retain his castles and authorized the construction of new fortresses. He even assigned him two hundred *morabetins* to defray the cost of
rebuilding Castellciutat.[44] As we will see later, these were terms that Arnau
would once again violate prior to their renewed reconciliation arranged by
the count-king in 1194.

Viscount Ponç III de Cabrera outdid Arnau de Castellbò by offending the
authority of both the count-king and the count of Urgell. Alfons, however,
was the first to declare war in response to these abuses. In November 1188,
just a few months after failing to renew his peace constitutions, Alfons
secured limited assistance from the count of Urgell "in this war that he has
against Ponç de Cabrera."[45] Ermengol's collaboration, however, was reluctant at best, resulting in a highly lopsided agreement in which the count-king
assumed most of the responsibility for engaging with the viscount. Alfons
was sufficiently suspicious of the count to make him swear not to form any
new "truce and peace" with Ponç during the one-year term of this accord,
which would commence at Easter.

It is evident from this agreement that Alfons and Ermengol each had different goals in mind at this moment. The count-king's central objective was
to secure Ermengol's permission to use Lleida as a military staging point
against Ponç's base at Àger to the north. Alfons would have the right to
use as many of Lleida's men as he needed and could also retain up to forty
Aragonese knights in the city during June and July, when he planned to campaign. Ermengol himself, however, was not required to contribute any military support to the enterprise, although he was entitled to a share of any

spoils if he did lend a hand. In return, Alfons would assist with Ermengol's
"war in Valencia" but could delay his collaboration until he had devoted this
upcoming year to engagement with Ponç. These respective objectives of the
count and count-king highlight the divergent implications of Ermengol's
successful peace of 1187 and Alfons's failed one the following year. In contrast to the count, who aspired to conduct this campaign into Valencia, the
count-king's ongoing internal struggles were distracting him from engaging
with Muslim territory. As a manner of advertising the peace provisions that
the counts of Urgell had refused to support, Alfons authorized Ermengol to
lodge grievances concerning "knights from the territory of the lord king"
accountable for malfeasance committed in accordance with "his peace and
truce." The concord also reveals their differing perspectives on Lleida's utility. For Alfons, the city was chiefly an asset for targeting this insubordinate
viscount to the north. For Ermengol, it served as an important gateway to
campaigning and conquest to the south.

Ermengol interpreted Alfons's support for his "war in Valencia" as coming in the form of castral positions and not simply auxiliary knights. In
June 1189, before the one-year term of this alliance had ended, Ermengol
pressed Alfons to render to him control of the well-positioned castle of
Gebut at the southern reaches of Lleida's district.[46] Rather than simply com-
plying with the count's request or establishing a compromise concerning
this particular castle, however, Alfons laid out a chain of conditional backup
measures involving neighboring castral districts. He promised Ermengol
that Ramon de Cervera, lord of Gebut, would perform homage to him
within two months upon his return from serving in the count-king's army
at Cervera. In assigning Gebut to Ermengol, Alfons reserved only his right
of *potestas* over the castle. If, however, the count-king ended up deciding not
to invest the count with this lordship, he would instead give him the castle
of Castelldans as a "free allod," and its lord, Ramon's nephew, Guillem IV
de Cervera, would perform homage to him for it. Anticipating that Guillem
might not be amenable to accepting Ermengol as Castelldans's overlord,
Alfons, as a last resort, appointed for the count to receive the strategically
vital castle of Mequinenza, at the confluence of the Ebro and Segre Rivers,
as a perpetual free allod "in exchange for the lordship (*senioratici*) of Gebut."

The intricacy of these arrangements, with all of their contingencies, was
not entirely of the count-king's making. The language of the charter suggests that Alfons's inability to force the Cervera family to submit to Ermengol's lordship necessitated these supplemental provisions. Ten years earlier,
in 1179, in partial fulfillment of Ramon Berenguer III's convention with the
Cervera family from 1119, Alfons had confirmed and made adjustments to

Guillem II de Cervera's lordship over Castelldans and Gebut, and Guillem had passed his rights to the latter castle to his son, Ramon, before his death around 1181. His other son, Guillem III, had received control of Castelldans and later transferred it to his son, Guillem IV.[47] It appears that this compli-cated chain of conditions did, in fact, run its course. Ermengol ended up with lordship over Mequinenza within the two-month time frame, as Alfons had promised. He was already exercising lordship over Mequinenza several months later, in September 1189, when he sold merchants from Tortosa an exemption from the *lleuda* there for two hundred *morabetins*.[48] As we will see below, in addition to refusing to support Ermengol and Alfons by cooperat-ing with this concord, Ramon de Cervera would soon join these rebellious viscounts in actively challenging the authority of both the count-king and count in other ways.

Additional agreements between the two rulers over the coming years manifested their growing shared commitment to conducting a coordinated assault on Ponç III de Cabrera. Ermengol's accord with Alfons, signed in Lleida in August 1191, was reminiscent of recent treaties against Navarre (e.g., those of Ágreda, Sangüesa, and Cazola) in that it planned out the conquest and distribution of Ponç's lands. Ermengol would obtain Ponç de Cabrera's castles and property pertaining to the viscounty of Àger within the county of Urgell, and Alfons was entitled to those from the viscounty of Cabrera "beyond Cervera in all of Catalonia."[49] A subsequent agreement, negotiated in April 1192, featured much more detailed language than ear-lier charters regarding the service Ermengol would owe as Alfons's man (*solidus*).[50] It emphasized twice that these responsibilities were expected as part of the service owed to one's lord. As part of his obligation to provide general military support ("hostes y cavalcadas"), Ermengol swore to help enforce the count-king's property rights and prerogatives among his knights and vassals ("hòmens propis"), likely a reference to Alfons's ongoing troubles with Ponç de Cabrera. Ermengol furthermore promised to conduct, with his own men, "peace and war" on the count-king's behalf against "Muslims and Christians" and to pledge his fidelity and take an oath "of the body of the said king and of his honor." In return, Alfons confirmed Ermengol's posses-sion of Mequinenza and Gebut in fief. He asserted his right to *potestas* for both castles but made no reservations regarding the appointment of their castellans. As further compensation, Ermengol received one thousand *solidi* annually from the *lleuda* collected from Lleida. Alfons also used the occasion to confirm Ermengol's "fiefs and allods from the city of Lleida" and Ascó as well as his rights to the castles of Aitona and Albesa. The agreement made clear that part of this compensation constituted reimbursement for property

Ermengol's family had lost when the Templars received their fifth shares of Lleida and Ascó from Ramon Berenguer IV. The count had good reason to minimize the perceived extent of these conferred rights so that Alfons would not be in a position to pressure him for even greater support.

Ermengol was more subdued when it came to other seigniorial agents within his county. Like the count-king, as the self-proclaimed defender of the peace over his lands, he wanted to be able to rely on the military resources present throughout the lordships of Urgell. Yet he avoided using this objective as a pretense for intervening in the internal affairs of seigniorial domains. In fact, for a price, Ermengol was willing to ignore certain disputes between his lords in which he was not directly involved. In 1190, for example, in return for a payment of nine hundred *solidi*, he promised the canons of the Augustinian priory of Solsona that he would not demand military service from their subjects in Solsona itself or from the house's extensive castral domains throughout the region for wars internal to the county, even if he fell into armed conflict with that town's primary lord, Ramon de Torroja. Ermengol stipulated that he would only call upon the priory to help defend the peace in the event that some powerful foreign invader entered the county.[51] The count offered a similar privilege to the residents of Solsona the following year for an even larger sum. In it, he agreed to safeguard their personal property and possessions. However, in anticipation of the inevitable damage of a siege against that town's lord, he would not consent to protect their town walls and fortifications. Instead, the residents would be held responsible for repairing or rebuilding them if Ermengol entered into a war with Ramon de Torroja. Ermengol also promised that, if this same Ramon fell into an isolated conflict with the bishop of Urgell, he would not to intervene to "cause any harm."[52] These measures illustrate how Ermengol differentiated such routine seigniorial disputes within his county from the threats presented by powerful, insubordinate barons such as the viscounts of Castellbò and Cabrera-Àger.

The apparent efficacy of such targeted efforts by ad hoc coalitions to engage with rebellious magnates may have helped encourage Alfons to take his systemic provisions for public order in Catalonia in a new direction. As reconciliations with Arnau de Castellbò and Ponç III de Cabrera were still pending, in November 1192 Alfons relocated the session to Barbastro, deep within Aragonese territory, and eliminated the mechanism of baronial consent.[53] Perhaps he was seeking to avoid a repeat of what had transpired at his failed peace assembly in 1188. Like any standard charter, the peace provisions produced on this occasion in 1192 were merely subscribed by a small number of Aragonese nobles along with archbishop of Tarragona, the sacrists of Barcelona and Vic, "and others of the court." In promulgating these statutes,

Alfons targeted a new audience: "the *prohoms* of both cities and towns and the populace" of Catalonia.[54]

While the involvement of bishops and vicars in earlier constitutions had implicitly signaled the importance of towns for the peace, here Alfons appears to have recognized explicitly, for the first time, the strategic importance of this growing constituency that was potentially more receptive to such curbs on violence and disorder. By grouping the magnates with the patricians and general populace as recipients of laws that did not require their consent, he was broadcasting a more ideologically potent and emboldened, if far less practicable, vision of comital-royal authority that built upon the concepts initially advanced by the *Usatges de Barcelona*: that all of them collectively, from commoner to baron, were subject to the rule of law delivered by the sovereign.[55] In his preamble to these peace constitutions of 1192, however, Alfons sought to draw attention away from these novel elements by construing the statutes as an authentic revival of the ancient "peace and truce" maintained by his predecessors. Those magnates who had rejected the peace "on account of their excessive eagerness and selfishness," Alfons maintained, were the ones guilty of destructive innovation.[56]

While these constitutions threatened to escalate the politicization of relations between the count-king and his magnates, they did not compromise Alfons's ongoing effort to subjugate the rebellious viscounts of Cabrera-Àger and Castellbò. Reconciliations with both of these agents took place at a "full" session of the court that was convoked at the monastery of Poblet in late August 1194, with significant baronial support. Ponç III de Cabrera and his son pledged their fidelity to the count-king and swore to respect his authority over their five castles.[57] Arnau de Castellbò, in the presence of Ermengol VIII and many other magnates, "placed himself under the control and power of Lord Alfons" and promised to remain faithful to him. This mode of reconciliation was telling because it served to unravel further the autonomy established by the count of Urgell via his independent peace constitutions. The ritual established that the viscount was, first and foremost, the count-king's man. The terms of their agreement largely restored the conventions arranged with Ermengol in 1190 discussed earlier. With Alfons serving as an intermediary, Arnau promised to answer for all of the complaints and pay for all of the damages suffered by the bishop and count of Urgell for "all injury and all bad things committed" by him and his men. He pledged two disputed castles to Ermengol and swore not to build or reconstruct fortifications without the count's consent or to exercise abusive or violent lordship on lands subject to the bishop and count.[58] In a separate instrument made the following day, Arnau committed to Ermengol *potestas* over nearly all of his castles in the Castellbò and Aguilar valleys as his "solid man" (*solidus*). He excluded only the castle of Sant Andreu in the Castellbò valley from the arrangement, without explanation or comment.[59]

Conflict under Pere

Ponç III de Cabrera and his son, Guerau IV, adhered to these conventions throughout Alfons's reign and subsequently renewed them as *convenientiae* with Pere in 1196 and 1199.[60] Arnau de Castellbò, however, did not honor the terms of his reconciliation for long. Soon, by the mid-1190s, he would be drawn into committing further violence against the bishop and count of Urgell with the Albigensian sympathizer Count Raymond-Roger of Foix.[61] The desecrations performed during these campaigns likely helped prompt Pere's renewal, in 1198, of his father's prior measures to defend the realms against heresy, which Alfons had issued at Lleida in 1194.[62] They may also have prompted the first of Pere's peace constitutions, delivered at Barcelona in April 1198.[63] Although Ermengol VIII intervened to defend the see of Urgell against further attack, this engagement did not distract him from attending to administrative duties to the south. He joined Pere in confirming Lleida's population charter, in 1196.[64] After making some adjustments to their division of property rights within Lleida in February 1200, Pere and Ermengol met again to confirm jointly the city's privileges yet again in April of that year.[65]

The election of a more energetic bishop, Bernat de Vilamurs, helped the see of Urgell establish better relations with Arnau de Castellbò, for the time being at least. Under Bernat's leadership, the cathedral was eventually able to come to a reconciliation with the viscount in 1201. Arnau, joined by his wife and daughter, pledged to pay reparations for "all injuries, damages, and evil deeds" inflicted against the church. He also confirmed the see's ownership of contested castles in his possession. He reestablished himself and his family, along with their knights, as the bishop's faithful servants for a minimum of fifteen years. They would perform military service for the see whenever called upon.[66]

Bishop Bernat also sought to exert control over the viscount's dynastic politics. Bernat appears to have shared Ermengol's greatest fear: that he would lose control over Arnau de Castellbò. Indeed, a looming threat was that Arnau might seek to ally his domains with the county of Foix by marrying his daughter, Ermessenda, to Raymond-Bernard, son of Count Raymond-Roger of Foix.[67] Bernat had Arnau promise that he would not carry out any such marriage alliance without first obtaining his prior consent. These concerns, it turned out, were well founded. Within months,

Arnau had broken most of these pledges by arranging this marriage alliance with Foix without episcopal consent, a move that soon led to renewed armed conflict with the bishop and count of Urgell.[68]

Empowered by their alliance, which they renewed in February 1200 while attending to their co-lordship in Lleida, Ermengol and Pere pursued diplomatic solutions with their shared enemies while leaving the door open to war, if necessary.[69] For example, even though Arnau de Castellbò continued to cause trouble through his alliance with the count of Foix, the count-king nevertheless continued to host him at court in the late 1190s.[70] With other nobles, such conciliatory tactics yielded only mixed results. For instance, Ramon de Cervera, the aforementioned lord of Gebut, responded to certain peace overtures that he did not view as antithetical to his autonomy. In April 1200, for instance, he conceded that he had acted unjustly toward the church of Osona by laying claim to its castle of L'Espelt. Pere witnessed and confirmed his renunciation for which Ramon received one hundred *aureos* from the church.[71] Ramon, however, continued to resist the count of Urgell's efforts to establish his ownership of castles held in fief by the noble that he had begun to treat as his own. Ermengol and Pere soon formed a new alliance specifically to address the security risk posed by Ramon's continuing insubordination. They only temporarily dissolved their standing agreement of mutual support in May 1200 so that the count-king could focus on renewing his peace and truce at the upcoming court session in June.[72] After Pere received broad noble support for these peace measures in July, he and Ermengol agreed to join forces against Ramon de Cervera to reestablish the count's *potestas* over Ramon's enfeoffed castles and lands.[73]

Ermengol was able to use his rights of lordship over Lleida to secure resources to fund this campaigning against Ramon de Cervera. In return for the count's confirmation of "all of its rights and possessions in Lleida and its district and in Urgell" in October 1201, the Templar Order paid Ermengol 250 *morabetins* and released a claim of 15,000 *solidi* it had been holding against him.[74] Ermengol and his allies soon managed to defeat Ramon de Cervera and his force of five thousand men at Agramunt in 1202.[75] Fighting within the Pyrenees nevertheless continued until February of the following year, when Ermengol's forces captured Arnau de Castellbò and Raymond-Roger of Foix, along with many of their knights. The reconciliation that would end their captivity took months to negotiate. In addition to owing a sizeable ransom, Raymond-Roger and his supporters would be responsible to pay and reimburse Ermengol for the cost of maintaining them in captivity, which amounted to twenty-five thousand *solidi*.[76] These arrangements were confirmed, with slight modifications, in a meeting at Lleida in August 1203 that was overseen by the count-king. Most of the ransom was to be delivered by Pedro Fernández de Castro, who entered into the service of the count of Urgell as early as 1199.[77] When he was finally released in early September, the count of Foix and his son once again took responsibility for the damages they had inflicted on the property and rights of the count and bishop of Urgell. They performed homage to Ermengol and swore to keep the peace as "faithful allies" (*amicos*) and respect their rights in the future.[78] Arnau de Castellbò owed a much smaller ransom but had to acknowledge his subordinate status and that Ermengol possessed the right of *potestas* over most of his castles.[79]

Ermengol and Elvira

In spite of these assurances, based on prior experience, Ermengol VIII and his supporters had reason to anticipate that trouble with these ambitious rivals would flare up yet again before too long. The risk of complications was heightened by the fact that Ermengol and his countess, Elvira Nuñez de Lara, remained childless.[80] Accordingly, soon after he had secured this latest peace, Ermengol set about reassessing his association with Elvira.

Although this was not the first time the couple had troubled themselves with their partnership, it was arguably the most serious. Following Ermengol's assumption of the county from his father almost twenty years earlier, he had taken steps to secure Elvira's position as countess and prepare for the transition of the county to his children or nearest relative in the event of his premature death. These measures largely dealt with Elvira's dower, which, as itemized in 1186, amounted to a sizeable ten thousand *morabetins* based on the castles of Agramunt, Ponts, Alòs de Balaguer, Linyola, and Bell-lloc, plus half of Ermengol's holdings in Lleida.[81] She would possess rights to the dower freely "for all of the days of your life with or without offspring" after which it would go to their children or return to Ermengol's family. Since these holdings represented the countess's own personal stake in the county, which would customarily fall under her control upon being widowed, they represented an ideal resource for establishing and defending her authority in her husband's absence.

Ermengol offered Elvira added assurances. On two consecutive days in late January 1188, with clear echoes of the definition of her dower, Ermengol had the individual male citizens of Agramunt and Ponts, over seventy in each locality, swear oaths to accept the countess as their lord for her lifetime following his death, regardless of whether she had borne Ermengol any children. These men swore to defend Elvira if anyone attempted to challenge her rights to Agramunt or Ponts. In entrusting urban citizens rather than his barons with these responsibilities, Ermengol was responding to the extraordinary urban growth and development of civilian collectives throughout Catalonia and aligning his dynastic goals with their shared interest in governmental stability.[82] He may also have been emulating the professions of homage Alfons had secured from urban communal collectives, such as that of Tortosa, at the outset of his unstable minority.[83] This activity was part of a trend that would surface again in Alfons's involvement of the towns for the first time at his peace assembly of 1192 and at subsequent such assemblies convoked by his son and grandson.[84] Unlike certain other lords, who viewed such communal regimes as detrimental to their authority and sought to suppress them, the count-king and his regents demonstrated how such collectives could serve as political assets.[85]

These oaths included language concerning the transition to the next generation. They made it clear that any children of the count and countess would naturally inherit their parents' rights. In the event that the couple lacked progeny and the count had left no will to obey, these men would ensure that the family's holdings were entrusted to Ermengol's closest relative.[86] Although these records of oaths survive only for these two communities, other localities pertaining to her dower or situated within the broader county probably made similar professions that are not reflected in extant documentation. The pair would have had an interest in rallying as much communal support as possible to offset any challenge presented by possible baronial usurpers.

Over a decade after these preparations, the couple was still engaged with similar issues, albeit with greater urgency due to the time that had passed. In 1203, still childless, they found themselves at a breaking point, with Ermengol seriously considering dismissing Elvira for another in his quest for an heir. In August of that year, as the viscount of Castellbò and count of Foix still remained in captivity, he met with the countess and a number of their mutual supporters in Lleida to make arrangements in the event that he decided to dissolve their marriage. Ermengol agreed that if he opted to dismiss Elvira, he would send her to Cardona, Oliola, or Puigverd. Under no circumstances would he imprison, defame, or harm her. However, two of her supporters, who were also men of the count, the Castilian noble Pedro Fernández de Castro and Viscount Guillem I de Cardona, pledged to defend Elvira if the count threatened her in any way.[87] Zurita reports that Pedro was a "gran señor en Galicia" descended from the count Pedro Fernández de Trava and that his sister was married to Ermengol VIII's cousin and rival, Guillem de Cabrera.[88] However, if Guillem de Cardona were to come to her defense, resulting in a "rift or tension" with Ermengol, he agreed that he would first have to give the count control of the castles he held from him. Similarly, even though Pedro Fernández held the castles of Montmagastre and Ponts per "recent" agreements (*convenientiae*) with Elvira, these holdings ultimately pertained to the count. Only Ponts pertained to Elvira's dower per the 1186 definition.[89] As a result, in the event of conflict with the count, the countess agreed that she would dissolve these *convenientiae*, thereby restoring Ermengol's rights to the holdings. Pedro Fernández would then have only his personal castle of Llorenç to use to assist her.[90]

In anticipation of being cast out by Ermengol, Elvira prepared to return to her family in Castile.[91] She may have been intending to become a sister of the Order of Calatrava when she donated to it all of her goods derived from her maternal and paternal lines in Castile-León on 21 August 1203. She stipulated that a portion of the incomes be used to maintain a priest who would pray for her as well as her parents and deceased relatives.[92] In addition to providing her with a protective place for her remaining days, this donation established the order as a defender of Elvira's property in the event that she were dismissed by Ermengol.[93]

Despite the seriousness of these preparations, by mid-September the couple had reconciled. They promised to treat one another properly and with fidelity as husband and wife and to respect each other's rights.[94] Although the agreement reestablishing their union does not indicate what motivated this shift, they had likely since discovered that Elvira was pregnant. Ermengol naturally could not have known that his wife would bear a daughter, Aurembiaix, and must have anticipated that he had a male successor on the way.[95] Accordingly, soon the count and countess were collaborating once again in their governance of their territories, possibly with an eye to Elvira's potential role as a key transitional figure in their heir's assumption of power. In a charter subscribed by Guerau IV de Cabrera in April 1204, for instance, Ermengol and Elvira together resolved their differences with the lord and citizens of Sanaüja and traded pledges of fidelity and support.[96]

Renewed Conflict

Leading up to the resolution of this marital crisis, Ermengol continued to be preoccupied with Viscount Arnau de Castellbò and Count Raymond-Roger of Foix. Following their capture, with Count-king Pere playing the role of intermediary, Ermengol had made arrangements in clear anticipation that Arnau would resist the terms of his release. He had appointed his noble supporter and creditor, Gombau de Ribelles, who was heavily invested in Ermengol and Pere's administration of the lower Segre region, to maintain guard over the viscount.[97] According to their convention signed in mid-August, Gombau was authorized to deliver Arnau to Pere only if the viscount first granted Ermengol and Urgell's bishop *potestas* over some of his castles within ten days. If he had not made arrangements concerning any of these castles by that date, then Arnau would instead suffer the less desirable outcome of being handed over to Ermengol.[98] For his part, the count-king moved to extend the count some assurances that he would handle the resolution in a judicious manner. He pledged to Ermengol, as his "man" (*homo*), "that all of the aforementioned [terms] should be observed for him, without ill will." As a symbol of his generosity as lord, Pere agreed to postpone his assumption of *potestas* over the castle of Mequinenza (positioned to the south of Lleida) for up to one year or until such time as Guillem IV de Cervera could secure it as castellan. Ermengol's possession of Mequinenza, which had originated in his aforementioned arrangement with Alfons in 1189, had developed into a source of embroiled conflict with Pere, who likely desired to regain control of it in order to support his planned campaigning into Valencia. Here the count-king promised not to exploit this situation with the viscount and count of Foix in order to pressure a more favorable outcome regarding that castle.[99]

Although Ermengol naturally had ambitions to profit, monetarily and with respect to his rights of lordship, from his victory over these rivals at Agramunt, he was also eager to secure a long-term solution to his conflicts with the viscount by impeding further collusion with the count of Foix. Following his release, Arnau had succumbed to pressure to ally himself more closely with the Ermengol dynasty by marrying Elissenda, Ermengol's niece and the daughter of the viscount Guillem of Cardona. In return, Ermengol had restored Arnau's infeudated castles and other properties for a probationary term of five years. Arnau and his men had then sworn to honor the count's rights of lordship. The victors even had Raymond-Roger of Foix join in, for good measure, with a pledge to ensure that Arnau and his supporters complied with the terms of the convention.[100] These arrangements were calculated to undo an existing betrothal between Arnau's daughter, Ermessenda, and Raymond-Roger's son, Raymond-Bernard that would have merged the Castellbò and Foix lines. As added protection, Ermengol made Arnau swear an oath never to execute this prior marriage arrangement when the viscount performed homage to him several weeks later.[101] A final safeguard against a Castellbò-Foix unification was made the following month, when Raymond-Roger agreed to marry his son to Ermengol's sister, Miracle. They mutually promised that neither Roger-Bernard nor any of the count of Foix's other sons would ever agree to marry Ermessenda or any other daughter of Arnau de Castellbò.[102] Guillem de Cardona and Ermengol established a formal contract of betrothal with Arnau de Castellbò in 1206, in which they presented him with a dowry for Elissenda of ten thousand *solidi*, "in accordance with the *fuero* and custom of our land." In return, Arnau presented a dower of equivalent value based on his property and rights held in the county of Cerdanya and named Pere as a *fideiussor*.[103] These arrangements succeeded in ushering in a period of relatively peaceful relations between these families. Between November 1206 and March 1207, for example, Ermengol oversaw the peaceful confirmation of the rights of lordship possessed by the new bishop of Urgell, Pere de Puigverd, to Arnau's holdings in the valleys of Caboet, San Juan, and Andorra and the viscount's participation as a supporter of the see of Urgell.[104] Arnau also fulfilled his expected role as a supporter of comital-royal initiatives, even when they did not align clearly with his interests as viscount. Later in 1207, for instance, he subscribed a royal privilege sheltering the canons of the see of Urgell from creditors seeking debts owed by their bishop.[105] This détente, however, was not to outlast Ermengol's lifetime. Despite his careful planning, the Castellbò and Foix families were able to stall these marriage arrangements until Ermengol's death in 1209. The ensuing turmoil regarding who would inherit the county of Urgell would liberate Arnau and Raymond-Roger to use their children to establish this feared marriage alliance, thereby effecting the long-anticipated merger of their households.[106]

Crises Following Ermengol VIII's Death

These careful precautions could not prevent the flare up of controversy with other parties following Ermengol VIII's death in 1209 without a male heir. Viscount Guerau IV de Cabrera advanced his claim to the county of Urgell based on his connection as Ermengol VII's grandson and Ermengol VIII's nephew. Like his father before him, Guerau was fully willing to take up arms in violation of comital-royal mandates and peace statutes in order to advance his interests.[107] The position of Countess Elvira and Aurembiaix in the face of the viscount's impending aggression in support of his claim was strengthened by the support of the count-king, who had continued to regard Ermengol as a close ally throughout the remainder of the count's life.[108] Already before Ermengol's death, the countess had wisely secured Pere's general support and protection of her position and property against all enemies twice, in 1205 and 1208.[109]

Other than the overcommitted count-king, what allies remained for the countess and her young daughter? It is unclear to what extent Pedro Fernández and Guillem de Cardona had continued to support Elvira following the

resolution of her marital conflicts with Ermengol in late 1203. Pedro Fernández's affiliation with the county may well have grown even stronger during
Ermengol's final years, if Zurita is correct that his son, Álvaro Fernández de
Castro, was already engaged to Aurembiaix by this point and thereby in place
to succeed Ermengol.[110] On the other hand, Pedro's daughter, Elo Pérez,
would soon marry Guerau de Cabrera, putting in question his allegiance to
the countess. An accord signed with the count-king in February 1206, roughly
three years before Ermengol's passing, raises further suspicions about Pedro
Fernández's plans for the future. It suggests that Pere had plans to extend what
he viewed as his suzerain rights to the county by supporting Pedro Fernández's own claims rather than those of his son, Álvaro, or future son-in-law,
Guerau. The count-king had pledged to assist the Castilian "in the acquisition
of the county of Urgell" on the condition that when Pedro obtained all "or a
greater share" of the county, he would hold it along with its most important
towns and castles in Lower Urgell and eastern Aragon (Calasanz, Santa Lecina,
Sant Llorenç, Balaguer, Ponts, Alòs de Balaguer) from Pere, subject to the
count-king's *potestas*. Ermengol neither witnessed nor subscribed the charter
and surely would not have consented to this alliance had he known about it.[111]

Although both parties stood to gain a great deal if their plans succeeded,
the count-king arguably secured the greatest benefits. He limited his military
support of Pedro to when he was personally "in Aragon and Catalonia,"
which was infrequent at that time. Furthermore, the agreement made it
clear that Pere intended to possess true lordship over the county and that he
saw this ownership as fully entitled by earlier transactions with the counts of
Urgell. Pedro would receive "the aforementioned County of Urgell *through
me . . . in accordance with the agreements and charters made between myself
and the count of Urgell* and his and our forebearers."[112] By this point, Pedro
had established himself as a dependable royal servant and officer who would
have been unlikely to stand in the way of the count-king's ambitions for
the county were their plans to materialize. He held outstanding royal debts
of over twenty thousand *morabetins* and had already assumed the position
of chief royal officer (*mayordomo*) in Aragon by early 1206.[113] These debts
remained unpaid and were later enlarged through additional borrowing by
the queen mother, Sancha, in 1208, to be financed by Pere's castles in Aragon
along with his incomes from Zaragoza, Teruel, and Calatayud.[114] A group of
Aragonese *ricos hombres* presented themselves as guarantors for these loans
and pledged to perform military service for the Castilian Order of Calatrava
should the count-king renege on his payment obligations. This move clearly
represented an effort to mobilize further support in defense of this key Castilian position against the Almohads.[115]

Subsequent moves by the count-king were seemingly aimed at promoting Pedro's standing. For example, on 27 May 1206, when he confirmed Lleida's consulate, mandating that the citizens remain faithful to the "Lord King, Count, and castellans of Lleida," the count-king invoked the "consent and counsel" of Pedro Fernández and castellan Guillem de Cervera but left out Ermengol, who did not subscribe the charter.[116] Although Pere had conferred unilaterally both the original authorization of Lleida's consulate in 1197 and the first confirmation in 1202, Ermengol's complete absence is suspicious due to the fact that he was present in Lleida at that time.[117] As was often the case for the overextended monarch, nothing was to come of these carefully mapped out ambitions.

Shortly before his death, Ermengol had made his own preparations to defend his daughter's and wife's rights to his county and other properties. He had forged agreements with Guillem IV de Cervera, lord of Juneda and Castelldans, and his uncle Ramon, lord of Gebut, investing them with fortifications and incomes in return for their pledges to join him against Guerau IV de Cabrera and all other enemies, save for the count-king and queen and one another.[118] Balancing out this noble support, Ermengol had mandated that the citizens of Linyola, Agramunt, and Ponts perform homage to Elvira and pledge to defend her and her authority over Urgell against any usurper or invader.[119] It is likely that these were deliberate repetitions of the oaths we know the citizens of Agramunt and Ponts made to the countess in 1188.

Other preparations by the count were far less effective, bordering on counterproductive. Although they were well-intended, the preparations made by Ermengol in his last will from August 1208 inadvertently weakened the defenses of his wife and daughter to maintain their control over his patrimony.[120] Ermengol appointed Aurembiaix as his primary heir, "countess of all of my land and the county of Urgell," whereas Elvira would only hold the county as regent to their daughter. The will recognized that Elvira would also possess her dower for her lifetime, but it valued at fifteen thousand *solidi*, which was a considerable reduction from what she had been awarded in 1186, when her *sponsalicium* was indicated as ten thousand *morabetins* or roughly sixty thousand *solidi*.[121] As a result, Elvira was less well equipped to defend herself and her daughter from these usurpers. Ermengol also paid a high price in land rights for apostolic protection for his county and its domains from Innocent III in hopes that it would provide for an uneventful transition of power to Aurembiaix and Elvira. However, as Damian Smith has noted, these valuable resources might have been better spent securing a stronger alliance with the count-king, as Elvira had much greater need of military than spiritual support at this moment.[122] Finally, Ermengol's will botched its well-meaning succession plan. First and foremost, Ermengol signaled Aurembiaix's weakness as the recipient of Urgell by holding out the hope that, before he could prepare another will, he might have a male child, who would then inherit the comital title and lands.[123] If Aurembiaix did end up inheriting the county, in the event of her death without legitimate offspring, Ermengol's elder sister, Marquesa, would become countess, followed by his younger sister, Miracle, and finally his more distant relative, Viscount Guillem de Cardona. When Ermengol drafted his will, he could not have anticipated that, by establishing his sister as next in line, he would thereby encourage her son, the Viscount Guerau IV de Cabrera, to proceed aggressively against Aurembiaix and Elvira in his efforts to claim Urgell for himself as the closest male heir.[124]

Opportunistic Intervention by Pere

The mounting threat presented by Guerau IV de Cabrera must have prompted Elvira, as regent, to turn to Pere for preemptive assistance within a year of her husband's death in 1209. At this point she had fewer allies to choose from than before, due to Guerau's own connections: Pedro Fernández, for example, was Guerau's brother-in-law.[125] There are signs that the inhabitants of the county were pessimistic that the young countess would prevail against this more seasoned, well established claimant. Indeed, in a relatively short space of time, Elvira and Aurembiaix had alarmingly already lost the support of some of the major towns in the county. The citizens of Agramunt and Linyola declared their support for the viscount, thus confirming that the homages received by Ermengol there had been ineffective in securing backing for his wife and daughter.[126]

Although the count-king did intervene on Elvira's behalf, there were signs that his true interest lay in fending off Guerau in order to harden his own overlordship over the county. Following his aforementioned accord with Pedro Fernández in 1206, Pere sought to capitalize on the countess's appeal as another means to establish his suzerain control over the county and its affiliated holdings. In a convention made in Lleida on the last day of October 1209, Elvira, in desperation, gave Pere full possession and use of the county of Urgell as well as her financial interests in the castles of Aitona and Artesa. Even though their agreement neglected to itemize other allodial holdings outside of the strict boundaries of the county, such as Lleida, later evidence we will consider below demonstrates that Pere would assert authority over these holdings on the basis of this transfer. In return for these donations and her performance of homage to the count-king, Elvira received his rights to Siurana and Seròs as well as a payment of five thousand *morabetins* that he would pay out over a five-year period.[127] Although Aurembiaix, as a minor, was not involved in the convention, Pere did agree to respect and defend her rights, as outlined in Ermengol's will, in a separate charter drafted that same day.[128] He may well have been sensitive about being seen by his nobles as overtly usurping the rights of the young countess, as Guerau de Cabrera was still threatening to do. Indeed, the count-king's barons remained generally opposed to many of the centralizing initiatives he had undertaken thus far in his reign. In particular, he faced continuing criticism over efforts to secure increased taxation to fund his mounting trans-Pyrenean campaigns as well as his longed-for expedition to Mallorca. This opposition had recently boiled over in 1205, resulting in the unprecedented (albeit unexecuted) concessions he granted his Catalan barons.[129] Indeed, such concerns likely encouraged his strategy of using Aurembiaix's rights of inheritance to his advantage.

Pere's negotiations with Elvira to undo Aurembiaix's tentative betrothal to Pedro Fernández's son, Álvaro, in order to secure her marriage to young Jaume and thereby absorb her rights to Urgell came to fruition in February of the following year, 1210.[130] The marriage arrangement between Jaume and Aurembiaix reveals plainly that Elvira's growing isolation and concerns over her and her daughter's future were the prime motivator in forging the new alliance. Aragonese and Catalonian barons swore oaths to uphold the count-king's pledges of Jaume's dower, which would consist of the entire county of Pallars and the castles and towns of Cervera, Camarasa, and Cubells. Such baronial consent seems to have been intended to uphold Elvira's and Aurembiaix's rights and security, as established by Ermengol's will and these marriage pledges, as well as approve the validity of the marriage alliance itself. The marriage would not take place until Aurembiaix was of sufficient age. In the event that the union remained unconsummated or did not produce children, Aurembiaix would retain all that she had been promised in Ermengol's will, which she carried into the marriage as her dowry. Any investments into the county and its holdings made by the future monarch, however, especially the redeeming of pledges, would have to be repaid.[131]

There are indications that Pere was positioning himself to take full advantage of this betrothal with respect to the county of Urgell and its peripheral holdings. Two years earlier, he had already taken the opportunity to reconfirm Lleida's population charter unilaterally in November, only weeks following Ermengol's death in 1209. An added possibility, which does not rule out the count-king's objectives in crafting the confirmation as he did, is that this enactment was requested by Lleida's citizenry in response to the changes in the composition of the town's lordship caused by Ermengol's death without a male heir.[132] The timing of this enactment seems far from accidental. For the very first time since Lleida's conquest by his grandfather, Pere had asserted himself as its primary jurisdictional lord. The citizens of Agramunt and Linyola, two of the communities that would soon side with the viscount in the revolt against Elvira, performed homage to Pere in early 1210, shortly following the marriage arrangements between Jaume and Aurembiaix.[133] Despite the fact that the dynastic merger with Ermengol's line remained tentative, the count-king's designated responsibility to defend the county and its peripheral holdings against the viscount, Guerau IV, invested him with the opportunity to assert his authority as peacemaker and de facto overlord within the county of Urgell.

In subjugating the citizenry of towns like Agramunt and Linyola in such a manner, the count-king was supposedly acting in the interests of Elvira and Aurembiaix. More than simply identifying these communities as supporters of the countess and count-king (as her protector), these acts of homage recalled the professions made by these same citizens to support the countess and her offspring in 1188 and 1206, discussed earlier. Those preparatory measures by Ermengol to secure communal support for his wife and descendants may not have succeeded in sheltering Elvira from noble opposition, but they did serve as building blocks for the countess to reconstruct her authority under the aegis of the count-king. At the same time, however, Pere, in his capacity as ruler, was the one to receive, personally, these professions of homage. Aside from forging direct bonds to him and augmenting the real implications of his personal authority within these localities, such professions of homage may have implied that Pere's controversial provisions for public order now applied within the long-independent lands of Urgell. As Bisson has observed, these collaborative acts by the countess and count-king had a transformative effect on these earlier attempts by Ermengol VIII to inject feudo-vassalic terminology of dependency into the development of communal collectives as a means to strengthen his hold over his county and shelter the succession to his authority from usurpation. Pere's reception of these professions of homage arguably undermined the utility of Ermengol's groundwork with these towns for promoting Urgell's independence and instead converted them to conform to "a model of royal power in the Crown of Aragon."[134]

Thus, while operating as a veritable surrogate for Elvira and Aurembiaix in governing Ermengol's lands, Pere was, at the same time, asserting himself as a primary protector and undermining Urgell's traditional independence.[135] Later, in the 1220s, when Aurembiaix's request for assistance in regaining control of the county was presented at Jaume I's court, her supporters argued that he was especially responsible for defending the rights of "widows and orphans."[136] But here Pere's intervention was justified by Elvira's act of donation alone. In the months following Ermengol's death, even though Pere had not numbered among the count's *manumissores*, he took personal responsibility for some of the pending donations she and Ermengol had once pledged or that he had provisioned for in his will.[137] In order to repay numerous debts owed to Guillem de Cervera amounting to twenty-four thousand *morabetins*, for example, Ermengol had pledged his rights to the castles and towns of Mequinenza, Aitona, and Santa Linya, plus all of his rights within Lleida.[138] That Pere and not Guillem IV de Cervera, who as Elvira's husband and primary creditor had the means to eliminate these debts, had inserted himself as the guarantor for these obligations within just weeks of Ermengol's death further signaled that the count-king was positioning himself to assume control over the county.[139]

Pere was indeed well suited to intervene in such matters for other reasons as well. Many of Ermengol's pledges concerned holdings or rights that were associated with the comital-royal patrimony in some manner. Ermengol's will, for example, had recognized debts owed to Pere Sasala and pledged in repayment the castle and town of Gebut, both of which were held from the count-king, and the grain house in Lleida.[140] Furthermore, Pere himself was busy at this same time managing debts from similar creditors. This aforementioned confirmation of the count's grants in November 1209, for instance, accompanied Pere's management of his own massive borrowings from Guillem de Cervera that totaled 21,500 *morabetins*. He arranged to repay the sum by pledging incomes from a wide range of holdings in Aragon and New Catalonia, including all of the revenues from the bailiwick of Lleida. Apart from the whole of the Conca de Barberà, all of the pledged castles and towns were situated in Lleida's general vicinity in the region organized around the lower Segre and Cinca Rivers. These included Pere's remaining rights to (and incomes from) Almacelles, Camarasa, Castelldans, Cubells, Fraga, Giminells, Masalcoreig, Mequinenza, San Esteban (de Litera), Seròs, Sucs, Tamarite (de Litera), Tarregà, and Zaidín.[141] Presumably, this right to Seròs excluded what he had recently donated to Elvira in exchange for the county of Urgell.

This list of pledged holdings must have been formulated through negotiation and appears to have been amenable to both parties for specific reasons. The logistics of collection by Guillem's bailiffs would have recommended such castles from the royal demesne that were within his sphere of activity around Cervera, Lleida, and Castelldans. Guillem de Cervera also obtained recognition of the *potestas* he already held over the castles of Mequinenza and Castelldans from prior concords involving both Ermengol and the king. In keeping with Pere's fiscal and administrative policy (maintained from his father's reign) of preserving the demesne in Old Catalonia, this transaction helps reveal the extent to which he had exhausted the other resources from Ramon Berenguer IV's conquests along the Ebro–Segre corridor.

Conventions devoted to organizing castle-holding within the county of Urgell also served as occasions for Pere to further his political objectives. Moments such as Arnau de Castellbò's profession of homage to the countess Elvira in June 1210, presided over and confirmed by the count-king, permitted Pere to safeguard her and her daughter's authority by co-opting potentially threatening barons while simultaneously securing his own relationships with these men and applying his self-promoted image as guardian of governmental order to the county. In this enactment, Elvira accepted Arnau's pledge of fidelity for the castles he had held from her deceased husband and received his oath that he would not try to harm her daughter's rights. In return, she promised that she would not appropriate his castles (or those of a number of castellans subjected to comital authority, who were present serving as witnesses) or assign them to the count-king, her daughter, Pedro Fernández, or any other party. Pedro Fernández's inclusion suggests that he remained the countess's protector despite his relation to Guerau de Cabrera and the dissolution of the marriage alliance between his son and Aurembiaix earlier that year. This list notwithstanding, Arnau had good reason to be chiefly concerned about the count-king's intervention. Elvira's reciprocal oath was reinforced by Pere's own pledge that, based on "faith and lordship (*seniorivo*) that we have in you [i.e., Arnau]," he would respect this convention with the countess and not force Arnau to render him, Aurembiaix, Pedro Fernández, or anyone else his castles "on account of that homage that you now make to the countess."[142] Although Arnau's oaths were directed at Elvira, he must have suspected that the count-king was the one presently exercising meaningful authority within Urgell.

Other moves by the count-king during this period do indeed go some way toward confirming Arnau's likely suspicions. Sparse evidence reveals that Pere was indeed attempting to assert his dominion over Urgell even as he was advocating for Elvira and Aurembiaix. Due to his son's marriage alliance with Aurembiaix, the count-king may not have seen his personal objectives regarding the county as incompatible with this advocacy. Furthermore, Pere's vision of his pan-comital, regalian authority may have led him to view his overarching sovereignty over the county as fully compatible with the rights exercised by the countess and her daughter.

Most tellingly, the count-king appears to have claimed the title of "count of Urgell" at this point. He asserted this status in new coinage he minted at Lleida during these transitional years following Ermengol VIII's death that bears the legend "PETRUS CO(ME)/URGEL."[143] As a low-value *denarius*, this coin issued by the count-king as the "count of Urgell" would have broad circulation, thereby further facilitating the broadcasting of the message of Pere's role in the county to a large subset of its residents. The slim possibility exists that Pere was asserting himself as "count" of Barcelona rather than of Urgell in this issue of coinage. Nevertheless, the very fact that he was issuing the coinage on his own authority would have made it a meaningful statement about his claims to rule over the county in any case.

There are some further considerations, however, that complicate this interpretation of the legend. First, although Pere sometimes added "count of Barcelona" to his primary title of "king of Aragon" in charters, he always asserted the title of king on the coinage he issued, which was compatible with his efforts to build his regalian authority throughout the Crown of Aragon.[144] By comparison, when Pedro Ansúrez had minted coinage in the county of Urgell that read "PETRVS COMES/VRGELLO (DOMIN)VS" in the early twelfth century, he was applying the title of "count" that derived from his lordship of Valladolid.[145] In contrast to the situation facing Elvira, Aurembiaix, and Pere a century later, Urgell already possessed a count when Pedro Ansúrez produced that coin—namely, Ermengol VI, for whom Pedro was serving as regent and protector, as we witnessed in chapter 2 above. That coinage accordingly presented Pedro only as "lord of Urgell," on Ermengol's behalf.

Historians such as Stephen Bensch have long recognized the "sovereign attributes" of coinage in Catalonia, as in other competitive political environments. As a corollary to Bensch's notion that a "separate coinage bolstered the independence of the counts . . . who could look back on a dynasty originally as illustrious as that of the counts of Barcelona," asserting control over the minting of another principality's coinage dealt a powerful blow to its independence.[146] Anna Balaguer has speculated that this particular act of minting the county's coinage at Lleida sparked opposition by the citizens of Agramunt, who held the traditional monopoly over the minting of Urgell's coinage.[147] When Pere, a monarch with a reputation for manipulating his own coinage, confirmed Lleida's privileges in 1210, he pledged to respect the general state of affairs maintained during Ermengol VIII's rule. He also promised specifically not to manipulate their coinage or to conduct minting elsewhere.[148] While these commitments by the count-king were an oblique admission of wrongdoing, they also served to confirm his authority over the county and further reinforced the bonds of fidelity with Agramunt's citizenry that Pere had recently transferred to himself. In addition to asserting his rights of lordship over the town by the very nature of these acts, the count-king implied that the entire county stood under his dominion: he exempted Agramunt's citizens from "new and old customs . . . through the entire county of Urgell and through all of the lands of our dominion."[149]

Such calculated maneuvers by the count-king to erode the traditional independence of the county and subject it to his claimed pan-Catalonian authority were likely to provoke conflict from other claimants. Pere anticipated problems with these men and, accordingly, made preparations to shift some of the likely burden of defense onto his barons. In November 1210, he commended administrative rights to the county of Urgell to Viscount Guillem de Cardona and his son Ramon Folc, as "our vassals" (*vassallis nostris*), for a limited term of five years.[150] As late as June of that year, Viscount Guerau IV de Cabrera appeared to remain on good terms with Pere. He continued to serve as a major creditor to the count-king and received incomes from numerous Aragonese towns in repayment of these outstanding loans.[151]

Nevertheless, according to Zurita, it was not long before Guerau sprang into action, during the summer of 1211. The viscount quickly invaded central and upper Urgell, taking possession of Balaguer and other towns and castles. The countess and her daughter reportedly took refuge in Lleida, under comital-royal protection.[152] The count-king mounted his defense swiftly and was already besieging Balaguer on 30 July 1211. He found time during this campaigning to, once again, assert his dominion over Urgell by granting the residents of Tremp a levy exemption very similar to what he had earlier awarded Agramunt.[153] Overwhelmed by this onslaught, Guerau appears to have fled from Balaguer, along with some of his knights as well as his wife and son, to the castle of Llorenç, where the count-king's men succeeded in capturing him. They imprisoned him in a fortification near Jaca.[154] In order to secure his release, Guerau agreed to invest Pere with "power" over his castles (Montsoriu, Montmagastre, Àger, Pinyana, and Finestres). He also confirmed that any future act of aggression would be punished by his reimprisonment and the permanent loss of all of his pledged castles.[155]

Pere used this victory as a justification for asserting further control over the county of Urgell. Rather than punishing Balaguer for its support of the viscount during this recent war, the count-king established a new relationship with the townspeople and assumed the role of benevolent patron, lawgiver, and jurisdictional lord.[156] He confirmed not only "all privileges, immunities, and franchises, and good customs which the count of Urgell of good memory conferred and conceded" to its citizens but also the new right to hold a weekly market and annual fair and novel protections against a host of levies and arbitrary seigniorial prerogatives that established his status as lawgiver to the community. Furthermore, in defining the nature of their exemption from the *cugucia* levy (collected in the event of a wife's adultery), Pere applied Lleida's provision that adulterers would be shamed publicly by being made to run naked through the streets but would suffer no financial penalty.[157] Such borrowing from a customary legal tradition of a town that had long been administered by the counts of Urgell under comital-royal overlordship was pragmatic. Even more importantly for the count-king's purposes, it suggested that Balaguer (and, by association, the wider county of Urgell) constituted part of the realms that stood under Pere's authority, despite the fact that it had stood under the independent, direct lordship of the Ermengol dynasty since its conquest. In awarding these prerogatives, Pere referred to local officials as if they belonged to him. For example, he exempted the citizens from having to undertake the ordeal by cold water or hot iron in any controversies they might have with "*our* knights and castellans of this town." He also directed, more formulaically, "all bailiffs and vicars and merinos and justices and other men of *ours*, present and future" to abide by these privileges. Pere inserted no language to suggest that he was governing on Elvira's or Aurembiaix's behalf, and neither the countess nor any of her noble supporters (aside from Guillem IV de Cervera) subscribed the document. Indeed, based simply on the charter's language, Balaguer seemed to be Pere's lordship without any limitations.[158]

By this point, the count-king had established a good track record of exercising lordship over the county, and this experience must have given him the confidence that his dynasty would continue to be able to assert itself similarly over future counts of Urgell once this period of crisis had passed. Already by January 1211, turning to his pressing trans-Pyrenean affairs, he had effectively dissolved the marriage agreement with Elvira that had betrothed Jaume and Aurembiaix by entering into another (ultimately unexecuted) arrangement. He had planned for his son to marry the daughter of Simon de Montfort, viscount of Beziers and Carcassonne. Once again, Guillem IV de Cervera was present to subscribe the agreement. As part of the arrangement, Pere granted Simon the city and lordship of Montpellier to possess until Jaume reached eighteen years of age.[159]

This enactment caused no apparent reduction in the count-king's control over Urgell, and the following year Pere was again busy making arrangements as the county's overlord. Reminiscent of his dealings with his mother over her dower, in October 1212 Pere came to a resolution with Dolça of Foix concerning her dower from her marriage with the long deceased Ermengol VII. Pere authorized Dolça to collect, for her lifetime, the incomes from most of the seigniorial rights and levies payable to his bailiffs in the towns of Menarguens, Balaguer, Albesa, and Albeda as well as an additional three thousand *solidi* annually from the *questia* levied in those towns. Illustrating that he also controlled the holdings deriving from Ermengol VIII that lay beyond Urgell's limits, he also conceded to Dolça "half of all of the incomes that Ermengol, count of Urgell, was accustomed to receive in Lleida." However, Pere was explicit about excluding from these donations any rights of lordship (including "homages of knights") to these towns. Signaling that these holdings pertained, without reservation, to his household, Pere further stipulated that following Dolça's death, all of these rights and incomes "would revert to us and our successors without any impediment." Because neither Viscount Guillem de Cardona nor Ramon Folc subscribed the charter, it is unclear whether their administration of the county, as established in 1210 for a five-year term, as discussed earlier, remained in force.[160]

By this point, Pere thus seems to have profited successfully from the political crises surrounding Ermengol VIII's death by securing effective and lasting control over his county and peripheral holdings. Even had he intended to honor Aurembiaix's rights of inheritance as stipulated in the count's will, her possession of her father's holdings would undoubtedly have been subject to comital-royal overlordship. These gains would be cast into doubt, however, by Pere's own succession crisis following his sudden death fighting the forces of this same Simon de Montfort at the battle of Muret in 1213. The political instability generated by this incident would empower Guerau IV de Cabrera to renew his offensive and secure control over most of the county of Urgell, this time without any noticeable comital-royal or baronial resistance.[161]

Rather than defending her claims to the county at this time, Aurembiaix would retire for some years to be with her mother's family in Castile. Here she would comply with the arrangements her father had made before his death, before the detour with Pere and Jaume, and marry Álvaro Fernández de Castro. This marriage in fact served to tighten further her association with Guerau de Cabrera. In addition to being her cousin via Ermengol VIII's sister, Marquesa, Guerau was now also her brother-in-law through his marriage to Álvaro's sibling, Elo Pérez. Some scholars have speculated that Aurembiaix was pressured by the Castro family, which frowned upon female governance, to defer to the viscount's claim.[162] As we will observe in part III below, Aurembiaix and her supporters would eventually intervene to oppose Guerau's efforts to be certified as count of Urgell at the royal court and reclaim her inheritance as stipulated in her father's will. This process would serve as an occasion for the future Jaume I, as he emerged from his minority, to build on the precedents established by his father in reasserting the suzerain rights over the county and securing greater rights over its peripheral holdings, such as Lleida.

Conclusions

In looking back over the trajectory of the reigns of Alfons and Pere explored over the last two chapters, we can now appreciate the lopsided influence of their administrative policies on the extent of the comital-royal patrimony within New Catalonia, in general, and along Catalonia's frontier with Islam, in particular, over the course of the later twelfth and early thirteenth centuries. The count-kings had largely overturned Ramon Berenguer IV's prioritization of Tortosa as a guarded frontier holding. Tortosa, as we have seen, had been the prized possession the count-prince had intended to preserve under his full control to help him maintain dominance over the southern frontier and to use to launch expeditions into northern Valencia. Although they may ultimately have taken it further than they ever intended, Alfons and Pere had engaged in this shift, in part at least, because they felt intense fiscal and political pressure to choose between Ramon Berenguer's prized front with Islam and other possessions that they deemed to be of greater relative importance and value. They leveraged or alienated Tortosa, the lower Ebro, and other parts of their demesne in order to retain their rights to Lleida and the lower Segre as well as to fund activity to the north and south of their realms. In the end, Pere's choice to leverage his few remaining holdings in New Catalonia appears to have been made reluctantly, as a necessary measure to secure additional financing for his ambitious and costly military projects. As a parallel example, inheriting his county and frontier ambitions from his father and grandfather, Ermengol VIII had similarly taken on huge debts in his persistent efforts to defend his comital rights against independent castellans and usurpers.

This fiscal need played into the hand of certain agents with the resources to provide this essential credit. By the time of Pere's death, Guillem IV de Cervera, for example, had assumed control, as pledges, of the majority of the count-king's and count of Urgell's lands within New Catalonia once so closely guarded by their predecessors. As one of young Jaume I's closest supporters and Countess Elvira of Urgell's new husband, Guillem benefited greatly from playing the part of a vital, stabilizing force and protector during these uncertain transitional years. In 1215, Elvira ceded Guillem control over the few holdings (Seròs and Siurana) she had received from Pere in exchange for the county of Urgell in 1209. They agreed that, upon Guillem's death, she would receive back these holdings, along with the castle and town of Cervera and a lump sum of ten thousand *morabetins*, for her maintenance. Guillem allayed his new wife's concerns about the adherence of his primary heirs to these stipulations by having his son, Ramon de Cervera, and nephew, Ramon d'Àger, perform homage to her.[163] Guillem joined a group of counselors that included the seneschal Guillem Ramon II de Montcada and Archbishop Espàreg of Tarragona, all of whom formally pledged to support the king during his minority.[164]

Even before Pere's death, the magnitude of this power vacuum, combined with the extent of this borrowing, emboldened Guillem de Cervera to assert his authority in unprecedented ways. Most tellingly, he proclaimed himself de facto lord of Lleida by minting his own coinage there that bore the legend "CERVERA."[165] Even as the count-king's political capital (and likely, his credit) experienced a resurgence following Las Navas de Tolosa in 1212, his efforts to strengthen his bonds of support with other powerful noble families served to diminish further the extent of the comital-royal domains and sow the seeds of progressive jurisdictional fragmentation in New Catalonia. Just months after this shared victory by Pere over the Almohads, the seneschal Guillem Ramon II de Montcada married Pere's daughter, Constança, whose sizeable dowry and personal holdings in the lower Segre region would develop into the Montcada barony of Aitona over the course of the thirteenth century. Her dowry included the castles and towns of Seròs (obtained from Guillem de Cervera by this time?), Aitona, and Soses.[166] In addition, she brought other holdings into the marriage: the castles and towns of Torres, Cabra (del Camp), Cubells, Camarasa, Vilagrassa, and other lordships within the Conca de Barberà.[167]

The problematic years of Jaume's minority and Aurembiaix's displacement would each be heavily shaped by the inability of their fathers to make good on their bold ambitions for their respective principalities. Both Pere and Ermengol VIII left behind enormous debts generated by their frustrated pursuits of greater authority and new conquests that invested noble families with unprecedented jurisdictional and financial rights at the expense of the royal and comital domains. The independence and integrity of Urgell, asserted at great financial and political cost by Ermengol, was largely undone by the actions Elvira undertook to defend herself and her daughter against Guerau IV de Cabrera. As famously recollected in Jaume's autobiographical *Llibre dels feits*, the difficulty years of his minority, when he was ensconced in the fortress of Monzón with "not even enough food for one day, so wasted and pledged was the land," seemed to be the direct result of the spendthrift policies of his father and grandfather, who had all but bankrupted the dynasty's finances while accomplishing little to prevent the growth of seigniorial control over comital-royal demesne lands.[168] Yet, although they were largely unsuccessful over the short term, these initiatives did begin to circulate powerful ideas concerning royal sovereignty, the validity of the count-king's provisions for public order, and royal general taxation rights that would be foundational for the aggrandizement of royal authority during the reigns of Jaume I and his successors over the thirteenth century.

❧ PART III

New Catalonia after Valencia

❧ CHAPTER 7

Repercussions of Further Conquest

Valencia and Tenurial Conditions in Catalonia

The situation of the dynasty in the years following Pere's death could not have been more precarious. Its treasury was depleted, and its fiscal outlook was burdened with debts owed to almost every societal sector in the kingdom. Its future king, Jaume, found himself secluded in the Templar castle of Monzón with only his regency, bolstered to some degree by the papacy, to shelter him from noble factions and other threats. Even upon emerging from his minority, Jaume would continue to face considerable obstacles in the long road to rebuilding the monarchy's stability. He would struggle to subject rebellious nobles throughout the realms to his authority. So, too, he would aspire to control interaction with Al-Andalus, while sheltering his realms from conflict with adjoining Muslim territories through well-calculated peace treaties and tributary relationships. Only gradually would the young king amass financial and military support from nobles, prelates, and urban populations sufficient to assist his expeditions against the Muslim-held Balearic Islands and kingdom of Valencia. His ability to control engagement along the frontier with Islam and thereby monopolize access to tribute, territory, and plunder would be integral to his capacity to stabilize his authority and establish dominion over powerful rivals.

In this final, two-chapter section, our scrutiny of Jaume's activity will reveal how his accomplishments and his less successful initiatives built upon the achievements and failures of his predecessors in unanticipated ways.

Jaume's reign, as we will see, was very much shaped by the legacies, institutions, traditions, and relationships forged, often inadvertently or uncon-
sciously, by his forebearers. Conquests managed during Alfons's reign had
indeed served to buffer the lower Ebro valley from Muslim attack and, in
turn, facilitated significant progress in the settlement and redevelopment
of the region. Yet both Alfons and Pere had also sacrificed comital-royal
control to fund their ambitions along the northern and southern fronts of
their realms. The capture of the Balearic Islands and Valencia in relatively
quick succession would supply Jaume and his successors with the lands and
incomes necessary to reassert authority over many of the alienated sectors
of the lower Ebro valley, domains over which certain lords had exercised
virtually autonomous authority in some cases. A variety of overlapping
phenomena served to place the lower Ebro valley within a novel administrative climate as it was transformed from the ill-defined frontier landscape
left from Ramon Berenguer IV's *repartiment* into a patchwork of delimited,
settled jurisdictional zones with specifically identified regional affiliations.
These included royal administrative development in the thirteenth century,
an emergent sovereign ruling ideology, the definition and assimilation of
the contiguous territories acquired in the push on Valencia, and repeatedly
altered divisions of Jaume's realms among his heirs.[1]

Under pressure from the incremental imposition of comital-royal regulations over long dislocated seigniorial domains, lords within New Catalonia
sought to maintain established prerogatives as well as to invoke new ones.
These novelties were often made in defiance of local privileges and exemptions awarded to earlier generations in order to promote settlement and
were done in hopes of increasing profit as well as slowing or reversing this
trend of centralization. These impulses by lords, and the expectations that
conditioned them, had deep roots within the conquered landscape. They
were linked to preconquest pledges and patterns of interaction, to the postconquest distribution of lands and jurisdictions by Ramon Berenguer IV,
and to the administrative strategies implemented by his successors that we
have already explored in detail in previous chapters of this book. As these
final pages will illustrate, in certain areas (notably, the Terra Alta, Ribera
d'Ebre, Fraga, Lleida, and Ribagorza) decades of local consolidation through
the issuance of population charters and customary laws also complicated
attempts to divide otherwise contiguous seigniorial landscapes through the
imposition of regional boundaries.

The imposition of comital-royal authority did make headway in the
lower Ebro and Segre valleys. In some cases—such as within the Templar
and lay lordships of the Terra Alta, Ribera d'Ebre, and Baix Segre—lords

reluctantly submitted to aspects of new administrative conditions. In other instances, such as the Templar-Montcada co-lordship of Tortosa, strong resistance to intervention ultimately culminated in the alienation of all jurisdictional rights to the Crown in return for more easily managed lordships elsewhere. As we will observe, the characteristics of the conquest, integration, and administration of these territories informed these administrative outcomes.

We will begin this chapter by tracing the convoluted route through which Jaume built upon the mixed records of his predecessors to secure his acquisition of new territories beyond the Ebro-Segre frontier. We will explore how the manner of his conquest influenced, and was informed by, the Crown of Aragon's political and territorial environment. Our attention will then turn to examining the extent to which the acquisitions of these vast territories noticeably prompted shifts in the tenurial conditions maintained by landlords in the former frontier lands of New Catalonia.

The next and final chapter to follow will continue this discussion by assessing how the political, dynastic, and territorial circumstances generated by the new conquests engendered novel conflicts (and breathed new life into existing ones) over borders and jurisdictional rights within the regions bounded by the Ebro and Segre River valleys. We will devote special attention to the monarchy's efforts to establish, recuperate, or expand its administrative prerogatives over a range of localities throughout Catalonia over the latter half of the thirteenth century that were, to some degree, motivated by New Catalonia's maturation and empowered by the monarchy's gains in wealth and prestige from its successes in the Balearic Islands and Valencia.

Territorial Advances and Development Preceding Valencia's Conquest

Before we turn to Jaume's successes, we should devote further attention to the efforts of the earlier count-kings that ultimately set the stage for Jaume's enterprises and helped condition how they would be managed. The conquest of new lands, beyond those taken or depopulated by Ramon Berenguer IV's expansive campaigns, not only permitted settlement projects along the militarized frontier line. They also naturally facilitated migration to the spaces within New Catalonia and Lower Aragon that were now less exposed to attack due to these recent territorial gains. Such more modest earlier enterprises did aid settlement efforts, in particular those to the southwest, along the Algars River, that had been frustrated by dangerous frontier conditions since the mid-twelfth century.

Although Alfons slowed his campaigning to the south following the Treaty of Cazola in 1179, he nevertheless led numerous small-scale expeditions that pushed deeper into northern Valencia in the 1180s and 1190s.[2] Catalano-Aragonese forces had closed in on important centers such as Morella and the coastal castle of Penyíscola, both of which would remain under Muslim control for decades to come. Olocau and Ulldecona fell before 1180, when they were granted to the Hospitallers,[3] and the castle of Polpís came under Templar lordship in 1190.[4] After the neighboring castles of Fredes, Bel, and Benifassà succumbed in the early 1190s, Alfons entrusted them to the see of Tortosa to both guard and settle.[5] Cabres also appears to have been taken by Christian forces in the 1190s and remained an important frontier outpost for striking Morella and other Muslim-held positions when Pere reassigned it in 1210.[6]

As we have already observed in previous chapters, Pere's resources were even more divided than those of Alfons between trans-Pyrenean and Peninsular interests. He tended to devote his attention to long-range raids and territorial expansion in western Valencia, away from the Mediterranean coast and accordingly relied more heavily on his magnates to organize and conduct their own expeditions.[7] The significant campaigns he did lead in the early thirteenth century tended to be delegated to lords and collectives. In 1210, for example, Pere assembled troops at Monzón and marched into Valencia to capture the castles of Ademuz, Castielfabib, and Sertella. The sponsorship of the Aragonese frontier bishops of Zaragoza, Huesca, and Tarazona as well as the Orders of the Temple and Hospital appears to have made the expedition possible.[8] Overall, however, Pere contributed relatively little to organizing further expansion and consolidation of the lower Ebro valley before his collaboration with Castile at Las Navas de Tolosa in 1212 that was followed by death the next year.[9] Instead, territorial gains primarily accomplished under Alfons had served to shelter Tortosa and the reaches of New Catalonia further from frontier danger. The utilization and development of lands along the Ebro valley and beyond its right bank did not have to await the additional buffering to be provided by Jaume's conquests.[10]

Preparations for and realization of these territorial gains generated a second wave of comital-royal jurisdictional allotments and settlement campaigns along the lower Ebro valley and extending up the Segre. Christian control beyond the right bank of the Ebro had been marginal during Ramon Berenguer IV's reign. The southern reaches of the Terra Alta had remained a no-man's-land, out of the grasp of the Templars and other lords established along the river's course. These campaigns orchestrated by Alfons secured Christian control along the Algars and Matarranya Rivers, enabling the extension of castral and settlement positions further beyond this stretch of the right bank of the Ebro.

The case of the castral district of Miravet, situated in the Terra Alta above the Ebro River valley, illustrates how establishing successful settlement, post-conquest, could be a complex, drawn-out enterprise. As a result of the insecure environment, the Templars had never been able to utilize much of the territory awarded to them by Ramon Berenguer IV's donation of Miravet from 1153.[11] Following these new campaigns, even while engaged in ending direct royal administration of vast territories along the frontier, Alfons responded to the order's apparent lack of progress by reassigning portions of Miravet's extensive district. Solidly within Miravet's stipulated boundaries, Rasquera had been issued a population charter by the Templars sometime in the 1160s. Alfons recovered and then realienated this lordship to the Hospitallers by 1171, possibly in remuneration for the order's military service the previous year.[12] Similarly, Alfons awarded Horta, which also lay within Miravet's original limits, a population charter in 1165, a short time before launching his first expeditions into Valencia.[13] These shifts accompanied other attempts by the count-king to draw settlers into a area. To the south of Miravet's domains, for example, Paüls obtained a settlement charter from Alfons in 1168.[14] The count-king also reclaimed the territory approaching the Algars River that lay further to the east. It appears that he initially generated a population charter for the settlement of Batea and Riu d'Algars on his own authority. After this measure saw little success, he instead decided to delegate the effort of population and defense of the two castles and their territories to Bernat Granell as local lord.[15]

In defending themselves against these encroachments, the Templars demanded that Alfons confirm the boundaries of Miravet outlined in his father's grant. When he eventually complied in 1182, these limits included Batea and the territory of the Algars River. Despite this concession, the order nevertheless had to pursue Bernat Granell, until 1187, when the count-king handed over to them his retained rights to the castles of Batea and Algars.[16] A second charter by the Templars in 1192, who had regained lordship over the town, does not necessarily signify that the count-king's original provision had failed. Instead, the order may have wished to establish new seigniorial prerogatives over present and future occupants.[17] Alfons's engagement, combined perhaps with the decreased danger of Muslim raiding, appears to have spurred the order to attempt to settle parts of its territories with greater tenacity. For instance, Gandesa, in between Batea and Miravet, received settlement charters from the Templars in 1192 and 1194.[18] In addition to reissuing failed charters, the order continued to license new loci for migration within the Terra Alta.[19] This case of Miravet exemplifies how, with further expansion and sporadic, often indecisive comital-royal oversight, the realization of territorial claims held by different seigniorial entities could be stalled by conflict and, in certain cases, left incomplete in spite of improving security.

The extensive domains of the Order of Calatrava originally included in its lordship of Alcañíz (in Lower Aragon), as outlined by a donation by Alfons in 1179, suffered similar erosion at the hands of Pere.[20] In 1205, the order sought to solidify territorial gains within the lordship by enfeoffing Berenguer de Cambrils and Dalmau de Canyelles with the castle of Calaceite, at the extreme limits of Alcañíz's domains, to guard and settle.[21] Dalmau subsequently divided a portion of his rights to the town between Sancho de Sariñena and Roderic de Bolea, granting them the castle but retaining the areas of Arenys and Lledó. He then sold these remaining rights to Berenguer de Cambrils.[22] A year later, Roderic and Sancho had already issued a population charter to Calaceite. They subsequently exercised their rights of lordship there actively for some time.[23] Berenguer, on the other hand, did not utilize Arenys and Lledó to the satisfaction of the order. Consequently, the commander of Alcañíz revoked his responsibility for the project, probably due to pressure from the count-king, but Berenguer appears to have resisted this order to surrender his lands. In 1209, he alienated his house's rights to these areas, along with "all claims and complaints we have against Berenguer de Cambrils," to Pere.[24] Rather than retain those holdings, however, the count-king shortly thereafter delegated lordship over the two castles, with their territories, resident populations, and rights to a weekly market, to the see of Tortosa, reserving "fidelity to us and our successors and reserving the rights of making peace and war against all Muslims."[25] Having inherited the order's continuing quarrels with Berenguer over these castles, the bishop of Tortosa decided to resolve the issue by enfeoffing him with the castle of Arenys in return for a quitclaim to Lledó.[26] Although the see of Tortosa's careful management of these lands likely pleased the count-king, it alarmed the neighboring bishop of Zaragoza, who feared that Tortosa would use these rights of lordship as an excuse to push out its shared diocesan boundary with Zaragoza. They eventually agreed to fix the limit at the Algars River, in 1210. As part of the agreement, and in line with its seigniorial ambitions, Tortosa secured from Zaragoza the churches of Cretas, Calaceite, Lledó, Arenys, and Algars.[27] Not surprisingly, consolidating land and rights commonly exposed overlapping boundaries between formerly unutilized lordships, often embroiling lords and sometimes settlers in protracted conflicts and bouts of litigation.[28]

Such experiences with Miravet and with these domains around Alcañíz were typical of these years. Many settlements that were nominally established but then languished in the postconquest period similarly witnessed vibrant development following this phase of further territorial expansion. In another illustration, Ramon Berenguer IV had granted Pere de Sentmenat the area known as Castles (now Alfara de Carles) after the conquest, yet not until the first decade of the thirteenth century do we have notice of an established population: the bishop of Tortosa referenced tithes and first fruits derived from cultivated lands, livestock, "labors of knights and peasants," and mills in Castles as well as the locality of Paüls to the north, which were affiliated under a single parochial church servicing the two centers.[29]

Territorial development could render a double benefit to an ecclesiastical lord like the see of Tortosa, which received both ecclesiastical taxes and seigniorial incomes. Such an increased incentive could explain why the bishop and chapter persistently agitated to establish communities on the see's lordships within its diocese, often without quibbling over seigniorial prerogatives and jurisdictional issues that arguably would have preoccupied other lords. In 1187, for example, the bishop of Tortosa rented land in Bitem, within the Templar-Montcada lordship and municipal district of Tortosa, on the condition that the tenant cultivate it (*ad plantandum*), in return for tithes and first fruits and simple recognition of his *senioraticum*, but did not make any of the common stipulations concerning seigniorial levies, judicial fines, and other jurisdictional issues.[30] In 1200, Pere granted the see responsibility over the settlement of Margalef after Ramon Sabater had done ostensibly nothing to carry out his license. The fact that Margalef was situated toward the northern limits of its diocese along the sheltered western edge of the Serra de Montsant must have made it a bigger potential prize for the revenue-starved see.[31] As a result of its entitlement to multiple streams of income from any locality within its diocese, the cathedral of Tortosa was less patient than lay lords when it came to the pace of settlement projects. When their attempt to establish three settler families in Figuera in 1205 stagnated or failed, for instance, the bishop and prior quickly followed up in 1207 with a grant to two different settlers on the condition that they build a house, establish a tenant, and help him exploit the land and reside there.[32]

Pere's sudden death, followed by Jaume's problematic minority, stalled additional territorial campaigns and the extension of further settlement into northern Valencia. Frontier lords lacked the initiative, resources, or authority to use their castral positions beyond the Ebro to advance on the nearby Andalusi strongholds of Morella, Borriana, and Penyíscola. These positions stood as a continuing threat to the security of Christian-held lands and an obstacle to further coastal expansion, which was eyed eagerly by the lords and citizens of Tortosa and greater Catalonia. In the meantime, these same lords benefited from the widened buffer between the Ebro valley and Muslim territory.

The eventual conquest of northern Valencia would bring extensive additional lands under Christian rule, neighboring the still sparsely populated territories of New Catalonia.[33] Alongside the usual need to entice migrants, the circumstances of the capture of the zone would further dictate that the lords of these new domains offer considerable exemptions. Such manipulations would potentially have significant implications for tenurial conditions to the north, as we will see.

Early Attempts on Northern Valencia

Innocent III was obliged to assist Jaume, as an orphan, during his minority, as the vicar of Christ, and because Pere's queen, Marie de Montpellier, had established the pope as her son's custodian in her will from 1213.[34] Innocent and his supporters were hard at work, in 1214, establishing key alliances with the rivals to the north of the realms that Jaume had inherited from the disputes that had culminated in his father's death. The pope also secured assurances, via Cardinal-legate Pietro Collivaccina da Benevento, from the young king's uncle, Count Sanç of Rosselló-Cerdanya, and Sanç's son, Nunyo Sanç, that they would not try to usurp the throne.[35] Along with Jaume's other uncle, the *infant* Ferran of Aragon, this father-son pair was arguably in the best position to support or disrupt Jaume's situation as monarch. Owing largely to this papal intervention, they would serve successively as his regents and *procuratores* during his minority.

This same cardinal-legal orchestrated the momentous meeting of the general court at Lleida that same year, at which the assembled representatives and stake-holders swore to uphold the peace and truce and to respect the king's authority. This was the occasion when Cardinal-legate Pietro established more concretely the guidelines for Count Sanç's regency.[36] After Sanç's considerable influence incurred criticism from numerous barons, however, the pope undertook more heavy-handed measures to stabilize the monarchy's governmental situation, in 1216.[37] He issued a bull that appointed seven counselors to assist the regent and king during the remaining years of the minority. He also wrote separate missives to Count Sanç requiring him to abide by the cardinal-legate's instruction in fulfilling his role as Jaume's *procurator* and to the barons of Aragon and Catalonia regarding their need to abide by the truce with Simon de Montfort.[38] Finally, Innocent addressed the castellans of the realms to urge them to support their lord king, whose welfare, he reminded them, was vital to the general well-being of the people.[39]

An extended truce with the Almohads of Valencia organized by Cardinal-legate Pierre de Douai before 1216 was serving to shelter the realms of the kingdom from Muslim raiding during Jaume's minority.[40] Nevertheless, the new pope, Honorius III, who received the pallium in July 1216, was far more insistent that the Crown of Aragon resume its campaigning against the Muslims, despite continuing political problems within the Aragonese realms. In 1222, for example, he issued a bull offering "favorem et subsidium" and a plenary indulgence to any who assisted the young king, as a faithful vassal of the Roman Church, against the Muslims. He noted that the "Muslims, whose land is known to be contiguous . . . are said to menace [Jaume] with repeated injuries."[41] Although the pope expressed trepidation over a Muslim assault, he implied that the best remedy for this vulnerability was to assume the offensive. Indeed, the true intent of his bull appears to have been to disrupt the truce by motivating an assault against Valencia.

Jaume and his supporters nevertheless resisted this pressure and made a concerted effort to hold the barons of the realms to preserve the peace with the Almohads so that the Crown could focus its attention on more pressing internal concerns. Later in 1222, for instance, the king prevented certain knights from making war against Valencia, including Gil García de Azagra by barring him from purchasing supplies in Aragon. Honorius failed to pressure Jaume to revoke his mandate and allow Gil García to mount his campaign.[42]

There were indeed compelling reasons to postpone hostilities with the Muslims at this time. Even before the young king emerged from his childhood residence at Monzón, Count Sanç and other supporters were desperately trying to manage the complicated fiscal and political difficulties left behind by Pere. In addition to being mired with the debts that we have already discussed in detail in part II above, the monarchy faced threats from various groups of barons within both Catalonia and Aragon.[43]

As we will examine further in the next chapter, following the deaths of Pere and Ermengol VIII of Urgell, Viscount Guerau IV de Cabrera responded to the withdrawal of Ermengol's daughter and sole direct descendant, Aurembiaix, to Castile by forcibly taking control of the county of Urgell. After organizing military resistance against this usurpation, Jaume and his supporters sought to manage the conflict by coming to terms with Guerau at meetings of the general court in 1217 and 1222.[44] The monarchy's goals regarding Guerau shifted over this period, however, as it sought to manage a much more serious conflict between Jaume's new regent, Nunyo Sanç, and

Guillem II de Montcada, viscount of Bearn.[45] A small disagreement between these men around 1217 had quickly developed into a war that drew in many of the most powerful barons in the region. Guillem initially allied with Pedro Fernández de Albarracín and Arnau de Castellbò as well as numerous Aragonese noble rebels, whereas Nunyo Sanç joined with the *infant* Ferran and Pedro de Ahonés. After he failed to get the factions to reconcile at a meeting of his general court in Monzón, Jaume was drawn deeper into the conflict and soon took Nunyo's side.[46]

As Guillem de Montcada and his allies prepared for hostilities, Nunyo Sanç, Count Sanç, the *infant* Ferran, and baronial supporters such as Ató de Foces, Blasc Maça, and Artau de Luna, gathered with Jaume to seek out additional aid against this coalition to prevent the situation from spiraling out of control.[47] The situation was rapidly growing more serious and embroiled, leading Jaume and his allies to reach out to Guerau IV de Cabrera on two occasions during 1223 to secure his assistance against the Montcada-led rebels.[48] Despite strengthening these vital alliances through these enactments, Jaume and Queen Leonor nevertheless fell prey to a treacherous plot orchestrated by the *infant* Ferran, who had turned against him by joining with Guillem de Montcada and his fellow rebels. The couple was forcibly sequestered by this group at Zaragoza for several weeks in the late spring of 1225.[49] After Jaume and his queen made a failed escape attempt, their captors forced them to agree to a ransom of 20,000 *morabetins* on 3 April. Once he had secured their release, however, Jaume sprang into action. He quickly regrouped at Lleida and, by the end of that month, was already in Tortosa organizing a new session of the general court and preparing his first expedition into northern Valencia that would target Penyíscola.[50]

Despite the progress Jaume and his supporters had made over these years of his minority, the campaign that they proposed at Tortosa was, by all accounts, premature and doomed from the start. Jaume was still a teenager at the time and had not made much headway in resolving his controversies with his barons in Aragon or Catalonia. On the other hand, papal pressure from Honorius III to resume hostilities remained strong, and the peace with Valencia had recently ended. Moreover, Jaume must have felt emboldened by his improving finances and determined to demonstrate his leadership abilities following his embarrassing incarceration at Zaragoza. His calculus may have been that a victory over the Muslims would help encourage his rebellious barons to desist in their resistance and recognize his leadership.[51]

Whereas earlier court sessions overseen by Jaume and his regency had chiefly attended to internal security issues regarding the weakening peace provisions inherited from Alfons and Pere, at Tortosa, in addition to readopting peace statutes, the king proclaimed a bold new agenda to the assembled nobles, prelates, and burghers.[52] "We have taken the cross to attack the barbarous nations," Jaume allegedly proclaimed, according to the court record. He used the occasion chiefly to solicit their support and advice "for advancing the cause of the cross."[53] This appears to have been the first instance when campaigning beyond the Ebro had been couched in terms of a crusade since the expeditions on Tarragona and Tortosa a century earlier as well as the first time that Jaume himself had assumed the crusader's cross.[54]

The king's choice of Tortosa as a venue was surely far from coincidental. A successful expedition into northern Valencia would have to rely on some degree of support from this city's lords and residents. Furthermore, the see of Tortosa's claim over a substantial portion of northern Valencia made the cathedral city a strategic place to announce a new phase of expansive campaigns couched in crusader language and symbolism. Jaume had indeed already begun planning an assault with the bishop and cathedral chapter of Tortosa by the time the court convened. The day before the meeting, he had prospectively granted the see the Valencian castles of Miravet and Sufera.[55] The bishop of Tortosa was sufficiently aware of the dangers of prospective grants to demand an additional charter from the king guaranteeing that these rights would be upheld, even if it came to light that Jaume's predecessors had already granted them to someone else.[56]

Over the next two months, Jaume spent time in Lleida, Barcelona, and Tortosa, where he succeeded in enlisting financial and military support for the expedition.[57] With such momentum established, he did not waste time transitioning from planning to launching his enterprise. By August 1225, Jaume and his knights were already laying siege to the coastal castle of Penyíscola.[58] During the campaign, probably as a means to encourage further support, he added to the bishop of Tortosa's entitled share by assigning him additional properties and castles and by confirming the enlarged limits of Tortosa's ancient diocese that included vast sections of still unconquered Valencia.[59] The see of Tortosa had long been impoverished due to its partial restoration and the slow settlement and economic development of its diocesan lands.[60] Jaume had the authority, as conqueror, to grant Tortosa control over portions of its diocesan territories as they were conquered, and the bishop may have been lobbying, in part, to secure these sorts of concessions. His effort appears to have yielded results. For instance, as the siege continued into September, Jaume invested the bishop with a property belonging to a Muslim resident to use to establish Penyíscola's first parochial church.[61] Jaume secured support from other parties by prospectively issuing them substantial castral and territorial holdings in the unconquered sectors of the region.[62] For instance, he prospectively issued the monastery of Poblet, another interested stakeholder based within New Catalonia, entitlements in Penyíscola, Cervera, Xivert, and Polpís in return for its aid.[63]

There were other factors working in Jaume's favor as he launched this initial campaign. He stood to benefit, for example, from infighting among the Muslims that was destabilizing their control over Valencia. Abū Zayd served as *walī* of Valencia and North Africa (Ifrīqiya), yet because of his reputation as a harsh and oppressive governor, his position was under threat from ʿAbdallāh b. Yaʿqūb al-Manṣur (known as al-ʿĀdil), son of the Almohad caliph al-Manṣūr and governor of neighboring Murcia.[64] In spite of these propitious developments, Jaume's forces nevertheless struggled to break through Penyíscola's defenses. Not surprisingly, the ambitious offensive suffered from insufficient support from the very barons he hoped that it would win over as well as from the military orders, who, despite their instrumental support of the king during these years, may have feared that a successful campaign would divert trade with Muslim lands away from the roads that ran by their lordships beyond the lower Ebro valley.[65] After approximately a month, Jaume lifted the siege and withdrew to Catalonia.[66]

Undeterred, the following year, in 1226, the king nevertheless doggedly pursued an alternate route that would draw on a different subset of supporters. This time, he planned an interior invasion from Teruel, in Aragon, but the outcome was even more disappointing than what had transpired with Penyíscola. Insubordination thwarted the expedition before it could even begin: Jaume was forced to postpone the effort when exceedingly few Aragonese knights responded to his call to arms.[67] Jaume could no longer ignore the indications that he would need to contend with these rebellious agents before seeking to engage further with his Muslim neighbors. These nobles openly rejected his authority by violating his laws, regulations, and prerogatives, taking oaths against him, and openly revolting.[68] Jaume cleverly used one problem to solve another by rewarding men who assisted in the suppression of these revolts with generous licenses to retain captured Muslim territory. After Blasco de Alagón joined other allies to help the king put a stop to noble incursions and bring about the downfall of the primary rebel, Pedro de Ahonés, for example, he received full rights to any castles he was able to conquer from Valencia.[69]

Even before this insidious baronial rebellion had been put down, Jaume's unsuccessful campaigning had nevertheless helped to advance his interests along this southern frontier. Overwhelmed by confrontation from both his Christian and Muslim neighbors, Valencia's ruler, Abū Zayd, soon agreed to pay the Crown an annual tribute of one-fifth of the revenues he derived from the territories under his governance on the condition that Jaume and his supporters cease launching expeditions into his lands.[70] As the impressive size of this tribute pledge suggests, Abū Zayd was in a precarious situation and desperate to relieve himself of pressure from the Christians along the northern frontier so that he could focus exclusively on his Muslim rivals. By this time, he had already lost his control of Ifrīqiya to al-ʿĀdil and the stability of his hold over Valencia itself was falling into question due to revolutionary activity at Onda led by Zayyān ibn Saʾd ibn Mardanīš, grandnephew of the "King Lobo" (Muḥammad ibn ʿAbd Allāh ibn Saʿd ibn Mardanīš), discussed earlier, who had governed Valencia and Murcia through 1172.[71]

Abū Zayd soon took the drastic measure of turning to his Christian aggressors for not just neutrality but active support against these rivals. In order to secure this additional aid, he reached out to the papacy and indicated that he wished to convert to Christianity and become a papal vassal.[72] As these negotiations were underway, Abū Zayd withdrew northward to Segorb early in 1229, and Valencia city quickly fell under the control of Zayyān ibn Saʾd ibn Mardanīš.[73] Abū Zayd soon met with the cardinal-legate to Iberia, Jean d'Abbeville, and followed through with his pledge to convert to Christianity. He then sought to align his own ambitions of restoring his rule over all of Valencia with Jaume's plans for conquest by signing an expansive treaty in Calatayud.[74] Given Abū Zayd's compromised situation at this point, it is not surprising that their arrangement was extremely lopsided in Jaume's favor. They arranged that all of Abū Zayd's remaining holdings, including the crucial castles of Penyíscola, Morella, Xèrica, and Segorb, would be enfeoffed to Jaume. The charter, furthermore, was unequivocal that Jaume was fully entitled to greater Valencia and could lay claim to any rights that Abū Zayd ended up regaining within the kingdom. Whereas Jaume would own fully any territory or castles he personally conquered from ibn Mardanīš, Abū Zayd would have to assign a one-fourth share of any areas he captured to the Christian king.

Apart from these auspicious diplomatic developments, Jaume's prospects against Valencia were on the rise due to progress in reconciling with his obstreperous Aragonese nobility. Although the assessment attributed to Jaume by the *Llibre dels feits* that "the cities of Aragon were all against me, save only Calatayud" was clearly an exaggeration, it is true that Jaume's noble opponents had allied with the bishop of Zaragoza and discontented townspeople in Zaragoza, Huesca, and Jaca.[75] These agents had drafted and signed an agreement on 13 November 1226 to form a "firm and perpetual friendship, association, and unification" against measures by the king and any party that wanted to "force or make violence against you . . . [or] make any exactions or marginalize your *fueros* and good customs."[76] In a second statement of alliance from later that same day, they manifested concern not only for their privileges but also for the state of safety in their realm.[77]

The following year, however, Jaume met with representatives of these dissidents at Alcalá to hear their complaints and seek to find some common ground.[78] Although he reprimanded the confederations for collaborating against him, he did not try to criminalize these actions. Instead, after they had submitted their documents of alliance and pledged to restore all of the royal property they had seized or damaged, he confirmed their *fueros* and swore off future attempts to marginalize their claimed rights.[79] The resolution of such conflicts in Aragon encouraged Jaume's reconciliation with other noble families in both Aragon and Catalonia. In Catalonia, he came to terms with the heads of the two branches of the Montcada family.[80] As we will see in the next chapter, Jaume also made progress with resolving an escalating dispute over rights to the county of Urgell in a fashion that would position him to reassert the royal dominance over the county that had narrowly escaped his father during the final years of his reign.

The Balearics and Valencia

The ability to push beyond the established frontiers of the kingdom relied on involvement throughout the realms. Not surprisingly, the support of the populations of Tortosa and Lleida, along with lay and ecclesiastical lords who held significant interests in the lower Ebro valley, was pronounced and consistent. These groups would accumulate and exercise substantial rights over lands acquired in Mallorca and Valencia—acquisitions that would affect the area's societal and administrative climates by further buffering the formerly exposed Ebro valley and enabling its inhabitants to invest and involve themselves in the obtained lands.

Despite the interest of certain Aragonese nobles in pushing ahead with the conquest of Valencia following their reconciliation with the king, Jaume had adopted a new primary objective. As we noted in chapter 2, Muslim pirates based in Balearic islands had been hampering Catalonian maritime commerce since the eleventh century.[81] After the ruler of Mallorca, Abū Yaḥyā, refused to return plunder taken during recent raiding against Catalonia-based ships, Jaume proposed to revive the dreams of his predecessors to conquer the islands, once and for all. The king had already been active in fostering Catalan maritime development by sheltering it from competition with other Mediterranean shippers. In 1227, for example, he forbade merchants from utilizing foreign ships departing from Barcelona if Catalonian ships traveling the same route were available.[82] Many of the Aragonese nobles refused to budge from their fixation on Valencia and thus declined to participate. At the *Cortes* of Zaragoza, held in July 1229 shortly before the fleet set sail, Jaume pressed them to, at the very least, respect the conditions of his imposed peace and truce. He made the case that these nobles could support the effort in their own way by not compromising the kingdom's public order during the campaign.[83]

Jaume ultimately found the support he needed for the venture, to compensate for this lack of Aragonese involvement, from Catalonia's three "estates." At the *Corts* of Barcelona in December 1228, the king received pledges of military aid and monetary support (in the form of the revived peace tax known as the *bovatge*).[84] Barcelona, Tortosa, and Tarragona agreed to supply ships, and these and other cities and towns in Catalonia also supplied militia forces.[85] Guillem II de Montcada, viscount of Bearn, Nunyo Sanç, and Hug, count of Empúries, along with other important nobles, pledged large forces of knights.[86]

Later that winter, Gregory IX elected to promote the effort as a holy war and authorized his legate, Jean d'Abbeville, to award indulgences to any army organized in northeastern Iberia to fight against the Muslims.[87] Jaume continued to campaign for support that year by promising a share of the conquered lands to knights who joined the coalition. The fleet sailed to Mallorca in September 1229. The force succeeded in capturing Palma de Mallorca by the end of the year and most of the rest of the island by the following May.[88] Acting upon a bull of crusade from Gregory IX, the archbishop-elect of Tarragona, Guillem de Montgrí, facilitated the capture of the neighboring islands of Eivissa and Formentera in 1235.[89] Following these successes, Guillem received these islands as royal fiefs.[90]

These victories confirmed Jaume's status as the head of a growing sea power, and other potentates in the western Mediterranean quickly took notice. The capture of these Balearic islands surely played a role in prompting Jaume's renewal of truces with the Genoese that dated back to their original alliance with Ramon Berenguer IV that had targeted Tortosa.[91] Like Ramon Berenguer, Jaume aspired to maintain the momentum established by these victories in order to press on and conquer Valencia. In a meeting with the king at Alcañíz in late 1231, Hug de Forcalquer, master of the Hospital, and Blasco de Alagón suggested that times were auspicious for conquering long-sought-after Valencia, "since God has guided you so well in this affair of Mallorca and in these islands."[92] Although Jaume was aware, according to the *Llibre dels feits*, that moving against Valencia could cost him the ground he had secured within the Balearic Islands, he nevertheless collaborated with these barons to plot a specific course of attack. They agreed to focus first on the coastal city and fortress of Borriana.[93] Lingering responsibilities in Mallorca, however, prevented Jaume from following through with this plan and instead encouraged him to continue collaborating with his Muslim allies. In January 1232, he made another pact with Abū Zayd, who pledged to Jaume the share of the revenues he had allegedly retained from the city of Valencia.[94]

It was only gradually, over the ensuing years, that Jaume was able to allocate increasing attention and resources to campaigning into northern Valencia while continuing his engagement with the Balearic Islands. He did so utilizing a combination of forces and resources, some of which were drawn from the former frontier lands of New Catalonia. According to Zurita, following Gregory IX's crusade bull against the new ruler of Valencia, the *Corts* of December 1232 supported another extraordinary *bovatge* levy in support of the mounting conquests of Valencia.[95] Some erosion of Muslim-held territory, settlements, and fortifications was left to local initiative, albeit with royal consent. In February 1233, Blasco de Alagón conquered Morella, south of Tortosa, in a largely independent campaign, and the municipal army of Teruel captured Ares. Jaume, Hug, and Blasco had identified both of these targets, "on this side of Valencia . . . which live on supplies from the plain of Borriana," at their meeting the previous year.[96] Shortly thereafter forces under royal command besieged and captured Borriana.[97] The *Llibre dels feits* and Zurita together highlight the involvement of Guillem IV de Cervera, lord of Juneda and Castelldans, Guillem I de Montcada, co-lord of Tortosa, and the militias of Lleida and Tortosa in this effort.[98]

Seeking, with mixed success, to attract trans-Pyrenean support to increase deployment of military resources in Valencia after Borriana's fall, Gregory IX counselled the archbishops of Bordeaux, Auch, Narbonne, and Tarragona to exhort the faithful to assist Jaume's campaigns, promising them plenary indulgences.[99] Despite the limited involvement of foreign troops, towns and castles in Borriana's plain and vicinity were isolated from the southern half of Muslim Valencia by this victory and threatened by continuing military activity from Jaume and his allies. These included Penyíscola, Castelló de la Plana, Polpís, Villafamés, Borriol, Alcalá de Xivert, Cervera, and Coves de Vinromà, all of which eventually surrendered to Catalonian and Aragonese forces.[100]

Negotiating surrenders was preferable to sieges not only because they underscored the authority and military efficacy of the victorious ruler. Such a strategy also naturally facilitated the retention of existing Andalusi infrastructure, populations, and local economies and raised the possibility that they could be put to work for the benefit of Christian-ruled society. The *Llibre dels feits*, for example, had Jaume opt to accept Borriana's surrender, among other reasons, because he was wary of squabbling between the Catalans, Aragonese, and foreigners fighting for him over the plunder in the city.[101] By securing this surrender, the king spared himself the needless disruption of the conquered environment, while preserving his role as the distributor of the captured property among his supporters.

Like his predecessors with their conquests, Jaume was naturally inclined to distribute these spoils of war liberally among his most valued supporters. These donations served as a means to enlist them in the defense of these acquisitions and to entice them to maintain their support for further campaigning into central and lower Valencia. Unlike his predecessors, however, Jaume was in a better position to resist fully alienating royal sovereign rights and interests over new lordships, even those conquered by nearly independent means, such as Morella by Blasco de Alagón. The *Llibre dels feits* recounts that Blasco pledged the town to the king after its capture and thenceforth held it in fief from him. The two formally reconfirmed and specified this relationship over Morella in 1235, around the same time that the king awarded Blasco with other holdings, such as the castles of Culla and Coves de Vinromà, in gratitude for his service against Morella.[102] In a separate agreement, Jaume then offered him a minor concession in return for promising not to violate his seigniorial prerogatives.[103]

After temporarily suspending further offensives in order to manage renewed disputes with rebellious nobles and delegates, including continuing problems with Viscount Ponç IV de Cabrera over the county of Urgell that we will discuss later, Jaume set to work organizing his supporters in order to capitalize on these territorial gains and extend his control beyond Castelló de la Plana.[104] In the first half of 1235, he met with prelates from the archdiocese at Tarragona and with essential constituencies at the *Corts* of Tarragona and *Cortes* of Zaragoza. At each of these gatherings, the king made a connection between his success as a military leader and his ruling authority over his realms. At the *Corts* in Tarragona, he reiterated how his subjects were obliged to support and abide by his royal peace regardless of their status: "peasants and villagers, whether of royal, ecclesiastical, or other religious lands, allodial or enfeoffed knights in war and peace, are under this peace and truce."[105] At the archdiocesan session, moreover, Jaume urged the bishops to use their powers of ecclesiastical censure to uphold the provisions of the peace and truce he had promulgated at the *Corts* of Barcelona in preparation for sailing to Mallorca.[106] About a month after these gatherings, adding further force to this political offensive, Gregory IX, in two separate papal bulls, threatened the resistant nobles with excommunication if they failed to assist their king in his efforts against the Muslims.[107] Gregory clearly sensed the danger presented by such widespread noble interference to Jaume's ambitions. He must have understood well the potential implications of the successful campaign of Valencia for the church's ongoing mission of restoration.

In anticipation of another phase of conquest, Jaume and the now converted Abū Zayd renewed their earlier peace in May 1236, which reestablished the former king and his sons as perpetual vassals of the king of Aragon and assigned them a collection of castles in fief.[108] At the *Cortes* of Monzón in October of that year, Jaume and the attendees again assumed "the Cross for conquering the kingdom of Valencia, for the exultation of the Christian faith."[109] This meeting represented a significant preparatory step in the latter half of the conquest of Valencia because it defined which collectives would contribute militia forces and thus benefit from the remainder of the enterprise. Present at Monzón was the expected host of citizen representatives from centers throughout Aragon: Zaragoza, Teruel, Daroca, Calatayud, Tarazona, Huesca, Jaca, and Barbastro. Tortosa and Lleida were notably the only Catalonian cities or towns to send delegates. Prelates and nobles from throughout both of the realms also attended the session.[110] Jaume promised notably the delegates, and anyone else who aided the effort, a share of the captured lands and formally committed himself to restoring and endowing the see of Valencia.[111]

In response to this assumption of the cross by Jaume and his nobles, Gregory IX called for preaching to promote the crusade against Valencia in the archdiocesan provinces of Tarragona, Narbonne, Aix, Arles, and Auch.[112] Because Jaume's ability to concentrate on the campaign continued to be plagued by noble insurrection, the pope encouraged prelates to use ecclesiastical censure to help stop the rebellions. He also extended apostolic protection over Jaume and his realms for the duration of the expedition.[113] Once the Christian forces camped at Puig de Cebolla outside of Valencia in April 1238, its ruler, Zayyān ibn Mardanīš, sought to offer Jaume castles and incomes to end the hostilities. Jaume, however, pushed on with mounting his siege which succeeded by September in forcing Zayyān ibn Mardanīš to surrender the city.[114]

In 1244, Jaume and Fernando III of Castile established the border between Valencia and Murcia with the Treaty of Almizra. This enactment ended the Aragonese king's official conquest, as he announced publicly at the *Cortes* of Huesca in 1247.[115] However, before Jaume could embark on further Mediterranean pursuits, as he aspired to do, he had to contend with considerable Muslim uprisings in Valencia. The first was led by "Albacor" (likely a Latinized version of al-Baqqār) in Alcoi. The second was a more widespread revolt instigated by AbīʿAbd Allāh b. Hudhayl, Muḥammad, known as al-Azraq, in the mountainous areas south of the city of Valencia.[116] Jaume and al-Azraq came to terms temporarily in 1245 when they signed a bilingual treaty that allowed the Muslim ruler to retain at least ten important castles.[117] Al-Azraq would use these fortifications to launch a much more devastating insurrection that would last more than a decade.[118] This conflict quickly grew serious enough to motivate Jaume to seek out a crusade bull to support his pacification efforts from Innocent IV in November 1248.[119] The discontented *mudéjares* of Valencia would continue to revolt under different leaders for the remainder of the thirteenth century. Although when Jaume later delegated oversight to his son, Pere II (r. 1276–85), he urged him to carry out a mass expulsion of the Muslims from the kingdom, Pere and his successors would nevertheless distinguish between loyal and rebellious Muslim subjects.[120] Not unlike the lower Ebro valley several generations earlier, successful conquest ushered in a painstaking process of pacification and defense. The consolidation of Valencia was likewise proving to be a long-term project with no quick or simple pathway to stability.

The Tenurial Implications of Consolidation and Further Territorial Expansion

These substantial new conquests facilitated the gradual transition of the lower Ebro valley from a Christian–Muslim frontier region into a Christian-administered landscape peopled by Christians, Jews, and Muslims.[121] More expansive and denser settlement prompted further shifts in landownership and practices of lordship. Most notably, as consolidation proceeded under Jaume's reign, this environment witnessed the further accumulation of holdings by the most powerful seigniorial families and associations, many of which had been invested in the region since the conquest.[122] The lay barony of Aitona, for example, which extended over a good portion of the lower Segre valley by the mid-thirteenth century and would be dominated by the Montcada family for centuries, was foreshadowed by Pere's alienation of castles over which Ramon Berenguer IV had retained direct lordship since the conquest and hardened during Jaume's tenure.[123] Similarly, the barony of Castellvell (later known as Entença) developed in the thirteenth century out of a conglomeration of castral territories along the Ebro River, between Tortosa and the confluence with the Segre. Composed chiefly of the settlements of Móra d'Ebre, Tivissa, Garcia, Pratdip, Marçà, and Falset, this barony took the form it would maintain for centuries in 1241, when Guillem d'Entença married Alamanda de Sant Martí, grandniece of Guillem de Castellvell, merging the Castellvell patrimony with the districts of Móra and Tivissa under Entença's lordship.[124]

For some time, however, the lands bounded by the lower Ebro and Segre valleys nevertheless conserved many of their characteristics from the post-conquest aftermath. Although the successful conquest of Valencia certainly buffered Tortosa and the lower Ebro valley with vast nominally Christian territories, the southern fringes of New Catalonia continued to border a vast, hostile landscape, as revealed by the aforementioned *mudéjar* revolts that Jaume and his supporters sought to suppress from the 1240s, with mixed success. The king clearly recognized conquered Valencia's latent insecurity and sought to enlist residents in the pacification and stabilization of these new lands and peoples. For example, seemingly identical in function to Ramon Berenguer IV's bounty provision in Tortosa's first settlement charter from 1149, in 1243 Jaume offered to reward its citizens for the discovery of Muslims up to the city of Valencia.[125]

It would be logical to presume that the desire of the new landlords of these captured lands below the nascent boundary between Catalonia and Valencia to attract Christian migrants would have exerted a powerful influence on the land market in the sectors of New Catalonia obtained before Jaume's invigorated campaigning commenced in the 1220s. The potential for an exodus of residents to the new territories could have had a pronounced influence on the settlement process and local land markets. Furthermore, the participation of numerous inhabitants of New Catalonia in the conquests would have entitled them to lands throughout both the Balearic Islands and Valencia that could have drawn them or their attentions away from their homelands. New Catalonian peasants willing to relocate in search of more favorable tenures naturally would have felt a stronger pull from contiguous lands in northern Valencia than from territories further afield in central or southern Valencia or in the islands. Enric Guinot's detailed research on settlement patterns demonstrates that the Christian populations taking root in the communities of northern Valencia as landlords or tenants consisted of a considerable number of settlers with names associating them with both New and Old Catalonia.[126] In contrast to the degradation of tenures in Old Catalonia following the accumulation of territory up to the Ebro valley in the mid-twelfth century, however, these acquisitions, together with other factors influencing the landed environment, inspired less dramatic adaptations of tenurial conditions in neighboring New Catalonia. We can work toward substantiating this general claim by examining the extent to which landlords who were active within the environments of New Catalonia sought to adapt tenurial conditions over the decades leading up to and following Jaume's conquests. As we will observe, there are indeed signs of a shift away from the terms and patterns established following the mid-twelfth-century conquests.

Peasant Servitude

The growing incidence of tenurial restrictions on peasants is a good measure of seigniorial assertiveness because it tends to be well recorded within the extant evidence. Starting in the second half of the twelfth century, some landlords in Old Catalonia sought to restrict the movement of their tenants for a variety of reasons, one of which was to inhibit migration to these new lands with their lower rents and enfranchisements.[127] Commendation charters from Old Catalonia in the early thirteenth century assigned status to peasants in accordance with their tenurial conditions, identifying them as *homines proprii* ("serfs") if they were subject to the *mals usos* ("bad customs") and had to make redemption payments to their lords to leave their tenures.[128] It is reasonable to suspect that certain lords in New Catalonia would have behaved similarly when confronted with the new territories made available by Valencia's capture that similarly threatened to draw away their tenants. While there is some weight to the characterization that New Catalonia as a whole manifested few cases of peasant servitude compared with the lands to the northeast, historians now generally view the boundary between the regions as only a rough and inconsistent indicator of lands containing free and servile tenures.[129] Agustí Altisent, for example, unearthed thirteenth-century evidence of commendation and servile dependence in the Conca de Barberà, close to Old and New Catalonia's traditional dividing line, the Llobregat River. Indications of the *mals usos* also recur in documentation from Santes Creus concerning the New Catalonian *comarques* of Conca de Barberà, Alt Penedès, Urgell, Tarragonès, Segarra, and Alt Camp.[130]

It is not altogether surprising that each region would feature diverse tenurial conditions and that degraded tenancies would not be strictly confined to Old Catalonia. Indeed, these regional designations within Catalonia were somewhat arbitrary and only retrospectively established in the thirteenth-century. When the jurist and canon of the see of Barcelona, Pere Albert, identified the Llobregat River as separating free and enserfed peasants in his *Commemoracions* (ca. 1250), he based his legal opinion on an evaluation of current tenurial conditions rather than on historical causes. He described how, to the northeast of the river, in Old Catalonia, "serfs (*homes solius*), who are not knights, are thus bound to their lords, and their sons are the vassals of their lords." To the southwest, in the land he called New Catalonia, "from the times of Ramon Berenguer [IV], . . . neither the sons of knights nor those of peasants are vassals of those magnates to whom their fathers were vassals unless . . . they have acceded to the feudal holding."[131] Although Pere Albert referred to the conqueror count-prince to account for

New Catalonia's creation, there is no indication that he viewed the capture of these lands from the Muslims as the primary cause of these differing regional attributes.[132]

A similar perspective informed the legislation now recognized by scholars as foundational for legitimizing seigniorial limitations on peasant mobility in Catalonia later in the thirteenth century.[133] The *Corts* of Barcelona in 1283 determined that lords could collect redemption payments from peasants wanting to relocate to royal lands if this practice was customary in their "lands or places," the law accordingly known as *En les terres o llocs*. Going a step beyond Pere Albert in its prioritization of custom, the assembly delimited the practice of reducing peasant freedom of mobility, yet not according to strict territorial boundaries. The legislation does not mention a single landmark or place-name. Instead, the legal designation would hinge on whether commendation that necessitated redemption was an established obligation for the tenancies in any given area.[134]

These retrospective legal maneuvers therefore do not, in themselves, account for the development of tenurial patterns within New Catalonia's landscapes. We need instead to take heed of the wide range of factors that influenced settlement in New Catalonia, guided the maturation of localized land markets, and thus conditioned diverse styles of lordship. Further from the boundary with Old Catalonia, toward more sparsely populated northern Valencia and Lower Aragon, seigniorial entitlement to the *mals usos* and other prerogatives that were understood to denote peasant servitude do not appear in the surviving evidence. A silence in the documentation, of course, does not rule out lordly abusiveness or even de facto conditions of servitude. Indeed, tenants in New Catalonia appear to have been aware that the settlement and insulation, through further conquest, of the territories they occupied could prompt the erosion of their customary franchises, just as lords in Old Catalonia had imposed upon their tenants during a period of reduced oversight without any legal justification at that time. Possibly out of competition for the best tenants or in order to demand higher lease rates, certain lords within New Catalonia offered guarantees to their residents that they would not behave like their counterparts to the northeast. A charter by the Templar Order from 1226, for example, exempted its tenants in Fontanet, near Lleida, from "servitude" (*servitutem*).[135] What this term *servitus* signified in this context is not fully clear. It was not one of the *mals usos* recognized by jurists but may have been intended to refer to marginalizing prerogatives in general. In any case, even if it was vague and legally unenforceable, the right to "servitude" was sufficiently valued so as to be itemized by castral lords in a number of thirteenth-century charters from throughout New Catalonia.

The sale of the castle of Raimat, near Lleida, in 1227, for instance, transferred the right to "all personal servitudes" to the purchasers.[136] And when
Alfons II's queen, Constança, transferred land in Vinexarop and Amposta,
outside Tortosa, with all its Christian and Muslim inhabitants to Pere Marini
in 1288, she included the imprecise right to "servitudes" among a number of
more specific abusive seigniorial prerogatives, including the *questia*.[137] The
sale of rights to the castle and domain of Torres de Segre in 1272, furthermore, granted the purchaser "whichever other exactions through which you
can institute servitude."[138]

These sparse examples notwithstanding, the majority of population charters and customary laws within New Catalonia continued to offer inhabitants
protections from the most feared of the *mals usos*.[139] The charter issued to
Rasquera and On by the Templars in 1206, for example, not only outlawed
the *mals usos* associated with *exorquia* (death without heirs), *intestia* (intestate
death), and *cugucia* (female adultery). It also referred to this ban as linked
to the "improvement of this place," which might come from the increased
migration and higher rents encouraged by such valued franchises.[140] The
Templars of Gardeny and Corbins permitted inhabitants of the neighboring settlements of Vilanova de la Barca, Aguilar, and Castellpagès (northeast of Lleida) freedom from *exorquia*, *intestia*, and *cugucia*, and then went
on to explain the practical significance of these stipulations: "if someone
dies intestate . . . let his sons or relatives inherit his goods just as if through
legitimate succession"; and "concerning *cugucias* just as is practice (*mos*) and
custom (*consuetudo*) [in] the city [of] Lleida, . . . let both [adulterers] run
through the village naked and chastised and [thereby] sustain no monetary
fines or disgrace to their honor."[141] This latter regulation thus utilized local
humiliation as a deterrent for adultery rather than property seizures or fines
benefiting the lords, as was typical in Old Catalonia.[142] Similar stipulations
appear in other Templar collections of customary laws from the region, such
as the *Costums d'Orta* for the village now known as Horta de Sant Joan, which
applied the *Usatges de Barcelona* as a supplement but also explicitly barred the
"usages which speak of *intestias*, *exorquias*, and *cugucias*."[143]

Another codification of customary law from the castellany of Miravet
indicated that judges could appeal to other influential legal collections including the thirteenth-century *Constitucions de Catalunya*, the *Usatges de Barcelona*,
and the *ius commune* ("a law common to all university-trained jurists," in
which Roman law was fused with canon law), save for legislation concerning "*cogucia*, *entestia*, or *exorquia* which one does not pay here."[144] Even large
donations to prominent religious institutions featured such exemptions. Alamanda d'Entença's grant of land in Móra d'Ebre to the Order of the Holy

Trinity in 1253, for example, barred *omni servitute* along with the *questia* and *toltas* from the order's lordship.[145] Other examples either left out the *mals usos* or exempted populations from them with blanket protections, such as the charter granted to Gandesa in 1194 barring "any other usage or service."[146] The contrast between the lack of specificity in these grants and the hyper-specificity in others already surveyed raises the likelihood that residents in certain localities felt at greater risk of suffering from the imposition of such seigniorial rights.

This diversity in tenurial conditions illustrates how lords in New Catalonia implemented varying seigniorial strategies. Because of the general absence of redemption throughout greater New Catalonia, landowners here who claimed abusive prerogatives ran the risk of losing tenants and would have had difficulty maintaining high occupancy.

Rents and Services

Landlords who wanted to keep their lands occupied naturally had to be attuned to the rental market and willing to adjust rents and other obliga-tions in order to continue to attract and retain tenants. Rent levels normally reflected the expected yield ratio for a given area of land. A major distinc-tion was between dry-farmed and irrigated lands. Whereas irrigated farms produced relatively consistent yields, dry-farmed plots in years with little precipitation could generate no harvests whatsoever.[147] The percentage of non-irrigated lands was low in the sectors of the alluvial plains along New Catalonia's numerous river valleys under cultivation, but those that were dry farmed naturally had to be subjected to dramatically lower rents.[148] Accord-ing to a contract dating from 1181, for example, one tenant had to render twelve times more rent for irrigated land than for the dry-farmed land he held from the Templars in Torrefarrera, near Lleida.[149] Environmental and infrastructural limitations were difficult for lords to ignore, even in cases of augmented control. In a revealing case from 1231, the Templars destroyed several small, dispersed settlements in the northern part of their domain in the Segrià to create the new, larger, fortified town of Castellnou (now Vilanova de Segrià). Despite the order's increased control over its tenants in this new scenario, it does not appear to have realized a significant increase in its collected rents.[150]

Given these market limitations on rental increases, many lords turned to other sources of revenue. In some villages or towns ruled by a single lord, settlement contracts created service monopolies that inhabitants were obli-gated to use or required the payment of special levies. In Rasquera and On, for instance, the Templars reserved *fabricas* (workshops), *furnos* (ovens) and all *molendinas* (mills).[151] Residents in these villages also had to render their lords a share of what they derived from the natural resources of the land: in this case, one-quarter of all slaughtered pigs, goats, deer and other game caught in the woods.[152] The bishop of Tortosa established similar monopolies in Lledó: as lord, he would keep one-sixteenth of all grain milled and one twenty-fifth of bread baked.[153] Apart from shares of the milling and baking, and levies for goods ferried across the Ebro at Miravet, the Templars required inhabitants in Rasquera and On to pay one *faneca* of wheat and one of barley for each parcel (*parellada*) held in tenure, above and beyond normal rents owed. Exercising its immunities from paying tithes and first fruits to the local cathedral, the Temple, like the sees of Tortosa and Lleida, could impose ecclesiastical taxes in the same manner as other seigniorial exactions. In Rasquera and On, for example, the Templars increased tithes on bread to one-fifth, without justification or additional comment, while maintaining first fruits and tithes on other produce at their traditional levels.[154]

Seigniorial Prerogatives of Force and Seizure

Given these motivations to increase services in spite of obstacles presented by the market for tenants and customary laws, it is not surprising to discover that certain lords throughout New Catalonia claimed abusive rights that did not number among the *mals usos*. The most widespread of these prerogatives were *toltas* and *forcias*, which granted landowners the use of arbitrary force and seizure in their exercise of lordship. Along with arbitrary levies, such as the *questia*, they appear to have been viewed informally by lords and tenants as identifiers for personal dependence derived from tenancy.[155] Jurists, however, did not consider these prerogatives to be indicative of degraded status because they were not common paired with redemption payments and therefore did not limit peasant mobility. Peasants on plots for which landlords claimed these abusive prerogatives therefore had the ability to escape this treatment if they had the means to relocate.[156]

There may be a connection between these rights to force and the seigniorial right to abuse peasants with impunity, later known as the *ius maletractandi*, that was first conceded at the peace assembly of Cervera in 1202, without any territorial limitations. In keeping with other erosions of the comital-royal peace during these years, safety guarantees would not apply to tenants on seigniorial lands that were not held from the count-king: "if lords have treated their peasants badly . . . , whether they are in the peace and truce or other lands, in no way are they to be held by the lord king in anything

unless they are in a fief of the lord king or religious lands."[157] Even though
Pere could not uphold a general public peace, he did seek to issue protections to individual settlements. When he granted a population charter to
Sant Jordi d'Alfama, a coastal settlement north of the Ebro delta, in 1201, for
example, the count-king declared that those who used violence or force (vim
et forciam) against the residents' property would also be guilty of treason (lèse
majesté).[158] He also sought to apply these protections to existing centers. In
1206, for instance, he safeguarded the market and goods of the inhabitants
of Cambrils, warning anyone who violated his concession that they would
"incur his ire and indignation."[159] Some lords in New Catalonia followed suit.
When the bishop of Tortosa issued a charter of settlement to Lledó, situated
near the Algars River, in 1210, he exempted its residents from any forcia.[160]
The Costums d'Orta included similar guarantees.[161]

Many other lords throughout New Catalonia, however, claimed and
counted as assets the rights of toltas and forcias, even for lands located to
the south and west of the Llobregat River. This evidence further demonstrates that lordship in the less buffered zones of the conquered landscape
had the potential to be aggressive and violent even without the imposition
of the notorious of the mals usos. Since claiming rights is not the same as
using them, it is difficult to demonstrate in most cases whether or how lords
used the privileges they itemized in these charters of exchange. However,
one overlooked charter may contain some rare frank discussion of the exercise of force—the inner workings of what Bonnassie has termed piraterie sei-
gneuriale.[162] In 1181, three decades from the conquest, Guillem IV de Cervera,
who held two-thirds of the castle of Garadella, near Castelldans, sold half his
estate to Pere Mascarell with "toltis et forciis." Ferrer de Castellnou held the
remaining one-third share, thus dividing the lordship into three. Since the
exercise of seigniorial rights to this castle was unusually complex, the charter
of sale went on to stipulate how these forcias should be exercised by Pere, the
new member of the partnership: "Let [a] forcia be created with the men who
will populate in this place. And if you are not able to make [a forcia] with these
men, then make that forcia jointly from your income and mine, and from
those [men] who in the future have joined with Ferrer de Castellnou." These
men could have been either subject knights or villagers who would serve in
the seigniorial band that would exercise forcias and other military services
required by the lords. The agreement goes on to explain that Pere would be
expected to hand over direction of the forcia for ten days and nights to Guillem or a delegate upon demand.[163] Another possible reading is that the forcia
was simply a war party or militia meant to combat enemies of the lords and

an obligation for the lordship's inhabitants to provide military service. It is also, of course, fully possible that these roles were not mutually exclusive.[164]

Toltas and *forcias*, often claimed alongside the right to military service and exclusively monetary seigniorial privileges, were generally relegated to rural spaces, villages and castral districts throughout New Catalonia. Mention of them in the context of urban lordships is rare. One prominent exception appears in Pere's *convenientia* with Ermengol VIII of Urgell from 1200. The count-king recognized the count's rights to "questiis, toltis vel forciis" in his allodial and enfeoffed shares of Lleida and its district.[165] This comital-royal acknowledgment of seigniorial rights of forcible seizure occurred two years before the *Corts* of Cervera established the *ius maletractandi*. For unexplained reasons, Pere was willing to concede these seemingly novel seigniorial impositions in this area, even though Ramon Berenguer IV and Alfons had never enumerated or mentioned them in earlier grants or confirmations of holdings in Lleida to the counts of Urgell. These seigniorial rights contrast sharply with the exemptions enjoyed by other communities, such as Tortosa. When Alfons alienated that town to the Templars in 1182, he indicated that *toltas* and *forcias* had never been asserted by him or his predecessors in the town.[166] Such prerogatives of urban lordship in Lleida, if they were in fact ever enjoyed, were exceptional and ephemeral. Lleida's customary laws, the *Consuetudines Ilerdenses* (1228), unequivocally exempted the citizens from "any *forcia* . . . in [their] possessions or persons" by "any lord or castellan or vicar or bailiff."[167]

Charter evidence from seigniorial castral domains in the vicinity of Lleida, however, illustrates how lay and religious lords alike continued to claim and conceptualize these rights. In 1233, for instance, Ponç de Santa Fe granted the monastery of Bellpuig de les Avellanes the tithes of the castle and town of Ares, also near Lleida, with all his "right" and *forcia*.[168] And in the aforementioned transfer of Torres de Segre from 1272, Jaume de la Roca, sacrist of the cathedral of Lleida and royal notary, sold to Martí de Vallebrera his third share of the waterway, castle, and town with a long list of entitlements, including *questias, toltas, forcias*, and rights to demand military service or redemption payments for it.[169] Such prerogatives became regular features of castral lordship that pervade documentation into the fourteenth century. In a case from 1320, for example, the executors of the will of Bonafonat de Vallebrera, citizen of Lleida, sold his castle of Almenarilla, located near Alcoletge, to another citizen of Lleida, one Jaume de Brau, itemizing a typical list of seigniorial rights pertaining to the fortification, including "toltis et forciis."[170]

Given the ubiquity of claims to *toltas* and *forcias* in these charters as part of increasingly formulaic lists of other castral prerogatives, only some of which appear to have been exercised in practice, it is difficult to know how significant they were for the quotidian conditions experienced by residents.[171] Other indications further complicate this quandary. In 1230, for instance, Constança de Montcada granted Ramon Berenguer d'Ager, for life, a sizeable collection of holdings to the north and south of Lleida, including the castles and towns of Aitona, Camarasa, Cubells, Montgai, and Seròs, all with full rights that included *toltas* and *forcias*. After detailing these prerogatives at length, however, Constança proceeded to revoke Berenguer's ability to utilize them. Lords like Constança may have been motivated to keep claims to valuable but potentially volatile seigniorial rights alive, even if they lacked the means or the will to employ them at that time.[172] In this case, limiting powers exercisable by her vassal could also have been a means of reinforcing Constança's claims to these holdings as overlord.

Although lords were, on the whole, assertive in introducing and maintaining these prerogatives, some were wary of acting on them without careful consideration. In 1258, a knight named Jordà de Peralta received the castle and town of Sucs, near Lleida, from Tomás de Sant Clement with "totam questiam vel forciam vel servicium." These rights came with strings attached, however, as Jordà promised not to utilize them without first receiving "special license" from his lord.[173] Tomás took a guarded approach to the infeudation of this holding. Jordà committed to rendering the castle and town to him upon request and swore that any homage he received from the men and castellan would not prejudice Tomás's prerogatives. Tomás thus seems to have recognized that the undue imposition of rights such as *forcias* could damage his investment and, as overlord, intended to micromanage their application. When the castle and town of Sucs were sold some years earlier, in 1235, to the royal notary Pere Sanç, the seigniorial prerogatives were itemized differently.[174]

Indications are that a subset of lords must have considered carefully whether and when to apply arbitrary rights of force and seizure. What Benito has noticed for the county of Barcelona, that "sometimes *toltas* and *forcias* practiced by castellans went accompanied by more sophisticated methods that reveal the importance of written custom in the regulation of agrarian relations," appears also to apply to New Catalonia.[175] It is from this vantage point that we can begin to understand how these sorts of prerogatives could coexist with the annual tenant obligations owed to the castral lord, delimited and regularized by territorial custom or contract. Even in less enfranchised Old Catalonia, lords did not possess an unfettered capacity to inflict their wills on their tenants. In addition to market conditions, which could deprive them of their tenants, lords had to contend with evolving legal frameworks that could regulate their domains, both well established and freshly settled.

Military Obligations

Given the danger commonly associated with proximity to Muslim-ruled lands, one might have expected settlement charters in the southern reaches of New Catalonia to impose greater obligations in terms of military services than in more sheltered areas further to the north. However, the situation was clearly more complicated. In the earliest charters granted to urban centers like Tortosa and Lleida, settlers were not obligated to perform military service.[176] Although, as we have seen, Ramon Berenguer IV did incentivize responsibilities for keeping the peace and defense by Christian inhabitants by offering a reward for the capture of "fugitive Muslims" along the frontier region, this service was not mandatory.[177] In general, comital-royal provisions for settlement in these territories through the reign of Pere rarely, if ever, mandated military service.[178] By contrast, certain population charters issued independently by lay and religious lords, from the late twelfth and early thirteenth centuries, did obligate settlers to perform military service. However, since such services were commonly expected from vassals throughout Catalonia and could have been directed equally at non-Muslim enemies, they cannot be directly linked to the frontier environment.[179]

The Templars were by far the most demanding lords in these territories when it came to military service. The order's population charter for Rasquera and On, for example, expected that settlers would perform military service against the Muslims whenever "when the lord king of the land or the lord master of the [Templars]" visited the area and demanded it.[180] Most charters issued by the Templars in New Catalonia during this period feature similar requirements for military responsibilities against Muslims.[181] When the order gave the locality of Pinell its second population charter in 1207, it not only required military service from the inhabitants and their progeny residing in the village (as had been stipulated, in 1198, in the first charter), but also claimed one-fifth of the booty this militia might seize while campaigning.[182]

Apart from the military orders, other lords occasionally expected military service, albeit with far less frequency, and only sometimes in accordance with the given lordship's proximity to the frontier. In 1210, the bishop of Tortosa retained rights to military service against Muslims during peace and war in the town of Lledó, past the Algars River at the reaches of Christian settlement at that time, and held the residents fully responsible for guarding the wider town, policing its walls and neighboring valleys, day and night, but not its castle.[183] When Pere entrusted Benifassà to Guillem de Cervera in 1208, he retained the right to draw upon its military resources at any time.[184] Like Benifassà, Ulldecona remained a border outpost through the first quarter of the thirteenth century and was far more exposed to Muslim attack than the Templar settlements around Miravet, for example. Yet when the noble, Ramon II de Montcada, co-lord of Tortosa, together with the master of the Hospitallers, granted a population charter to Ulldecona's settlers in 1222, he issued them "the good customs and liberties of Tortosa" and specified no military obligations.[185] When it came to the imposition of military obligations, the habits and objectives of the landlord were arguably more significant that the settlement's proximity to Muslim territory.

Some Templar houses did eventually lift military requirements along with other unpopular impositions, likely in order to attract and retain occupants. In 1226, the Templars of Gardeny granted their tenants in Fontanet an exemption from payment of the *questia* as well as from military service.[186] A monetary levy adjusted in accordance with one's personal property, the *questia* was imposed by the sovereign or lord on his subjects without any regularity. As Benito has argued, the arbitrary nature of the *questia* helps explain how it came to be viewed as an identifier for territorial lordship and personal dependence based on tenancy. According to Benito, this designation accounts for why, at the peace assembly held in Tortosa in 1225, the king banned royal officers and knights from demanding the *questia* on wheat from anyone other than their own subjects. Indeed, from the beginning of the thirteenth century, freedom from this levy became one of the most desired exemptions among tenants.[187] Like the *questia*, the contribution to defense that was demanded of residents was in effect another form of seigniorial income, in the form of a service or, increasingly, monetary redemption from service, and was not necessarily tied to the frontier. In a suggestive case from 1293, Joan Puig, lord of Paüls, established new terms of settlement for his residents that assigned to them the responsibility of guarding the castle in lieu of any offensive military service requirements. With local opportunities for raiding into Andalusi-held lands and engaging with Muslim troops long past by the time of this enactment, these duties must have been considerably more valuable to the lord and presumably were more palatable to the inhabitants of Paüls as well.[188]

Enfranchisement and Customary Law

As these military service requirements and other obligations imposed by landlords illustrate, the volatility of the postconquest land market tended to complicate the persistence of customary franchises. These dynamics had the potential to work to the disadvantage of tenants. In 1182, for example, when Alfons gave all of his jurisdictional rights in Tortosa "to [the Templar Order's] lordship (*dominium*) and power (*potestatem*) . . . retain[ing] nothing for myself," he had renounced his own right to claim the *mals usos* and military service, some of which had already been expressly outlawed by Tortosa's population charter, but stipulated nothing about limitations on the Templars' ability to impose them.[189] When Pere echoed this renunciation in 1209, he added a much more comprehensive list of potential levies and services to be enjoyed by the order, excluding *malum servicium* and exclusively comital-royal levies such as the *bovatge* and *monedatge*.[190] The *bovatge* was a general tax initially timed with the comital-royal peace constitutions that developed, by Pere's reign, into an accession-tax, whereas the *monedatge* was intended to support the "redemption of the money."[191] We have no way of knowing Pere's true intentions in generating this list, but it seems likely that the Templars were concerned to enhance their ability to profit from the lordship as much as possible while limiting the monarchy's capacity to make monetary demands on their subjects following the purchase.[192] The creation of a document that barred the count-king from imposing services in Tortosa that he and his predecessors had never enjoyed there may well have distorted the Templars' understanding of the prerogatives they would be entitled to there as lords. Indeed, these early exchanges could have served to aggravate the subsequent disputes between the seigniorial regime and Tortosa's citizens.

Despite considerable legal and logistical obstacles, lords in New Catalonia did seek to increase their authority and control either by encroaching on exemptions and privileges of the inhabitants, sometimes by reissuing population charters or by establishing new centers of settlement with contracts that supported greater seigniorial prerogatives. In contrast to Old Catalonia, only scant evidence from New Catalonia demonstrates whether or how lords enacted plans to erode rights in existing communities.[193] To return again to Tortosa as an illustration of this phenomenon, during the thirteenth century both the *universitas* of citizens and the Templars, sought to reinterpret, to their respective advantages, local customs that had evolved from Ramon Berenguer IV's original population charter and subsequent associated comital-royal privileges. These opposing readings fomented this decades-long dispute that was only resolved in a settlement demanding significant concessions from both sides.[194] The unauthorized *Consuetudines Dertusenses*, which had been compiled over the course of decades by the citizens' *universitas*, without seigniorial involvement, did include several additional exemptions as well as general freedom from "anything that could be termed a servitude" from the lords as well as from the count-king, queen, and vicar.[195] These exemptions were later suppressed, however, when the collection was revised and codified, by a seigniorial tribunal, into the *Costums de Tortosa* in the 1270s.[196]

Since Tortosa's customary laws and privileges had been inherited from the count-kings and not established by the current jurisdictional lords, they must have appeared to the new constituted seigniorial regime as especially unwarranted and deleterious to the financial viability of the lordship. Furthermore, the lords' affiliation with extensive holdings elsewhere in Catalonia, where such exemptions were not common, likely increased their distaste for the exemptions enjoyed by these citizens. For the seigniorial regime, the differences between conditions in Tortosa and their expectations as the incoming jurisdictional authorities must have helped to justify their decision to pursue litigation to challenge elements of the customary privileges of the citizens. As the legal scholar Rafael Gibert once wrote, this was a collision between two diametrically opposed "medieval conceptions of law, seigniorial and municipal."[197] Only after decades of conflict did these sides come to terms in a resolution that permanently handicapped the seigniorial regime's ability to exercise the powers of jurisdiction and taxation to which it felt entitled. This outcome likely encouraged the Templars and Montcadas to cooperate with the Crown's efforts to purchase full jurisdictional rights in the 1290s, which enabled them to shift their capital long tied up in Tortosa to less encumbered domains elsewhere.[198]

Conditions within lordships located elsewhere in New Catalonia similarly were forged in reference to a wider context. Both seigniorial and comital-royal settlement projects featured enfranchisements similar to those of centers created in the aftermath of the conquest. For example, when Pere issued the aforementioned population charter to Sant Jordi d'Alfama in 1201, he reimposed "those liberties which Ramon Berenguer . . . gave . . . the inhabitants of Tortosa."[199] Royal population charters would continue to invoke this influential corpus of privileges and customs even at the end of the thirteenth century. In 1294, for instance, Jaume II instructed Bernat de Llibiá, the royal bailiff in Tortosa, to populate Font del Perelló and grant settlers the franchises and liberties held by the citizens of Tortosa.[200]

The monarchy was not alone in this tendency to reuse customary legal compilations. Throughout the period of consolidation, many lords also opted to borrow from existing bodies of customary law rather than generating their own. In one typical case from 1185, the bishop of Tortosa granted a population charter to the residents of Cabacés, granting them full access to the resources of the area under the condition that they continue to reside and work there. He reserved tithes, first fruits, judicial fines, the town oven and mill, and some additional property, along with claiming additional unstipulated rights according to "custom in the castle of Móra [d'Ebre]."[201]

As we saw earlier with his settlement provisions for Ulldecona, Ramon II de Montcada also utilized the customary laws of his co-lordship of Tortosa in his settlement projects in the early thirteenth century, even though they were already a source of conflict with the citizens in that town. For example, his charter to Pere Nebot to populate and otherwise develop Fullola, in the northern outskirts of Tortosa, into a castral center, applied those same customary laws.[202] Far from conclusive evidence that Ramon was attached to these customs, their application to Ulldecona could have been the result of demands of settlers that they be allowed to use that popular collection, with its coveted prerogatives and enfranchisements. Their appeal would have been further strengthened by the new center's proximity to Tortosa, which would likely be a major source of Ulldecona's settlers. Even if the customs of Tortosa had contained elements Ramon would have preferred to omit from future settlement projects, he could not ignore the utility of applying Tortosa's customs, which had the added benefit of linking together, jurisdictionally, his domains in the lower Ebro region and facilitating their socioeconomic interdependence.

While there are no known examples in New Catalonia of Templar houses redeploying entire legal corpuses without alteration, the order sometimes imposed customs that had been established and developed in nearby settlements under its lordship. For instance, the Templars settled Camposines under the customs of Ascó, modifying only the seigniorial rents payable by the residents, whereas Gandesa received the *Costums d'Orta*.[203] Indeed, when Horta's customary laws were codified in the later thirteenth century, certain of its residents requested to use Lleida's customs but were refused by Templar lords who demanded that they use Horta's own laws.[204] Although Lleida's customary legal tradition continued to exert an influence on the local laws at Horta and Gandesa, the collections remained distinct.

Despite clear borrowings from Lleida's comital-royal customs in Horta's resulting legal collection, the body of laws manifests seigniorial influences that are worth examining.[205] The regulations described by the *Costums d'Orta* paint a vivid picture of the mixed conditions of settler rights and seigniorial prerogatives experienced on these rural domains.[206] Residents were free to settle disputes informally among themselves (c. 8), and could elect judges for certain cases, with seigniorial approval (15). However, the local Templar commander and his bailiff reserved the right to judge all formal judicial proceedings (8, 10, 11, 16). Fines were payable exclusively to the commander or his bailiffs (8 and 11) and were exacted for a range of offences (34–37, 40), including blasphemy (19). Those convicted of heresy would be burned, and their property would be assumed by the order (79). Bread that was sold under weight would be seized by the lords. Third-time offenders would have their stalls locked in the castle or be fined twenty-five *solidi* by the commander (24). If the citizens rang the bells at the wrong time they would be fined fifteen *solidi* (26). Markets were not to be held without the commander's prior approval (29). Since the seigniorial court stood as the sole judicial body, its rules and regulations were stipulated with considerable attention to detail (48–63, 70, 72–77). There was no recognition of royal authority in the *Costums d'Orta* and notably no legal mechanism by which residents could bypass or even challenge the order's authority.

When it came to Muslim residents, lords faced an added risk that was not normally an issue with Christian tenants. Seeking to change the conditions of tenancy in order to increase revenues or seigniorial control could prompt *mudéjares* to relocate not simply to other lordships but away from Christian lands altogether.[207] Landlords accordingly had good reason to tread especially carefully with this category of tenant. Within areas that had built up a relatively high density of habitation, however, some lords nevertheless sought to reduce or eliminate altogether some of the exemptions enjoyed by most *mudéjar* tenants since the conquest. In 1258, for example, the Hospitallers of Amposta established new and considerably less favorable settlement terms for their Muslim community in nearby l'Aldea. The agreement offered religious and judicial rights similar to those arranged with the Muslims of Tortosa and the Ribera d'Ebre a century earlier, but also reduced the mobility and self-determination of the residents in the community.[208] Whereas the Muslims of the Ribera d'Ebre (like those of Tortosa) theoretically enjoyed complete freedom of movement according to their charter of settlement, those inhabiting l'Aldea were granted mobility sufficient only to sustain their commercial activities. And they were not permitted to leave the Hospitallers' lordship without authorization.[209] There are no explicit indications that the residents of l'Aldea were required to make redemption payments, however, and the agreement does not stipulate how they were to secure the right to relocate and elect a different lord.[210] These inhabitants were also subject to a host of new levies and services: labor services (*azofra*), which had been outlawed by these earlier charters, amounting in l'Aldea to one day a month laboring personally and with their beasts for the Hospitallers; novel taxes on goats and animals hunted in the district; and one-fourth of all produce and one-fifth of all land sold, in addition to various other annual payments absent from the earlier agreements.

Just as the privileges for Christian populations could fall under seignio-rial scrutiny and potentially suffer erosion, the provisions and protections of surrender treaties and postconquest settlement charters remained in force for *mudéjar* communities only so long as inhabitants were willing to fight to protect them. By the thirteenth century, *mudéjar* communities had learned the intricacies of Catalano-Aragonese juridical culture sufficiently to know to demand numerous confirmations of their privileges from their Templar lords.[211] Tellingly, after the Templar Order was dissolved and its lordships of the Ribera d'Ebre fell under the control of the Hospitallers, on numerous occasions during the fourteenth century its Muslims communities success-fully countered attempts by the order to encroach on their customary privi-leges and exemptions.[212]

The Dynamics and Impact of Comital-Royal Centralization

Comital-royal weakness had made it possible for lords to subvert the peace and truce to manipulate tenurial conditions with relative impunity under the reigns of Alfons and Pere and during Jaume's troubled minority.[213] Alfons's public-peace provisions of 1173 were notably scaled back at sessions in Girona in 1188 and Barbastro in 1192.[214] Under Alfons's successors, the mon-archy's ability to guarantee peace and access to public justice for all suffered further setbacks. At the peace assembly at Barcelona in 1200, for example, Pere loosened restrictions established by Alfons that threatened malefactors who injured persons on public roads with lèse majesté, but exempted from these restrictions knights making war and masters detaining runaway *homi-nes proprii*.[215] Public-peace provisions over roads were not stipulated again until the *Corts* of Lleida in 1214, during Jaume's minority, although this new king soon conceded similar exceptions to lords in 1218 and 1225.[216] By the late twelfth and early thirteenth centuries, castellans whose families had held remote castles for generations had the potential to benefit from diminishing general standards of public order, which removed large sectors of the popu-lation from the limited protections, offered by access to the royal courts, against seigniorial abuse and degradation of status.[217]

Once Jaume emerged from his minority, he began to work against this *status quo*, with the vital assistance of his former regents and other sup-porters. The resulting gradual recovery of authority, however tentative and insecure, prompted lords to defend their accustomed increased autonomy. The regalian ideology promoted by the *Usatges de Barcelona* informed the continual promotion from the 1220s onward, in assemblies and constitutions, of the theory that all inhabitants in the king's realms were protected by and bound to uphold the king's peace in cooperation with local royal officials.[218]

According to Bisson, Jaume was heir to the idea that "justice was at the heart of the king's . . . conception of power," and unlike his predecessors, he was finally in a stronger position to act on it by developing more robust and policed provisions for public order.[219] The assembly he convoked at Tarragona in 1235 delivered a statement explaining the implications of this peace meant for his most vulnerable subjects: "peasants and villagers, whether of royal, ecclesiastical, or other religious lands, allodial or enfeoffed knights in war and peace, are under this peace and truce . . . with all of their property."[220] Even though they were developed later in Jaume's reign, Pere Albert's *Commemoracions* nevertheless provide a window onto this king's operative conception of authority during these formative years. Pere Albert's corpus was far from a simple, unprejudiced attempt to "gather up the Catalonian feudal practice of his time."[221] In drawing on Roman legal concepts from the *ius commune* and prioritizing Jaume's goal of centralization, the text served to promote the principle of overarching royal authority.[222] As Susan Reynolds has suggested generally for high medieval western Europe, the "new emphasis on the ruler's authority is generally associated with the study of Roman law."[223] Pere Albert's project was therefore far less innocuous and theoretical than it might appear. The *Commemoracions* were engaged in confirming, defining, and thus delimiting seigniorial prerogatives, while subordinating them to royal ones whenever possible. One example of how even apparent setbacks could nevertheless serve Jaume's agenda is this aforementioned development of legally sanctioned peasant servitude during the thirteenth century. The lords to the north and east of the Llobregat River were able to impose tenurial restrictions on their nonknightly tenants as *homes solius* under Jaume's watch, thus legally binding them to the soil. This development, however, empowered the king to borrow from this same logic and use it against these lords by claiming that these same lords were similarly his *homes solius* and thus subject to his authority as *princeps terrae*.[224]

Such potent expressions of royal authority by the midpoint of Jaume's reign should not imply that the monarch enjoyed untrammeled success in the pursuit of his aims without any setbacks. Indeed, the frequent reiteration of peace constitutions during Jaume's reign suggests that the application of the royal peace continued to weather significant opposition. Lords throughout the realms ardently resisted the notion that these royal regulations affected their domains and tenants and that they were obliged to cooperate in upholding them.[225]

Not content to advance royal authority by means of theoretical provisions alone, Jaume and his advisors promoted pronounced administrative development in the offices of the royal court and in those of local delegates (vicars, bailiffs) based in municipalities. From the 1220s, Jaume also started to recover some of the jurisdictional authority in New Catalonia that had been alienated under his predecessors.[226] For example, in addition to making arrangements to assume full lordship over Lleida, the king also acquired new property in Tortosa and successfully lobbied the lords there to permit him to install a local bailiff there in 1247.[227] By the 1280s, Pere II was attempting to exert his control over vicar, *paers*, and lower officials in the city in order to conduct royal business.[228] He had also begun directing officials based in both Catalonia and Aragon to regulate tenants on the long-autonomous seigniorial domains of the Terra Alta and Ribera d'Ebre: most significantly, the lay baronies of Flix and Entença and the military-order lordships of Horta, Miravet, and Ascó. These jurisdictional developments would culminate in the monarchy recovering vast territorial holdings throughout lower New Catalonia by the end of the thirteenth century.[229]

Seigniorial resistance did manage to slow or block, for a time, the centralizing influence of the *ius commune*. Under pressure in 1243, Jaume banned the use of Roman law in secular courts throughout his realm, in preference to local customary laws and the regalian yet familiar *Usatges de Barcelona*, as well as judicial common sense.[230] This order, which helped shelter seigniorial jurisdiction from royal intervention, was reiterated at the *Corts* of Barcelona in 1251.[231] It is important to recognize that such measures could arguably only impede one dimension of this legal corpus. Since the "*ius commune* was used to provide legal rules when no statute or custom provided otherwise," it was also "influential even where it was not immediately authoritative." Thus, even when it was legally restrained, the *ius commune* could still exert influence on local laws of the land (*ius proprium*) and on the theoretical formulations of jurists such as Pere Albert.[232]

In the light of these engagements over the *ius commune*, it is not surprising that these previously discussed thirteenth-century charters from the vicinity of Lleida also awarded lords a monopoly on justice that threatened to deprive tenants of recourse to nonseigniorial courts and rights over purportedly royal levies such as the *bovatge* and *monedatge*.[233] When Guillem de Cardona and his wife sold Pere Bosch and his family the castle of Raimat, near Lleida, for three thousand *morabetins* in 1227, along with *questias*, *toltas* and *forcias*, and *servitutes*, they itemized as pertaining to the lordship "all jurisdiction" with *bannos* (the rule of law) and *districtiones* (the coercive power accompanying the exercise of judicial authority).[234] The Bosch family then sold their rights to the holding to the aforementioned royal notary, Pere Sanç, in two separate transactions in 1231 and 1232. These subsequent charters of sale were even more explicit in defining the judicial capacities that pertained to Raimat's lord, claiming the right to hear "all cases, civil and criminal," that is, *merum et mixtum imperium* or high and low justice.[235]

In asserting their rights to the *monedatge* and *bovatge* levies, these lords may have been seeking to challenge the imposition of royal taxation within their domains. These prerogatives appear within lists of other seigniorial entitlements (such as *questias, toltas, forcias*, military service, and general "usaticis") without further comment or any mention of the king. In the later twelfth century, the count-kings had seized upon the *monedatge* and *bovatge* to culti- vate as general taxes—what some scholars have interpreted as a major step in the development of a cohesive "feudal state."[236] Whereas the *monedatge* was "ransomed" by the monarchy to redeem the coinage for the general welfare, the *bovatge* was transformed (according to comital-royal definition) from a "purchase of peace" to a "public necessity" imposed upon the accession of the monarch or in other times of extraordinary expenditure, such as military campaigns.[237]

The count-kings' efforts to escalate these levies into general taxation, tied to the peace provisions and likewise pervading Catalonia, had faltered in the face of opposition from barons who must have viewed these attempts as unwelcome novelties. In the peace constitutions established at Girona in 1188, for example, Alfons had sworn not to impose "anything on the occa- sion of the *bovatge* or the arrangement of peace" on anyone living between Salses, Tortosa, and Lleida.[238] No matter what the monarchy may have intended for these levies, rights to impose the *bovatge* and *monedatge* had not remained exclusively comital-royal preserves. Rather, other self-proclaimed independent magnates, such as the counts of Empúries, had continued to collect them, as did lesser lords, sometimes based on recent donations by the money-hungry count-kings themselves.[239]

The enjoyment of these sorts of prerogatives by lords had not been very uncommon or controversial in the twelfth and early thirteenth centuries. It was only later, as Jaume developed and implemented the centralizing gov- ernmental principles that had been roughly sketched by Ramon Berenguer IV and his successors, that the sharing of these rights appeared to be so illegitimate and improper. Indeed, during the phases of the *repartiment* and royal withdrawal from New Catalonia, before the development of comital peace legislation increased conflict between comital-royal public and sei- gniorial private authority, the count-kings had viewed seigniorial rights later understood to be harmful to royal prerogatives as tolerable and perhaps even normative. Within several years of Tortosa's capture, for instance, Ramon Berenguer IV had assigned the city's restored episcopal see the right to exercise "full jurisdiction" as well as collect the *bovatge*, *monedatge*, and other levies on some of its domains.[240] When Alfons, together with his baron, Pere de Subirachs, had invested three knights with the castellany of Paüls in the foothills of Els Ports, to the west of Tortosa, in 1168, for example, he had granted them sweeping rights to exercise justice and collect a range of levies including the *questia*, *bovatge*, and *monedatge*, as well as *forcias*.[241]

We lack evidence to confirm that the rights of *bovatge* or *monedatge* claimed in other lordships within New Catalonia (such as by the aforementioned Bosch family of Raimat) derived similarly from comital-royal donation. Indeed, these prerogatives could have had other origins. They could have been claimed autonomously by lords within the unregulated twelfth-century environment or even invoked more recently in opposition to thirteenth-century royal advances under Jaume. Increasing royal reliance on such levies under Jaume and his sons in the thirteenth century and efforts to impose them without prior authorization by the *Corts* continued to incur stiff seigniorial resistance. Given this context of opposition, these castral lords, in defying royal mandates by claiming these taxation rights for themselves, could have been seeking to make a statement about the competency of seigniorial jurisdiction as well as to enhance the autonomy of their domains, if the rights were indeed exercised. These prerogatives thus would have represented a challenge to the king's claim that, as "king of the land" (*princeps terrae*), he represented the chief guarantor of public safety and welfare and that his pervasive prerogatives permeated seigniorial jurisdictions. A more innocuous possibility is that lords were simply seeking to protect their ability to collect these levies within their domains in satisfaction of royal demands. These rights then would have rendered the lords as collaborators rather than competitors with the royal fiscal demands. But claims to exercise these rights in their domains, even in the name of the king, should not have empowered lords to pass their own obligations on to the residents of their domains, since the formulaic clauses of promulgation of the *bovatge*, expressed from the reign of Jaume, explicitly ruled out the applicability of "charters of franchise" for the levy.[242]

Even if certain lords did not assert these prerogatives for themselves, they could still help their taxed residents voice their opposition. The lords of Tortosa, for example, appear never to have claimed the right to the *bovatge*, but, at the same time, were clearly not assisting the Crown with its collection. In 1280, however, only three years after the settlement of their long dispute over customary exemptions with the seigniorial regime, when the wounds from that hard-fought series of battles must still have been fresh, the city's *universitas* directed a delegate to the seigniorial court administered by the Montcadas and Templars to complain that the *bovatge* demanded by the king threatened to impoverish the citizenry. The delegate was to request that the lords support the *universitas*'s appeal "with beneficial advice" and help protect the *universitas*'s property and merchandise against the demands of royal officials as they went about their daily lives, hopefully "with the consent of the king."[243] Neither "usurpers" nor facilitators of the imposition of the *bovatge*, the lords of Tortosa here were acting as civilian advocates. Such a role was probably founded on mutual self-interest. Since it was not their levy, the lords in fact had an incentive to assist the citizens, conserving local resources for their own seigniorial prerogatives. The incident illustrates the difficulty the monarchy could face in seeking to assert prerogatives within lordships it did not directly administer.

Once Jaume II purchased jurisdiction over Tortosa in the early 1290s, the citizenry changed its strategy, which generated new challenges for the monarchy. In addition to claiming customary immunity from the *bovatge*, the *universitas* argued, in 1298, that as former occupants of a Templar lordship, its members should benefit from that order's traditional exemption from the levy.[244] The stalemate remained unresolved less than a year later, with certain residents blocking the royal porter's entry to the city to prevent him from trying to collect the tax. Representatives argued that especially because the citizens were loyal royal subjects, always "prepared to defend the right of the lord king in everything," the "privileges and immunities and the customs of the city of Tortosa [had been] granted and observed for a long time by the predecessors of the lord king." Since the city had never paid the *bovatge*, they asserted, these demands violated "the rights, privileges and customs of Tortosa."[245] Echoing to some degree the experiences of the Templars and Montcadas after receiving jurisdiction over Tortosa from the count-prince and count-kings in the twelfth century, the Crown's attempt to impose this tax within this new jurisdiction was thus plagued by the customs established or intensified within the context of many decades of seigniorial administration.

Conclusions

These examples further illustrate the antagonism inherent in the lord–tenant relationship. Irrespective of a given landscape's state of postconquest consolidation, these parties were engaged in a zero-sum game over jurisdictional rights and the productive capacity of the land. This is not to suggest, however, that changes in the territorial environment prompted by progressive, gradual migration over time or by the acquisition of neighboring lands were not usually significant in influencing the dynamics between lords and tenants. As we have seen with the influence of successful campaigning into northern Valencia on New Catalonia, territorial accumulation could engender demographic and economic variations within neighboring lands and thereby stimulate significant changes within local land markets.

Customary franchises that hindered a lord's modulation of the tenurial conditions of his domains in tune with the dynamics of the local market put pressure on that relationship and encouraged the lord (whether he be a lowly castellan or the king himself) to seek to make changes.[246] Indeed, this aforementioned body of castral documentation from around Lleida demonstrates how certain lords were able to commandeer local resources that were not explicitly protected by custom. Common use of natural resources (*ademprivium* or *empriu*) had been standard in earlier settlement charters and customary legal collections but appears as an exclusive seigniorial prerogative in many of these later exchanges. One representative transfer dating from 1227 itemized the rights of the lord of the castle of Raimat, including wells, meadows (*prata*), mountains and plains, all lands in general (populated or unpopulated), all waters and waterways (including, explicitly, rivers), riverbanks, rocks, trees, timber (or firewood), turf and game (*venationes*), as well as wastelands (*garrigas*).[247] Along with redemption, rights of *empriu* were addressed in the *Corts* of 1283, where "ancient" custom was again defined as the determinant for legitimate current practice.[248] Scholars have noticed that seigniorial and royal rights of *empriu* in New Catalonia, along with the kingdoms of Mallorca and Valencia, in general remained governed by settlement charters and foral laws, while in much of Old Catalonia, excluding the Vall d'Aran, Pallars, and Andorra, ancient custom usually served as the primary guide.[249]

These tendencies nevertheless left assertive lords throughout Catalonia room to maneuver, particularly in localities like Raimat that had never been awarded explicit customary protections of communal rights. This distinction between zones with and without established franchises safeguarding the enjoyment of *empriu* and other entitlements would help define relations between lords and residents in this environment for generations to come. In the late sixteenth century, for instance, the new lords of Maldà (near Lleida) and the Vall d'Aran (in the Pyrenees of Old Catalonia) both claimed *empriu* at the expense of their tenants. This move occurred around the time the residents of Tortosa, by contrast, received another confirmation of their twelfth-century privileges, which included full rights to the natural resources of the city and district.[250] Catalonia thus remained a landscape that was simultaneously dynamic and static. New Catalonia's customary traditions, which had generally been forged during the earliest phases of settlement, continued to delimit and variegate tenurial conditions even as the course of consolidation and the push into new lands in northern Valencia and beyond applied new pressures on its urban and rural environments.

✣ CHAPTER 8

The Impact of Conquest and Consolidation on Jurisdiction and Administration

As discussed in the previous chapter, notwithstanding ongoing security concerns, successful expansion into Valencia did serve to shelter New Catalonia progressively, thereby facilitating its economic development and demographic growth. It also made these once peripheral lands seem closer to the Crown of Aragon's core and thus presumably more desirable to landlords and settlers alike. Perceived relative proximity could not erase, however, the institutional imprints left behind by the intricate, individuated, and multifaceted histories of conquest and settlement that had been experienced by different zones and localities within these territories.

By integrating Tortosa and Lleida as *marcae*, for example, Ramon Berenguer IV had avoided designating where the boundaries between Aragon and Catalonia would divide the new territories. This maneuver had enabled him to avoid the issue of officially assigning these districts to either principality yet also instituted an ambiguity that would repeatedly spark conflict in future years. Both Lleida and Fraga were fully implicated in the dispute. While Aragonese claims over Tortosa were never voiced, parts of its wider district were also affected by the controversy.[1] In the immediate aftermath of the conquests, as we have seen, Count-prince Ramon Berenguer IV had chosen to invent for Tortosa and Lleida new sets of privileges and provisional customary laws rather than imposing available collections of *fueros* affiliated with other centers and regions. Such a designation further disconnected these new centers from neighboring Catalonian and Aragonese societies in terms of their legal traditions.[2] In both Tortosa and Lleida, these charters had come to represent the most important constitutional bases of their individual extensive local customary laws. These legal corpuses, in turn, grew increasingly influential throughout their surrounding regions as other lords applied them to new settlement projects.[3]

The additional territories acquired during Alfons's rule raised the stakes and complicated the resolution of the issue, but the creation of an outright conflict awaited further regional centralization in the thirteenth century. Following the conquest of Valencia, the kingdom of Aragon and principate of Catalonia developed increasingly capable administrative capacities and sought to impose their respective rules of law and financial demands on their common frontier. Local populations, lords, and the monarchy were caught in an ongoing struggle to define the entire length of the border from Ribagorza, through the Litera and the districts of Lleida and Fraga, and into the lower Ebro valley bounded by the Terra Alta and Ribera d'Ebre. The boundary issue continued to afflict some areas as late as the fifteenth century, in most cases because the monarchy and other authorities had difficulty reconciling different indicators of regional adherence. Local determinants, such as the customary law implemented at the time of settlement, often conflicted with royal designations, which themselves were inconsistent, as well as with the present inclinations of resident populations and local lords.

This final chapter of the book continues the discussion from the previous chapter of the repercussions of the conquest on tenurial conditions within Catalonia's former frontier zones. It commences with a detailed examination of these boundary disputes that were at least partly fomented by long-awaited success in the consolidation of these conquered lands together with general advances in administrative capacity throughout both Catalonia and Aragon. To conclude the chapter, and as a means to begin bringing the book to a close, we will then turn to studying the means by which the monarchy and its officials sought to establish or recuperate administrative and jurisdictional rights over seigniorial or baronial entities. Although areas throughout Catalonia experienced this phenomenon, it was especially notable within the former frontier lands of New Catalonia. As we will see, the pace and course of the monarchy's pursuit of jurisdictional rights tended to be motivated chiefly by its concerns regarding the activity of certain lords, its sense of the increased relative proximity of formerly peripheral lands, and its heightened awareness of the empowering implications of its claimed regalian authority throughout Catalonia.

The Cinca and Segre Rivers

When Alfons had promulgated his peace and truce at the *Corts* of Fondarella in 1173, he implied that Lleida and Tortosa, with their respective districts, sat outside of Aragonese territory. He left ambiguities, however, surrounding the border issue that his successors later had to address.[4] In Andalusi times, Fraga had been a dependency of Lleida. It became an independent municipality under Christian rule by default, and Alfons appears to have believed that Fraga should pertain to Aragon even though Lleida had fallen under Catalonia's sphere of influence. Although Fraga did sit well within Lleida's diocesan boundaries, so did much unquestionably Aragonese territory, including the archdeaconates of Barbastro, Terrantona, and Benasque. Furthermore, ecclesiastical delimitations tended not to figure in disputes concerning secular administrative jurisdictions.[5] The imposition of an Aragonese collection of customs and legal privileges, the *fueros* of Huesca, and the grant of the center to Catalonia-based Arnau Mir de Pallars as an *honor* similarly provided unclear indications regarding Fraga's status.[6]

Administrative dealings in the early thirteenth century perpetuated this ambiguity. At the *Corts* celebrated in Lleida in 1214, for example, the cardinal legate, acting in the name of the young king, renewed the peace to be observed by all the nobles, barons, knights, citizens, and burghers of all of Catalonia to the Cinca River. Although this statement appeared to confirm Lleida's inclusion within Catalonia, it had unclear implications for Fraga's status, seated as it was on the left, or eastern, bank of the Cinca.[7] The *Cortes* of Daroca in 1229, however, proved a complete reversal. *Prohoms* from Lleida and men representing all of Fraga ("toto concilio de Fraga") joined knights and representatives from other cities and towns across the kingdom of Aragon. They all performed homage to the *infant* Alfons as heir to the throne of the kingdom of Aragon. According to the record of the meeting, Aragon was delimited by Ariza to the west and the Segre River to the east. In addition to representatives from Lleida and Fraga and numerous Aragonese nobles, attendees from numerous Aragonese towns subscribed the charter documenting the meeting, including Ejea (de los Caballeros), Zaragoza, Huesca, Tarazona, Calatayud, Daroca, Ariza, Aranda, Teruel, Pertusa, Ricla, Luna, Ayerbe, Almudévar, and Barbastro. Out of more than fifteen town delegations, the men from Lleida were the only attendees from a center that had traditionally fallen under Catalonia's influence.[8] Taken together, these two gatherings suggest a continuing lack of a consensus regarding the regional jurisdictional circumstances of towns along the corridor between these two rivers.

Far from clarifying these ambiguities, future dealings by the monarchy worsened the situation. Jaume was still married to Leonor of Castile when the *Cortes* of Daroca met in 1228.[9] At that time, the couple was in the process of establishing their newborn son, Alfons, as heir to the kingdom of Aragon, thereby revoking the right to Aragon held up to that point by Jaume's uncle, the *infant* Ferran. Ferran ultimately submitted to this arrangement when he participated in the homage ceremonies at this same meeting of the *Cortes* at Daroca and swore his fidelity to Jaume, Leonor, and Alfons. In making this assignment, however, the royal family did not clarify the extent of Alfons's received rights by precisely defining the limits of the kingdom. The boundary ambiguity that had persisted during the *infant* Ferran's tenure as the kingdom's overlord was allowed to survive this transition to the young Alfons.

Jaume soon ended his marriage with Leonor and took Violant of Hungary as his queen, in 1235. The offspring from this new union would complicate not only dynastic politics but also the jurisdictional statuses of these conquered territories.[10] When he revised his will in 1244, Jaume reverted to the stance originally adopted at the aforementioned *Corts* of 1214 and established once and for all, "perpetuam et inviolabilem firmitatem," that the border between Aragon and Catalonia lay along the Cinca River and not the Segre.[11] According to Zurita, Catalan attendees of the *Corts* of Barcelona had helped push the king toward this shift. For their part, the Aragonese, joined by the *infant* Alfons of Aragon, naturally felt that they had been wronged by Jaume's alteration, which robbed their kingdom of valuable territory to which it had long been entitled.[12] Contemporary evidence, however, has not surfaced to support Zurita's justification. It seems more likely that the king made the deviation from what had been agreed at Daroca in 1228 to accommodate his growing dynasty. Not long before Jaume prepared this updated will, Violant had given birth to two sons, Pere and Jaume, in 1240 and 1243 respectively, whereas the king's relations with his assertive first son to Leonor, the *infant* Alfons, had further soured. Indeed, on this same day in 1244 that the king reasserted the boundary at the Cinca River, he also promoted Pere's standing by making him heir to the county of Barcelona along with the rest of Catalonia.[13]

In an interesting development that was supportive of these same goals, Jaume then moved to alter the official documentary record of the *Cortes* of Daroca. Still on that same day in 1244, he redefined that session of the *Cortes* as a meeting of bishops, nobles, and councils "of cities of Aragon and among other men of the city of Lleida," presumably so as not to imply that Lleida was part of that kingdom.[14] In a clarifying passage that seems to have been intended chiefly for Alfons's and his contingent's consumption, Jaume emphasized that

> we did not give our son [i.e., Alfons] either the city of Lleida or the territory from the Segre to the Cinca, nor did we propose to do this, nor did we bear anything of the kind in our mind . . . although it is possible it was understood this way by some on account of too much subtlety, malice, ignorance . . . and if this was committed by us through word or deed, then we revoke and completely annul it.[15]

This added language made the king's alteration of Catalonia's boundaries unambiguous and thus served to preempt any complaints or objections by Alfons or his Aragonese partisans.

Given Lleida's prominent place in Jaume's statement, it is surprising that a subset of its citizens initially resisted this reassignment by refusing to perform homage to Pere as their new lord. The cause of this response remains an enigma. Possibly these citizens were concerned about the repercussions this shift in lordship might have on their economic relations with neighboring Aragonese territory. Or perhaps they sought to take advantage of tension within the comital-royal household to secure concessions from the king and their city's new overlord. Whatever their goals, these citizens did succeed in getting the king's attention and bringing him to the bargaining table. When Jaume confirmed this designation and Pere's inheritance in September 1246, he appointed judges to hear the dispute between the citizens of Lleida and Pere over "rendering [him, as count and lord of Catalonia from the Salses to the Cinca] the sacrament of fidelity and homage."[16] The sources, however, do not appear to indicate what, if anything, these citizens ultimately gained from this hearing.

Although this group of citizens of Lleida must have had good political reasons for resisting this profession of homage and fealty, it also must have been the case that because Lleida lay at the shared limits of two increasingly delimited and centralized sociopolitical units, Catalonia and Aragon, the city naturally felt an attraction from either side. By the mid-thirteenth century, indications are understandably mixed that Lleida's inhabitants and local sentiment were decidedly "Catalan" in terms of their cultural or political identities. Even though their historical interpretations do seem to have been shaped by anachronistic and nationalistic sentiments, Soldevila, Valls i Taberner, and Lladonosa nevertheless may have been at least partly correct in contending that Lleida was "Catalan" by language and law if by that they meant that its populations spoke early Catalan and had a legal tradition influenced more by Visigothic Law and the *Usatges de Barcelona* than by Aragonese *fueros*.[17] It is more difficult, however, to support the theory that that the cultural and ethno-political identifications of Lleida's residents informed their engagement with these conflicts over jurisdictional lines.[18]

Indeed, as we have seen earlier in this book, Lleida and its surrounding area had been conquered by a mixture of Catalonian, Aragonese, and non-Peninsular troops and settled by a similarly diverse pool of migrants who, not surprisingly, maintained aspects of their respective cultures for generations. In the decades following the conquest, Lleida's Christian residents, and the emergent institutions that had been produced by the transition to Christian rule, established connections with neighboring areas and urban centers, irrespective of whether they were on Aragonese or Catalonian territory.[19] As with Tortosa, Lleida's customary law evolved out of a new tradition initiated by Ramon Berenguer IV's settlement charter and manifested Catalonian influences such as a dependence on the *Liber Iudicorum* and the *Usatges de Barcelona*. Yet, at the same time, other enduring facets of Lleida's local culture were tied to neighboring Aragonese centers. In 1249, for example, just years after reassigning Lleida to Catalonia, Jaume issued a charter allowing the inhabitants of Aragonese Jaca to paint their houses in the color and style used in both (Aragonese) Huesca and (Catalonian) Lleida.[20]

The king might have been surprised and disappointed to learn, over the coming years, that the Cinca River, although a convenient territorial marker, remained problematic and would require further alteration. Fraga, for example, sat on the river's left, or eastern, bank and therefore technically at this point should have pertained to Catalonia. Nevertheless, it persisted insecurely as an Aragonese settlement until conflict over its inclusion within the vicariate of Lleida necessitated another jurisdictional definition. In 1281, Pere II ruled that men of Fraga who committed crimes west of the right bank of the Cinca River, where the *fueros* and peaces and truces of Aragon applied, would be judged by the *sobrejuntero* of Aragon rather than by the vicar of Lleida. Crimes committed east of the Cinca, however, would fall under that vicar's jurisdiction and be judged by the *Usatges de Barcelona* as well as Catalonia's peaces and truces.[21]

This ruling furthered the monarchy's agenda of imposing regional territorial laws such as the *Fueros de Aragón* and the *Usatges de Barcelona* onto the landscapes checkered with distinct local customary laws, via the definition of vicarial jurisdictions. Outside of their immediate districts and subject localities, Fraga's *fueros*—a mélange of customary laws drawn from Huesca and Lleida—would, from this point forward, have no authority. The king's judgment made little headway, however, in resolving definitively Fraga's dilemma of being an ostensibly Aragonese town within Catalonia's legal limits. This continuing ambiguity may explain why Fraga's status as an Aragonese center could again be challenged in the 1360s, when Pere III "the Ceremonious" entertained an inquiry over whether "Fraga and its *tenentia* are within the limits of Catalonia."[22] Pere III again upheld Fraga's Aragonese status in 1379 when he ruled that "the town of Fraga is governed according to the *Fueros de Aragón* and not according to the *Constitucions de Catalunya*." Such determined intervention did not prevent the issue from surfacing yet again, a century later, at the *Cortes* of 1460.[23]

Further north, the county of Ribagorza found itself in a similar, albeit less embroiled, conundrum. Although an Aragonese territory according to its legal tradition, Ribagorza found itself separated from the kingdom of Aragon by the course of the Cinca River.[24] Despite being granted the *Fueros de Aragón*, Ribagorza officially stood under Catalonian jurisdiction until its inhabitants complained to Pere II about the situation in 1284. The issue nevertheless remained unresolved until stakeholders brought it to the attention of Jaume II (r. 1291–1327) at the *Cortes* of 1300 and 1305. Over the next two decades, as further claims were voiced by the justice of Aragon, this king rendered a series of decisions that supported Ribagorza's designation as Aragonese. He upheld the claim that the county should fall under direct Aragonese jurisdiction despite lying within the legal boundaries of the Catalonian vicariate of Pallars.[25] The establishment of diocesan boundaries and ecclesiastical jurisdictional rights was also contentious during this extended period of consolidation but was not colored by sectarian territorial boundaries. Just as vacillations over Fraga's status had not impacted its place within the diocese of Lleida, so too the archdeaconate of Ribagorza, along with that of Benasque, remained under the authority of the bishop of Lleida.[26]

The Right Bank of the Ebro River

Ramon Berenguer IV's ambiguous incorporation of the *taifas* of Tortosa and Lleida as frontier zones known as *marcae* left for future generations the equally complex task of determining the territorial division of the lower Ebro valley and northern Valencia, especially along the Terra Alta and Ribera d'Ebre. In contrast to the aforementioned ambiguities regarding the division between Aragon and Catalonia along the lower Cinca and Segre valleys, Aragonese populations had comparatively stronger claims to territory beyond the Ebro's right bank. These assertions were based on papally confirmed rights to conquest received by the Aragonese monarchy during its independent period before the union with Barcelona as well as on that monarchy's own temporary territorial gains. As we observed in part I, Alfonso I of Aragon had briefly conquered some of these claimed lands in the 1130s before losing them to the Muslim counterattack.[27]

Ramon Berenguer IV had neither addressed the issue of Aragonese claims to the lower Ebro nor issued settlement charters to indicate where he imagined the boundary might lie. The details of a number of settlement projects in the area sponsored by Alfons were supportive of Aragonese influence yet did not clearly indicate that he and his advisors were aware or advocates of Aragonese claims to the right bank of the lower Ebro. He issued the *fueros* of Zaragoza to the communities of Paüls and Horta in the mid-1160s just as he was preparing campaigns that relied heavily on military forces based in Aragon.[28] Tellingly, in his charter to Horta de Sant Joan, Alfons indicated that the castle and its limits pertained to him through his rights to the kingdom of Aragon.[29] Horta's charter furthermore manifests similarities to the settlement charter granted by Ramon Berenguer IV to Aragonese Alcañiz several years earlier, in 1157.[30] Modeling aspects of Horta's settlement project on what had been recently given to a locality positioned closer to the Aragonese heartlands could have been a strategy to attract Aragonese migrants to Horta via Alcañiz or from other centers within Aragon. Indeed, given his reliance on Aragonese forces at this time, the count-king (and his advisors) may have viewed Aragonese migration into this zone as an effective means to accelerate its consolidation, rendering it more defensible as well as a better staging point for offensive campaigning. There is no evidence, however, to suggest that the Crown intended for these arrangements to establish enduring jurisdictional entitlements to the lower Ebro valley.

Subsequent seigniorial population charters deviated from these comital-royal measures by implanting non-Aragonese foral traditions in the zone. These actions complicated the status of the Ebro River as the shared boundary line between Catalonia and Aragon. As we noted earlier in chapter 7, certain Templar settlement projects in this zone manifested faint connections with Lleida's customary legal tradition. After the Templars acquired lordship over Horta, they imposed new settlement conditions on any existing inhabitants and all future migrants to the town in 1192.[31] Although the order did not openly acknowledge any dependency on Lleida and the charter did not sufficiently detail Horta's customs for us to be able to recognize a clear linkage to Lleida's local law, the settlement terms did stipulate that Horta's residents were to use weights and measures from Lleida to pay the seigniorial levies. Horta's customs soon became a recognized independent collection, and this lack of a connection to any influential Aragonese collections alone problematized any effort to demonstrate Aragon's entitlement to the area based on foral traditions. Within two months of Horta's charter, the populators of Gandesa, "within the district of Miravet," were subjected to the authority of the Templar houses of Gardeny and Corbins, both near Lleida, yet granted customs "just as the populators of Horta have."[32]

There are no indications that the Templars were interested in questioning the identification of the Ebro as a boundary between Catalonia and Aragon. Rather, it is likely that their engagement with customary legal issues was chiefly targeted at promoting the settlement of their domains and facilitating their seigniorial control over these domains. Issuing Horta and Gandesa the same sets of local laws and privileges, even though these settlements came to be governed by separate Templar *comandas* (Horta and Miravet, respectively), must have furthered these same objectives. The Templar Order did not apply this same family of customary laws to all of its settlements in the area but instead seems to have utilized different traditions to promote collaboration and networking between otherwise separate domains. The town of Camposines, for example, received a population charter from the Templars in 1209 that established a link with the castral domains of Ascó, some ten kilometers to the north. In addition to being subjected to Ascó's customary laws, Camposines's residents had to pay their annual seigniorial levy to the castle of Ascó using its own proprietary system of measures.[33] Furthermore, the customs of the Templar domain of Miravet, codified in 1319, exhibit clear influences from the *Usatges de Barcelona*.[34] The Templars were unusual in this tendency to innovate with the foral traditions they applied to their settlement projects. Although most other lords pursuing settlement projects within the Terra Alta and Ribera d'Ebre at this time preferred to apply well-known collections that had developed under the oversight of other authorities, they did mimic the Templar Order in their preference for Catalonia-derived bodies of customary law. The barony of Flix, for example, utilized the customs of Tortosa, and the barony of Castellvell/Entença applied both the *Usatges de Barcelona* and *Constitucions de Catalunya*.[35]

As with conflicts over the position of the border along the Segre and Cinca Rivers, the seeds for the jurisdictional disputes over the territory past the right bank of the lower Ebro were planted early on but did not fully develop until the mid-thirteenth century. Although Jaume's apportioning of the realms among his heirs did play a major role in worsening these conflicts, the successful conquest of Valencia also intensified the situation by raising the stakes through the addition of vast new territories. Already by the early 1230s, an intensive push to settle northern Valencia by distinct seigniorial agents within Catalonia and Aragon had disseminated a range of foral traditions across the region. Although the *fueros* of Zaragoza were, by far, the most widespread, being applied to more than thirty settlements, the customs of Lleida also grew influential as they were granted to nearly ten centers. The customs of Tortosa and Barcelona were each only issued to one settlement: San Lucas de Ulldecona (21 Mar. 1274) and Moncófar (1 Jan. 1255), respectively.[36] By the early 1240s, Jaume had begun promulgating the primitive customs of Valencia that were increasingly applied to settlement projects and soon presented as the new universal law of the kingdom. Catalonian and Aragonese lords with Valencian domains resisted pressure to adopt these new legal norms, however, and instead persisted in using their own foral traditions for existing as well as new settlements throughout the later thirteenth and fourteenth centuries.[37]

Queen Violant gave birth to a third son, Ferran, in 1245, and this addition to the dynasty fomented a series of redistributions that brought new jurisdictional inconsistencies to light. Jaume prepared another new will in 1248, which detailed the boundaries between Catalonia, Aragon, and Valencia as it divided the realms among his sons.[38] Pere received Catalonia and Mallorca, and Jaume obtained the kingdom of Valencia, which left young Ferran with Rosselló, Montpellier, and Cerdanya. This will determined that Catalonia's borders with Valencia and Aragon would follow Tortosa's historic district from the coast along the Ulldecona River, pass along the Traseras to Miravet, and then follow the course of the Ebro to Mequinenza and the junction with the Cinca.[39]

Not surprisingly, Catalonian and Aragonese contingents (along with their developing regional administrations) found different aspects of this new will to be objectionable. Among Catalonia's stakeholders, the lords of the lower Ebro valley were naturally the most affected by the king's redefinition. Because the will assigned to Aragon territory between the Algars and Ebro Rivers, it severed the otherwise contiguous Templar lordships of Ascó, Horta, and Miravet, as well as the lay baronies of Flix and Entença, thereby eroding lands many had long presumed fell within Catalonia's provisional limits.[40] Although implicated groups must also have harbored strong feelings about the division along the Ulldecona River, which curtailed the southward extension of Tortosa's district, said to have extended as far as Benifassà as late as 1208, we lack evidence of any objections concerning this sector of the imposed boundary.[41]

For Aragonese stakeholders and their titular overlord, the *infant* Alfons, this distribution had greater negative effects on their interests than did Valencia's established limits. By granting the kingdom of Valencia to the *infant* Jaume, the king's will cut Aragon off from avenues of further interaction with and expansion into Muslim-ruled territory that had helped fuel its development over the past two centuries. In the words of Ángels Masià de Ros, the division threatened to landlock Aragon, thus turning it into "a new Navarre."[42] Thirteenth-century Aragonese society must have been unimaginable to its nobility and other elites without its frontier with Islam. According to Zurita, deteriorating relations between the king and the *infant* Alfons, backed by his Aragonese nobles, culminated in his temporary disinheritance.[43]

The premature death of Jaume's youngest son, Ferran, necessitated yet another reallocation in 1251. Although this new arrangement did not deviate from the boundaries proposed in 1248, it nevertheless exacerbated the king's already enflamed relations with his eldest son, Alfons. The *infant* Jaume obtained Ferran's full entitlement to Rosselló, Montpellier, and Cerdanya, whereas the others' shares were left unchanged.[44] Two years later, however, King Jaume made a surprising reversal by transferring entitlement to the kingdom of Valencia from the young Jaume to Alfons.[45] Just days later, Alfons's confirmation of the rights of his half-brothers, solidifying his reception of the kingdom, reestablished Catalonia's boundaries as running from the sea along the limits of Tortosa and the course of the Ebro up to the Cinca River.[46] In 1257, Jaume ordered the citizens of Valencia to recognize Alfons as heir in place of the *infant* Jaume. At the same time, he required Jaume to absolve the Valencians of their oath of fidelity to him that they had performed when he had been heir to their kingdom.[47]

Alfons's demise in 1260, however, necessitated yet another division, effected in 1262, which for the first time united the monarchy's Peninsular territories under one heir. Jaume's second son, Pere, received the territorial Aragon, Valencia, and Catalonia. Jaume was left with the Balearic Islands, Conflent, Cerdanya, Roussillon, and Montpellier.[48] In September, the king ordered the inhabitants of the lands obtained by *Infant* Jaume to recognize him as heir.[49] In November, he related this new division to the residents of Valencia and required them to render homage to Pere.[50] King Jaume reconfirmed this same division in 1270 without notable alterations.[51] He maintained the grouping yet again, in 1275, when he decreed that Pere's heir, Alfons, would inherit Aragon, Valencia, and Catalonia in the event that Pere predeceased him.[52]

This unification of Catalonia and Aragon under one heir had the potential to heighten tension over the selection of the lower Ebro as a boundary marker. As the new king, Pere II supported attempts by Aragonese officials to impose upon the largely independent lords of the Terra Alta and Ribera d'Ebre: most importantly, the lay baronies of Flix and Entença and the Templar/Hospitaller lordships of Horta, Miravet, and Ascó.[53] Although Pere's stance on the boundary issue remains unclear from the extant evidence, the unification appears to have facilitated the implementation of Aragonese administrative claims. The king may have supported the enlargement of Aragon's territories at Catalonia's expense. On the other hand, there are signs that administrative development had been moving in this direction even before Pere assumed the throne. Aragonese interests in asserting its jurisdictional and taxation rights over the Ebro's right bank had already accelerated with the consolidation of the administrative units of the *juntas* around 1260.[54]

These trends culminated in Pere's announcement, in March 1278, of Aragon's rights to even greater limits than had been suggested by Jaume's numerous divisions. He claimed that the limits of Zaragoza's *junta* ran along the right bank of the Ebro past Tortosa to the sea and then along the Ulldecona River and the upper boundary of Morella's district.[55] Despite this proclamation, Zaragoza's *sobrejuntero* nevertheless appears to have restricted his claims to the disputed territory assigned to Aragon in Jaume's royal divisions, thus respecting the established limits of Tortosa's district.

It is possible that Pere and his advisors tacitly supported Aragon's claims to the zone not necessarily because they believed in the validity of the underlying argument but because the jurisdictional shift could serve as a mechanism for reducing the autonomy of the powerful seigniorial entities within the affected territories. At the same time, Pere's legal experts must have understood the traditional legal principle that jurisdictional rights hinged on whatever law the lands in question had been granted when settled. They would have anticipated, and would soon learn by experience, that revoking legally obtained and long-ingrained administrative entitlements was no simple matter. Accordingly, in 1278, after the royal justice of Morella had sought to compel the men of Gandesa and other inhabitants of the Templar *batllia* of Miravet as well as those of the Templar *comanda* of Horta to use the *fueros* of Aragon and swear fidelity to him, Pere warned him to do so only if it agreed with the customs the inhabitants had been granted when settled there. The fact that these populations had not been granted Aragonese *fueros* when established by the Templars a century or so earlier made it extremely difficult for these Aragonese agents to impose their new regulations on them. In this case, Pere warned the justice of Morella that he would have to present written evidence supporting his case in court before he could resume his attempts to impose these administrative demands.[56]

In future years, Pere would seek to utilize this same *sobrejuntero* position to penetrate the tight control the Templars had developed over these lands since the late twelfth century. Their offensive concentrated on both taxation and jurisdictional prerogatives. In 1280, for example, Pere collaborated with the *sobrejuntero* in an effort to collect a levy known as the *quinta* to be paid on mules within the districts of Miravet and Ascó.[57] They developed even more of a determined focus on eroding the order's jurisdictional autonomy. Within a short time, with ample royal support, the *sobrejuntero* had installed local royal officials to serve as parallel *sobrejunteros* in localities within the region. Pere encouraged his officials to seek pretenses for intervening to adjudicate even minor offenses or crimes involving the Templar lords. In June 1282, the king ordered the lieutenant of the *sobrejuntero* of Horta to detain a Muslim of Ascó who had violently attacked a Templar brother.[58] Surprisingly, rather than resisting this mandate in order to manage the situation internally, the Templars cooperated fully with the royal investigation and permitted the brother's complaint to be handled by royal officials. It is possible that, at this point, the order still felt sufficiently secure and did not view these overtures by the Crown as a threat to its traditional jurisdictional prerogatives. The following year, Pere continued this trend of intervention when he commanded the *sobrejunteros* of Zaragoza and Horta to investigate a case of some dead Muslims discovered in Miravet.[59] Here again, no sign of any effort by the order to block this intrusion by royal administration has surfaced in the extant documentation.

These examples of cooperation by this Templar *comanda* were by no means exceptional. Indeed, neighboring *comandes* were similarly submitting to pressure from Pere and his officials. A month after the attack on the Templar brother, for example, in July 1282, Pere informed the nearby Templar lordship of Ascó that the *sobrejuntero* of Zaragoza had appointed the Muslim *alcaydus* of Tortosa to investigate and judge the dispute that Ascó's commander had lodged against a Muslim named Aliono Ferrer. On this occasion, Pere was especially direct and warned the Templar official not to take justice into his own hands.[60] Later that same summer, at the end of August, likely in response to pressure by royal officials, the master of the Templar Order, with the full consent of the commander of Ascó and other brothers of the *comanda*, confirmed the privileges originally granted by Ramon Berenguer IV and others to the Christians and Muslims constituting the *universitas* of Ascó. These residents also gained the right to appeal seigniorial cases before the royal curia of Zaragoza so long as they first notified the Templar lords.[61] Subsequent to this ruling, appeals from these localities were indeed heard by the curia of Zaragoza, with royal oversight.[62]

On the whole, inhabitants of the region appear to have benefited from this new juridical climate. Evidence suggests that they took advantage of this heightened access to royal governance in order to subvert the ingrained seigniorial judicial and administrative monopolization. In 1293, for example, the *universitas* of Ascó warned its lord, the Templar commander of Ascó, that if he continued to violate its privileges and ignore its grievances, the citizens would appeal to the curia of Zaragoza for intervention.[63] On the other hand, although they clearly enjoyed this protections and enhanced maneuverability, these Templar tenants made it clear that they did not support the campaign to subjugate their region to Aragonese jurisdiction that would run counter to their foral traditions. Indeed, in 1290, the men of Ascó and Miravet lodged a complaint with the *sobrejuntero* of Zaragoza that they should not form part of the *junta* of Alcañíz or any other Aragonese *junta* because they had been settled by the customs of Lleida, did not use the *fueros* of Aragon, and "are of Catalonia."[64] In spite of such vocal opposition, the *sobrejuntero* nevertheless continued his campaign to subjugate these lands to Aragonese jurisdiction. In 1308, in response to complaints lodged by the men of Gandesa, Jaume II ordered the *sobrejuntero* of Zaragoza to desist in his attempts to force them to submit to his *junta*'s administration. At the same time, the king formally confirmed their established use of the customary laws of Lleida and mandated that his officials respect these traditional practices.[65]

It is less evident that these residents supported their Templar lords' opposition to the taxation demanded by royal administrators. They may well have felt ambivalent because of the likelihood that any taxes denied to royal administrators would instead by collected by their lords in some form or another. For their part, the Templars of the region naturally rejected the Crown's taxation attempts as illegitimate. They deemed it to be a violation of their basic privileges, regardless of whether their lordships were deemed as falling under Catalonian or Aragonese oversight. In 1306, for example, Berenguer de Sant Just, commander of Miravet and Torres de Segre, issued a protest with the royal bailiff of Tortosa, who had been appointed as inquisitor by the king. He alleged that the *batllia* of Miravet had never been subject to the royal levy of the *cena* in either Catalonia or Aragon and had always enjoyed immunity.[66]

By the early fourteenth century, the lords and inhabitants of the Templar *comandes* of the Terra Alta and Ribera d'Ebre appear to have succeeded in thwarting any shift to Aragonese jurisdiction. Based as they were on Alfonso's conquests and a small number of twelfth-century settlement grants that had imposed Aragonese *fueros*, Aragonese claims to these lands had fallen short when compared with so many decades of continuous use of Catalonian customary laws. Although other seigniorial entities with a presence within these contested lands followed a similar trajectory, in some cases a positive outcome took more time to materialize. The lay baronies of Flix and

Entença, for instance, established their entitlement to adhere to Catalonia by the late thirteenth or early fourteenth century, even though their domains extended past the Ebro's right bank.[67] The lordships of Miravet, Ascó, and Horta, however, which fell under Hospitaller control upon the dissolution of the Templars, did not decisively realize their Catalonian designation until the second half of the fourteenth century.[68] In due course, this sector of the boundary between Catalonia and Aragon came to be recognized as following the course of the Algars River rather than that of the Ebro. Even though Aragonese administrators had failed in their attempts to shift this border with Catalonia to a further marker, their efforts did have lasting benefits for the monarchy in facilitating its attempts to compromise the jurisdictional autonomy of some of the most important lordships in the region.

Reclaiming Royal Administration over the Consolidated Landscape

Such episodes serve as an indication of how the monarchy's growing administrative capabilities and corresponding ambition to build its centralized authority would make the autonomy many lords of the Ebro and Segre valleys had developed in the postconquest environment considerably harder to sustain. Whether they fell under Catalonian or Aragonese jurisdiction, lords had begun to acknowledge reluctantly that, in this developing climate, their subjects would enjoy some degree of access to royal justice and, accordingly, that the monarchy's officials would intrude in their lordships' affairs. Certain lords nevertheless preserved significant administrative prerogatives that the monarchy was unable to revoke. Most notably, even though Jaume I had asserted the exclusive royal right to justice over capital crimes (*merum imperium*) within the kingdoms of Valencia and Aragon in the mid-thirteenth century, the Templar *comandas* of the Ebro valley and certain lay barons, such as the Montcadas of the barony of Aitona in the Baix Segre, all retained the competency to judge civil as well as capital cases (*merum et mixtum imperium*).[69] Jaume II went so far as to appeal to Boniface VIII for the right to *merum imperium* within the ecclesiastical lordships of his realms in 1297, but his request was flatly denied by the pope. The Templars managed to retain these judicial rights until their dissolution in the fourteenth century.[70] Such discrepancies between royal policy and local practice would continue to persist despite sporadic strong opposition from the monarchy.

Alongside efforts to impose administrative rights, the monarchy simultaneously engaged in assuming direct control over a subset of these autonomous domains, many of which had once pertained to the royal patrimony but had been alienated by earlier monarchs. In this final section of this chapter, we will examine both how the monarchy pursued these lands and how certain lords maneuvered, sometimes successfully, to oppose this agenda.

Tortosa and the Lower Ebro River Valley

Tortosa serves as a good example of the monarchy's efforts to change local conditions in order to generate greater income and be consistent with circumstances elsewhere in the realm. From the mid-thirteenth century, the Crown had manifested a clear interest in finally asserting certain long-established prerogatives in the alienated royal lordship of Tortosa, such as imposing bailiffs and other officials, demanding exclusive royal rights of jurisdiction and taxation over Muslims and Jews, and asserting rights to collect various royal levies.[71] Through an arrangement in 1247 with the Templars, Jaume had raised his share of the revenues of Tortosa to more than one-third.[72] The agreement, however, explicitly denied the king a jurisdictional presence in the city. While the Templars conceded to Jaume the right to maintain a bailiff there who would collect the Crown's incomes, they made it clear that this official would have no jurisdictional or coercive powers. Some of the incomes and rights pertaining to the king and queen in 1247 were identical to those itemized in the memorials of 1182 and 1184 that we discussed earlier, in chapter 5. These included the same half of fishing and hunting rights in Tortosa when the king and queen were present, which raises the possibility that they had never been lost. Any judicial matter involving the king's property would be handled by the Templar bailiff, who would render to the king's agent any derived judicial awards or penalties.[73]

Royal designs on the city became more apparent, and more problematic for the seigniorial regime, around 1271. The Templars lodged a complaint concerning moves the king had made to secure not only additional rents and rights in the city but also increased jurisdictional capacities.[74] The king had argued that he should have the right to maintain a royal bailiff there (with full rights, rather than the limited ones outlined in the agreement of 1247) and maintain a presence in the *zuda*. Neither co-lord Ramon de Montcada nor one of his delegates, moreover, was to take up residence in the *zuda* whenever the royal bailiff was absent. Tortosa's castle was the seat of the seigniorial regime and its court: the imposition of a royal administrator there represented a significant threat to seigniorial authority. The king also asserted his rights over aspects of Tortosa's population and local economy previously enjoyed by the co-lords, particularly concerning religious minorities. He asserted that all

Jews and Muslims pertained to him, a concept that was gradually developing into standard royal policy, and warned against the lords taxing the Jews and Muslims of the city beyond the accustomed two hundred *solidi*. The Templars protested these royal actions, defending their rights and those of the Montcadas in the city and rejecting Jaume's claims as illegitimate novelties.[75]

Since their accession to jurisdictional lordship in the late twelfth century, the Templars had diligently worked to fortify their dominance over Tortosa, grappling at times with other power holders in the city and region. By the mid-thirteenth century, they had established their primacy and did not experience significant opposition from other lords. Most notably, the order had subjugated the Montcadas by the turn of the thirteenth century, establishing them as vassals for the rights they held within Tortosa. Sources have not survived to inform us of the institution of this vassalage, but we do know that the Montcadas, at times, resisted this designation. On several occasions, the Templars chastised their co-lord vassals for exercising undue independence and encroaching on the order's prerogatives as overlord, particularly in their relations with the *universitas* of citizens.[76] On the other hand, the Montcada lords are known to have assumed a leadership role within the lordship on occasion. In 1256, for example, Guillem I de Montcada independently recognized that, due to an earlier convention involving his family, the Templars, the king, and traders from Valencia, Zaragoza's merchants were perpetually exempt from the *lleuda* and *pedatge* levies on the goods they trafficked within Tortosa. They instead would pay, directly to the co-lords' bailiff, a sixtieth part of the value of their goods. Guillem appears to have directed his animated pledge to defend Zaragoza's right to enjoy this privilege at the Templar Order and the Crown, neither of which had representatives subscribe the enactment.[77]

Despite such occasional moments of empowerment, overall the seigniorial prerogatives enjoyed by the Montcadas since the first decades following the conquest were eroding under pressure from multiple sources by the 1290s. In November 1293, another unique and symbolic privilege held by the Montcadas throughout their time as jurisdictional lords in Tortosa was under threat by the *universitas*. The Montcadas had appointed the vicars of Tortosa since the late twelfth century. Yet, despite reception of the vicar's oath of office by the noble or his bailiff, the family had not noticeably exercised controls or undue influence over the office. The municipal government (*Paeria*) conducted many of its duties in tandem with the vicar. At this point in its development, the *universitas* sought to end the disjunction of an informally defined vicar cooperating with elements of the recently institutionalized municipal administration. Montcada was not resistant to the concept of reestablishing the "vicar in the vicariate of Tortosa." Accordingly, the *universitas* took full responsibility from the noble over the exercise of justice using this reformulated vicariate. It furthermore pledged that the powers of the *Paeria* would not be undercut by the change.[78]

Although the Montcadas had retained only a minority one-third share of the *zuda* since the late twelfth century, they exercised full control over the castle by holding the Templars' two-third share in fief from the order. This arrangement had served the co-lords for many years. On 17 January 1293, however, the Templars exercised their right to assume control of the fortification. The incident is curious and illustrates how delegates could struggle with drastic administrative shifts. Montcada's knight, Guillem de Perexens, was manning the *zuda* for the noble when a notary and the Templar commander of Tortosa arrived with letters from the master of the Templars in Aragon and Catalonia and Guillem de Montcada himself ordering Perexens to submit to the demand and surrender the castle. The order had given the knight the required ten days' notice of the revocation of the fief, and full compliance was now past due, the letters of the commander and noble agreed, for compliance. Even though Guillem de Montcada did not dispute the Temple's right to the *zuda*, Guillem de Perexens was nevertheless reluctant to comply with these commands. Despite the presentation of these authorized letters as well as a further letter from Montcada proffered by the notary and commander, Perexens argued that he did not feel sufficiently authorized or prepared to relinquish his post.[79] Soon, however, the order secured control of the castle. This radical deviation from decades of co-lordship may have been preparatory for the order's transfer of its jurisdictional rights within the city to the Crown the following year.

Leading up to Tortosa's acquisition, the monarchy had been successful in acquiring seigniorial strongholds in the town's vicinity. In 1280, for instance, Pere II acquired the castle and town of Amposta from the Hospitallers in exchange for the castles and towns of Gallur in Aragon and Onda in Valencia. The associated charter declares that the king had been planning the transfer for some time and that it had been designed for the "comfort" and "utility" of the Hospitallers.[80] It is possible that this was in reference to the disputes that had flared up between Amposta and the seigniorial regime of Tortosa in the late 1270s that the Crown had intervened to manage.[81] Royal lordship over Amposta was defined by a settlement charter issued by Pere II in 1282. Alfons II (r. 1285–91) issued an expanded charter to the town in 1286.[82] Despite their loss of jurisdictional lordship in the region, the Hospitallers retained all their churches in Amposta along with all rights to tithes and first fruits from their lands within the diocese of Tortosa. The frequent conflicts between the co-lords of Tortosa, Templars and Montcadas, and the citizens' collective (*universitas*) throughout the thirteenth century had made Amposta a continued source of concern and considerably less profitable than the lords likely hoped.[83] The troubled history of this lordship likely encouraged the order to consider an exchange with the monarchy for seigniorial rights elsewhere.

In keeping with the expansion of royal administration over the course of the thirteenth century, intervention by the monarchy had increased within spaces such as Tortosa despite its lack of rights of direct lordship.[84] Since its installation in 1247, the Crown's office of bailiff there continued to serve as an important channel for royal engagement with its fiscal interests within Tortosa and the wider region.[85] This bailiff not only serviced the monarchy's properties within the center, but also ensured that it received its share of its seigniorial entitlements.[86] In 1276, for instance, Pere II ordered Tortosa's Templar commander to give the monarchy's share of the incomes from the city's municipal court to his bailiff.[87] The king even used this bailiff to pay off loans that he owed to Tortosa's co-lords, such as the thirty-thousand *solidi* debt he arranged to repay Ramon de Montcada from the monarchy's incomes from Tortosa in 1278.[88] Other officers also played a role. Documents from the following years record the increasing presence of royal officials, such as the porter who visited Tortosa numerous times in 1290 to collect taxes demanded by the Crown.[89] Not surprisingly, these efforts often provoked tenacious resistance from the residents. The *universitas* frequently resisted the collection of the *bovatge* and the *lleuda*, among other obligations demanded by the Crown.[90]

When the monarchs sought to override the seigniorial regime's administration in order to promote royal prerogatives or interests, they often reached out to local officials or inhabitants directly via correspondence. For example, by ordering the citizens of Tortosa and other Templar subjects in "towns" and "places" under the order's lordship to perform homage to the master of the Templars in Aragon and Catalonia as their "lord" in 1273, Jaume asserted his capacity as Catalonia's overlord to manage seigniorial authority.[91] Jaume also intruded to confirm the customs and privileges of the city that were detrimental to the prerogatives of the seigniorial regime.[92] Pere II maintained this effort to circumvent Templar-Montcada authority and establish the precedent of royal approval into Tortosa's local environment by confirming civilian customary laws and exemptions that conflicted with seigniorial objectives and revenues.[93] He also directly confronted the co-lords on numerous occasions to warn them not to infringe on his rights over Tortosa's inhabitants, as defined by the *Usatges de Barcelona*.[94]

Although Jaume's son, Pere II, and first grandson, Alfons II, continued this pursuit of expanded administrative rights in and around Tortosa, the most strategic and effective advocate proved to be his other grandson, Jaume II.[95] With little likelihood of future Catalano-Aragonese acquisition of Andalusi territory, Jaume II and his administrators attempted to recuperate territorial concessions and reduce the privileges of major beneficiaries of the policies of his predecessors. Thanks to the Crown's recuperation of Amposta, new settlement projects, and significant gains within Tortosa, Jaume II came to power in 1291 with a firm, established foothold in the Ebro region.[96] Resumption of direct lordship over Tortosa would earn the young king full control over the Ebro delta, which had grown into a vital hub for Peninsular and Mediterranean mercantilism.[97]

Although the acquisition of Tortosa certainly suited this later thirteenth-century royal agenda, it is unclear whether Jaume II first brought up the issue of the transfer. Sources do not confirm whether the monarchy understood the Templar lordship over Tortosa to be in crisis and sought to use this state of affairs to its advantage in realizing its desires for control in the lower Ebro region.[98] After decades of resistance by the civilians to seigniorial authority, the order was now willing to alienate its jurisdictional responsibilities back to the Crown. In September 1294, Templar representatives officially exchanged the order's share of jurisdiction in Tortosa for the northern Valencian castles and towns of Penyíscola, Ares, and Coves de Vinromà.[99] The Templars took care to ensure that their jurisdictional control over these new holdings would be more ironclad than it had been within Tortosa. Accordingly, within a few years of the exchange, the order demanded royal confirmation of its right to exercise undiluted *merum et mixtum imperium* within these domains.[100] Despite their exodus from jurisdictional lordship, the Templars nevertheless maintained a presence in Tortosa and continued to operate as prominent landlords under royal administration.[101]

Once the exit of the Templars from Tortosa had been confirmed, the assumption of the remaining minority share by the Montcadas was all but assured. Jaume II was probably not interested in managing a situation of co-lordship, nor is it likely the Montcadas would have wanted to cling to their rights in Tortosa, had this been a possibility. Shortly after the Templars executed their transaction, Guillem II de Montcada exchanged his rights to Tortosa and its *zuda* to the monarchy for the Aragonese castles and towns of Ballobar and Zaidín.[102] Jaume II desired to reestablish straightforward royal dominion over fiscal administration as well, negotiating the purchase or renunciation of other interests in Tortosa. In 1296, for example, the king acquired the share of Tortosa's *lleuda* held by the citizens of Narbonne since the comital *repartiment*, thus erasing another facet of Tortosa's legacy of conquest.[103]

The monarchy sought to establish good relations with the city's elites and *universitas*, in sharp contrast with the activity of Tortosa's co-lords over the past decades. The royal treasury had already discovered the possibilities offered by elite urbanites in helping to finance the monarchy's aspirations.[104] Indeed, Tortosa would play an important role in the Mediterranean policies of Jaume II and his successors. In particular, its status as a breadbasket for the kingdom made controlling the town all the more advantageous for the Crown.[105] The monarchy had asserted control over exports of grain and other commodities from Tortosa and its surrounding area over the latter half of the thirteenth century, well before its assumption of lordship over the city.[106]

The year after the exchange, Jaume II reaffirmed Tortosa's civilian privileges and ensured its citizens that the homage they owed to him would not violate their customary laws.[107] Around the same time, he granted Tortosa the right to hold an annual festival in honor of Sant Bertomeu for fifteen consecutive days in perpetuity and confirmed and expanded the city's rights to hold a periodic market.[108] He also sought to stimulate Tortosa's sea commerce by awarding it the same exemptions that would benefit Barcelona. A year after assuming lordship, Jaume II granted franchises to the merchants of both cities in the kingdom of Sicily.[109] Despite this auspicious start, not surprisingly, the shift to royal lordship did not make Tortosa's citizens any less resistant to taxation, and they continued to exploit every pretext available to them to evade these alleged obligations. The monarchy, for example, continued to struggle to collect the *bovatge*. A year after the king rejected the citizens' claim of exemption in 1298, the royal porter complained that the residents had blockaded the city's bridge in order to prevent his attempts to collect the tax.[110]

The Crown's assumption of Tortosa stimulated its efforts to develop settlement within the lower Ebro area. Just months after finalizing the exchange with the city's former co-lords, Jaume II authorized his newly invested bailiff of Tortosa to populate nearby Font del Perelló.[111] Some years later, he issued a charter to Galera, also in Tortosa's vicinity.[112] Tortosa's development into a center of royal governance for the region facilitated, but did not guarantee the success of, efforts to impose on seigniorial domains in its vicinity. In 1304, for example, the king ordered his officers to collect the *herbatge* from lands in the district of Tortosa. The Templar commander of Tortosa, however, successfully challenged the mandate by demonstrating to the vicar of Tortosa and the Ribera d'Ebre that his order had received their lands from the king himself as exempt allods.[113] Preoccupied as he was with other matters throughout the kingdom, Jaume II's involvement in the Ebro delta zone could not have been as attentive as the resident lords he had displaced, in spite of the presence of dedicated royal officials. He progressively enfeoffed his holdings within the town over the duration of his reign. This style of rulership fostered the growth of municipal organizations and the further empowerment of local magnates as they expanded to fill the administrative vacuum within the city.[114]

The County of Urgell

The Crown's dogged and painstaking, yet ultimately successful effort to assert its dominance over the independent county of Urgell over the course of the thirteenth century was heavily conditioned by the institutional groundwork and patterns of interaction that we have already detailed in previous chapters.[115] Jaume I's challenges in managing and profiting from the conflict between the rival claimants to Urgell, the viscounts of Cabrera-Àger and the last remnants of the Ermengol dynasty, only grew more difficult during his own tumultuous minority following his father's sudden death at Muret in 1213. As we started to witness in chapter 6, since Ermengol VIII's demise, Viscount Guerau IV de Cabrera had alleged that his rights to the county trumped those of Ermengol's only child, Aurembiaix, even though his were indirect, primarily because he was male. Guerau's mother, Marquesa, was a daughter of Ermengol VII, making him a nephew of Ermengol VIII and Aurembiaix's cousin.[116] Aurembiaix was the only other serious claimant to the county. She was the daughter and sole heir of Ermengol VIII and Elvira Nuñez de Lara, who had since remarried with one of Jaume's most important supporters and creditors, Guillem IV de Cervera, lord of Juneda and Castelldans.[117] After Aurembiaix retired to Castile following her father's death in 1209, she eventually fulfilled her marriage arrangement to Álvaro Fernández de Castro. In the meantime, Viscount Guerau capitalized on both her absence and the financial and political instability of Jaume's minority by occupying the county of Urgell by force and claiming the title of count.[118] Although Elvira and Guillem de Cervera both remained in Catalonia, and despite their designated roles as Aurembiaix's protectors, they do not appear to have intervened at all to resist Guerau's actions. Elvira herself may have doubted that Aurembiaix would return to Catalonia, for when she issued her will in 1220, she notably assigned Aurembiaix properties in Galicia and Castile but nothing in Catalonia or Aragon.[119]

Despite Aurembiaix's absence, Jaume's regent, Count Sanç of Rosselló-Cerdanya and various supporters nevertheless fought for the young king and countess against this usurpation. Most notable among these supporters were the seneschal Guillem Ramon II de Montcada, Ramon II de Montcada, Guillem IV de Cervera, and the men of Balaguer, Linyola, and Agramunt, who remained loyal to the Ermengol line. Eventually, after Urgell's castles and towns had suffered much damage in the scantly documented engagement, Guerau de Cabrera agreed to attend a meeting of the general court convoked at the nine-year-old king's residence at Monzón in 1217.[120] Among the assembled barons, prelates, and municipal delegates, Guerau and Jaume traded oaths that sought to stabilize the conflicts regarding Urgell, once and for all. The agreement tried to address and move beyond past wrongs and prevent future conflicts by making detailed stipulations regarding all of the possible outcomes. Both sides released all claims against one another for any damage they had caused during their fighting. Guerau agreed to commit to the king possession of Agramunt, Balaguer, Linyola, and Albesa, among other unnamed "castles, towns, and possessions."

With Jaume's control over the parts of county that Guerau had captured thus secured, the men turned to plotting out the future of the county and managing Aurembiaix's competing claim, despite her continued absence. In this case, the planning was clearly weighted in favor of the viscount, presumably because he was present and still possessed the means to reinitiate conflict to the detriment of Jaume and his supporters. Guerau committed to transmit to Jaume two large sums within the coming two years: twenty-four thousand *morabetins* and fifty thousand *solidi*.[121] During this period, all hostilities would cease. If, during those two years when the viscount would be paying the king, the young countess failed to return or to make these same payments in lieu of the viscount, Guerau would obtain the county of Urgell as his free allod and Aurembiaix would be left with neither her title nor her lands. Jaume further promised that neither he nor his successors would try to make any exceptions that would deprive Guerau of his received rights. If, on the other hand, Aurembiaix returned with sufficient funds to repay both the king and viscount, she tellingly would not resume control of her entire county. Although she would retain the title of countess and most of her ancestral comital lands, she would be utterly defenseless against the viscount who would nevertheless receive eight of Urgell's most important castles as his allodial possessions within forty days: Agramunt, Balaguer, Ponts, Linyola, Oliana, Albesa, Menàrguens, and Albelda. Adding insult to injury, Jaume promised the viscount that he would retain no right to *potestas* or infeudations that would compromise Guerau's use of those fortifications. The concord also addressed the circumstances of a critical castle in the Ribagorza, Montmagastre, which was held by Guillem IV's son, Ramon de Cervera, and determined that, if the viscount paid the expected sums to the king within two years, Ramon would have to perform homage to Guerau, thereby recognizing his lordship.[122]

Although the structuring of this 1217 agreement clearly reflected the monarchy's desperate financial situation, since the king would collect these large payments regardless of the outcome, it did not meaningfully build on Pere's calculated efforts during the final decade of his reign to establish control over the county. The unevenness of the terms suggests that, even though Jaume and his regents were successful in bringing Guerau to the bargaining table, they were not able to dictate terms that favored royal authority. No matter which party prevailed, the viscount would enjoy full entitlement to these castles, and the concord made no stipulations regarding the king's overarching authority within Catalonia or sovereign commitment to uphold the peace and truce and secure public order. Given the fragility of Jaume's hold over the kingdom during his minority and Guerau's capacity to destabilize the situation further, the king and his regents may have had little choice but to give the viscount a deal that he would accept and postpone provoking him until Jaume was older and the monarchy had attained a stronger position.

Aurembiaix did not return from Castile to fulfill the demands of the agreement, whereas the viscount appears to have satisfied the king's demands and thus secured control of Urgell.[123] After realizing his claim, however, Guerau became embroiled in violent hostilities with Jaume and his supporters yet again, necessitating another peace accord in December 1222.[124] The record of this peace provides the only clues regarding what had transpired during these intervening years between 1217 and 1222. Based on its contents, it is likely that Jaume and his supporters had attempted to alter the most unfavorable aspects of the 1217 peace accord, in particular the promise that Guerau would hold both Urgell and his viscounty of Cabrera as allods with no feudal obligations to the king. With the monarchy's progressive stabilization over the intervening years, Jaume and his regency may have developed second thoughts about assigning Guerau such a high degree of autonomy. The fact that this new count of Urgell consented, in 1222, to hold both his county and viscounty as fiefs from the king and ceremonially rendered homage to the king suggests that Guerau had not prevailed in these engagements. This new peace revisited another important aspect of the 1217 concord. Notably, even though Guerau had assumed control of Urgell and the title of count, the parties agreed that Aurembiaix had not forfeited her claim even though the two-year period scheduled in the prior peace had long since elapsed. Jaume and Guerau both acknowledged that Aurembaix would still be able to recover the county whenever she returned, without any stipulated end date, so long as she paid thirty thousand *morabetins*, which was roughly equivalent to what Jaume had mandated in 1217.[125]

Within months of this dramatic adjustment of the terms of Guerau's possession of both Urgell and his viscounty, Jaume found himself relying on this former troublemaker for support against men who had once ranked among his closest supporters. As we observed in the previous chapter, Guillem de Montcada's disagreement with Nunyo Sanç quickly grew into a major rebellion against the Crown.[126] In response, Jaume and his supporters tried to add Guerau de Cabrera to their list of allies by establishing a new agreement regarding Urgell in April 1223.[127] It turned out that Guerau had his own motivations for allying with the king's faction, for he himself was in need of assistance with an internal matter. Two major figureheads within the Montcada family who remained on good terms with the king and his regent, the seneschal Guillem Ramon II de Montcada and Ramon II de Montcada, had usurped some territory that pertained to the county of Urgell. Jaume and Queen Leonor jointly promised to intervene to have these lands returned to Guerau within a month on the condition that he pay them nine thousand *morabetins*. In return, Guerau agreed to assist the royal couple, Nunyo Sanç, and their other allies with their shared conflict against Viscount Guillem II de Montcada of Bearn, Arnau de Castellbò, and the other rebels. Although Guerau and Jaume were already bound to assist one another through the infeudation of the county that had been stipulated in their 1222 peace accord, their own history of conflict, combined with the urgency of these situations, recommended this targeted arrangement. If Jaume were unable to adhere to the one-year timeframe, Guerau would still need to render the nine thousand *morabetins*, but Jaume would accelerate matters by using his authority as king to oblige the inhabitants of the county to assist Guerau, "just as their true lord" (*tamquam domino suo vero*), with the ousting of the usurpers. He furthermore promised not to forge any truces or peaces with the Montcadas until they had been dislodged from the county. Similarly, Guerau took a special oath of fidelity in support of the king in this matter, according to the *fueros* of Aragon.[128]

As the campaign against this rebel Guillem II de Montcada and his supporters grew more embroiled, with combat and castle sieges, Jaume, with his uncle, cousin, and baronial allies, renewed their pledges of mutual support with Guerau de Cabrera in October 1223.[129] Now that Guerau numbered among one of Jaume's close allies during a time of crisis, he earned other benefits that likely would have been inconceivable several years earlier. Most notably, as Jaume confirmed at a meeting of his general court in Barbastro in April 1224, he had entrusted Guerau with undiluted lordship over Lleida, fully enfranchised, and "without any retention . . . except for fidelity and only right justice."[130] Although the king did not stipulate how Guerau had acquired these prerogatives, they must have derived from his inheritance of Ermengol VIII's comital title, which had been associated with rights of lordship in Lleida since the conquest, as we have seen.

Throughout this period of continued instability, Guerau IV de Cabrera and his sons, Ponç IV and Guerau, worked to harden their control over Urgell and their associated viscounties.[131] For almost a decade by this point, they had not experienced serious competition for their family's entitlement to these domains. Although she appears to have remained in Castile continuously during this period, starting in the mid-1220s Aurembiaix started to take greater interest in the properties and rights she should have inherited from her father. In 1226, for example, while still in Toledo and without claiming the title of countess, she transferred the right to possess the castle and town of Montmagastre, as a free allod, to one of her most loyal supporters, Ramon de Peralta, in recognition of his past services.[132] As we witnessed earlier, the 1217 concord between Jaume's regency and Guerau de Cabrera had determined that the viscount would receive the homage of Ramon de Cervera for his possession of Montmagastre in recognition of Guerau's lordship as the count of Urgell so long as he satisfied the required payments to the king within the scheduled two-year period. This enactment by Aurembiaix does not stipulate what had happened to Ramon de Cervera's rights to the castle or make mention of any rights of lordship claimed or exercised by the viscount of Cabrera. Rather, it implies that Ramon de Peralta would not face any opposition in realizing these transferred entitlements. Aurembiaix also arranged to repay Ramon de Peralta a debt of five thousand *morabetins* by allowing him to collect from the incomes of her castles and towns of Gavasa, Puig-roig, Rocafort, and Pelegrí as their enfeoffed lord for his lifetime if she ended up with no heirs. If she did succeed in having children in the future, however, Ramon would need to relinquish control of these holdings to them.[133]

The motivations behind Aurembiaix's transition from Castile to Catalonia in the late 1220s are undocumented. However, there are reasons to believe that the death of Elvira, the decline of the Lara family in Castile during the reign of Fernando III, and Aurembiaix's separation from Álvaro Fernández de Castro, likely due to their failure to produce offspring, each played a role.[134] This distancing from the Castro family notably would have severed one of Aurembiaix's ties of consanguinity to the Cabrera family and, along with Elvira's passing, may have liberated her to choose her own path and ignore family pressure for the first time. She likely also received encouragement from her stepfather, Guillem de Cervera, who remained one of Jaume's closest supporters.[135]

There are other enactments from this time period that provide further indications of this shift to Catalonia. Although, in 1228, Aurembiaix established that she might join the Castilian Order of Santiago in the future and made arrangements to be buried there, around that same time she also piously granted the order all of the holdings in Galicia and León that she had inherited from her mother.[136] She also, reclaiming the title of countess of Urgell for possibly the first time in her adult life, transferred all of the lands she had inherited from her mother in Castilian Bretavillo to her cousin, Nuño Pérez, in July 1228.[137]

In opting to pursue, at long last, her claim to her inheritance from Ermengol VIII, Aurembiaix (and her advisors) must have been aware that she was in for a major battle against the Cabreras, who had been tightening their control over the Urgell for the past two decades. Although men like Ramon de Peralta might have been able to assist her using the few castles that had escaped the Cabreras's control, she required a more capable patron. King Jaume was an obvious albeit risky choice, as his father had been for her mother, Elvira. Although his bold ascendancy following the trials and tribulations of his minority had rendered him an even more formidable ally, Aurembiaix must have remembered or at least have recalled stories of how Pere had opportunistically sought to secure control over Urgell during his final years. Indeed, Jaume had good reasons to capitalize on Aurembiaix's vulnerability by using this opportunity to oust the Cabreras and establish new means by which to secure more complete control over Ermengol VIII's patrimony. Having Aurembiaix as countess was clearly preferable to leaving the Cabreras in possession of the county and worth some of the king's precious resources and political capital as he plotted further expeditions against the Muslims. Especially if she remained a single woman, Aurembiaix as ruler of Urgell would be substantially more vulnerable and far less likely to resist royal oversight.

As the *Llibre dels feits* explains, with the assistance of Guillem de Cervera and Ramon de Peralta, as her primary supporters, and Guillem Sasala, a Bologna-trained lawyer, as her advocate, Aurembiaix began to construct her legal claim to the county as Ermengol VIII's closest relative and sole surviving descendant, which Guillem Sasala prepared to deliver on her behalf at royal court.[138] The king had to follow the correct legal procedure in order to divest the Cabrera family of its possession of Urgell in fief, which was not illegitimate but had, in fact, already been established and ratified by Jaume's regency in the aforementioned agreements of 1222 and 1223. As the king's vassal, Ponç IV de Cabrera (r. ca. 1227–43) was legally obliged to respond to his summons.[139] The law dictated that, if he failed to report to the royal curia after three citations, Ponç would forfeit his fiefs. After Jaume's first call to court went unanswered, Ponç decided to respond to the second citation by sending Guillem de Cardona to serve as his procurator. The two sides presented arguments and debated before the king and the other attendees assembled at the general court in Lleida. Guillem conveyed Ponç's surprise at being challenged by Aurembiaix after holding Urgell for so many years without incident, whereas Guillem Sasala urged the king to proceed against the count if he still failed to appear after being asked a third time to address Aurembiaix's charges.[140] According to the *Llibre dels feits*, the king was only swayed to support a military campaign to divest the Cabrera family of Urgell in a subsequent meeting of his court at his steward's house. After Guillem Sasala reminded the king of his obligation to render justice to the needy, above all "widows and orphans," Guillem de Cardona assured the entire court that the Cabreras would not give up Urgell unless forced, and the two sides began to prepare for battle.[141]

Once the Cabreras's procurator had escalated the conflict by informing the court that there could be no peaceful outcome if Aurembiaix's claim were upheld, Jaume, Aurembiaix, and their respective advisors got to work structuring their partnership. In an agreement formulated in Lleida on the first of August 1228, the countess agreed to transfer to the king, as his perpetual, allodial property, all of her inherited rights to Lleida, either enfeoffed or allodial. Jaume clearly wanted undiluted control over Lleida, which had eluded his predecessors since the conquest, and this may have been one of the non-negotiable conditions for his support of the countess. Although Jaume was more compliant when it came to Aurembiaix's possession of Urgell, he nevertheless carefully engineered the terms to support a high degree of control over the county and to create a pathway to its eventual absorption by the monarchy. In return for Jaume's help with wresting control of Urgell from Ponç de Cabrera, Aurembiaix promised to give the king her county and hold it from him and his successors in perpetuity as a fief. In addition to this infeudation, Jaume and his advisors were careful to build legally binding vulnerabilities into the agreement. He identified nine strategically essential castles over which he would have the right of *potestas*: Agramunt, Linyola, Menàrguens, Balaguer, Albesa, Ponts, Oliana, Calassanç, and Albelda.[142] The countess would not have to hand over to the king, under any circumstances, Urgell's remaining castles, however. Although no money changed hands, Jaume agreed to forgive the debt of twenty-four thousand *morabetins* that

Ermengol VIII had owed to Guillem IV de Cervera at the time of his death and over which King Pere had taken responsibility.[143] As added insurance against the king's loss of control over the fief, Aurembaix promised not to marry without Jaume's consent. To ensure that their arrangement would not be disrupted by other dealings before its fulfillment, the countess also agreed not to make any obligations regarding the county (aside from drafting her will) before the king had wrested her nine castles from the Cabreras's control.

With this alliance established and Jaume now fully invested in realizing Aurembiaix's claim to the county, the king and his men rapidly conducted their campaign against Ponç IV de Cabrera's key positions, from late September through early November 1228.[144] As companies from both Catalonia and Aragon assembled over the following weeks, the growing force under the command of the king and his barons secured one castle or fortified town after the next: Albelda, Tamarit, Menàrguens, Linyola, Balaguer, Agramunt, Ponts, and Oliana. If the *Llibre dels feits* can be believed, the king's army experienced little resistance. Soon, agents loyal to Aurembiaix had effectively secured control of the entire county.[145]

Even before this campaign against the Cabreras had concluded, however, in late October, Aurembiaix was already preparing to assume rule over the county by meeting with the king at Agramunt to revisit their arrangement from a few months earlier. She needed to prepare for the likely event that she would face further challenges from Ponç or other claimants so long as she remained unmarried or without some sort of male protector.[146] The countess reconfirmed her donation of her county to the king on the condition that she hold it from him in fief and save for his "power" over the aforementioned nine castles. She also repeated her donation of her share of the city of Lleida as a free allod, again on the condition that Jaume satisfy her father's debts with Guillem de Cervera amounting to thirty thousand *morabetins*. There appears to have been some concern that the looming effort to conquer Mallorca would interfere with the campaign to take the county. Thus, Aurembiaix imposed the condition that, if the assault on Mallorca materialized and prevented the king's forces from securing her remaining two castles of Calassanç and Ponts, Jaume would complete the effort within thirty days of the conclusion of that expedition.[147]

In other respects, the negotiations ventured into territory that the pair had not explored in their earlier arrangement. In addition to a new payment of three thousand *morabetins*, she proposed to assign to Jaume her residual rights to a series of holdings that did not fall within the official limits of the county: the castles of Fraga, Montclús, Vilella, Vallobar, Albatal, Estada, Estadella,

Saidí, and Pomar.[148] She attached some unusual conditions to this new group of donations. She proposed to bind herself to Jaume in some fashion on the condition that he would not be permitted to leave her unless he found a wife with whom to rule who had a patrimony that was larger and more lucrative than her county of Urgell. He would be entitled to her county as well as all of these other possessions, in perpetuity, if Aurembiaix joined a religious order or died before him. However, if they had a child together, then that child would receive all of these donations, plus the counties of Cerdanya and Conflent and the Berguedà, after Jaume's death and hold them in fief from the new king. If that child never reached adulthood or died without progeny, however, then all of these domains would revert entirely to the Crown.

Soldevila may have been the first to suggest that these terms of the agreement sought to structure a relationship of concubinage (*amistançament*) between Aurembiaix and Jaume, the practice more widely known as *barragania*.[149] More recent scholarship has questioned this characterization, however. Although some of the terms were reminiscent of Pere's marriage arrangements for Jaume and Aurembiaix two decades earlier, the countess and king, who remained married to Queen Leonor at the time, were clearly not discussing marriage. Rather, the arrangement operated more as a stabilizing feudal agreement (or *convenientia*) that the countess apparently sought, unsuccessfully, to gender and sexualize.[150] Jaume's pledges that appear later in the document, tellingly, do not echo any of these elements of Aurembiaix's proposal. Instead, he only swore to uphold the aspects of the agreement that would have been familiar in any *convenientia* between two men. His focus was exclusively on the properties and entitlements that she had assigned him, his role in defending her from her enemies and reestablishing her control over her county, and receiving her profession of homage, which, as described from the king's perspective, notably lacks any signs of feminization. Jaume thus seemingly refused to collaborate in her effort to intensify and perpetuate this feudal partnership by masculinizing his role as lord and feminizing her vassalage.[151] Jaume was indeed discontented with Leonor by this time, and, by April 1229, his advisors would already be at work to annul their marriage.[152] Nevertheless, the king seems to have believed that he had little to gain, strategically, from attaching himself to Aurembiaix as anything other than her lord. He had already secured all of the control over her county and other lands from the routine elements of this agreement that he and his advisors presumably desired.

These two agreements with the king, in August and October, may have garnered Aurembiaix an opportunistic protector, but they did relatively little to mitigate her vulnerability as a female ruler who lacked both a husband and an heir. In fact, Jaume's unreceptiveness to Aurembiaix's proposal to establish him as her male protector and father to her heir could have been a serious miscalculation on his part. It motivated her to seek out a more secure union with a male partner that threatened to disrupt her arrangement with Jaume while rendering her less exposed and thus more independent as countess. The fact that Aurembiaix began to seek out a husband is therefore not surprising. The speed in which she found one, however, was quite unexpected. Within a year, just months after Jaume had begun the process to divorce Leonor, Aurembiaix was already married to the *infante* Pedro de Portugal.[153]

Far from being arranged or sanctioned by the king, as the October 1228 concord required, this unanticipated union threatened to undo the monarchy's careful planning to assume control over the county of Urgell and its succession. As part of their marriage arrangements in July 1229, Aurembiaix pledged to grant the *infante* her county for his lifetime or until they could produce an heir.[154] Jaume soon engaged with both parties in an effort to preserve his rights to the county. First, he secured another donation of the county from Aurembiaix in October of that year.[155] Second, he obtained Pedro's promise, in April 1231, to permit Aurembiaix to follow through with her arrangements with the king and later, in September of that same year, his quitclaim for any entitlement to the county or her other holdings.[156] The latter agreement took place only a month after Aurembiaix had unexpectedly died, a turn of events that complicated the situation considerably. The *infante* nevertheless appears to have withheld certain rights that took Jaume longer to resolve. It was not until 1244 that the king finally obtained all of Pedro's residual interest in the county in exchange for a number of his most important lordships in northern Valencia: the castles and towns of Morella, Morvedre, Almenara, Segorb, and Castelló de la Plana.[157] This transfer was yet another example of Jaume utilizing peripheral holdings recent secured via conquest to assume direct control over domains situated near the core of his realms.

During this time when Jaume was still seeking to eradicate the *infante* Pedro's residual rights to the county, he also continued his fight against the claims of Ponç IV de Cabrera, who had been emboldened by Aurembiaix's demise, in 1231.[158] This time, rather than asserting his entitlement to Urgell by making ultimatums and quickly resorting to arms, Ponç wisely employed the proper legal channels. Ponç's case was now more difficult for the king to dismiss, following Aurembiaix's death without offspring. In open defiance of the king's decision to dispossess him, Ponç had continued claiming the title of count of Urgell even before her death.[159] For his part, Jaume had delayed coming to terms with Ponç and even antagonistically pawned all of the Cabrera family's properties in Camarasa and Cubells to his long-time supporter Berenguer de Finestres in 1235.[160] Finally, when there was no further room for delay, Jaume agreed to a resolution, in 1236, that was far less favorable for him than his 1228 agreement with Aurembiaix. Jaume acknowledged Ponç's rightful possession of the county and other holdings such as Lleida, and, in return, Ponç had to recognize the king's supreme dominion as monarch.[161]

This new line of counts wasted no time seeking to weaken or eliminate altogether the extent of their subjugation to the monarchy by a variety of means. In an effort to emphasize his family's connections with the defunct ancient line of the Ermengols and no doubt hearken back to the days when Urgell had been fully independent from royal oversight, Ponç had named his eldest son Ermengol. Ermengol IX died suddenly, however, only months after his father, in 1243.[162] His brother, Álvar (r. 1243–68), next became count, and he again reestablished this connection by naming his son Ermengol.[163] This Ermengol X (r. 1268–1314) was the product of Álvar's controversial second marriage to the daughter of Roger-Bernard II of Foix, and disputes over his legitimacy would complicate the early years of his reign as count and lead to conflict with Jaume and his son, Pere II, over the dominion they were supposed to exercise over the county.[164] Ermengol X eventually allied with his grandfather, the count of Foix, as well as with the viscount of Cardona, the count of Pallars, and other magnates in a revolt took shape in the late 1270s.[165] These barons sought to increase their independence by taking advantage of Pere's absence from Catalonia to suppress the rebellion of Valencia's *mudéjares*. The king nevertheless managed to regroup and challenge the rebels in an intensive campaign.[166] Lleida's *prohoms* and nobles had suffered the devastation of their fields by the counts of Foix and Urgell and subsequently represented a strong base of support for the king during his operation against these rebellious barons, who had established themselves at nearby Balaguer.[167] Pere II solicited aid for the attack from these same *prohoms* in addition to other townsmen and vassals, recalling the *Princeps Namque* provision of the *Usatges de Barcelona* that all men, "both knights and foot soldiers," come to aid the king when his authority was challenged in this way.[168] He also expected assistance from his subjects in the form of extraordinary taxation, such as the *peita* he requested from numerous Aragonese towns in June 1278 to help him overcome the "many injuries inflicted on us, our lordship (*dominacio*), and the men of our land by these barons of Catalonia."[169] When Balaguer was besieged and, at last, taken by the royal forces, and the rebels were held accountable for "contemptibly" coordinating their treasonous plot with the "devastation of the perfidious Muslims" and were required to hand over control of all of their enfeoffed castles.[170] Notwithstanding this outcome, Ermengol X eventually regained his authority, but his insubordination had induced the monarchy to assert even greater direct authority over castles and towns of the county of Urgell as well as to keep a closer watch on the wayward count of Urgell for the remainder of his life. When Ermengol died in 1314, Jaume II ended the control of the viscounts of Cabrera over the county and finally added Urgell to the royal patrimony.[171]

Lleida and the Lower Segre River Valley

In sharp contrast to Tortosa, Lleida had remained under royal overlordship since Jaume's arrangement with Countess Aurembiaix of Urgell in 1228, governed by municipal officials in tandem with royal officers. The curia of Lleida collaborated with the royal bailiff and vicar, which were both filled by royal appointment. Jaume had already personally intervened in the city's governance as he emerged from his minority, in 1224, by confirming its privileges, promising to be a judicious and watchful overlord, and halting the collection of illegal levies on wheat by his bailiffs.[172] As he sought to emerge from the fiscal crisis handed down to him by his father, he mimicked the practices of his predecessors by contracting loans from these bailiffs that they would then repay from the incomes of the bailiwick. In 1222, for example, when he had just emerged from fighting with Guerau IV de Cabrera, the king confirmed a large debt in *morabetins* owed to Lleida's bailiff, Ramon de Ramon.[173] The following year, as he engaged in the war with Viscount Guillem II de Montcada of Bearn and his allies, Jaume recognized owing this same bailiff a further sum that Ramon de Ramon was to collect from Lleida's *monedatge*. His regent, Nunyo Sanç, served as guarantor for the loan.[174] The king would continue to engage in such transactions for the remainder of his reign.[175]

Although the 1228 transfer had left the king with full lordship, Ramon II de Montcada retained certain jurisdictional rights in Lleida originally enfeoffed to him by the count of Urgell.[176] Jaume appears to have respected this arrangement, perhaps because Ramon was also one of his closest allies. The king even permitted the transfer of this fief to Ramon's son, Guillem I de Montcada, after Ramon and his cousin, this same Guillem II de Montcada, viscount of Bearn, died in the assault on Mallorca.[177]

In 1255, however, given Lleida's increasing royal administrative importance as the center of a vicariate, Jaume decided to strip seigniorial agents altogether from Lleida's jurisdictional environment. In exchange for renouncing their enfeoffed rights to lordship in Lleida, Guillem I de Montcada and his son Ramon III received full lordship, in fief according to the *Usatges de Barcelona*, to Fraga, which Jaume had regained from seigniorial control earlier in his reign.[178] Two years later, the king completed this purge by purchasing Ramon I de Cervera's enfeoffed control over Lleida's curia and local exercise of justice for fifteen thousand *morabetins*. Ramon had inherited these rights from his father, Guillem V, and grandfather, Guillem IV.[179] Alongside the Montcadas, the Cerveras had dominated Lleida's local administration as agents of the count-kings and counts of Urgell since the aftermath of the conquest. Through these moves, Jaume had nearly reversed the divisions of jurisdictional authority at Lleida perpetrated by the distributions and alienations of his predecessors. Only the residual rights of the counts of Urgell remained, which were eventually recovered by the Crown in the early fourteenth century, as discussed above.

Fraga and the Lower Cinca River Valley

As we have seen, especially during the early years of his reign, Jaume I faced times of insecurity and weakness. Like his predecessors, even during times of empowerment and stability, he continued relied on various supporters to rule and conquer, a dependency that necessitated leveraging or enfeoffing of the existing royal patrimony in addition to sharing entitlement to new acquisitions. Yet, arguably more than his father and grandfather, Jaume's use of royal lands and rights was calculated and supported his strategy of jurisdictional accumulation: in particular, he never sacrificed direct administrative control over either Tortosa or Lleida in order to raise capital.[180] Rather, he tended to make sure of peripheral assets, as he had done to regain full control over Lleida. The lordship of Fraga, with its surrounding territories in the lower Cinca valley, serves as an illuminating example of this tactic and its (sometimes unwanted) repercussions. As mentioned, the Montcada family had received Fraga in fief from Jaume in 1255. In 1266, this same king pledged his remaining royal rights there to secure a loan from Ramon III de Montcada for ten thousand *solidi* to finance his war with the king of Granada.[181] This investiture and subsequent enlargement would prove to be surprisingly difficult for the monarchy to reverse.

The fact that Ramon III had received these rights of lordship in fief theoretically made them more vulnerable to alteration or revocation by the Crown, compared with Tortosa's haphazard alienation, for example, and furthermore subjected the noble's administrative practices to royal oversight.[182] In April 1289, Alfons II had his administrator, the vicar of Lleida, intervene to hold Ramon accountable for his forcible seizure of the *aldea* of Peñalba and its unjust separation, for the purposes of taxation and other contributions, from the city of Fraga.[183] These alleged offenses were especially serious because they ran counter to royal decree: Peñalba had been consigned to Fraga's limits in a judgment delivered by Jaume in 1232.[184] Following a process at the court of Lleida, Alfons made it clear that in light of these offenses, he intended to exercise *potestas* over Fraga's castle and dissolve the infeudation that Jaume and the Montcadas had established in 1255. He transferred responsibility over Fraga's administration to the royal vicar in Lleida.[185] When Ramon died, however, it provided his heir, Guillem II, with a means to distance himself from the scandal and seek to reestablish his family's rights to Fraga on stable footing. Guillem pledged to the citizens to undo all of the wrongs his father had committed with respect to Peñalba. He also sought to repair his father's legacy by explaining that he had confessed a desire to make amends to the bishop of Tortosa during his final days.[186] The same day, Guillem and his mother were able to convince the king to reinvest them with lordship over Fraga according to the *Constitucions de Catalunya* and the *Usatges de Barcelona*.[187]

These negotiations were accompanied by the granting of privileges by the restored lords of Fraga to the local *universitas*, adjusting taxation and pledging to honor royal privileges and, in turn, confirming rights to "all other lordship and jurisdiction that we have . . . in the town and district of Fraga and [over] all inhabitants for any reason."[188] The residents thus managed to interject their interests into this royal-seigniorial conflict in order to obtain valuable confirmations from the Montcadas.[189] In 1294, as the reconciliation was still being resolved, Fraga's citizens, with the king's oversight, also secured renewed exemptions from levies such as *questias* and *peytas* and unpopular seigniorial uses such as *toltas* and *forcias*.[190] For his part, the king sought to capitalize on this popular agitation within the lordship to add pressure on the Montcadas to satisfy his demand for sizeable damages of ten thousand *solidi*.[191] Yet there were no signs that these understandably opportunistic citizens were clamoring for royal administration to displace their noble lords. In January 1290, for example, Alfons was forced to address his complaint to Guillem II when the men of Fraga refused to form a militia and aid the king in his effort to punish the *universitas* of citizens in Lleida for themselves ignoring the call issued by his general court.[192] The monarchy eventually purchased lordship over Fraga in the 1330s, but this opportunity was only made available to the king due to a disruption within the local Montcada dynasty. Prior to Guillem de Montcada's death around 1326, he had remained highly defensive regarding his independence in administering Fraga.[193]

Conclusions

As a means to bringing this chapter, and book, to a close, it is worth reflecting further on these successive cycles of conquest, delegation, and repossession that we have addressed in detail throughout the foregoing pages. It is no simple task to account for the timing of such shifts toward recuperation and direct governance in these areas, which in some cases reversed trends that had been in place for generations. During the final years of Jaume I's rule and the reigns of Pere II, Alfons II, and Jaume II, royal objectives had to adapt to narrowed prospects for further territorial conquest of neighboring lands and instead pursue new modes of growth and development within the wider arenas of the Peninsula and Mediterranean. As part of this transfer of attention away from organizing further Peninsular conquests, these monarchs increasingly concentrated on enhancing the development and exploitation of lands they had already captured and whose consolidation was already in process.

This new climate encouraged the renegotiation of long-ingrained relationships, patterns, and institutions that we have seen emerge throughout this book. For example, during the reigns of Jaume I's successors, the royal relationship with the international military orders underwent significant, albeit gradual, changes. As we have witnessed in earlier chapters, Ramon Berenguer IV and his successors had co-opted the Templars and Hospitallers in their offensives from the mid-twelfth century. Such self-serving patronage emulated the alliances that Alfonso I of Aragon had first developed with both homegrown and international military orders when he was seeking to energize his campaigning into the Ebro valley in the early decades of the twelfth century.[194] Those partnerships had served their purpose by supporting the conquest as well as successive painstaking phases of consolidation. Alfons I, Pere I, and Jaume I (during the first part of his reign) each relied heavily on the orders and certain barons to scale back the drain on comital-royal resources to manage these frontier lands. In time, these beneficiaries of this withdrawal would profit greatly as the improved conditions of the land permitted more substantial settlement and economic development and the generous tax exemptions and other entitlements they had received from the count-kings enabled them to capture a larger share of their growing revenues.

As we have seen, over the course of the thirteenth century, the monarchy developed greater capacity to govern these territories, especially once the door to the Crown's longstanding trans-Pyrenean ambitions had been closed, once and for all. Additional territorial gains, moreover, further insulated former frontier centers like Tortosa: decreasing costs of defense matched with progressively denser settlement helped to enhance their profitability. At the same time, the Templar and Hospitaller houses throughout Europe as a whole were undergoing a complicated period of transition and redefinition. Scholars view the close of the thirteenth century as the end of the great age of monastic expansion in Europe when orders were obliged to reexamine their relationships to societies that had, on the whole, changed dramatically over the past several generations. The Templar and Hospitaller houses within the Crown of Aragon, in particular, struggled to adapt to the changed climate pervading the realms and, most pressingly, to the growing competitiveness of the monarchy toward them.[195] Most notably, the monarchy increasingly sought to restrict or eliminate these orders' traditional privileges and exemptions. At the same time, to make matters worse, the finances of local houses were being pinched by increasing demands for aid by houses in the Holy Land.[196] For the Templar Order, this changing tide would culminate in Jaume II's decision, following the French king's condemnation of the order, to dismantle the Templar establishment in his realms, beginning in earnest in 1308.[197] Although the Hospitallers (alongside the newly founded Order of Montesa) would actually benefit from the Templar Order's dissolution, they did not escape unscathed and had to adapt to a series of novel limitations imposed by the Crown, resulting in significant financial difficulties from the first quarter of the fourteenth century onward.[198]

Over the course of the thirteenth century, the divergence in the monarchy's treatment of seigniorial autonomies within the former frontier lands of New Catalonia and the more recently captured Valencian territories widened. As we have seen, the Templars and Hospitallers, along with important Catalonia-based noble families such as the Montcadas, came to hold substantial lands and rights in the kingdom of Valencia. Not only did the monarchy repay these collaborators in the military campaigns with lands and, in turn, rely on them to manage settlement, reorganize the vast remaining Muslim populations, and defend the new kingdom from internal and outside attack. It also increased their holdings there by exchanging them in this effort to regain control of these formerly leveraged and alienated lands along the Ebro Valley, as we have observed. The Templars furthermore obtained some of their holdings in Valencia through purchase.[199] Even before it developed significantly its Mediterranean agenda, the monarchy had naturally made greater use of the military orders in more peripheral regions that were in greater need of military assistance. This phenomenon supplemented these other factors in drawing the presence of these orders away from the heartlands of the Crown of Aragon.

In spite of these enhancements in the purview of royal administration in various localities that we have detailed in parts II and III of this study, lords continued to defend their ingrained judicial prerogatives with considerable vigor and ingenuity. In addition to the retention of rights of *merum et mixtum imperium* described earlier, certain lords even managed to fend off royal attempts to secure the right of appeal. The Templars of Horta, for example, established in 1296 that judgments by the local commander should be appealed to the provincial master, thereby circumventing royal courts altogether.[200] Indeed, the idealized paradigm maintained by the Crown's inner circle of a pervasive and standardized system of justice emanating from the royal curia rarely described reality outside of the domains under direct control. For instance, before the Crown purchased jurisdiction over Tortosa from its seigniorial regime, in addition to struggling to maintain a robust administrative presence, it also had difficulty providing its residents with access to royal justice. In 1282, Pere II confidently informed the *prohoms* and *universitas* of Tortosa that that litigants wishing to appeal their cases in Tortosa should first refer them to "our vicar" based in the city and subsequently direct them to the royal curia for judgment. These judicial prerogatives, he claimed, "ought to pertain to us because of regalian jurisdiction."[201] As a seigniorial appointee at that time, however, Tortosa's vicar did not view himself, or behave, as a royal delegate. And even if a resident had possessed the means to appeal directly to royal court, the regime maintained by the co-lords likely would have resisted any verdict delivered by the Crown.[202] There are no indications the monarchy was successful in making these legal channels available within Tortosa before its assumption of jurisdictional lordship a decade later. More often than not, judicial access, like many of the prerogatives and amenities asserted by the Crown, required royal overlordship.

Although lords thus still possessed the means to deflect certain efforts by the monarchy to undercut their local authority, and even though the monarchy perpetuated such jurisdictional dislocation by funding its resumption of direct authority in one area with withdrawals elsewhere, the overall trend was nevertheless toward increasing royal authority and administrative presence. Over the course of the fourteenth century, seigniorial incomes from jurisdictional lordships throughout the realms and collective baronial political capital were insufficient to stay the monarchy's encroachment, and the same trend of royal acquisition of alienated lordships and reimposition of jurisdiction witnessed in Lleida, the Terra Alta and Ribera d'Ebre, and Tortosa subsequently affected other zones.[203] After a cycle of conquest, royal administrative retreat, and seigniorial consolidation, the Crown increasingly found itself invested with the means to emerge from the shadow of victory and begin to realize, albeit gradually and inconsistently, the governmental ambitions of the eleventh- and twelfth-century counts and count-kings.

APPENDIX

Dynastic Succession of the Counts of Urgell

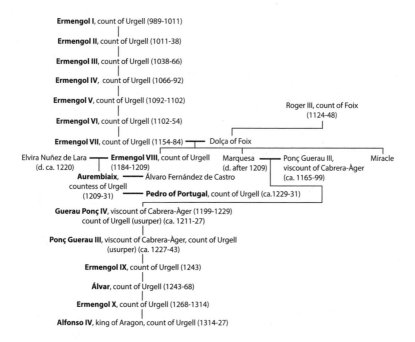

Note: In general, only figures mentioned in the text are included in these tables. The dates reflect reigns and certain marriages and offspring have been omitted. The names of successive title-holders have been bolded.

Dynastic Succession of the Kings of Aragon

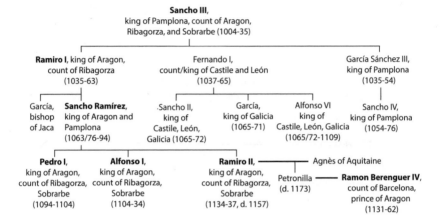

Sancho III,
king of Pamplona, count of Aragon,
Ribagorza, and Sobrarbe (1004-35)

Ramiro I, king of Aragon,
count of Ribagorza
(1035-63)

Fernando I,
count/king of Castile and León
(1037-65)

García Sánchez III,
king of Pamplona
(1035-54)

García,
bishop
of Jaca

Sancho Ramírez,
king of Aragon and
Pamplona
(1063/76-94)

Sancho II,
king of
Castile, León,
Galicia (1065-72)

García,
king of Galicia
(1065-71)

Alfonso VI
king of
Castile, León, Galicia
(1065/72-1109)

Sancho IV,
king of Pamplona
(1054-76)

Pedro I,
king of Aragon,
count of Ribagorza,
Sobrarbe
(1094-1104)

Alfonso I,
king of Aragon,
count of Ribagorza,
Sobrarbe
(1104-34)

Ramiro II,
king of Aragon,
count of Ribagorza,
Sobrarbe
(1134-37, d. 1157)

Agnès of Aquitaine

Petronilla
(d. 1173)

Ramon Berenguer IV,
count of Barcelona,
prince of Aragon
(1131-62)

Dynastic Succession of the
Counts of Barcelona and Count-Kings of Barcelona/Aragon

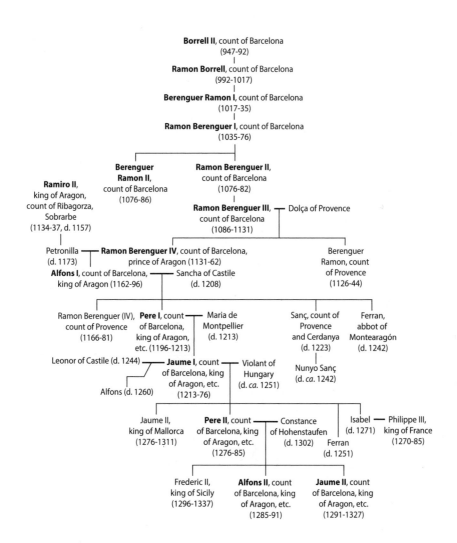

Notes

Abbreviations, Naming, and Coinage

1. See, generally, A. Balaguer, *Història de la moneda dels comtats catalans* (Barcelona: Societat Catalana d'Estudis Numismàtics, 1999).

Introduction

1. ACA, C, Procesos en cuarto, 1296B (May 1296).

2. See O. R. Constable, *Housing the Stranger in the Mediterranean World: Lodging, Trade, and Travel in Late Antiquity and the Middle Ages* (Cambridge: Cambridge University Press, 2003), esp. 158–200.

3. E.g., the monarchy paid for the share of the *lleuda* levy that the Narbonnese had held since the conquest. ACA, C, pergs. J II, no. 706 (12 Oct. 1296).

4. R. Bartlett, *The Making of Europe: Conquest, Colonization, and Cultural Change* (Princeton, NJ: Princeton University Press, 1993), 307.

5. Bartlett, *The Making of Europe*, 309.

6. N. Berend, "The Expansion of Latin Christendom," in *The Central Middle Ages, 950–1320*, ed. D. Power (Oxford: Oxford University Press, 2006), 178. See also C. Wickham, "Making Europes," *New Left Review* I: 208 (1994): 133–43, and M. Borgolte, *Europa entdeckt seine Vielfalt, 1050–1250* (Stuttgart: E. Ulmer, 2003).

7. Bartlett, *The Making of Europe*, 307–8, 309.

8. Bartlett, *The Making of Europe*, 307.

9. For a brief overview, see T. N. Bisson, *The Medieval Crown of Aragon: A Short History* (Oxford: Clarendon Press, 1986). For a detailed analysis, see J. Salrach, *El procès de feudalització: segles III–XII*, Història de Catalunya 2 (Barcelona: Edicions 62, 1998), 255–398, and A. J. Kosto, "Aragon and the Catalan Counties Before the Union," in *The Crown of Aragon: A Singular Mediterranean Empire*, ed. F. Sabaté (Leiden and Boston: Brill, 2017), 70–91.

10. See L. García-Guijarro Ramos, "Reconquest and the Second Crusade in Eastern Iberia: The Christian Expansion in the Lower Ebro Valley," in *The Second Crusade: Holy War on the Periphery of Latin Christendom*, ed. J. T. Roche and J. Møller Jensen (Turnhout: Brepols, 2015), 219–55, who has taken a similar approach in stressing the importance of viewing the conquest of Tortosa (alongside that of Lleida) within its long-term local context rather than as a sudden gain produced by the Second Crusade.

11. Primarily for the sake of expediency, previous work has tended to organize temporal frontier development into uniform phases. E.g., B. Catlos, *The Victors and the Vanquished: Christians and Muslims of Catalonia and Aragon, 1050–1300*

(Cambridge: Cambridge University Press, 2004), 119, who identifies "three general stages of settlement and social development . . . in the formerly Muslim-dominated territories of the Ebro watershed": occupation, which "involved the consolidation of Christian administration and the end of the period of military uncertainty vis-à-vis the Muslims" and lasted from the conquests until the 1180s; settlement, which "saw the retreat of the frontier with Islam, demographic consolidation and expansion, the elaboration of local *fueros*, the granting of more *cartas pueblas*, and the seigniorialization of land tenure" and lasted from the 1150s to 1230s; and finally entrenchment, when Christians began to become the numerical majority, which began with the battle of Las Navas de Tolosa (1212) and ended with the capture and pacification of the kingdom of Valencia. E. Rodríguez-Picavea, "The Frontier and Royal Power in Medieval Spain: A Developmental Hypothesis," *Medieval History Journal* 8 (2005): 281–92, breaks frontier development into four phases and recognizes unevenness between different frontiers but less so within frontier regions: the military phase, the economic phase (when the conquering society reorganized the landscape "according to its own guidelines"), the cultural phase (characterized by the genesis of "a mental frontier" whereby the conquerors redefine the cultural belonging of this space), and the political-administrative phase (when a "socio-political unit is in a position to gain sovereignty over the land it occupies").

12. J. Torró, "Viure del botí: La frontera medieval com a parany historiogràfic," *Recerques: història, economia, cultura* 43 (2001): 31.

13. See P. Bonnassie and P. Guichard, "Les communautés rurales en Catalogne et dans le pays valencien (IXe milieu XIVe siècle)," in *Les communautés villageoises en Europe occidentale du Moyen Âge aux Temps modernes: Quatrièmes journées internationales d'histoire, Centre culturel de l'abbaye de Flaran, 8–10 septembre 1982* (Auch: Comité départemental du tourisme du Gers, 1984), 88.

14. P. Freedman, *The Origins of Peasant Servitude in Medieval Catalonia* (Cambridge: Cambridge University Press, 1991), esp. 135–39.

15. E.g., J. M. Font Rius, "La comarca de Tortosa a raíz de la reconquista cristiana (1148): notas sobre su fisonomía político-social," in his *Estudis sobre els drets i institucions locals en la Catalunya medieval: Col·lectanea de treballs del Professor Dr. Josep Mª Font i Rius amb motiu de la seva jubilació acadèmica* (Barcelona: Universitat de Barcelona, 1984), 75–92, and Font Rius, "La reconquista de Lérida y su proyección en el orden jurídico," in his *Estudis sobre els drets i institucions locals en la Catalunya medieval*, 55–74. J. E. García i Biosca, *Els orígens del terme de Lleida: la formació d'un territori urbà (s. XI i XII)* (Lleida: Diario "La Mañana," 1995) studies how Lleida's postconquest municipal boundaries mirrored the city's preconquest Andalusi district.

16. T. N. Bisson, "'Statebuilding' in the Medieval Crown of Aragón," in *XVe Congreso de Historia de la Corona de Aragón: El poder real en la Corona de Aragón (Siglos XIV–XVI) (Jaca, 20–25 de septiembre de 1993). Actas*, vol. 1.1 (Zaragoza: Departamento de Educación y Cultura, 1996), 144.

17. Bisson, "'Statebuilding' in the Medieval Crown of Aragón," 147.

18. See P. Limerick, "The Adventures of the Frontier in the Twentieth Century," in *The Frontier in American Culture*, ed. J. R. Grossman (Berkeley: University of California Press, 1994), 67–102, and N. Berend, *At the Gate of Christendom: Jews, Muslims, and "Pagans" in Medieval Hungary* (Cambridge: Cambridge University Press, 2001), chap. 1.

19. Berend, *At the Gate of Christendom*, 16.

20. E.g., ACA, C, pergs. P I, no. 308 (26 Nov. 1208); L. Pagarolas, *Els Templers de les terres de l'Ebre de Jaume I fins a l'abolició de l'Orde (1213–1312)*, 2 vols. (Tarragona: Diputació Provincial de Tarragona, 1999), vol. 2, doc. 213, which is placed in context and analyzed in chapter 5 below.

21. F. J. Turner, *The Frontier in American History* (New York: Henry Holt, 1921), 38.

22. Torró, "Viure del botí," 14. See M. Zimmermann, "Le rôle de la frontière dans la formation de la Catalogne (IX–XIIème siècle)," in *Las sociedades de frontera en la España medieval. Aragon en la Edad Media: Sesiones de trabajo. II seminario de historia medieval* (Zaragoza: Universidad de Zaragoza, 1993), 7–29 and F. Sabaté, "La frontière catalane (X^e–XIIe siècles): perception, altérité, pouvoir et mémoire," in *Ériger et borner diocèses et principautés au Moyen Âge: Limites et frontières*, vol. 2, *Histoire et Civilisations*, ed. N. Baron, S. Boissellier, F. Clément, and F. Sabaté (Villeneuve d'Ascq: Presses Universitaires du Septentrion, 2017), 185–218, esp. 195–205.

23. E.g., A. Virgili, *Ad detrimentum Yspanie: la conquesta de Ṭurṭūša i la formació de la societat feudal (1148–1200)* (Valencia: Universitat Autònoma de Barcelona, Servei de Publicacions, 2001); C. Stalls, *Possessing the Land: Aragon's Expansion into Islam's Ebro Frontier under Alfonso the Battler, 1104–1134* (Leiden: Brill, 1995); R. I. Burns, *The Crusader Kingdom of Valencia: Reconstruction on a Thirteenth-Century Frontier*, 2 vols. (Cambridge, MA: Harvard University Press, 1967).

24. For some useful overviews with attention to this growing critique, see A. Novikoff, "Tolerance in Intolerance in Medieval Spain: An Historiographic Enigma," *Medieval Encounters* 11 (2005): 7–36; M. Soifer, "Beyond *Convivencia*: Critical Reflections on the Historiography of Interfaith Relations in Christian Spain," *Journal of Medieval Iberian Studies* 1 (2009): 19–35; and K. B. Wolf, "Convivencia in Medieval Spain: A Brief History of an Idea," *Religion Compass* 3 (2008): 72–85. Scholars are also questioning the historiographical notion of simplistic coexistence in Muslim-ruled society. See E. Manzano Moreno, "Qurtuba: Some Critical Considerations of the Caliphate of Córdoba and the Myth of 'Convivencia,'" in *Reflections on Qurtuba in the 21st Century* (Madrid: Casa Árabe, 2013), 111–32.

25. E.g., Catlos, *The Victors and the Vanquished*; P. Ortega Pérez, *Musulmanes en Cataluña: las comunidades musulmanas de las encomiendas templarias y hospitalarias de Ascó y Miravet (siglos XII–XIV)* (Barcelona: Consejo Superior de Investigaciones Científicas, 2000); M. Meyerson, *Jews in an Iberian Frontier Kingdom: Society, Economy, and Politics in Morvedre* (Leiden: Brill, 2004); I. O'Connor, *A Forgotten Community: The Mudejar Aljama of Xàtiva, 1240–1327* (Leiden: Brill, 2003).

26. The bibliography is too extensive to list in full here, but important examples include Burns, *Crusader Kingdom of Valencia*; M. T. Ferrer i Mallol, *La frontera amb l'Islam en el segle XIV: cristians i sarraïns als país Valencia* (Barcelona: Consell Superior d'Investigacions Científiques, 1988); M. T. Ferrer i Mallol, *Organització i defensa d'un territori fronterer: la governació d'Oriola en el segle XIV* (Barcelona: Consell Superior d'Investigacions Científiques, 1990); E. Guinot Rodríguez, *Els fundadors del Regne de València: repoblament, antroponímia i llengua a la València medieval* (Valencia: E. Climent, 1999); and E. Guinot Rodríguez, *Els límits del regne: el procés de formació territorial del País Valencià medieval, 1238–1500* (Valencia: Edicions Alfons el Magnànim, 1995). This weighting toward the later Middle Ages is especially noticeable when it comes to the study of tolerated Jews and Muslims. E.g., R. I. Burns, *Islam under the Crusaders: Colonial Survival in the Thirteenth-Century Kingdom of Valencia* (Princeton,

NJ: Princeton University Press, 1973); R. I. Burns, *Medieval Colonialism: Postcrusade Exploitation of Islamic Valencia* (Princeton, NJ: Princeton University Press, 1975); J. Boswell, *The Royal Treasure: Muslim Communities under the Crown of Aragon in the Fourteenth Century* (New Haven: Yale University Press, 1977); M. T. Ferrer i Mallol, *Els sarraïns de la corona catalano-aragonesa en el segle XIV: segregació i discriminació* (Barcelona: Consell Superior d'Investigacions Científiques, 1987).

27. A. García Sanjuán has written widely on the problems of the historiographical concept of the *Reconquista*. See his "Rejecting al-Andalus, Exalting the Reconquista: Historical Memory in Contemporary Spain," *Journal of Medieval Iberian Studies* 10 (2018): 127–45; "Al-Andalus en la historiografía nacionalcatólica Española: Claudio Sánchez Albornoz," *eHumanista* 37 (2017): 305–28; "La persistencia del discurso nacionalcatólico sobre el medievo peninsular en la historiografía Española actual," *Historiografías* 12 (2016): 132–53; and *La conquista islámica de la Península Ibérica y la tergiversación del pasado* (Madrid: Marcial Pons Historia, 2013).

28. The list of relevant studies is too large to be surveyed comprehensively here. Perhaps most foundational among twentieth-century frontier scholarship was C. Sánchez-Albornoz's *Despoblación y repoblación del Valle del Duero* (Buenos Aires: Instituto de Historia de España, 1966), akin to G. Duby's *La société aux XIᵉ et XIIᵉ siècles dans la région mâconnaise* (Paris: A. Colin, 1953) for the structure and methodology of future study of feudal society. Although its central thesis is no longer accepted, the study continues to influence current research and inspire colloquia devoted to the problems surrounding territorial expansion, such as *Despoblación y colonización del Valle del Duero (siglos VIII–XX), IVᵒ Congreso de Estudios Medievales* (Ávila: Fundación Sánchez-Albornoz, 1995). Sánchez-Albornoz believed Spain's frontier past has colored indelibly its character across history. The broader phenomenon of Christian expansion in Iberia has been surveyed by S. de Moxó, *Repoblación y sociedad en la España cristiana medieval* (Madrid: Ediciones Rialp, S.A., 1979). See also E. Manzano Moreno, "The Creation of a Medieval Frontier: Islam and Christianity in the Iberian Peninsula, Eighth to Eleventh Centuries," in *Frontiers in Question: Eurasian Borderlands, 700–1700*, ed. D. Power and N. Standen (New York: St. Martin's Press, 1999), 32–54. For an insightful comparison of Iberia's engagements with those in Hungary and Poland, see N. Berend, "Défense de la Chrétienté et naissance d'une identité: Hongrie, Pologne et péninsule Ibérique au Moyen Âge," *Annales. Histoire, Sciences Sociales*, 58ᵉ année, no. 5 (2003): 1009–27.

29. See M. F. Ríos Saloma, *La Reconquista: una construcción historiográfica (siglos XVI–XIX)* (Madrid: Marcial Pons, Ediciones de Historia, 2011), 87–94, and Sabaté, "La frontière catalane (Xᵉ–XIIᵉ siècle)," 185–89.

30. For the military orders, see L. Pagarolas, *La comanda del Temple de Tortosa: primer període (1148–1213)* (Tortosa: Institut d'Estudis Dertosenses, 1984); Pagarolas, *Els Templers*; and M. Bonet Donato, *La orden del Hospital en la Corona de Aragón: poder y gobierno en la Castellanía de Amposta (ss. XII–XIV)* (Madrid: Consejo Superior de Investigacion Científicas, 1994). J. Serrano Daura has written numerous detailed studies on the Templar houses and local baronies within the Terra Alta, including *Senyoriu i municipi a la Catalunya Nova (segles XII–XIX): comandes de Miravet, d'Orta, d'Ascó i de Vilalba i baronies de Flix i d'Entença*, 2 vols. (Barcelona: Fundació Noguera, 2000). For local urban history, see E. Fabregat, *Burgesos contra senyors: la lluita per la terra a Tortosa*

(1148–1299) (Tortosa: Generalitat de Catalunya and Arxiu Comarcal de les Terres de l'Ebre, 2006) and F. Sabaté, *Història de Lleida*, vol. 2, *Alta edat mitjana* (Lleida: Pagès, 2003). Two aging city/*comarca*-based local histories, E. Bayerri, *Historia de Tortosa y su comarca*, 8 vols. (Tortosa: Imprenta moderna de Algueró y Baiges, 1933–60) and J. Lladonosa, *Història de Lleida* (Tàrrega: F. Camps Calmet, 1972–74), are important exceptions and remain useful, even though they tend to rely chiefly on published sources and are not well documented.

31. See Torró, "Viure del botí," 6–12, who contends that the Eurocentrism of much medieval frontier research has been inspired by Turner's discredited thesis.

32. T. W. Barton, *Contested Treasure: Jews and Authority in the Crown of Aragon* (University Park: Pennsylvania State University Press, 2015). See also T. W. Barton, "Muslims in Christian Countrysides: Reassessing Exaricus Tenures in Eastern Iberia," *Medieval Encounters* 17 (2011): 233–320, which considers how an Andalusi form of land tenure was maintained in diversely adapted forms under Christian rule.

33. For now, see T. W. Barton, "Constructing a Diocese in a Post-Conquest Landscape: A Comparative Approach to the Lay Possession of Tithes," *Journal of Medieval History* 35 (2009): 1–33.

Chapter 1. *Parias* and Churches along the Eleventh-Century Frontier

1. See, for example, B. A. Catlos, "Accursed, Superior Men: Ethno-Religious Minorities and Politics in the Medieval Mediterranean," *Comparative Studies in Society and History* 56, no. 4 (2014): 844–69.

2. Consider R. d'Abadal, *Els primers comtes catalans: Història de Catalunya. Biografies catalanes*, vol. 1 (Barcelona: Vicens-Vives, 1985), 193. Sunyer II, who ruled over the coastal county of Empúries, situated to the north of Barcelona, some distance from the frontier, launched an independent naval expedition along the southeastern coast of al-Andalus around 891.

3. See M. Zimmermann, "Le concept de Marca Hispanica et l'importance de la frontière dans la formation de la Catalogne," in *La marche supérieure d'al-Andalus et l'occident chrétien*, ed. P. Sénac (Madrid: Casa de Velázquez, 1988), 41–42.

4. This is the mode of discourse that Brian Catlos has labeled "ecumenian" because it is "moralizing, and expresses itself dogmatically and rigidly, through the language of doctrine, principle, eternal truth, and opposition to compromise." See *Muslims of Medieval Latin Christendom, c. 1050–1614* (Cambridge: Cambridge University Press, 2014), 527.

5. ACL, *Llibre Vert*, fol. 1v.

6. Catlos, *Muslims*, 525, argues that any actor was capable of multiple modes of discourse and registers of expression. See T. Deswarte, *Une Chrétienté romaine sans pape: l'Espagne et Rome (586–1085)* (Paris: Classiques Garnier, 2010), 320–28.

7. *El "Llibre Blanch" de Santas Creus: cartulario del siglo XII*, ed. F. Udina Martorell, Textos y estudios de la Corona de Aragón 9 (Barcelona: Consejo Superior de Investigaciones Científias, 1947), doc. 9 (11 Jan. 1038). For numerous further examples, see F. Sabaté, "Occuper la frontière du nord-est péninsulaire (X^e–XIIe siècles)," *Entre Islam et Chrétienté. La territorialisation des frontières, XIe–XVIe siècles*, ed. S. Boissellier, F. Fernandes, and I. Cristina (Rennes: Presses Universitaires de Rennes, 2015), 88–96.

8. See P. Bonnassie, *La Catalogne du milieu du Xe à la fin du XIe siècle: croissance et mutations d'une société*, 2 vols. (Toulouse: Association des publications de l'Université de Toulouse-Le Mirail, 1975–76), 1:355; C. Vela Aulesa, "L'Àndalus en la política de Barcelona i la Corona d'Aragó (segle XI–1213)," in *Tractats i negociacions diplomàtiques de Catalunya i de la Corona catalanoaragonesa a l'edat mitjana, vol. I.2: Tractats i negociacions diplomàtiques amb els regnes peninsulars i l'Àndalus (segle XI–1213)*, ed. M. T. Ferrer i Mallol and M. Riu i Riu (Barcelona: Institut d'Estudis Catalans, 2018), 117–80 (esp. 117–24); and J. Mestre and F. Sabaté, *Atles de la "Reconquesta": la frontera peninsular entre els segles VIII i XV* (Barcelona: Edicions 62, 1998), 12–13. On this phenomenon of migration, see Salrach, *El procès de feudalització*, 238, 255–57; P. Freedman, *The Diocese of Vic: Tradition and Regeneration in Medieval Catalonia* (New Brunswick: Rutgers University Press, 1983), 3; and Jarrett, *Rulers and Ruled*, 87–89. Compare F. Sabaté, *L'expansió territorial de Catalunya (segles IX–XII): conquesta o repoblació?* (Lleida: Servei de publicacions, Universitat de Lleida, 1996), 28. Bonnassie, *La Catalogne du milieu du Xe à la fin du XIe siècle*, 1:440 discusses the expansion of the arable in this context.

9. See D. Wasserstein, *The Rise and Fall of the Party-Kings: Politics and Society in Islamic Spain, 1002–1086* (Princeton, NJ: Princeton University Press, 1985), 40–43, and M. Makki, "The Political History of al-Andalus (92/711–897/1492)," in *The Legacy of Muslim Spain*, ed. S. K. Jayyusi, 2nd ed. (Leiden: Brill, 1994), 3–87 (esp. 41–45).

10. M. Sánchez Martínez, "La expedición de Al-Manṣūr contra Barcelona en el 985 según las fuentes árabes," in *Catalunya i França meridional a l'entorn de l'any mil*, ed. X. Barral et al. (Barcelona: Generalitat de Catalunya, Departament de Cultura, 1991), 293–301.

11. See J. Bowman, *Shifting Landmarks: Property, Proof, and Dispute in Catalonia around the Year 1000* (Ithaca: Cornell University Press, 2004), 19–20, G. Feliu, *La presa de Barcelona per Almansor: història i mitificació* (Barcelona: Institut d'Estudis Catalans, 2007), and Makki, "Political History of al-Andalus," 42–44.

12. See S. Sobrequés, *Els grans comtes de Barcelona*, Història de Catalunya, Biografies catalanes vol. 2 (Barcelona: Editorial Vicens-Vives, 1961), 4–6, and Wasserstein, *Rise and Fall of the Party-Kings*, 43; L. Seco de Lucena, "New Light on the Military Campaigns of Al-manzor," *Islamic Quarterly* 14 (1970): 126–42; and L. Molina, "Las campañas de Almanzor a la luz de un nuevo texto," *Al-Qanṭara* 2 (1981): 209–63.

13. See D. Lomax, *The Reconquest of Spain* (London: Longman, 1978), 47, and O. R. Constable, "Regulating Religious Noise: The Council of Vienne, the Mosque Call and Muslim Pilgrimage in the Late Medieval Mediterranean World," *Medieval Encounters* 16 (2010): 64–95.

14. Makki, "Political History of al-Andalus," 45.

15. See J. Jarrett, *Rulers and Ruled in Frontier Catalonia, 880–1110: Pathways of Power* (Suffolk: Boydell, 2010), esp. chap. 3.

16. See Mestre and Sabaté, *Atles de la "Reconquesta,"* 32–33.

17. Wasserstein, *Rise and Fall of the Party-Kings*, 6, and Makki, "Political History of al-Andalus," 45–46. For a revisionist take on the involvement of Berbers and other North African groups in these affairs, see B. Catlos, *Kingdoms of Faith: A New History of Islamic Spain* (New York, Basic Books, 2018), esp. part III.

18. C. Gómez-Rivas, *Law and the Islamization of Morocco under the Almoravids: The Fatwās of Ibn Rushd al-Jadd to the Far Maghrib* (Leiden: Brill, 2014), esp. 26–39, 76–84, and 104–12. See J. Bosch Vilá, *Los Almorávides* (Granada: Universidad de Granada,

1956); A. S. Baadj, *Saladin, the Almohads and the Banū Ghāniya* (Leiden: Brill, 2015), esp. 154–73 (on Yaḥya ibn Ghāniya); A. J. Fromherz, *The Almohads: The Rise of an Islamic Empire* (New York: Palgrave Macmillan, 2010); and A. Bennison, *The Almoravid and Almohad Empires* (Edinburgh: Edinburgh University Press, 2016), esp. 54–61, 74–78.

19. Makki, "Political History of al-Andalus," 46.

20. See Wasserstein, *Rise and Fall of the Party-Kings*, 55–81.

21. Makki, "Political History of al-Andalus," 48–49. See Lomax, *Reconquest of Spain*, 48, and A. G. Chejne, *Muslim Spain: Its History and Culture* (Minneapolis: University of Minnesota Press, 1974), 50.

22. See Makki, "Political History of al-Andalus," 47–49.

23. See Wasserstein, *Rise and Fall of the Party-Kings*, 83–98.

24. See Catlos, *The Victors and the Vanquished*, 54.

25. E. Lévi-Provençal, *Histoire de l'espagne musulmane*, 3 vols. (Paris: Maisonneuve, 1950), 3:57.

26. See J. Safran, *Defining Boundaries in al-Andalus: Muslims, Christians, and Jews in Islamic Iberia* (Ithaca: Cornell University Press, 2013), 172–73.

27. See *Catalunya Romànica*, 27 vols. (Barcelona: Portic, 1985–98), 26:38–39 (Baix Ebre) and 24:29–31 (Segrià), respectively.

28. See J. Lomba Fuentes, "El pensamiento filosófico en la Marca Superior," in *La marche supérieure d'al-Andalus et l'occident chrétien*, ed. Sénac, 177–88; J. Bosch Vilá, *El oriente árabe en el desarrollo de la cultura de la Marca Superior* (Madrid: Imprenta y Editorial Maestre, 1954); and M. Grau Monserrat, "Contribución al estudio del estado cultural del Valle del Ebro en el siglo XI y principios del XII," *Boletín de la Real Academia de Buenas Letras de Barcelona* 27 (1957–58): 227–72.

29. Wasserstein, *Rise and Fall of the Party-Kings*, 136, and see 100–115; M. J. Viguera Molins, *Reinos de taifas y las invasiones Magrebíes (al-Andalus del XI al XIII)* (Madrid: Editorial Mapfre, 1992), 59–64, 75–88.

30. A. Turk, *El reino de Zaragoza en el siglo XI de Cristo (V de la Hégira)* (Madrid: Instituto Egipcio de Estudios Islámicos, 1978), 65–80 and 123–44. See R. Miravall, *Madīna Turtūxa: introducció a la Tortosa islàmica* (Tortosa: Dertosa, 1999), 168–76, and C. E. Bosworth, *New Islamic Dynasties: A Chronological and Genealogical Manual* (Edinburgh: Edinburgh University Press, 1996), chap. 2.17.

31. Wasserstein, *Rise and Fall of the Party-Kings*, 88–89 and 96.

32. The term *paria* derives either from the Arabic *bara'* (to be free or cleared of a debt) or *bara'* (to donate, give, or concede): O. R. Constable, *Trade and Traders in Muslim Spain: The Commercial Realignment of the Iberian Peninsula, 900–1500* (Cambridge: Cambridge University Press, 1994), 9n14.

33. Consider *El "Llibre Blanch" de Santas Creus*, ed. Udina Martorell, doc. 9 (11 Jan. 1038).

34. *El "Llibre Blanch" de Santas Creus*, ed. Udina Martorell, doc. 16 (18 June 1076).

35. Salrach, *El procès de feudalització*, 299 and 345–50. Compare Jarrett, *Rulers and Ruled*, esp. 129–43. See F. Sabaté, "La castralització de l'espai en l'estructuració d'un territori conquerit (Urgell, Pla d'Urgell, Garrigues, i Segrià)," *URTX: Revista Cultural de l'Urgell* 11 (1989): 9–16.

36. *Els pergamins de l'Arxiu Comtal de Barcelona, de Ramon Borrell a Ramon Berenguer I*, ed. J. M. Salrach et al., 3 vols. (Barcelona: Fundació Noguera, 1999), vol. 2, doc. 530 (26 Nov. 1058).

37. *Els pergamins de l'Arxiu Comtal de Barcelona, de Ramon Borrell a Ramon Berenguer I,* ed. Salrach et al., vol. 2, doc. 479 (12 Nov. 1056).

38. Bonnassie, *La Catalogne du milieu du Xe à la fin du XIe siècle,* 2:666–69.

39. See Lomax, *Reconquest of Spain,* 58.

40. R. Menéndez Pidal, *España del Cid,* 2 vols. (Madrid: Editorial Plutarco, 1929), 1:132–34.

41. Menéndez Pidal, *España del Cid,* 1:285–90 and Turk, *El reino de Zaragoza en el siglo XI de Cristo,* 122–44. See Salrach, *El procès de feudalització,* 345–50, and below.

42. See Menéndez Pidal, *España del Cid,* 1:378–89, and R. Fletcher, *The Quest for El Cid* (Oxford: Oxford University Press, 1989), 158–59.

43. *Els pergamins de l'Arxiu Comtal de Barcelona, de Ramon Borrell a Ramon Berenguer I,* ed. Salrach et al., vol. 2, doc. 523 ([1 July ca. 1058]). See A. Kosto, "The Elements of Practical Rulership: Ramon Berenguer I of Barcelona and the Revolt of Mir Geribert," *Viator* 47, no. 2 (2016): 67–94.

44. Catlos, *Muslims,* 527, would situate these attitudes within the "ecumenian register of expression or rhetoric."

45. *The Song of Roland: An Analytical Edition,* ed. and trans. G. J. Brault, 2 vols. (University Park: Pennsylvania State University Press, 1978). See R. W. Southern, *Western Views of Islam in the Middle Ages* (Cambridge, MA: Harvard University Press, 1962); G. Johnson, "Muhammad and Ideology in Medieval Christian Literature," *Islam and Christian-Muslim Relations* 11 (2000): 333–46; and J. Tolan, *Medieval Christian Perceptions of Islam: A Book of Essays* (New York: Garland, 1996). For a recent consideration of theological texts, see F. Quinn, *The Sum of All Heresies: The Image of Islam in Western Thought* (Oxford: Oxford University Press, 2008). For further reflections on the representation of Muslims in the *Song of Roland,* see S. Conklin Akbari, *Idols in the East: European Representations of Islam and the Orient, 1100–1450* (Ithaca: Cornell University Press, 2009), 209–16.

46. See Zimmermann, "Le rôle de la frontière dans la formation de la Catalogne," 18 and below in this chapter.

47. See D. Urvoy, "Sur l'évolution de la notion de ǧihād dans l'Espagne musulmane," *Mélanges de la Casa de Velazquez* 9 (1973): 335–71 (at 344–59), and B. Kedar, *Crusade and Mission: European Approaches towards the Muslims* (Princeton, NJ: Princeton University Press, 1988), 86–87.

48. Wasserstein, *Rise and Fall of the Party-Kings,* 280.

49. Wasserstein, *Rise and Fall of the Party-Kings,* 280.

50. Wasserstein, *Rise and Fall of the Party-Kings,* 281.

51. Bonnassie, *La Catalogne du milieu du Xe à la fin du XIe siècle,* 1:443.

52. For what follows, see Bonnassie, *La Catalogne du milieu du Xe à la fin du XIe siècle,* 2:554–74, and Salrach, *El procès de feudalització,* 292–99, 312–24.

53. See Bonnassie, *La Catalogne du milieu du Xe à la fin du XIe siècle,* vol. 2, chaps. 10–12. On this apparent breakdown of authority, see T. N. Bisson, "The 'Feudal Revolution,'" *Past & Present* 142 (1994): 6–42, with responses by D. Barthélemy and S. White in *Past & Present* 152 (1996): 196–205 and 205–23, respectively. See also Bisson's rebuttal in *Past & Present* 155 (1997): 208–25, and C. Wickham's submission to the debate in *Past & Present* 155 (1997): 196–208. For an updated picture, see P. Benito, *Senyoria de la terra i tinença pagesa al comtat de Barcelona (segles XI–XIII)* (Barcelona:

Consell Superior d'Investigacions Científiques, 2003), 102–11, and T. N. Bisson, *The Crisis of the Twelfth Century: Power, Lordship, and the Origins of European Government* (Princeton, NJ: Princeton University Press, 2009), 57.

54. Bonnassie, *La Catalogne du milieu du Xe à la fin du XIe siècle*, 2:645–46.

55. ACL, A 659 [Caj. 181, Paqu. 8, no. 269 (Castillón), no. 1706 (Barnola)] (5 Nov. 1050); E. Corredera, *El archivo de Ager y Caresmar* (Balaguer: Artes Gráficas Romeu, 1978), no. 32 and appendix doc. 3. On *potestas* and the related prerogative of *statica* (lodging rights), see A. Kosto, *Making Agreements in Medieval Catalonia: Power, Order, and the Written Word, 1000–1200* (Cambridge: Cambridge University Press, 2001), 92–94.

56. For both charters, see Corredera, *El archivo de Ager y Caresmar*, no. 44 and appendix no. 4 (17 Oct. 1058).

57. Sobrequés, *Els grans comtes de Barcelona*, 43–45.

58. Zimmermann, "Le rôle de la frontière dans la formation de la Catalogne," 18. Zimmermann likely based his account on *Els pergamins de l'Arxiu Comtal de Barcelona, de Ramon Borrell a Ramon Berenguer I*, ed. Salrach et al., vol. 3, doc. 841bis, a list of Ramon's complaints against Arnau.

59. *Els pergamins de l'Arxiu Comtal de Barcelona, de Ramon Borrell a Ramon Berenguer I*, ed. Salrach et al., vol. 3, doc. 843bis ([1047 / 1071]). Other *querimoniae* decry the breaking of peaces but do not mention Muslims: e.g., docs. 917–20. Their *convenientia* of 9 Dec. 1072 (doc. 851) and other agreements that played a role in resolving their dispute (e.g., doc. 922), do not mention the episode. Compare Catlos, *The Victors and the Vanquished*, 84.

60. *Els pergamins de l'Arxiu Comtal de Barcelona, de Ramon Borrell a Ramon Berenguer I*, ed. Salrach et al., vol. 3, doc. 843bis.

61. Zimmermann, "Le rôle de la frontière dans la formation de la Catalogne," 18.

62. Bonnassie, *La Catalogne du milieu du Xe à la fin du XIe siècle*, 2:560–73, 692–701.

63. See Bonnassie, *La Catalogne du milieu du Xe à la fin du XIe siècle*, 2:574–95.

64. See Sabaté, *L'expansió territorial de Catalunya*, 68–86.

65. P. Bonnassie, "The Formation of Catalan Feudalism and Its Early Expansion (to *c.* 1150)," in P. Bonnassie, *From Slavery to Feudalism in South-Western Europe*, trans. J. Birrell (Cambridge: Cambridge University Press, 1991), 156–57.

66. P. Bonnassie, "The Survival and Extinction of the Slave System in the Early Medieval West (Fourth to Eleventh Centuries)," in Bonnassie, *From Slavery to Feudalism in South-Western Europe*, 1–59 (at 56–59). See Freedman, *Origins of Peasant Servitude*, 62–64.

67. Bonnassie, *La Catalogne du milieu du Xe à la fin du XIe siècle*, 1:256 and 513. See T. W. Barton, "Lords, Settlers, and Shifting Frontiers in Medieval Catalonia," *Journal of Medieval History* 36 (2010): 227–48.

68. Freedman, *Origins of Peasant Servitude*, 89–118.

69. Kosto, *Making Agreements in Medieval Catalonia*, 74–77, and see Bonnassie, *La Catalogne du milieu du Xe à la fin du XIe siècle*, vol. 2, chap. 13.

70. *Els pergamins de l'Arxiu Comtal de Barcelona, de Ramon Borrell a Ramon Berenguer I*, ed. Salrach et al., vol. 2, doc. 388 ([1041 / 1050]).

71. See chapter 2 below for further on this development.

72. *Els pergamins de l'Arxiu Comtal de Barcelona, de Ramon Borrell a Ramon Berenguer I*, ed. Salrach et al., vol. 2, doc. 588 (13 Jan. 1060). See Sobrequés, *Els grans comtes*,

50; Vela Aulesa, "L'Àndalus en la política de Barcelona i la Corona d'Aragó (segle XI–1213)," 138; and A. Virgili, "Els *Fills* de Tamarit (L'origen medieval de les localitats del Baix Gaià)," *Estudis Altafullencs* 25 (2001): 7–22 (13).

73. ACA, C, pergs. Extrainvenatrio, no. 3271 [1038–1065]; *Els pergamins de l'Arxiu Comtal de Barcelona, de Ramon Berenguer II a Ramon Berenguer IV*, ed. Baiges et al., vol. 1, doc. 39. I would date this transaction toward the end of this range, in the 1060s, due to the fact that it stands as evidence of the count's emergence from the governmental crisis that had plagued his regime during the early decades of his reign.

74. ACA, C, pergs. RB II, no. 9 (12 Nov. 1076); *Els testaments dels comtes de Barcelona i dels reis de la Corona d'Aragó: de Guifré Borrell a Joan II*, ed. A. Udina i Abelló (Barcelona: Fundació Noguera, 2001), doc. 10; *Els pergamins de l'Arxiu Comtal de Barcelona, de Ramon Berenguer II a Ramon Berenguer IV*, ed. I. J. Baiges et al., 4 vols. (Barcelona: Fundació Noguera, 2010), vol. 1, doc. 63; *Liber Feudorum Maior: Cartulario real que se conserva en el Archivo de la Corona de Aragón*, ed. F. Miquel Rosell, 2 vols. (Barcelona: Consejo Superior de Investigaciones Científicas, 1945), vol. 1, doc. 492.

75. *Els pergamins de l'Arxiu Comtal de Barcelona, de Ramon Berenguer II a Ramon Berenguer IV*, ed. Baiges et al., vol. 1, doc. 126 [1076–81].

76. The bibliography on the nature of this exchange is immense. For the Ebro valley in particular, see the often-overlooked J. Vernet, "El Valle del Ebro como nexo entre Oriente y Occidente," *Boletín de la Real Academia de Buenas Letras de Barcelona* 23 (1950): 249–86.

77. Bonnassie, *La Catalogne du milieu du Xe à la fin du XIe siècle*, 1:443. S. Bensch, *Barcelona and Its Rulers, 1096–1291* (Cambridge: Cambridge University Press, 1995), 88–121, demonstrates that disruptions caused by the end of *paria* payments at the end of the eleventh century helped bring about a significant slowdown in Barcelona's regional economy that was not reversed until several decades into the twelfth century.

78. See Constable, *Trade and Traders in Muslim Spain*, 38–42; T. Glick, *Islamic and Christian Spain in the Early Middle Ages*, 2nd ed. (Leiden: Brill, 2005), 132–33; and J. M. Lacarra, "Acerca de las fronteras en el valle del Ebro (siglos VIII–XII)," *En la España Medieval* 4 (1984): 181–91.

79. Bonnassie, *La Catalogne du milieu du Xe à la fin du XIe siècle*, 1:379.

80. J. M. Lacarra, "Dos tratados de paz y alianza entre Sancho el de Peñalén y Moctádir de Zaragoza (1069–1073)," in his *Colonización, parias, repoblación, y otros estudios* (Zaragoza: Anubar, 1981), 92.

81. Constable, *Trade and Traders in Muslim Spain*, 45–46.

82. See Constable, *Trade and Traders in Muslim Spain*, 47, and C. Alsina, G. Feliu, and L. Marquet, *Pesos, Mides i Mesures del Països Catalans* (Barcelona: Curial, 1990), 114–243.

83. E.g., *Codice diplomatico della repubblica di Genova*, ed. C. Imperiale Sant'Angelo, 3 vols. (Rome: Tipografia del Senato, 1936–42), vol. 1, doc. 195 (17 Apr. 1149), a treaty between Genoa and Pisa, assigning to the Genoese rights for fifteen years throughout the Mediterranean.

84. See S. Bensch, "From Prizes of War to Domestic Merchandise: The Changing Face of Slavery in Catalonia and Aragon, 1000–1300," *Viator* 25 (1994): 63–93, and Catlos, *The Victors and the Vanquished*, 221.

85. *Usatges de Barcelona: el codi a mitjan segle XII. Establiment del text llatí i edició de la versió catalana del manuscrit del segle XIII de l'arxiu de la d'Aragó de Barcelona*, ed. J. Bastardas i Parera, Col·lecció textos i documents 6, 2nd ed. (Barcelona: Fundació Noguera, 1991), nos. 100–102. See D. J. Kagay, "The Essential Enemy: The Image of the Muslim as Adversary and Vassal in the Law and Literature of the Medieval Crown of Aragon," in *Western Views of Islam in Medieval and Early Modern Europe: Perception of Other*, ed. D. R. Blanks and M. Frassetto (London: St. Martin's Press, 1999), 121–22. This law code also sought to regulate enslaved Muslim captives under Christian lordship: *Usatges de Barcelona*, ed. Bastardas, no. 93.

86. For further on the context of the promulgation of the *Usatges*, see chapter 4 below.

87. See I. S. Robinson, *The Papacy, 1073–1198: Continuity and Innovation* (Cambridge: Cambridge University Press, 1990), esp. chaps. 4, 8, and 9.

88. Deswarte, *Une Chrétienté romaine sans pape*, finds that Iberian bishops and lay rulers through the tenth century for the most part acted independently of papal directives. See also his "Rome et la spécificité catalane: la papauté et ses relations avec la Catalogne et Narbonne (850–1030)," *Revue Historique* 294 (1995): 3–43. P. F. Kehr, *Das Papsttum und der katalanische Prinzipat bis zur Vereinigung mit Aragon* (Berlin: Verlag der Akademie der Wissenschaften, in Kommission bei Walter de Gruyter, 1926), trans. into Catalan by R. d'Abadal i de Vinyals as *El Papat i el principat de Catalunya fins a la unió amb Aragó* (Barcelona: Fundació Patxot, 1931), viewed this influence as varying from pontificate to pontificate. See J. M. Laliena Corbera, "Problemas historiográficos de la Edad Media aragonesa: una revisión crítica," *Argensola: Revista de Ciencias Sociales del Instituto de Estudios Altoaragoneses* 113 (2003): 13–35.

89. On Sancho's reign, see, generally, D. Buesa Conde, *El Rey Sancho Ramírez* (Zaragoza: Guara, 1978).

90. A. I. Lapeña Paúl, *Sancho Ramírez: rey de Aragón, y su tiempo, ¿1064?–1094, y rey de Navarra, 1075–1094* (Gijón: Ediciones Trea, 2004), 73–112, details this enduring relationship. See also L. García-Guijarro Ramos, "El Papado y el reino de Aragón en la segunda mitad del siglo XI," *Aragón en la Edad Media* 18 (2004): 245–64.

91. Consider Urban II's letter to Pedro I of Aragon: *Liber Feudorum Maior*, ed. Miquel Rosell, vol. 1, doc. 5 (16 Apr. 1095). See D. Smith, "¿Soli Hispani? Innocent III and Las Navas de Tolosa," *Hispania Sacra* 51 (1999): 489–512.

92. See García-Guijarro Ramos, "El Papado y el reino de Aragón en la segunda mitad del siglo XI," 257–64.

93. García-Guijarro Ramos, "El Papado y el reino de Aragón en la segunda mitad del siglo XI," 250.

94. P. Sénac, *La frontière et les hommes (VIIIᵉ–XIIIᵉ siècle): le peuplement musulman au nord de l'Ebre et les débuts de la reconquête aragonaise* (Paris: Maisonneuve et Larose, 2000), 354–55. See P. F. Kehr, "Cómo y cuándo se hizó Aragón feudatario de la Santa Sede," *Estudios de Edad Media de la Corona de Aragón* 1 (1945): 300–306.

95. *Documentos correspondientes al reinado de Sancho Ramírez: desde MLXIII hasta MLXXXXIII años: documentos reales prcedentes de la real casa y monasterio de San Juan de la Peña*, ed. J. Salarrullana de Dios and E. Ibarra, 2 vols. (Zaragoza: M. Escar, 1904–13), vol. 1, doc. 3.

96. See García-Guijarro Ramos, "El Papado y el reino de Aragón en la segunda mitad del siglo XI," 248–52.

97. Robinson, *The Papacy*, 304.

98. See C. Vela Aulesa, "La política ibèrica de Barcelona i la Corona d'Aragó (segle XI–1213)," in *Tractats i negociacions diplomàtiques de Catalunya i de la Corona catalanoaragonesa a l'edat mitjana, vol. I.2: Tractats i negociacions diplomàtiques amb els regnes peninsulars i l'Àndalus*, ed. Ferrer i Mallol and Riu i Riu, 19–116 (20–21 and 130–31).

99. It is not known precisely why the Aragonese did not participate in the campaign. It may have been due to the fact that Sancho Ramírez had only recently assumed the throne. See P. Boissonade, "Cluny, la papauté et la premiére grande croisade international contre les sarrasins d'Espagne: Barbastro (1064–1065)," *Revue des questions historiques* 60 (1932): 257–301, and compare V. Cantarino, "The Spanish Reconquest: A Cluniac Holy War against Islam?" in *Islam and the Medieval West*, ed. K. I. Semaan (Albany: State University of New York Press, 1980), 82–109, and A. Ferreiro, "The Siege of Barbastro, 1064–65: A Reassessment," *Journal of Medieval History* 9 (1983): 129–44.

100. L. Villegas-Aristizábal, "Norman and Anglo-Norman Interventions in the Iberian Wars of the Reconquest before and after the First Crusade," in *Crusading and Pilgrimage in the Norman World*, ed. P. Oldfield and K. Hurlock (Woodbridge: Boydell, 2015), 103–21.

101. Sancho Ramírez also arranged to marry the sister of Count Ebles de Roucy, who soon after, with papal approval, undertook a military campaign in Iberia. See J. F. O'Callaghan, *Reconquest and Crusade in Medieval Spain* (Philadelphia: University of Pennsylvania Press, 2003), 27.

102. In 1089, for example, Urban II confirmed Aragon's feudatory status and excused King Pedro I from the five-hundred-*mancus* annual payment; an indication that the papacy was focused primarily on the symbolic value of its papal suzerainty. Pedro, however, in reestablishing the enfeoffment of his kingdom with Urban II in 1095, pledged anew this customary tribute to the papacy. In return, the pope reestablished his protection over the kingdom. See Sénac, *La frontière et les hommes*, 355–56.

103. See, generally, B. Rosenwein, *To Be the Neighbor of St. Peter: The Social Meaning of Cluny's Property, 909–1049* (Ithaca: Cornell University Press, 1989), 144–201.

104. J. Martínez de Aguirre, "Arquitectura y soberanía: la catedral de Jaca y otras empresas constructivas de Sancho Ramírez," *Anales de Historia del Arte, Volumen Extraordinario* 2 (2011): 181–249, esp. 209–10.

105. Consider Kehr, *Das Papsttum und der katalanische Prinzipat bis zur Vereinigung mit Aragon*, 54, who wrote that, at the close of Urban II's pontificate, "Katalanien steht damals in dem Komplex der päpstlichen Politik durachaus an zweiter Stelle. Kastilien und Aragon stehen in Vordergrund."

106. Indeed, the Milanese chronicler Arnulf reports that Alexander had feared Hildebrand so much that he would do nothing without his approval. See H. E. J. Cowdrey, *Gregory VII, 1073–1085* (Oxford: Clarendon Press, 1998), 70.

107. A. Ubieto Arteta, "La introducción del rito romano en Aragón y Navarra," *Hispania Sacra* 1 (1948): 299–324.

108. See U.-R. Blumenthal, *The Investiture Controversy: Church and Monarchy from the Ninth through the Twelfth Century*, trans. U.-R. Blumenthal (Philadelphia: University of Pennsylvania Press, 1988), 115–20.

109. See Deswarte, *Un Chrétienté romaine sans pape*, 418–84.

110. E.g., *La documentación pontificia hasta Inocencio III (965–1216)*, ed. D. Mansilla, Monumenta hispaniae vaticana, sección: registros 1 (Rome: Instituto Español de Estudios Eclesiásticos, 1955), docs. 9, 10, 12.

111. *La documentación pontificia hasta Inocencio III*, ed. Mansilla, doc. 6 (30 Apr. 1073). In another letter from 1077, he espoused similar ideas: doc. 13 (28 June 1077).

112. L. McCrank, "Restoration and Reconquest in Medieval Catalonia: The Church and Principality of Tarragona, 971–1177" (PhD diss., University of Virginia, 1974), 206.

113. See Salrach, *El procès de feudalització*, 356.

114. Sobrequés, *Els grans comtes de Barcelona*, 122. See P. F. Kehr, "Das Papsttum und die Königreiche Navarra und Aragon bis zur mitte des Jahrhunderts," *Abhandlungen der Preussischen Akademie der Wissenschaft. Phil. hist. Klasse* 4 (1928); translated into Castilian as "El Papado y los reinos de Navarra y Aragón hasta mediados del siglo XII," *Estudios de Edad Media de la Corona de Aragón* 2 (1946): 104–39.

115. Salrach, *El procès de feudalització*, 345.

116. McCrank, "Restoration and Reconquest in Medieval Catalonia," 180. See also L. McCrank, "Restauración canonica e intento de Reconquista de la sede Tarraconense (1076–1108)," *Cuadernos de Historia de España* 61–62 (1977): 148–53.

117. McCrank, "Restoration and Reconquest in Medieval Catalonia," 209, has argued that the three primary motives behind the donation were to preserve the frontier for future Catalonian expansion, to block claims by Alfonso VI of Castile-León against Berenguer Ramon's regency, and to accelerate papal recognition of Tarragona's metropolitan authority and official restoration.

118. The document is published in the appendices to E. Flórez et al., *España sagrada: Theatro geographico-histórico de la iglesia de España*, 56 vols. (Madrid: A. Marin, 1771–1908), vol. 25, and in E. Flórez, *Las memorias eclesiasticas antiguas de la santa iglesia de Tarragona* (Madrid: J. Rodriguez, 1859), appendix 11 (212–13): "per manus principis apostolorum Petri et eius vicarii domini Urbani secundi papae et successorum eius." This charter of donation, enigmatically, transferred to the pope castles and territories that were not yet under Barcelona's control, including the still unoccupied city of Tarragona. Berenguer Ramon and his advisors must have hoped that subjecting intended zones of conquest to papal suzerainty would make them off limits to rivals.

119. E.g., a letter from Urban II to King Pedro in 1095 urging him to continue his campaigns to conquer lands from the Muslims. *Liber Feudorum Maior*, ed. Miquel Rosell, vol. 1, doc. 5 (16 Apr. 1095).

120. *Colección diplomática de la catedral de Huesca*, ed. A. Durán Gudiol, 2 vols. (Zaragoza: Escuela de Estudios Medievales, Instituto de Estudios Pirenaicos, 1965–69), vol. 1, doc. 38 (17 Feb. 1074).

121. E.g., when Gregory VII wrote to Sancho Ramírez of Aragon about electing a successor to the see of Huesca. *La documentación pontificia hasta Inocencio III*, ed. Mansilla, doc. 11 (24 Jan. 1075). This policy would be maintained in the twelfth century after Aragon's union with the county of Barcelona.

122. See Barton, "Constructing a Diocese in a Post-Conquest Landscape" and my forthcoming *From the Hands of the Infidels: The Christianization of Islamic Landscapes in Europe*. For a broader treatment on the problem within the German Empire during this same time period, see J. Eldevik, *Episcopal Power and Ecclesiastical Reform in the German Empire: Tithes, Lordship, and Community, 950–1150* (Cambridge: Cambridge University Press, 2012), esp. chaps. 5 and 6.

123. McCrank, "Restoration and Reconquest in Medieval Catalonia," 65. See also Salrach, *El Procès de feudalització*, 246.

124. Scholars have long recognized this duality. See, e.g., J. F. O'Callaghan, *A History of Medieval Spain* (Ithaca: Cornell University Press, 1975), 488–90.

125. R. Konetzke, "Probleme der Beziehungen zwischen Islam und Christentum im spanischen Mittelalter," *Miscellanea Medievalia* 1 (1962): 219–58. See Bartlett, *The Making of Europe*, 11–13.

126. See McCrank, "Restoration and Reconquest in Medieval Catalonia," 75.

127. See McCrank, "Restoration and Reconquest in Medieval Catalonia" and Sobrequés, *Els grans comtes de Barcelona*, 120–24, and compare E. Morera, *Tarragona cristiana: historia del arzobispado de Tarragona y del territorio de su provincia (Cataluña la Nueva)*, 2 vols. (Tarragona: Diputació Provincial de Tarragona, 1897), 1: 325–96.

128. Compare McCrank, "Restoration and Reconquest in Medieval Catalonia," 250.

129. See McCrank, "Restoration and Reconquest in Medieval Catalonia," 66–94. There were two other earlier attempts, in 856 and 886.

130. McCrank, "Restoration and Reconquest in Medieval Catalonia," 95–96.

131. McCrank, "Restoration and Reconquest in Medieval Catalonia," 98–101.

132. For what follows, see also McCrank, "Restauración canonica e intento de Reconquista," 160–75.

133. McCrank, "Restoration and Reconquest in Medieval Catalonia," 183.

134. McCrank, "Restoration and Reconquest in Medieval Catalonia," 170–72. See Gregory VII's letter to the bishop of Girona concerning the problematic archbishop: *La documentación pontificia hasta Inocencio III*, ed. Mansilla, doc. 15 (2 Jan. 1079).

135. *La documentación pontificia hasta Inocencio III*, ed. Mansilla, docs. 25 and 26 (10 Oct. 1088).

136. Revising Kehr, McCrank, "Restoration and Reconquest in Medieval Catalonia," 183, has argued convincingly that the interpolated bull of 1088 demonstrates that the push for reform originated as a grassroots campaign in Catalonia rather than as a papal agenda. On Berenguer de Lluçà's career, see Freedman, *Diocese of Vic*, 29–35.

137. See O'Callaghan, *History of Medieval Spain*, 489, and McCrank, "Restoration and Reconquest in Medieval Catalonia," 219.

138. Flórez et al., *España sagrada*, vol. 28, appendix 18, 295–97. See McCrank, "Restoration and Reconquest in Medieval Catalonia," 219. Freedman, *Diocese of Vic*, 30–37, discusses the implications for Vic of Berenguer's appointment as archbishop.

139. McCrank, "Restoration and Reconquest in Medieval Catalonia," 103.

140. *La documentación pontificia hasta Inocencio III*, ed. Mansilla, doc. 31 [1090], Urban II's document to his legate (Rainerius). See McCrank, "Restoration and Reconquest in Medieval Catalonia," 191–93.

141. See McCrank, "Restoration and Reconquest in Medieval Catalonia," 195–203.

142. *La documentación pontificia hasta Inocencio III*, ed. Mansilla, doc. 32 (1 Jul. 1091). See McCrank, "Restauración canonica e intento de Reconquista," 183–203.

143. See P. Bertran, "Ermengol d'Urgell: l'obra d'un bisbe del segle XI," in *La transformació de la frontera al segle XI: Reflexions des de Guissona arran del IX centenari de la consagració de l'església de Santa Maria*, ed. F. Sabaté (Lleida: Institut d'Estudis Ilerdencs, 2000), 93–109. See Freedman, *Diocese of Vic*, 20–25, on Vic's system of *levitate*, and Bertran, "Ermengol d'Urgell," 109–12, on Urgell.

144. Already within a year of issuing his approval, Urban II wrote to Archbishop Berenguer to urge him to effect Tarragona's restoration. He also counseled him to

respect Toledo's primacy over his province. *La documentación pontificia hasta Inocencio III*, ed. Mansilla, doc. 33 (25 Apr. 1092).

Chapter 2. Competition along the Frontier

1. *Diplomatari d'Alguaire i del seu monestir santojoanista de 1076 a 1244*, ed. J. Alturo i Perucho (Barcelona: Fundació Noguera, 1999), doc. 1 (June 1075).

2. A. Ubieto Arteta, *Historia de Aragón*, 8 vols. (Zaragoza: Anubar, 1981–89), 1:8, S. Barton, *A History of Spain*, 2nd ed. (New York: Palgrave MacMillan, 2009), 55, and Turk, *El reino de Zaragoza en el siglo XI de Cristo*, 164–68.

3. See Stalls, *Possessing the Land*, 14.

4. *Historia Roderici vel gesta Roderici Campidocti*, in *Chronica Hispana Saeculi XII*, ed. E. Falque Rey (Turnhout: Brepols, 1990), 56–57. See Sénac, *La frontière et les hommes*, 400–401, and Menéndez Pidal, *España del Cid*, 1:297–98.

5. This attempt is similar to what Castile was later able to do to the Crown of Aragon's hopes for further southward acquisition under Jaume II around the turn of the fourteenth century. By securing its right to Murcia, Castile blocked the Crown of Aragon, effectively diverting its expansion into the Mediterranean. See J. Hinojosa Montalvo, *Jaime II y el esplendor de la Corona de Aragón* (San Sebastián: Nerea, 2006), 189.

6. *Documentos para el estudio de la reconquista y repoblación del Valle del Ebro*, ed. J. M. Lacarra, 2 vols. (Zaragoza: Anubar, 1982–85), vol. 1, doc. 14 (3 May 1093).

7. *Crónica de San Juan de la Peña*, ed. A. Ubieto Arteta (Valencia: Caja de Ahorros y Monte de Piedad de Zaragoza, Aragón y Rioja, 1961), 58. Translated as *The Chronicle of San Juan de la Peña: A Fourteenth-Century Official History of the Crown of Aragon*, trans. L. Nelson (Philadelphia: University of Pennsylvania Press, 1991), 20.

8. X. Eritja Ciuró, *De l'almunia a la turris: organització de l'espai a la regió de Lleida (segles XI–XIII)* (Lleida: Edicions de la Universitat de Lleida, 1998), 57–59.

9. See McCrank, "Restauración canonica e intento de Reconquista," 224–32.

10. *Cronica de San Juan de la Peña*, ed. Ubieto Arteta, 58–65 (*Chronicle of San Juan de la Peña*, trans. Nelson, 20–23) and the *Chronicon Rotense*, in *Viage literario á las iglesias de España*, ed. Jaime Villanueva, 22 vols. in 11 (Madrid: Real Academia de la Historia, 1821–1902), vol. 15, doc. 60 (334). See Sénac, *La frontière et les hommes*, 409–11, 415–17 and Turk, *El reino de Zaragoza en el siglo XI de Cristo*, 179–85, for details on these campaigns.

11. F. Sabaté, *El territori de la Catalunya medieval: percepció de l'espai i divisió territorial al llarg de l'Edat Mitjana* (Barcelona: R. Dalmau, 1997), 40.

12. E.g., ACA, C, pergs. Extrainvenario, no. 3279; *Els pergamins de l'Arxiu Comtal de Barcelona, de Ramon Berenguer II a Ramon Berenguer IV*, ed. Baiges et al., vol. 1, doc. 34 [ca. 15 July 1063].

13. *Liber feudorum maior*, ed. Miquel Rosell, vol. 1, doc. 148 (5 Sept. 1058); *Marca hispanica sive limes hispanicus*, ed. P. de Marca and E. Baluze (Paris: Muguet, 1688), doc. 257. See P. de Bofarull y Mascaró, *Los condes de Barcelona vindicados, y cronologia y genealogia de los reyes de España considerados como soberanos independientes de su marca*, 2 vols. (Barcelona: Imprenta de J. Oliveres y Monmany, 1836), vol. 2, 78.

14. ACA, C, pergs. Extrainvenario, no. 3519; *Els pergamins de l'Arxiu Comtal de Barcelona, de Ramon Berenguer II a Ramon Berenguer IV*, ed. Baiges et al., vol. 1, doc. 40

[1039–65]: "ipsa paria que hodie conventa est tibi de Hispania vel que in antea per meum consilium adquisieris."

15. ACA, C, pergs. Extrainvenario, no. 4726; *Els pergamins de l'Arxiu Comtal de Barcelona, de Ramon Berenguer II a Ramon Berenguer IV*, ed. Baiges et al., vol. 1, doc. 66 [1066–76]: "sine ullo locro de suo avere si ipse per suam bonam volumptatem non vult ei dare, si ipse per suam bonam volumptatem non vult ei dare." See Vela Aulesa, "L'Àndalus en la política de Barcelona i la Corona d'Aragó (segle XI–1213)," 131. In an extensive section of the agreement, the counts resolved to settle their future differences resulting from the *convenientia* through an intricate system of trials by battle.

16. On the Cid's relationship with al-Muqtadir, see Fletcher, *The Quest for El Cid*, 133–34.

17. ACA, C, pergs. RB II, no. 69 [1076–81]; doc. 126; See Bofarull, *Los condes vindicados*, 2:109–10; Kosto, *Making Agreements*, 130; and Vela Aulesa, "L'Àndalus en la política de Barcelona i la Corona d'Aragó (segle XI–1213)," 139. See chapter 1 above for discussion of the *parias* treated in this charter.

18. Eritja, *De l'almunia a la turris*, 15 and 22–23. The name Mascançà derives from the Andalusi administrative zone, the fahs Maskiján. See *La Péninsule ibérique au moyen-âge d'après le Kitāb ar-rawḍ al-mi'ṭār fī ḥabar al-akṭār d'Ibn 'Abd al Mun'im al-ḥimyari: Text arabe des notices relatives à l'Espagne, au Portugal e au sud-ouest de la France*, ed. and trans. É. Lévi-Provençal (Leiden: Brill, 1938), 157. Fahs denoted a valley or agricultural plain.

19. See F. Foguet i Boreu, "Notícia sobre la colonització del fahs Maskigan," *Mascançà* 8 (2017): 31–36.

20. García i Biosca, *Els orígens del terme de Lleida*, figs. 2 and 3, 109–10, provides useful reconstructions of the castral and territorial expansion around these centers. See also *L'Islam i Catalunya*, ed. M. Miquel and M. Sala (Barcelona: Museu d'Història de Catalunya, 1998), 180, for an excellent map of advancement along the counties of Urgell, Osona, and Barcelona in the late tenth to mid-eleventh centuries, as well as Bonnassie, *La Catalogne du milieu du Xᵉ à la fin du XIᵉ siècle*, 1:439–40.

21. García i Biosca, *Els orígens del terme de Lleida*, 109–10.

22. Corredera, *El archivo de Ager y Caresmar*, appendix doc. 6 (22 Apr. 1079).

23. See Eritja, *De l'almunia a la turris*, 20–21, for a map of the fortifications across the plain of Mascançà toward Corbins and Balaguer in the later eleventh century.

24. X. Mora Giné, *Un poble del comtat d'Urgell: Alberola* (Lleida: Universitat de Lleida, 2010), 33–34.

25. See chapter 3 below. *El cartulario de Tavérnoles*, ed. J. Soler Garcia (Castellón de la Plana: Sociedad Castellonense de Cultura, 1961), doc. 47 (26 May 1091), and *Cartas de población y franquicia de Cataluña*, ed. J. M. Font Rius, 2 vols. in 3 (Madrid: Consejo Superior de Investigaciones Científicas, 1969–83), vol. 1.1, doc. 56 (31 Oct. 1139). P. Bertran, "Notes sobre els origens d'unes poblaciones urgellenques: la Fuliola, Bolú i Bellcaire als segles XI i XII," *Ilerda* 42 (1981): 237–72, also reproduces these texts.

26. *Diplomatari de Santa Maria de Poblet (960–1177)*, ed. A. Altisent (Barcelona: Abadia de Poblet and Generalitat de Catalunya, 1995), doc. 43 (9 Apr. 1094).

27. P. Sanahuja, *Història de la ciutat de Balaguer*, 2nd ed. (Balaguer: Excel.lentíssim Ajuntament de Balaguer, 1984), 99.

28. Sanahuja, *Història de la ciutat de Balaguer*, 99–108. Most of these castles were eventually captured by the viscount of Girona and Lower Urgell, Guerau Ponç II, in 1115/16. See below.

29. For a brief overview on Ermengol VI's activity, see B. F. Reilly, "Prince into Mercenary: Count Armengol VI of Urgel, 1102–1154," *Journal of Military History* 2 (2004): 39–52. A fuller account, especially of Ermengol's dealings in Castile-León, is provided by S. Barton, "The Count, the Bishop, and the Abbot: Armengol VI of Urgel and the Abbey of Valladolid," *English Historical Review* 111 (1996): 85–103. On Pedro Ansúrez's career, see B. F. Reilly, "The Rediscovery of Count Pedro Ansúrez," in *Cross, Crescent and Conversion: Studies on Medieval Spain and Christendom in Memory of Richard Fletcher*, ed. S. Barton and P. Linehan (Leiden: Brill, 2008), 109–26.

30. Sanahuja, *Història de la ciutat de Balaguer*, 110. See J. Rodríguez Fernández, *Pedro Ansúrez* (León: Imprenta Provincial, 1966), 70–73.

31. ACA, pergs. RB III, no. 95; *Liber Feudorum Maior*, ed. Miquel Rosell, vol. 1, doc. 159 (3 Nov. 1105), in which Pedro assumes the title of "comes Urgellensi."

32. *Colección diplomática de la catedral de Huesca*, ed. Durán Gudiol, vol. 1, doc. 109 ([1105–1110]).

33. *Liber Feudorum Maior*, ed. Miquel Rosell, vol. 1, doc. 160 ([1109?]).

34. *Colección diplomática de Pedro I de Aragón y Navarra*, ed. A. Ubieto Arteta (Zaragoza: Consejo Superior de Investigaciones Científicas, 1951), 25–27. See B. F. Reilly, *The Kingdom of León-Castilla under King Alfonso VI, 1065–1099* (Princeton, NJ: Princeton University Press, 1988), 323–24.

35. "Els documents, dels anys 1101–1150, de l'Arxiu Capitular de la Seu d'Urgell," ed. C. Baraut, *Urgellia* 9 (1988–89), 7–312, doc. 1261 (12 July 1110). Compare Sanahuja, *Història de la ciutat de Balaguer*, 110.

36. Eritja, *De l'almunia a la turris*, 18.

37. P. Sénac, "Peuplement et habitats ruraux dans la Marche Supérieure d'al-Andalus: l'Aragon," *Actes des congrès de la Société des historiens médiévistes de l'enseignement supérieur public* 21, no. 1 (1990): 27–38. Some seventy-five *almuniae* are mentioned for the sector around Monzón in an agreement between Sancho Ramírez and Ramon Dalmacio, bishop of Roda, over the tithes and first fruits dating from 1089. ACL, *Llibre Vert*, fols. 14v–15v. The first documentary use of *almunia* dates from 1078 for a zone neighboring the county of Urgell: *Liber Feudorum Maior*, ed. Miquel Rosell, vol. 1, doc. 165. Eritja, *De l'almunia a la turris*, 18n38, hypothesizes this particular *almunia* might have been located at Torregrossa.

38. Stalls, *Possessing the Land*, 25, also notes this lack of involvement.

39. *Liber Feudorum Maior*, ed. Miquel Rosell, vol. 1, doc. 410 (27 May 1113), in which Ramon Berenguer III established Guerau Ponç II de Cabrera, viscount of Girona and Lower Urgell, with the castle of Montplau in fief in return for a pledge of fidelity and military service. See Sobrequés, *Els grans comtes de Barcelona*, 142–43 and 169. For detail on Guerau Ponç's involvement in the county of Urgell, see Sanahuja, *Història de la ciutat de Balaguer*, 114–15 and 118. Guerau's father, Ponç Guerau I, had sworn an oath of fidelity for the castles of Blanes, Argimon, and Cabrera before 1106. ACA, C, pergs. RB III, no. 20 (undated); *Els pergamins de l'Arxiu Comtal de Barcelona, de Ramon Berenguer II a Ramon Berenguer IV*, ed. Baiges et al., vol. 2, doc. 361. See J. Coll i Castanyer, "Els vescomtes de Girona," *Annals de l'Institut d'estudis geronins* 30 (1988–89): 64, as well as Kosto, *Making Agreements in Medieval Catalonia*, 220–21.

40. For Anglesola, see *Liber Feudorum Maior*, ed. Miquel Rosell, vol. 1, doc. 165 (26 June 1079); for Tàrrega, see docs. 171 and 172 (5 Feb. 1058, and [1058], respectively).

McCrank, "Restoration and Reconquest in Medieval Catalonia," 309, notes that as a result of incorporating the front with Lleida, Ramon Berenguer III carefully defined Tarragona's western borders for the first time.

41. Sobrequés, *Els grans comtes de Barcelona*, 159.

42. See C. Servatius, *Paschalis II. (1099–1118): Studien zu Seiner Person und Seiner Politik* (Stuttgart: Anton Hiersemann, 1979), 137–45. For what follows on this campaign, see McCrank, "Restauración canonica e intento de Reconquista," 203–24.

43. *Papsturkunden in Spanien: vorarbeiten zur Hispania Pontificia*, vol. 1, *Katalanien*, ed. P. F. Kehr (Berlin: Weidmannsche Buchhandlung, 1926), doc. 23 (1089–91). See McCrank, "Restoration and Reconquest in Medieval Catalonia," 264.

44. Villanueva, *Viage literario*, vol. 6, appendix 39, docs. 1 and 2.

45. Villanueva, *Viage literario*, vol. 6, appendix 39, docs. 1 and 2. See McCrank, "Restoration and Reconquest in Medieval Catalonia," 255–56.

46. *Diplomatari de la cartoixa de Montalegre*, ed. X. Pérez i Gómez (Barcelona: Fundació Noguera, 1998), doc. 44. See Virgili, *Ad detrimentum Yspanie*, 37. See McCrank, "Restoration and Reconquest in Medieval Catalonia," 252–53.

47. See McCrank, "Restoration and Reconquest in Medieval Catalonia," 250.

48. *La documentación pontificia hasta Inocencio III*, ed. Mansilla, doc. 32 (1 Jul. 1091).

49. Flórez et al., *España sagrada*, vol. 25, appendix 11 (1090–1091).

50. See McCrank, "Restoration and Reconquest in Medieval Catalonia," 244.

51. See P. Benito i Montclús, "Fams i caresties a la Mediterrània occidental durant la baixa edat mitjana: El debat sobre 'les crisis de la crisi,'" *Recerques: història, economia, cultura* 49 (2004): 179–94.

52. "Els documents, dels anys 1093–1100, de l'Arxiu Capitular de la Seu d'Urgell," ed. C. Baraut, *Urgellia* 8 (1986–87): 7–149, doc. 1102 (20 Mar. 1093).

53. Villanueva, *Viage literario*, vol. 6, appendix 39, docs. 1–2. See McCrank, "Restauración canonica e intento de Reconquista," 212.

54. These ships first had to assist Alfonso VI of Castile-León with his planned siege of Balansiya, a coastal town located in southern Valencia. Caffaro, *De captione Almerie et Tortuose*, ed. Luigi Tommaso Belgrano, *Annali Genovesi di Caffaro e de suoi continuatori* (Rome: Tipografia del Senato, 1890), 13. See Virgili, *Ad detrimentum Yspanie*, 36, and McCrank, "Restoration and Reconquest in Medieval Catalonia," 260.

55. ACA, C, pergs RB II, no. 48; *Els pergamins de l'Arxiu Comtal de Barcelona, de Ramon Berenguer II a Ramon Berenguer IV*, ed. Baiges et al., vol. 1, doc. 113 (10 Dec. 1080).

56. Ibn al-Qanā, cited by Menéndez Pidal, *España del Cid*, 1:416–18; 2:778; Aḥmad ibn Muḥammad al-Maqqarī, *Kitāb nafh al-tīb*, in *The History of the Mohammedan Dynasties in Spain*, trans. P. de Gayangos, 2 vols. (London: Oriental Translation Fund, 1840–43), 2:38–39, confuses the king of Aragon with the count of Barcelona. Compare McCrank, "Restoration and Reconquest in Medieval Catalonia," 283.

57. Menéndez Pidal, *España del Cid*, 1:463–94. Sulaymān ibn Hūd was the last of Tortosa's independent *taifa* rulers before the zone fell under the influence of the Almoravids. See Miravall, *Madīna Turtūxa*, 176–81.

58. Flórez et al., *España sagrada*, 42:102. On this reference, see also Bayerri, *Historia de Tortosa*, 6:739, and Morera, *Tarragona cristiana*, 1:371. For an overview, see Bayerri, *Historia de Tortosa*, 6:738–51.

59. AHN, Códices, no. 662B, *Cartulario de Ulldecona*, 3–6; *Cartulario de "Sant Cugat" del Vallés*, ed. J. Rius y Serra, 3 vols. (Barcelona: Consejo Superior de Investigaciones Científicas, 1945–47), vol. 2, doc. 765 (10 Jan. 1097).

60. P. Artigués and M. Villalbí, "L'adaptació estructural del Castell d'Amposta al món feudal," in *IV Congreso de Arqueología Medieval Española* (Alicante: Asociación Española de Arqueología Medieval, 1993), 2:451–53, and M. Villalbí, T. Forcadell, and M. C. Montañés, "El castell d'Amposta: resultats d'unes excavacions urbanes," *I Congrés d'Arqueologia Medieval i Moderna a Catalunya* (Igualada: Associació Catalana per la Recerca en Arqueologia Medieval, 2000), 90–99.

61. See McCrank, "Restoration and Reconquest in Medieval Catalonia," 262, and Sobrequés, *Els grans comtes de Barcelona*, 152.

62. ACA, C, pergs. RB III, no. 51 (21 Jan. 1097); *Els pergamins de l'Arxiu Comtal de Barcelona, de Ramon Berenguer II a Ramon Berenguer IV*, ed. Baiges et al., vol. 2, doc. 296. See F. Cheyette, "The 'Sale' of Carcassonne to the Counts of Barcelona (1067–1070) and the Rise of the Trencavels," *Speculum* 63 (1988): 826–64, esp. 863–64; J. Shideler, *A Medieval Catalan Noble Family: The Montcadas, 1000–1230* (Berkeley: University of California Press, 1983), 96–97; Bartlett, *The Making of Europe*, 90; and Kosto, *Making Agreements in Medieval Catalonia*, 98–99.

63. Flórez et al., *España sagrada*, vol. 42, appendix 1 (6 May 1097) and appendix 2 (confirmation). See Bayerri, *Historia de Tortosa*, 6:740–43, 742n2; McCrank, "Restoration and Reconquest in Medieval Catalonia," 264–65; and Kosto, *Making Agreements in Medieval Catalonia*, 220. Papal confirmation: *Cartulario de "Sant Cugat" del Vallés*, ed. Rius y Serra, vol. 2, doc. 774, and *Papsturkunden in Spanien*, ed. Kehr, doc. 29 (1 Dec. 1098).

64. Compare McCrank, "Restoration and Reconquest in Medieval Catalonia," 263.

65. Compare McCrank, "Restoration and Reconquest in Medieval Catalonia," 259.

66. See Salrach, *El procès de feudalització*, 351, and Sobrequés, *Els grans comtes de Barcelona*, 152–53.

67. E.g., Ermengol VI's grant, under the oversight of Pedro Ansúrez, to the church of Santa Maria in the castle of Solsona of a number of fortifications near Balaguer (Castelló, Os, Tartareu, and Santa Linya) in 1105/6. *Diplomatari de l'arxiu diocesà de Solsona (1101–1200)*, ed. A. Bach Riu and R. Sarobe i Huesca, 2 vols. (Barcelona: Fundació Noguera, 2002), vol. 1, doc. 50.

68. Reilly, *Kingdom of León-Castilla under King Alfonso VI*, 318, 323–24, 356–58. See Stalls, *Possessing the Land*, 29.

69. Sanahuja, *Història de la ciutat de Balaguer*, 142.

70. ACA, C, pergs. RB III, no. 222 (15 Feb. 1120); *Els pergamins de l'Arxiu Comtal de Barcelona, de Ramon Berenguer II a Ramon Berenguer IV*, ed. Baiges et al., vol. 2, doc. 518.

71. "Els documents, dels anys 1101–1150, de l'Arxiu Capitular de la Seu d'Urgell," ed. Baraut, doc. 1240 (1106), and Arxiu Capitular de Solsona, *Cartulari* 2, fols. 30v–31r (1122).

72. Kosto, *Making Agreements in Medieval Catalonia*, 229–30. See Sanahuja, *Història de la ciutat de Balaguer*, 122–23.

73. Lladonosa, *Història de Lleida*, 111.

74. ACA, C, pergs. RB III, no. 207; *Col·lecció diplomàtica de la casa del Temple de Gardeny (1070–1200)*, ed. R. Sarobe i Huesca, 2 vols., Diplomataris 16–17 (Barcelona:

Fundació Noguera, 1998), vol. 1, doc. 3 (5 June 1118); *Liber Feudorum Maior*, ed. Miquel Rosell, vol. 1, doc. 166; *Els pergamins de l'Arxiu Comtal de Barcelona, de Ramon Berenguer II a Ramon Berenguer IV*, ed. Baiges et al., vol. 2, doc. 501. Compare García i Biosca, *Els orígens del terme de Lleida*, 215n6. See the discussion of disputes over these castles with Arnau Berenguer's son in chapter 4 below.

75. ACA, C, pergs. RB III, no. 208; *Els pergamins de l'Arxiu Comtal de Barcelona, de Ramon Berenguer II a Ramon Berenguer IV*, ed. Baiges et al., vol. 2, doc. 502; *Liber Feudorum Maior*, ed. Miquel Rosell, vol. 1, doc. 186. See Kosto, *Making Agreements in Medieval Catalonia*, 255–56.

76. Tàrrega: *Cartas de población*, ed. Font Rius, vol. 1.1, doc. 48 (1116). Balaguer: *Cartas de población*, ed. Font Rius, vol. 1.1, doc. 50 (1118). Compare McCrank, "Restoration and Reconquest in Medieval Catalonia," 313, and Sobrequés, *Els grans comtes de Barcelona*, 160.

77. See C. Laliena Corbera, "*Larga stipendia et optima praedia*: Les nobles francos en Aragon au servisse d'Alphonse le Batailleur," *Annales du Midi* 112 (2000): 149–69. On the roles played by *chansons de geste* and chivalric romances, see S. Vander Elst, *The Knight, the Cross, and the Song: Crusade Propaganda and Chivalric Literature, 1100–1400* (Philadelphia: University of Pennsylvania Press, 2017), esp. 11–50.

78. See Stalls, *Possessing the Land*, 28, and Ubieto Arteta, *Historia de Aragon*, 1:142–43.

79. ADM, Entença, L. 18, no. 550 (Rotlle no. 67, Fotograma no. 115) (11 Jan. 1103), using the *fueros* of Monzón.

80. Sobrequés, *Els grans comtes de Barcelona*, 165. *Gesta comitum Barcinonensium: Cròniques Catalanes*, ed. L. Barrau Dihigo and J. Massó Torrents (Barcelona: Institut d'Estudis Catalans, 1925), c. 16, 37–38.

81. Miravall, *Madīna Turtūxa*, 180–81.

82. See Wasserstein, *Rise and Fall of the Party-Kings*, 286–89.

83. Menéndez Pidal, *España del Cid*, 2:578–82; Lomax, *Reconquest of Spain*, 73–75; Catlos, *Kingdoms of Faith*, 244–48.

84. See McCrank, "Restauración canonica e intento de Reconquista," 233–43.

85. *Cartulario de "Sant Cugat" del Vallés*, ed. Rius y Serra, doc. 794, 2:449 (9 May 1107).

86. See Sobrequés, *Els grans comtes de Barcelona*, 154, and Lomax, *Reconquest of Spain*, 81.

87. *La documentación pontificia hasta Inocencio III*, ed. Mansilla, doc. 47.

88. Miravall, *Madīna Turtūxa*, 180.

89. P. Balañà, *Musulmans a Catalunya (713–1153): assaig de sintési orientativa* (Sabadell: AUSA, 1993), 113, 117. See Stalls, *Possessing the Land*, 25; Catlos, *Kingdoms of Faith*, 249; Mestre and Sabaté, *Atles de la "Reconquesta,"* 29; Viguera Molins, *Reinos de taifas y las invasiones Magrebíes*, 178; and *Catalunya Romànica*, 24:31.

90. See Balañà, *Musulmans a Catalunya (713–1153)*, 113–15, and Lomax, *Reconquest of Spain*, 68.

91. Servatius, *Paschalis II*, 142.

92. See Kehr, *Das Papsttum und der katalanische Prinzipat bis zur Vereinigung mit Aragon*, 59–60. J. Martí Bonet, *Oleguer: servent de les esglésies de Barcelona i Tarragona* (Barcelona: Arxiu Diocesà de Barcelona, 2003). Orderic Vitalis, *Ecclesiasticae Historiae Libri*

tredecim. The Ecclesiastical History of Orderic Vitalis, ed. and trans. M. Chibnall, 6 vols. (Oxford: Oxford University Press, 1969–80), 6:274–75, mentions Oleguer's preaching.

93. See Sobrequés, *Els grans comtes de Barcelona*, 148–50.

94. See U. Vones-Liebenstein, *Saint-Ruf und Spanien: Studien zur Verbreitung und zum Wirken der Regularkanoniker von Saint-Ruf in Avignon auf der Iberischen Halbinsel (11. und 12. Jahrhundert)*, 2 vols. (Turnhout: Brepols, 1996), 1:411–45.

95. See M. Parker, "Pisa, Catalonia, and Muslim Pirates: Intercultural Exchanges in the Balearic Crusade of 1113–1115," *Viator* 45, no. 2 (2014): 77–100; Sobrequés, *Els grans comtes de Barcelona*, 152–55; and Salrach, *El procès de feudalització*, 351–52.

96. Compare McCrank, "Restoration and Reconquest in Medieval Catalonia," 353n17. See the *Vita Prima of Oleguer*, 5: Flórez et al., *España sagrada*, vol. 29, appendix 21.

97. W. J. Purkis, *Crusading Spirituality in the Holy Land and Iberia, c. 1095–c. 1187* (Woodbridge: Boydell, 2008), 168.

98. See F. Cheyette, *Ermengard of Narbonne and the World of the Troubadours* (Ithaca: Cornell University Press, 2001), 87–95.

99. O. R. Constable, "Genoa and Spain in the Twelfth and Thirteenth Centuries: Notarial Evidence for a Shift in Patterns of Trade," *Journal of Economic History* 19 (1990): 637.

100. *Liber Maiolichinus de gestis pisanorum illustribus*, ed. C. Calisse, Fonti per la Storia d'Italia 29 (Rome: Tip. del Senato, 1904), 137–40. See Parker, "Pisa, Catalonia, and Muslim Pirates," 86–89.

101. Purkis, *Crusading Spirituality*, 168.

102. See Parker, "Pisa, Catalonia, and Muslim Pirates," 89–90.

103. Sobrequés, *Els grans comtes de Barcelona*, 155.

104. For what follows, see Sobrequés, *Els grans comtes de Barcelona*, 155–56, and McCrank, "Restoration and Reconquest in Medieval Catalonia," 297–300.

105. See Cheyette, *Ermengard of Narbonne*, 83–87.

106. See Parker, "Pisa, Catalonia, and Muslim Pirates," 91–92.

107. *La documentación pontificia hasta Inocencio III*, ed. Mansilla, doc. 50 (23 May 1116). See Sobrequés, *Els grans comtes de Barcelona*, 157. Compare McCrank, "Restoration and Reconquest in Medieval Catalonia," 299.

108. *La documentación pontificia hasta Inocencio III*, ed. Mansilla, doc. 50.

109. See C. de Ayala Martínez, *Sacerdocio y reino en la España altomedieval: iglesia y poder político en el Occidente peninsular, siglos VII–XII* (Madrid: Sílex, 2008), 390–98.

110. Flórez et al., *España sagrada*, vol. 29, appendix 21. See McCrank, "Restoration and Reconquest in Medieval Catalonia," 298–303, and F. Fita, "Concilios de Gerona, Segovia, y Tuy en 1117 y 1118," *Boletín de la Real Academia de Historia* 48 (1906): 501–9.

111. *Liber Feudorum Maior*, ed. Miquel Rosell, vol. 1, doc. 211 (16 May 1119). See Sobrequés, *Els grans comtes de Barcelona*, 169. For a detailed examination of Bernat Amat's activity as viscount, see F. Rodríguez Bernal, *Els vescomtes de Cardona al segle XII. Una història a través dels seus testaments* (Lleida: Universitat de Lleida, 2009), 23–47. This Bernat Amat was a descendant of the Bernat Amat de Claramunt who received that castles of Tamarit and Ullastrell from Ramon Berenguer I in 1060. See chapter 1 above.

112. See E. Juncosa Bonet, *Estructura y dinámicas de poder en el señorio de Tarragona (1118–1462)* (Barcelona: Consejo Superior de Investigaciones Científicas, 2015), 87–88.

113. D. Smith, "The Abbot-Crusader: Nicholas Breakspear in Catalonia," in *Adrian IV, the English Pope, 1154–1159: Studies and Texts*, ed. B. Bolton and A. Duggan (Aldershot: Variorum, 2003), 33.

114. *Cartas de población*, ed. Font Rius, vol. 1.1, doc. 49 (23 Jan. 1118).

115. Flórez et al., *España sagrada*, vol. 25, appendix 16. See Bisson, *Medieval Crown of Aragon*, 27. Compare McCrank, "Restoration and Reconquest in Medieval Catalonia," 306–10. Vitalis, *Ecclesiasticae Historiae*, ed. and trans. Chibnall, 13.5, 6:403, describes Tarragona's desolate state during this period.

116. For Provence, see *Liber Feudorum Maior*, ed. Miquel Rosell, vol. 2, docs. 875–878 (1 Feb. 1112, 3 Feb. 1112, 13 Jan. 1113, and [1113]). M. Aurell, *Les noces du comte: mariage et pouvoir en Catalogne (785–1213)* (Paris: Publications de la Sorbonne, 1995), 394–95, and Sobrequés, *Els grans comtes de Barcelona*, 157–58 and 162.

117. See Sobrequés, *Els grans comtes de Barcelona*, 162–64.

118. Balañà, *Musulmans a Catalunya (713–1153)*, 117.

119. Virgili, *Ad detrimentum Yspanie*, 39, and Sénac, *La frontière et les hommes*, 425, among others, make this identification. See Parker, "Pisa, Catalonia, and Muslim Pirates," 92. R. Pita Mercè, *Lérida árabe* (Lleida: Dilagro, 1974), hypothesized that Abū Hilāl was an independent Almoravid governor in Lleida who was fighting a civil war with Tortosa. See also García i Biosca, *Els orígens del terme de Lleida*, 46–47.

120. It is clear that the count would be holding these family members as hostages to guarantee Abū Hilāl's faithful compliance with the terms of the agreement. See Kosto, *Making Agreements in Medieval Catalonia*, 128, and A. Kosto, *Hostages in the Middle Ages* (Oxford: Oxford University Press, 2012), 9–19.

121. ACA, C, RB III, no. 229 (14 Nov. 1120); *Els pergamins de l'Arxiu Comtal de Barcelona, de Ramon Berenguer II a Ramon Berenguer IV*, ed. Baiges et al., vol. 2, doc. 525; *Documentos para el estudio de la reconquista y repoblación del Valle del Ebro*, ed. Lacarra, vol. 1, doc. 69. See Virgili, *Ad detrimentum Yspanie*, 39–40. Compare Villanueva, *Viage literario*, 16:4, and appendix doc. 1.

122. This is evidenced by the settlement charter granted by Alfonso I (ADM, Entença, L. 18, no. 550), mentioned earlier. Zurita writes that the count of Urgell took the castle of Alcolea in 1123 and used it to launch campaigns against Lleida and Fraga before entrusting it to Iñigo Galíndez, lord of Sos. J. Zurita, *Anales de la Corona de Aragón*, ed. Á. Canellas López, 8 vols. (Zaragoza: Institución "Fernando el Católico," 1967–77), 1.47, 1:155.

123. See above for contextual information on the taking of these castles. *Liber Feudorum Maior*, ed. Miquel Rosell, vol. 1, doc. 186. Albesa, as we have seen, was conquered later, and therefore does not appear to have been rendered as described here. Setting aside the possibility of forgery, it is reasonable that, by these donations, the qā'id of Lleida was authorizing Ramon Berenguer III's prior seizure of these fortifications. McCrank, "Restoration and Reconquest in Medieval Catalonia," 318–19, is thus too quick to accept the validity of these castle donations without qualification. See *Els castells catalans*, 6 vols. (Barcelona: R. Dalmau, 1967–79), 6.2:849.

124. ACA, C, RB III, no. 229.

125. J. Salarrullana de Dios, "El reino moro de Afraga y las últimas campañas y muerte del Batallador," republished in his *Estudios historicos acerca de la ciudad de Fraga*, 2 vols. (Fraga: Ayuntamiento de Fraga, 1989–90), 1:23–118. See J. Miret y Sans, "Alfonso el Batallador en Fraga, en 1122," *Boletín de la Real Academia de Buenas Letras de Barcelona* 11, no. 48 (1912): 542, and the interpretations by Stalls, *Possessing the Land*, 46, and Ubieto Arteta, *Historia de Aragón*, 1:146. Compare García i Biosca, *Els orígens del terme de Lleida*, 138n168.

126. A. Huici Miranda, *Historia musulmana de Valencia y su región: novedades y rectificaciones*, 3 vols. (Valencia: Ayuntamiento de Valencia, 1970), 3:80–82. B. F. Reilly, *The Kingdom of León-Castilla under Queen Urraca, 1109–1126* (Princeton, NJ: Princeton University Press, 1982), 170–73, hypothesizes regarding these preparations and the motives that prompted them. See Stalls, *Possessing the Land*, 47–48, and Sabaté, *Història de Lleida*, 2:181–82.

127. Miret y Sans, "Alfonso el Batallador en Fraga, en 1122," 541: a grant by Alfonso I (1122), "in villa que dicitur Fraga," republished in *Colección diplomática de Alfonso I de Aragón y Pamplona, 1104–1134*, ed. J. A. Lema Pueyo (San Sebastián: Editorial Eusko Ikaskuntza, 1990), doc. 119, and *Documentos para el estudio de la reconquista y repoblación del Valle del Ebro*, ed. Lacarra, vol. 1, doc. 314. Scholars disagree on the timing and extent of Fraga's conquest. Compare *Documentos para el estudio de la reconquista y repoblación del Valle del Ebro*, ed. Lacarra, 1:130n1, with Stalls, *Possessing the Land*, 48. See Ubieto Arteta, *Historia de Aragón*, 1:167. Miret y Sans, "Alfonso el Batallador en Fraga, en 1122," 545, following Salarrullana, argued that "es lo cierto que Fraga y Gardeny estaban occupados por el rey de Aragón en 1123." Compare also J. M. Lacarra, "La reconquista y repoblación del valle del Ebro," in his *Estudios dedicados a Aragón: Colectánea de sus trabajos que, en su homenaje y memoria edita la Facultad de Filosofía y Letras y su área de Historia Medieval* (Zaragoza: Universidad de Zaragoza, 1987), 217.

128. *Colección diplomática de Alfonso I de Aragón y Pamplona*, ed. Lema Pueyo, doc. 121 (May 1123) and doc. 118 (1123). Zurita, *Anales de la Corona de Aragón*, ed. Canellas López, 1.47, 1:155.

129. See Zurita, *Anales de la Corona de Aragón*, ed. Canellas López, 1.47, 1:155.

130. García i Biosca, *Els orígens del terme de Lleida*, 138, suggests that the battle of Corbins (see below) was the result of poor relations between Barcelona and the qāʾid of Lleida after Ramon Berenguer III had failed to shield his tributary from Aragonese assault. One charter reported that the rulers engaged in a duel in an effort to settle their conflicting claims. *Documentos para el estudio de la reconquista y repoblación del Valle del Ebro*, ed. Lacarra, vol. 1, doc. 90 (Mar. 1123). Although there is no evidence to prove that Alfonso's forces even besieged Lleida, scholars widely assume the Aragonese mounted some sort of attack. J. M. Lacarra, *Alfonso el Batallador* (Zaragoza: Guara, 1978), 80–81, hypothesizes that Alfonso was forced to lift the siege after losing a battle to Ramon Berenguer III.

131. A. Ubieto Arteta, "La reconquista y repoblación de Alcañiz," *Teruel* 9 (1953): 37–55. See J. M. Font Rius, "Notas sobre algunas cartas pueblas de la región oriental aragonesa," *Anuario de historia del derecho español* 41 (1971): 724–38.

132. Sobrequés, *Els grans comtes de Barcelona*, 163–65. See McCrank, "Restoration and Reconquest in Medieval Catalonia," 319–21.

133. *Liber Feudorum Maior*, ed. Miquel Rosell, vol. 2, doc. 520 (13 Oct. 1122). This *convenientia* was primarily dedicated to renewing Ponç's vassalage to Ramon Berenguer for the castles of Ceret and Molins within the counties of Cerdanya and Besalú. The agreement also made explicit mention of the castles of Pavià and Estopiñán, which Ponç may have controlled through his ties to the aforementioned viscount of Girona and Lower Urgell, Guerau Ponç II de Cabrera. See Sobrequés, *Els grans comtes de Barcelona*, 170–72. Ponç's oath is also preserved as ACA, C, pergs. RB III, no. 241b (13 Oct. 1122); *Liber Feudorum Maior*, ed. Miquel Rosell, vol. 2, doc. 521; *Els pergamins de l'Arxiu Comtal de Barcelona, de Ramon Berenguer II a Ramon Berenguer IV*, ed. Baiges et al., vol. 3, doc. 539. Compare García i Biosca, *Els orígens del terme de Lleida*, 142. Kosto, *Making Agreements in Medieval Catalonia*, 244, documents how some of the terms of this agreement later became embroiled of conflict further on in Ramon Berenguer III's reign (in 1127) as well as at the beginning of Ramon Berenguer IV's rule. Because the frontier military relationship described by this 1122 agreement was never fully enacted, these later disputes focused on other issues between the two rulers.

134. Villanueva, *Viage literario*, 16:2.

135. See Parker, "Pisa, Catalonia, and Muslim Pirates," 94, for thoughts on how the failure of the campaign to conquer Mallorca in 1115 may have played a role in this shift.

136. *La documentación pontificia hasta Inocencio III*, ed. Mansilla, doc. 62 (2 Apr. [1121–24]). See McCrank, "Restoration and Reconquest in Medieval Catalonia," 313.

137. *La documentación pontificia hasta Inocencio III*, ed. Mansilla, doc. 62. *Sacrorum conciliorum: nova et amplissima collectio*, ed. G. D. Mansi et al., 53 vols. (Paris: H. Welter, 1901–27), vol. 21, col. 284, Canon 10: *Eis qui Hierosolymam proficiscuntur*. See McCrank, "Restoration and Reconquest in Medieval Catalonia," 320–21.

138. See McCrank, "Restoration and Reconquest in Medieval Catalonia," 321.

139. Sanahuja, *Història de la ciutat de Balaguer*, 125–26. See also M. J. Viguera Molins, *Aragón musulmán: La presencia del Islam en el Valle del Ebro* (Zaragoza: Mira Editores, 1988), 241, and Sabaté, *Història de Lleida*, 183.

140. McCrank, "Restoration and Reconquest in Medieval Catalonia," 323, relying on the *Vita Prima* of Oleguer. The *Cronicon Dertusense II* (Villanueva, *Viage literario*, 5:237) reports that many Christians died at Corbins. See Zurita, *Anales de la Corona de Aragón*, ed. Canellas López, 1.49, 1:160–61.

141. Sanahuja, *Història de la ciutat de Balaguer*, 126.

142. Zurita, *Anales de la Corona de Aragón*, ed. Canellas López, 1.49, 1:160–61.

143. A. Giménez Soler, *La Edad Media en la Corona de Aragón*, 2nd ed. (Barcelona: Editorial Labar, 1944), 101–2.

144. Sobrequés, *El grans comtes de Barcelona*, 173.

145. See Stalls, *Possessing the Land*, 51.

146. R. Jiménez de Rada, *Historia de Rebus Hispanie sive Historia Gothica*, ed. J. Fernández Valverde, Corpus Christianorum, Continuatio Medievalis 72 (Turnhout: Brepols, 1987), 4.11. See Ubieto Arteta, *Historia de Aragón*, 1:180–87.

147. McCrank, "Restoration and Reconquest in Medieval Catalonia," 324–25. C. Devic and J. Vaissete, *Histoire générale de Languedoc*, 15 vols. (Toulouse: Édouard Privat, 1872–92), 3:667–68.

148. See L. McCrank, "The Foundation of the Confraternity of Tarragona by Archbishop Oleguer Bonestruga, 1126–1129," *Viator* 9 (1978): 157–77; reprinted in his *Medieval Frontier History in New Catalonia* (Ashgate: Variorum, 1996), Essay III.

149. Flórez et al., *España sagrada*, vol. 28, appendix 22, and Villanueva, *Viage literario*, vol. 5, doc. 46. See McCrank, "Restoration and Reconquest in Medieval Catalonia," 325–27.

150. Sobrequés, *Els grans comtes de Barcelona*, 166.

151. ACA, C, pergs. RB III, no. 293 (28 Nov. 1127). *Codice diplomatico della repubblica di Genova*, ed. Imperiale de Sant'Angelo, vol. 1, doc. 46.

152. ACA, C, pergs. RB III, no. 293.

153. The first recorded noncomital donation in Tarragona dates from October 1128. Flórez et al., *España sagrada*, vol. 28, appendix 23. See McCrank, "Restoration and Reconquest in Medieval Catalonia," 328.

154. Vitalis, *Ecclesiasticae Historiae*, ed. and trans. Chibnall, 13.2, 6:394–97. *Cartulario de "Sant Cugat" del Vallés*, ed. Rius y Serra, vol. 3, doc. 912. See McCrank, "Restoration and Reconquest in Medieval Catalonia," 340.

155. *Liber Feudorum Maior*, ed. Miquel Rosell, vol. 1, doc. 211 (16 May 1119). *El "Llibre Blanch" de Santas Creus*, ed. Udina Martorell, doc. 38 (9 Mar. 1134).

156. *Cartas de población*, ed. Font Rius, vol. 1.1, doc. 51 (14 Mar. 1129). See Juncosa Bonet, *Estructura y dinámicas de poder en el señorio de Tarragona*, 89–94.

157. *Cartas de población*, ed. Font Rius, vol. 1.1, doc. 51. See McCrank, "Restoration and Reconquest in Medieval Catalonia," 367.

158. McCrank, "Restoration and Reconquest in Medieval Catalonia," 367.

159. Sobrequés, *Els grans comtes de Barcelona*, 167, and L. McCrank, "Norman Crusaders in the Catalan Reconquest: Robert Burdet and the Principality of Tarragona, 1129–55," *Journal of Medieval History* 7 (1981): 67–82.

160. Robert's later charter of franchise to the inhabitants of Tarragona from 1149 describes this earlier visit and the exemptions awarded by the prince: *Cartas de población*, ed. Font Rius, vol. 1.1, doc. 73 (3 Sep. 1149). See *Cartas de población*, ed. Font Rius, vol. 1.1, doc. 52 [posterior to 14 Mar. 1129]. See also McCrank, "Restoration and Reconquest in Medieval Catalonia," 369–70.

161. Morera, *Tarragona Cristiana*, 1:395, based on ibn 'al-Abbar's *Complementum Libri Assila*.

162. See J. F. Utrilla, "Los grupos aristocráticos aragonenses en la época de la gran expansión territorial del reino (1076–1134): poder, propiedad y mentalidades," in *De Toledo a Huesca: Sociedades medievales en transición a finales del siglo XI (1080–1100)*, ed. C. Laliena and J. F. Utrilla (Zaragoza: Institución "Fernando el Católico," 1998), 167–97, and McCrank, "Restoration and Reconquest in Medieval Catalonia," 379–80.

163. ADM, Entença, L. 15, no. 401 (Rotlle no. 40, Fotograma no. 509) (28 July 1131).

164. Lacarra, *Alfonso el Batallador*, 105. See Stalls, *Possessing the Land*, 53–54.

165. *Liber Feudorum Maior*, ed. Miquel Rosell, vol. 1, doc. 6 (31 Oct. 1131).

166. Sabaté, *Història de Lleida*, 183–86.

167. *Documentos para el estudio de la reconquista y repoblación del Valle del Ebro*, ed. Lacarra, vol. 1, doc. 221 (Jan. 1133); doc. 223 (Mar. 1133) suggests that Alfonso had lost Godall by that time. See Ubieto Arteta, *Historia de Aragón*, 1:189.

168. *Documentos para el estudio de la reconquista y repoblación del Valle del Ebro*, ed. Lacarra, vol. 1, doc. 224 (June 1133).

169. See Bisson, *Medieval Crown of Aragon*, 16.

170. "Els documents, dels anys 1101–1150, de l'Arxiu Capitular de la Seu d'Urgell," ed. Baraut, doc. 1425 (8 Feb. 1133).

171. McCrank, "Restoration and Reconquest in Medieval Catalonia," 369–70. See also Flórez et al., *España sagrada*, 25:126. See Lacarra, *Alfonso el Batallador*, 128–31, and Sénac, *La frontière et les hommes*, 180–83, 426–29.

172. Ibn al-Khaṭīb, *Kitāb a'māl al-a'lām*, ed. and trans. R. Castrillo (Madrid: Instituto Hispano-Árabe de Cultura, 1983), 152.

173. *Chronica Adefonsi Imperatoris*, in *Chronica Hispana Saeculi XII*, ed. E. Falque, J. Gil, and A. Maya (Turnhout: Brepols, 1990), 1.51.

174. *Chronica Adefonsi Imperatoris*, ed. Falque, Gil, and Maya, 1.51–53. Other sources deviate from the *Chronica*'s narrative. See Lacarra, *Alfonso el Batallador*, 130–31. Various Muslim chroniclers describe the siege and its aftermath in varying levels of detail. See Ibn al-Aṯir, *al-Kāmil fī al-tārīḥ*, trans. E. Fagnan, *Annales du Maghreb et de l'Espagne* (Algiers: A. Jourdan, 1898), 554–55, and *Al-Ḥimyari*, *Kitāb al-Rawḍ al-Mi'ṭār*, trans. in *Péninsule Ibérique au Moyen Âge d'après le Kitāb ar-rawḍ al-mi'ṭār*, ed. and trans. Lévi-Provençal, 31–32.

175. See Sénac, *La frontière et les hommes*, 428.

176. Sénac, *La frontière et les hommes*, 429, based on *Documentos para el estudio de la reconquista y repoblación del Valle del Ebro*, ed. Lacarra, vol. 1, doc. 283 (1134). See also Lacarra, *Alfonso el Batallador*, 135–37.

177. *Documentos para el estudio de la reconquista y repoblación del Valle del Ebro*, ed. Lacarra, vol. 1, doc. 281 (Aug. 1134). See Sénac, *La frontière et les hommes*, 429.

178. Zurita, *Anales de la Corona de Aragón*, ed. Canellas López, 1.52, 1:165–69. See Lacarra, "La reconquista y repoblación del valle del Ebro" and Sénac, *La frontière et les hommes*, 429.

179. See L. Villegas-Aristizábal, "Spiritual and Material Rewards on the Christian–Muslim Frontier: Norman Crusaders in the Valley of the Ebro in the First Half of the Twelfth Century," *Medievalismo* 27 (2017): 367.

180. See B. F. Reilly, *The Kingdom of León-Castilla under King Alfonso VII, 1126–1157* (Philadelphia: University of Pennsylvania Press, 1998), esp. 41–60.

181. Compare Catlos, *The Victors and the Vanquished*, 92.

Chapter 3. Unification and Conquest

1. N. Jaspert, "*Capta est Dertosa, clavis Christianorum*: Tortosa and the Crusades," in *The Second Crusade: Scope and Consequences*, ed. J. Phillips and M. Hoch (Manchester: Manchester University Press, 2001), 95.

2. Sénac, *La frontière et les hommes*, 433, and see Reilly, *Kingdom of León-Castilla under King Alfonso VII*, 46–47.

3. E. Lourie, "The Will of Alfonso, 'El Batallador,' King of Aragon and Navarre: A Reassessment," *Speculum* 50 (1975): 635–51. Compare A. J. Forey, "The Will of Alfonso I of Aragon and Navarre," *Durham University Journal* 73, no. 1 (n.s. 42, no. 1) (1980): 59–65, and Lourie's response, "The Will of Alfonso I of Aragon and Navarre: A Reply to Dr. Forey," *Durham University Journal* 77, no. 2 (n.s. 46, no. 2) (1984–85): 165–72.

4. See, generally, A. I. Lapeña Paúl, *Ramiro II de Aragón: el rey monje (1134–1137)* (Gijón: Ediciones Trea, 2008).

5. R. del Arco, "Referencias a acaecimientos históricos en las datas de documentos Aragoneses de los siglos XI y XII," *Estudios de Edad Media de la Corona de Aragón*

3 (1947–48): 291–354, doc. 82 (1 Oct. 1134). See Zurita, *Anales de la Corona de Aragón*, ed. Canellas López, 1.53, 1:170–75. For Alfonso's will, see *Liber Feudorum Maior*, ed. Miquel Rosell, vol. 1, doc. 6 (Oct. 1131).

6. D. Smith, "The Men Who Would Be Kings: Innocent II and Spain," in *Pope Innocent II (1130–43)*, ed. J. Doran and D. Smith (London: Routledge, 2016), 188.

7. See S. McDougall, "The Monk-King and the Abbess-Countess: Dynastic Lineage in Twelfth-Century Aragon and Boulogne," in *Boundaries in the Medieval and Wider World: Essays in Honour of Paul Freedman*, ed. T. W. Barton, S. McDonough, S. McDougall, and M. Wranovix (Turnhout: Brepols, 2017), 109–26, and *Royal Bastards: The Birth of Illegitimacy, 800–1230* (Oxford: Oxford University Press, 2016), 190–201.

8. The so-called Pact of Vadoluengo: *Colección de documentos inéditos del Archivo de la Corona de Aragón*, ed. P. de Bofarull y Mascaró et al., 42 vols. (Barcelona, 1847–1973), vol. 4, doc. 150. *Chronica Adefonsi Imperatoris*, ed. Falque, Gil, and Maya, 1.62. See A. J. Martín Duque, "La restauración de la monarquía navarra y las órdenes militares (1134–1194)," *Príncipe de Viana* 63 (2002): 852–54.

9. *Colección de documentos inéditos del Archivo de la Corona de Aragón*, ed. de Bofarull y Mascaró et al., vol. 4, doc. 150.

10. See H. Grassotti, "Homenaje de García Ramírez a Alfonso VII," *Príncipe de Viana* 25 (1964): 57–66.

11. Del Arco, "Referencias a acaecimientos históricos en las datas de documentos Aragoneses de los siglos XI y XII," doc. 84 (10 June 1135). See Zurita, *Anales de la Corona de Aragón*, ed. Canellas López, 1.54–55, 1:176–84 and I. Álvarez Borge, *Cambios y alianzas: La política regia en la frontera del Ebro en el reinado de Alfonso VIII de Castilla (1158-1214)* (Madrid: Consejo Superior de Investigaciones Científicas, 2008), 349.

12. See Sénac, *La frontière et les hommes*, 432–33.

13. See S. de Vajay, "Ramire II le Moine, roi d'Aragon et Agnès de Poitou dans l'histoire et dans la légende," in *Mélanges offerts à René Crozet*, ed. P. Gallais and Y.-J. Riou (Poitiers: Société d'études médiévales, 1966), 727–50.

14. See Smith, "The Men Who Would Be Kings," 185–89.

15. *Papsturkunden in Spanien*, ed. Kehr, doc. 50 (1135/36). See Kehr, "El Papado y los reinos de Navarra y Aragón hasta mediados del siglo XII," 162–63. See Lourie, "The Will of Alfonso I of Aragon and Navarre," 165, and Reilly, *Kingdom of León-Castilla under King Alfonso VII*, 54–55.

16. See *Chronica Adefonsi Imperatoris*, ed. Falque, Gil, and Maya, 1.62.

17. Ubieto Arteta, *Historia de Aragón*, 5:132–33.

18. ACA, C, pergs. RB IV, no. 86 (11 Aug. 1137); *Documentos de Ramiro II de Aragón*, ed. A. Ubieto Arteta (Zaragoza: Anubar, 1988), doc. 110; *Liber Feudorum Maior*, ed. Miquel Rosell, vol. 1, doc. 7; confirmed as ACA, C, pergs. RB IV, no. 87; *Documentos de Ramiro II*, ed. Ubieto Arteta, doc. 114 (27 Aug. 1137). This arrangement utilized the juridical tradition of *casamiento en casa*. See A. Ubieto Arteta, *Los esponsales de la reina Petronila y la creación de la corona de Aragón* (Zaragoza: Diputación General de Aragón, 1987), 61–63. Ramiro later defined the limits of his realm (*Documentos de Ramiro II*, ed. Ubieto Arteta, doc. 113). Compare Sénac, *La frontière et les hommes*, 433, and see P. Schramm, "Ramon Berenguer IV," in *Els primers comtes-reis*, ed. E. Bagué, J. Cabestany, and P. Schramm (Barcelona: Vicens-Vives, 1980), 30.

19. ACA, C, pergs. RB IV, no. 86; *Documentos de Ramiro II*, ed. Ubieto Arteta, doc. 110.

20. *Chronica Adefonsi Imperatoris*, ed. Falque, Gil, and Maya, 1.70.

21. Del Arco, "Referencias a acaecimientos históricos en las datas de documentos Aragoneses de los siglos XI y XII," doc. 87 (28 Oct. 1136).

22. Del Arco, "Referencias a acaecimientos históricos en las datas de documentos Aragoneses de los siglos XI y XII," doc. 89 (5 Dec. 1137). See Zurita, *Anales de la Corona de Aragón*, ed. Canellas López, 2.2, 1:195.

23. See Sénac, *La frontière et les hommes*, 434.

24. ACA, C, pergs. RB IV, no. 86; *Documentos de Ramiro II*, ed. Ubieto Arteta, doc. 113 ([Aug. 1137]).

25. See Sénac, *La frontière et les hommes*, 431–32. The charters edited in *Documentos de Ramiro II*, ed. Ubieto Arteta, track Ramiro's activity during his reign.

26. See *Documentos de Ramiro II*, ed. Ubieto Arteta, doc. 120 (10 Mar. 1144), issued by Ramiro alone, as "king," with Ramon Berenguer as "king of Aragon."

27. ACA, C, pergs. RB IV, no. 159 (27 Nov. 1143); *Col·lecció diplomàtica*, ed. Sarobe, vol. 1, doc. 9, in which Ramon Berenguer entitles himself "Dei gratia regni dominator Aragonensis." He soon adopted "princeps," which became his standard title. See J. M. Lacarra, "Alfonso II El Casto, Rey de Aragón y Conde de Barcelona," in *VII Congrès d'Història de la Corona d'Aragó*, 3 vols. (Barcelona: Institución "Fernando el Católico," 1963), 1:95–120 (103–7), and Schramm, "Ramon Berenguer IV," 17–18.

28. J. Miret y Sans, *Les cases de Templers y Hospitalers en Catalunya* (Barcelona: Impr. de la Casa Provincial de Caritat, 1910), 13–14, based on ACA, AGP, Arm. 3: Cervera, perg. no. 359 (1111). M. L. Ledesma Rubio, *Templarios y hospitalarios en el Reino de Aragón* (Zaragoza: Guara, 1982), 26, questions this early date. See Bonet Donato, *La orden del Hospital en la Corona de Aragón*, 9–10, and compare McCrank, "Restoration and Reconquest in Medieval Catalonia," 319.

29. A. J. Forey, *The Templars in the* Corona de Aragón (London: Oxford University Press, 1973), 6–9. Compare Miret y Sans, *Les cases de Templers y Hospitalers*, 15–17.

30. *Diplomatari d'Alguaire i del seu monestir santojoanista*, ed. Alturo, doc. 3 (July 1134).

31. *Cartulaire général de l'Ordre du Temple, 1119?–1150: Recueil des chartes et des bulles relatives à l'Ordre du Temple*, ed. J. A. d'Albon (Paris: H. Champion, 1922), doc. 100 (14 July 1130 or 1131). Compare Miret y Sans, *Les cases de Templers y Hospitalers*, 23–24, and Forey, *Templars in the* Corona de Aragón, 8. Ramon Berenguer III's will suggests that the count did not execute these arrangements: *Cartulaire général de l'Ordre du Temple*, ed. d'Albon, 28–29, doc. 38; *Liber Feudorum Maior*, ed. Miquel Rosell, vol. 1, doc. 493.

32. ACA, C, pergs. RB IV, no. 14 (19 Oct. 1132); *Col·lecció diplomàtica de la casa del Temple de Barberà (945–1212)*, ed. J. M. Sans i Travé (Barcelona: Generalitat de Catalunya, Departament de Justícia, 1997), doc. 27. See Forey, *Templars in the* Corona de Aragón, 16.

33. ACA, C, pergs. RB IV, no. 28; *Les constitucions de Pau i Treva de Catalunya (segles XI–XIII)*, ed. G. Gonzalvo i Bou, Textos jurídics catalans, Lleis i Costums II 3 (Barcelona: Generalitat de Catalunya, Departament de Justícia, 1994), doc. 11 (15 Apr. 1134).

34. ACA, C, pergs. RB IV, no. 27 (3 Jan. 1135); *Col·lecció diplomàtica de la casa del Temple de Barberà*, ed. Sans i Travé, doc. 28.

35. Forey, *Templars in the* Corona de Aragón, 17.

36. *Documentos para el estudio de la reconquista y repoblación del Valle del Ebro*, ed. Lacarra, vol. 1, doc. 173. See Ubieto Arteta, *Historia de Aragón*, 1:168–71, and Stalls, *Possessing the Land*, 52–53.

37. *Diplomatari d'Alguaire i del seu monestir santojoanista*, ed. Alturo, doc. 3 (July 1134).

38. H. Nicholson, *The Knights Templar: A Brief History of the Warrior Order* (London: Constable & Robinson, 2010), 102.

39. ACA, C, pergs. RB IV, no. 28; *Les constitucions de Pau i Treva de Catalunya*, ed. Gonzalvo i Bou, doc. 11.

40. See Forey, *Templars in the* Corona de Aragón, 20.

41. See Forey, *Templars in the* Corona de Aragón, 21, and J. M. Sans i Travé, "La introducció de l'orde del Temple a Catalunya i la seva organització," in *Actes de les primeres jornades sobre els ordes religioso-militars als països catalans (segles XII–XIX): Montblanc, 8–10 de novembre de 1985* (Tarragona: Diputació de Tarragona, 1994), 19–23. Identical renunciations are contained in ACA, C, pergs. RB IV, no. 116; *Colección de documentos inéditos del Archivo de la Corona de Aragón*, ed. de Bofarull y Mascaró et al., vol. 4, doc. 32. The Hospitallers' compromise was also recorded separately as *Liber Feudorum Maior*, ed. Miquel Rosell, vol. 1, doc. 12. The patriarch subsequently authorized the accord: *Liber Feudorum Maior*, ed. Miquel Rosell, vol. 1, doc. 10 (29 Aug. 1141).

42. E.g., Chalamera was captured in April 1141 (*Documentos para el estudio de la reconquista y repoblación del Valle del Ebro*, ed. Lacarra, vol. 1, doc. 304). A new *tenente* held Monzón and Alcolea de Cinca in May: Ubieto Arteta, *Historia de Aragon*, 1:219. Compare Catlos, *The Victors and the Vanquished*, 106.

43. ACA, C, pergs. RB IV, no. 159 (27 Nov. 1143). *Col·lecció diplomàtica*, ed. Sarobe, vol. 1, doc. 9.

44. ACA, AGP, Arm. 23: Comunes, perg. no. 97, doc. 2. *Col·lecció diplomàtica*, ed. Sarobe, vol. 1, doc. 28.

45. Confirmation by Pope Hadrian IV: *Regesta Pontificum Romanorum*, ed. P. Jaffé et al., 2 vols. (Graz: Akademische Druck- und Verlagsanstalt, 1956), no. 10161, 2:117, "Catholicorum principum" (20 Mar. 1156); *Diplomatari de la catedral de Tortosa (1062–1193)*, ed. A. Virgili, Diplomataris 11 (Barcelona: Fundació Noguera, 1997), doc. 64. See Schramm, "Ramon Berenguer IV," 19–20.

46. See Forey, *Templars in the* Corona de Aragón, 23.

47. ACA, C, pergs. RB IV, no. 159.

48. *Colección de documentos inéditos del Archivo de la Corona de Aragón*, ed. de Bofarull y Mascaró et al., vol. 4, doc. 153.

49. See *Diplomatari d'Alguaire i del seu monestir santojoanista*, ed. Alturo, doc. 4 (27 Nov. 1143; copy from 12 Sept. 1401).

50. See A. J. Forey, "The Military Orders and the Spanish Reconquest in the Twelfth and Thirteenth Centuries," *Traditio* 40 (1984): 197–234.

51. Lomax, *Reconquest of Spain*, 107–8.

52. ACA, C, pergs. RB IV, no. 73, and *Colección de documentos inéditos del Archivo de la Corona de Aragón*, ed. de Bofarull y Mascaró et al., vol. 4, doc. 22 (28 Dec. 1136).

53. Sabaté, *L'expansió territorial de Catalunya*, 87. See Glick, *Islamic and Christian Spain*, 85–86.

54. See F. Sabaté, "Organització administrativa i territorial del comtat d'Urgell," in *El Comtat d'Urgell*, ed. F. Sabaté (Lleida: Universitat de Lleida, 1995), 26–27.

55. *Cartas de población*, ed. Font Rius, vol. 1.1, doc. 56 (31 Oct. 1139).

56. E.g., *Cartas de población*, ed. Font Rius, vol. 1.1, doc. 57 (29 Dec. 1139).

57. *Col·lecció diplomàtica*, ed. Sarobe, vol. 1, doc. 8 (25 Mar. 1142).

58. *Cartas de población*, ed. Font Rius, vol. 1.1, doc. 60 (28 Jan. 1143).

59. *Cartas de población*, ed. Font Rius, vol. 1.1, doc. 63, and *Diplomatari de Santa Maria de Poblet*, ed. Altisent, doc. 105 (12 Aug. 1146).

60. *Col·lecció diplomàtica*, ed. Sarobe, vol. 1, docs. 15 and 16 (before 26 Oct. 1147 and 28 Oct. 1147).

61. *Cartas de población*, ed. Font Rius, vol. 1.1, doc. 107 (26 Sept. 1157).

62. See P. Toubert, "L'incastellamento aujourd'hui: quelques réflexions en marge de deux colloques," in *"L'Incastellamento": Actas de las reuniones de Girona (26–27 Noviembre 1992) y de Roma (5–7 Mayo 1994)*, ed. M. Barceló and P. Toubert (Rome: École Française de Rome, 1998), xi–xviii, and C. Wickham, "L'incastellamento e i suoi destini undici anni dopo il *Latium* di P. Toubert," in *Structures de l'habitat et occupation du sol dans les pays méditerranéens: les méthodes et l'apport de l'archéologie extensive*, ed. G. Noyé, Castrum 2 (Rome: Casa de Velázquez, 1988), 411–20.

63. See Eritja, *De l'almunia a la turris*, 20–21.

64. *Cartas de población*, ed. Font Rius, vol. 1.1, doc. 64 (13 Apr. 1147).

65. *Diplomatari de l'arxiu diocesà de Solsona*, ed. Bach Riu and Sarobe, vol. 1, doc. 318. See A. Virgili, "Conqueridors i colons a la frontera: Tortosa, 1148–1212," *Recerques: història, economia, cultura* 43 (2001): 47–49, and C. Batet i Company, *Castells termenats i estratègies d'expansió comtal: La Marca de Barcelona als segles X–XI* (Vilafranca del Penedès: Institut d'Estudis Penedesencs, 1996).

66. Ubieto Arteta, *Historia de Aragon*, 1:219.

67. *Colección diplomática de la catedral de Huesca*, ed. Durán Gudiol, vol. 1, doc. 139 (May 1147) and doc. 140 (June 1147). See Zurita, *Anales de la Corona de Aragón*, ed. Canellas López, 2.6, 1:206.

68. AHN, Clero: Poblet, c. 1999, no. 15; *Diplomatari de Santa Maria de Poblet*, ed. Altisent, docs. 106 and 107 (28 Dec. 1146).

69. AHN, Clero: Poblet, c. 2000, no. 6 (22 Aug. 1148); *Diplomatari de Santa Maria de Poblet*, ed. Altisent, doc. 115.

70. *Cartas de población*, ed. Font Rius, vol. 1.1, doc. 64 (13 Apr. 1147).

71. ACA, AGP, Arm. 7: Espluga Calba, perg. no. 7 (14 Sept. 1147); *Col·lecció diplomàtica*, ed. Sarobe, vol. 1, doc. 14.

72. AHN, Clero: Poblet, c. 2000, nos. 3 and 9; *Diplomatari de Santa Maria de Poblet*, ed. Altisent, doc. 112 (8 June 1147), containing a valuable irrigation canal (*cequia*). On the reuse of Andalusi irrigation systems, see T. Glick, *From Muslim Fortress to Christian Castle: Social and Cultural Change in Medieval Spain* (Manchester: Manchester University Press, 1995), 152–53.

73. *Colección de documentos inéditos del Archivo de la Corona de Aragón*, ed. de Bofarull y Mascaró et al., vol. 4, doc. 50 (17 Feb. 1146).

74. AHN, Clero: Poblet, c. 2000, no. 6 (22 Aug. 1148); *Diplomatari de Santa Maria de Poblet*, ed. Altisent, doc. 115.

75. See Forey, *Templars in the Corona de Aragón*, 24; McCrank, "Restoration and Reconquest in Medieval Catalonia," 313; and F. Codera, *Decadencia y desaparición*

de los Almoravides en España (Zaragoza: Tip. de Comas hermanos, 1899), 123–25. For general information on ibn Mardanīš, "El Rey Lobo," see Huici Miranda, *Historia musulmana de Valencia y su región*, 1:129–70. See below in this chapter as well as chapter 5.

76. See, e.g., A. Loriente, *L'horitzó andalusi de l'antic Portal de Magdalena* (Lleida: Ajuntament de Lleida, 1990), 45–46. For context, see J. E. García Biosca, J. Giralt, A. Loriente, and J. Martínez, "La gènesi dels espais urban andalusins (segles VIII–X): Tortosa, Lleida i Balaguer," in Miquel and Sala, *L'Islam i Catalunya*, 137–65.

77. See García-Guijarro Ramos, "Reconquest and the Second Crusade in Eastern Iberia," 255.

78. See G. Constable, "The Second Crusade as Seen by Contemporaries," *Traditio* 9 (1953): 237. Compare García-Guijarro Ramos, "Reconquest and the Second Crusade in Eastern Iberia," 230–34, who critiques Constable, Jaspert, and others for overemphasizing the importance of crusading in Tortosa's conquest.

79. In his detailed list of collaborators, Zurita identifies the counts of Urgell and Pallars, the viscount of Gavarret and Bearn, Gomez (lord of Jaca and Ayerbe), Artal (lord of Alagón), Poncio (lord of Calatayud), Sancho Enecón (lord of Daroca), Fortún Aznárez (castellan of Tarazona), Galín Jiménez (castellan of Belchite), Pelegrín (castellan of Alquézar), Fortún Dat (castellan of Barbastro), Pedro de Rueira (master of the Templars and lord of Monzón and Corbins), and the seneschal Guillem Ramon II de Montcada. Zurita, *Anales de la Corona de Aragón*, ed. Canellas López, 2.9, 1:213–14.

80. See A. Virgili, *"Angli cum multis aliis alienigenis:* Crusade Settlers in Tortosa (Second Half of the Twelfth Century)," *Journal of Medieval History* 35 (2009): 297–312, and R. Miravall, *Immigració britànica a Tortosa (segle XII)* (Barcelona: R. Dalmau, 1980). For further on French settlement, see C. Batlle, "Els francesos a la Corona d'Aragó," *Anuario de Estudios Medievales* 10 (1980): 362. L. Villegas-Aristizábal, "Anglo-Norman Intervention in the Conquest and Settlement of Tortosa, 1148–1180," *Crusades* 8 (2009): appendix A, 84–129, provides a detailed register of Anglo-Norman landholding. See also his "Spiritual and Material Rewards on the Christian–Muslim Frontier," 362–67.

81. See Lomax, *Reconquest of Spain*, 107, and Villegas-Aristizábal, "Norman and Anglo-Norman Interventions in the Iberian Wars of the Reconquest."

82. ACA, C, pergs. RB IV, nos. 202 and 233; *Col·lecció diplomàtica*, ed. Sarobe, vol. 1, doc. 17 (25 May 1148). *Liber Feudorum Maior*, ed. Miquel Rosell, vol. 1, doc. 161. This charter had been drafted in reference to prior *convenientiae*. See Kosto, *Making Agreements in Medieval Catalonia*, 219–33.

83. See C. Biarnés Biarnés, *Moros i moriscos a la Ribera d'Ebre (710–1615)* (Barcelona: Rafael Dalmau, 1972), 28. *Diplomatari de la catedral de Tortosa (1062–1193)*, ed. Virgili, doc. 28 (5 Aug. 1151) may indicate that Ascó had already been captured by 1151. J. M. Font Rius, "La carta de seguridad de Ramón Berenguer IV a las morerías de Ascó y Ribera del Ebro (siglo XII)," in *Homenaje a Don José Maria Lacarra de Miguel en su jubilación del Profesorado* (Zaragoza: Anubar, 1977), 267n17, however, argued that this charter was an anticipatory grant.

84. ACA, C, pergs. RB IV, no. 202; *Col·lecció diplomàtica*, ed. Sarobe, vol. 1, doc. 17 (25 May 1148). See T. N. Bisson, "The Problem of Feudal Monarchy: Aragon, Catalonia and France," in his *Medieval France and Her Pyrenean Neighbours: Studies in Early Institutional History* (London and Ronceverte, WV, 1989), 243.

85. ACA, C, pergs. RB IV, no. 189a; *Els pergamins de l'Arxiu Comtal de Barcelona, de Ramon Berenguer II a Ramon Berenguer IV*, ed. Baiges et al., vol. 3, doc. 852; *Colección de documentos inéditos del Archivo de la Corona de Aragón*, ed. de Bofarull y Mascaró et al., vol. 4, doc. 51 (3 Aug. 1146).

86. G. B. Doxey, "Christian Attempts to Conquer the Balearic Islands, 1015–1229" (PhD diss., University of Cambridge, 1991), 234.

87. García-Guijarro Ramos, "Reconquest and the Second Crusade in Eastern Iberia." See Sabaté, *El territori de la Catalunya medieval*, 382–83, and Virgili, *Ad detrimentum Yspanie*, 46–58.

88. See, generally, Cheyette, *Ermengard of Narbonne*, 88–90, and S. Orvietani Busch, *Medieval Mediterranean Ports: The Catalan and Tuscan Coasts, 1100 to 1235* (Leiden: Brill, 2001), esp. 216–26.

89. *Liber iurium reipublicae Genuensis*, ed. E. Ricotti, Historiae patriae monumenta 7.1 (Turin: E. regio typographeo, 1839–1955), docs. 39 and 40.

90. *Codice diplomatico della repubblica di Genova*, ed. Imperiale de Sant'Angelo, vol. 1, doc. 83 (July 1138). *Liber iurium reipublicae Genuensis*, ed. Ricotti, docs. 54–56 and 81–82.

91. See Caffaro, *Annales Ianuenes*, ed. Belgrano, *Annali Genovesi di Caffaro e de suoi continuatori*, 1:24–26.

92. *Codice diplomatico della repubblica di Genova*, ed. Imperiale de Sant'Angelo, vol. 1, docs. 124 and 125 (both 1143). Compare *Liber iurium reipublicae Genuensis*, ed. Ricotti, docs. 87 and 88.

93. J. Gil, "Carmen de expugnatione Almariae urbis," *Habis* 5 (1974): 62.

94. *Codice diplomatico della repubblica di Genova*, ed. Imperiale de Sant'Angelo, vol. 1, doc. 126 (3 Sept. 1143).

95. Devic and Vaissete, *Histoire générale du Languedoc*, 3:754–56. See Lomax, *Reconquest of Spain*, 92.

96. For an overview, see J. B. Williams, "The Making of a Crusade: The Genoese Anti-Muslim Attacks in Spain, 1146–1148," *Journal of Medieval History* 23 (1997): 30–53.

97. *Chronica Adefonsi Imperatoris*, ed. Falque, Gil, and Maya, 2.51.

98. Caffaro, *De captione Almerie et Tortuose*, ed. Belgrano, 79.

99. Caffaro, *Annales Ianuenses*, ed. Belgrano, 33–34. See S. Epstein, *Genoa and the Genoese, 958–1528* (Chapel Hill: University of North Carolina Press, 1996), 49.

100. Cheyette, *Ermengard of Narbonne*, 94.

101. Caffaro, *De captione Almerie et Turtuose*, ed. Belgrano, 86.

102. *Codice diplomatico della repubblica di Genova*, ed. Imperiale de Sant'Angelo, vol. 1, doc. 167 (Sept. 1146).

103. Caffaro, *De captione Almarie et Turtuose*, ed. Belgrano, 79. See Williams, "The Making of a Crusade," 33, 48. See also Epstein, *Genoa and the Genoese*, 50, and Constable, "The Second Crusade as Seen by Contemporaries," 228n80.

104. *Poem of Almería* in the *Chronica Adefonsi Imperatoris*, ed. Falque, Gil, and Maya, lines 255 (Urgell), 275 (Navarre), and 330 (Barcelona, Pisa, Genoa, Guilhem VI de Montpellier). Caffaro, *De captione Almerie et Tortuose*, ed. Belgrano, 83, noted that García Ramírez of Navarre and Ermengol VII of Urgell were sent as legates for the Christian force to negotiate terms of surrender with the Muslims of Almería.

See Virgili, *Ad detrimentum Yspanie*, 55–58. Compare Parker, "Pisa, Catalonia, and Muslim Pirates," 95.

105. *Codice diplomatico della repubblica di Genova*, ed. Imperiale de Sant'Angelo, vol. 1, docs. 168, 169 (1146, possibly in September); ACA, C, pergs. RB IV, sin fecha, nos. 6 and 10 (undated); *Els pergamins de l'Arxiu Comtal de Barcelona, de Ramon Berenguer II a Ramon Berenguer IV*, ed. Baiges et al., vol. 3, docs. 854 and 855. See Kosto, *Making Agreements in Medieval Catalonia*, 99, and J. Ruíz Doménec, "Génova y Barcelona en el siglo XII: la structura básica de su realidad," *Saggi e documenti* 4 (1983): 48–50.

106. *Codice diplomatico della repubblica di Genova*, ed. Imperiale de Sant'Angelo, vol. 1, doc. 169. See Virgili, *Ad detrimentum Yspanie*, 50–53.

107. *Codice diplomatico della repubblica di Genova*, ed. Imperiale de Sant'Angelo, vol. 1, doc. 166. Compare Constable, "The Second Crusade as Seen by Contemporaries," 227n73. See R. Hiestand, "Reconquista, Kreuzzug und heiliges Grab: Die Eroberung von Tortosa 1148 im Lichte eines neuen Zeugnisses," *Gesammelte Aufsätze zur Kulturgeschichte Spaniens* 31 (1984): 155–56. ·

108. Caffaro, *De captione Almarie et Turtuose*, ed. Belgrano, 80, 86 (not to enter battle without the direction and permission of the consuls), and 87 (not to leave Tortosa before the conquest had been completed).

109. ACA, C, pergs. RB IV, sin fecha, no. 22; *Els pergamins de l'Arxiu Comtal de Barcelona, de Ramon Berenguer II a Ramon Berenguer IV*, ed. Baiges et al., vol. 3, doc. 856.

110. Caffaro, *De captione Almarie et Turtuose*, ed. Belgrano, 84.

111. *Codice diplomatico della repubblica di Genova*, ed. Imperiale de Sant'Angelo, vol. 1, doc. 182 (5 Nov. 1147). As Genoa's vassal in Almería, Ottone swore to be faithful, to maintain at least three hundred men there, and to exempt the people from Liguria from levies. Almería would fall to the Almohads in 1157. See Lomax, *Reconquest of Spain*, 93.

112. Caffaro, *De captione Almarie et Turtuose*, ed. Belgrano, 84–85.

113. See Constable, "The Second Crusade as Seen by Contemporaries," 237.

114. *De expugnatione Lyxbonensi (The Conquest of Lisbon)*, ed. and trans. C. W. David, 2nd ed. (New York: Columbia University Press, 2001), claims 164 ships met at Dartmouth in May of 1147. See H. V. Livermore, "The *Conquest of Lisbon* and Its Author," *Portuguese Studies* 6 (1990): 1–16, who argues that the crusaders did not stop in Lisbon accidentally or whimsically but had formulated plans earlier to participate. Compare with S. B. Edgington, "The Capture of Lisbon: Premeditated or Opportunistic?," in *The Second Crusade*, ed. Roche and Møller Jensen, 257–72. Another important source, the "Lisbon Letter," published in S. B. Edgington, "The Lisbon Letter of the Second Crusade," *Historical Research* 69 (1996): 328–339, trans. by S. B. Edgington, "Albert of Aachen, St Bernard and the Second Crusade," in Phillips and Hoch, *The Second Crusade*, appendix 1, 61–67, put the number of crusaders at two hundred. Surviving evidence, however, does not indicate what portion of the crusader fleet stopped to fight against Tortosa. Caffaro, *De captione Almarie et Turtuose*, ed. Belgrano, 86, only vaguely described this flank of the invading force: "Angli namque, una cum militibus Templi et cum multis aliis alienigenis." A source that was unknown to G. Constable ("Note on the Route of the Anglo-Flemish Crusaders," *Speculum* 28 [1953]: 525–26) indicates that the participants were predominately

English but also derived from other places: D. Jaime Pascual, *Sacrae antiquitatis Cataloniae monumenta*, vol. 8, Biblioteca de Catalunya, MS 577, p. 10, as cited by Hiestand, "Reconquista, Kreuzzug und heiliges Grab," 156–57. Ramon Berenguer IV issued a charter that also hinted at this diverse composition when it recalled the siege. *L'arxiu antic de Santa Anna de Barcelona del 942 al 1200*, ed. J. Alturo i Perucho, 3 vols. (Barcelona: Fundació Noguera, 1985), vol. 1, doc. 268 (2 Nov. 1149): "et ex devota petitione peregrinorum ex littoribus hinc inde maris interfluentis Angliam et terras citramarinas venientium tunc temporis existentium in obsidione Tortosae cum reliquo exercitu."

115. *Codice diplomatico della repubblica di Genova*, ed. Imperiale de Sant'Angelo, vol. 1, doc. 195 (17 Apr. 1149).

116. *Codice diplomatico della repubblica di Genova*, ed. Imperiale de Sant'Angelo, vol. 1, doc. 194 (Apr. 1149). M. Pagès i Paretas, "Restes de pintura mural a la catedral de Gènova que representaven la conquesta de Tortosa," *Recerca* 2 (1998): 227–32.

117. *Codice diplomatico della repubblica di Genova*, ed. Imperiale de Sant'Angelo, vol. 1, doc. 196 (June 1149).

118. On 27 Jan. 1149. M. Gual Camarena, "Precedentes de la Reconquista valenciana," *Estudios Medievales* 1, no. 5 (1952): 218.

119. *Codice diplomatico della repubblica di Genova*, ed. Imperiale de Sant'Angelo, vol. 1, docs. 191 (Jan. 1149) and 193 (Feb. 1149).

120. *Codice diplomatico della repubblica di Genova*, ed. Imperiale de Sant'Angelo, vol. 1, doc. 243 (Nov. 1153). This exodus was part of a general withdrawal by the Genoese from its once robust partnership with the Catalans that would continue into the thirteenth century. See M. T. Ferrer i Mallol, "Catalans i Genovesos durant el segle XIII. El declivi d'una amistat," *Anuario de Estudios Medievales* 26 (1996): 783–823.

121. See Virgili, *Ad detrimentum Yspanie*, 60–72.

122. The date of the conquest is recorded as either 24 or 25 October in numerous chronicles. The *Chronicon Barcinonense I*, in Flórez et al., *España sagrada*, 28:323, has the earlier date. See Lladonosa, *Història de Lleida*, 122. For context, see H. Kennedy, *Muslim Spain and Portugal: A Political History of al-Andalus* (Abingdon: Routledge, 1996), 202–3.

123. See Zurita, *Anales de la Corona de Aragón*, ed. Canellas López, 2.14, 1:221–22. Ponç II de Cervera, viscount of Bas, established Guerau Segura at the castle of l'Espluga in an enactment dated to 30 March 1151, in which Guerau pledged to aid in the defense of the castle and to reside there after Siurana fell: AHN, Clero: Poblet, c. 1993, no. 7; *Diplomatari de Santa Maria de Poblet*, ed. Altisent, doc. 135. Scholars believe that Ramon Berenguer and his allies launched a campaign from Tortosa in the direction of Miravet around 1152. This is confirmed by del Arco, "Referencias a acaecimientos históricos en las datas de documentos Aragoneses de los siglos XI y XII," doc. 100 (1152). Forces under the command of Bertran de Castellet, with the assistance of Guillem II de Cervera, captured Siurana and Prades in 1153. See Miret y Sans, *Les cases de Templers y Hospitalers*, 80; *Cartas de población*, ed. Font Rius, 1.2:759 (Siurana), and 793 (Miravet); and Serrano Daura, *Senyoriu i municipi a la Catalunya Nova*, 1:40. See L. McCrank, "The Lost Kingdom of Siurana: Highland Resistance by Muslims to Christian Conquest and Assimilation in the Twelfth Century," in *On the Social Origins of Medieval Institutions: Essays in Honor of Joseph F. O'Callaghan*, ed. D. J. Kagay and T. M. Vann (Leiden: Brill, 1998), 115–48.

NOTES TO PAGES 88–91   331

331

124. Zurita, *Anales de la Corona de Aragón*, ed. Canellas López, 2.8, 1:211.

125. ACB, Libri Antiquitatum, fol. 10v, doc. 21 (15 Oct. 1148).

126. J. Miret y Sans, "Los ciutadans de Barcelona en 1148," *Boletín de la Real Academia de Buenas Letras de Barcelona* 17, no. 67 (1917): 137–38. See Miret y Sans, at 139–40, and Sabaté, *Història de Lleida*, 195.

127. *Diplomatari de l'arxiu diocesà de Solsona*, ed. Bach Riu and Sarobe, vol. 1, doc. 322 (15 Oct. 1148).

128. "Els documents, dels anys 1101–1150, de l'Arxiu Capitular de la Seu d'Urgell," ed. Baraut, doc. 1504 ([1137–49]).

129. E.g., numerous loans from the Montcada family: *Colección de documentos inéditos del Archivo de la Corona de Aragón*, ed. de Bofarull y Mascaró et al., vol. 4, docs. 51, 55, 141, 144, and 154.

130. ACA, C, pergs. RB IV, no. 214 (1 July 1149); *Colección de documentos inéditos del Archivo de la Corona de Aragón*, ed. de Bofarull y Mascaró et al., vol. 4, doc. 59.

131. *Papsturkunden in Spanien*, ed. Kehr, doc. 57 (25 July 1149); dating proposed by Lacarra, "Alfonso II El Casto," 111.

132. Del Arco, "Referencias a acaecimientos históricos en las datas de documentos Aragoneses de los siglos XI y XII," doc. 97 (Feb. 1151).

133. See Barton, *Contested Treasure*, 33–36.

134. ACA, C, pergs. RB IV, no. 189A; *Colección de documentos inéditos del Archivo de la Corona de Aragón*, ed. de Bofarull y Mascaró et al., vol. 4, doc. 51 (3 Aug. 1146).

135. "Quapropter vos" (22 June 1152). *Regesta Pontificum Romanorum*, ed. Jaffé et al., 2:80, no. 9594. See D. Smith, "A Golden Rose and the Deaf Asp that Stoppeth Her Ears: Eugenius III and Spain," in *Pope Eugenius III: The Cistercian Pope, 1145–1153*, ed. A. Jotischky and I. Fonnesberg-Schmidt (Abingdon: Routledge, 2017), 219–42.

136. *Papsturkunden in Spanien*, ed. Kehr, doc. 70 (24 Sept. [1153–54]).

137. ACA, C, pergs. RB IV, no. 229; *Colección de documentos inéditos del Archivo de la Corona de Aragón*, ed. de Bofarull y Mascaró et al., vol. 4, doc. 63 (Sept. 1150). See *Fiscal Accounts of Catalonia under the Early Count-Kings (1151–1213)*, ed. T. N. Bisson, 2 vols. (Berkeley: University of California Press, 1984), 1:62.

138. ACA, C, pergs. RB IV, no. 241; *Diplomatari de la catedral de Tortosa (1062–1193)*, ed. Virgili, doc. 28 (5 Aug. 1151).

139. Miret y Sans, "Los ciutadans de Barcelona en 1148," 138.

140. ACA, C, pergs. RB IV, no. 16; *Fiscal Accounts*, ed. Bisson, vol. 2, doc. 4 ([first week of June 1156–25 Apr. 1157]). For context and a summary of this document, see also J. Ventura, *Alfons "El Cast": el primer comte-rei* (Barcelona: Editorial Aedos, 1961), 57–59.

141. *Liber Feudorum Maior*, ed. Miquel Rosell, vol. 1, doc. 29 (27 Jan. 1151). Ramon Berenguer IV and Alfonso VII reaffirmed their alliance of Tudillén by arranging the marriage of Ramon's son to Alfonso's daughter in 1156 (*Liber Feudorum Maior*, ed. Miquel Rosell, vol. 1, doc. 30). These arrangements were later adjusted by the Treaty of Cazola, *Liber Feudorum Maior*, ed. Miquel Rosell, vol. 1, doc. 35 (20 Mar. 1179), on which see chapter 5 below. See A. Büschgens, *Die politischen Verträge Alfons' VIII. von Kastilien (1158–1214) mit Aragón-Katalonien und Navarra: Diplomatische Strategien und Konfliktlösungen im mittelalterlichen Spanien* (Frankfurt am Main: P. Lang, 1995), 116–26 and 243–48.

142. *Liber Feudorum Maior*, ed. Miquel Rosell, vol. 1, doc. 28 (21 Feb. 1141). See Lacarra, "Alfonso II El Casto," 110–11, and Aurell, *Les noces du comte*, 280–87 and 371–75.

143. ACA, C, pergs. RB IV, no. 189A (3 Aug. 1146); *Els pergamins de l'Arxiu Comtal de Barcelona, de Ramon Berenguer II a Ramon Berenguer IV*, ed. Baiges et al., vol. 3, doc. 852.

Chapter 4. Aftermaths

1. See *Catalunya Romànica*, 24:49, 52–59, and X. Eritja Ciuró, "Estructuració feudal d'un nou territori al segle XII: l'exemple de Lleida," in *El feudalisme comptat i debatut: formació i expansió del feudalisme català*, ed. M. Barceló, G. Feliu, A. Furió, M. Miquel, and J. Sobrequés (Valencia: Universitat de València, 2003), 293–314.

2. *Col·lecció diplomàtica*, ed. Sarobe, vol. 1, doc. 39 (14 July 1152).

3. The count retained two-thirds of the remaining district after subtracting the Templar Order's fifth, with one-third of the remainder going to Ermengol VI of Urgell. Lladonosa, *Història de Lleida*, 128–39, represents the most comprehensive study of Lleida's comital *repartiment*. Lladonosa's unsystematic survey lists forty-three comital donations. See Sabaté, *Història de Lleida*, 215–31.

4. See Virgili, *Ad detrimentum Yspanie*, 89–90, 100 (map of the comital sector), and 101–2, noting thirty-five direct comital donations in Tortosa.

5. *Fiscal Accounts*, ed. Bisson, 1:59.

6. Bisson, *Crisis of the Twelfth Century*, 328. See R. F. Berkhofer III, *Day of Reckoning: Power and Accountability in Medieval France* (Philadelphia: University of Pennsylvania Press, 2004), esp. chap. 2, for further on the emergence of the idea of accountability.

7. *Fiscal Accounts*, ed. Bisson, 1:25–29 (quote at 25).

8. E.g., *Diplomatari de la catedral de Tortosa (1062–1193)*, ed. Virgili, docs. 18, 133, 186, 358, and 389.

9. *Fiscal Accounts*, ed. Bisson, vol. 2, doc. 144 (24 Apr. 1149).

10. See *Cartas de población*, ed. Font Rius, vol. 1.1, doc. 95 (5 June 1154).

11. See Ponç's will: *Diplomatari de la catedral de Tortosa (1062–1193)*, ed. Virgili, doc. 190; *Fiscal Accounts*, ed. Bisson, vol. 2, doc. 145 (7 May 1168). On Bertran de Castellet, see *Diplomatari de la catedral de Tortosa (1062–1193)*, ed. Virgili, docs. 36 (27 Jan. 1153), 80 (24 May 1157), and 210 (20 Dec. 1170).

12. T. N. Bisson, "Feudalism in Twelfth-Century Catalonia," in his *Medieval France and Her Pyrenean Neighbours: Studies in Early Institutional History* (London: Hambledon Press, 1989), 161. For what follows, see N. Jaspert, "Bonds and Tensions on the Frontier: The Templars in Twelfth-Century Western Catalonia," in *Mendicants, Military Orders, and Regionalism in Medieval Europe*, ed. J. Sarnowsky (Aldershot: Ashgate, 1999), 26–36.

13. Sabaté, *El territori de la Catalunya medieval*, 30–33. The regime would continue to refer to Tortosa and Lleida in this manner until the reign of Pere I. See Schramm, "Ramon Berenguer IV," 23.

14. See Zimmermann, "Le rôle de la frontière dans la formation de la Catalogne," and "Le concept de Marca Hispanica." See Sabaté, *El territori de la Catalunya medieval*, 30–33.

15. See T. N. Bisson, "The Rise of Catalonia: Identity, Power and Ideology in a Twelfth-Century Society," in his *Medieval France and Her Pyrenean Neighbours*, 140; "Feudalism in Twelfth-Century Catalonia," 164–65; and *Crisis of the Twelfth Century*, 374. Bonnassie, *La Catalogne du milieu du Xe à la fin du XIe siècle*, 2:711–28, limits the original nucleus of texts to seven out of 175 articles. J. Bastardas i Parera, *Sobre la problemàtica dels Usatges de Barcelona* (Barcelona: Reial Acadèmia de Bones Lletres de Barcelona, 1977), presents hypothetical reconstructions of the text compiled ca. 1150.

16. *Usatges de Barcelona*, ed. Bastardas, c. 59, 60, 68, 71.

17. See chapter 5 below, and A. Kosto, "The Limited Impact of the *Usatges de Barcelona* in Twelfth-Century Catalonia," *Traditio* 56 (2001): 53–88.

18. See Serrano Daura, *Senyoriu i municipi a la Catalunya Nova*, 1:61, and A. Virgili, "Acerca del quinto templario: La orden del Temple y los Condes de Barcelona en la conquista de al-Andalus," *Anuario de Estudios Medievales* 27 (1997): 775–802.

19. *Col·lecció diplomàtica*, ed. Sarobe, vol. 1, doc. 9 (27 Nov. 1143).

20. Sabaté, *El territori de la Catalunya medieval*, 32–33, and Font Rius, "La comarca de Tortosa a raíz de la reconquista cristiana," 105–6. *Colección de documentos inéditos del Archivo de la Corona de Aragón*, ed. de Bofarull y Mascaró et al., vol. 4, doc. 43. See Forey, *Templars in the* Corona de Aragón, 26.

21. ACA, C, pergs. RB IV, no. 261 (24 Aug. 1153); *Colección de documentos inéditos del Archivo de la Corona de Aragón*, ed. de Bofarull y Mascaró et al., vol. 4, doc. 77; and *Col·lecció diplomàtica*, ed. Sarobe, 1:143–45, doc. 54. See E. Rodón Binué, *El lenguaje tecnico del feudalismo en el siglo XI en Cataluña: contribución al estudio del latín medieval* (Barcelona: Consejo Superior de Investigaciones Científicas, 1957), 135–36, and Serrano Daura, *Senyoriu i municipi a la Catalunya Nova*, 1:9 (map), 45–46.

22. *Liber instrumentorum memorialium: Cartulaire des Guillems de Montpellier*, ed. A. Germain (Montpellier: J. Martel, 1884–86), doc. 95, 1:179 (12 Dec. 1146).

23. Caffaro, *De captione Almerie et Tortuose*, ed. Belgrano, 31–32. *Liber instrumentorum memorialium*, ed. Germain, vol. 1, doc. 98 (Nov. 1182). See Devic and Vaissete, *Histoire générale du Languedoc*, 3:739–40; Constable, "The Second Crusade as Seen by Contemporaries," 231–32n99; A. Lewis, "The Guillems de Montpellier: A Sociological Appraisal," *Viator* 2 (1972): 161–62; and Virgili, *Ad detrimentum Yspanie*, 59. See *Llibre dels feits del rei en Jaume*, ed. J. Bruguera, 2 vols., Els Nostres Clàssics, Col·lecció B 10–11 (Barcelona: Fundació Jaume I, Editorial Barcino, 1991), c. 2–4, 2:7–10.

24. See Sabaté, "La frontière catalane (X^e–XIIe siècles)," 205–6.

25. ACA, C, pergs. RB IV, no. 202; *Col·lecció diplomàtica*, ed. Sarobe, vol. 1, doc. 17 (25 May 1148). See Font Rius, "La Reconquista de Lérida," 57, and R. Gras i d'Esteva, *Història de la Paheria de Lleida* (Lleida: La Paeria, 1988), 51–52.

26. Alfons I's confirmation in 1187 repeated features of the agreement. See ACA, C, pergs. A I, no. 455 (4 June 1187); *Alfonso II Rey de Aragón, Conde de Barcelona y Marqués de Provenza: Documentos (1162–1196)*, ed. A. I. Sánchez Casabón, Fuentes históricas aragonesas 23 (Zaragoza: Institución Fernando el Católico, 1995), doc. 443. See below as well as the discussion in the next chapter.

27. Kosto, *Making Agreements in Medieval Catalonia*, 88–89.

28. Consider *Usatges de Barcelona*, ed. Bastardas, c. 26 (p. 30).

29. See *Col·lecció diplomàtica*, ed. Sarobe, 1:46–66, and Lladonosa, *Història de Lleida*, 128–29.

30. ACA, C, pergs. RB IV, no. 189A; *Liber Feudorum Maior*, ed. Miquel Rosell, vol. 1, doc. 462 (3 Aug. 1146). *Codice diplomatico della repubblica di Genova*, ed. Imperiale de Sant'Angelo, vol. 1, doc. 169. On Genoese activity within Tortosa, see *L'arxiu antic de Santa Anna de Barcelona del 942 al 1200*, ed. Alturo i Perucho, vol. 1, docs. 267 (Nov. [1149]) and 268 (2 Nov. [1148]). See Forey, *Templars in the* Corona de Aragón, 24–25.

31. Chief supporters of comital authority occupied the office of seneschal or *dapifer*. The Montcada family monopolized it from the mid-eleventh century. See Shideler, *A Medieval Catalan Noble Family*, 5 and 10, and A. Pladevall, "Els senescals dels comtes de Barcelona durant el segle XI," *Anuario de Estudios Medievales* 3 (1966): 111–30.

32. *Diplomatari de la catedral de Tortosa (1062–1193)*, ed. Virgili, doc. 18 ([29 July 1149]). See Virgili, *Ad detrimentum Yspanie*, 75–81, with a map of the division on 77.

33. ACA, C, pergs. RB IV, no. 266; *Liber Feudorum Maior*, ed. Miquel Rosell, vol. 1, doc. 463; *Codice diplomatico della repubblica di Genova*, ed. Imperiale de Sant'Angelo, vol. 1, docs. 243 and 244. See Epstein, *Genoa and the Genoese*, 52–53, and Virgili, *Ad detrimentum Yspanie*, 80–81. The Genoese retained their Ebro island, exemptions, all *almuniae* and towers, and residency rights between the *Portu Veneris* and the *Portum Monacum*. The "Genoese" district endured: e.g., ACT, Ardiaca Major II, 61 (15 Apr. 1294). In 1230, Jaume I recognized to the Genoese consul that he still owed Genoa over fourteen thousand pounds. *Documentos de Jaime I de Aragón*, ed. A. Huici Miranda and M. D. Cabanes Pecourt, 5 vols. (Valencia: Anubar Ediciones, 1976–88), vol. 1, doc. 132 (June 1230). See Virgili, *Ad detrimentum Yspanie*, 81, and Font Rius, "La comarca de Tortosa a raíz de la reconquista cristiana," 81–85.

34. ACA, C, pergs. RB IV, no. 189; *Liber Feudorum Maior*, ed. Miquel Rosell, vol. 1, doc. 464; *Colección de documentos inéditos del Archivo de la Corona de Aragón*, ed. de Bofarull y Mascaró et al., vol. 4, doc. 51. See Pagarolas, *Els Templers*, 1:151–57, and Shideler, *A Medieval Catalan Noble Family*, 88–93, 108n63 (for the dating), and compare at 199. The *Carta divisionis civitatis Dertuse* suggests that the count-prince retained most of these Genoese rights: *Diplomatari de la catedral de Tortosa (1062–1193)*, ed. Virgili, doc. 18. See Virgili, *Ad detrimentum Yspanie*, 87.

35. The infeudation is reflected in lists of *honores* from 1157. See J. Salarrullana de Dios, "Fronteras o límites de Aragón y Cataluña en los tiempos medievales," republished in his *Estudios historicos acerca de la ciudad de Fraga*, 1:135n302. See also Zurita, *Anales de la Corona de Aragón*, ed. Canellas López, 2.20, 1:66.

36. *Col·lecció diplomàtica*, ed. Sarobe, vol. 1, doc. 29 (20 May 1150). See Rodón Binué, *El lenguaje técnico del feudalismo en el siglo XI en Cataluña*, 141–42. Compare Virgili, *Ad detrimentum Yspanie*, 89, who argues that *hereditas* was used similarly to *honor*. *Hereditas* signified a heritable allod: E.g., *Col·lecció diplomàtica*, ed. Sarobe, vol. 1, doc. 29 (20 May 1150). See Rodón Binué, *El lenguaje técnico del feudalismo en el siglo XI en Cataluña*, 135–36.

37. See Sabaté, "La frontière catalane (X^e–XIIe siècles)," 206–7.

38. *Diplomatari de la catedral de Tortosa (1062–1193)*, ed. Virgili, doc. 16 (29 May [1149]).

39. *El "Llibre Blanch" de Santas Creus*, ed. Udina Martorell, doc. 50 (1 Jan. 1151). Compare with *Diplomatari de la catedral de Tortosa (1062–1193)*, ed. Virgili, doc. 46 (1 Oct. 1154).

40. See Virgili, *Ad detrimentum Yspanie*, 150–53, and J. W. Brodman, "'Exceptis militibus et sanctis': Restrictions upon Ecclesiastical Ownership of Land in the Foral Legislation of Medieval Castile and Valencia," *En la España medieval* 15 (1992): 63–76. See e.g. ACA, GPC, Arm. 11: Gardeny, perg. no. 1930 (12 Aug. 1157); *Col·lecció diplomàtica*, ed. Sarobe, vol. 1, doc. 76, and *Diplomatari de la catedral de Tortosa (1062–1193)*, ed. Virgili, doc. 46 (1 Oct. 1154).

41. Lladonosa, *Història de Lleida*, compiles lists of distributions for Lleida: 130–33, 134–37, 140–51, 152–57, 156–61.

42. See chapter 5 below.

43. AHN, Órdenes Militares, c. 686, no. 2 (8 Jan. 1151); *Cartulaire général de l'Ordre du Temple*, ed. d'Albon, doc. 553. Forey, "The Military Orders and the Spanish Reconquest," 200. See A. J. Forey, "The Militarisation of the Hospital of St John," *Studia Monastica* 26 (1984): 75–89. Compare S. Garcia Larragueta, "La orden del Hospital en la crisis del imperio hispánico del siglo XII," *Hispania* 12 (1952): 496, and Bonet Donato, *La orden del Hospital en la Corona de Aragón*, 3n12.

44. ACA, C, pergs. RB IV, no. 317; *Colección de documentos inéditos del archivo general de la Corona de Aragón*, ed. de Bofarull y Mascaró et al., vol. 4, doc. 94, and *Diplomatari d'Alguaire i del seu monestir santojoanista*, ed. Alturo, doc. 8 (1157).

45. See Kosto, *Making Agreements in Medieval Catalonia*, 255.

46. Anglesola: ACA, pergs. RB II, no. 41 (26 June 1079); *Liber Feudorum Maior*, ed. Miquel Rosell, vol. 1, doc. 165. Corbins and Alcoletge: ACA, C, pergs. RB III, no. 207 (5 June 1118); *Liber Feudorum Maior*, ed. Miquel Rosell, vol. 1, doc. 166.

47. ACA, C, pergs. RB IV, no. 275 (4 Oct. 1154); *Els pergamins de l'Arxiu Comtal de Barcelona, de Ramon Berenguer II a Ramon Berenguer IV*, ed. Baiges et al., vol. 4, doc. 982. See Serrano Daura, *Senyoriu i municipi a la Catalunya Nova*, 1:80–83.

48. "Els documents, dels anys 1101–1150, de l'Arxiu Capitular de la Seu d'Urgell," ed. Baraut, doc. 1502, and *Diplomatari d'Alguaire i del seu monestir santojoanista*, ed. Alturo, doc. 5 (7 July 1149). See *Catalunya Romànica*, 24:115–16.

49. ACA, C, pergs. A I, no. 434; *Diplomatari d'Alguaire i del seu monestir santojoanista*, ed. Alturo, doc. 55 (Nov. 1186). See the next chapter for further discussion.

50. ACA, C, Reg. 9, fol. 18v (5 Feb. 1158 and 5 Feb. 1258); *Colección de documentos inéditos del Archivo de la Corona de Aragón*, ed. de Bofarull y Mascaró et al., vol. 4, doc. 93. See Serrano Daura, *Senyoriu i municipi a la Catalunya Nova*, 1:80–90.

51. *Diplomatari de la catedral de Tortosa (1062–1193)*, ed. Virgili, doc. 48 (18 Oct. 1154).

52. See A. Virgili, "El monestir de Santes Creus i Tortosa (segles XII–XIII)," *Resclosa* 7 (2002): 35–45; L. McCrank, "The Cistercians of Poblet as Medieval Frontiersmen: An Historiographic Essay and Case Study," in *Estudios en homenaje a Don Claudio Sánchez-Albornoz en sus 90 años: Anexos de Cuadernos de Historia de España* (Buenos Aires: 1983), 2:313–61 (reprinted in his *Medieval Frontier History in New Catalonia*, Essay VII); and L. McCrank, "The Frontier of the Spanish Reconquest and the Land Acquisitions of the Cistercians of Poblet, 1150–1276," *Analecta Cisterciensia* 29 (1973): 57–78 (reprinted in his *Medieval Frontier History*, Essay V).

53. ACL, *Llibre Vert*, fols. 16v–17r (30 Oct. 1149). *Diplomatari de la catedral de Tortosa (1062–1193)*, ed. Virgili, docs. 13 (31 Dec. 1148) and 28 (5 Aug. 1151). Archbishop Bernat became interim bishop: *Diplomatari de la catedral de Tortosa (1062–1193)*, ed. Virgili, doc. 13 (31 Dec. 1148).

54. *Diplomatari de la catedral de Tortosa (1062–1193)*, ed. Virgili, doc. 64 (20 Mar. [1156]).

55. See, generally, Barton, *Contested Treasure*, chap. 1.

56. The literature on this subject is vast. For a representative sampling, see Catlos, *The Victors and the Vanquished*, chap. 1; Virgili, *Ad detrimentum Yspanie*, chap. 3; and, for the thirteenth century, Burns, *Islam under the Crusaders*, chap. 6.

57. AHN, Órdenes Militares, c. 636, no. 1; J. M. Font Rius, "La carta de seguridad de Ramon Berenguer IV a las morerías de Ascó i Ribera de Ebro," in *Homenaje a Don José Maria Lacarra de Miguel en su jubilación del profesorado*, 2 vols. (Zaragoza: Anubar, 1977), 1: 282–83. Muslim communities in Ascó, Flix, Móra d'Ebre, García, Maçalefa, Castellón and Tivissa are explicitly included in the agreement. Zaragoza's charter has not survived.

58. For Tortosa's surrender treaty, see ACA, C, pergs. RB IV, no. 209 (31 Dec. 1148); *Els pergamins de l'Arxiu Comtal de Barcelona, de Ramon Berenguer II a Ramon Berenguer IV*, ed. Baiges et al., vol. 3, doc. 876. For a summary of the provisions of the charter, J. Serrano Daura, "La carta de seguretat dels sarraïns de Tortosa, de 1148," in *Les cartes de població cristiana i de seguretat de jueus i sarraïns de Tortosa (1148/1149): actes de les jornades d'estudi commemoratives del 850è aniversari de la seva concessió, Tortosa, 14, 15 i 16 de maig de 1999*, ed. J. Serrano Daura (Barcelona: Universitat Internacional de Catalunya, 2000), 115–24.

59. ACT, Cartulari 6, fol. 12r–v (ca.1153–ca.1158); *Diplomatari de la catedral de Tortosa (1062–1193)*, ed. Virgili, doc. 34.

60. AHN, Órdenes Militares, c. 636, no. 1. ACA, C, pergs. RB IV, no. 209.

61. See, e.g., Glick, *From Muslim Fortress to Christian Castle*, 115–24, and Catlos, *The Victors and the Vanquished*, 189–91.

62. Sabaté, *El territori de la Catalunya medieval*, 123–24.

63. Glick, *Islamic and Christian Spain*, 115, defines *alfoz* as "the immediate rural environs controlled by a town (synonymous with Romance *término*)." An *aldea*, from *dai'a*, country estate or hamlet, denoted a dependent peripheral settlement.

64. *Cartas de población*, ed. Font Rius, vol. 1.1, doc. 126 (Jan. 1165), awarding the Christian settlers the right to utilize the Aragonese *fueros* of Zaragoza.

65. *Diplomatari de la catedral de Tortosa (1062–1193)*, ed. Virgili, doc. 28 (5 Aug. 1151).

66. ACL, *Llibre Vert*, fols. 16v–17v (30 Oct. 1149); *Diplomatari de la catedral de Tortosa (1062–1193)*, ed. Virgili, doc. 19.

67. See chapter 3 above.

68. *Diplomatari de la catedral de Tortosa (1062–1193)*, ed. Virgili, doc. 64 (20 Mar. 1156).

69. *Diplomatari de la catedral de Tortosa (1062–1193)*, ed. Virgili, doc. 301 (28 Nov. 1178).

70. See Sabaté, *Història de Lleida*, 371.

71. Sabaté, *Història de Lleida*, 216.

72. *Diplomatari de la catedral de Tortosa (1062–1193)*, ed. Virgili, doc. 52 (22 Jan. 1155).

73. *Diplomatari de la catedral de Tortosa (1062–1193)*, ed. Virgili, doc. 95 (27 Dec. 1158). See J. Corominas, *Onomasticon cataloniae*, 8 vols. (Barcelona: Curial Ed.

Catalanes, 1989–97), 7:408–10. The Premonstratensians later refounded the house of Vallclara in another locality: see *Cartulari de Poblet: edició del manuscrit de Tarragona*, ed. E. Toda (Barcelona: Institut d'Estudis Catalans, 1938), docs. 133 (27 Oct. 1189), 146 (20 Oct. 1204), and 147 (10 June 1196). See L. McCrank, "The Fiscal Autonomy of the Post-Restoration Church of Tarragona: An Audit of the *Rationes decimarum Hispaniae* (1279–1280)," in his *Medieval Frontier History*, Essay IX, 256.

74. *Diplomatari de la catedral de Tortosa (1062–1193)*, ed. Virgili, doc. 96 (2 Jan. 1159).

75. *Diplomatari de la catedral de Tortosa (1062–1193)*, ed. Virgili, doc. 139 (9 Mar. 1164).

76. *Diplomatari de la catedral de Tortosa (1062–1193)*, ed. Virgili, docs. 301 (28 Nov. 1178) and 380 (9 May 1185).

77. AHN, Códices, no. 662B, *Cartulario de Ulldecona*, 153–54.

78. R. Sarobe, "L'evolució socioeconòmica de Rosselló de Segrià: De la repoblació a la consolidació (1149–1260)," in *Territori i societat a l'Edat Mitjana: història, arqueologia, documentació: I (1997)*, ed. J. Bolòs and J. Busqueta (Lleida: Universitat de Lleida, 1997), 191–202, and Eritja, *De l'almunia a la turris*, 59–61.

79. See Sabaté, *El territori de la Catalunya medieval*, 94–104.

80. Sabaté, *Història de Lleida*, 218–19. Also Eritja, *De l'almunia a la turris*, esp. 59–64, and "Entre la Lleida andalusí i la feudal (segles XI–XII): Un model d'explotació rural," in *Paisatge i societat a la Plana de Lleida a l'Edat Mitjana*, ed. J. Bolòs (Lleida: Universitat de Lleida, 1993), 23.

81. ADM, Entença, L. 21, no. 377 (7 Sept. 1154). See *Cartas de población*, ed. Font Rius, 1.2:759.

82. ACA, C, pergs. A I, no. 122 (6 Mar. 1173); *Alfonso II*, ed. Sánchez Casabón, doc. 139.

83. *Cartas de población*, ed. Font Rius, vol. 1.1, doc. 133 (Feb. 1168).

84. See *Cartas de población*, ed. Font Rius, 1.2:760.

85. ACA, C, pergs. A I, no. 122.

86. *Cartas de población*, ed. Font Rius, vol. 1.1, doc. 75 (30 Nov. 1149). See *Cartas de población*, ed. Font Rius, 2:493. Virgili, *Ad detrimentum Yspanie*, 26 (map), 27.

87. ACA, C, pergs. RB IV, no. 202; *Col·lecció diplomàtica*, ed. Sarobe, vol. 1, doc. 17.

88. *Cartas de población*, ed. Font Rius, vol. 1.1, doc. 79.

89. AML, Reg. 1372, *Llibre Verd Petit*, fol. 143v; Gras, *Història de la Paheria*, appendix 1; García i Biosca, *Els orígens del terme de Lleida*, 219–20.

90. García i Biosca, *Els orígens del terme de Lleida*, 24–42, esp. 37–38. Compare Gras, *Història de la Paheria*, 53–55.

91. AML, Reg. 1372, fol. 145v.

92. García i Biosca, *Els orígens del terme de Lleida*, 215–16. See also *Catalunya Romànica*, 24:47–48.

93. Eritja, *De l'almunia a la turris*, 62.

94. See Sabaté, *Història de Lleida*, 217–21.

95. See Catlos, *The Victors and the Vanquished*, 112–17. J. M. Lacarra, *Historia del reino de Navarra en la edad media* (Pamplona: Caja de Ahorros de Navarra, 1975), 180–83. Compare Stalls, *Possessing the Land*, 83.

96. See chapter 5 below for further discussion of this case.

97. ACA, GPC, Códices, no. 115, *Cartulari de Tortosa*, fol. 70r, no. 227; Pagarolas, *La comanda del Temple de Tortosa*, doc. 130 (8 June 1209).

98. ACA, GPC, Códices, no. 115, *Cartulari de Tortosa*, fol. 75, no. 246 (1 June 1210).

99. See, e.g., *Cartulario de "Sant Cugat" del Vallés*, ed. Rius y Serra, vol. 2, doc. 579 (20 June 1045), *Diplomatari de la catedral de Tortosa (1062–1193)*, ed. Virgili, doc. 48 (18 Oct. 1154), docs. 153 (2 June 1165) and 268 (11 Aug. 1175). For similar documents from elsewhere in the Peninsula, e.g. Coimbra, see L. Ventura, "Os seguins: Uma família de francos na Coimbra do século XII," in *Mundos medievales: espacios, sociedades y poder. Homenaje al Profesor José Ángel García de Cortázar y Ruiz de Aguirre*, ed. B. Arízaga Bolumburu et al., 2 vols. (Santander: Editorial Universidad Cantabria, 2014), 1:915–26.

100. R. García-Velasco Bernal, "'Alā fūr Tuṭīla': Jews and Muslims in the Administrative Culture of Post-Conquest Tudela, c.1118–1220," *Al-Masāq* 29, no. 3 (2017): 253.

101. See Sénac, *La frontière et les hommes*, 449–56; Virgili, *Ad detrimentum Yspanie*, 99; and Villegas-Aristizábal, "Anglo-Norman Intervention in the Conquest and Settlement of Tortosa," 76. See also A. Virgili, "War and Booty as Incentives for Emigration: Tortosa and al-Andalus (12th–13th Centuries)," in *From Al-Andalus to the Americas (13th-17th Centuries): Destruction and Construction of Societies*, ed. T. F. Glick et al. (Leiden: Brill, 2018), 103–29.

102. Catlos, *The Victors and the Vanquished*, 113. See J. M. Lacarra, "Introducción al estudio de los mudejares aragoneses," *Aragón en la Edad Media* 2 (1979): 10–13.

103. *El "Llibre Blanch" de Santas Creus*, ed. Udina Martorell, doc. 72 (1 Aug. 1156).

104. Compare J. Utrilla Utrilla and J. C. Esco Samperiz, "La población mudéjar en la Hoya de Huesca (siglos XII y XIII)," in *Actas del III Simposio Internacional de Mudejarismo* (Teruel: Instituto de Estudios Turolenses, 1986), 190.

105. *Diplomatari de la catedral de Tortosa (1062–1193)*, ed. Virgili, doc. 118 (23 June 1161). See also doc. 195 (5 Dec. 1168).

106. *Diplomatari de la catedral de Tortosa (1062–1193)*, ed. Virgili, doc. 157 (10 Jan. 1166).

107. *Diplomatari de la catedral de Tortosa (1062–1193)*, ed. Virgili, doc. 307 (16 Apr. 1179).

108. AHN, Clero: Poblet, c. 1999, perg. 15B; *Diplomatari de Santa Maria de Poblet*, ed. Altisent, doc. 107 (28 Dec. 1146).

109. *Diplomatari de Santa Maria de Poblet*, ed. Altisent, doc. 168 (14 Mar. 1167).

110. *Diplomatari de la catedral de Tortosa (1062–1193)*, ed. Virgili, doc. 30 (1 Mar. 1152).

111. See Sabaté, *Història de Lleida*, 280.

112. E.g., *Diplomatari de la catedral de Tortosa (1062–1193)*, ed. Virgili, doc. 97 (8 Feb. 1159).

113. *Diplomatari de la catedral de Tortosa (1062–1193)*, ed. Virgili, doc. 295 (22 May 1178).

114. *Diplomatari de la catedral de Tortosa (1062–1193)*, ed. Virgili, doc. 360 (20 Mar. 1184).

115. *Diplomatari de la catedral de Tortosa (1062–1193)*, ed. Virgili, doc. 201 (1 Oct. 1169).

116. *Cartulari de Poblet*, ed. Toda, doc. 189 (21 Dec. 1198).

117. *Diplomatari de la catedral de Tortosa (1062–1193)*, ed. Virgili, doc. 44, and *Col·lecció diplomàtica*, ed. Sarobe, vol. 1, doc. 59 (21 Aug. 1154).

118. ACL, *Llibre Vert*, fols. 361v–362r (June 1190).

119. *Diplomatari de la catedral de Tortosa (1062–1193)*, ed. Virgili, doc. 47 (17 Oct. 1154). See also doc. 56 (6 Apr. 1155).

120. Bisson, "The Rise of Catalonia," 152; Kosto, *Making Agreements in Medieval Catalonia*, 279–80.

121. For some examples, see Barton, *Contested Treasure*, 29–30.

122. *Fiscal Accounts*, ed. Bisson, 1:24–25.

123. F. Sabaté, "Judici entre el comte Ramon Berenguer IV i Bernat d'Anglesola," *Ilerda "Humanitats"* 49 (1991): 139–40. See also M. Riu, "El feudalismo en Cataluña," in *I Congreso de Estudios Medievales: En torno al feudalismo hispánico* (Ávila: Fundación Sánchez-Abornoz, 1989), 373–91. For similar struggles in Castile, see R. Pastor de Togneri, "La conquista cristiana de Castilla la Nueva y el desarrollo de las estructuras feudales," in *I Congreso de Historia de Castilla-La Mancha*, vol. 5, *Musulmanes y Cristianos: la implantación del feudalismo* (Valladolid: Junta de Comunidades de Castilla-La Mancha, 1988), 127–36.

124. *Liber Feudorum Maior*, ed. Miquel Rosell, vol. 1, doc. 462 (3 Aug. 1146). The *Usatges de Barcelona*, ed. Bastardas, c. 80 (us. 105), established this court as competent to judge such disputes.

125. ACA, C, pergs. RB IV, no. 189; *Liber Feudorum Maior*, ed. Miquel Rosell, vol. 1, docs. 464 and 465. See Fabregat, *Burgesos contra senyors*, 33–42.

126. Compare Shideler, *A Medieval Catalan Noble Family*, 197.

127. See J. Nelson, "Dispute Settlement in Carolingian West Francia," in *The Settlement of Disputes in Early Medieval Europe*, ed. W. Davies and P. Fouracre (Cambridge: Cambridge University Press, 1986), 59–61, and R. McKitterick, "Introduction: Sources and Interpretation," in *The New Cambridge Medieval History, c. 500–700*, ed. R. McKitterick (Cambridge: Cambridge University Press, 1995), 15–16.

128. The office of *mostassaf* derived from the Arabic *muḥtasib*. F. Corriente, *Dictionary of Arabic and Allied Loanwords: Spanish, Portuguese, Catalan, Gallician and Kindred Dialects* (Leiden: Brill, 2008), 160. See M. T. Ferrer i Mallol, "Els redemptors de captius: Mostolafs, eixees o alfaquecs (segles XII–XIII)," *Medievalia* 9 (1990): 85–106.

129. *Liber Feudorum Maior*, ed. Miquel Rosell, vol. 1, doc. 464.

130. *Fiscal Accounts*, ed. Bisson, 1:120, estimates that royal domains within Catalonia were producing around one hundred thousand *solidi* annually by the end of Alfons's reign.

131. *Liber Feudorum Maior*, ed. Miquel Rosell, vol. 1, doc. 465.

132. *Liber Feudorum Maior*, ed. Miquel Rosell, vol. 1, doc. 465. The judges may have been drawing here on the legal concept of "mora trahit periculum" that was evolving during this period. The influential canon lawyer Huguccio, who was active in the later twelfth century, wrote, "Nam mora modici temporis non trahit hic ad se periculum." Huguccio, D.100 c.1 v. *retinuierit*, Admont MS 7, fol. 126r, as cited by K. Pennington, "The Making of a Decretal Collection: The Genesis of *Compilatio tertia*," in his *Popes, canonists and texts, 1150–1550* (Aldershot: Variorum, 1993), Essay VIII, 84n50.

133. See E. Klein, *Jews, Christian Society, and Royal Power in Medieval Barcelona* (Ann Arbor: University of Michigan Press, 2006), chap. 1, and Barton, *Contested Treasure*, chap. 2.

134. See, e.g., *Diplomatari de la catedral de Tortosa (1062–1193)*, ed. Virgili, doc. 138 (22 Jan. 1164).

135. See T. N. Bisson, "The Problem of Feudal Monarchy: Aragon, Catalonia, and France," in his *Medieval France and Her Pyrenean Neighbours*, 245.

136. On Bernat's career, see *Fiscal Accounts*, ed. Bisson, 1:64–65.

137. *Liber Feudorum Maior*, ed. Miquel Rosell, vol. 1, doc. 465.

138. See S. White, "The Politics of Fidelity: Hugh of Lusignan and William of Aquitaine," in *Georges Duby: L'écriture de l'Histoire*, ed. C. Duhamel-Amado and G. Lobrichon (Brussels: De Boeck Supérieur, 1996), 223–30, and Shideler, *A Medieval Catalan Noble Family*, 101.

139. E.g., ACA, GPC, Arm. 11: Gardeny, perg. no. 2121 (26 May 1156); *Col·lecció diplomàtica*, ed. Sarobe, vol. 1, doc. 66. ACA, C, pergs. RB IV, no. 266; *Colección de documentos inéditos del Archivo de la Corona de Aragón*, ed. de Bofarull y Mascaró et al., vol. 4, doc. 78 (Nov. 1153).

140. ACA, C, pergs. RB IV, no. 11; *Colección de documentos inéditos del archivo general de la Corona de Aragón*, ed. de Bofarull y Mascaró et al., vol. 4, doc. 115; *Col·lecció diplomàtica*, ed. Sarobe, vol. 1, doc. 108 (Jan.–June 1162). See Sabaté, "Judici," 131.

141. Sabaté, "Judici," 140.

142. ACA, C, pergs. RB IV, no. 11; *Col·lecció diplomàtica*, ed. Sarobe, vol. 1, doc. 108.

143. ACA, C, pergs. RB II, no. 41 (26 June 1079); *Liber Feudorum Maior*, ed. Miquel Rosell, vol. 1, doc. 165.

144. ACA, C, pergs. RB IV, no. 11; *Col·lecció diplomàtica*, ed. Sarobe, vol. 1, doc. 108.

145. ACA, C, pergs. RB III, no. 207 (5 June 1118); *Liber Feudorum Maior*, ed. Miquel Rosell, vol. 1, doc. 166.

146. ACA, C, pergs. RB III, no. 207 (5 June 1118); *Liber Feudorum Maior*, ed. Miquel Rosell, vol. 1, doc. 166.

147. See *Fiscal Accounts*, ed. Bisson, 1:97. ACA, C, pergs. RB III, no. 174.

148. See A. J. Kosto, "The *Liber feudorum maior* and the Counts of Barcelona: The Cartulary as an Expression of Power," *Journal of Medieval History* 27 (2001): 1–22; T. N. Bisson, "Ramon de Caldes (*c.* 1135–1199): Dean of Barcelona and Royal Servant," in *Medieval France and Her Pyrenean Neighbours*, 187–98; and chapter 6 below.

149. ACA, C, pergs. RB IV, no. 159 (27 Nov. 1143); *Col·lecció diplomàtica*, ed. Sarobe, vol. 1, doc. 9.

150. Berenguer later appointed his son to hold Corbins from the Templars: *Col·lecció diplomàtica*, ed. Sarobe, vol. 2, doc. 397 (3 Jan. 1182).

151. *Usatges de Barcelona*, ed. Bastardas, c. 59 (us. 62), 94–95.

152. ACA, C, pergs. RB IV, no. 11; *Col·lecció diplomàtica*, ed. Sarobe, vol.1, doc. 108.

153. See T. N. Bisson, "The Crisis of the Catalonian Franchises (1150–1200)," in *La formació i expansió del feudalisme català*, ed. J. Portella i Comas, special issue, *Estudi general* 4–5 (1985–86): 153–63; B. Garí, "Las 'querimoniae' feudales en la documentació catalana del siglo XII (1131–1178)," *Medievalia* 5 (1984): 39; and J. M. Salrach,

"Agressions senyorials i resistències pageses en el procés de feudalització (segles IX–XII)," in *Revoltes populars contra el poder de l'estat* (Barcelona: Generalitat de Catalunya, Departament de Cultura, 1992), 11–29.

Chapter 5. Repositioning within the Lower Ebro Valley

1. See D. Abulafia, *The Western Mediterranean Kingdoms, 1200–1500: The Struggle for Dominion* (London: Longman, 1997), esp. chap. 2. For what follows, see Barton, "Lords, Settlers, and Shifting Frontiers," 209–14.

2. ACA, C, pergs. A I, no. 13 (confirmed 11 Oct. 1162, dictated by count 4 Aug. 1162); *Els testaments dels comtes de Barcelona*, ed. Udina i Abelló, doc. 13. *Gesta comitum Barcinonensium*, ed. Barrau Dihigo and Massó Torrents, 5:9. Zurita, *Anales de la Corona de Aragón*, ed. Canellas López, 1.19, 1:236. Frederick Barbarossa confirmed Barcelona's claims to Provence: *Liber Feudorum Maior*, ed. Miquel Rosell, vol. 2, doc. 902 (18 Aug. 1162).

3. See J. Á. Sesma Muñoz, "Aragón y Cataluña," in *Historia de España Ramón Menéndez Pidal*, vol. 9, *La Reconquista y el proceso de diferenciación política (1035–1217)*, ed. M. Á. Ladero Quesada et al. (Madrid: Espalsa-Calpe, 1998), pp. 661–752.

4. E.g., *Liber Feudorum Maior*, ed. Miquel Rosell, vol. 1, doc. 16 (4 Apr. 1152).

5. See, e.g., ACA, C, pergs. RB IV, no. 214.

6. E.g., *Documentos de Ramiro II*, ed. Ubieto Arteta, docs. 12 (1149), 122 (1153), and 123 (23 May 1154).

7. *Liber Feudorum Maior*, ed. Miquel Rosell, vol. 1, doc. 16 (4 Apr. 1152). Pere was betrothed to Sancha of Castile upon the confirmation of the Treaty of Tudillén in 1156: *Liber Feudorum Maior*, ed. Miquel Rosell, vol. 1, doc. 30 (May 1156). See Zurita, *Anales de la Corona de Aragón*, ed. Canellas López, 2.20, 1:239–40. Compare Aurell, *Les noces du comte*, 375. Alfons later assumed Pere's place after breaking his engagement to Princess Mahaut of Portugal. See A. Ubieto Arteta, "Un frustrado matrimonio de Alfonso II de Aragón," in *VII Congrés d'Història de la Corona d'Aragó*, 2:263–68.

8. On this birth year, see Ubieto Arteta, *Historia de Aragón*, 5:181–84, and "De nuevo sobre el nacimiento de Alfonso II de Aragón," *Estudios de Edad Media de la Corona de Aragón* 6 (1956): 203–9. See also A. Ubieto Arteta, "El nacimiento de Alfonso II de Aragón," *Estudios de Edad Media de la Corona de Aragon* 4 (1950): 419–25, and J. F. Cabestany, "Alfons el Cast," in Bagué, Cabestany, and Schramm, *Els primers comtes-reis*, 59. Compare F. Soldevila, "La data de naixença d'Alfons II d'Aragó, primer de Catalunya," in *Homenaje a Don Ramón Carande*, 2 vols. (Madrid: Sociedad de Estudios y Publicaciones, 1963), 1:299–310.

9. *Liber Feudorum Maior*, ed. Miquel Rosell, vol. 1, doc. 31 (Feb. 1158).

10. ACA, C, pergs. A I, no. 13 (11 Oct. 1162) (*Els testaments dels comtes de Barcelona*, ed. Udina i Abelló, doc. 13).

11. Zurita, *Anales de la Corona de Aragón*, ed. Canellas López, 1.20, 1:239–40; *Diplomatari de la catedral de Tortosa (1062–1193)*, ed. Virgili, doc. 129 (17 Feb. 1163); and *Gesta comitum Barcinonensium*, ed. Barrau Dihigo and J. Massó Torrents, 9:12–13. See Ventura, *Alfons "El Cast,"* 87. Compare McCrank, "Restoration and Reconquest in Medieval Catalonia," 447–48.

12. Petronilla later alluded to this name change in her will: *Liber Feudorum Maior*, ed. Miquel Rosell, vol. 1, doc. 17 (18 June 1164); *Colección de documentos inéditos del*

Archivo de la Corona de Aragón, ed. de Bofarull y Mascaró et al., vol. 4, doc. 146. See Zurita, *Anales de la Corona de Aragón*, ed. Canellas López, 2.20, 1:240; Ubieto Arteta, *Historia de Aragón*, 5:184–86; and Kehr, "El Papado y los reinos de Navarra y Aragón hasta mediados del siglo XII," 175.

13. See J. Caruana Gómez, "Itinerario de Alfonso II de Aragón," *Estudios de Edad Media de la Corona de Aragón* 7 (1962): 75.

14. E.g., *Alfonso II*, ed. Sánchez Casabón, docs. 2–3, 5–9.

15. See J. Caruana Gómez, "Sobre el nacimiento de Alfonso II de Aragón," *Teruel* 11 (1954): 5–32.

16. *Alfonso II*, ed. Sánchez Casabón, doc. 1 (Aug. 1162).

17. Zurita, *Anales de la Corona de Aragón*, ed. Canellas López, 2.20, 1:238–40, provides a summary. ACA, C, pergs. A I, no. 13 (11 Oct. 1162); *Els testaments dels comtes de Barcelona*, ed. Udina i Abelló, doc. 13. See Caruana Gómez, "Itinerario de Alfonso II," 78–79.

18. *Cartas de población*, ed. Font Rius, vol. 1.1, doc. 120; *Alfonso II*, ed. Sánchez Casabón, doc. 9 (7 Feb. 1163).

19. See Caruana Gómez, "Itinerario de Alfonso II," 79–80.

20. *Diplomatari de la catedral de Tortosa (1062–1193)*, ed. Virgili, doc. 129 (17 Feb. 1163).

21. ACA, C, pergs. A I, no. 2 (27 Sep. 1162); *Alfonso II*, ed. Sánchez Casabón, doc. 4, a renewal of Ramon Berenguer IV's Treaty of Tudillén with Alfonso VII necessitated by the split of Castile and León in 1157. See H. Sirantoine, *Imperator Hispaniae: les idéologies impériales dans le royaume de León, IX–XII siècles* (Madrid: Casa de Velázquez, 2012), esp. 309–73, on Castilian-Leonese imperial ideology.

22. *Papsturkunden in Spanien*, ed. Kehr, docs. 95 (7 Dec. 1162) and 108 (26 July 1163).

23. See Lacarra, "Alfonso II El Casto," 112–20.

24. Alfons used these words in his letter to Louis VII of France (cited below). See A. Ubieto Arteta, "La aparición del falso Alfonso I el Batallador," *Argensola: Revista de Ciencias Sociales del Instituto de Estudios Altoaragoneses* 38 (1958): 29–38; M. Defourneaux, "Louis VII et le souverains espagnols: L'enigme du 'pseudo-Alphonse,'" in *Estudios dedicados a Menéndez Pidal* (Madrid: Consejo Superior de Investigaciónes Científicas, Patronato Marcelino Menéndez y Pelayo, 1956), 6:647–61; and G. Lecuppre, *L'imposture politique au moyen âge: la seconde vie des rois* (Paris: Presses Universitaires de France, 2005), 249–50, 256–57, 300–301.

25. A. C. Floriano, "Fragmentos de unos viejos anales (1089–1196): Transcripción y análisis paleográfico. Crítica histórica," *Boletín de la Real Academia de la Historia* 94 (1929): 153–54.

26. Jiménez de Rada, *Historia de Rebus Hispaniae*, ed. Fernández Valverde, 7.3, 224.

27. *Crónica de los Estados Peninsulares: Texto del siglo XIV*, ed. A. Ubieto Arteta (Granada: Universidad de Granada, 1955), 128.

28. R. de Huesca et al., *Teatro histórico de las iglesias del reyno de Aragón*, 9 vols. (Pamplona: J. M. de Ezquerro, 1780–1807), vol. 7, appendix 16 (at 485) (Mar. 1175 or 1176), followed by other donations to the monastery (Huesca et al., *Teatro histórico de las iglesias del reyno de Aragón*, 7:314–15). See Bisson, "The Rise of Catalonia," 146.

29. Ubieto Arteta, "La aparición del falso Alfonso I el Batallador," doc. 2 (at 38) (late 1178–early 1179); see 34–36.

30. Floriano, "Fragmentos de unos viejos anales," 153–54.

31. See M. de Riquer, *Los trovadores: historia literaria y textos*, 2 vols., 2nd ed. (Barcelona: Planeta, 1992), 2:683–84.

32. "Pois lo gens terminis floritz," in *The Poems of the Troubadour Bertran de Born*, ed. and trans. W. D. Paden Jr., T. Sankovitch, and P. H. Stäblein (Berkeley: University of California Press, 1986), 265–72. In "Qan vei pels vergiers despleiar" (at 274–80), he claimed to have "sung [his *sirvente*] to the king of Navarre and spread it throughout Castile." See M. de Riquer, "La littérature provençale à la cour d'Alphonse II d'Aragon," *Cahiers de civilisation médiévale* 2 (1959): 177–201.

33. See *Les poesies del trobador Guillem de Berguedà: text, traducció, introducció i notes*, ed. M. de Riquer (Barcelona: Quaderns Crema, 1996). See chapter 6 below for details on conflicts with Arnau de Castellbò.

34. M. de Riquer, "El trovador Giraut del Luc y sus poesías contra Alfonso II de Aragón," *Boletin de la Real Academia de Buenas Letras de Barcelona* 23 (1950): 217–19. See Forey, *Templars in the* Corona de Aragón, 29.

35. *Les poesies del trobador Guillem de Berguedà*, ed. de Riquer; Bisson, *Crisis of the Twelfth Century*, 433–34.

36. See M. Cabré, "Italian and Catalan Troubadours," in *The Troubadours: An Introduction*, ed. S. Gaunt and S. Kay (Cambridge: Cambridge University Press, 1999), 134–35.

37. E.g., in 1163, when Alfons invested Pere de Avellá with the responsibility of fortifying and populating Vilanova de Prades. *Cartas de población*, ed. Font Rius, vol. 1.1, doc. 121; *Alfonso II*, ed. Sánchez Casabón, doc. 11 (24 Feb. 1163).

38. *Cartas de población*, ed. Font Rius, vol. 1.1, doc. 126 (Jan. 1165). On Aragon's entitlement to this zone, see Serrano Daura, *Senyoriu i municipi a la Catalunya Nova*, 1:101–2; *El conflicte catalanoaragonès pel territori de la Ribera d'Ebre i de la Terra Alta, en els segles XIII i XIV* (Ascó: Ajuntament d'Ascó, 1997); and chapter 8 below.

39. *Cartas de población*, ed. Font Rius, vol. 1.1, doc. 134 (26 July 1168).

40. *Cartas de población*, ed. Font Rius, vol. 1.1, doc. 119; *Alfonso II*, ed. Sánchez Casabón, doc. 12 (Feb. 1163). See *Cartas de población*, ed. Font Rius, 1.2:745–47.

41. *Diplomatari d'Alguaire i del seu monestir santojoanista*, ed. Alturo, doc. 12 (Jan. 1163).

42. *Diplomatari de la catedral de Tortosa (1062–1193)*, ed. Virgili, doc. 141 (11 May 1164).

43. *Cartas de población*, ed. Font Rius, vol. 1.1, doc. 126 (Jan. 1165).

44. *Col·lecció diplomàtica*, ed. Sarobe, vol. 1, doc. 237 (3 Oct. 1173).

45. *Cartas de población*, ed. Font Rius, vol. 1.1, doc. 123 (Dec. 1163).

46. *Cartas de población*, ed. Font Rius, vol. 1.1, doc. 122 (13 Nov. 1163). See *Cartas de población*, ed. Font Rius, 1.2:707–8.

47. *Cartas de población*, ed. Font Rius, vol. 1.1, doc. 130 (22 Mar. 1166).

48. *Fiscal Accounts*, ed. Bisson, 1:76.

49. See Bensch, *Barcelona and Its Rulers*, 206–8.

50. See chapter 2 above.

51. See Juncosa Bonet, *Estructura y dinámicas de poder en el señorio de Tarragona*, 95–107.

52. *Alfonso II*, ed. Sánchez Casabón, doc. 10 (13 Feb. 1163).

53. See McCrank, "Restoration and Reconquest in Medieval Catalonia," 450.

54. *Fiscal Accounts*, ed. Bisson, vol. 2, doc. 18 ([*c.* 1165]). See *Fiscal Accounts*, ed. Bisson, 1:74–76.

55. *Col·lecció diplomàtica*, ed. Sarobe, vol. 1, doc. 171 (Oct. 1167).

56. ACA, C, pergs. A I, no. 58 (1 July 1168); *Fiscal Accounts*, ed. Bisson, vol. 2, doc. 20.

57. *Fiscal Accounts*, ed. Bisson, 1:80. See, e.g., *Col·lecció diplomàtica*, ed. Sarobe, vol. 1, docs. 211, 237, 238, 252, 280, and 302.

58. E.g., he and two other officers received the *almunia* of La Llitera from Alfons in 1168. AHN, Códices no. 992B, fols. 105v–106r (Nov. 1168); *Diplomatari de Santa Maria de Poblet*, ed. Altisent, doc. 338.

59. ACA, C, pergs. A I, no. 310 (12 Jan.? 1180); *Fiscal Accounts*, ed. Bisson, vol. 2, doc. 35.

60. *Fiscal Accounts*, ed. Bisson, 1:82.

61. ACA, C, pergs. A I, no. 60 (11 Sept. 1168); *Fiscal Accounts*, ed. Bisson, vol. 2, doc. 21.

62. See F. Soldevila and F. Valls i Taberner, *Història de Catalunya*, 2nd ed. (Barcelona: Selecta, 1968), 1:201.

63. ACA, C, pergs. A I, no. 62 (5 Nov. 1168); *Alfonso II*, ed. Sánchez Casabón, doc. 56. See A. Altisent, "Seguint el rastre de Guerau de Jorba i el seu llinatge," *Aplec de treballs* 1 (1978): 33–83.

64. ACA, C, pergs. A I, no. 64 (19 Dec. 1168); *Alfonso II*, ed. Sánchez Casabón, doc. 58.

65. *Gesta comitum Barcinonensium*, ed. Barrau Dihigo and Massó Torrents, 9:14 ([*c.* 1160s]). See J. Aurell, *Authoring the Past: History, Autobiography, and Politics in Medieval Catalonia* (Chicago: University of Chicago Press, 2012), 122–25, and Barton, *Contested Treasure*, 8.

66. Zurita, *Anales de la Corona de Aragón*, ed. Canellas López, 2.25, 1:251.

67. See chapter 2 above. *Cartas de población del reino de Aragón en los siglos medievales*, ed. M. L. Ledesma Rubio (Zaragoza: Institución "Fernando el Católico," 1991), doc. 83 (Nov. 1157). Zurita, *Anales de la Corona de Aragón*, ed. Canellas López, 2.25, 1:251–52. Compare Gual Camarena, "Precedentes de la Reconquista valenciana," 227–28.

68. See Cabestany, "Alfons el Cast," 82.

69. ACA, C, pergs. A I, no. 85 (4 July 1170); *Alfonso II*, ed. Sánchez Casabón, doc. 90. See Shideler, *A Medieval Catalan Noble Family*, 111.

70. ACA, C, pergs. A I, no. 88, and *Liber Feudorum Maior*, ed. Miquel Rosell, vol. 1, doc. 32 (July 1170); *Alfonso II*, ed. Sánchez Casabón, doc. 92. See Kosto, *Hostages in the Middle Ages*, 30–31.

71. ACA, C, pergs, A I, no. 146; *Alfonso II*, ed. Sánchez Casabón, doc. 161 (18 Jan. 1174). See Cabestany, "Alfons el Cast," 80.

72. See Burns, *Crusader Kingdom of Valencia*, 1:45–53.

73. See H. Kennedy, *Muslim Spain and Portugal: A Political History of al-Andalus* (London and New York: Longman, 1996), chap. 9, and O'Callaghan, *A History of Medieval Spain*, 236–37.

74. Lomax, *Reconquest of Spain*, 112–15. J. M. Lacarra, "El Rey Lobo de Murcia y la formación del señorío de Albarracín," in *Estudios dedicados a Menendez Pidal*, 3 vols.

(Madrid: Consejo Superior de Investigaciónes Científicas, 1950–62), 3:515–26, esp. 519–20.

75. Gual Camarena, "Precedentes de la Reconquista valenciana," 195–96. For further on this order, see A. J. Forey, "The Order of Mountjoy," *Speculum* 46 (1971): 257–62.

76. *Diplomatari d'Alguaire i del seu monestir santojoanista*, ed. Alturo, doc. 20 (Apr. 1171).

77. AHN, *Códices* no. 649B, doc. 261; *Alfonso II*, ed. Sánchez Casabón, doc. 106 (April 1170).

78. Zurita, *Anales de la Corona de Aragón*, ed. Canellas López, 2.32, 1:268.

79. See *Crónica general de España: Crónica de la Provincia de Murcia*, ed. J. Bisso (Madrid: Rubio, Grilo y Vitturi, 1870), 38.

80. ACA, C, pergs. A I, no. 105; *Alfonso II*, ed. Sánchez Casabón, doc. 107 (4 May 1171). See Kosto, *Hostages in Medieval Europe*, 159.

81. Zurita, *Anales de la Corona de Aragón*, ed. Canellas López, 2.35, 1:275. *Liber Feudorum Maior*, ed. Miquel Rosell, vol. 1, doc. 33, dated "in obsidione super Concam."

82. O'Callaghan, *A History of Medieval Spain*, 239–40.

83. Zurita, *Anales de la Corona de Aragón*, ed. Canellas López, 2.32, 1:268–69. See Cabestany, "Alfons el Cast," 84. Ágreda: ACA, C, pergs. A I, no. 402 (21 Jan. 1186); *Alfonso II*, ed. Sánchez Casabón, doc. 421.

84. ACA, C, pergs. A I, no. 288 (Mar. 1179/80); *Alfonso II*, ed. Sánchez Casabón, doc. 287.

85. AHN, Clero: Poblet, c. 2024, no. 8 (Feb. 1176); *Diplomatari de Santa Maria de Poblet*, ed. Altisent, doc. 548.

86. Gual Camarena, "Precedentes de la Reconquista valenciana," 198.

87. AHN, Clero: Poblet, c. 2024, no. 9 (Feb. 1176); *Diplomatari de Santa Maria de Poblet*, ed. Altisent, doc. 549.

88. ACA, C, pergs. A I, no. 700 (Dec. 1194); *Alfonso II*, ed. Sánchez Casabón, doc. 628.

89. ACT, Comú del Bisbe i Capitol, no. 4 (28 Nov. 1178); "Colección de cartas pueblas," ed. Ramón de Maria. Confirmation by Jaume: ACT, Cartulari 8, fols. 28r–30r, Cartulari 9A, pp. 131–34; ACA, C, Cartas Reales Diplomáticas, J I, no. 86 (27 Apr. 1225); *Documentos de Jaime I*, ed. Huici and Cabanes, vol. 1, doc. 66. See Burns, *Crusader Kingdom of Valencia*, 1:42–45.

90. *Diplomatari de la catedral de Tortosa (1062–1193)*, ed. Virgili, doc. 301 (28 Nov. 1178). "Colección de cartas pueblas," ed. P. Ramón de Maria, *Boletín de la Sociedad Castellonense de Cultura* 16 (1935): 385–88.

91. On the contribution by nonroyal initiatives, see Zurita, *Anales de la Corona de Aragón*, ed. Canellas López, 2.40, 1:285.

92. ACA, C, pergs. A I, no. 268B (20 Mar. 1179); *Alfonso II*, ed. Sánchez Casabón, doc. 281. See Zurita, *Anales de la Corona de Aragón*, ed. Canellas López, 2.37, 1:279. See also Ventura, *Alfons "El Cast,"* 192–95 and Álvarez Borge, *Cambios y alianzas*, 43.

93. ACA, C, pergs. A I, no. 268B. See Cabestany, "Alfons el Cast," 85.

94. Gual Camarena, "Precedentes de la Reconquista valenciana," 200.

95. AHN, *Códices*, no. 662B, pp. 153–54, at 154 (1 Aug. 1180); *Alfonso II*, ed. Sánchez Casabón, doc. 308. AHN, *Códices*, no. 649B, *Cartulario de Ulldecona*, doc. 127,

pp. 126–27 ([Aug 1180]); *Alfonso II*, ed. Sánchez Casabón, doc. 307. See Zurita, *Anales de la Corona de Aragón*, ed. Canellas López, 2.38, 1:283.

96. ACA, C, pergs. A I, no. 538 (Jan. 1190); *Alfonso II*, ed. Sánchez Casabón, doc. 503; *Col·lecció diplomàtica*, ed. Sarobe, vol. 2, doc. 543. The aforementioned *sirvente* of Giraut del Luc made this claim. Jaume later recaptured it: ACA, C, pergs. J I, no. 269 (3 Sept. 1225) and AHN, Clero: Poblet, c. 2141, no. 16 (5 Sept. 1225); *Documentos de Jaime I*, ed. Huici and Cabanes, vol. 1, docs. 71 and 72. See J. Miret y Sans, *Itinerari de Jaume I* (Barcelona: Institut d'Estudis Catalans, 1918), 56. See Forey, *Templars in the Corona de Aragón*, 28–29.

97. *Cartas de población*, ed. Font Rius, vol. 1.1, doc. 202 (Apr. 1195).

98. *Cartas de población*, ed. Font Rius, 1.2:804.

99. *Diplomatari de la catedral de Tortosa (1062–1193)*, ed. Virgili, doc. 379 (Apr. 1185).

100. *Alfonso II*, ed. Sánchez Casabón, doc. 149 (7 Sep. 1190).

101. *The Latin Chronicle of the Kings of Castile*, trans. J. F. O'Callaghan (Tempe, AZ: Arizona Center for Medieval and Renaissance Studies, 2002), 28–29. See Cabestany, "Alfons el Cast," 86–87; Lomax, *Reconquest of Spain*, 118–23; O'Callaghan, *Reconquest and Crusade*, 61–62.

102. See D. Smith, *Innocent III and the Crown of Aragon: The Limits of Papal Authority* (Burlington, VT: Ashgate, 2004), 95–99, 111–15.

103. See Smith, *Innocent III and the Crown of Aragon*, 15–17, 43–53. Compare E. Bagué, "Pere El Catòlic," in Bagué, Cabestany, and Schramm, *Els primers comtes-reis*, 107–27.

104. Smith, *Innocent III and the Crown of Aragon*, 43–47.

105. *La documentación pontificia hasta Inocencio III*, ed. Mansilla, doc. 318 (16 June 1205). See Smith, *Innocent III and the Crown of Aragon*, 40, 50–51, and Baadj, *Saladin*, 159–60.

106. *La documentación pontificia hasta Inocencio III*, ed. Mansilla, doc. 321 (16 June 1205).

107. *Cartas de población del reino de Aragón en los siglos medievales*, ed. Ledesma Rubio, doc. 152; *Pedro el Católico, Rey de Aragón y Conde de Barcelona (1196–1213): Documentos, Testimonios y Memoria Histórica*, ed. M. Alvira Cabrer, 6 vols., Fuentes Históricas Aragonesas 52 (Zaragoza: Consejo Superior de Investigaciónes Científicas, 2010), vol. 1, doc. 323 (30 Apr. 1203).

108. *Pedro el Católico*, ed. Alvira Cabrer, vol. 1, doc. 328bis (6 Jun. 1202).

109. ACA, C, pergs. P I, no. 167 (5 Oct. 1203); *Cartas de población del reino de Aragón en los siglos medievales*, ed. Ledesma Rubio, doc. 145; *Pedro el Católico*, ed. Alvira Cabrer, vol. 2, doc. 404.

110. Gual Camarena, "Precedentes de la Reconquista valenciana," 208–10, Zurita, *Anales de la Corona de Aragón*, ed. Canellas López, 2.60, 1:331–32. See Smith, *Innocent III and the Crown of Aragon*, 89–92. Compare J. Miret y Sans, "Itinerario del rey Pedro I de Cataluña, II en Aragón (1196–1213)," *Boletín de la Real Academia de Buenas Letras de Barcelona* 6, no. 24 (1907): 511–12. See chapter 7 below.

111. *Pedro el Católico*, ed. Alvira Cabrer, vol. 3, doc. 1082bis (22 Sept. 1210).

112. ACA, C, pergs. P I, no. 370 (19 Sept. 1210); Pagarolas, *Els Templers*, doc. 134; *Pedro el Católico*, ed. Alvira Cabrer, vol. 3, doc. 1082. ACA, C, pergs. P I, no. 372 (23 Oct. 1210); *Pedro el Católico*, ed. Alvira Cabrer, vol. 3, doc. 1087. See below for detailed discussion of these transactions.

113. ACA, C, pergs. P I, no. 410 (5 Nov. 1211). See Gual Camarena, "Precedentes de la Reconquista valenciana," 210n120.

114. ACA, C, pergs. P I, no. 413 (6 Dec. 1211); *Pedro el Católico*, ed. Alvira Cabrer, vol. 3, doc. 1223.

115. ACA, C, pergs. P I, no. 416; *Pedro el Católico*, ed. Alvira Cabrer, vol. 3, doc. 1247. See J. Miret y Sans, "Itinerario del Rey Pedro I de Cataluña, II en Aragón (1196–1213)," *Boletín de la Real Academia de Buenas Letras de Barcelona* 7, no. 25 (1907): 30. AHN, Órdenes Militares, c. 479, no. 20 (22 Jan. 1213). The Templars gained holdings in Lower Aragon by absorbing the Order of the Holy Redeemer, including Cantavieja: AHN, Órdenes Militares, c. 651, no. 1 (29 Nov. 1212); *Pedro el Católico*, ed. Alvira Cabrer, vol. 3, doc. 1412.

116. AHN, Códices, no. 1126B, fol. 89r (26 Aug. 1210).

117. *Fiscal Accounts*, ed. Bisson, 1:129–33, and Smith, *Innocent III and the Crown of Aragon*, 95–99.

118. What follows builds on Barton, *Contested Treasure*, 38–53.

119. ACA, C, pergs. A I, no. 58 (1 July 1168); *Fiscal Accounts*, ed. Bisson, vol. 2, doc. 20. For an example of one of these standard sales, see ACA, C, pergs. A I, no. 25 (9 Sept. 1165); *Fiscal Accounts*, ed. Bisson, vol. 2, doc. 16.

120. ACA, C, pergs. A I, no. 67 (20 May 1169); *Fiscal Accounts*, ed. Bisson, vol. 2, doc. 22.

121. ACA, C, pergs. A I, no. 200 (25–31 Mar. 1175); *Fiscal Accounts*, ed. Bisson, vol. 2, doc. 26; *Alfonso II*, ed. Sánchez Casabón, doc. 192.

122. ACA, C, pergs. A I, no. 179 (26 Aug. 1175); *Fiscal Accounts*, ed. Bisson, vol. 2, doc. 28.

123. *Fiscal Accounts*, ed. Bisson, vol. 2, doc. 27 ([Mar. ca. 1174–75]). See P. Orti Gost, "La primera articulación del estado feudal en Cataluña a través de un impuesto: el bovaje (ss. XII–XIII), *Hispania* 61, no. 3 (2001): 967–98. See also Barton, *Contested Treasure*, 39–40, 59–60.

124. AHN, Órdenes Militares, c. 607, no. 10; *Alfonso II*, ed. Sánchez Casabón, doc. 316 (26 Nov. 1180). The value was established by the first 1175 loan.

125. *El "Llibre Blanch" de Santas Creus*, ed. Udina Martorell, doc. 235; *Alfonso II*, ed. Sánchez Casabón, doc. 310 (8 Sept. 1180).

126. *El "Llibre Blanch" de Santas Creus*, ed. Udina Martorell, doc. 246; *Alfonso II*, ed. Sánchez Casabón, doc. 330 (30 Oct. 1181).

127. See Jaspert, "Bonds and Tensions on the Frontier," 36–44.

128. ACA, GPC, Códices, no. 197, *Cartulari de Gardeny*, fol. 49v, doc. 111 (2 Nov. 1159); *Col·lecció diplomàtica*, ed. Sarobe, vol. 1, doc. 92.

129. *Diplomatari de la catedral de Tortosa (1062–1193)*, ed. Virgili, doc. 45 (Oct. 1154).

130. ACA, GPC, Arm. 11: Gardeny, perg. no. 2205 (16 June 1158); *Col·lecció diplomàtica*, ed. Sarobe, vol. 1, doc. 83.

131. *Diplomatari de la catedral de Tortosa (1062–1193)*, ed. Virgili, doc. 135 (20 Nov. 1163).

132. *Diplomatari de la catedral de Tortosa (1062–1193)*, ed. Virgili, doc. 136 (7 Dec. 1163).

133. *Diplomatari de la catedral de Tortosa (1193–1212)*, ed. A. Virgili, Diplomataris 25 (Barcelona: Fundació Noguera, 2001), doc. 515 (15 Oct. 1194).

134. ACA, GPC, Arm. 11: Gardeny, perg. no. 244 (25 July 1158); *Col·lecció diplomàtica*, ed. Sarobe, vol. 1, doc. 84.

135. Virgili, *Ad detrimentum Yspanie*, 156–57 (fig. 6) and 158–59 (fig. 7, table 13).

136. F. Sabaté, "Il mercato della terra in un paese nuovo Lerida nella seconda metà del XII secolo," *Rivista di Storia dell'Agricoltura* 43/1 (2003): 57–90 (70).

137. ACA, GPC, Arm. 11: Gardeny, perg. no. 1786 (29 Aug. 1174); *Col·lecció diplomàtica*, ed. Sarobe, vol. 1, doc. 255. See Forey, *Templars in the* Corona de Aragón, 215. Fields within the Crown of Aragon were measured in *fanecades, cafizades,* and *jovades,* with six *fanecades* to the *cafizada* and six *cafizades* to the *jovada.* A *fanecada* was the amount of land (roughly an acre and a half) one could plant with a *faneca* (from the Arabic, *fanîqa,* "sack") or bushel of seed. See T. Glick, *Irrigation and Society in Medieval Valencia* (Cambridge, MA: Harvard University Press, 1970), 15–16.

138. ACA, GPC, Arm. 11: Gardeny, perg. no. 1978 (29 July 1153); *Col·lecció diplomàtica*, ed. Sarobe, vol. 1, doc. 52.

139. Freedman, *Origins of Peasant Servitude*, 103–18.

140. J. Bolòs, "Paisatge i societat al 'Segrià' al segle XIII," in Bolòs, *Paisatge i societat a la Plana de Lleida a l'edat mitjana,* 71. See also his "Changes and Survival: The Territory of Lleida (Catalonia) after the Twelfth-Century Conquest," *Journal of Medieval History* 27 (2001): 323–24.

141. The parcels were usually one *parellada,* which could amount to as much as ten hectares. See Bolòs, "Paisatge i societat," 58, as well as his "Changes and Survival," 324–28.

142. See Serrano Daura, *Senyoriu i municipi a la Catalunya Nova,* 1:508.

143. Compare Jaspert, "Bonds and Tensions on the Frontier," 45.

144. *Diplomatari de la catedral de Tortosa (1193–1212),* ed. Virgili, doc. 577 (31 Dec. 1198).

145. ACA, C, pergs. A I, no. 6 (25 Apr. 1163).

146. ACA, C, pergs. A I, no. 153 (18 June 1174); *Alfonso II,* ed. Sánchez Casabón, doc. 170.

147. ACA, C, pergs. A I, no. 299 (Sept. 1180); *Alfonso II,* ed. Sánchez Casabón, doc. 313.

148. ACA, GPC, Códices, no. 115, *Cartulari de Tortosa,* fol. 86v, no. 275 (Feb. 1182); *Alfonso II,* ed. Sánchez Casabón, doc. 324; *Die Juden im Christlichen Spanien,* ed. Y. Baer (Berlin: Akademie-Verlag, 1929–36), doc. 48. See Barton, *Contested Treasure,* 45.

149. ACA, C, pergs. A I, no. 326 (Mar. 1182); *Alfonso II,* ed. Sánchez Casabón, doc. 339. See Forey, *Templars in the* Corona de Aragón, 27–28, and Pagarolas, *Els Templers,* 1:157–58.

150. The last comital-royal bailiff appears to have been withdrawn around 1186. See *Cartulari de Poblet,* ed. Toda, doc. 38 (Nov 1186). For context, see A. M. Aragó Cabañas, "La institución 'baiulus regis' en Cataluña en la época de Alfonso el Casto," *VII Congreso de Historia de la Corona de Aragón,* 3 vols. (Barcelona: Diputación provincial, 1962), 3: 137-42, and *Fiscal Accounts,* ed. Bisson, 1:68–71.

151. ACA, C, pergs. A I, no. 326; *Alfonso II,* ed. Sánchez Casabón, doc. 339·

152. See Barton, *Contested Treasure,* 65; Shideler, *A Medieval Catalan Noble Family,* 11–12; Virgili, *Ad detrimentum Yspanie,* 187–88; *Fiscal Accounts,* ed. Bisson, 1:66–68. For information on the norms of the office within Catalonia in general, see J. Lalinde Abadía, *La jurisdicción real inferior en Cataluña ("corts, veguers, batlles")* (Barcelona: Ayuntamiento de Barcelona, 1967), 174–75, and J. Lalinde Abadía, "El 'curia' o 'cort' (una magistratura medieval mediterránea)," *Anuario de Estudios Medievales* 4 (1967):

NOTES TO PAGES 158-161

240–44. For documentation referring to successive vicars within Tortosa, see Pagarolas, *La comanda del Temple de Tortosa*, doc. 107 (1195); *Diplomatari de la catedral de Tortosa (1193–1212)*, ed. Virgili, docs. 577 (1198) and 722 (1209); and Pagarolas, *La comanda del Temple de Tortosa*, docs. 119 (1200) and 135 (1211).

153. ACA, C, pergs. A I, no. 326; *Alfonso II*, ed. Sánchez Casabón, doc. 339. These rights appear to have been fully itemized in a supplementary convention that is now lost.

154. ACA, C, pergs. A I, no. 328 (1 May 1182); Pagarolas, *Els Templers*, vol. 2, doc. 206; *Alfonso II*, ed. Sánchez Casabón, doc. 347.

155. ACA, C, pergs. A I, no. 362 (Jan. 1184); *Alfonso II*, ed. Sánchez Casabón, doc. 382; and *Liber Feudorum Maior*, ed. Miquel Rosell, vol. 1, doc. 467.

156. *Diplomatari de la catedral de Tortosa (1062–1193)*, ed. Virgili, doc. 381 (27 May 1185); Pagarolas, *La comanda del Temple de Tortosa*, doc. 87.

157. ACA, C, pergs. A I, no. 146 (18 Jan. 1174); *Alfonso II*, ed. Sánchez Casabón, doc. 161. The dower was termed the *donatio propter nupcias* or *sponsalicium*.

158. Smith, *Innocent III and the Crown of Aragon*, 21.

159. Compare *Fiscal Accounts*, ed. Bisson, 1:98n75.

160. *Fiscal Accounts*, ed. Bisson, 1:98n75. The omission of some of Alfons's domains from the list could be a sign that he wished to limit her dower to this subset of his patrimony.

161. See Bensch, *Barcelona and Its Rulers*, 264–65. J. Lalinde Abadía, "Los pactos matrimoniales catalanes (esquema histórico)," *Anuario de la historia del derecho español* 33 (1963): 133–266. Compare Smith, *Innocent III and the Crown of Aragon*, 21–23.

162. See C. Johnson, "Marriage Agreements from Twelfth-Century Southern France," in *To Have and To Hold: Marrying and Its Documentation in Western Christendom, 400–1600*, ed. P. L. Reynolds and J. Witte Jr. (Cambridge: Cambridge University Press, 2007), 221–23.

163. See Pagarolas, *Els Templers*, 1:157. The queen managed her own property unilaterally. In 1190, she established settlers in a place called Montsant neighboring Castelldans, Ascó, and Cabacés, an act subscribed by her own bailiff that lacked any involvement by the count-king. *Cartas de población*, ed. Font Rius, vol. 1.1, doc. 185 (26 May 1190); *Diplomatari de la catedral de Tortosa (1062–1193)*, ed. Virgili, doc. 441.

164. M. T. Ferrer i Mallol, *Entre la paz y la guerra: la Corona catalano-aragonesa y Castilla en la Baja Edad Media* (Barcelona: Consejo Superior de Investiaciones Científicas, 2005), 14–15; J. González, *El reino de Castilla en la época de Alfonso VIII*, 3 vols. (Madrid: Consejo Superior de Investiaciones Científicas, 1960), 1: 820–34.

165. ACA, C, pergs. A I, no. 454 (May 1187); *Alfonso II*, ed. Sánchez Casabón, doc. 442.

166. Alfons's will of 1194 would later refer to these donations to the dower as still unfulfilled. See below and compare Aurell, *Les noces du comte*, 470.

167. *Alfonso II*, ed. Sánchez Casabón, doc. 520 (7 Sept. 1190). ACA, C, pergs. A I, no. 585 (May 1191); *Alfonso II*, ed. Sánchez Casabón, doc. 533, established the alliance with Sancho I of Portugal and Alfons IX of León against Castile. See Ferrer i Mallol, *Entre la paz y la guerra*, 15.

168. AHN, Clero: Poblet, c. 2055, no. 14; see *Fiscal Accounts*, ed. Bisson, 1:258. Ramon was listed as the *baiulus domine regine* or *baiulus Siurane* in 1194–95, 1197, and perhaps 1200. See *Fiscal Accounts*, ed. Bisson, 1:275.

169. ACA, C, pergs. A I, Extrainventario nos. 2613 and 2616; *Fiscal Accounts*, ed. Bisson, vol.2, doc. 78 and 79 ([Nov. 1189–Feb. 1190]).

170. ACA, C, pergs. A I, no. 700 (Dec. 1194); *Alfonso II*, ed. Sánchez Casabón, doc. 628. See Pagarolas, *Els Templers*, 1:159.

171. Bisson viewed this allocation by Alfons as a sign that his pledge on Ascó had been repaid by this time. He also suggested that the 1182 arrangement remained intact and that Alfons's will intended for his half share of the revenues and retained demesnes to be used to satisfy these disbursements. See *Fiscal Accounts*, ed. Bisson, 1:224, 230.

172. ACA, C, pergs. A I, no. 700 (Dec. 1194); *Alfonso II*, ed. Sánchez Casabón, doc. 628. See Pagarolas, *Els Templers*, 1:159.

173. This practice of establishing the queen mother as regent (for the standard period) was common throughout western Europe. See A. Poulet, "Capetian Women and the Regency: The Genesis of a Vocation," in *Medieval Queenship*, ed. J. C. Parsons (New York: St. Martins Press, 1993), 93–94, and T. Earenfight, *The King's Other Body: María of Castile and the Crown of Aragon* (Philadelphia: University of Philadelphia Press, 2010), 44–45. Pere was born in 1177 or 1178: *Pedro el Católico*, ed. Alvira Cabrer, vol. 1, doc. 1 (Apr./July 1177/78) from the *Chronicon Dertusense II*. See J. Ventura, *Pere El Catòlic i Simó de Montfort* (Barcelona: Aedos, 1960), 41–42.

174. *Pedro el Católico*, ed. Alvira Cabrer, vol. 1, doc. 154 (20 May 1198). See Smith, *Innocent III and the Crown of Aragon*, 22.

175. *Pedro el Católico*, ed. Alvira Cabrer, vol. 1, doc. 402 ([Sept. 1203?]).

176. See *Pedro el Católico*, ed. Alvira Cabrer, vol. 1, doc. 40 (24 Apr. 1196), Zurita, *Anales de la Corona de Aragón*, ed. Canellas López, 2.47, 1:298–300, and *Gesta comitum Barcinonensium*, ed. Barrau Dihigo and Massó Torrents, p. 15.

177. AHN, Clero: Poblet, c. 2062, no. 5 (Apr. 1196); *Alfonso II*, ed. Sánchez Casabón, doc. 657.

178. Final reference as *infant*: *Fiscal Accounts*, ed. Bisson, vol. 2, doc. 102; *Pedro el Católico*, ed. Alvira Cabrer, vol. 1, doc. 42 (6 May 1196).

179. E.g., AML, Fons Municipal, perg. no. 10 = *Pedro el Católico*, ed. Alvira Cabrer, vol. 1, doc. 45 (May 1196); *Pedro el Católico*, ed. Alvira Cabrer, vol. 1, docs. 46 (May 1196) and 47 (14 May 1196). She did not subscribe or approve his donation to the Templars: AHN, Órdenes Militares, c. 654, no. 22 (14 May 1196); *Pedro el Católico*, ed. Alvira Cabrer, vol. 1, doc. 47 (14 May 1196).

180. ACA, C, pergs. P I, no. 7 (May 1196); *Pedro el Católico*, ed. Alvira Cabrer, vol. 1, doc. 50.

181. ACA, C, pergs. P I, no. 7.

182. AHN, Órdenes Militares, c. 582, nos. 44 and 45 (6 June 1196); *Pedro el Católico*, ed. Alvira Cabrer, vol. 1, doc. 53. Later that year, he shifted his plans to Poblet, like his father. *Pedro el Católico*, ed. Alvira Cabrer, vol. 1, doc. 235 (13 Apr. 1200). *Cartulari de Poblet*, ed. Toda, docs. 29 (Feb. 1175) and 30 (Dec. 1190).

183. *Pedro el Católico*, ed. Alvira Cabrer, vol. 1, docs. 56 and 57; *Papsturkunden in Spanien*, ed. Kehr, docs. 268 and 269 (both 7 Aug. 1196).

184. *Pedro el Católico*, ed. Alvira Cabrer, vol. 1, doc. 201 (13 May 1199); Smith, *Innocent III and the Crown of Aragon*, doc. 1. *Pedro el Católico*, ed. Alvira Cabrer, vol. 1, doc. 245 (5 May 1200); *La documentación pontificia hasta Inocencio III*, ed. Mansilla, doc. 228; Smith, *Innocent III and the Crown of Aragon*, doc. 3.

185. See L. García-Guijarro Ramos, "The Aragonese Hospitaller Monastery of Sigena: Its Early Stages, 1188–c.1210," in *Hospitaller Women in the Middle Ages*, ed. A. Luttrell and H. J. Nicholson (Aldershot: Ashgate, 2006), 115–17. See Smith, *Innocent III and the Crown of Aragon*, 15n15. Sancha's earliest appearance as a Hospitaller sister: *Pedro el Católico*, ed. Alvira Cabrer, vol. 2, doc. 415 (1 Dec. 1203); M. Alvira Cabrer and D. J. Smith, "Política antiherética en la Corona de Aragón: Una carta inédita del Papa Inocencio III a la reina Sancha (1203)," *Acta historica et archaeologica mediaevalia* 27–28 (2006–7): 65–88, doc. 2.

186. ACA, C, pergs. P I, no. 84 (7 Feb. 1200); *Fiscal Accounts*, ed. Bisson, vol. 2, doc. 103; *Pedro ed Católico*, ed. Alvira Cabrer, vol. 1, doc. 225.

187. ACA, C, pergs. P I, no. 87 (19 Apr. 1200); *Pedro el Católico*, ed. Alvira Cabrer, vol. 1, doc. 237.

188. Subsequent evidence suggests that Sancha subsequently exercised lordship over at least some of these holdings. In 1203, for example, she joined Pere and Ramon de Cervera in authorizing Cervera's consulate. *Pedro el Católico*, ed. Alvira Cabrer, vol. 2, doc. 369 (8 Feb. 1203).

189. ACA, C, pergs. P I, no. 98; *Pedro el Católico*, ed. Alvira Cabrer, vol. 1, doc. 261 (26 Sept. 1200). See M. de Pano y Ruata, *La santa reina Doña Sancha, hermana hospitalaria, fundadora del monasterio de Sijena* (Zaragoza: Berdejo Casanal, 1943), 67–68.

190. Where Pere assigned the rents from Seròs to repay a five-thousand-*masmudines* loan, he indicated that three thousand *solidi* of that revenue stream had to be reserved for the queen mother: ACA, C, pergs. P I, no. 87; *Pedro el Católico*, ed. Alvira Cabrer, vol. 1, doc. 237 (19 Apr. 1200).

191. *Pedro el Católico*, ed. Alvira Cabrer, vol. 2, doc. 395bis (7 Aug. 1203).

192. Pagarolas, *La comanda del Temple de Tortosa*, doc. 116, and *Diplomatari de la catedral de Tortosa (1193–1212)*, ed. Virgili, doc. 578 (1 Jan. 1199). See Forey, *Templars in the* Corona de Aragón, 29.

193. ACA, GPC, Arm. 4: Tortosa, perg. no. 85; Pagarolas, *La comanda del Temple de Tortosa*, doc. 57 (15 Mar. 1200).

194. Pere still retained some taxation rights in Tortosa. In a convention between the Templars and Ramon II de Montcada from later in 1202, the noble complained that the commander was collecting the *questia* that he had been enlisted to levy on the count-king's behalf. ACA, GPC, Códices, no. 115, *Cartulari de Tortosa*, fol. 9, no. 28; Pagarolas, *La comanda del Temple de Tortosa*, doc. 122 (13 June 1202).

195. ACA, GPC, Códices, no. 115, *Cartulari de Tortosa*, fols. 46v–47r, no. 144; Pagarolas, *La comanda del Temple de Tortosa*, doc. 121 (15 Jan. 1202).

196. ACA, C, pergs. P I, no. 257; *Diplomatari de la catedral de Tortosa (1193–1212)*, ed. Virgili, doc. 678 (5 Apr. 1207). *Diplomatari de la catedral de Tortosa (1193–1212)*, ed. Virgili, doc. 667 (5 Jan. 1206). See ACA, GPC, Arm. 11: Gardeny, perg. no. 1939 (28 Apr. 1192); *Col·lecció diplomàtica*, ed. Sarobe, vol. 2, doc. 592; *Fiscal Accounts*, ed. Bisson, fol. 2, doc. 159. See *Fiscal Accounts*, ed. Bisson, 1:241, 266. Guillem was serving Sancha by 1201, but his activity in Tortosa did not predate mid-1202. ACA, C, pergs. P I, no. 108. Later, he engaged in property transfers in Lleida without any designation as bailiff: *Diplomatari de la catedral de Tortosa (1193–1212)*, ed. Virgili, docs. 618 and 619 (both 11 May 1202).

197. ACA, C, pergs. P I, no. 139 (3 July 1202); Pagarolas, *La comanda del Temple de Tortosa*, doc. 121; *Pedro el Católico*, ed. Alvira Cabrer, vol. 1, doc. 337. See Forey, *Templars in the* Corona de Aragón, 30.

198. See Forey, *Templars in the* Corona de Aragón, 30.

199. ACA, C, pergs. P I, no. 201 (Jan. 1204); *Fiscal Accounts*, ed. Bisson, vol. 2, doc. 108; *Pedro el Católico*, ed. Alvira Cabrer, vol. 2, doc. 428. Pere also obtained rights to tithes owed by the Order of the Holy Redeemer, which stood under Templar jurisdiction: *Pedro el Católico*, ed. Alvira Cabrer, vol. 2, doc. 600 (8 Mar. 1206).

200. *Pedro el Católico*, ed. Alvira Cabrer, vol. 2, doc. 601 (9 Mar. 1206).

201. ACA, C, pergs. P I, no. 313; *Fiscal Accounts*, ed. Bisson, vol. 2, doc. 122 (16 Feb. 1209).

202. Notice of her death: *Pedro el Católico*, ed. Alvira Cabrer, vol. 2, doc. 824 (9 Nov. 1208).

203. *Pedro el Católico*, ed. Alvira Cabrer, vol. 2, doc. 820 (27 Oct. 1208). See also her will: doc. 823 (6 Nov. 1208).

204. AHN, Clero: Poblet, c. 2097, no. 1 (29 Jan. 1209).

205. ACA, C, pergs. P I, no. 308; Pagarolas, *Els Templers*, vol. 2, doc. 213 (26 Nov. 1208). See G. Gonzalvo i Bou and M. Salas, "Guillem IV de Cervera, Cavaller i Monjo de Poblet," *Anuario de Estudios Medievales* 28 (1998): 405–18.

206. ACA, C, pergs. P I, no. 308. See Barton, *Contested Treasure*, 37–38.

207. See González, *El reino de Castilla en la época de Alfonso VIII*, 3: 179–86.

208. Smith, *Innocent III and the Crown of Aragon*, 40–41.

209. Smith, *Innocent III and the Crown of Aragon*, 42, 60–63. See also *Fiscal Accounts*, ed. Bisson, 1:123, and Ferrer i Mallol, *Entre la paz y la guerra*, 15.

210. Smith, *Innocent III and the Crown of Aragon*, 36–40.

211. For a detailed chronology and analysis of these developments, see Smith, *Innocent III and the Crown of Aragon*, 60, 70–78. See also, D. Smith, *Crusade, Heresy, and Inquisition in the Lands of the Crown of Aragon* (Leiden: Brill, 2010), 31–32.

212. See Smith, *Innocent III and the Crown of Aragon*, 79–95, and E. Jenkins, *The Mediterranean World of Alfonso II and Peter II of Aragon (1162–1213)* (New York: Palgrave Macmillan, 2012), 94–95.

213. *Cartas de población*, ed. Font Rius, vol. 1.1, doc. 227 (22 Nov. 1208).

214. *Cartas de población*, ed. Font Rius, vol. 1.1, doc. 202 (Apr. 1195).

215. See Forey, *Templars in the* Corona de Aragón, 30, and Pagarolas, *Els Templers*, 1:162–64. See Aurell, *Les noces du comte*, 357.

216. AHN, Clero: Poblet, c. 2099, no. 7 (3 Nov. 1209); *Fiscal Accounts*, ed. Bisson, vol. 2, doc. 128; *Pedro el Católico*, ed. Alvira Cabrer, vol. 3, doc. 964.

217. Pagarolas, *La comanda del Temple de Tortosa*, doc. 130 (8 June 1209). One of these *algeziras*, called "Moled," appears in other documentation, which is suggestive that the Pinyols did not obtain all of the islands but rather a significant portion of their parcels from the queen mother. See *Diplomatari de la catedral de Tortosa (1062–1193)*, ed. Virgili, docs. 388 (29 July 1185) and 394 (14 Mar. 1186). Ramon II de Montcada may not have been a completely impartial judge, as his family had held investments in this area. In 1186, his father, Ramon I, had donated to the altar of Sant Pere in the cathedral of Tortosa a field in "Moled," which pertained to the see. *Diplomatari de la catedral de Tortosa (1062–1193)*, ed. Virgili, doc. 394 (14 Mar. 1186).

218. The rental contract survives: *Diplomatari de la catedral de Tortosa (1193–1212)*, ed. Virgili, doc. 642 (15 May 1204).

219. ACA, GPC, Códices, no. 115, *Cartulari de Tortosa*, fol. 75, no. 246 (1 June 1210); *Pedro el Católico*, ed. Alvira Cabrer, vol. 3, doc. 1050 (1 June 1210).

220. *Diplomatari de la catedral de Tortosa (1193–1212)*, ed. Virgili, doc. 586 (20 Apr. 1199). The see already held land in this area. In 1185, the *cambrer* of Tortosa sold to the sacrist his honor in Moled. *Diplomatari de la catedral de Tortosa (1062–1193)*, ed. Virgili, doc. 388 (29 July 1185).

221. ACA, GPC, Códices, no. 115, *Cartulari de Tortosa*, fol. 75, no. 246.

222. ACA, C, pergs. P I, no. 370 (19 Sept. 1210); Pagarolas, *Els Templers*, doc. 134; *Pedro el Católico*, ed. Alvira Cabrer, vol. 3, doc. 1082.

223. AHN, Órdenes Militares, c. 636, no. 5 (23 Oct. 1210); *Pedro el Católico*, ed. Alvira Cabrer, vol. 3, doc. 1087.

224. See Forey, *Templars in the* Corona de Aragón, 30.

225. ACA, C, Reg. 310, fol. 35r–v (3 Nov. 1210); Pagarolas, *Els Templers*, vol. 2, doc. 215.

226. Regarding the king's death at Muret, see Bagué, "Pere El Catòlic," 127–42; M. Alvira Cabrer, *12 de septiembre de 1213: el jueves de Muret* (Barcelona: Ariel, 2002); and L. W. Marvin, *The Occitan War: A Military and Political History of the Albigensian Crusade, 1209–1218* (Cambridge: Cambridge University Press, 2008), 158–95. See M. Pegg, *The Corruption of Angels: The Great Inquisition of 1245–1246* (Princeton, NJ: Princeton University Press, 2001), chap. 2, and M. Costen, *The Cathars and the Albigensian Crusade* (Manchester: Manchester University Press, 1997), 127.

227. ACA, C, pergs. J I, no. 39 (and other copies) (23 Mar. 1215); Pagarolas, *Els Templers*, vol. 2, doc. 1. Compare Shideler, *A Medieval Catalan Noble Family*, 200–201.

228. ACA, GPC, Códices, no. 115, *Cartulari de Tortosa*, fol. 50v; Pagarolas, *Els Templers*, vol. 2, doc. 2.

229. The following year, a community of monks was already in residence there. See *Cartas de población*, ed. Font Rius, 1.2:804.

230. Pagarolas, *La comanda del Temple de Tortosa*, doc. 135 (23 July 1211).

231. ACA, GPC, Códices, no. 115, *Cartulari de Tortosa*, fol. 73r; Pagarolas, *Els Templers*, vol. 2, doc. 10 (and see 1:165).

232. See chapter 7 below for further discussion of changes to tenurial conditions within New Catalonia during the thirteenth century.

233. Sabaté, *El territori de la Catalunya medieval*, 247–66.

234. Bensch, *Barcelona and Its Rulers*, 209.

Chapter 6. Lleida and the County of Urgell

1. See Sabaté, "Organització administrativa i territorial del comtat d'Urgell." Lleida's disconnection from this frontier could also explain why Pere agreed to release its citizens requested from any obligations to construct, arm, or harbor warships of any kind in 1196. AML, Fons Municipal, perg. no. 12 (30 Nov 1196); *Pedro el Católico*, ed. Alvira Cabrer, vol. 1, doc. 70.

2. See Barton, *Contested Treasure*, 64–68, and Jaspert, "Bonds and Tensions on the Frontier," 41–43.

3. ACA, C, pergs. P I, no. 425 (1 June 1213); *Pedro el Católico*, ed. Alvira Cabrer, vol. 4, doc. 1519.

4. ACA, C, pergs. RB IV, nos. 202 and 233; *Col·lecció diplomàtica*, ed. Sarobe, vol. 1, doc. 17 (25 May 1148). *Liber Feudorum Maior*, ed. Miquel Rosell, vol. 1, doc. 161.

5. For examples of typical joint enactments, consider AML, Fons Municipal, perg. no. 9 = AML, reg. 1372, Llibre Vert Petit, fol. 145r-v (undated, in which Alfons and Ermengol VIII license a weekly market in Lleida), and AML, Fons Municipal, perg. no. 10 (3 Aug. 1196, in which Pere and Ermengol VIII confirmed Lleida's privileges, franchises, and "good uses"); *Pedro el Católico*, ed. Alvira Cabrer, vol. 1, doc. 45. For illustrative unilateral enactments by the count-kings, consult AML, Fons Municipal, perg. no. 5 = AML, reg. 1372, *Llibre Vert Petit*, fols. 107v-108r (22 Oct. 1173, in which Alfons confirmed the franchises and good uses of the city conceded by Ramon Berenguer IV), and AML, Fons Municipal, perg. no. 7 (Mar 1191, in which Alfons promised to the citizens and *prohoms* of Lleida full use of the neighborhoods, streets, and plazas of the city without any interference).

6. See Shideler, *A Medieval Catalan Noble Family*, 102, and chapter 5 above.

7. ACA, C, pergs. A I, no. 260; *Alfonso II*, ed. Sánchez Casabón, doc. 276; *Liber Feudorum Maior*, ed. Miquel Rosell, vol. 1, doc. 188 (1 Jan. 1179). See Lladonosa, *Història de Lleida*, 289–90.

8. ACA, C, pergs. A I, no. 455 (4 June 1187); *Alfonso II*, ed. Sánchez Casabón, doc. 443.

9. Zurita, *Anales de la Corona de Aragón*, ed. Canellas López, 2.40, 1:285. See D. de Monfar y Sors, *Historia de los condes de Urgel*, 2 vols. (Barcelona: J. E. Monfort, 1853), 1:415–16.

10. Monfar, *Historia de los condes de Urgel*, 1:418–21 (at 420); also *Colección de documentos inéditos del Archivo de la Corona de Aragón*, ed. de Bofarull y Mascaró et al., 9:433–37. For his earlier will, see "Els documents, dels anys 1151–1190, de l'Arxiu Capitular de la Seu d'Urgell," ed. C. Baraut, *Urgellia* 10 (1990–91): 7–349, doc. 1621 (3 Aug. 1167).

11. J. Miret y Sans, *Investigación histórica sobre el vizcondado de Castellbó* (Barcelona: J. Puigventos, 1900), 101. For what follows regarding Ponç III and Guerau IV, see F. Fité, *Reculls d'història de la vall d'Àger. I – Període antic i medieval* (Àger: Centre d'Estudis de la Vall d'Àger, 1985), 218–23, and 224–25, respectively.

12. See Bisson, *Crisis of the Twelfth Century*, 504.

13. *Les constitucions de Pau i Treva de Catalunya*, ed. Gonzalvo i Bou, doc. 15 (1173). See Bisson, *Crisis of the Twelfth Century*, 504–5.

14. See Ventura, *Alfons "El Cast,"* 228, and Fité, *Reculls d'història de la vall d'Àger*, 219.

15. ACA, C, pergs. A I, no. 412 (Apr. 1186); *Alfonso II*, ed. Sánchez Casabón, doc. 423. See Monfar, *Historia de los condes de Urgel*, 1:422.

16. Smith, *Crusade, Heresy, and Inquisition*, 94–95. For what follows, see C. Baraut, "La senyoria d'Andorra: Segles IX–XIII," *Urgellia* 11 (1992–93): 264–67; S. Sobrequés, *Els barons de Catalunya*, Història de Catalunya, Biografies catalanes vol. 3 (Barcelona: Vicens-Vives, 1989), 46–47; C. Baudon de Mony, *Relations politiques des comtes de Foix avec la Catalogne jusqu'au commencement du XIVe siècle*, 2 vols. (Paris: A. Picard et fils, 1896), 1:106–8.

17. *Cartulari de la vall d'Andorra, segles IX–XIII*, ed. C. Baraut, 2 vols. (Andorra: Conselleria d'Educació i Cultura del Govern d'Andorra, 1988–90), vol. 1, doc. 80 (3 July 1185).

18. *Cartulari de la vall d'Andorra*, ed. Baraut, vol. 1, docs. 82 (25 Sept. 1185) and 83 (1185–86).

19. *Cartulari de la vall d'Andorra*, ed. Baraut, vol. 1, doc. 112 (inventory of documents from 1236–41).

20. *Cartulari de la vall d'Andorra*, ed. Baraut, vol. 1, doc. 84 (1 May 1186).

21. *Cartulari de la vall d'Andorra*, ed. Baraut, vol. 1, doc. 85 (21 May 1186).

22. ACA, C, pergs. A I, no. 412.

23. See G. Gonzalvo i Bou, "La Pau i Treva de l'any 1187 per al comtat d'Urgell i vescomtat d'Àger," *Ilerda "Humanitats"* 48 (1990): 157–74, and Fité, *Reculls d'història de la vall d'Àger*, 219–20. For similar conduct by the counts of Empúries, see S. Bensch, "Three Peaces of Empúries (1189–1220)," *Anuario de Estudios Medievales* 26 (1996): 583–603.

24. See G. Gonzalvo i Bou, "El Comtat d'Urgell i la Pau i Treva," in Sabaté, *El Comtat d'Urgell*, 71–88.

25. *Les constitucions de Pau i Treva de Catalunya*, ed. Gonzalvo i Bou, doc. 16 (19 May 1187), c. 1.

26. *Les constitucions de Pau i Treva de Catalunya*, ed. Gonzalvo i Bou, doc. 16, c. 12.

27. *Les constitucions de Pau i Treva de Catalunya*, ed. Gonzalvo i Bou, doc. 16, c. 9.

28. E.g., *Usatges de Barcelona*, ed. Bastardas, c. 59. See chapter 4 above. *Les constitucions de Pau i Treva de Catalunya*, ed. Gonzalvo i Bou, doc. 15, c. 16 and 17.

29. *Les constitucions de Pau i Treva de Catalunya*, ed. Gonzalvo i Bou, doc. 16, c. 11.

30. Sabaté, "Organització administrativa i territorial del comtat d'Urgell," 48–49.

31. *Les constitucions de Pau i Treva de Catalunya*, ed. Gonzalvo i Bou, doc. 16, c. 12.

32. Bisson, *Crisis of the Twelfth Century*, 504.

33. ACA, C, pergs. A I, Extrainventario no. 3465; T. N. Bisson, "The War of the Two Arnaus: A Memorial of the Broken Peace in Cerdanya (1188)," in *Miscel·lània en homenatge al P. Agustí Altisent* (Tarragona: Diputació de Tarragona, 1991), 99 and 103–4.

34. *Layettes du trésor des chartes*, ed. A. Teulet et al., 5 vols. (Paris: Henri Plon, 1863–1909), doc. 94 (5:32–33). See Bisson, "War of the Two Arnaus," 99.

35. *Liber Feudorum Maior*, ed. Miquel Rosell, vol. 2, docs. 621 and 622, and Baudon de Mony, *Relations politiques des comtes de Foix avec la Catalogne*, vol. 2, docs. 20 and 21 (6 Sept. 1188).

36. *Liber Feudorum Maior*, ed. Miquel Rosell, vol. 2, docs. 623 and 624, and Baudon de Mony, *Relations politiques des comtes de Foix avec la Catalogne*, vol. 2, docs. 22 and 23 (9 Sept. 1188). See Baudon de Mony, *Relations politiques des comtes de Foix avec la Catalogne*, 1:109–10.

37. ACA, C, pergs. A I, Extrainventario no. 3465.

38. *Liber Feudorum Maior*, ed. Miquel Rosell, vol. 2, doc. 621.

39. *Les constitucions de Pau i Treva de Catalunya*, ed. Gonzalvo i Bou, doc. 17 (13 Aug. 1188), c. 7, 14, 17, 19.

40. *Les constitucions de Pau i Treva de Catalunya*, ed. Gonzalvo i Bou, doc. 17, c. 20.

41. See Bisson, *Crisis of the Twelfth Century*, 507–8.

42. Bisson, *Crisis of the Twelfth Century*, 505.

43. Baudon de Mony, *Relations politiques des comtes de Foix avec la Catalogne*, vol. 2, doc. 23 (Apr. 1190).

44. P. de la Marca, *Marca hispanica sive limes hispanicus* (Paris: Muguet, 1688; repr. Barcelona: Base, 1972), cols. 1380–82. See Baraut, "La senyoria d'Andorra," 267, and Baudon de Mony, *Relations politiques des comtes de Foix avec la Catalogne*, 1:109–11.

45. ACA, C, pergs. A I, no. 512 (Nov. 1188); *Alfonso II*, ed. Sánchez Casabón, doc. 481.

46. ACA, C, pergs. A I, no. 523 (June 1189); *Alfonso II*, ed. Sánchez Casabón, doc. 498. See Fité, *Reculls d'història de la vall d'Àger*, 220–21. Notably, no one from the Cervera family subscribed the agreement.

47. *Liber Feudorum Maior*, ed. Miquel Rosell, vol. 1, docs. 186 (5 June 1119) and 188 (1 Jan. 1179).

48. ACTE, perg. no. 699, Diversorum II, no. 63.2; ACTE, perg. no. 1470, Escatró, Mequinensa, no. 32 (24 Sept. 1189).

49. *Alfonso II*, ed. Sánchez Casabón, doc. 541 (Aug. 1191). Compare Monfar, *Historia de los condes de Urgel*, 1:423–24, and see Fité, *Reculls d'història de la vall d'Àger*, 222.

50. ACA, C, pergs. A I, no. 621; *Alfonso II*, ed. Sánchez Casabón, doc. 553 (7 Apr. 1192). Catalan version: ACA, AGP, Arm. 14: Corbins, perg. no. 84; *Col·lecció diplomàtica*, ed. Sarobe, vol. 2, doc. 589 (Apr. 1192).

51. D. Costa y Bafarull, *Memorias de la ciudad de Solsona y su iglesia*, 2 vols. (Barcelona: Balmes, 1959), 1:272–75 (21 Sept. 1190). *Els castells catalans*, 7:90, 100–101.

52. *Diplomatari de l'arxiu diocesà de Solsona*, ed. Bach Riu and Sarobe, vol. 2, doc. 534 (3 Dec. 1191).

53. See Bisson, *Crisis of the Twelfth Century*, 509, and "Rise of Catalonia," 148–49.

54. *Les constitucions de Pau i Treva de Catalunya*, ed. Gonzalvo i Bou, doc. 18 (Nov. 1192).

55. See *Usatges de Barcelona*, ed. Bastardas, c. 59, and chapter 4 above.

56. *Les constitucions de Pau i Treva de Catalunya*, ed. Gonzalvo i Bou, doc. 18: "Nulli ex vobis credimus venire in dubium iam longuis retro temporibus ante pacium novarum constitucionem, quas comuni assensu procerum nostrorum et magnatum feceramus, sed postea, ad nimiam eorundem instanciam et importunitatem, apud Barchinonem, in celebri curia in irritum deduximus, paces inquam Domini seu treugas ab illustrissimis predecessoribus nostris, Barchinone comitibus constitutas fuisse, quod eciam ipsa Usaticorum scriptura manifeste declarat."

57. *Liber Feudorum Maior*, ed. Miquel Rosell, vol. 1, docs. 412–14 (28 Aug. 1194). See Bisson, *Crisis of the Twelfth Century*, 505, and Monfar, *Historia de los condes de Urgell*, 1:416–17.

58. Baudon de Mony, *Relations politiques des comtes de Foix avec la Catalogne*, vol. 2, doc. 24 (27 Aug. 1194).

59. Baudon de Mony, *Relations politiques des comtes de Foix avec la Catalogne*, vol. 2, doc. 25 (28 Aug. 1194).

60. ACA, C, pergs. P I, no. 66; *Pedro el Católico*, ed. Alvira Cabrer, vol. 1, doc. 203; *Liber Feudorum Maior*, ed. Miquel Rosell, vol. 1, doc. 416. *Liber Feudorum Maior*, ed. Miquel Rosell, vol. 1, doc. 415 ([Apr. 1196]). See Monfar, *Historia de los condes de Urgell*, 1:418, Fité, *Reculls d'història de la vall d'Àger*, 222–24, and Sobrequés, *Els barons de Catalunya*, 38. Guerau also submitted various castles to Pere: *Pedro el Católico*, ed. Alvira Cabrer, vol. 1, doc. 267 (17 Dec. 1200). See Ubieto Arteta, *Historia de Aragon*, 4:722 and 753.

61. See Baraut, "La senyoria d'Andorra," 268–69, and Smith, *Crusade, Heresy, and Inquisition*, 91–93. This violence paralleled earlier aggression against the bishopric by Viscount Pere Ramon de Castellbò: "Els documents, dels anys 1101–1150, de l'Arxiu Capitular de la Seu d'Urgell," ed. Baraut, doc. 1508 (1114–50).

62. *Alfonso II*, ed. Sánchez Casabón, doc. 621 (Oct. 1194). ACL, *Llibre Vert*, fols. 38r–39r (Feb. 1198); *Pedro el Católico*, ed. Alvira Cabrer, vol. 1, doc. 128.

63. *Les constitucions de Pau i Treva de Catalunya*, ed. Gonzalvo i Bou, doc. 19 (1 Apr. 1198).

64. AML, Fons Municipal, perg. no. 10; *Pedro el Católico*, ed. Alvira Cabrer, vol. 1, doc. 45 (May 1196). During this same period, Ermengol also unilaterally confirmed the customary privileges held by his own town of Agramunt: *Cartas de población*, ed. Font Rius, vol. 1.1, doc. 209 (27 Feb. 1198), a confirmation of *Cartas de población*, ed. Font Rius, vol. 1.1, doc. 122 (13 Nov. 1163) which added exemptions from various arbitrary seigniorial exactions (*questias, toltas*, and *forcias*).

65. *Col·lecció diplomàtica*, ed. Sarobe, vol. 2, doc. 747; *Pedro el Católico*, ed. Alvira Cabrer, vol. 1, doc. 227 (Feb. 1200), in which Alfons consigned to Ermengol a one-third interest in his workshops in the parish of Sant Llorenç of Lleida and half of the one thousand *solidi* from the *lleuda* that the count-king had since repurchased. AML, Fons Municipal, perg. no. 16; *Pedro el Católico*, ed. Alvira Cabrer, vol. 1, doc. 240 (26 Apr. 1200). Ermengol and the Pere used this same occasion to rule that property owners in Lleida who did not pay their taxes would lose their citizenship.

66. Baudon de Mony, *Relations politiques des comtes de Foix avec la Catalogne*, vol. 2, doc. 26 (11 Apr. 1201). See also *Cartulari de la vall d'Andorra*, ed. Baraut, vol. 1, docs. 93–95 (all dated 11 Apr. 1201), 96 (1 May 1201), and 97 (11 Aug. 1201).

67. Baudon de Mony, *Relations politiques des comtes de Foix avec la Catalogne*, 1:121–25 and 130–32. See also Smith, *Crusade, Heresy, and Inquisition*, 95–96.

68. Baudon de Mony, *Relations politiques des comtes de Foix avec la Catalogne*, 1:125. See also Miret y Sans, *Investigación histórica*, 150, and Smith, *Crusade, Heresy, and Inquisition*, 96. See *Les constitucions de Pau i Treva de Catalunya*, ed. Gonzalvo i Bou, doc. 18 (Nov. 1192), discussed earlier in this chapter.

69. *Col·lecció diplomàtica*, ed. Sarobe, vol. 2, doc. 747; *Pedro el Católico*, ed. Alvira Cabrer, vol. 1, doc. 227 (Feb. 1200). See Sobrequés, *Els barons de Catalunya*, 21.

70. For example, Arnau subscribed the count-king's mediation of the jurisdictional disputes between the Templars and citizens of Tortosa in 1199. Pagarolas, *La comanda del Temple de Tortosa*, doc. 116 (1 Jan. 1199).

71. *Pedro el Católico*, ed. Alvira Cabrer, vol. 1, doc. 239 (19 Apr. 1200)

72. ACA, C, pergs. P I, no. 89 (May 1200); *Pedro el Católico*, ed. Alvira Cabrer, vol. 1, doc. 247. The document credits multiple prior agreements for generating this alliance.

73. *Les constitucions de Pau i Treva de Catalunya*, ed. Gonzalvo i Bou, doc. 20 (9 July 1200). ACA, C, pergs. P I, no. 93 (July 1200); *Pedro el Católico*, ed. Alvira Cabrer, vol. 1, doc. 253.

74. ACA, C, pergs. P I, no. 119 (30 Oct. 1201).

75. Sobrequés, *Els barons de Catalunya*, 21.

76. ACA, C, pergs. P I, no. 155 (2 July 1203); Baudon de Mony, *Relations politiques des comtes de Foix avec la Catalogne*, vol. 2, doc. 27. Raymond-Roger agreed to render Ermengol six of his knights as hostages as sureties for the ransom. See Zurita, *Anales de la Corona de Aragón*, ed. Canellas López, 2.48–49, 1:302–5. ACA, C, pergs. P I, no. 156 (2 July 1203).

77. ACA, C, pergs. P I, no. 71 (15 Oct. 1199). See Baudon de Mony, *Relations politiques des comtes de Foix avec la Catalogne*, 1:126, and Smith, *Innocent III and the Crown of Aragon*, 188.

78. ACA, C, pergs. P I, no. 162 (7 Sept. 1203); Baudon de Mony, *Relations politiques des comtes de Foix avec la Catalogne*, vol. 2, doc. 30 (7 Sept. 1203). The broader peace, with this performance of homage, was executed in a separate charter: ACA, C, pergs. P I, no. 166 (Sept. 1203); Baudon de Mony, *Relations politiques des comtes de Foix avec la Catalogne*, vol. 2, doc. 32.

79. ACA, C, pergs. P I, no. 159 (Aug. 1203); *Pedro el Católico*, ed. Alvira Cabrer, vol. 2, doc. 398; Baudon de Mony, *Relations politiques des comtes de Foix avec la Catalogne*, vol. 2, doc. 28.

80. For an overview on Elvira's identity, see D. Domingo, *A la recerca d'Aurembiaix d'Urgell* (Lleida: Edicions de la Universitat de Lleida, 2000), 18–21.

81. ACA, C, pergs. A I, no. 405 (6 Feb. 1186).

82. See Bensch, *Barcelona and Its Rulers*, 170–83.

83. See the beginning of the previous chapter.

84. See T. N. Bisson, "Poder escrit i successió al comtat d'Urgell (1188–1210)," *Acta historica et archaeologica mediaevalia* 20–21 (1999–2000): 193, and see above in this chapter.

85. See P. Freedman, "An Unsuccessful Attempt at Urban Organization in Twelfth-Century Catalonia," *Speculum* 54 (1979): 479–91, and "Another Look at the Uprising of the Townsmen of Vic (1181–1183)," *Acta Mediaevalia* 20–21 (2000): 177–86.

86. ACA, C, pergs. A I, nos. 472 and 470 (26 Jan. 1188 and 27 Jan. 1188); Bisson, "Poder escrit," docs. 1 and 2.

87. ACA, C, pergs. P I, no. 160 (Aug. 1203). Compare Aurell, *Les noces du comte*, 356–57, and Monfar, *Historia de los condes de Urgel*, 1:432. Concerning Pedro's activity, including these interactions with Urgell, see González, *El reino de Castilla en la época de Alfonso VIII*, 1:331–36. See also Domingo, *A la recerca d'Aurembiaix d'Urgell*, 72–73.

88. Zurita, *Anales de la Corona de Aragón*, ed. Canellas López, 2.57, 1:325–26.

89. See Aurell, *Les noces du comte*, 356.

90. Pedro Fernández had recently received this castle: ACA, C, pergs. P I, no. 151 (15 Apr. 1203).

91. For a detailed analysis of her extended family within the Castilian context, see S. R. Doubleday, *The Lara Family: Crown and Nobility in Medieval Spain* (Cambridge, MA: Harvard University Press, 2001).

92. See J. de las Heras, *La orden de Calatrava: religión, guerra y negocio* (Madrid: Edaf, 2008), 126–28.

93. AHN, Órdenes Militares, c. 456, no. 50 (21 Aug. 1203); Domingo, *A la recerca d'Aurembiaix d'Urgell*, doc. 2.

94. ACA, C, pergs. P I, no. 163 (13 Sept. 1203); Domingo, *A la recerca d'Aurembiaix d'Urgell*, doc. 4. Monfar, *Historia de los condes de Urgel*, 1:432. Compare Aurell, *Les noces du comte*, 356n3.

95. Domingo, *A la recerca d'Aurembiaix d'Urgell*, 27.

96. ACA, C, pergs. P I, no. 185 (Apr. 1204); Domingo, *A la recerca d'Aurembiaix d'Urgell*, doc. 3.

97. In 1199, Ermengol VIII had granted Gombau one thousand *solidi* annually for life in rents from his seigniorial grain incomes from Lleida in return for services he had performed for him: AHN, Clero: Poblet, c. 2070, no. 12 (Jan. 1199); *Pedro el*

Católico, ed. Alvira Cabrer, vol. 1, doc. 190. Later that year, Gombau and his relations appeared as major creditors to the Crown. Pere confirmed that he owed them ten thousand *solidi* and would repay the debt beginning on the upcoming Michelmas pending the family's choice of properties to hold as pawns. The Templars of Monzón and Gardeny and other supporters presented themselves to the family as sureties ("obstaticos") for the debt in Lleida. ACA, C, pergs. P I, no. 67 (19 June 1199); *Pedro el Católico,* ed. Alvira Cabrer, vol. 1, doc. 206. See Monfar, *Historia de los condes de Urgel,* 1:427.

98. ACA, C, pergs. P I, no. 157 (16 Aug. 1203).

99. ACA, C, pergs. P I, no. 159 (Aug. 1203); *Pedro el Católico,* ed. Alvira Cabrer, vol. 2, doc. 398.

100. ACA, C, pergs. P I, no. 161 (7 Sept. 1203); Baudon de Mony, *Relations politiques des comtes de Foix avec la Catalogne,* vol. 2, doc. 29.

101. ACA, C, pergs. P I, no. 165 (30 Sept. 1203); Baudon de Mony, *Relations politiques des comtes de Foix avec la Catalogne,* vol. 2, doc. 31.

102. ACA, C, pergs. P I, no. 168 (1 Oct. 1203); Baudon de Mony, *Relations politiques des comtes de Foix avec la Catalogne,* vol. 2, doc. 33.

103. *Pedro el Católico,* ed. Alvira Cabrer, vol. 2, doc. 602 (17 Mar. 1206).

104. Baudon de Mony, *Relations politiques des comtes de Foix avec la Catalogne,* vol. 2, doc. 35 (13 Nov. 1206). ACA, C, pergs. P I, no. 254; Baudon de Mony, *Relations politiques des comtes de Foix avec la Catalogne,* vol. 2, doc. 34 (18 Mar. 1207). See Baraut, "La senyoria d'Andorra," 273–74.

105. *Pedro el Católico,* ed. Alvira Cabrer, vol. 2, doc. 707 (8 Sept. 1207).

106. The date of Raymond-Bernard's and Ermessenda's marriage remains unknown. The couple's first surviving enactment dates from 1226, when Arnau de Castellbò's death required them to perform homage to Bishop Pere de Puigverd of Urgell for their holdings as the new viscounts. *Cartulari de la vall d'Andorra,* ed. Baraut, vol. 1, doc. 107 (22 Nov. 1226). See Baraut, "La senyoria d'Andorra," 275, and R. Viader, *L'Andorre du IXe au XIVe siècle: Montagne, féodalité et communautés* (Toulouse: Presses Universitaires du Mirail, 2003), 126.

107. Such potential for aggression did not preclude relatively harmonious relations with Ermengol in the years leading up to his death, however. In 1205, for example, Guerau de Cabrera, as he prepared to depart for a campaign launched from Castile, established his mother, Marquesa, as his heiress, under Ermengol's and Pere's combined protection. See *Pedro el Católico,* ed. Alvira Cabrer, vol. 2, doc. 439 (2 Feb. 1205).

108. Ermengol VIII participated in the following grants concerning New Catalonia during his final year: *Pedro el Católico,* ed. Alvira Cabrer, vol. 2, docs. 856 (23 Jan. 1209), 868 (13 Feb. 1209), 872 (20 Feb. 1209), 885 (2 Apr. 1209), 886 (3 Apr. 1209), 890 (13 Apr. 1209).

109. The earlier convention no longer survives; we have only a summary of its contents: *Pedro el Católico,* ed. Alvira Cabrer, vol. 2, doc. 524 (Apr. 1205). ACA, C, pergs. P I, no. 289 (8 May 1208); *Pedro el Católico,* ed. Alvira Cabrer, vol. 2, doc. 779. See Fité, *Reculls d'història de la vall d'Àger,* 224.

110. Zurita, *Anales de la Corona de Aragón,* ed. Canellas López, 2.47, 1:325, relying on unidentified "antiguas memorias," asserted that the two had been engaged since

1203. We possess no contemporary evidence of this betrothal, and the marriage, as we shall see below, did not take place until 1212. Given our redating of Aurembiaix's birth to 1203, the arrangement must have taken place somewhat later.

111. ACA, C, pergs. P I, no. 223 (10 Feb. 1206); *Pedro el Católico*, ed. Alvira Cabrer, vol. 2, doc. 597. See *Fiscal Accounts*, ed. Bisson, 1:124.

112. ACA, C, pergs. P I, no. 223; *Pedro el Católico*, ed. Alvira Cabrer, vol. 2, doc. 597 (my italics).

113. The count-king recognized an outstanding debt of 27,267 *morabetins* around the same time that Pedro began to appear as *mayordomo*. ACA, C, pergs. P I, no. 232 (6 May 1206); *Pedro el Católico*, ed. Alvira Cabrer, vol. 2, doc. 616 and docs. 622 and 623 (both May 1206). J. Lalinde Abadía, *La gobernación general en la Corona de Aragón* (Madrid: Consejo Superior Investigaciones Científicas, 1963), 13–14, views the *mayordomo* as roughly equivalent to the Catalonian seneschal.

114. ACA, C, pergs. P I, no. 301 (18 Aug. 1208); *Pedro el Católico*, ed. Alvira Cabrer, vol. 2, doc. 800.

115. See E. Rodríguez-Picavea Matilla, "Monarquia castellana: Alfonso VIII y la orden de Calatrava," in *II Curso de Cultura Medieval, Aguilar de Campoo, 1–6 Octubre 1990, Seminario: Alfonso VIII y su época*, ed. J. Nuño González (Madrid: Centro de Estudios del Románico, 1992), 370–72. For further background on Pedro and the Castro family, see González, *El reino de Castilla en la época de Alfonso VIII*, 1:333–34, and Domingo, *A la recerca d'Aurembiaix d'Urgell*, 72–73.

116. AML, Reg. 1372, *Llibre Vert Petit*, fol. 114 (27 May 1206); *Pedro el Católico*, ed. Alvira Cabrer, vol. 2, doc. 631.

117. AML, Fons Municipal, perg. no. 13 (20 Sept. 1197). AML, Reg. 1372, *Llibre Vert Petit*, fol. 112 (19 Sept. 1202); *Pedro el Católico*, ed. Alvira Cabrer, vol. 1, doc. 348. AML, Fons Municipal, perg. no. 17 (27 May 1206); *Pedro el Católico*, ed. Alvira Cabrer, vol. 2, doc. 630. More notable still is the fact that Archbishop Berenguer of Narbonne, Guillem Durfort, Guillem de Cervelló, and Guillem IV de Cervera all subscribed the privilege.

118. Monfar, *Historia de los condes de Urgell*, 1:429, dating the agreements with Ramon and Guillem to 3 Feb. and 4 May, respectively. These charters appear to be lost.

119. ACA, C, pergs. P I, nos. 238, 239, and 240 (all 17 Aug. 1206). Bisson, "Poder escrit," docs. 3–5. See Monfar, *Historia de los condes de Urgel*, 1:432.

120. ACA, C, pergs. P I, no. 303 (30 Aug. 1208); Domingo, *A la recerca d'Aurembiaix d'Urgell*, doc. 5; Monfar, *Historia de los condes de Urgel*, 1:434. The will fails to indicate the properties on which this sum had been based throughout their marriage. Domingo, *A la recerca d'Aurembiaix d'Urgell*, 35–36, provides a summary. Regarding the count's death, see *Pedro el Católico*, ed. Alvira Cabrer, vol. 3, doc. 958 (16 Sept. to 31 Nov. 1209) and Miret, *Investigación histórica*, 174–75.

121. ACA, C, pergs. A I, no. 405. For the conversion, see Bensch, *Barcelona and Its Rulers*, 412–13, and Balaguer, *Història de la moneda dels comtats catalans*, 84–85.

122. Smith, *Innocent III and the Crown of Aragon*, 86.

123. Zurita, *Anales de la Corona de Aragón*, ed. Canellas López, 2.57, 1:325, clarifies that Aurembiaix would inherit her father's rights in Ribagorza (consisting of nine castles), while her brother would inherit the comital title and lands. Elvira would still receive all that she had been promised in the will.

124. Guerau IV de Cabrera's status as Marquesa's son is confirmed by two charters identified by Monfar, *Historia de los condes de Urgel*, 1:416–17 (22 Oct. 1186 and 14 Mar. 1195).

125. Zurita, *Anales de la Corona de Aragón*, ed. Canellas López, 2.57, 1:326.

126. Monfar, *Historia de los condes de Urgel*, 1:439–40.

127. ACA, C, pergs. P I, nos. 343 and 345 (both 31 Oct. 1209); *Pedro el Católico*, ed. Alvira Cabrer, vol. 3, docs. 959 and 960. She may have been drawing on these rights when she repaid debts of 1,300 *morabetins* to Guillem Renardi with wheat and barley from the vicinity of Prades: ACA, pergs. P I, no. 395 (8 June 1211). See Fité, *Reculls d'història de la vall d'Àger*, 224–25.

128. ACA, C, pergs. P I, no. 344 (31 Oct. 1209); *Pedro el Católico*, ed. Alvira Cabrer, vol. 3, doc. 961.

129. T. N. Bisson, "An 'Unknown Charter' for Catalonia (1205)," in his *Medieval France and Her Pyrenean Neighbours*, 211–12. Bisson, *Crisis of the Twelfth Century*, 514, notes that "there is no sign that this *magna carta* was ever promulgated, let alone observed."

130. ACA, C, pergs. P I, no. 378 (Feb. 1210); *Pedro el Católico*, ed. Alvira Cabrer, vol. 3, doc. 1016.

131. ACA, C, pergs. P I, no. 378. See Miret y Sans, "Itinerario del Rey Pedro I de Cataluña," 20n1, and Miret y Sans, *Itinerari de Jaume I*, 16.

132. AML, Fons Municipal, perg. no. 1 (Jan. 1150, conf. 11 Nov. 1209); *Cartas de población*, ed. Font Rius, vol. 1.1, doc. 79; and Gras, *Història de la Paheria*, 225–27.

133. ACA, C, pergs. P I, no. 356; *Pedro el Católico*, ed. Alvira Cabrer, vol. 3, doc. 1019 (1 Mar.–18 Apr. 1210). ACA, C, pergs. P I, no. 357 (5 Mar. 1210); *Pedro el Católico*, ed. Alvira Cabrer, vol. 3, doc. 1020.

134. Bisson, "Poder escrit," 194.

135. J. Villanueva, *Memorias cronológicas de los condes de Urgel*, ed. C. Cortès and E. Corredera Gutiérrez (Balaguer: Ayuntamiento de Balaguer, 1976), 205, noted Elvira's absence in the administrative sources for the county following her conventions with the count-king.

136. *Llibre dels feits*, ed. Bruguera, c. 36, 2:46–47. Regarding the authorship and Islamic influences on this text, see R. I. Burns, "The King's Autobiography: The Islamic Connection," in his *Muslims, Christians and Jews in the Crusader Kingdom of Valencia* (Cambridge: Cambridge University Press, 1984), 285–88.

137. For example, he confirmed their donations to the church of Solsona and monastery of Poblet. *Pedro el Católico*, ed. Alvira Cabrer, vol. 3, doc. 1018 (1 Mar. 1210) and AHN, Clero: Poblet, c. 2109, no. 7 (5 May 1213); *Pedro el Católico*, ed. Alvira Cabrer, vol. 4, doc. 1503.

138. Ermengol had confirmed and ordered his wife to repay these debts in his final will from 1208 discussed above: ACA, C, pergs. P I, no. 303 (30 Aug. 1208).

139. ACA, C, pergs. P I, no. 346 (2 Nov. 1209); *Pedro el Católico*, ed. Alvira Cabrer, vol. 3, doc. 963.

140. ACA, C, pergs. P I, no. 303.

141. AHN, Clero: Poblet, c. 2099, no. 7 (3 Nov. 1209); *Fiscal Accounts*, ed. Bisson, vol. 2, doc. 128; *Pedro el Católico*, ed. Alvira Cabrer, vol. 3, doc. 964.

142. ACA, C, pergs. P I, no. 366; *Pedro el Católico*, ed. Alvira Cabrer, vol. 3, doc. 1051 (June 1210). Domingo, *A la recerca d'Aurembiaix d'Urgell*, 49, makes a similar observation. See Baudon de Mony, *Relations politiques des comtes de Foix avec la Catalogne*, 1:138.

143. A. M. Balaguer, "Redescoberta del diner comtal urgellès de Pere el Catòlic," *Acta Numismàtica* 12 (1982): 167–72.

144. M. Crusafont i Sabater, *Numismática de la corona catalano-aragonesa medieval* (Madrid: Editorial Vico, 1982), 78–79 and 212–13 (nos. 143–45).

145. Balaguer, "Redescoberta del diner comtal urgellès," 168–69.

146. S. Bensch, "Lordship and Coinage in Empúries, ca. 1080–ca.1040," in *The Experience of Power in Medieval Europe*, ed. R. F. Berkhofer, A. Cooper, and A. J. Kosto (Aldershot: Ashgate, 2005), 86.

147. See Balaguer, "Redescoberta del diner comtal urgellès," 170–71, and Balaguer, *Història de la moneda dels comtats catalans*, 242. On Agramunt's history of coinage, see P. Bertran, "Notes sobre l'origen i expansió de la moneda d'Agramunt," *Urgellia* 3 (1980): 307–18. Ermengol later donated tithes to Poblet received by him in money coined at Agramunt "or in any other place in my entire county": AHN, Clero: Poblet, c. 54, no. 10; AHN, Clero: Poblet, c. 2093, nos. 8–10 (6 Apr. 1208).

148. ACA, C, pergs. P I, no. 355; *Cartas de población*, ed. Font Rius, vol. 1.1, doc. 231; *Pedro el Católico*, ed. Alvira Cabrer, vol. 3, doc. 1017 (1 Mar. 1210). See J. Botet i Sisó, *Les monedes catalanes: estudi y descripció de les monedes carolingies, comtals, senyorials, reyals y locals propries de Catalunya*, 3 vols. (Barcelona: Puvill, 1976), 1:150–51.

149. ACA, C, pergs. P I, no. 355.

150. ACA, C, pergs. P I, no. 374 (6 Nov. 1210); *Fiscal Accounts*, ed. Bisson, vol. 2, doc. 129, *Pedro el Católico*, ed. Alvira Cabrer, vol. 3, doc. 1092. See Monfar, *Historia de los condes de Urgel*, 1:443–44, and *Fiscal Accounts*, ed. Bisson, 1:133.

151. ACA, C, pergs. P I, no. 365 (13 June 1210); *Pedro el Católico*, ed. Alvira Cabrer, vol. 3, doc. 1053.

152. Zurita, *Anales de la Corona de Aragón*, ed. Canellas López, 2.57, 1:326. Compare Aurell, *Les noces du comte*, 357.

153. Miret y Sans, "Itinerario del Rey Pedro I de Cataluña," 25.

154. ACA, C, pergs. P I, no. 404 (10 Sept. 1211); *Pedro el Católico*, ed. Alvira Cabrer, vol. 3, doc. 1193. See Domingo, *A la recerca d'Aurembiaix d'Urgell*, 50. Innocent III later chided the king for occupying the castle of Corçà during the conflict without authorization from the monastery of Àger. Smith, *Innocent III and the Crown of Aragon*, doc. 15 (20 Apr. 1211). Compare Zurita, *Anales de la Corona de Aragón*, ed. Canellas López, 2.57, 1:326.

155. ACA, C, pergs. P I, Extrainventario no. 3652 ([Sept. 1211]); *Pedro el Católico*, ed. Alvira Cabrer, vol. 3, doc. 1194.

156. *Cartas de población*, ed. Font Rius, vol. 1.1, doc. 234 (16 Sept. 1211). See Zurita, *Anales de la Corona de Aragón*, ed. Canellas López, 2.57, 1:326.

157. For further on *cugucia*, see Freedman, *Origins of Peasant Servitude*, 17.

158. *Cartas de población*, ed. Font Rius, vol. 1.1, doc. 234 (my italics). See Sanahuja, *Història de la ciutat de Balaguer*, 149.

159. ACA, C, pergs. P I, no. 379 (27 Jan. 1211); *Pedro el Católico*, ed. Alvira Cabrer, vol. 3, doc. 1113. See Miret y Sans, *Itinerari de Jaume I*, 16.

160. Compare ACA, C, pergs. P I, no. 374 (6 Nov. 1210); *Fiscal Accounts*, ed. Bisson, vol. 2, doc. 129; *Pedro el Católico*, ed. Alvira Cabrer, vol. 3, doc. 1092.

161. Monfar, *Historia de los condes de Urgel*, 1:452–53.

162. See, e.g., Domingo, *A la recerca d'Aurembiaix d'Urgell*, 74.

163. For the 1209 agreement, see ACA, C, pergs. P I, no. 345. ACA, C, pergs. J I, no. 31 (13 Jan. 1215).

164. ACA, C, pergs. J I, no. 66 (15 Sept. 1216). See chapter 7 below for further details.

165. This coin also has the words "PAX V(O)B(I)S." Balaguer, *Història de la moneda dels comtats catalans*, 242. See Balaguer, "Redescoberta del diner comtal urgellès," and Crusafont, *Numismática de la corona catalano-aragonesa medieval*, 64–65.

166. ACA, C, pergs. P I, nos. 431 and 430 (7 Nov. 1212) (*Pedro el Católico*, ed. Alvira Cabrer, vol. 3, docs. 1400–1401), and 432 (8 Nov, 1212). Versions of these first two charters are also held at the Medinacelli ducal archive: ADM, Montcada, L. 21, no. 7; L 24, nos. 21, 15; L.16, no. 38.

167. ACA, C, pergs. P I, no. 433 (13 Nov. 1212); *Pedro el Católico*, ed. Alvira Cabrer, vol. 3, doc. 1404.

168. *Llibre dels feits*, ed. Bruguera, c. 11, 2:15. See Bensch, *Barcelona and Its Rulers*, 209–11.

Chapter 7. Repercussions of Further Conquest

1. On these fundamental administrative changes, see R. I. Burns, *Society and Documentation in Crusader Valencia* (Princeton, NJ: Princeton University Press, 1985), 15–57. See also M. Vanlandingham, *Transforming the State: King, Court, and Political Culture in the Realms of Aragon (1213–1387)* (Leiden: Brill, 2002). For further on the emergence and full expression of the monarchy's ideology of sovereignty, see Barton, *Contested Treasure*, esp. 55–82, and S. F. Cawsey, *Kingship and Propaganda: Royal Eloquence and the Crown of Aragon, c.1200–1450* (Oxford: Oxford University Press, 2002).

2. See chapter 5 above for further contextualization of these gains.

3. Olocau: AHN, Códices, no. 649B, no. 143 [Aug. 1180]; *Alfonso II*, ed. Sánchez Casabón, doc. 307. Ulldecona: AHN, Órdenes Militares, c. 686, no. 4 (1 Aug. 1180); *Alfonso II*, ed. Sánchez Casabón, doc. 308.

4. ACA, C, pergs. A I, no. 538 (Jan. 1190); *Col·lecció diplomàtica*, ed. Sarobe, vol. 2, doc. 543.

5. *Cartas de población*, ed. Font Rius, vol. 1.1, doc. 202 (Apr. 1195).

6. AHN, Códices, no. 1126B, fol. 89r (26 Aug. 1210).

7. The count-king had granted the bishop of Zaragoza all the Muslim-held castles he could conquer within the year. ACA, C, pergs. P I, no. 413 (6 Dec. 1211).

8. See Gual Camarena, "Precedentes de la Reconquista valenciana," 208–10; Zurita, *Anales de la Corona de Aragón*, ed. Canellas López, 2.60, 1:331–32. This expedition is not evidenced by contemporary documentation or the itinerary reconstructed by Miret y Sans, "Itinerario del rey Pedro I de Cataluña," who believes Zurita is incorrect in his dating, that the king marched instead on Languedoc at this time and that the offensive took place at a later date. The Hospitallers were prospectively awarded the castle and town of Cabañas and the mosques of Borriana for their participation. See Gual Camarena, "Precedentes de la Reconquista valenciana," 210n120.

9. Bagué, "Pere El Catòlic," 127–42.

10. Compare *Cartas de población*, ed. Font Rius, 2:128.

11. ACA, C, pergs. RB IV, no. 261 (24 Aug. 1153); *Col·lecció diplomàtica*, ed. Sarobe, vol. 1, doc. 54.

12. *Cartas de población*, ed. Font Rius, vol. 1.1, doc. 142 (before 1171); see 1.2:797–98. The order obtained "iure hereditario."

13. *Cartas de población*, ed. Font Rius, vol. 1.1, doc. 126 (Jan. 1165).

14. *Cartas de población*, ed. Font Rius, vol. 1.1, doc. 134 (26 July 1168). Alfons issued the settlement the *fueros* of Zaragoza, manifesting early Aragonese ambitions to draw the boundary with Catalonia closer to the course of the Ebro River, rather than along the Algars where it was ultimately established. See J. Serrano Daura, *La delimitació dels territoris de la Batllia de Miravet i de la Comanda d'Orta amb el de la ciutat de Tortosa, als segles XII al XIV* (Gandesa: Consell Comarcal de la Terra Alta, 1999), 28–29.

15. *Cartas de población*, ed. Font Rius, vol. 1.1, docs. 164–65 (30 Oct. 1181), which reconciles these two seemingly contradictory settlement charters by suggesting that Alfons subsequently redated his first population charter. See *Cartas de población*, ed. Font Rius, 1.2:798.

16. *Cartas de población*, ed. Font Rius, 1.2:798–99.

17. *Cartas de población*, ed. Font Rius, vol. 1.1, doc. 190 (10 Jan. 1192).

18. *Cartas de población*, ed. Font Rius, vol. 1.1, doc. 191 (13 Mar. 1192) and doc. 196 (Apr. 1194).

19. E.g., in 1209, the preceptor of the Ribera d'Ebre granted settlement terms to the existing inhabitants of Camposines, south of Ascó. *Cartas de población*, ed. Font Rius, vol. 1.1, doc. 228 (2 Mar. 1209).

20. Zurita, *Anales de la Corona de Aragón*, ed. Canellas López, 2.28, 1:256–59. ACA, C, pergs. A I, no. 288B; *Alfonso II*, ed. Sánchez Casabón, doc. 279 (Mar. 1179 or 1180).

21. See *Cartas de población*, ed. Font Rius, 1.2:805–6.

22. *Diplomatari de la catedral de Tortosa (1193–1212)*, ed. Virgili, doc. 674 (20 Sept. 1206) and doc. 376 (20 Sept. 1206).

23. *Cartas de población del reino de Aragón en los siglos medievales*, ed. Ledesma Rubio, doc. 150 (Apr. 1207). The Order of Calatrava regained direct lordship over the town sometime before 1278, when it issued a more extensive population charter establishing greater seigniorial prerogatives. See doc. 222 (18 Apr. 1278).

24. *Diplomatari de la catedral de Tortosa (1193–1212)*, ed. Virgili, doc. 714 (4 Apr. 1209).

25. *Diplomatari de la catedral de Tortosa (1193–1212)*, ed. Virgili, doc. 716 (13 Apr. 1209); *Cartas de población*, ed. Font Rius, vol. 1.1, doc. 229; *Cartas de población del reino de Aragón en los siglos medievales*, ed. Ledesma Rubio, doc. 155. The count-king placed people and their goods going to and from the market under his protection and *guidaticum*. At nearly the same time, the bishop also independently secured rights to the two localities held by Maria, widow of Bernat Ballester, thus consolidating unencumbered rights of lordship. Evidence of how Bernat accumulated these rights has not surfaced. In return, Maria received houses and two *parellades* of land in Lledó and one in Arenys. Maria and her son, Guillem, opted to join the cathedral chapter community as spiritual sister and brother in return for food and clothing. If Guillem married, he would lose the privileges of maintenance but would retain usufruct over the three *parellades* of land until his death. *Diplomatari de la catedral de Tortosa (1193–1212)*, ed. Virgili, docs. 715 (12 Apr. 1209) and 717 (13 Apr. 1209).

26. *Diplomatari de la catedral de Tortosa (1193–1212)*, ed. Virgili, doc. 718 (15 Apr. 1209).

27. *Diplomatari de la catedral de Tortosa (1193–1212)*, ed. Virgili, doc. 732 (13 June 1210).

28. In 1210, for example, the bishop of Tortosa met with the lord of Camarles to resolve his boundary with the see's neighboring domain of Granadella. *Diplomatari de la catedral de Tortosa (1193–1212)*, ed. Virgili, doc. 686 (6 May 1207).

29. *Diplomatari de la catedral de Tortosa (1193–1212)*, ed. Virgili, doc. 754. The zone was significant enough for the cathedral to send or maintain a bailiff there.

30. *Diplomatari de la catedral de Tortosa (1062–1193)*, ed. Virgili, doc. 413 (1 July 1187).

31. *Diplomatari de la catedral de Tortosa (1193–1212)*, ed. Virgili, doc. 597 (17 Apr. 1200).

32. *Diplomatari de la catedral de Tortosa (1193–1212)*, ed. Virgili, doc. 661 (12 Nov. 1205) and doc. 682 (20 Jan. 1207). See also the example of Arenys and Lledó discussed earlier.

33. For an overview of the course of conquest and colonization in Valencia, see Burns, *Crusader Kingdom of Valencia*, 1:5–7, and R. Ferrer Navarro, *Conquista y repoblación del Reino de Valencia* (Valencia: Promoción Cultura Valenciana-del Senia al Segura, 1999), 25–44.

34. Smith, *Innocent III*, 145, identifies a host of further reasons motivating the pope to shepherd the young king.

35. E.g., *La documentación pontificia hasta Inocencio III (965-1216)*, ed. Mansilla, docs. 515 (15 Jan. 1214) and 516 (23 Jan. 1214). See Smith, *Innocent III*, 149.

36. *Les constitucions de Pau i Treva de Catalunya*, ed. Gonzalvo i Bou, doc. 23; *Llibre dels feits*, ed. Bruguera, c. 11, 2:15. See F. Soldevila, *Els primers temps de Jaume I* (Barcelona: Institut d'Estudis Catalans, 1968), 67–82.

37. See Soldevila, *Els primers temps*, 85–99.

38. *La documentación pontificia hasta Inocencio III (965–1216)*, ed. Mansilla, docs. 554 [Feb.–Jul. 1216] and 565 [Mar.–16 Jul. 1216].

39. ACA, Bulas, Innocent III, leg. 3, no. 25; *La documentación pontificia hasta Inocencio III (965–1216)*, ed. Mansilla, no. 537 (23 Jan. 1216); Soldevila, *Els primers temps*, 100–101. For Aragon, the counselors were Bishop García Frontín of Tarazona and the nobles Jimeno Cornel and Pedro de Ahonés. For Catalonia, they were Archbishop Espàreg of Tarragona, the nobles Guillem IV de Cervera and Viscount Guillem I de Cardona, and the master of the Templar Order for Iberia, Guillem de Mont-rodon.

40. *La documentación pontificia hasta Inocencio III (965–1216)*, ed. Mansilla, no. 537 refers to these arrangements.

41. *La documentación pontificia de Honorio III (1216–1227)*, ed. D. Mansilla, Monumenta hispaniae vaticana, sección: registros 2 (Rome: Instituto Español de Estudios Eclesiásticos, 1965), doc. 404 (15 June 1222).

42. *La documentación pontificia de Honorio III (1216–1227)*, ed. Mansilla, doc. 419 (22 Nov. 1222). Jaume's actions were nothing personal against this knight or his order. In fact, Gil García served with Jaume at Borriana, for which he received a royal property grant in 1235 and appears to have fallen during the siege of Valencia in 1238. *Privilegios reales de la orden de Montesa en la Edad Media: catálogo de la serie existente en el Archivo Histórico Nacional*, ed. A. L. Javierre Mur (Madrid: Junta Técnica de Archivos, Bibliotecas y Museos, 1945), doc. 51 (2 Jan. 1235). Later, during the siege of Valencia city, when Gil García's widow was dying, Jaume offered to settle her debts in recompense for the couple's past services. *Documentos de Jaime I*, ed. Huici and Cabanes, vol. 2, doc. 272 (1238).

43. T. N. Bisson, "The Finances of the Young James I (1213–1228)," in his *Medieval France and Her Pyrenean Neighbours*, 351–92.

44. ACA, C, pergs. J I, no. 78 (19 June 1217); *Documentos de Jaime I*, ed. Huici and Cabanes, vol. 1, doc. 2. ACA, C, pergs. J I, no. 205 (21 Dec. 1222); *Documentos de Jaime I*, ed. Huici and Cabanes, vol. 1, doc. 39.

45. Count Sanç withdrew from his position as primary regent in 1217. See Soldevila, *Els primers temps*, 139–40 and 148–55.

46. *Llibre dels feits*, ed. Bruguera, c. 20, 2:22–24. See Zurita, *Anales de la Corona de Aragón*, ed. Canellas López, 2.78, 1:392–93, and Soldevila, *Els primers temps*, 203–4.

47. *Llibre dels feits*, ed. Bruguera, c. 21, 2:24–25. Soldevila, *Els primers temps*, 204–5.

48. ACA, C, pergs. J I, no. 211 (19 Apr. 1223); *Documentos de Jaime I*, ed. Huici and Cabanes, vol. 1, doc. 43. Domingo, *A la recerca d'Aurembiaix*, 68. For the second conord, in October 1223, see Soldevila, *Els primers temps*, 210n41.

49. *Llibre dels feits*, ed. Bruguera, c. 22, 2:27–28. See Zurita, *Anales de la Corona de Aragón*, ed. Canellas López, 2.79, 1:395–96 and Soldevila, *Els primers temps*, 212–17.

50. *Llibre dels feits*, ed. Bruguera, c. 23–25, 2:28–31, and Soldevila, *Els primers temps*, 217–19.

51. See Bisson, "The Finances of the Young James I (1213–1228)," 367–74.

52. See chapter 6 above and Barton, *Contested Treasure*, 59–63.

53. Compare Shideler, *A Medieval Catalan Noble Family*, 150–54. *Cortes de los antiguos reinos de Aragón y de Valencia y Principado de Cataluña*, 27 vols. (Madrid: Real Academia de la Historia, 1896–1922), 1:102 (28 Apr. 1225).

54. See R. I. Burns, "The Many Crusades of Valencia's Conquest (1225–1280): An Historiographical Labyrinth," in Kagay and Vann, *On the Social Origins of Medieval Institutions*, 167–77.

55. ACT, Cartulari 8, fols. 28r–30r = ACT, Cartulari 9A, pp. 131–34 = ACA, C, Cartas Reales Diplomáticas, J I, no. 86 (27 Apr. 1225).

56. *Documentos de Jaime I*, ed. Huici and Cabanes, vol. 1, doc. 66; see also doc. 65. Compare P. Ramón de María, "Don Poncio de Torrella y el asedio de Peñíscola," *Boletín de la Sociedad Castellonense de Cultura* 18 (1943): 271–74. See R. Miravall, *Ponç de Torrella, bisbe dels tortosins* (Barcelona: Rafael Dalmau, DL, 1972) and Burns, *Crusader Kingdom of Valencia*, 1:43–44.

57. Miret y Sans, *Itinerari de Jaume I*, 55.

58. See Miret y Sans, *Itinerari de Jaume I*, 56–57, and Soldevila, *Els primers temps*, 221–25.

59. ACT, Cartulari 8, fols. 134v–135v (13 Aug. 1225). *Documentos de Jaime I*, ed. Huici and Cabanes, vol. 1, doc. 70. ACA, C, pergs. J I, no. 269 = ACT, Cartulari 8, fols. 24v–27v (3 Sept. 1225); *Documentos de Jaime I*, ed. Huici and Cabanes, vol. 1, doc. 71. Regarding Tortosa's ancient diocesan limits, see L. Vazquez de Parga, *La division de Wamba: Contribución al estudio de la historia y geografia eclesiasticas de la edad media española* (Madrid: Consejo Superior de Investigaciones Científicas, 1943), 83.

60. See Barton, "Constructing a Diocese in a Post-conquest Landscape," 7–10.

61. *Documentos de Jaime I*, ed. Huici and Cabanes, vol. 1, doc. 73 (10 Sept. 1225).

62. E.g., ACA, C, Reg. 309, fol. 45r (21 Sept. 1225); Gual Camarena, "Precedentes de la Reconquista valenciana," doc. 65. ACA, C, pergs. J I, no. 288 (10 Apr. 1226), regarding a loan in support of the siege.

63. AHN, Clero: Poblet, c. 2141, no. 16 (5 Sept. 1225); *Documentos de Jaime I*, ed. Huici and Cabanes, vol. 1, doc. 72.

64. See Baadj, *Saladin*, 168–70.

65. A. Ubieto Arteta, *Orígenes del Reino de Valencia*, 2 vols. (Valencia: Anubar, 1975), 1:95. B. Desclot, *La Crònica de Bernat Desclot o Llibre del Rey en Pere d'Aragó e dels seus antecessors*, c. 13, in *Les quatre grans croniques*, ed. Ferran Soldevila, with philological revision by J. Bruguera and historical revision by M. T. Ferrer i Mallol, vol. 2, Memóries de la secció històrico-arqueològica 80 (Barcelona: Institut d'Estudis Catalans, 2008). See also Ferrer Navarro, *Conquista y repoblación del Reino de Valencia*, 25–27, and J. Torró, *El naixement d'una colònia: Dominació i resistència a la frontera valenciana (1238–1276)* (Valencia: Universitat de València, 2006), 43.

66. Documents during the siege range from 13 August and 21 September: *Documentos de Jaime I*, ed. Huici and Cabanes, vol. 1, docs. 62 (misdated to 1224) and 70–73.

67. See *Llibre dels feits*, ed. Bruguera, c. 25–26, 2:30–36. See Soldevila, *Els primers temps*, 239–41.

68. See D. Kagay, "Structures of Baronial Dissent and Revolt under James I (1213–76)," *Mediaevistik* 1 (1988): 62, 66, and 72.

69. *Documentos de Jaime I*, ed. Huici and Cabanes, vol. 1, doc. 85 (14 July 1226). *Llibre dels feits*, ed. Bruguera, c. 27–29, 2:34–38. See Soldevila, *Els primers temps*, 242–55.

70. *Llibre dels feits*, ed. Bruguera, c. 25, 2:30–32. See Soldevila, *Els primers temps*, 241–42. Compare Ubieto Arteta, *Orígenes del Reino de Valencia*, 1:39, and Miret y Sans, *Itinerari de Jaume I*, 57–58.

71. Baadj, *Saladin*, 169. See chapter 5.

72. See O'Callaghan, *Reconquest*, 90.

73. O'Callaghan, *Reconquest*, 90 and 99, and Burns, *Islam under the Crusaders*, 33–34. *Crónica latina de los reyes de Castilla*, ed. M. D. Cabanes Pecourt (Zaragoza: Anubar, 1985), c. 54. See al-Maqqarī, *The History of the Mohammedan Dynasties in Spain*, trans. Gayangos, 8.4, 2:334.

74. ACA, C, pergs. J I, no. 373 (20 Apr. 1229); *Documentos de Jaime I*, ed. Huici and Cabanes, vol. 1, doc. 119.

75. *Llibre dels feits*, ed. Bruguera, c. 28, 2:35–36.

76. ACA, C, pergs. J I, no. 308 (13 Nov. 1226). See Soldevila, *Els primers temps*, 245–49.

77. ACA, C, pergs. J I, no. 309 (13 Nov. 1226); Soldevila, *Els primers temps*, 256–57 publishes the document.

78. See Soldevila, *Els primers temps*, 259–72, for a detailed contextual accounting.

79. *Documentos de Jaime I*, ed. Huici and Cabanes, vol. 1, doc. 91 (1 Apr. 1227). See *Llibre dels feits*, ed. Bruguera, c. 30–33, 2:18–21, and Shideler, *A Medieval Catalan Noble Family*, 155–57. Ferran, the *infant* of Aragon, and the bishop of Zaragoza negotiated their case with Jaume a day earlier: ACA, C, pergs. J I, no. 322 (31 Mar. 1227). The bishop of Lleida, archbishop of Tarragona, and master of the Templars presided over the meeting as *iurati*. *Llibre dels feits*, ed. Bruguera, c. 30–33, 2:38–43, has a colorful description of Jaume's reconciliation with these Aragonese barons, led by Ferran who asked for the king's forgiveness for him and Viscount Guillem II de Montcada. Shideler, *A Medieval Catalan Noble Family*, 155–57, judiciously reconstructs the episode, but fails to note that Ferran and the bishop of Zaragoza,

representing the other nobles, negotiated their case with Jaume the day before the king issued his reconciliation, as indicated by ACA, C, pergs. J I, no. 322 (31 Mar 1227).

80. See Shideler, *A Medieval Catalan Noble Family*, 155 and charts 1, 2, and 4 of the appendix. These familial branches were represented by Guillem II de Montcada, viscount of Bearn and lord of Montcada and Castellvell, and Ramon II de Montcada, co-lord of Tortosa and enfeoffed lord of Lleida (with his brother, Guillem Ramon II Seneschal).

81. See chapter 3 above.

82. *Documentos de Jaime I*, ed. Huici and Cabanes, vol. 1, doc. 96 (12 Oct. 1227).

83. *Vidal Mayor: Traducción aragonesa de la obra In Excelsis Dei Thesauris de Vidal de Canellas*, ed. G. Tilander, 3 vols. (Lund: Håkan Ohlssons Boktryckeri, 1956), vol. 2, 8.4 (2 July 1229). For examinations of how these conflicts continued, see J. C. Wilman, *Jaime I "El Conquistador" and the Barons of Aragon, 1244–1267: The Struggle for Power* (Ann Arbor: University Microfilms International, 1987) and L. González Antón, *Las uniones aragoneses y las Cortes del reino (1283–1301)*, 2 vols. (Zaragoza: Consejo Superior de Investigaciones Científicas, Escuela de Estudios Medievales, 1975).

84. ACA, C, pergs. J I, no. 365 (23 Dec. 1228). *Colección de documentos inéditos del Archivo de la Corona de Aragón*, ed. de Bofarull y Mascaró et al., vol. 6, doc. 16, and *Documentos de Jaime I*, ed. Huici and Cabanes, vol. 1, doc. 113. Desclot, *Crònica*, ed. Soldevila, c. 14. See O'Callaghan, *Reconquest*, 90–91. We have already discussed earlier impositions of this so-called peace tax. See especially chapters 5 and 6 above. During this same visit to Barcelona, Jaume acknowledged to the bishops of his realm that their aid in the fight against the Muslims was free and voluntary. ACA, C, pergs. J I, no. 363 (21 Dec. 1228); *Documentos de Jaime I*, ed. Huici and Cabanes, vol. 1, doc. 110.

85. See, e.g., ACA, C, pergs. J I, no. 429 (11 July 1231). See J. Powers, "Two Warrior-Kings and Their Municipal Militias: The Townsman-Soldier in Law and Life," in *The Worlds of Alfonso the Learned and James the Conqueror: Intellect and Force in the Middle Ages*, ed. R. I. Burns (Princeton, NJ: Princeton University Press, 1985), 95–129 (esp. 120).

86. *Llibre dels feits*, ed. Bruguera, c. 49–56, 2:59–67.

87. *Les registres de Grégoire IX*, ed. L. Auvray et al., 4 vols. (Paris: A. Fontemoing and E. de Boccard, 1863–1955), vol. 1, no. 268 (12 Feb. 1229).

88. ACA, C, pergs. J I, no. 124 (28 Aug. 1229 and 18 Sept. 1229). Compare A. Santamaría Arández, "La expansión político-militar de la Corona de Aragón bajo la dirección de Jaime I: Baleares," in *Jaime I y su época: X Congreso de Historia de la Corona de Aragón*, 2 vols. (Zaragoza: Institución "Fernando el Católico," 1979), 1:91–146, and O'Callaghan, *Reconquest*, 91–92. Ramon II de Montcada, co-lord of Tortosa, and Guillem II de Montcada, viscount of Bearn, helped lead the offensive. Both fell in battle. *Llibre dels feits*, ed. Bruguera, c. 36–37, 2:46–48.

89. Compare Burns, "The Many Crusades of Valencia's Conquest," 167–72, with P. Guichard, *Les musulmans de Valence et la Reconquête: XIᵉ–XIIIᵉ siècles*, 2 vols. (Damas: Institut français de Damas, 1990–91), 2:397.

90. O'Callaghan, *Reconquest*, 92; Burns, "The Many Crusades of Valencia's Conquest," 174; and *Llibre dels feits*, ed. Bruguera, c. 115–26, 2:120–28.

91. ACA, C, pergs. J I, no. 403 (28 July 1230). *Documentos de Jaime I*, ed. Huici and Cabanes, vol. 1, doc. 133.

92. *Llibre dels feits*, ed. Bruguera, c. 127, 2:128.

93. *Llibre dels feits*, ed. Bruguera, c. 128–31, 2:128–30.

94. ACA, C, pergs. J I, no. 480 (30 Jan. 1232).

95. Zurita, *Anales de la Corona de Aragón*, ed. Canellas López, 3.15, 1:478–79. O'Callaghan, *Reconquest*, 100–101, differentiates this bull summarized by Zurita from the extant bull that survives in Barcelona: ACA, C, Bulas, leg. 5, no. 10 (10 Mar. 1232); *Regesta de letras pontificias del Archivo de la Corona de Aragón*, ed. F. J. Miquel Rosell (Madrid: Cuerpo Facultativo de Archiveros, 1945), no. 92.

96. *Llibre dels feits*, ed. Bruguera, c. 130, 2:129–30, and Zurita, *Anales de la Corona de Aragón*, ed. Canellas López, 3.15, 1:481–82. See *Llibre dels feits*, ed. Bruguera, c. 132, 2:131 (on the capture of Ares) and c. 136, 2:65 (on Morella). See also Powers, "Two Warrior-Kings and Their Municipal Militias," 121–22.

97. *Documentos de Jaime I*, ed. Huici and Cabanes, vol. 1, docs. 181–82 (5 June and 15 July 1233). See Torró, *El naixement d'una colònia*, 44. Years later, for example, the king recalled the service of Tortosa's citizens in Borriana's capture and accordingly awarded them enfranchisement from the *lleuda* and *pedatge* commerce levies throughout Aragon and Catalonia. ACTE, perg. no. 394, Privilegis I, no. 25 (22 Jul. 1269).

98. Zurita, *Anales de la Corona de Aragón*, ed. Canellas López, 3.16, 1:486. See *Llibre dels feits*, ed. Bruguera, c. 157, 2:149.

99. *Les registres de Grégoire IX*, ed. Auvray et al., vol. 1, nos. 1490 and 1491 (both 9 Aug. 1233).

100. See O'Callaghan, *Reconquest*, 100, 100n5.

101. *Llibre dels feits*, ed. Bruguera, c. 177–78, 2:163–64.

102. ACA, C, pergs. J I, no. 644 (1 May 1235).

103. ACA, C, pergs. J I, no. 643. *Documentos de Jaime I*, ed. Huici and Cabanes, vol. 1, doc. 219 (11 May 1235).

104. See Kagay, "Structures of Baronial Dissent."

105. Tarragona: *Cortes de los antiguos reinos*, docs. 18 (7 Feb. 1235) and 19 (17 Mar. 1235), 1:123–27, and 127–33. Zaragoza: *Vidal Mayor*, vol. 2, 8.5 (18 Mar 1235).

106. *Cortes de los antiguos reinos*, doc. 18, c. 23 (1:127).

107. *Les registres de Grégoire IX*, ed. Auvray et al., vol. 2, nos. 2527 (24 Apr. 1235) and 2528 (25 Apr. 1235).

108. ACA, C, pergs. J I, no. 678 (28 May 1236); *Documentos de Jaime I*, ed. Huici and Cabanes, vol. 1, doc. 236.

109. *Documentos de Jaime I*, ed. Huici and Cabanes, vol. 1, doc. 239 (28 Oct. 1236).

110. See P. López Elum, *Los orígenes de los "Furs de València" y de las cortes en el siglo XIII* (Valencia: P. López Elum, 1998), 32.

111. *Documentos de Jaime I*, ed. Huici and Cabanes, vol. 1, doc. 239.

112. *Les registres de Grégoire IX*, ed. Auvray et al., vol. 2, no. 4070 (9 Feb. 1238).

113. *Les registres de Grégoire IX*, ed. Auvray et al., vol. 2, no. 4116 (5 Mar. 1238). See O'Callaghan, *Reconquest*, 103.

114. ACA, C, pergs. J I, no. 734 (28 Sept. 1238). See Burns, *Islam under the Crusaders*, 35–36.

115. *Documentos de Jaime I*, ed. Huici and Cabanes, vol. 2, doc. 388 (26 Mar. 1244), essentially confirming the Treaty of Cazola (1179). The *Cortes* of Huesca: *Fueros, observancias, y actos de corte del reino de Aragón*, ed. P. Savall y Dronda and

S. Penén y Dehesa, 2 vols. (Zaragoza: El Justicia de Aragón, 1886), vol. 1, prologue. Crusade indulgence: ACA, Bulas, leg. 8, no. 20 (18 Mar. 1246). R. I. Burns, "The Loss of Provence: King James's Raid to Kidnap Its Heiress (1245); Documenting a Legend," in *XII Congrès d'histoire de la Couronne d'Aragon*, 3 vols. (Montpellier: Soc. Archéologique, 1987–1988), 3:230, doc. 18. Jaume was planning an expedition to Constantinople; see O'Callaghan, *Reconquest*, 107.

116. See R. I. Burns, "The Crusade against Al-Azraq: A Thirteenth-Century Mudejar Revolt in International Perspective," *American Historical Review* 93 (1988): 80–106, and O'Callaghan, *Reconquest and Crusade*, 107–8.

117. See R. I. Burns and P. E. Chevedden, *Negotiating Cultures: Bilingual Surrender Treaties on the Crusader-Muslim* (Leiden: Brill, 1999), 6–8, chaps. 2 and 3.

118. Torró, *El naixement d'una colònia*, 46–67, provides a detailed account of the rise and fall of the insurrection.

119. *Llibre dels feits*, ed. Bruguera, c. 364, 2:276–77. See Desclot, *Crònica*, ed. Soldevila, c. 49. *La documentación pontificia de Inocencio IV (1243–1254)*, ed. A. Quintana Prieto (Rome: Instituto español de historia eclesiástica, 1987), doc. 558 (13 Nov. 1248).

120. *Llibre dels feits*, ed. Bruguera, c. 564, 2: 385–86: "que gitàs tots los moros del dit regne de València, per ço con eren tots traydors e havien-nos-ho donat a conèxer moltes vegades, que, nós faén bé a ells." See Catlos, *Muslims of Medieval Latin Christendom*, 73–74.

121. The following pages draw on Barton, "Lords, Settlers, and Shifting Frontiers," 219–49.

122. See chapter 5 above for discussion of earlier phases of this phenomenon.

123. See M. Monjo, *Sarraïns sota el domini feudal: La baronia d'Aitona al segle XV* (Lleida: Universitat de Lleida, 2004), 38–40.

124. See J. Ciurana i Sans, *La baronia d'Entença, capital Falset: de Cambrils-Hospitalet de l'Infant a Mequinensa, del Coll de la Teixeta a l'Ebre, un estat multisecular (segles XII–XIX)* (Reus: J. Ciurana i Sans, 2002); M. Romero Tallafigo, "El señorío catalán de los Entenza a la luz de la documentación existente en el Archivo Ducal de Medinaceli (Sevilla), años 1173–1324," *Historia-Instituciones-Documentos* 4 (1977): 577, doc. 15; and Serrano Daura, *Senyoriu i municipi a la Catalunya Nova*, 69–77.

125. *Cartas de población*, ed. Font Rius, vol. 1.1, doc. 75 (30 Nov. 1149). ACTE, perg. no. 538, Privilegis V, no. 5 (28 Dec. 1243).

126. Guinot Rodríguez, *Els fundadors del Regne de València*, 136–54 and 264–65. Compare Ferrer Navarro, *Conquista y repoblación del Reino de Valencia*, 282–96.

127. Freedman, *Origins of Peasant Servitude*, 135–39.

128. Freedman, *Origins of Peasant Servitude*, 122, 131.

129. See P. Freedman, "The Llobregat as a Frontier in the Thirteenth Century," in *Miscel·lània en homenatge al P. Agustí Altisent*, 109–18.

130. Freedman, *Origins of Peasant Servitude*, 136–37. For definitions and discussion of these *mals usos*, see Freedman, *Origins of Peasant Servitude*, 17, and E. Hinojosa, *El régimen señorial y la cuestión agraria en Cataluña durante la edad media* (Madrid: Suárez, 1905), 165–94.

131. *Costums de Catalunya entre senyors i vassalls*, in *Usatges de Barcelona i Commemoracions de Pere Albert*, ed. J. Rovira i Ermengol, Els Nostres classics, Col·lecció A 43–44 (Barcelona: Barcino, 1933), 180–81, c. 35. See E. Ferran i Planas, *El jurista Pere Albert*

i les Commemoracions (Barcelona: Universitat Pompeu Fabra, 2006), 231, and *Customs of Catalonia between Lords and Vassals*, ed. and trans. D. Kagay (Tempe: Arizona Center for Medieval and Renaissance Studies, 2002), xxxv–xliv, who provides the above translation (at 33).

132. See P. Freedman, "Cowardice, Heroism and the Legendary of Catalonia," *Past & Present* 121 (1988): 3–28.

133. Freedman, *Origins of Peasant Servitude*, 119–21.

134. *Cortes de los antiguos reinos*, 1:147, doc. 22, no. 17.

135. ACA, GPC, Arm. 11: Gardeny, perg. no. 107 (5 Feb. 1226). Compare ACA, GPC, Arm. 11: Gardeny, perg. no. 724 (25 Dec. 1257). The order also pledged not to require military service. See below for further discussion of military service requirements and exemptions.

136. ACL, L 670 (15 June 1227): "scilicet dominicaturas domos servitutesque omnes personales et omnes iurisdicionem."

137. ACT, Cartulari 8, fols. 164v–165bis recto; ACT, Cartulari 9, fols. 141v–142r (7 Oct. 1288): "omnibus iuribus et quibuscumque aliis questiis cenis serviciis angariis servitutibus et cuiuslibet conditionis ademprivis." See below for discussion of the *questia*.

138. ACA, GPC, Arm. 19: Torres de Segre, perg. no. 1 (9 May 1272): "et quibuslibet aliis exaccionibus cuiuslibet feceris servitutum."

139. See Freedman, *Origins of Peasant Servitude*, 91–99.

140. P. Ortega Pérez, "Un nuevo documento repoblacional de la Ribera d'Ebre (Tarragona): la carta de población de Rasquera (1206)," in *Miscel·lania en homenatge al P. Agusti Altisent*, 527.

141. *Cartas de población*, ed. Font Rius, vol. 1.1, doc. 236 (26 Apr. 1212).

142. For a comparison with the *Furs* of Valencia, see D. Nirenberg, *Communities of Violence: The Persecution of Minorities in the Middle Ages* (Princeton, NJ: Princeton University Press, 1996), 132.

143. *Els costums d'Orta (1296): estudi introductori i edició*, ed. J. Serrano Daura (Horta de Sant Joan: Ajuntament d'Horta de Sant Joan, 1996), no. 9. See below in this chapter for further on these customary laws.

144. *Les costums de Miravet*, ed. F. Valls Taberner (Tarragona: Col·legi d'Advocats de Tarragona, 2006), 30, c. 129. On the *ius commune*, see R. H. Helmholz, *The Spirit of Classical Canon Law* (Athens: University of Georgia Press, 1996), 20.

145. ACT, Cartulari 2, fols. 47v–48r (19 Oct. 1253).

146. *Cartas de población*, ed. Font Rius, vol. 1.1, doc. 196 (Apr. 1194). See also the second charter granted to Pinell: doc. 222 (15 Mar. 1207).

147. Consider the discussion on irrigation in the Iberian Mediterranean environment by P. Horden and N. Purcell, *The Corrupting Sea: A Study of Mediterranean History* (Oxford: Oxford University Press, 2000), 237–57. They suggest that the use of irrigation to create a summer growing season has been overestimated by scholars, and that systems were usually implemented to regulate and extend the spring and fall growing seasons.

148. See Bolòs, "Paisatge i societat," 49.

149. ACA, GPC, Códices no. 197: *Cartulari de Gardeny*, fols. 78v–79, no. 198 (28 Feb. 1181); *Col·lecció diplomàtica*, ed. Sarobe, vol. 1, doc. 372. The source does not stipulate whether the rented land contained equal shares of irrigated and dry land.

150. Bolòs, "Paisatge i societat," 53–44. *Cartas de población*, ed. Font Rius, vol. 1.1, doc. 256 (29 Aug. 1231).

151. Ortega Pérez, "Un nuevo documento repoblacional," 527.

152. Ortega Pérez, "Un nuevo documento repoblacional." This became a standard seigniorial imposition. For example, Joan Puig claimed it for his lordship of Paüls. *Cartas de población*, ed. Font Rius, vol. 1.1, doc. 356 (18 Nov. 1294).

153. *Cartas de población*, ed. Font Rius, vol. 1.1, doc. 232 (13 Oct. 1210).

154. Ortega Pérez, "Un nuevo documento repoblacional," 527.

155. Benito, *Senyoria*, 425.

156. See Freedman, *Origins of Peasant Servitude*, 81; Benito, *Senyoria*, 418; and Rodón Binué, *El lenguaje técnico del feudalismo en el siglo XI en Cataluña*, 121–22 and 244–45.

157. *Les constitucions de Pau i Treva de Catalunya*, ed. Gonzalvo i Bou, doc. 21, c. 2 (Sept. 1202). "Religious lands" probably did not encompass the domains of the military orders. The *Corts* of 1283, e.g., distinguished between prelates and the military orders: *Les constitucions de Pau i Treva de Catalunya*, ed. Gonzalvo i Bou, doc. 22, c. 6.

158. *Cartas de población*, ed. Font Rius, vol. 1.1, doc. 215 (24 Sept. 1201).

159. *Cartas de población*, ed. Font Rius, vol. 1.1, doc. 221 (31 May 1206).

160. *Cartas de población*, ed. Font Rius, vol. 1.1, doc. 232 (13 Oct. 1210).

161. *Els costums d'Orta*, ed. Serrano Daura, 78, c. 16.

162. See Bonnassie, *La Catalogne du milieu du Xe à la fin du XIe siècle*, 2:590–95, and Hinojosa, *El régimen señorial*, 195–220.

163. ACA, GPC, Arm. 23: Comunes, perg. no. 45 (30 Mar. 1181). There is a slight possibility that the actor here was Guillem III de Cervera, who died around this same year.

164. On *forcia*, consider ACA, GPC, Códices no. 115: *Cartulari de Tortosa*, fol. 52r, no. 159 (3 Nov. 1196).

165. ACA, GPC, Arm. 11: Gardeny, perg. no. 1903; *Col·lecció diplomàtica*, ed. Sarobe, vol. 2, doc. 747 (Feb. 1200).

166. ACA, C, pergs. A I, no. 326 (Mar. 1182); *Alfonso II*, ed. Sánchez Casabón, doc. 339, later codified as *Costums de Tortosa*, ed. J. Massip (Barcelona: Fundació Noguera, 1996), 1.1.5.

167. *Els costums de Lleida: documents de l'Arxiu Municipal de Lleida*, ed. J. Busqueta i Riu, Col·lecció Guillem Botet (Lleida: Paeria, Ajuntament de Lleida, 1999), 77, fol. 70r–v.

168. ACL, L 2171 (13 Jan. 1223).

169. ACA, GPC, Arm. 19: Torres de Segre, perg. no. 1 (9 May 1272): "cum questiis toltis forciis et ademprivis et cum iusticiis caoniis firmamentis . . . cum exercitu penitus sive redempcionibus exercituum et hostibus ac cavalcatis et cum bovaticis monedaticis."

170. ACL (uncataloged), c. 154, c. 1, no. 21 (29 Aug. 1320).

171. Hinojosa, *El régimen señorial*, 120.

172. ACA, GPC, Arm. 23: Comunes, perg. no. 73 (24 July 1230). See Shideler, *A Medieval Catalan Noble Family*, 132.

173. ACL, L 3794 and L 3795 (18 Apr. 1258).

174. ACL, L 671 (12 Sept. 1235).

175. Benito, *Senyoria*, 418.

176. *Cartas de población*, ed. Font Rius, vol. 1.1, docs. 75 (30 Nov. 1149) and 79 (Jan. 1150).

177. Captures made on the northern left bank of the Ebro river up to Tarragona were to be awarded only one *morabetin*, while those made between the southern right bank and Ulldecona would earn two. *Cartas de población*, ed. Font Rius, vol. 1.1, doc. 75.

178. For example, the charter issued by Pere to Sant Jordi d'Alfama in 1201 called for no military obligations. *Cartas de población*, ed. Font Rius, vol. 1.1, doc. 214 (24 Sept. 1201).

179. The *convenientiae* between Alfons and Pere and the counts of Urgell discussed in chapter 6 above had established the obligation of their vassals to perform military service against Muslim as well as Christian enemies. In the agreement with Pere, Ermengol VIII of Urgell promised "quod faciam ego et successores mei per vos et per successores vestros pacem et guerram sarracenis et Christianis de me et de meis militibus et hominibus et de terra mea." AGP, Arm. 11: Gardeny, pergs., no. 1903 (Feb. 1200); *Col·lecció diplomàtica*, ed. Sarobe, vol. 2, doc. 747.

180. Ortega Pérez, "Un nuevo documento repoblacional," 527.

181. For example, the two charters for Gandesa from 1192 and 1194 have identical language. *Cartas de población*, ed. Font Rius, vol. 1.1, docs. 191 and 196: "exercitum super gentem sarracenorum." The charter issued to Batea called for "exercitus et cavalcatas." *Cartas de población*, ed. Font Rius, vol. 1.1, doc. 219 (25 Nov. 1205).

182. The first charter issued to Pinell reads "cavalcadas exercitus super sarracenos." *Cartas de población*, ed. Font Rius, vol. 1.1, doc. 209 (27 Feb. 1198), The second charter, *Cartas de población*, ed. Font Rius, vol. 1.1, doc. 222 (15 Mar. 1207), has "Retinemus ibi in vos et in omnem proieniem vestram ibi comorantem exercitus quando domnus rex vel domnus magister noster in terra paganorum intraverit, et quintam partem de rebus a vobis ibi adquisitis."

183. *Cartas de población*, ed. Font Rius, vol. 1.1, doc. 232 (13 Oct. 1210).

184. *Cartas de población*, ed. Font Rius, vol. 1.1, doc. 227 (22 Nov. 1208). See chapter 5 above.

185. *Cartas de población*, ed. Font Rius, vol. 1.1, doc. 242 (11 Apr. 1222). This was Ramon de Montcada II, who died in 1229. See Shideler, *A Medieval Catalan Noble Family,* chart 1.

186. ACA, GPC, Arm. 11: Gardeny, perg. no. 107 (5 Feb. 1226).

187. *Les constitucions de Pau i Treva de Catalunya*, ed. Gonzalvo i Bou, doc. 25, c. 21 and Benito, *Senyoria de la terra*, 421–26. Pronouncements on the *questia* in later assemblies tended to focus primarily on ecclesiastical immunity from the levy: e.g. the constitution issued at Tarragona in 1235 (*Les constitucions de Pau i Treva de Catalunya*, ed. Gonzalvo i Bou, doc. 27, c. 20). On the *questia* and related levies in the context of the thirteenth and fourteenth-century crown, see Vanlandingham, *Transforming the state*, 122–23.

188. *Cartas de población*, ed. Font Rius, vol. 1.1, doc. 356 (16 May 1293).

189. Compare Virgili, *Ad detrimentum Yspanie*, 183 and Fabregat, *Burgesos contra senyors*, 76. For background, see Jaspert, "Bonds and tensions on the frontier," 26–36. Alfons made the same stipulations for the castle and town of Ascó, which were also transferred to Templar lordship on this occasion, as discussed earlier in chapter 5. ACA, C, pergs. A I, no. 326 (Mar. 1182); *Alfonso II*, ed. Sánchez Casabón, doc. 339.

190. AHN, Órdenes Militares, c. 608, no. 29 (20 Feb. 1209); *Pedro el Católico*, ed. Alvira Cabrer, vol. 2, doc. 872. See Smith, *Innocent III*, 83 and T. N. Bisson, "Sur les origines du monedatge: quelques textes inedits," in his *Medieval France and Her Pyrenean Neighbours*, 325–38.

191. See Bisson, *The Medieval Crown of Aragon*, 55–57, and refer to the further discussion of these levies later in this chapter.

192. See below and P. Orti Gost, "La primera articulación del estado feudal en Cataluña a través de un impuesto: el bovaje (ss. XII–XIII)," *Hispania*, 61 (2001), 967–98 (at 977–86).

193. For example, according to Massip, in their struggle against the citizens of Tortosa, the Templars reissued a revised population charter that enhanced the order's prerogatives. See J. Massip, "La carta de població del territori de Tortosa, i el Temple," *Actes de les primeres jornades sobre els ordes religioso-militars als països catalans (segles XII–XIX) (Montblanc, 8–10 de Novembre de 1985)* (Tarragona: Diputació de Tarragona, 1994), 43–53 and J. Massip, *La gestació de les Costums de Tortosa* (Tortosa: Consell Intercomarcal de les Terres de l'Ebre, 1984), 73–79. Many other historians read the evidence as merely a reinterpretation rather than deliberate manipulation of the customary tradition, and some have suggested that this "Templar version" is simply the result of a scribal error. See Pagarolas, *Els Templers*, 1:208–9.

194. See J. M. Font Rius, "El procés de formació de les Costums de Tortosa," in his *Estudis sobre els drets i institucions locals en la Catalunya medieval*, 141–62, and T. W. Barton, "Jurisdictional Conflict, Strategies of Litigation, and Mechanisms of Compromise in Thirteenth-Century Tortosa," *Recerca* 14 (2012): 201–48. Fabregat, *Burgesos contra senyors*, esp. 81–145, offers a fresh reading of the conflicts with an eye to rights over common lands rather than simply jurisdiction. We discussed this transition to Templar lordship in detail in chapter 5 above.

195. *Costums de Tortosa*, ed. J. Massip (Barcelona: Fundació Noguera, 1996), 8, 1.1.5: "quitis e deliures d'ost, de cavalcada, d'encalç, de cenes, de questa, de toltes, de forçes, de leudes, de peatges, d'acaptes, de pes e de mesuratge."

196. *Costums de Tortosa*, ed. Massip, 8, 1.1.5: "de mesuràgie, de carnàgie, d'erbàgie, de beuràgie e de tota altra cosa que servitut pusca ésser nomenada, que no·n són tengutz de fer a rey ne a regina, ne a lurs fils, ne a hereus d'éls, ne al Temple, ne al lignàgie de Moncada, ne a nul veguer de Tortosa." Barton, "Jurisdictional Conflict, Strategies of Litigation, and Mechanisms of Compromise," 233–44, describes the process of review and codification.

197. R. Gibert, *Historia general de derecho Español* (Granada: Imp. F. Román, 1968), 106.

198. For further details on this transaction and its implications, see Pagarolas, *Els Templers*, 1:243–52; Fabregat, *Burgesos contra senyors*, 147–51; Barton, *Contested Treasure*, 157–60; and chapter 8 below.

199. *Cartas de población*, ed. Font Rius, vol. 1.1, doc. 214 (24 Sept. 1201). Fabregat, *Burgesos contra senyors*, 93–95, views this charter as evidence that Pere was acting on his ruling of 1199 defending the persistence of Tortosa's customary exemptions against erosion by that city's lords. At 126–29, he traces the later spread of the uses of Tortosa into surrounding areas.

200. *Cartas de población*, ed. Font Rius, vol. 1.1, doc. 357 (18 Nov. 1294). Bernat, in turn, issued these privileges formally to eighty-four residents of Font de Perelló about a month later: *Cartas de población*, ed. Font Rius, vol. 1.1, doc. 358 (16 Dec. 1294). It is certainly significant that this enterprise coincided with the monarchy's assumption of lordship over Tortosa that same year.

201. *Diplomatari de la catedral de Tortosa (1062–1193)*, ed. Virgili, doc. 380 (5 May 1185).

202. *Cartas de población*, ed. Font Rius, vol. 1.1, doc. 226 (30 Aug. 1208). It is possible that Ramon II de Montcada here intended for Tortosa's laws to govern Nebot's own activity as land and castle-holder rather than the tenants he established there.

203. *Cartas de población*, ed. Font Rius, vol. 1.1, docs. 228 (2 Mar. 1209) and 191 (13 Mar. 1192), respectively.

204. See *Els costums d'Orta*, ed. Serrano Daura, esp. 46–62. See also J. Cots i Gorchs, "Les *Consetuds* d'Horta (avui Horta de Sant Joan) a la ratlla del Baix Aragó," *Estudis Universitaris Catalans* 15 (1930): 304–23, and M. T. Tatjer Prat, "L'administració de justícia segons el dret d'Orta," in *Actes de les Jornades d'Estudi sobre els Costums de la Batllia de Miravet* (Gandesa: Consell comarcal de la Terra Alta, Diputació de Tarragona, 2001), 103–19. See *Els costums d'Orta*, ed. Serrano Daura, 74.

205. *Costums d'Orta*, ed. Serrano, 74–103.

206. See *Costums d'Orta*, ed. Serrano, 75.

207. For fourteenth-century examples of *mudéjar* emigration from one seigniorial domain to another, see Ortega Pérez, *Musulmanes en Cataluña*, 23n19. We possess this evidence because lords tracked these movements. Ortega Pérez notes that lords appear to have traded *mudéjar* settlers on occasion.

208. See chapter 4 above for discussion of the charter for Ribera d'Ebre. For further on the case of l'Aldea, see Fabregat, *Burgesos contra senyors*, 135–39.

209. *Cartas de población*, ed. Font Rius, doc. 303 (Feb. 1258). For obvious reasons, no promise was made to these Muslims that they would never be subject to any Christian. Ramon Berenguer IV had unrealistically made this pledge to the Muslims of Tortosa in 1148: ACA, C, pergs. RB IV, no. 209 (31 Dec. 1148).

210. Although certain *mudéjar* communities may have felt some pressure from religious authorities to emigrate to Muslim-ruled lands, it is difficult to ascertain the degree to which immigration to (or emigration from) Christian lands was influenced by religious ideologies. See R. I. Burns, "Immigrants from Islam: The Crusaders' Use of Muslims as Settlers in Thirteenth-Century Spain," *American Historical Review* 80 (1975), 21–42, and M. A. Fierro, "La emigración en el Islam: conceptos antiguos, nuevos problemas," *Awrāq* 12 (1991), 11–41. For considerations regarding a later period, see K. A. Miller, "Muslim Minorities and the Obligation to Emigrate to Islamic Territory: *Fatwās* from Fifteenth-Century Granada," *Islamic Law and Society* 7 (2000), 256–88 and *Guardians of Islam. Religious Authority and Muslim Communities of Late Medieval Spain* (New York: Columbia University Press, 2008), 20–43.

211. According to *Cartas de población*, ed. Font Rius, 1.2:803, confirmations of the original comital-royal charter of security were made by the Templars in 1276,

1282 and 1293, and possibly subsequently. See Catlos, *Victors*, 123 and 140–42, for additional examples.

212. See *Cartas de población*, ed. Font Rius, 1.2:803, and Ortega Pérez, *Musulmanes en Cataluña*, esp. 166–79.

213. See T. N. Bisson, "The Organized Peace in Southern France and Catalonia, ca. 1140–ca. 1233," in Bisson, *Medieval France and Her Pyrenean Neighbours*, 233, and Barton, *Contested Treasure*, 59–64.

214. *Les constitucions de Pau i Treva de Catalunya*, ed. Gonzalvo i Bou, docs. 17 (13 Aug. 1188) and 18 (Nov. 1192).

215. *Les constitucions de Pau i Treva de Catalunya*, ed. Gonzalvo i Bou, doc. 20, c. 11 (9 July 1200). Compare with doc. 15, c. 11 (1173) and doc. 18, c. 5 (Nov. 1188).

216. Freedman, *Origins of Peasant Servitude*, 112–14. See generally Soldevila, *Els primers temps*, 131–37.

217. Bisson, "Problem of Feudal Monarchy," 244.

218. See Ferran i Panas, *El jurista Pere Albert*, 145–54; J. Lalinde Abadía, *La jurisdicción inferior en Cataluña (Corts, veguers, batlles)* (Barcelona: Ayuntamiento de Barcelona, 1966), 72–79; and Sabaté, *El territori de la Catalunya medieval*, 172–80.

219. Bisson, *Crisis of the Twelfth Century*, 373.

220. Tarragona: *Les constitucions de Pau i Treva de Catalunya*, ed. Gonzalvo i Bou, doc. 27 (7 Feb. 1235) and doc. 28, c. 1 (17 Mar. 1235) (quoted). Assemblies in Aragon devote more attention to the dependence owed by nobles to the king: e.g., *Vidal Mayor*, ed. Tilander, vol. 2, 8.5 (Zaragoza, 1235).

221. J. M. Font Rius, "El desarrollo general del derecho en los territorios de la Corona de Aragón (siglos XII–XIV)," in *VII Congreso de historia de la corona de Aragón*, 3 vols. (Barcelona: Talleres de Viuda de Fidel Rodríguez Ferrán, 1964), 1:316.

222. R. H. Helmholz, *The Spirit of Classical Canon Law* (Athens: University of Georgia Press, 1996), 20.

223. S. Reynolds, *Kingdoms and Communities in Western Europe, 900–1300* (Oxford: Oxford University Press, 2001), 46.

224. Ferran i Planas, *El jurista Pere Albert*, 243.

225. *Les constitucions de Pau i Treva de Catalunya*, ed. Gonzalvo i Bou, docs. 24 (1218), 25 (1225), 26 (1228), 27 (1235), 28 (1235), 29 (1251), 30 (1257).

226. See Lalinde Abadía, *La jurisdicción inferior*, 79–88, and Sabaté, *El territori de la Catalunya medieval*, 172–80, 227–45.

227. For Lleida, see Barton, *Contested Treasure*, 55–57. For Tortosa, see Barton, *Contested Treasure*, chap. 2.

228. See Barton, *Contested Treasure*, chaps. 4 and 5.

229. See chapter 8 below.

230. See M. Turull i Rubinat and O. Oleart i Piquet, *Història del dret espanyol* (Barcelona: Universitat de Barcelona, 2000), 33, and Vanlandingham, *Transforming the State*, 96–100.

231. *Les constitucions de Pau i Treva de Catalunya*, ed. Gonzalvo i Bou, doc. 29, c. 3 (1251). The order also banned the *ius commune* and the *Liber iudicorum* (Romanized Visigothic law).

232. Font Rius, "El desarrollo general del derecho," 315–18.

233. See Hinojosa, *El régimen señorial*, 120–28.

234. ACL, L 670 (15 June 1227). Guillem was the son of Viscount Guillem I de Cardona and would later serve as Ponç IV de Cabrera's procurator at Jaume I's court in 1228. See chapter 8 below.

235. ACL, L 721 (23 Oct. 1231) and ACL, L 668 (18 Oct. 1232).

236. Orti Gost, "La primera articulación," 972–77.

237. Bisson, "Organized Peace," 303 and 309; Bisson, "Sur les origines du monedatge"; and Bisson, *Medieval Crown of Aragon*, 73. See also A. M. Balaguer, "Sobre els orígens de l'impost del monedatge a Catalunya (segles XI–XII)," *Glaux* 7 (1991): 791–802, and Orti Gost, "La primera articulación," 986–90.

238. *Les constitucions de Pau i Treva de Catalunya*, ed. Gonzalvo i Bou, doc. 17, c. 23 (13 Aug. 1188).

239. See Bensch, "Lordship and Coinage in Empúries," 83–86.

240. *Diplomatari de la catedral de Tortosa (1062–1193)*, ed. Virgili, doc. 52 (22 Jan. 1155).

241. *Cartas de población*, ed. Font Rius, vol. 1.1, doc. 134 (26 July 1168).

242. Orti Gost, "La primera articulación," 990–94.

243. ACTE, pergs. no. 229, Comú III, 15 (23 Oct. 1280).

244. ACTE, pergs. no. 187, Comú II, 25 (31 Aug. 1298).

245. ACTE, pergs. no. 202, Comú II, 46D (2 May 1299).

246. See V. Farías Zurita, "El medio natural en una sociedad señorializada: composición, explotación y apropiación del incultum en la Catalunya del noreste (siglos X–XIII)," in *El medio natural en la España medieval: Actas del I Congreso sobre ecohistoria e historia medieval*, ed. J. Clemente Ramos (Cáceres: Universidad de Extremadura, 2001), 277–99.

247. ACL, L 670 (15 June 1227). A charter concerning Aitona, Seròs, and other holdings had a similar list, but added prerogatives to regulate and levy fishing, ovens, beasts of burden (*iumentum*), ferry transport, roads, and forests: ACA, GPC, Arm. 23: Comunes, perg. no. 73 (24 July 1230). Seigniorial population charters from the thirteenth century established similar prerogatives: e.g., *Cartas de población*, ed. Font Rius, vol. 1.1, doc. 318 (27 Mar. 1270). The thirteenth-century confrontations between the *universitas* and lords of Tortosa concerned the residents' rights to *empriu*. See Fabregat, *Burgesos contra senyors*, 97–106, 114–18.

248. *Cortes de los antiguos reinos*, vol. 1, doc. 22, c. 37.

249. J. Bringué i Portella and M. Sanllehy i Sabi, "Boscos, pastures i ramaderia," in *Història agrària dels països catalans*, vol. 3, *Edat moderna*, ed. E. Giralt, J. Salrach, and E. Serra (Barcelona: Fundació Catalana per la recerca, 2008), 171–233.

250. Bringué i Portella and Sanllehy i Sabi, "Boscos, pastures i ramaderia," 172–73.

Chapter 8. The Impact of Conquest and Consolidation on Jurisdiction and Administration

1. See Lacarra, "Alfonso II El Casto," 116–18.

2. See J. Busqueta, "Sobre la carta de poblament de Lleida (1150): l'herència de Tortosa," in *Les cartes de població cristiana*, ed. Serrano Daura, 199–212. Consider R. Piña Homs, "La carta de Tortosa i la seva projecció en el Regne de Mallorca," in *Les cartes de població cristiana*, ed. Serrano Daura, 213–23. See Serrano Daura, *Senyoriu i*

municipi a la Catalunya Nova, 1:139–41. The *Consuetudines Ilerdenses* (1228) identified Visigothic law as a resource after the *Usatges de Barcelona*: see *Els costums de Lleida*, ed. Busqueta, fol. 92, pp. 113–14.

3. See Barton, "Lords, Settlers, and Shifting Frontiers," 223–24, 233–34 and chapter 7 above.

4. *Cortes de los antiguos reinos*, doc. 5, 1:56.

5. See *Catalunya Romànica*, 24:70 (map).

6. Salarrullana de Dios, "Fronteras o límites de Aragón y Cataluña," 135n302, 141. See also Zurita, *Anales de la Corona de Aragón*, ed. Canellas López, 2.20, 1:66, and 3.36, 1:535.

7. *Cortes de los antiguos reinos*, vol. 1, doc. 14.

8. AML, Fons Municipal, perg. no. 308 (6 Feb. 1229).

9. AML, Privilegis reials, no. 308 (6 Feb. 1228). See T. N. Bisson, "A General Court of Aragon (Daroca, 1228)," in Bisson, *Medieval France and Her Pyrenean Neighbours*, 31–48 (with an edition of the source at 41–46).

10. AML, Fons Municipal, perg. no. 308. Compare À. Masià de Ros, "La cuestión de los límites entre Aragón y Cataluña: Ribagorza y Fraga en tiempos de Jaime II," *Boletín de la Real Academia de Buenas Letras de Barcelona* 22 (1949): 165, and Miret y Sans, *Itinerari de Jaume I*, 166. See also Zurita, *Anales de la Corona de Aragón*, ed. Canellas López, 3.40, 1:545–46 (with numerous inaccuracies).

11. ACA, C, pergs. J I, no. 935 (21 Jan. 1244). *Documentos de Jaime I*, ed. Huici and Cabanes, vol. 2, doc. 364. See Serrano Daura, *El conflicte*, 69, and Masià de Ros, "Cuestion de los límites entre Aragón y Cataluña," 165.

12. Zurita, *Anales de la Corona de Aragón*, ed. Canellas López, 3.40, 1:545–46.

13. *Documentos de Jaime I*, ed. Huici and Cabanes, vol. 2, doc. 365 (21 Jan. 1244).

14. ACA, C, pergs. J I, no. 937 (21 Jan. 1244); *Documentos de Jaime I*, ed. Huici and Cabanes, vol. 2, doc. 366.

15. ACA, C, pergs. J I, no. 937.

16. ACA, C, pergs. J I, nos. 1054 and 1055 (24 Sept. 1246). *Documentos de Jaime I*, ed. Huici and Cabanes, vol. 2, docs. 439 and 440.

17. Soldevila and Valls i Taberner, *Història de Catalunya*, 1:180–85.

18. Compare Lladonosa, *Història de Lleida*, 290–91.

19. See A. Virgili, "Gent nova: la colonització feudal de la Catalunya Nova (segles XII–XIII)," *Butlletí de la Societat Catalana d'Estudis Històrics* 21 (2010): 77–102 (esp. 91–97).

20. *Documentos de Jaime I*, ed. Huici and Cabanes, vol. 2, doc. 488 (30 Mar. 1249).

21. Edited by Salarrullana de Dios, "Fronteras o límites de Aragón y Cataluña," 139–40 (13 Aug. 1281).

22. Salarrullana de Dios, "Fronteras o límites de Aragón y Cataluña," 162–65.

23. Edited by Salarrullana de Dios, "Fronteras o límites de Aragón y Cataluña," 167–70 and 171 (for the fifteenth-century inquiry).

24. Zurita, *Anales de la Corona de Aragón*, ed. Canellas López, 3.63, 1:552.

25. ACA, C, Reg. 47, fol. 54 (10 Aug. 1284); ACA, C, Reg. 236, fol. 11v (27 July 1305); and ACA, C, Reg. 222, fol. 18v (5 Sept. 1322); Masià de Ros, "Cuestion de los límites entre Aragón y Cataluña," docs. 1, 2, and 5, respectively. See Masià de Ros, "Cuestion de los límites entre Aragón y Cataluña," 171.

26. See Sabaté, *Història de Lleida*, 244, and *Catalunya Romànica*, 24:70.

27. See Serrano Daura, *El conflicte*, 61.

28. *Cartas de población*, ed. Font Rius, vol. 1.1, docs. 126 (Jan. 1165, Horta) and 134 (26 July 1168, Paüls).

29. *Cartas de población*, ed. Font Rius, vol. 1.1, doc. 126.

30. Font Rius, "Notas sobre algunas cartas pueblas de la región oriental aragonesa," 733–35.

31. *Cartas de población*, ed. Font Rius, vol. 1.1, doc. 190 (10 Jan. 1192).

32. *Cartas de población*, ed. Font Rius, vol. 1.1, doc. 191 (13 Mar. 1192).

33. *Cartas de población*, ed. Font Rius, vol. 1.1, doc. 228 (2 Mar. 1209).

34. See chapter 7 above.

35. See Serrano Daura, *Senyoriu i municipi a la Catalunya Nova*, 2:1144–45.

36. M. Gual Camarena, "Contribución al estudio de la territorialidad de los fueros de Valencia," *Estudios de la Edad Media de la Corona de Aragón* 3 (1947–48): 262–89 (chart at 272–73, map at 280–81).

37. See Gual Camarena, "Contribución al estudio de la territorialidad de los fueros de Valencia," 269, and López Elum, *Los orígenes de los "Furs de València,"* 38–49. The *Furs* would not be officially promulgated until 1261.

38. Zurita, *Anales de la Corona de Aragón*, ed. Canellas López, 3.43, 1:551–53. *Furs de València*, c. 1 (boundaries), ed. López Elum, *Los orígenes de los "Furs de València,"* 109. See Guinot Rodríguez, *Els límits del regne*, 25–35.

39. Masià de Ros, "Cuestión de los límites entre Aragón y Cataluña," 167. See Guinot Rodríguez, *Els límits del regne*, 47–51 (Catalonia), and 51–63 (Aragon).

40. Ecclesiastical and secular domains could openly conflict. As we saw earlier, in chapter 7, the sees of Tortosa and Zaragoza agreed to establish their boundaries along the Algars River in 1210 without exerting influence on the dispute: *Diplomatari de la catedral de Tortosa (1193–1212)*, ed. Virgili, doc. 732 (13 June 1210).

41. AHN, Clero: Poblet, c. 2096, no. 6 (22 Nov. 1208). *Cartes de poblament medievals valencianes*, ed. E. Guinot Rodríguez (Valencia: Servei de Publicacions de la Presidència, 1991), doc. 1.

42. Masià de Ros, "Cuestión de los límites entre Aragón y Cataluña," 167.

43. Zurita, *Anales de la Corona de Aragón*, ed. Canellas López, 3.45, 1:562.

44. Zurita, *Anales de la Corona de Aragón*, ed. Canellas López, 3.46, 1:564–65, and ACA, C, pergs. J I, no. 1244 (26 Mar. 1251); *Documentos de Jaime I*, ed. Huici and Cabanes, vol. 3, doc. 562. Alfons's confirmation: ACA, C, pergs. J I, no. 1267 (21 Nov. 1251).

45. ACA, C, pergs. J I, no. 1846 (20 Sept. 1253). *Documentos de Jaime I*, ed. Huici and Cabanes, vol. 3, doc. 626.

46. ACA, C, pergs. J I, no. 1347 (23 Sept. 1253).

47. ACA, C, Reg. 9, fol. 30v (both 29 Aug. 1257); *Documentos de Jaime I*, ed. Huici and Cabanes, vol. 3, docs. 750 and 751. Earlier that year, Jaume had increased the *infant's* stake in the Balearic Islands: *Documentos de Jaime I*, ed. Huici and Cabanes, vol. 3, doc. 724 (11 Jan. 1257).

48. ACA, C, pergs. J I, no. 1720 (21 Aug. 1262).

49. ACA, C, Reg. 12, fol. 70r (10 Sept. 1262); *Documentos de Jaime I*, ed. Huici and Cabanes, vol. 4, doc. 1290.

50. *Documentos de Jaime I*, ed. Huici and Cabanes, vol. 4, docs. 1297 and 1298 (7 Nov. 1262).

51. ACA, C, pergs. J I, no. 2018 (27 Mar. 1270).

52. ACA, C, pergs. J I, no. 2252 (19 Nov. 1275); *Diplomatari de Pere el Gran 1*, ed. Cingolani, doc. 38.

53. Compare Serrano Daura, *El conflicte*, 70.

54. Serrano Daura, *El conflicte*, 66.

55. ACA, C, Reg. 44, fol. 146r; Serrano Daura, *El conflicte*, doc. 1.

56. ACA, C, Reg. 41, fol. 19r (24 Nov. 1278); Serrano Daura, *El conflicte*, doc. 2.

57. ACA, C, Reg. 48, fol. 3r (20 Apr. 1280); Serrano Daura, *El conflicte*, doc. 4.

58. ACA, C, Reg. 59, fol. 19r (29 June 1282); Serrano Daura, *El conflicte*, doc. 5.

59. ACA, C, Reg. 62, fol. 2r (15 Aug. 1283); Serrano Daura, *El conflicte*, doc. 11. In this instance, the *sobrejuntero* was misidentified as the *supravicarius*.

60. ACA, C, Reg. 59, fol. 28r (12 July 1282); Serrano Daura, *El conflicte*, doc. 6.

61. AHN, Órdenes Militares, c. 636, no. 12 (27 Aug. 1282); Serrano Daura, *El conflicte*, doc. 7.

62. E.g., ACA, C, Reg. 85, fol. 12v (25 Apr. 1290); Serrano Daura, *El conflicte*, doc. 12.

63. AHN, Órdenes Militares, c. 636, no. 14 (15 June 1293); Serrano Daura, *El conflicte*, doc. 15.

64. ACA, C, Reg. 81, fol. 176v (1 Aug. 1290); Serrano Daura, *El conflicte*, doc. 13.

65. ACA, C, Reg. 142, fol. 153r (both 19 Aug. 1308); Serrano Daura, *El conflicte*, docs. 17 and 18.

66. AHN, Órdenes Militares, c. 610, no. 79 (8 Dec. 1306); Serrano Daura, *El conflicte*, doc. 16.

67. See Serrano Daura, *El conflicte*, 94–95.

68. See Serrano Daura, *El conflicte*, 89–91, and 93–94.

69. Monjo, *Sarraïns sota el domini feudal*, 41–42. Serrano Daura, *Senyoriu i municipi a la Catalunya Nova*, 1:412–13. Forey, *Templars in the* Corona de Aragón, 130–31.

70. Forey, *Templars in the* Corona de Aragón, 131.

71. See Bonet Donato, *La orden del Hospital en la Corona de Aragón*, 50–59.

72. ACA, C, pergs. J I, no. 1083 (28 July 1247); *Documentos de Jaime I*, ed. Huici and Cabanes, vol. 2, doc. 467. See Pagarolas, *Els Templers*, 1:243–44, and Barton, *Contested Treasure*, chap. 2.

73. *Documentos de Jaime I*, ed. Huici and Cabanes, vol. 2, doc. 467.

74. ACA, GPC, Arm. 4: Tortosa, perg. no. 43 (27 Aug. 1271); Pagarolas, *Els Templers*, vol. 2, doc. 116.

75. See Barton, *Contested Treasure*, 128–30.

76. See ACTE, perg. no. 136, Castellania i Templers II, no. 21; Massip, *La gestació de les costums de Tortosa*, doc. 9.

77. ACA, C, pergs. J I, 1454 (1 Jul. 1256).

78. ACA, C, pergs. J II, no. 300 (2 Nov. 1293).

79. ACA, C, pergs. J II, no. 194 (17 Jan. 1293). Pagarolas, *Els Templers*, vol. 2, doc. 169.

80. ACTE, perg. no. 139, Castellania i Templers, II, no. 32 = ACA, C, pergs. P II, no. 222 (7 Dec. 1280); *Diplomatari de Pere el Gran 1. Cartes i Pergamins (1258-1285)*, ed. S.

M. Cingolani (Barcelona: Fundació Noguera, 2011), doc. 237. See *Cartas de población*, ed. Font Rius, vol. 1.1:784–85.

81. See ACA, C, Reg. 40, fols. 68r (20 Feb. 1278) and 72r (1 Mar. 1278); Reg. 66, fol. 117r (10 Jun. 1286); Pagarolas, *Els Templers*, vol. 2, doc. 152.

82. *Cartas de población*, ed. Font Rius, vol. 1.1, docs. 346 (28 May 1282) and 350 (29 Mar. 1286).

83. See Pagarolas, *Els Templers*, 1:149–218.

84. See Barton, *Contested Treasure*, chap. 5.

85. See, e.g., ACA, C, pergs. P II, no. 57 (21 Aug 1277); *Diplomatari de Pere el Gran 1*, ed. Cingolani, doc. 97, in which the king assigned Ramon Guàrdia, serving as royal bailiff over both Tortosa and Penyíscola, responsibility over Penyíscola's saltworks. Shortly thereafter, Ramon enlisted a resident of Tortosa to build and operate new salt works on the king's behalf. ACA, C, pergs. P II, no. 58 (25 Aug 1277); *Diplomatari de Pere el Gran 1*, ed. Cingolani, doc. 98.

86. Jaume often authorized his bailiff in Tortosa to repay debts and expenses from the Crown's rents from the city: E.g., ACA, C, Reg. 20, fol. 229v–30r (both 22 Mar. 1274), fol. 194r (26 Dec. 1274), fol. 273v (23 Jul. 1275), fol. 332r (22 Mar. 1276); Reg. 22, fol. 72v (23 Jul. 1276).

87. ACA, C, Reg. 38, fol. 54v (12 Oct. 1276); Pagarolas, *Els Templers*, vol. 2, doc. 131. Consider also ACA, C, Reg. 41, fol. 103v (12 Jul. 1279); Pagarolas, *Els Templers*, vol. 2, doc. 137, in which Pere II orders the Templar commander to cede to the royal bailiff the Crown's share of the *monedatge* collected within Tortosa. The king engaged frequently with the co-lords over their sharing in the collection of this tax: e.g., ACA, C, Reg. 40, fol. 58r (14 Jan. 1278).

88. ACA, C, Reg. 40, fol. 65r (18 Feb. 1278).

89. E.g., ACTE, perg. no. 264, Comú III, no. 171 (7 July 1290).

90. See chapter 7 above. For conflict over the *bovatge*, see, e.g., ACTE, perg. no. 201, Comú II, no. 46C (23 Oct. 1280), ACTE, perg. no. 229, Comú III, no. 15 (23 Oct. 1281), ACTE, perg. no. 199, Comú II, no. 46A (13 Nov. 1286). For the *lleuda*, see ACA, C, Reg. 444, fol. 222r (6 Apr. 1282).

91. ACA, C, pergs. J I, no. 2153 (12 Apr. 1273); Pagarolas, *Els Templers*, vol. 2, doc. 122.

92. See Fabregat, *Burgesos contra senyors*, 102–4, and Barton, "Jurisdictional Conflict, Strategies of Litigation, and Mechanisms of Compromise," 213–15.

93. E.g., ACA, C, Reg. 39, fol. 171v (8 Mar. 1277), and ACTE, perg. no. 539, Privilegis V, no. 6 (25 Dec. 1283).

94. E.g., ACA, C, Reg. 39, fol. 128r (24 Dec. 1276).

95. See A. Luttrell, "The Aragonese Crown and the Knights Hospitallers of Rhodes: 1291–1350," *English Historical Review* 76 (1961): 1–19, esp. 3. For examples, see Bonet Donato, *La orden del Hospital en la Corona de Aragón*, 59–69.

96. E.g., Jaume II ratified his father's exchange in 1298: Bayerri, *Historia de Tortosa*, 7:643 and 643n1, and *Llibre de Privilegis de la vila de Ulldecona*, ed. E. Bayerri (Tortosa: Imprenta Blanch, 1951), doc. 5 (fols. 2r–5v). See Bonet Donato, *La orden del Hospital en la Corona de Aragón*, 292.

97. Pagarolas, *Els Templers*, 1:243–45. See Orvietani Busch, *Medieval Mediterranean Ports*, 79–80.

98. Compare Pagarolas, *Els Templers*, 1:245–46.

99. ACTE, perg. no. 138, Castellania i Templers II, no. 31 (15 Sept. 1294); Pagarolas, *Els Templars*, vol. 2, doc. 172. See ACTE, paper nos. 1933 and 292, Privilegis, III, nos. 23 and 27 (21 Sept. 1294). See L. Pagarolas, "La fi de l'orde del Temple a Tortosa: La permuta de 1294," *Anuario de Estudios Medievales* 28 (1998): 269–91.

100. ACA, C, pergs. J I, no. 766 (2 Feb. 1297): "ab mer imperi e ab mixt imperi e ab totes altres jurisdictions."

101. ACTE, perg. no. 115, Castellania i Templers I, no. 10, and ACA, C, pergs. J II, no. 398 (24 Sept. 1294). See J. Fuguet Sans, "Fortificacions menors i altre patrimoni retingut pels Templers a Tortosa després de la permuta de 1294," *Anuario de Estudios Medievales* 28 (1998): 293–309.

102. ACTE, perg. no. 474, Privilegis III, no. 17 = ACA, C, Reg. 194, fols. 79r–82r = ADM, Montcada, L. 16, no. 21 = ADM, Montcada, L. 10, no. 21 (7 Oct. 1294). As proof of execution, the Montcadas soon obtained the castle of Saidí—ACA, C, pergs. J II, no. 428 (19 Oct. 1294)—and exercised lordship over Villovar: ADM, Montcada, L. 16, no. 22 (6 Apr. 1315). See Barton, *Contested Treasure*, 199–200.

103. ACA, C, pergs. J II, no. 706 (12 Oct. 1296). See the court case related to this purchase that was discussed in the introduction.

104. Pagarolas, *Els Templers*, 1:244. This status was recognized by R. Muntaner, *Crònica*, c. 178, in *Les quatre grans cróniques*, ed. F. Soldevila, with philological revision by J. Bruguera and historical revision by M. T. Ferrer i Mallol, vol. 3, Memóries de la secció històrico-arqueològica 86 (Barcelona: Institut d'Estudis Catalans, 2011). See Pagarolas, *Els Templers*, 1:244n2, and consider Muntaner, *Crònica*, ed. Soldevila, c. 36, 44, 46, 48, 112, 223, and 277.

105. E.g., ACA, C, Reg. 40, fol. 12r (18 Aug. 1277); Pagarolas, *Els Templers*, vol. 2, doc. 134, in which Pere ordered the Templar commander, Co-lord Ramon III de Montcada, and the *prohoms* and other officials of Tortosa to permit a merchant from Fraga to take a quantity of wheat from the city freely. See also ACA, C, Reg. 39, fols. 203v (13 Jun. 1277), 219r (6 Jul. 1277), and 234r (28 Jul. 1277) in which he forbade Tortosa's officials to export grain to Valencia owing to the troubles with the revolting *mudéjares* there. See ACA, C, Reg. 44, fol. 244r (22 Dec. 1284), in which Pere authorized merchants from Barcelona to purchase flax, tallow, and pitch from Tortosa despite his embargo on these commodities. Shortly thereafter, he simultaneously managed trade prohibitions for Tortosa and Lleida: ACA, C, Reg. 44, fol. 125v (30 Jan 1285).

106. See A. Curto, *La intervenció municipal en l'abastament de blat d'una ciutat catalana: Tortosa, segle XIV* (Barcelona: Fundació Salvador Vives Casajuana, 1988).

107. ACTE, perg. no. 551, Privilegis V, no. 67 (5 Jan. 1295) and no. 435, Privilegis II, no. 27 (29 Jan. 1295).

108. ACTE, perg. no. 275, Consolat i Fira, no. 36 (29 Jan. 1295). ACTE, perg. no. 269, Consolat i Fira, no. 4 (29 Jan. 1295).

109. ACTE, perg. no. 528, Privilegis IV, no. 24 (25 Feb. 1295); ACTE, perg. no. 541, Privilegis V, no. 8. See J. N. Hillgarth, "The Problem of a Catalan Mediterranean Empire, 1229–1327," *English Historical Review*, Supplement 8 (1975): iii–iv, 1–54; republ. in his *Spain and the Mediterranean in the Later Middle Ages: Studies in Political and Intellectual History* (Aldershot: Ashgate Variorum, 2003), Essay II.

110. ACTE, perg. no. 187, Comú II, no. 25 (31 Aug. 1298). ACTE, perg. no. 202, Comú II, no. 46D (3 May 1299).

111. *Cartas de poblacón*, ed. Font Rius, vol. 1.1, doc. 357 (28 Nov. 1294). Charter to Font de Perelló: doc. 358 (16 Dec. 1294).

112. *Cartas de poblacón*, ed. Font Rius, vol. 1.1, doc. 367 ([1303–21]).

113. ACA, GPC, Arm. 4: Tortosa, perg. no. 57 (26 Aug. 1304). Pagarolas, *Els Templers*, vol. 2, doc. 203.

114. Among numerous examples, Ramon de Sentmenat recognized that he held a hospice in the *zuda* and incomes from the local market in fief from the king in 1305: ACA, C, Reg. 25, fol. 266v (22 Jun. 1305). In 1322, Guillem Pinyol performed homage to Jaume II for Cardò and Sallent, in the district of Tortosa, which he held in fief from the king according to the *Usatges de Barcelona* and "consuetudines Catalonie." ACA, C, Reg. 25, fol. 295v (23 Jun. 1322). On municipal development, see Curto, *La intervenció municipal en l'abastament de blat d'una ciutat catalana*, 69–98; F. Sabaté, "El veguer i la vegueria de Tortosa i la Ribera d'Ebre al segle XIV," *Recerca* 2 (1998): 115–51 (esp. 115–25); and J. Vidal Franquet, *Les obres de la ciutat: L'activitat constructiva i urbanística de la universitat de Tortosa a la baixa edat mitjana* (Barcelona: Publicacions de l'Abadia de Montserrat, 2008), 41–119.

115. The best general account remains Soldevila, *Els primers temps*, 187–201 and 273–97.

116. Lladonosa, *Història de Lleida*, 304–5. See Fité, *Reculls d'història de la vall d'Àger*, 224–25.

117. See Lladonosa, *Història de Lleida*, 304–8; Shideler, *A Medieval Catalan Noble Family*, 156; and Sabaté, "Organització administrativa i territorial del comtat d'Urgell," 38–39.

118. See Domingo, *A la recerca d'Aurembiaix d'Urgell*, doc. 14 (May 1225), in which Álvaro and "mea mulier la condesa Don Orembiax" perform a joint donation.

119. ACA, C, pergs. J I, no. 148 (26 Jul. 1220); Domingo, *A la recerca d'Aurembiaix d'Urgell*, doc. 11.

120. The *Llibre dels feits* does not mention this stage of the conflict, but these details can be inferred from the resolution made at the *Cortes* of Monzón in 1217 discussed below: ACA, C, pergs. J I, no. 78 (19 June 1217); *Documentos de Jaime I*, ed. Huici and Cabanes, vol. 1, doc. 2. This record singles out the important role played by Viscount Guillem I de Cardona in arranging the meeting. Soldevila, *Els primers temps*, 116–18, thoroughly analyzes the list of attendees. Zurita, *Anales de la Corona de Aragón*, ed. Canellas López, 2.59, 2:367, mentions that other business was conducted at the meeting, including the concession of the *bovatge*, regarding which no contemporary documentation survives. The *Llibre dels feits*, ed. Bruguera, c. 14, 2:17, appears to make brief mention of this meeting of the court but provides no details regarding what transpired there. See Soldevila, *Els primers temps*, 121.

121. ACA, C, pergs. J I, no. 78. For summaries of the enactment, see Soldevila, *Els primers temps*, 118–20 and Domingo, *A la recerca d'Aurembiaix d'Urgell*, 66–67. See also Fité, *Reculls d'història de la vall d'Àger*, 225. The amounts of the sums are not explained in the document, but Domingo hypotheses that the first payment was "la quantitat que devia Elvira a Pere I per l'execució del testament d'Ermengol VIII," which we discussed in chapter 6 above: ACA, C, pergs. P I, no. 303 (2 Nov. 1209); *Pedro el Católico*, ed. Alvira Cabrer, vol. 3, doc. 963. This possibility is unlikely given that the arrangement explicitly excluded the debts owed to Guillem IV de Cervera and the county's other creditors: "et excludantur pignora G. de Cervaria et aliorum creditorum." It

does also make exception for the "convention" made between Ermengol VIII and Alfons, but, here again, these outstanding obligations were not linked to the sums to be paid by Guerau IV or Aurembiaix.

122. ACA, C, pergs. J I, no. 78.

123. See Domingo, *A la recerca d'Aurembiaix d'Urgell*, 71–79, for an accounting of Aurembiaix's activity in Castile. Compare Miret y Sans, *Investigación sobre el vizcondado de Castellbó*, 108, who claimed that she retired to a monastery in Lleida during these years.

124. ACA, C, pergs. J I, no. 205 (21 Dec. 1222); *Documentos de Jaime I*, ed. Huici and Cabanes, vol. 1, doc. 39. The record makes specific mention of the destruction of the castles of Castelló and Pineda. See Domingo, *A la recerca d'Aurembiaix d'Urgell*, 67, and Soldevila, *Els primers temps*, 199–201.

125. Since the general rate of change during this period was one *morabetin* to nine Catalonian *solidi*, the combined payment of twenty-four thousand *morabetins* and fifty thousand *solidi* that had been stipulated in 1217 was roughly equal to this sum of thirty thousand *morabetins*.

126. *Llibre dels feits*, ed. Bruguera, c. 20, 2:22–24. See Zurita, *Anales de la Corona de Aragón*, ed. Canellas López, 2.78, 1:392–93, and Soldevila, *Els primers temps*, 203–4.

127. ACA, C, pergs. J I, no. 211 (19 Apr. 1223); *Documentos de Jaime I*, ed. Huici and Cabanes, vol. 1, doc. 43. Domingo, *A la recerca d'Aurembiaix d'Urgell*, 68.

128. ACA, C, pergs. J I, no. 211.

129. Soldevila, *Els primers temps*, 205–10. For the charter of renewal, see Soldevila, *Els primers temps*, 209–10 and 210n41.

130. AML, Reg. 1372, *Llibre Vert Petit*, fol. 99v–102r (9 Apr. 1224); *Documentos de Jaime I*, ed. Huici and Cabanes, vol. 1, doc. 50.

131. There are no signs that Guerau IV passed on his titles to or full control over Urgell, Cabrera, or Àger until his death. He continued to make enactments regarding Urgell and his other domains as "Count of Urgell and Viscount of Cabrera," with Ponç appearing only as "his son" and no formal title until 1227. E.g., ACA, C, pergs. J I, no. 304 (18 Aug. 1226): "Geraldus dei gratia comes Urgelli at vicecomes Caprarie et ego Poncetus eius filius." Compare Fité, *Reculls d'història de la vall d'Àger*, 226, who maintained that Guerau passed control to his sons around 1224. He has been followed by Domingo, *A la recerca d'Aurembiaix d'Urgell*, 68–69. Aurembiaix's 1228 donation of Lleida, discussed further below, still refers to Ponç as "filius Geraldi" but identifies him as the agent who "detinet de comitatu Urgelli." ACA, C, pergs. J I, no. 357 (1 Aug. 1228). According to Fité, by 1227, Guerau had joined the Templars and taken up residence at Gardeny. Ponç's wife, Maria, adopted the title of countess of Urgell in a transaction from July of that year. See Domingo, *A la recerca d'Aurembiaix d'Urgell*, 89n218.

132. ACA, C, pergs. J I, no. 292 (1 May 1226), Domingo, *A la recerca d'Aurembiaix d'Urgell*, doc. 15. She identified herself solely as "dompne Orenbiax." See Domingo, *A la recerca d'Aurembiaix d'Urgell*, 78.

133. *Llibre dels feits*, ed. Bruguera, c. 34, 2:44, mentions this agreement as part of the countess's arrangements with Jaume to regain control over the county. The chronicle indicates that Ramon de Peralta refused to surrender the castle until Aurembiaix arrived and then gave her control of Montmagastre but retained control over these four other castles.

134. See Domingo, *A la recerca d'Aurembiaix d'Urgell*, 77–79.

135. Domingo, *A la recerca d'Aurembiaix d'Urgell*, 85.

136. Domingo, *A la recerca d'Aurembiaix d'Urgell*, docs 18 (Aug. 1228) and 21 (undated). See Domingo, *A la recerca d'Aurembiaix d'Urgell*, 81–84.

137. Domingo, *A la recerca d'Aurembiaix d'Urgell*, doc. 16 (Jul. 1228).

138. *Llibre dels feits*, ed. Bruguera, c. 34, 2:43–44. Supposedly Bishop Berenguer d'Erill of Lleida, numerous barons present at the meeting, and the *prohoms* of Lleida all recommended Guillem Sasala as her legal representative. She assigned him payment using taxation rights she had retained from the city of Lleida worth around two hundred *solidi* at the time. See Domingo, *A la recerca d'Aurembiaix d'Urgell*, 89–90.

139. The *Llibre dels feits* states that the king summoned Guerau IV, but scholars widely recognize that it meant Ponç IV, who had inherited his father's title by this point.

140. *Llibre dels feits*, ed. Bruguera, c. 35, 2:45–46.

141. *Llibre dels feits*, ed. Bruguera, c. 36, 2:46–47. See Soldevila, *Els primers temps*, 274–78.

142. ACA, C, pergs. J I, no. 357 (1 Aug. 1228); *Documentos de Jaime I*, ed. Huici and Cabanes, vol. 1, doc. 102; Domingo, *A la recerca d'Aurembiaix d'Urgell*, doc. 17. See Soldevila, *Els primers temps*, 279–81.

143. ACA, C, pergs. P I, no. 303 (30 Aug. 1208). See chapter 6 above.

144. Domingo, *A la recerca d'Aurembiaix d'Urgell*, 90. For the dating, see Miret y Sans, *Itinerari de Jaume I*, 71–73.

145. *Llibre dels feits*, ed. Bruguera, c. 37–46, 2:47–56. See Domingo, *A la recerca d'Aurembiaix d'Urgell*, 90–92, and, for a detailed accounting of the entire campaign, Soldevila, *Els primers temps*, 273–97. The chronicle relates how, as these primary castles and secondary fortifications were delivered by the royal host to the countess, Aurembiaix entrusted them to the men of her inner circle and their delegates. E.g., she entrusted Ramon Berenguer d'Àger with the castle and town of Santa Linya in November. ACA, C, pergs. J I, no. 362 (10 Nov. 1228); Domingo, *A la recerca d'Aurembiaix d'Urgell*, doc. 20. Ramon Berenguer was involved in the campaigning and had been recommended to take possession of Balaguer when it was captured: *Llibre dels feits*, ed. Bruguera, c. 44, 2:54. He represented an important ally because he guarded over the monastery of Sant Pere d'Àger by holding many of the monastery's castles in the region, and thus had the means to menace the Cabreras at the core of their ancestral domains (Domingo, *A la recerca d'Aurembiaix d'Urgell*, 90).

146. ACA, C, pergs. J I, no. 389 (23 Oct. 1228); Soldevila, *Els primers temps*, 298–300; Domingo, *A la recerca d'Aurembiaix d'Urgell*, doc. 19.

147. This reference to Mallorca has prompted theories that the document could have been modified a year later, in 1229, closer to that expedition. See Soldevila, *Els primers temps*, 287–95 and Domingo, *A la recerca d'Aurembiaix d'Urgell*, 96–97.

148. See the territorial map of the county of Urgell in Sabaté, "Organització administrativa i territorial del comtat d'Urgell," 28–29. She did not stipulate the extent of her interest in each of these holdings. Some of them, e.g. Fraga (on which, see below in this chapter), must have been marginal based on the shares that we know were held by other parties.

149. See Soldevila, *Els primers temps*, 292–93.

150. Domingo, *A la recerca d'Aurembiaix d'Urgell*, 98–99; M. Shadis, "'Received as a Woman': Rethinking the Concubinage of Aurembiaix of Urgell," *Journal of Medieval*

Iberian Studies 8 (2016): 38–54. We discussed this earlier marriage contract in chapter 6 above.

151. See Domingo, *A la recerca d'Aurembiaix d'Urgell*, 99, and Shadis, " 'Received as a Woman,' " 48–49.

152. As evidenced by a letter to the pope from the legate concerning the possibility of a divorce: ACA, C, pergs. J I, no. 375 (29 Apr. 1229). Eventually, as we discussed earlier in this chapter, Jaume did successfully annul his marriage, but his son with Leonor, Alfons, was pronounced legitimate, although he died in 1260 before he could inherit the throne. Jaume married Violant of Hungary in 1235. See ACA, C, pergs. J I, no. 635 (1235), a letter to Jaume from the king of Hungary concerning the marriage alliance.

153. For their first marriage contract, see ACA, C, pergs. J I, no. 381 (11 July 1229); Domingo, *A la recerca d'Aurembiaix d'Urgell*, doc. 23.

154. A second charter built upon the aforementioned marriage agreement from earlier in July: ACA, C, pergs. J I, nos. 380 (15 July 1229); Domingo, *A la recerca d'Aurembiaix d'Urgell*, doc. 24. Her will, performed in August 1231, reiterated this same pledge. ACA, C, pergs. J I, no. 431 (11 Aug. 1231); Domingo, *A la recerca d'Aurembiaix d'Urgell*, doc. 27.

155. ACA, C, pergs. J I, no. 389 (22 Oct. 1229).

156. Domingo, *A la recerca d'Aurembiaix d'Urgell*, doc. 25 (23 Apr. 1231). ACA, C, pergs. J I, no. 438 (29 Sept. 1231); *Documentos de Jaime I*, ed. Huici and Cabanes, vol. 1, doc. 159; and Domingo, *A la recerca d'Aurembiaix d'Urgell*, doc. 28. This quitclaim was especially important due to stipulations of Aurembiaix's will from August of that same year (see above). See Domingo, *A la recerca d'Aurembiaix d'Urgell*, 101–2.

157. ACA, C, pergs. J I, no. 961 (18 Aug. 1244); *Documentos de Jaime I*, ed. Huici and Cabanes, vol. 2, doc. 394. In a supplemental agreement enacted the following day, the *infante* agreed to return to Jaume his received holdings in Valencia, along with some additional holdings in Evissa, if he died without an heir. ACA, C, pergs. J I, no. 962 (19 Aug. 1244); *Documentos de Jaime I*, ed. Huici and Cabanes, vol. 2, doc. 395.

158. ACA, C, pergs. J I, no. 624 (21 Jan. 1236); *Documentos de Jaime I*, ed. Huici and Cabanes, vol. 1, doc. 231.

159. For examples of Ponç using the comital title from as early as 1229, see Fité, *Reculls d'història de la Vall d'Àger*, 227.

160. ACL, A 460 (3 Mar 1235). Berenguer de Finestres had served in the campaign the king led against the Cabreras in 1228 discussed above. See, e.g., *Llibre dels feits*, ed. Bruguera, c. 41, 2:51, where he played a notable role during the capture of Balaguer.

161. ACA, C, pergs. J I, no. 624 (21 Jan. 1236).

162. Fité, *Reculls d'història de la Vall d'Àger*, 228.

163. Fité, *Reculls d'història de la Vall d'Àger*, 229–30. Even after Álvar had assumed control of the county, Ponç's widow, Maria, continued to employ the title of countess and furthermore was able to draw on important holdings within the county to satisfy her deceased husband's remaining debts. In 1244, for example, she assigned repayment of obligations to Ramon de Castluç by pledging him the castle and town of Gebut, which she held in fief from Guillem I de Montcada, co-lord of Tortosa. If Guillem opposed the arrangement, Maria and her son, Ermengol, authorized the pawning of their castle and town of Oliana. ACL, A 698 (24 Nov 1244).

164. Fité, *Reculls d'història de la Vall d'Àger*, 230–31. As one manifestation of this conflict, in 1283, two related knights, Ramon and Ramon Arnau de Castelló, sided

with Pere II against Ermengol X in recognition that the count had violated his *conveniencias* with the king. ACA, C, pergs. P II, no. 383 (16 Dec. 1283); *Diplomatari de Pere el Gran 1*, ed. Cingolani, doc. 362.

165. Jaume anticipated this conflict as early as 1271, when he warned the bailiffs, *prohoms, universitati* and paers of Agramunt, Lleida, Menàrguens, Albelda and other centers to assist in the defense of various fortifications against forces under the command of count of Urgell's son: ACA, C, Reg. 18, fol. 86v (27 Dec. 1271). In 1274, he circulated a letter to urban officials throughout Aragon and Catalonia, telling them to prepare for the "war that we believe to have in Catalonia": ACA, C, Reg. 18, fol. 62r–v (8 Sept. 1274).

166. Fité, *Reculls d'història de la Vall d'Àger*, 231–32.

167. F. Carreras y Candi, "Caciquisme polítich en lo segle XIII (Continuació)," *Boletín de la Real Academia de Buenas Letras de Barcelona 5*, no. 18 (1905): 70; see also 77–78.

168. ACA, C, Reg. 48, fol. 52. See Fité, *Reculls d'història de la Vall d'Àger*, 232. For detail, see F. Carreras y Candi, "Caciquisme polítich en lo segle XIII (Continuació)," *Boletín de la Real Academia de Buenas Letras de Barcelona 5*, no. 19 (1905): 134–43, who edited the king's letter at 141. The same day he also similarly appealed for aid from the archbishop of Tarragona, the bishops of Barcelona, Girona, Tortosa, Urgell, Zaragoza, Osca, and Lleida, the abbots of Poblet and Montearagón, the chapter of Tarazona, the masters of the Temple and Hospital, and the commanders of Montalbán and Alcañíz. The literature on the *Princeps Namque* is considerable. See D. J. Kagay, "The Defense of the Crown of Aragon during the War of the Two Pedros (1356–1366)," in *The Hundred Years War (Part II): Different Vistas*, ed. L. J. A. Villalon and D. J. Kagay (Leiden: Brill, 2008), 185–210; D. J. Kagay, "*Princeps namque*: Defense of the Crown and the Birth of the Catalan State," *Mediterranean Studies* 8 (1999): 55–87; and T. W. Barton, "Resisting the Call to Arms in Medieval Catalonia," in *Boundaries in the Medieval and Wider World*, ed. Barton et al., 24–44.

169. ACA, C, Cartas Reales Diplomáticas, P II, no. 17 = ACA, C, Reg. 22, fol. 85r (5 Jun. 1278); *Diplomatari de Pere el Gran 1*, ed. Cingolani, doc. 117.

170. For the judgment, see ACA, C, pergs. P II, no. 266 (23 Aug. 1281); *Diplomatari de Pere el Gran 1*, ed. Cingolani, doc. 260. Carreras y Candi, "Caciquisme polítich en lo segle XIII (Continuació)," 134–43 provides an overview.

171. Fité, *Reculls d'història de la Vall d'Àger*, 233–38. He granted the county to his second son, *Infant* Alfons. See Sabaté, "Organització administrativa i territorial del comtat d'Urgell," 39.

172. AML, Reg. 1372, *Llibre Vert Petit*, fol. 99v–102r and 102r–103r (both 9 Apr. 1224); *Documentos de Jaime I*, ed. Huici and Cabanes, vol. 1, docs 50 and 51.

173. E.g., ACA, C, pergs. J I, no. 204 (10 Dec. 1222); *Documentos de Jaime I*, ed. Huici and Cabanes, vol. 1, doc. 38. See Lladonosa, *Història de Lleida*, 330.

174. E.g., ACA, C, pergs. J I, no. 216 (11 Jul. 1223); *Documentos de Jaime I*, ed. Huici and Cabanes, vol. 1, doc. 46.

175. E.g., ACA, C, Reg. 16, fol. 164v (14 May 1269), in which the king recognized that he owed Dominic de Cardona over sixteen thousand *solidi* and authorized him to collect it from the rents of Lleida. The same day, Jaume did an accounting with his bailiff of Lleida, Guillem de na Montagut, and confirmed his right to retain over three thousand *solidi* from his bailiwick. ACA, C, Reg. 16, fol. 165v.

176. For the earlier history of the Montcada family's involvement, see Shideler, *A Medieval Catalan Noble Family*, 212–15.

177. See Shideler, *A Medieval Catalan Noble Family*, 158, *Llibre dels feits*, ed. Bruguera, c. 62–66, 2:74–78, and chapter 7 above.

178. ACA, C, pergs. J I, no. 1423 (27 Sept. 1255) and ACA, C, pergs. J I, no. 903/2 (11 Oct. 1255). In preparation for this transfer, Guillem I de Montcada and his heir, Ramon III de Montcada, had already sworn to uphold the *fueros*, privileges, and enfranchisements awarded to them by Jaume and his predecessors: ACA, C, pergs. J I, no. 903/3 (20 Aug. 1255). See Salarrullana de Dios, "Fronteras o límites de Aragón y Cataluña," 152–59.

179. ACA, C, pergs. J I, no. 1481 (11 July 1257). Ramon identifies himself as son of Folc de Ponteves (Guillem V de Cervera) in the agreement.

180. Jaume's successors would also maintain this discipline. E.g., when Pere II needed funds to repay a large debt of over thirty-one thousand *solidi* owed to Ramon III de Montcada, lord of Fraga, he employed the standard practice of assigning the nobleman revenues collected by the bailiff of Lleida over the next two years. ACA, C, pergs. P II, no. 298 (15 Apr. 1282); *Diplomatari de Pere el Gran 1*, ed. Cingolani, doc. 279.

181. ACA, C, Reg. 14, fol. 69v (13 Feb. 1266); Salarrullana de Dios, "Fronteras o límites de Aragón y Cataluña," 161.

182. ACA, C, Reg. 44, fol. 171v (24 Feb. 1280). For the mandate concerning Tortosa's Jews, discussed earlier, see ACA, C, Reg. 44, fol. 194v (18 Dec. 1280). For context and analysis, refer to Barton, *Contested Treasure*, 196–203.

183. ACA, C, Reg. 81, fols. 78v–79r (5 Apr. 1289). The specifics of these offenses are detailed in the concession by Guillem II de Montcada from the following year, discussed below. *Libro de privilegios de Fraga y sus aldeas*, ed. G. Redondo Veintemillas and E. Sarasa Sánchez, 2 vols., facsimile ed. (Zaragoza: Cortes de Aragón, 1999), fols. 30v–31r (19 Aug. 1290).

184. *Libro de privilegios de Fraga y sus aldeas*, ed. Redondo Veintemillas and Sarasa Sánchez, fols. 24v–26r (19 Sept. 1232).

185. ACA, C, Reg. 81, fol. 126r–v (8 June 1289). He justified this revocation of the fief on the grounds that Ramon had not satisfied his necessary service obligations to the Crown, presumably by ruling the city unjustly.

186. *Libro de privilegios de Fraga y sus aldeas*, ed. Redondo Veintemillas and Sarasa Sánchez, fols. 30v–31r (19 Aug. 1290).

187. *Libro de privilegios de Fraga y sus aldeas*, ed. Redondo Veintemillas and Sarasa Sánchez, fols. 28v–30v (19 Aug. 1290).

188. *Libro de privilegios de Fraga y sus aldeas*, ed. Redondo Veintemillas and Sarasa Sánchez, fol. 31r–v (20 Aug. 1289) and fols. 2r–6r (26 Aug. 1290) (quoted).

189. *Libro de privilegios de Fraga y sus aldeas*, ed. Redondo Veintemillas and Sarasa Sánchez, fol. 31r–v (20 Aug. 1290).

190. ACA, C, Reg. 194, fol. 47r, *Libro de privilegios de Fraga y sus aldeas*, ed. Redondo Veintemillas and Sarasa Sánchez, fols. 12v–13v (25 Aug. 1294). See chapter 7 above for further discussion of these undesirable impositions.

191. *Libro de privilegios de Fraga y sus aldeas*, ed. Redondo Veintemillas and Sarasa Sánchez, fol. 31r–v (20 Aug. 1290).

192. ACA, C, Reg. 81, fol. 24r (30 Jan. 1290).

193. For further details, see Barton, Contested Treasure, esp. 202–3.

194. See chapter 3 above.

195. Forey, *Templars in the* Corona de Aragón, 61. For the case of Spain, see also J. Perez de Urbel, *Los monjes españoles en la edad media*, 2 vols. (Madrid: Imprenta de E. Maestre, 1933–34), vol. 2. This is a familiar theme to medievalists and has been developed at length elsewhere. Forey, *Templars in the* Corona de Aragón, 61, lists other germane sources.

196. Forey, *Templars in the* Corona de Aragón, 356 and J. Bronstein, *The Hospitallers and the Holy Land: Financing the Latin East, 1187–1274* (Woodbridge: Boydell, 2005), 100–102.

197. Forey, *Templars in the* Corona de Aragón, 356–64. See generally A. J. Forey, *The Fall of the Templars in the Crown of Aragon* (Aldershot: Ashgate, 2001), 156–96.

198. See Forey, *The Fall of the Templars*, esp. 238.

199. Forey, *Templars in the* Corona de Aragón, 61–62.

200. Forey has found evidence of the application of these prescriptions. See Forey, *Templars in the* Corona de Aragón, 132. Their general tenor is clearly present in the *Costums* of Horta issued that same year. See *Els costums d'Orta*, ed. Serrano Daura, esp. c. 10, p. 78.

201. ACA, C, Reg. 46, fol. 64v (28 Feb. 1282). See Forey, *Templars in the* Corona de Aragón, 132.

202. See Barton, *Contested Treasure*, chap. 5, for numerous examples of the monarchy's mixed success in its efforts to commandeer local officers to carry out its administrative tasks.

203. See, e.g., the comprehensive study by M. T. Ferrer i Mallol, "El patrimoni reial i la recuperació dels senyorius jurisdiccionals en els estats catalano-aragonesos a la fi del segle XIV," *Anuario de Estudios Medievales* 7 (1970–71): 351–491.

✍ SELECT BIBLIOGRAPHY

Note: Due to space constraints, this bibliography does not include any of the secondary literature that is referenced throughout the preceding pages. Readers should refer to the initial citations for each work, which contain complete reference information. A complete bibliography is available online at https://hdl.handle.net/1813/64626

Unpublished Primary Sources

Archivo Ducal de Medinaceli [ADM] (Arxiu Montserrat Tarradellas i Macià, Abadía de Poblet)
    Entença
    Montcada
Archivo Historico Nacional [AHN] (Madrid)
    Clero: Poblet, Sección de Sellos
Códices: nos. 649B, 662B (*Cartulario de Ulldecona*), 992B, 1126B
    Órdenes Militares
Arxiu Capitular de Lleida [ACL] (Lleida)
    Pergamins: Àger [A], Lleida [L]
    Llibre Vert
Arxiu Capitular de Solsona (Solsona)
Cartulari 2
Arxiu Capitular de Tortosa [ACT] (Tortosa)
    Cartularis 2, 8, 9A
    Pergamins: Ardiaca Major II, Comú del Bisbe i Capitol, Comú del Capítol I
Arxiu de la Catedral de Barcelona [ACB] (Barcelona)
Libri Antiquitatum
Archivo de la Corona de Aragón [ACA] (Barcelona)
    Cancillería Real
      —Bulas
      —Cartas Reales Diplomáticas: Jaime I [J I], Pedro II [P II]
      —Pergaminos: Ramon Berenguer II [RB II], Ramon Berenguer III [RB III], Ramon Berenguer IV [RB IV], Alfonso I [A I], Pedro I [P I], Jaime I [J I], Pedro II [P II], Jaime II [J II]
      —Extrainventario: Alfonso I [A I], Pedro I [P I]
      —Procesos en cuarto, no. 1296B
      —Registros 9, 12, 14, 41, 44, 46, 47, 48, 59, 62, 81, 85, 142, 194, 222, 236, 309, 310
    Gran Priorato de Cataluña de la Orden de San Juan de Jerusalén [GPC]

Sección 1ª—Pergaminos: Armario nos. 3 (Cervera), 4 (Tortosa), 7 (Espluga
Calba), 11 (Gardeny), 14 (Corbins), 19 (Torres de Segre), 23 (Comunes)
Sección 2ª—Códices: no. 115 (*Cartulari de Tortosa*)
Arxiu Històric Comarcal de les Terres del Ebre [ACTE] (Tortosa)
Pergamins
Paper
Arxiu Municipal de Lleida [AML] (Lleida)
Fons Municipal: pergamins
Manuscrits:
Reg. 1372, *Llibre Vert Petit*

Published Primary Sources

al-Aṯir, Ibn. *al-Kāmil fī al-tārīḫ*. Trans. Edmond Fagnan. *Annales du Maghreb et de l'Espagne*. Algiers: A. Jourdan, 1898.

Alfonso II Rey de Aragón, Conde de Barcelona y Marqués de Provenza: Documentos (1162–1196). Ed. Ana I. Sánchez Casabón. Fuentes históricas aragonesas 23. Zaragoza: Institución Fernando el Católico, 1995.

al-Maqqarī, Aḥmad ibn Muḥammad. *Kitāb nafh al-ṭīb*, in *The History of the Mohammedan Dynasties in Spain*. Trans. Pascual de Gayangos. 2 vols. London: Oriental Translation Fund, 1840–43.

L'arxiu antic de Santa Anna de Barcelona del 942 al 1200. Ed. Jesús Alturo i Perucho. 3 vols. Barcelona: Fundació Noguera, 1985.

Caffaro. *De captione Almerie et Tortuose*. Ed. Luigi Tommaso Belgrano. In *Annali Genovesi di Caffaro e de suoi continuatori*, vol. 1, *Dal MXCIX al MCCXCIII*, 77–90. Genoa: Tipografia del R. Istituto Sordo-Muti, 1890.

Cartas de población del reino de Aragón en los siglos medievales. Ed. M. L. Ledesma Rubio. Zaragoza: Institución "Fernando el Católico," 1991.

Cartas de población y franquicia de Cataluña. Ed. José María Font Rius. 2 vols. in 3. Madrid: Consejo Superior de Investigaciónes Científicas, 1969–83.

Cartes de poblament medievals valencianes. Ed. E. Guinot Rodríguez. Valencia: Servei de Publicacions de la Presidència, 1991.

Cartulaire général de l'Ordre du Temple, 1119?–1150: Recueil des chartes et des bulles relatives à l'Ordre du Temple. Ed. J. A. d'Albon. Paris: H. Champion, 1922.

Cartulari de la vall d'Andorra, segles IX–XIII. Ed. C. Baraut, 2 vols. Andorra: Conselleria d'Educació i Cultura del Govern d'Andorra, 1988–90.

Cartulari de Poblet: edició del manuscrit de Tarragona. Ed. Eduardo Toda. Barcelona: Institut d'Estudis Catalans, 1938.

Cartulario de "Sant Cugat" del Vallés. Ed. J. Rius y Serra. 3 vols. Barcelona: Consejo Superior de Investigaciones Científicas, 1945–47.

El cartulario de Tavérnoles. Ed. J. Soler Garcia. Castellón de la Plana: Sociedad Castellonense de Cultura, 1961.

Chronica Adefonsi Imperatoris. In *Chronica Hispana Saeculi XII*, ed. E. Falque, J. Gil, and A. Maya, 109–248. Turnhout: Brepols, 1990.

Codice diplomatico della repubblica di Genova. Ed. Cesare Imperiale de Sant'Angelo. 3 vols. Rome: Tipografia del Senato, 1938–42.

"Colección de cartas pueblas." Ed. P. Ramón de María. *Boletín de la Sociedad Castellonense de Cultura* 16 (1935): 385–88.

Colección de documentos inéditos del Archivo de la Corona de Aragón. Ed. Próspero de Bofarull y Mascaró et al. 42 vols. Barcelona, 1847–1973.

Colección diplomática de Alfonso I de Aragón y Pamplona, 1104–1134. Ed. J. A. Lema Pueyo. San Sebastián: Editorial Eusko Ikaskuntza, 1990.

Col·lecció diplomàtica de la casa del Temple de Gardeny (1070–1200). Ed. Ramon Sarobe i Huesca. 2 vols. Diplomataris 16–17. Barcelona: Fundació Noguera, 1998.

Colección diplomática de la catedral de Huesca. Ed. Antonio Durán Gudiol. 2 vols. Zaragoza: Escuela de Estudios Medievales, Instituto de Estudios Pirenaicos, 1965–69.

Colección diplomática de Pedro I de Aragón y Navarra. Ed. Antonio Ubieto Arteta. Zaragoza: Consejo Superior de Investigaciones Científicas, 1951.

Les constitucions de Pau i Treva de Catalunya (segles XI–XIII). Ed. Gener Gonzalvo i Bou. Textos jurídics catalans, Lleis i Costums II 3. Barcelona: Generalitat de Catalunya, Departament de Justícia, 1994.

Cortes de los antiguos reinos de Aragón y de Valencia y Principado de Cataluña. 27 vols. Madrid: Real Academia de la Historia, 1896–1922.

Costums de Catalunya entre senyors i vassals. In *Usatges de Barcelona i Commemoracions de Pere Albert,* ed. J. Rovira i Ermengol, Els Nostres classics, Col·lecció A 43–44. Barcelona: Barcino, 1933.

Els costums de Lleida: documents de l'Arxiu Municipal de Lleida. Ed. J. Busqueta i Riu. Col·lecció Guillem Botet. Lleida: Paeria, Ajuntament de Lleida, 1999.

Les costums de Miravet. Ed. Ferran Valls Taberner. Tarragona: Col·legi d'Advocats de Tarragona, 2006.

Costums de Tortosa. Ed. J. Massip. Barcelona: Fundació Noguera, 1996.

Els costums d'Orta (1296): estudi introductori i edició. Ed. Josep Serrano Daura. Horta de Sant Joan: Ajuntament d'Horta de Sant Joan, 1996.

Crónica de los Estados Peninsulares: Texto del siglo XIV. Ed. Antonio Ubieto Arteta. Granada: Universidad de Granada, 1955.

Crónica de San Juan de la Peña. Ed. A. Ubieto Arteta. Valencia: Caja de Ahorros y Monte de Piedad de Zaragoza, Aragón y Rioja, 1961. Translated as *The Chronicle of San Juan de la Peña: A Fourteenth-Century Official History of the Crown of Aragon,* trans. L. Nelson. Philadelphia: University of Pennsylvania Press, 1991.

Crónica latina de los reyes de Castilla. Ed. M. D. Cabanes Pecourt. Zaragoza: Anubar, 1985.

Customs of Catalonia between Lords and Vassals. Ed. and trans. Donald Kagay. Tempe: Arizona Center for Medieval and Renaissance Studies, 2002.

De expugnatione Lyxbonensi (The Conquest of Lisbon). Ed. and trans. C. W. David. 2nd ed. New York: Columbia University Press, 2001.

Desclot, Bernat. *La* Crònica *de Bernat Desclot o Llibre del Rey en Pere d'Aragó e dels seus antecessors.* In *Les quatre grans croniques,* ed. Ferran Soldevila, with philological revision by J. Bruguera and historical revision by M.T. Ferrer i Mallol, vol. 2,

Memóries de la secció històrico-arqueològica 80. Barcelona: Institut d'Estudis Catalans, 2008.

Diplomatari d'Alguaire i del seu monestir santojoanista de 1076 a 1244. Ed. J. Alturo i Perucho. Barcelona: Fundació Noguera, 1999.

Diplomatari de la cartoixa de Montalegre. Ed. X. Pérez i Gómez. Barcelona: Fundació Noguera, 1998.

Diplomatari de la catedral de Tortosa (1062–1193). Ed. Antoni Virgili. Diplomataris 11. Barcelona: Fundació Noguera, 1997.

Diplomatari de la catedral de Tortosa (1193–1212). Ed. Antoni Virgili. Diplomataris 25. Barcelona: Fundació Noguera, 2001.

Diplomatari de l'arxiu diocesà de Solsona (1101–1200). Ed. Antoni Bach Riu and Ramon Sarobe i Huesca. 2 vols. Barcelona: Fundació Noguera, 2002.

Diplomatari de Pere el Gran 1. Cartes i Pergamins (1258–1285). Ed. Stefano M. Cingolani. Diplomataris 62. Barcelona: Fundació Noguera, 2011.

Diplomatari de Santa Maria de Poblet (960–1177). Ed. Agustí Altisent, 1 vol. to date. Barcelona: Abadia de Poblet and Generalitat de Catalunya, 1995.

La documentación pontificia de Honorio III (1216–1227). Ed. Demetrio Mansilla. Monumenta hispaniae vaticana, sección: registros 2. Rome: Instituto Español de Estudios Eclesiásticos, 1965.

La documentación pontificia de Inocencio IV (1243–1254). Ed. Augusto Quintana Prieto. Rome: Instituto español de historia eclesiástica, 1987.

La documentación pontificia hasta Inocencio III (965–1216). Ed. Demetrio Mansilla. Monumenta hispaniae vaticana, sección: registros 1. Rome: Instituto Español de Estudios Eclesiásticos, 1955.

Documentos correspondientes al reinado de Sancho Ramírez: desde MLXIII hasta MLXXXXIII años: documentos reales prcedentes de la real casa y monasterio de San Juan de la Peña. Ed. José Salarrullana de Dios and Eduardo Ibarra. 2 vols. Zaragoza: M. Escar, 1904–13.

Documentos de Jaime I de Aragón. Ed. Ambrosio Huici Miranda and María de los Desamparados Cabanes Pecourt. 5 vols. Valencia: Anubar Ediciones, 1976–88.

Documentos de Ramiro II de Aragón. Ed. A. Ubieto Arteta. Zaragoza: Anubar, 1988.

Documentos para el estudio de la reconquista y repoblación del Valle del Ebro. Ed. J. M. Lacarra. 2 vols. Zaragoza: Anubar, 1982–85.

"Els documents, dels anys 1093–1100, de l'Arxiu Capitular de la Seu d'Urgell." Ed. Cebrià Baraut. *Urgellia* 8 (1986–87): 7–149.

"Els documents, dels anys 1101–1150, de l'Arxiu Capitular de la Seu d'Urgell." Ed. Cebrià Baraut. *Urgellia* 9 (1988–89): 7–312.

"Els documents, dels anys 1151–1190, de l'Arxiu Capitular de la Seu d'Urgell." Ed. Cebrià Baraut. *Urgellia* 10 (1990–91): 7–349.

Fiscal Accounts of Catalonia under the Early Count-Kings (1151–1213). Ed. Thomas N. Bisson. 2 vols. Berkeley: University of California Press, 1984.

Fueros, observancias, y actos de corte del reino de Aragón. Ed. Pascual Savall y Dronda and Santiago Penén y Dehesa. 2 vols. Zaragoza: El Justicia de Aragón, 1886.

Gesta comitum Barcinonensium: Cròniques Catalanes. Ed. Louis Barrau Dihigo and Jaume Massó Torrents. Barcelona: Institut d'Estudis Catalans, 1925.

Historia Roderici vel gesta Roderici Campidocti. In *Chronica Hispana Saeculi XII*, ed. E. Falque Rey, J. Gil, and A. Maya, 1–98. Turnhout: Brepols, 1990.

Ibn al-Khatīb. *Kitāb a'māl al-a'lām*. Ed. and trans. Rafaela Castrillo. Madrid: Instituto Hispano-Árabe de Cultura, 1983.

Jiménez de Rada, Rodrigo. *Historia de Rebus Hispaniae sive Historia Gothica*. Ed. Juan Fernández Valverde. Corpus Christianorum, Continuatio Medievalis 72. Turnhout: Brepols, 1987.

Die Juden im Christlichen Spanien. Ed. Yitzhak Baer. Berlin: Akademie-Verlag, 1929–36.

The Latin Chronicle of the Kings of Castile. Trans. J. F. O'Callaghan. Tempe, AZ: Arizona Center for Medieval and Renaissance Studies, 2002.

Layettes du trésor des chartes. Ed. Alexandre Teulet et al. 5 vols. Paris: Henri Plon, 1863–1909.

Liber Feudorum Maior: Cartulario real que se conserva en el Archivo de la Corona de Aragón. Ed. Francisco Miquel Rosell. 2 vols. Barcelona: Consejo Superior de Investigaciones Científicas, 1945–47.

Liber instrumentorum memorialium: Cartulaire des Guillems de Montpellier. Ed. A. Germain. Montpellier: J. Martel, 1884–86.

Liber iurium reipublicae Genuensis. Ed. E. Ricotti. Historiae patriae monumenta 7.1. Turin: E. regio typographeo, 1839–1955.

Liber Maiolichinus de gestis pisanorum illustribus. Ed. C. Calisse. Fonti per la Storia d'Italia 29. Rome: Tip. del Senato, 1904.

Libro de privilegios de Fraga y sus aldeas. Ed. Guillermo Redondo Veintemillas and Esteban Sarasa Sánchez. 2 vols. Facsimile Edition. Zaragoza: Cortes de Aragón, 1999.

El "Llibre Blanch" de Santas Creus: cartulario del siglo XII. Ed. Frederic Udina Martorell. Textos y estudios de la Corona de Aragón 9. Barcelona: Consejo Superior de Investigaciones Científicas, 1947.

Llibre dels feits del rei en Jaume. Ed. Jordi Bruguera. 2 vols. Els Nostres Clàssics, Col·lecció B 10–11. Barcelona: Fundació Jaume I, Editorial Barcino, 1991.

Llibre dels feits del rei en Jaume o Crònica de Jaume I. In *Les quatre grans croniques*, ed. Ferran Soldevila, with philological revision by J. Bruguera and historical revision by M.T. Ferrer i Mallol, vol. 1, Memóries de la secció històrico-arqueològica 73. Barcelona: Institut d'Estudis Catalans, 2007.

Llibre de Privilegis de la vila de Ulldecona. Ed. Enrique Bayerri. Tortosa: Imprenta Blanch, 1951.

Marca hispanica sive limes hispanicus, ed. P. de Marca and E. Baluze. Paris: Muguet, 1688.

Muntaner, Ramon. *Crònica*. In *Les quatre grans cróniques*, ed. Ferran Soldevila, with philological revision by J. Bruguera and historical revision by M.T. Ferrer i Mallol, vol. 3, Memóries de la secció històrico-arqueològica 86. Barcelona: Institut d'Estudis Catalans, 2011.

Papsturkunden in Spanien: vorarbeiten zur Hispania Pontificia, vol. 1, *Katalanien*. Ed. Paul F. Kehr. Berlin: Weidmannsche Buchhandlung, 1926.

Pedro el Católico, Rey de Aragón y Conde de Barcelona (1196–1213): Documentos, Testimonios y Memoria Histórica. Ed. Martín Alvira Cabrer. 6 vols. Fuentes Históricas Aragonesas 52. Zaragoza: Consejo Superior de Investigaciónes Científicas, 2010.

La Péninsule ibérique au moyen-âge d'après le Kitāb ar-rawḍal-miʻṭār fī ḥabar al-akṭār d'Ibn 'Abd al Mun'im al-Ḥimyari. Text arabe des notices relatives à l'Espagne, au Portugal e au sud-ouest de la France. Ed. and trans. Évariste Lévi-Provençal. Leiden: Brill, 1938.

Els pergamins de l'Arxiu Comtal de Barcelona, de Ramon Berenguer II a Ramon Berenguer IV. Ed. Ignasi J. Baiges et al. 4 vols. Barcelona: Fundació Noguera, 2010.

Els pergamins de l'Arxiu Comtal de Barcelona, de Ramon Borrell a Ramon Berenguer I. Ed. Josep M. Salrach et al. 3 vols. Barcelona: Fundació Noguera, 1999.

The Poems of the Troubadour Bertran de Born. Ed. and trans. W. D. Paden Jr., T. Sankovitch,and P. H. Stäblein. Berkeley: University of California Press, 1986.

Les poesies del trobador Guillem de Berguedà: text, traducció, introducció i notes. Ed. Martin de Riquer. Barcelona: Quaderns Crema, 1996.

Privilegios reales de la orden de Montesa en la Edad Media: catálogo de la serie existente en el Archivo Histórico Nacional. Ed. A. L. Javierre Mur. Madrid: Junta Técnica de Archivos, Bibliotecas y Museos, 1945.

Regesta de letras pontificias del Archivo de la Corona de Aragón. Ed. Francisco J. Miquel Rosell. Madrid: Cuerpo Facultativo de Archiveros, 1945.

Regesta Pontificum Romanorum. Ed. P. Jaffé et al. 2 vols. Graz: Akademische Druck- und Verlagsanstalt, 1956.

Les registres de Grégoire IX. Ed. L. Auvray et al. 4 vols. Paris: A. Fontemoing and E. de Boccard, 1863–1955.

Sacrorum conciliorum: nova et amplissima collectio. Ed. G. D. Mansi et al. 53 vols. Paris: H. Welter, 1901–27.

The Song of Roland: An Analytical Edition. Ed. and trans. G. J. Brault. 2 vols. University Park: Penn State University Press, 1978.

Els testaments dels comtes de Barcelona i dels reis de la Corona d'Aragó: de Guifré Borrell a Joan II. Ed. A. Udina i Abelló. Barcelona: Fundació Noguera, 2001.

Usatges de Barcelona: el codi a mitjan segle xii. Establiment del text llatí i edició de la versió catalana del manuscrit del segle XIII de l'arxiu de la d'Aragó de Barcelona. Ed. Joan Bastardas i Parera. Col·lecció textos i documents 6. 2nd ed. Barcelona: Fundació Noguera, 1991.

Vidal Mayor: Traducción aragonesa de la obra In Excelsis Dei Thesauris de Vidal de Canellas. Ed. Gunnar Tilander. 3 vols. Lund: Håkan Ohlssons Boktryckeri, 1956.

Vitalis, Orderic. Ecclesiasticae Historiae Libri tredecim. The Ecclesiastical History of Orderic Vitalis. Ed. and trans. M. Chibnall. 6 vols. Oxford: Oxford University Press, 1969–80.

Zurita, Jerónimo. Anales de la Corona de Aragón. Ed. Angel Canellas López. 8 vols. Zaragoza: Institución "Fernando el Católico," 1967–77.

✷ INDEX

Names and terms beginning with "al-" are indexed under the main part of the word. For added clarity, dating and biographical information is provided for certain individuals.

Muḥammad ibn Abī ʿĀmir al-Manṣūr, 17–19
al-Mundhir ibn Aḥmad, 20, 21, 41
al-Muqtadir. *See* Aḥmad ibn Sulaymān
Murcia, 28, 67, 73, 80, 81, 87, 91, 143, 144, 146, 147, 224, 225, 230
Muret, Battle of (1213), 206
Muslim-Christian interactions on eleventh-century frontier, 15–39; comital control, struggles for, 23–29; dissolution of Umayyad caliphate and rise of *taifa* states, 18–23; economic effects, 23, 29–30; final conquests of Tortosa/Lleida and, 70; holy war theories, development of, 23; al-Manṣūr, raids of, 17–19; papacy and, 16, 22–23, 28, 30–35; *parias* or tribute payments, 20–22, 23, 25, 26, 27, 28–29, 34; restoration of churches and dioceses, 16–17, 34–38; unclaimed land, donations of/independent settlement on, 17, 26–28
Muslims: Alfons I's relationship with, 137; conquest of Valencia/Balearic Islands and accommodations with, 221, 224–25, 228, 230, 231; uprisings in postconquest Valencia, 230–31, 232. *See also* Almoravids/Almohads; Andalus; *mudéjar* communities; *specific individuals*
al-Muʾtamin of Zaragoza, 21

Nájima, Treaty of (1158), 134, 144
Narbonne, 1–2, 35–38, 58, 64, 83, 228, 230, 274–75, 297n3
Narbonne, Council of (1127), 64
Navarre: Alfons I/Pere I and, 146, 160, 163, 169, 186; Sangüesa, Treaty of (1169), with Aragon, 143, 144, 186; in Treaty of Tudillén (1151), 91, 143
New Catalonia, 4–6, 9–10, 76, 97, 120, 132, 140–41, 151, 155, 174, 201, 207–8, 214–16, 228, 232–45, 249–51, 253–54. *See also* territorial expansion of Catalonia
Noguera Ribagorzana River, 53–55, 77, 139
Norman fighters, use of, 28, 32, 54, 65, 66
Nunyo Sanç, count of Rosselló-Cerdanya, 220, 221–22, 227, 279, 287

Old Catalonia, 6, 27, 97–98, 120, 140, 155, 202, 232–35, 240–41, 243, 253
Oleguer Bonestruga, bishop/archbishop of Barcelona/Tarragona, 57, 58, 60, 62–66, 73, 75
Ottone di Bonvillano (Genoese delegate), 87, 329n111

papacy: authority construction in conquered landscapes and, 107; competition and collaboration along Upper Frontier and, 42, 49, 50, 52, 56, 57, 59, 62, 63, 64, 67; minority of Jaume I and, 213, 220–21; Muslim-Christian interactions on eleventh-century frontier and, 16, 22–23, 28, 30–35; in reigns of Alfons I and Pere I, 136, 144, 148, 163, 164, 165, 362n154; suzerainty over Iberian leaders, 31–34, 59, 148, 307n88, 308n102, 309n118; unification of Barcelona/Aragon and conquest of Tortosa/Lleida, 72, 73, 76, 87, 90; Valencia and Balearic Islands, conquest of, 222, 227–31. *See also specific popes*
parias or tribute payments: competition and collaboration along Upper Frontier and, 43, 46, 55, 61; etymology of *parias*, 303n32; Muslim-Christian interactions on eleventh-century frontier and, 20–22, 23, 25, 26, 27, 28–29, 34; from Sancho Ramírez of Aragon to papacy, 31; Tortosa, *mudéjar* community of, 156; unification of Barcelona/Aragon and conquests of Lleida/Tortosa, 80, 90; from Valencia, 28, 143, 144, 145–46, 224–25
Paschal II (pope; formerly Cardinal-legate Rainer of Bleda), 49, 56, 57, 59–60
peace and truce. *See* peace constitutions
peace constitutions, 178, 180–84, 187–89, 247, 250
Peace of God, 180
peasant servitude. *See* Catalonia, extent of peasant servitude within
Pedro I, king of Aragon and Pamplona, 16, 30–31, 42, 47, 68, 308n102, 309n119
Pedro Ansúrez, "count" of Urgell, 46–47, 53, 203, 315n67
Pedro de Ahonés, 222, 224, 365n39
Pedro de Portugal *(infante,* husband of Aurembiaix, countess of Urgell), 285, 386n157
Pedro Fernández de Albarracín, 222
Pedro Fernández de Castro, 191, 192–93, 195–99, 202, 358n90
Pedro Fernández de Trava, 192
Pedro Ruiz de Azagra, 144, 146
Peire Vidal (troubadour), 137
Pere I, count-king of Aragon: authority construction after conquests of Tortosa/Lleida and, 114, 115, 132; comital-royal weakness under, 247; Ermengol VIII of Urgell and conflicts with viscount